A Guide to Writing in English as a Second or Foreign Language: An Annotated Bibliography of Research and Pedagogy

Dan J. Tannacito

Indiana University of Pennsylvania

Teachers of English to Speakers of Other Languages, Inc.

Teachers of English to Speakers of Other Languages, Inc.
1600 Cameron Street, Suite 300
Alexandria, Virginia 22314 USA
Tel 703-836-0774 ● Fax 703-836-7864

Copyright © 1995 by Teachers of English to Speakers of Other Languages, Inc. (TESOL).

All rights reserved. Copying or further publication of the contents of this work are not permitted without permission of TESOL, except for limited "fair use" for educational, scholarly, and similar purposes as authorized by U.S. Copyright Law, in which case appropriate notice of the source of the work should be given.

ISBN 939791-60-9

In Memoriam

Mother and Father

PREFACE

Writing in a second language is a new field. The field is largely a response to the need for writing instruction for non-native students entering and traversing educational systems in English-speaking countries in unprecedented numbers in recent years. The rapid growth of this field especially in North America is evident from the steady increase in the number of talks and papers devoted to writing in English as a second or foreign language (ESL/EFL) at the annual conference of Teachers of English as a Second Language (TESOL). Textbooks, scholarly monographs, and guides for new teachers devoted specifically to this area have appeared in increasing numbers. The publication in 1992 of *Second Language Writing,* a refereed journal, marks the maturing of scholarly communication in the field.

It may be debated whether writing in English as an additional language is properly a branch of applied linguistics, English, composition studies, literacy, or foreign language education. Certainly, those who author papers, publications, and textbooks are themselves housed in a wide variety of departments and divisions, reflecting the diversity of their own advanced degrees. They serve populations enrolled in equally diverse educational contexts and levels. Perhaps, then, we may start, with the assumption that the field of writing in English as a second/foreign language is interdisciplinary in nature. Wherever they work, however, more and more teachers and scholars are identifying themselves as ESL/EFL writing specialists.

The importance of writing in English as a second/foreign language was prompted more than two decade ago by changes internal to the profession of English language teaching. TESOL began expanding its concerns from the oral to the written language of second language users during the late 1960s when, generally, it also began shifting from behavioral to cognitive and communicative assumptions and methods of teaching. At the same time, the rise of English composition outside of TESOL (mainly in English Departments) throughout the 1970s and 1980s and the increasing prominence of native English-speaker (NES) composition research and pedagogy influenced the pace and development of the field of ESL/EFL writing. Perhaps only toward the end of the 1980s can it be said that the field became independent of NES composition with its own set of instructional and research questions as well as institutional mechanisms for the education of students, teachers, and researchers in ESL/EFL writing.

Scope

This bibliography offers ESL/EFL specialists and non-specialists a comprehensive annotated listing of scholarship in the field through the end of 1993 with a few exceptions. It includes nearly 3500 references which taken together comprehensively treat writing in English as a foreign or second language at all educational levels. It includes entries which focus on how non-native speakers write in English, how they learn to write in English, how ESL and NES composition students compare, how English is taught in contexts where it is used as a second or a foreign language, as well as textbooks and materials devoted to support writing in a second/foreign language. The earliest entry is dated 1937; the most recent is 1994.

This bibliography cites both published and unpublished works. Published works include six sources described below. Textbooks are included. Those unpublished works included are mostly conference talks and papers which have been presented at the national or international level as well as dissertations and theses. No films, videotapes, or sound recordings are referenced. It also excludes review articles except those that define movements in the field or survey a series of works on a topic. Finally, only citations in the English language are included.

Sources

This guide accesses works from six main sources: bibliographies, monographs or textbooks, periodicals, dissertations and theses, conference papers, and government clearinghouses.

Bibliographies

A number of partial bibliographies have been used to identify relevant citations. The earliest lists include sparse references to ESL/EFL writing (Ohannessian, 1964, 1966; Shen & Crymes, 1965; Robinson, 1969). More substantive annotated bibliographies covering ESL/EFL writing appeared in bibliographies comprehensively covering TESOL (Goldstein 1975). The most thorough bibliographic report specialized on research about ESL writing is Schecter & Harlau, 1991. However, the most comprehensive coverage of ESL/EFL writing to date has been the serial publication *Longman Bibliography of Composition and Rhetoric, 1984-85,* which since 1987 has been entitled the *CCCC Bibliography of Composition and Rhetoric.* While indispensable hitherto, the *CCCC Bibliography* is limited to secondary and higher educational levels. It also overlooks a significant number of published and unpublished citations in each year's work in ESL/EFL writing. Recently, the *Journal of Second Language Writing* began publishing three times per year (1993-) a cumulative, serial bibliography of the year's work . Each issue selects and summarizes 20-30 references to "theoretically grounded reports of research and discussions of central issues." This work serves a timely function analogous to Larsen's annual bibliography of native English composition which has appeared annually in *Research in the Teaching of English* for many years.

Monographs/Textbooks

One of the main sources of published material on writing in English as a second or foreign language are commercial publishers and university presses. Only recently have monographs begun to appear in this field (Jacobs, 1982). Monographs include books singly or multiply authored (Raimes, 1983; Straton, Shuy, Peyton, & Reed, 1988; Edelsky, 1989; Swales, 1990; Leki, 1992), collections that bring together previously published essays, articles, and papers (McKay, 1984; Cumming, 1994), anthologies of original research (Connor & Kaplan, 1987; Connor & Johns, 1990; Kroll, 1990; Hamp-Lyons, 1993; Carson & Leki, 1993), and creative ideas in pedagogy (Johnson & Roen, 1989; Reid, 1993). All monographs were studied first-hand, except a recent volume by Belcher & Braine (1994) which was unavailable before going to press. While the appearance of monographs are recent developments in the field, there is a longer tradition of textbook publication in ESL/EFL writing. The compiler relied on written information about textbooks provided by publishers and cross-checked their information against information provided in *Books in Print*.

Periodicals

A steadily increasing amount of scholarly and pedagogical information on ESL/EFL writing has begun to appear in professional journals in the US, Canada, Britain, and Australia. This study utilized the *CCCC Bibliography* journal list, supplemented by periodicals devoted exclusively to TESOL, applied linguistics, and foreign language education in order to search for relevant citations. Articles on ESL/EFL writing regularly appear in: *Annual Review of Applied Linguistics, Applied Linguistics, College ESL, English Teaching Forum, ELT Journal, English for Specific Purposes, ESP Journal, Journal of Second Language Writing, Language Learning, Modern Language Journal, Research in the Teaching of English, Studies in Second Language Acquisition, TESL Canada Journal, TESOL Journal,* and *TESOL Quarterly*.

Dissertation Abstracts

Dissertation research has contributed significantly to the development of ESL/EFL writing as a field (Krapels, 1990; Silva, 1993). The main source for dissertation citations included in this bibliography is *Dissertation Abstracts International (DAI)*, although not all degree-granting institutions list their dissertations in *DAI*. Since *DAI* abstracts are at least 300 words in length and provide institutional information, entries here are adapted from *DAI* and intended to direct readers to *DAI* for fuller treatment.

Some master's theses are included but not all of these are annotated. Master's theses are incompletely and inconsistent listed in reference works. A few are included in *DAI*, and some in one of several series devoted to master's programs (e.g., *Master's in Education*). Many that are listed do not include abstracts. In recent years, fewer and fewer master's degrees have included a thesis requirement.

Conference Papers

All unpublished talks and papers on ESL/EFL writing that have been presented at the annual conventions of TESOL, CCCC, NAFSA, NCTE, AERA and the Second Language Research Forum among other conferences have been included. This bibliography digests the author provided titles and abstracts from convention handbooks. In some cases (e.g., AERA, CCCC) no abstracts are available. Although papers are listed in convention catalogues, in a very small percentage of cases a few may never have been presented at the conference mentioned. The merit of including unpublished work in this bibliography lies in providing indications of work in an area of interest, trends, and areas of concentration. Perhaps also it may help reduce duplication of effort in conference presentations and publications.

Resources in Education

The ERIC microfiche system, especially the ERIC Clearinghouse on Foreign Languages and Linguistics (ERIC/FLL) and the ERIC Clearinghouse on Reading and Communication Skills (ERIC/RCS), is a repository for research reports, talks and papers on ESL/EFL writing among other materials. Some documents have been submitted directly while others deposited subsequent to presentation at conferences. Copies of materials which may subsequently become published as articles in journals or as monographs are sometimes included. In a few cases publications now out of print are reproduced in ERIC. But duplication of entries has been avoided as much as possible. It should be remembered that articles or papers which appear in ERIC are manuscripts and may be altered from previous presentations as conference talks or even from subsequent publications. The six digit ERIC ED number is included at the end of entries in this bibliography for those citations accessible in the ERIC system.

Criteria

Several criteria have been relied upon in the compilation of this bibliography.

Comprehensiveness

Items are included when the primary concern is with ESL/EFL writing or as in the case of studies on literacy when ESL writing is a main concern of the topic. The intention of this bibliography is to include as many references through 1993 as possible in order to provide teachers and researchers with a ready reference to the field of ESL/EFL writing. There are, no doubt, some references that have eluded this collection.

Relevance

The widest possible interpretation of what is ESL/EFL writing is assumed. Relevance is left in the first instance to the authors who are cited here. Hence, articles on spelling and computers may figure equally with those concerned with revision or errors. No effort has been made to select items for inclusion based on how relevant or current the citation may be to teachers or to researchers. Readers may determine the relevance of citations for their own purposes.

Reference Value

Some textbooks now out of print as well as historically remote articles or papers unlikely to be available from their authors are included for their unique reference value.

Annotations

Nearly all entries in this bibliography are annotated from the works directly or from author abstracts. The main exceptions are papers from conferences which publish no abstracts (e.g., *Conference on College Composition and Communication*) and some master's theses. Other omissions of annotations have been persistently unavailable. Digests of abstracts from *DAI* and ERIC are provided.

Annotations aim to provide a reader with the thesis, argument, point, finding, purpose, or major organization of the citation in question. Generally annotations are relatively brief, ranging from 25-75 words per entry. Relative length is not necessarily an indication of importance. Annotations are longer if giving more detail makes a difference in communicating the meaningfulness of the item. Also, one citation sometimes covers more information than another and consequently needs more space. Nonetheless, annotations are meant to be descriptive rather than evaluative. An effort is made to avoid criticism, praise, and partisanship about an entry in order to let the user judge the content's value. While no description in language can be totally free of value, these annotations restrict interpretation and inference to what is necessary for the most general audience to understand.

Classification

A choice was made early in this research not to produce a classified bibliography but rather to list entries alphabetically and to classify the corpora by means of multiple descriptor labels at the end of each entry. This contrasts with the technique used by Lindemann (1987; 1988; 1989) and her successors, e.g. Hawisher & Selfe (1991; 1992; 1993). In a new field with no standard structure of topics, it seems preferable to let the data of citations establish the categories rather than to impose those used to describe native-speaker composition. Categories attempt to aid readers rather than to pigeonhole studies, as Silva & Reichelt (1993; 1994) in their recent bibliographies of research articles suggest. Many studies, however, defy single categorization; hence, readers are better served with an indication of multiple categories in order to facilitate searching topics.

The compilation of this bibliography was aided by a computer program, Pro-Cite, dedicated to bibliographic management. While this program is not without its flaws, it certainly enabled ready access to and consistent manipulation of an unwieldy database. The format of each citation conforms to the reference style of the *Publication manual of the American Psychological Association* (Fourth Edition).

Lists

The preliminary material in this volume include two lists. The list of abbreviations gives the acronyms used in citations, titles, or abstracts. The list of country/languages is intended to show at a glance which languages or countries are explicitly treated in the citations included in this volume to the extent that it is determinable from the content. All languages and countries listed are also included in the "Index of Subjects." A journal list is not provided since it is more convenient for the reader to have the full title in each entry.

Indexes

Each entry begins with a unique entry number and ends with a descriptor line for the purpose of accessing citations through two indexes provided at the end of this work. The "Index of Names" lists all primary and secondary authors of every monograph, article, document, and paper cited herein. In addition, the editors of anthologized collections in which articles and essays appear are also included.

The Index of Subjects includes every entry at least once and most entries usually several times. Where an entry has multiple descriptors, the entry is listed under each descriptor in the index. Users of this volume can search individual topics comprehensively by using one or more key words or phrases in the subject index.

Acknowledgments

This compilation of this bibliography began in the early 1980s as support materials for doctoral courses in Rhetoric & Linguistics. I'm grateful to IUP for a semester sabbatical in 1992 which provided the time needed to make the bibliography comprehensive. Several professional organizations: AERA, CAL, NAFSA, and TESOL -- kindly made their archives available. As a visiting scholar, I was able to use the library at the University of Pittsburgh, thanks to arrangements by Professors Michael Helfand and Phillip Smith. A special thanks are due to more than twenty leading ESL/EFL writing scholars (who will remain unnamed) for kindly reviewing for accuracy and inclusiveness a preliminary list of annotated citations of their own research and writing. Several graduate students who worked as my research assistants in the Rhetoric & Linguistics Ph.D. program at IUP during the last ten years deserve my gratitude for their help searching out references and collecting and digesting printed abstracts. I would especially single out Dr. Jacinta Thomas for her assistance with this project. Gail McCawley, Lori Renwick, and Lucinda Strong have my thanks for typing and editorial work on the indexes. I am also grateful to TESOL and the editorial staff for patience in producing this work. Of course, all errors or omissions are my own responsibility.

Since I anticipate updating this volume periodically, I would welcome responses for improving the next version. Readers are welcome to call to my attention errors in this volume, material that might have been missed in this volume, and provide suggestions that would make this tool more useful in the future. Responses can be sent to my attention at: English Department, Indiana University of Pennsylvania, Indiana, PA 15705 USA or by e-mail (DJT@grove.iup.edu).

Pittsburgh, PA
September 1994

Language/Country List

- Amer-Indian
- Arabic
- Asian
- Bantu
- Bolivia
- Brazil
- Cambodian
- Chinese
- Creole
- Dutch
- Ethiopian
- Finnish
- French
- German
- Greek
- Gujuarti
- Haitian
- Hebrew
- Hindi
- Hispanic
- Hmong
- Hungarian
- India
- Indo-Chinese
- Indonesian
- Iranian/Persian
- Italian
- Japanese
- Korean
- Malawi
- Malay
- Mali
- Marathi
- Nigerian
- Norwegian
- Papua New Guinean
- Phillipines
- Polish
- Portugese
- Punjabi
- Russian
- Samoa
- Senegal
- Singaporean
- Sri Lankean
- Swedish
- Tagalog
- Thai
- Tonga
- Turkish
- Vietnamese
- West Indian
- Zairean
- Zimbabwe

List of Abbreviations

AERA-American Educational Research Association
ASL-American Sign Language
BIA-Bureau of Indian Affairs
CAL-Center for Applied Linguistics
CILT-Center for Information on Language Teaching
CCCC-Conference on College Composition and Communication
EFL-English as a foreign language
EAP-English for Academic Purposes
ESL-English as a second language
ERIC-Educational Resources Information Center
ESP-English for Specific Purposes
ETS-Educational Testing Service
ELT-English Language Teaching
IATEFL-International Association of Teachers of Foreign Languages
IELTS-International English Language Testing Service
FSP-functional sentence perspective
IEA-International Education Achievement
IIE-Institute for International Education
IEP-intensive English program
GRE-Graduate Record Examination
L1-first language
L2-second language
LEA-language experience approach
LEP-limited English proficiency
LOR- Length of residence
MBTI-Meyer-Briggs Type Indicator
MELAB-Michigan English Language Assessment Battery
NS- native speaker
NNS-non-native speaker
NES-native English speaker
NNES-non-native Engish speaker
NAFSA-National Association of Foreign Student Affairs
NCTE-National Council of Teachers of English
PTS- primary trait scoring
SCA-Speech Communication Association
SLEP-Second Language English Proficiency
TAS-Test of Ability to Subordinate
TESOL-Teachers of English to Speakers of Other Languages
TEFL-Teaching English as a foreign language
TESL-Teaching English as a second language
TWE-Test of Written English
TOEFL-Test of English as a Foreign Language
TSA-topical structure analysis
WAC- writing across the curriulum

Guide to Writing in English as a Second or Foreign Language: An Annotated Bibliography of Research and Pedagogy

A

1. Abadir, L. A. (1977). *A contrastive analysis of English and Farsi with a suggested program in ESL for Persian students.* Unpublished master's thesis, Hunter College, CUNY, New York, NY.
    Contrastive Rhetoric/Persian/Programs.

2. Abdan, A. A. (1984). The effect of sentence combining on the written syntactic maturity, overall writing quality, and reading comprehension of EFL Saudi students. *Dissertation Abstracts International, 44*(11), 3307A.
    Examines the effect of sentence-combining exercises on syntactic maturity, writing proficiency, and reading comprehension of EFL Saudi students. Results indicate that sentence-combining exercises promote syntactic maturity and writing quality but do not effect reading comprehension. Suggests incorporating these exercises into EFL composition courses in Saudi Arabia.
    Arabic/Sentence Combining.

3. Abdulaziz, H. T., & Shenkarow, E. (1986). *Write it right: Beginning handwriting and composition for students of ESL.* Englewood Cliffs, NJ: Prentice Hall Regents.
    Text is designed for ESL students literate in their own language, but who have little or no familiarity with English or the Roman alphabet. It begins with basic handwriting instructions, then advances to vocabulary, sentence structure, and finally, to paragraph development.
    Beginners/Handwriting/Textbook.

4. Abi-Naer, J., & Sitko, B. (1992, March). *Teaching writing in a native American reservation school.* Paper presented at the 26th Annual TESOL Convention, Vancouver, BC.
    Describes progress of a three-year study of writing instruction in an Indian reservation high school in which collaborative planning and revising after feedback are taught.
    Amer-Indian/Secondary School/Collaboration.

5. Aboderin, A. O. (1984, March). *Writing practices and writing needs of Nigerian secondary school students: A survey.* Paper presented at the 18th Annual TESOL Convention, Houston, TX.
    Failure on English certificate examinations may be attributed to writing instruction which neglects the practical aspects of student lives as well as modern techniques of composing.
    Errors/Secondary School/Nigerian.

6. Abraham, R. G. (1981). The relationship of cognitive style to the use of grammatical rules by Spanish-speaking ESL students in editing written English. *Dissertation Abstracts International, 42*(9), 3892A.
    An examination of multiple tasks by Spanish-speaking students finds that greater

accuracy occurs in writing than in speaking, confirming the role of monitoring proposed by Krashen and others. Different patterns occur in correlations of performance variables and cognitive style and attitude measures.
Spanish/Editing/Speaking-Writing Relations.

7. Abu-Humos, O. M. (1993). Interlingual and cross-modalities relationships of first and second language of adult EFL Arab speakers. *Dissertation Abstracts International*, *53*(9), 3129A-3130A.
A study of 20 Arabic-speaking first-year university students finds a moderately strong interlingual correlation between English and Arabic writing skills. Also finds a moderately strong correlation between speaking and writing in English and speaking and writing in Arabic.
Arabic/L1-L2 Comparison/Speaking-Writing Relations.

8. Abunowara, A. M. (1983). *Contrastive analysis of Arabic and English passive structures*. Unpublished master's thesis, Colorado State University.
Contrastive Rhetoric/Arabic.

9. Achiba, M., & Kuromiya, Y. (1983). Rhetorical patterns extant in the English compositions of Japanese students. *JALT Journal*, *5*, 1-13.
An analysis of 130 compositions by Japanese EFL students seems to support the CA hypothesis in that Japanese L1 compositions exhibit a preponderance of indirect style whereas their English L2 compositions are predominantly linear in organizational style.
Japanese/Contrastive Rhetoric/L1-L2 Comparison.

10. Ackert, P. (1986). *Please write: A beginning composition text for students of ESL*. Englewood Cliffs, NJ: Prentice Hall.
Teaches students how to use given information to compose correct English sentences and then organize them into paragraphs.
Beginners/Textbook.

11. Acton, W. (1984). Some pragmatic dimensions of ESL writing tutorials. *TECFORS*, *7*(3), 1-7. [ERIC ED 267 581].
Discusses how language learners need oral, interpersonal skills to discuss their writing, elicit and respond to criticism, and learn to self-edit.
Social/Speaking-Writing Relations.

12. Acuna, D. S. (1986). English as a second language (ESL) development: An investigation into the relationship of the students' reading comprehension and writing ability at the college level in Puerto Rico. *Dissertation Abstracts International*, *47*(4), 1201A.
Studies the relationship of reading comprehension level, syntactic maturity, and overall writing proficiency of Spanish-speaking college students across three semesters of ESL instruction. Results suggest reading/writing connection and pedagogical implications.
Hispanic/Reading-Writing Relations.

13. Adams, C. (1989). *Beginning language students can write: Integrating the language experience chart and process writing*. Unpublished M.A.T. thesis, the School for International Training, Brattleboro, VT. [ERIC ED 313 904]

Offers a lesson-by-lesson plan for beginning students that combines the language experience approach and process writing.
LEA/Beginners.

14. Adams, J., & Dwyer, M. (1982). *English for academic uses*. Englewood Cliffs, NJ: Prentice-Hall.
A writing workbook for advanced students who want to learn how to use English in an academic context. The book features chapters on topic sentences, paragraph unity, definition, supporting material, grammar, and vocabulary. Also includes material on note-taking, outlining, summarizing, and proofreading.
Advanced/University/Textbook.

15. Adams, K., & Adams, J. (1985). Write, read and edit! ESL theory in the basic writing curriculum. *The Writing Instructor*, *4*, 116-122.
Tries to show how Krashen's ideas apply to developmental students and basic writing instruction.
Reading-Writing Relations/Editing.

16. Adamson, H. D. (1993). *Academic competence: Theory and classroom practice: Preparing ESL students for content courses* NY: Longman.
Discusses research on ESL students in precourses, i.e. temporary participation in regular credit courses. Reports only limited involvement with writing.
Content.

17. Adjakey, K. M. (1990). Second language speakers as translators: Implications for linguistic theory and second language acquisition. *Dissertation Abstracts International*, *50*(9), 2877A.
Finds that knowledge of subject matter, of discourse as well as both ideology and ideolect influence language proficiency in tests.
Translation.

18. Afghari, A. (1984). Grammatical errors and syntactic complexity in three discourse categories: An analysis of English compositions written by Persian speakers. *Dissertation Abstracts International*, *45*(3), 771A.
Investigates the explanatory, expressive and persuasive writing of ESL students and studies the correlation of task and (1) total number of errors; (2) proportion of interlingual and intralingual errors; (3) syntactic complexity; (4) number of errors and syntactic maturity. Results show (1) that task influences language -- expressive compositions showed more syntactic complexity and grammatical errors (2) correlation between grammatical errors and T-unit length.
Errors/Syntactic Development/Persian.

19. Aghbar, A. A. (1993, April). *Functional grammar for the ESL writing class*. Paper presented at the 27th Annual TESOL Convention, Atlanta, GA.
Discusses how to use functional grammar in order to teach clear and coherent prose.
Grammar.

20. Aghbar, A. A. (1991, March). *Writing activities for critical thinking in content-based instruction*. Paper presented at the 25th Annual TESOL Convention, New York, NY.

Discusses the contribution of different writing activities to the development of critical thinking.
Cognition/Instruction.

21. Aghbar, A. A. (1990, October). *Fixed expressions in written texts: Implications for assessing writing sophistication*. Paper presented at the English Association of Pennsylvania State System Universities, Shippensburg, PA. [ERIC ED 329 125].
Claims that the use of formulaic language is an important aspect of ESL writing proficiency.
Style.

22. Aghbar, A. A. (1984, March). *Read comp: A useful addition to placement test batteries*. Paper presented at the 18th Annual TESOL Convention, Houston, TX.
For fast and reliable results, advocates testing students' abilities to write from memory after reading a paragraph.
Assessment/Reading-Writing Relations.

23. Aghbar, A. A. (1983a). Guided impressionistic scoring of ESL compositions. *WATESOL Working Papers*, *1*, 36-52. [ERIC ED 242 195].
Describes an adaptation of an impressionistic scoring method for placement of ESL students and presents a correlational study of its reliability.
Evaluation/ Assessment.

24. Aghbar, A. A. (1983b, March). *Grid-based impressionistic scoring of ESL compositions*. Paper presented at the 17th Annual TESOL Convention, Toronto, BC.
Demonstrates a method (based on Pritchard, 1980) of scoring compositions.
Evaluation.

25. Aghbar, A. A., & Alam, M. (1992, March). *Teaching the writing process through full dyadic writing*. Paper presented at the 26th Annual TESOL Convention, Vancouver, BC.
Discusses how to teach the writing process through full dyadic writing.
Process Instruction/Collaboration.

26. Aghbar, A. A., & Trump, K. (1985). When theory and intuition meet: An approach to composition instruction. *WATESOL Working Papers*, *2*, 26-37. [ERIC ED 267 587].
In the form of dialogue, authors address topics such as self-confidence in writing, non-judgmental conditions for writing practice, the uses of free-writing, finding a balance between the "what" and the "how" of composition, generating ideas for writing, and reducing writer's block.
Instruction.

27. Aguas, E. F. (1964). English composition errors of Tagalog speakers and implications for analytical theory. *Dissertation Abstracts International*, *25*(6), 3561.
Classifies sentence level errors in compositions by 300 Tagalog-speaking learners of English across grade levels from elementary through university. Errors in the use of verbs and prepositions were the most frequent.
Tagalog/Errors.

28. Ahn, B. (1990). The effect of errors on native speaker comprehension in written English discourse of Korean students. *Dissertation Abstracts International*, *51*(10),

3347A.
English composition samples produced by Korean college students were evaluated by undergraduate native speakers using a four-point scale. Little reason is found to associate reader perception and writer intention. Moreover, errors of lexical choice are, apparently, less comprehensible than discourse or sentence level errors.
Error Gravity/Korean.

29. Ahrens, C. O. (1985). Comparing composition skills of native and non-native born students at the junior high school level
Depending on their length of residence in the U.S., students are shown to differ significantly in the quality of their essays and the syntactic complexity of their writing.
Secondary School/NS-NNS Comparisons.

30. Aitches, M., & Shreve, D. H. (1983, March). *Teaching composition, rhetoric, and logic in the ESL classroom: Setting it up for success*. Paper presented at the 17th Annual TESOL Convention, Toronto, BC.
Focuses on teaching writing beyond the paragraph level to high intermediate and advanced ESL students.
Advanced.

31. Alam, M. B. (1989). Using shadow stories to elicit EFL/ESL writing. *English Teaching Forum, 27*(3), 50-51.
Suggests engaging learners in writing responses to conventional stories presented to them with deliberate changes, i. e. shadow stories.
Narration.

32. Alamansa, A. (1986, March). *Why and how to use conference-centered writing*. Paper presented at the 20th Annual TESOL Convention, Anaheim, CA.
Advocates conferencing as efficient and effective use of teacher's time.
Conferencing.

33. Albertini, J. (1993). Critical literacy, whole language, and the teaching of writing to deaf students: Who should dictate to whom? *TESOL Quarterly, 27*, 59-73.
Analyzes journal entries of 87 college-aged German deaf students and the autobiographical essays of 87 U.S. deaf college students. Finds that their prior instruction emphasized narrow conceptions of literacy and inaccurate assumptions about language learning. Advocates use of whole language approaches to writing for deaf second language students.
Hearing-Impaired/German.

34. Albrechtsen, D., Evensen, L. S., Lindeberg, A. C., & Linnarud, M. (1991). Analyzing developing discourse structure: The NORDWRITE Project. In R. Phillipson, E. Kellerman, L. Selinker, M. Sharwood Smith, & M. Swain (Eds.), *Foreign/second language pedagogy research: A commemorative volume for Claus Faerch* (pp. 79-91). Clevedon, ENG: Multilingual Matters.
The NORDWRITE project aims to describe coherence in the written interlanguage of EFL learners from grades 8 to university level in four Nordic countries (Norway, Sweden, Finland, and Denmark) and, ultimately to suggest strategies for the teaching of EFL writing. Report summarizes the general approach

and aims of the pilot phase.
Coherence/Cohesion.

35. Al-Falahi, H. A. (1982). The relationship between discourse universals and discourse structure of English and Arabic. *Dissertation Abstracts International, 42*(7), 3135A.

Examines discourse structure syntagmatically and paradigmatically and the four aims of discourse or discourse universals -- expression, literature, reference, and persuasion -- in English and Arabic. Findings indicate: (1) that conceptual patterns in both languages occur in combination at different hierarchical levels; (2) parallel forms in both languages use similar combination of conceptual forms; (3) discourse is recursive not linear.
Arabic/Discourse Analysis.

36. Alhaidari, A. O. (1992). How Arab students summarize English prose and how they revise their summaries. *Dissertation Abstracts International, 52*(10), 3568A-3569A.

A think aloud analysis of Saudi ESL students summarizing and revising summaries shows a moderate awareness of summarization rules (Brown & Day, 1983), moderate language monitoring, but little metacognitive planning. Revisions tended to make meaning clearer and more accurate.
Arabic/Summary Writing/Revision.

37. Ali, H. A. (1990). A process-based approach to teaching written English to first-year university students in Lebanon: An exploratory study. *Dissertation Abstracts International, 50*(10), 3170A.

Reports result of an experiment comparing teaching methodologies for fourteen weeks at a Lebanese university. Performance of subjects treated with a "process approach" was judged significantly better than those receiving a "product" control approach. The following four characteristics of the successful treatment are identified: writing as meaning making, reading for writing, speaking for writing, and multiple drafting.
Process Instruction/University/Arabic.

38. Al-Jabr, A. M. (1987). Cohesion in text differentiation: A study of English and Arabic. *Dissertation Abstracts International, 49*(1), 51A.

Finds that English prefers economy in the use of cohesive devices, while Arabic largely coheres through the redundant effect created by the high frequency of most pronominal co-reference and lexical repetition.
Cohesion/Arabic.

39. Al-Jubouri, A. J. R. (1984). The role of repetition in Arabic argumentative discourse. In J. M. Swales, & H. Mustafa (Eds.), *English for Specific Purposes in the Arab world* (pp. 99-117). Birmingham, UK: University of Aston, Language Studies Unit.

Outlines some aspects of the nature and function of repetition in written argumentative discourse of contemporary standard Arabic. Finds built-in mechanisms for repetition at multiple levels of text.
Cohesion/Arabic.

40. Allaei, S. K. (1992, March). *Portfolio assessment of ESL writing: Integrating process and product*. Paper presented at the 26th Annual TESOL Convention, Vancouver,

BC.
    Argues that a portfolio approach frees teachers from justifying grades on individual pieces and develops student awareness of writing processes.
    Assessment/Portfolios.

41. Allaei, S. K., & Connor, U. M. (1991a). Exploring the dynamics of cross-cultural collaboration in writing classrooms. *The Writing Instructor, 10*, 19-28.
    Discusses impediments to using collaborative groups in ESL classrooms. These stem from inter-ethnic and cross-cultural differences as well as the influence of prior cultural knowledge about text-shaping and reader-writer roles. Recommends consciousness-raising and special preparation about peer response.
    Collaboration/Culture.

42. Allaei, S. K., & Connor, U. M. (1991b). Using performative assessment instruments with ESL student writers. In L. Hamp-Lyons (Ed.), *Assessing second language writing in academic contexts* (pp. 227-240). Norwood, NJ: Ablex.
    Introduces performative assessment, designed to describe ESL writing in relation to specific tasks and discourse demands. Explores potential use for diagnostic and classroom purposes.
    Assessment.

43. Allaei, S. K., & Connor, U. M. (1989, March). *Performative writing assessment: Combining assessment and instruction.* Paper presented at the 23rd Annual TESOL Convention, San Antonio, TX.
    Describes performative assessment as a diagnostic tool and guide for the revising process.
    Assessment/Revision.

44. Allahyari, K. H. (1988, March). *ESL research papers on the computer: A process approach.* Paper presented at the 39th Annual CCCC Meeting, St. Louis, MO.
    Research Writing/Computers.

45. Allen, V. F. (1983, March). *Writing as a route to reading: A technique to increase comprehension.* Paper presented at the 17th Annual TESOL Convention, Toronto, BC.
    Shows ways to guide the composing of sentences so as to facilitate comprehension of grammatically complex reading.
    Reading--Writing Relations

46. Allen, V. F. (1978a). Using the written language creatively. *Modern Language Journal, 62*, 407-410.
    Discusses the use of books, concrete experiences, and poetry as springboards to creative writing in the foreign language classroom. Examples are given for each of the techniques.
    Creative Writing.

47. Allen, V. F. (1978b). Writing. In D. Ilyin, & T. Tragardh (Eds.), *Classroom practices in adult ESL* (pp. 176-177). Washington, DC: TESOL.
    Advises teachers to carefully control topic, purpose, and scope of student writing.
    Adult Education/Control.

Reading-Writing Relations/Control.

48. Allen, V. F., & Hudelson, S. (1986, March). *Speaking and writing: Helping LEP children make the connection.* Paper presented at the 20th Annual TESOL Convention, Anaheim, CA.

Shows how oral language supports composition and how writing creates new purposes for speaker.

Speaking-Writing Relations/Elementary.

49. Allen, V. F., Peyton, J. K., Samway, K. D., & Urzua, C. (1987, March). *Young children composing: A web of interconnecting elements.* Paper presented at the 21st Annual TESOL Convention, Miami Beach, FL.

Colloquium on current research into the writing processes of elementary school children.

Children/Process Research.

50. Allen, V. G. (1991). Teaching bilingual and ESL children. In J. Flood, J. M. Jensen, D. Lapp, & J. R. Squire (Eds.), *Handbook of research on teaching the English language arts* (pp. 356-364). NY: Macmillan.

Summarizes general research on second language acquisition with a focus on second language literacy. Points out that second language learners draw upon their L1 print knowledge when writing in L2.

Children/Literacy.

51. Allen, W. P. (1981). A controlling frame for paragraph development. *TESL Reporter, 14*(3), 55-56.

Claims that paragraph development in American English is "more direct than in some other languages." Presents model exercises dealing with topic and supporting sentences and summary conclusion. Students complete the model for various stories and paragraphs.

Paragraph/Control.

52. Allison, D. (1986). Training learners to prepare short written answers. *ELT Journal, 40*, 27-32.

Suggests ideas to link composition class activities to content courses.

Academic Writing/Content.

53. Allison, D., & Cheung, E. (1990, April). *"Good" and "poor" writing and writers: Studying individual performance as a part of test validation.* Paper presented at the Annual Meeting of the SEAMEO Regional Language Center Seminar, Singapore.

Investigates the validity of criteria for marking essays by arts faculty students at the University of Hong Kong.

Assessment/Rating.

54. Allwright, J. (1988). Don't correct -- reformulate! In P. C. Robinson (Ed.), *Academic writing: Process and product* (pp. 109-116). London: Modern English Publications/British Council.

Finds the concept of reformulation essential to foster autonomy in editing ESL academic writing. Discusses a pedagogical strategy for the teacher who wants to reformulate a single learner text in class.

Academic Writing/Revision/Reformulation.

55. Allwright, R. (1988). Investigating reformulation as a practical strategy for the teaching of academic writing. *Applied Linguistics*, 9, 236-256.

   Studies the use of reformulation as a strategy for the teaching of writing. The strategy generates a rich database of writing samples which permit the pursuit of a number of precise research questions.

   Revision/Reformulation.

56. Almeida, J. C. P. (1984). The interplay of cohesion and coherence in native and non-native written academic discourse. *Dissertation Abstracts International*, 46(5), 1263A.

   Studies cohesion at discourse level in writing of students in their native language (Portugese) and in a non-native language (English), using Halliday and Hasan's taxonomy of cohesion. Results indicate that more successful written discourse in the native language uses: (1) more explicit logical relations; (2) more organized sequences of events; (3) longer distance between cohesive items; (4) and fewer exophoric ties.

   Cohesion/Coherence/Portuguese.

57. Alptekin, C. (1988). Chinese formal schemata in ESL composition. *British Journal of Language Teaching*, 26(2), 112-116.

   Describes how features of the classical Chinese world view are reflected in compositions written by 42 Chinese graduate students at an American university. Finds that the majority used "a non-linear rhetorical organization," complementary propositions with yin-yang attributes, analogies based on relational thinking, and a global perspective where argumention was expected.

   Chinese/Contrastive Rhetoric/Schema.

58. Alptekin, C., & Alptekin, M. (1983). The role of content schemata in ESL composition. *TESL Reporter*, 16(4), 63-66.

   Discusses the need for teachers to be cross-culturally informed as readers of ESL compositions.

   Culture/Schema.

59. Alt, R. R., & Kirkland, M. L. (1973). *Steps to composition: A pre-composition workbook for students of English as a second language*. Washington, DC: Georgetown University Press.

   Textbook with a variety of exercises provides 28 chapters on grammatical constructions leading to individual chapters on writing dialogues and paragraphs.

   University/Grammar/Textbook.

60. Alvarez, R. S. (1977). *An analysis of the writing errors of five adult ESL students*. Unpublished master's thesis, Hunter College, CUNY, New York, NY.

   Error Analysis.

61. Aly, M. S. (1992). A descriptive study of four EFL teachers' treatment of writing errors and their feedback in an Arab country. *Dissertation Abstracts International*, 53(2), 429A.

   Analyzes questionnaires, interviews, texts written by Arab learners, and feedback from four Arab EFL instructors to determine how teachers and students responded to each other. Finds that teachers treated errors in isolation from global

aspects of learner's text and acted in an authoritative role, thus limiting feedback about errors.
Errors/Feedback/Arabic.

62. Amato, K. (1992). Pluralism and its discontents: Tutor training in a multicultural university. *Writing Lab Newsletter, 17*(4), 1-6.
Points out how half the clientele at a university writing center are non-native speakers, very few of whom have either training in linguistics or TESOL or prior experience with ESL students.
Writing Center/Tutoring.

63. Amiri, P. M. (1979). An adaptation of Aristotelian rhetoric for teaching English persuasive themes to Iranian college students. *Dissertation Abstracts International, 40*(3), 1315A.
Examines five types of contemporary persuasion using Aristotelian norms, an Aristotelian framework and a Persian framework, and constructs a workable syllabus for teaching persuasive writing in English for Persian college students.
Persuasion/Persian.

64. Amiri, P. M. (1976). *Teaching English composition to Iranian college students: An historical perspective.* Unpublished master's thesis, University of Texas, Austin, TX.
Persian/University.

65. Ammon, P. (1985). Helping children to write in English as a second language: Some observations and some hypotheses. In S. W. Freedman (Ed.), *The acquisition of written language: Response and revision* (pp. 65-84). Norwood, NJ: Ablex.
Examines the writing development of children learning English as a second language. Concludes that a top-down approach in an instructional program rich in communicative purposes and which involves a lot of writing tasks leads to greater writing development.
Hispanic/Children.

66. Anakasiri, S. (1987). Indicators of quality in second language written communication. *Dissertation Abstracts International, 48*(3), 583A.
Examines three factors related to the quality of writing -- syntactic complexity, global and local errors, and cohesion -- in order to determine which one relates to the overall quality of compositions as judged by native speakers. The results confirm that the length of the text is not a significant indicator of quality but that subordination and cohesion (i.e., reference cohesive ties, substitutions) are the main factors in the quality judgments by native speakers.
Errors/Syntactic Development/Evaluation.

67. Anderson, D., & Montalvan, R. (1992, March). *The teaching of writing: Workshops for teacher trainers.* Workshop presented at the 26th Annual TESOL Convention, Vancouver, BC.
Describes a 55-hour workshop for teacher trainers in the Phillipines on the teaching of writing.
Teacher Preparation/Phillipines.

68. Anderson, K. H. (1986). A synthesis of rhetoric and grammar in an English as a second language writer's handbook. *Dissertation Abstracts International, 47*(6), 2059A.

   Illustrates how current ESL composition texts and grammar handbooks separate grammatical material from very restricted rhetorical material. Proposes, and illustrates through sample chapters, an ESL writer's handbook that overcomes this deficiency by integrating the grammatical and the rhetorical.

   Rhetoric/Grammar/Materials.

69. Anderson, K. H. (1981, March). *Primary trait scoring: New approaches to evaluating ESL compositions.* Paper presented at the 15th Annual TESOL Convention, Detroit, MI.

   Finds PTS method superior to holistic scoring in that it enables instructors to grade specifically on one writing task and students to focus on a specific rhetorical context.

   Evaluation/Scoring.

70. Anderson, M. L., & Wrase, J. (1976, March). *What's REALLY basic about teaching composition to foreign students?* Paper presented at the 27th Annual CCCC Meeting, Philadelphia, PA. [ERIC ED 130 532].

   Uses two sample compositions to illustrate similarities and differences between paragraphing by NS and NNS writers.

   NS-NNS Comparisons/Paragraph.

71. Anderson, P. L. (1981, March). *The use of editing to teach composition to adults.* Paper presented at the 15th Annual TESOL Convention, Detroit, MI.

   Exposure and analysis of English passages help ESL students internalize norms for English prose.

   Editing.

72. Anderson, P. L. (1980a, November). *Cohesion as an index for written and oral composition of ESL learners.* Paper presented at the Annual Meeting of the Midwest Modern Language Association, Minneapolis, MN. [ERIC ED 198 529].

   Examines the use of cohesion in the spoken and written narratives of ESL adult learners using Halliday & Hasan's system. While more devices were found in oral than written data, cohesion frequency analysis correlated inconsistently with holistic writing and TOEFL scores. Does not recommend using cohesion analysis for analyzing discourse of ESL writers.

   Cohesion/Speaking-Writing Relations.

73. Anderson, P. L. (1980b). The relationship between observed and elicited oral and written language of adult learners of English as a second language. *Dissertation Abstracts International, 41*(5), 1983A.

   Studies: (1) relationship between students', instructors', and observers' perceptions of student ability in ESL; (2) relationship of holistic evaluation and frequency of cohesive ties in oral and written language; (3) relationship between indices used in study and TOEFL scores; (4) relationship between oral and written language; (5) relationship of perception indices and evaluation indices. Results show differential perceptions of language ability by teachers and students. While oral and

written language differ in amount of cohesion devices, they do not relate significantly to TOEFL scores. Cohesion frequency and holistic scores do not always correlate.
Speaking-Writing Relations/Cohesion.

74. Anderson, P. J. (1977). *Intersentential cohesion of texts as written by learners of English as a second language.* Unpublished master's thesis, University of Kansas, Lawrence, KS.
Cohesion.

75. Anderson, R. (1988). Overwriting and other techniques for success with academic articles. In P. C. Robinson (Ed.), *Academic writing: Process and product* (pp. 151-158). London: Modern English Publications/British Council.
A working scientist reviews some of the circumstances and factors that go into the overelaborate use of language by academic and professional writers. Links this "overwriting" with personal display and in-group style. Suggests that ESP teachers collaborate with subject specialists to articulate the implicit rules of language use in the field of writing scientific reports.
ESP/Academic Writing/Style.

76. Angelis, P. J. (1975a). Sentence combining, error analysis, and the teaching of writing. In M. K. Burt, & H. C. Dulay (Eds.), *On TESOL '75: New directions in second language learning, teaching, and bilingual education* (pp. 292-299). Washington, DC: TESOL.
Endorses a cognitive approach to the teaching of writing with the addition of error analysis and sentence-combining.
Approaches.

77. Angelis, P. J. (1975b, April). *Sentence-combining, error analysis, and the teaching of writing.* Paper presented at the 9th Annual TESOL Convention, Los Angeles, CA. [ERIC ED 103 882].
Argues for a special approach unique to college ESL writing that combines a "thinking process concept" with error analysis and sentence-combining.
Error Analysis/Sentence Combining.

78. Angioletti, P. J. (1978). *Teaching ESL writing to Chinese students.* Unpublished master's thesis, Hunter College, CUNY, New York, NY.
Contrastive Rhetoric/Chinese.

79. Antia, B. (1985). Rockin', rollin', and writin': Using fan letters in the ESL classroom. *TESL Canada Journal, 3*(1), 72-73.
Suggests for motivational value that students write fan letters to favorite pop/rock singers.
Motivation/Letter Writing.

80. Appel, G. (1986). L1 and L2 narrative and expository discourse production: A Vygotskyan analysis. *Dissertation Abstracts International, 47*(12), 4373A.
Analyzes the oral recall protocols of narrative and expository texts by native and non-native speakers of English, using the quantitative procedures of L2 research paradigm and qualitative features of Vygotskyan methodology. Findings show that there are no absolute differences between L1 and L2 speakers and that differences are largely task-dependent.

Narration/Exposition/NS-NNS Comparisons.
81. Arani, M. T. (1985). Error analysis: The types and the causes of the major structural errors made by Iranian university students when writing expository and imaginative prose. *Dissertation Abstracts International, 46*(12), 3634A.
Finds seriousness is not necessarily related to frequency in a sample of 891 errors among 10 major categories types in compositions written by Iranian subjects.
Error Analysis/Persian.
82. Arapoff-Cramer, N. (1978, April). *Workshop in creative writing for the ESL/EFL student*. Paper presented at the 12th Annual TESOL Convention, Mexico City, Mexico.
Outlines a creative writing curriculum for intermediate level ESL/EFL students.
Creative Writing/Intermediate.
83. Arapoff-Cramer, N. (1977, April). *Generative rhetoric in the ESL/EFL writing program*. Paper presented at the 11th Annual TESOL Convention, Miami Beach, FLA.
Advocates using Christensen's rhetorical procedure (1963) rather than transformational sentence-combining because the former addresses the making of discourse rather than individual sentences.
Generative Rhetoric/Methods.
84. Arapoff-Cramer, N. (1975). Towards a hierarchical sequencing of writing situations. In R. Crymes, & W. E. Norris (Eds.), On *TESOL '74: Selected papers from the 8th Annual TESOL convention* (pp. 171-177). Washington, DC: TESOL.
Presents a hierarchically ordered curriculum for writing based on H. D. Brown's cognitive model of language learning.
Curriculum.
85. Arapoff-Cramer, N. (1974, March). *Toward a hierarchical sequencing of writing situations*. Paper presented at the 8th Annual TESOL Convention, Denver, CO.
Suggests how to devise a series of problems that enable students to analyze topics hierarchically in order to create new ideas in writing.
Invention.
86. Arapoff, N. (1969). Discover and transform: A method of teaching writing to foreign students. *TESOL Quarterly, 3*, 297-304.
Claims that learning to speak is different from learning to write. Suggests a discover and transform method which uses reading to teach writing.
Reading-Writing Relations.
87. Arapoff, N. (1968). Controlled rhetoric frames. *English Language Teaching Journal, 23*(1), 27-36.
Provides a grid to control student choice of content and rhetoric in successive sentences on a teacher-provided topic.
Control/Rhetoric.
88. Arapoff, N. (1967a, April). Writing: A thinking process. Paper presented at the 1st TESOL Convention, Miami Beach, FL.
See next item.

See next item.
Cognition.

89. Arapoff, N. (1967b). Writing: A thinking process. *TESOL Quarterly, 1*, 33-39.
Claims that learning to write is different from other language skills. Suggests a curriculum based on writing three types of expository prose: reporting, organizing, explaining, and evaluating.
Curriculum/ Cognition.

90. Arcinegas, M., & Vincent, A. (1992, March). *Process-based writing for ESL students: Is there a difference?* Paper presented at the 26th Annual TESOL Convention, Vancouver, BC.
Compares the difference in using a process based approach with elementary and secondary school native and non-native students.
NS-NNS Comparisons/Elementary/Secondary School.

91. Ard, J. (1981, March). *Use of bilingual dictionaries in ESL composition.* Paper presented at the 15th Annual TESOL Convention, Detroit, MI.
Reports case studies that mention how bilingual dictionaries are actually used by ESL students in composing.
Lexis/Dictionaries.

92. Arena, L. A. (1983). Accuracy vs. fluency revisited for the advanced ESL composition class. In R. J. DiPietro, & W. E. Frawley (Eds.), *The First Delaware Symposium on Language Studies: Selected papers* (pp. 316-324). Newark, DE: University of Delaware Press.
Re-evaluates the traditional orientation of ESL composition and proposes that fluency should be fostered without accepting inaccuracy. Gives several solutions to problems associated with an emphasis on fluency.
Advanced/Accuracy/Fluency

93. Arena, L. A. (1975a). A method for improving the writing skills of foreign students in University-level expository English composition courses. In M. K. Burt, & H. C. Dulay (Eds.), *On TESOL '75: New directions in second language learning, teaching, and bilingual education* (pp. 281-291). Washington, DC: TESOL.
Presents a clause analysis (similar to T-unit analysis) that purports to define objectively the structural style of expository writing. Also suggests that sentence embedding is not characteristic of all languages (e.g., Farsi and Hebrew).
Objective Measures/Style.

94. Arena, L. A. (1975b, March). *"Structural fingerprinting": A method for the improvement of writing skills of foreign students in university level expository composition courses.* Paper presented at the 9th Annual TESOL Convention, Los Angeles, CA.
Describes a writer's idiolect in terms of the type, number, and frequency of clause usage. Reports expected frequency for the basic types in expository writing as: 50% transitive clauses; 20% intransitive; 20% equational; and 10% passive.
Style/Syntactic Structures.

95. Arkin, M. (1982). *Tutoring ESL students: A guide for tutors (and teachers) in the subject areas.* NY: Longman.

volume focuses on problems in all skills areas.
Tutoring.

96. Arnaudet, M. L., & Barrett, M. E. (1984). *Approaches to academic reading & writing*. NY: Prentice-Hall Regents.
Provides a guide to intensive analytic reading of academic prose and the writing skills needed to succeed with academic writing assignments.
University/Advanced/Textbook.

97. Arnaudet, M. L., & Barrett, M. E. (1981). *Paragraph development: A guide for students in a second language*. Englewood Cliffs, NJ: Prentice-Hall Regents.
This writing textbook focuses on the paragraph. Topic sentences, supportive evidence, and unity are emphasized.
Advanced/Textbook.

98. Arndt, V. (1993). Response to writing: Using feedback to inform the writing process. In M. N. Brock, & L. W. Walters (Eds.), *Teaching composition around the Pacific Rim: Politics and pedagogy* (pp. 90-116). Clevedon, ENG: Multilingual Matters.
Claims that the use of feedback is essential in the teaching of writing. Examines teachers' and students' perceptions of effective feedback and suggests ways to promote the effective use of feedback in a writing class.
Feedback.

99. Arndt, V. (1987a). First and foreign language composing: A protocol-based study. In T. Bloor, & J. Norrish (Eds.), *Written language: Papers from the Annual Meeting of the British Association for Applied Linguistics*. London: CILT.
Reports results from a comparative, protocol-based study of six Chinese EFL graduate students. Two versions of an academic essay for a Chinese and an English audience were written. Finds several approaches to generating ideas, but inadequate coherence strategies, an absence of a metacognitive critical perspective, and an incomplete personal commitment to meaning.
Chinese/NS-NNS Comparisons.

100. Arndt, V. (1987b). Six writers in search of texts: A protocol-based study of L1 and L2 writing. *ELT Journal, 41*, 257-267.
Proposes protocol analysis as a teaching tool helpful in diagnosing writers' deficiencies. Explores the writing processes of postgraduate EFL students in China and suggests the need of more help by students with the demands of writing-as-text.
Assessment/Chinese/Graduate Students.

101. Aron, H.(1989, March). *Double-entry notebooks: Successful technique for reading/writing classes*. Paper presented at the 23rd Annual TESOL Convention, San Antonio, TX.
Discusses how to use a journal technique for ESL classes.
Reading-Writing Relations.

102. Aron, H., & Jeannet, J. (1992, March). *Writing the research paper: Procedures, promises, and pitfalls*. Paper presented at the 26th Annual TESOL Convention, Vancouver, BC.
Describes an approach to teaching research writing at a liberal arts college.
Research Writing.

Research Writing.

103. Arthur. B. (1983, March). *Teaching independence to advanced EFL writers*. Paper presented at the 17th Annual TESOL Convention, Toronto, BC.

Describes self-editing strategies, developing independent awareness and successful error correction.

Editing/Advanced.

104. Arthur, B. (1980). Short-term changes in EFL composition skills. In C. Yorio, K. Perkins, & J. Schachter (Eds.), *On TESOL '79* (pp. 330-342). Washington, DC: TESOL.

Examines changes in writing of lower-intermediate ESL adult learners during an eight-week period. Thirteen ESL teachers ranked a sample of 152 timed, in-class compositions written by 14 lower-intermediate adult students. Students improved their writing speed and vocabulary size during the test period. Length of each composition was the best predictor of teacher ranking. A single composition is not a reliable basis for judging the writing ability of a student.

Assessment/Intermediate.

105. Asaad, S. B. (1985). The construction and validation of a multiple-choice and a performance test of communicative writing abilities for the EFL classroom. *Dissertation Abstracts International*, 45(9), 2880A.

Develops and examines the validity of a multiple-choice and a performance test in assessing the communicative writing ability of Arabic-speaking EFL students. Results suggest that the writing performance test and an analytic scoring procedure are objective in evaluation, while the multiple-choice test does not measure receptive writing ability.

Assessment.

106. Ascher, A. (1993). *Thinking about editing: An ESL writer's guide*. Boston: Heinle & Heinle.

A grammar-editing guide for self-editing for academic purposes.

Textbook/Editing.

107. Asenavage, K., & Connor, U. M. (1993, April). *Social interaction, peer collaboration, and the ESL writing process*. Paper presented at 44th Annual Convention of CCCC, San Diego, CA.

Peer Response.

108. Atatri, O. F. (1984a). A contrastive analysis of Arab and American university students' strategies in accomplishing written English discourse functions: Implications for EFL. *Dissertation Abstracts International*, 44(10), 3047A.

Hypothesizes that the stylistic problems of Arab students in composition are caused by different communicative strategies like introducing a broad statement instead of a topic sentence or elaborating one topic frame and not the others. Adopts a functional approach to data analysis which confirms the hypothesis that the writing strategies of Arab students run counter to native readers' expectations.

Arabic/Speaking-Writing Relations.

109. Atari, O. F. (1984b). Oral style strategies in EFL written discourse. In I. Abu-Salim, & J. Owens (Eds.), *Proceedings of the Third Annual Linguistics Conference* (pp. 35-

006].
Finds support in an analysis of EFL essays for the transfer of stylistic strategies typical of spoken Arabic. Suggests that teachers engage in questioning and requests for specific information in order to cultivate specificity in the written English of Arab learners.
Arabic/Speaking-Writing Relations.

110. Atkinson, D., & Hedgcock, J. (1990, March). *Effects of extensive genre-specific reading on L2 writing*. Paper presented at the 24th Annual TESOL Convention, San Francisco, CA.
No significant results were found for the genre hypothesis (Smith 1988) that written competence in a genre is only acquired through a combination of extensive genre-specific reading and an integrative approach to a discourse community which communicates in that genre.
Reading-Writing Relations.

111. Auerbach, B., & Snyder, B. (1983). *Paragraph patterns*. NY: Harcourt Brace Jovanovich.
An eclectic writing textbook exclusively devoted to paragraphs, emphasizing different rhetorical modes, pre-writing strategies, sentence-combining, and editing.
Intermediate/University/Textbook.

112. Auerbach, E. R. (1992). *Making meaning, making change: Participatory curriculum development for adult ESL literacy*. Language in Education: Theory & Practice 78. Washington, DC: ERIC/LE. [ERIC ED 356 688].
Relevant for the ESL teacher who needs to provide reading and writing for an adult population, this guide examines how to serve the needs of literacy limited students and develop a curriculum around themes with a participatory approach.
Literacy/Adult Education.

113. Aungprethep, C. (1989). The self-reported composing experiences of four Thai ESL writers. *Dissertation Abstracts International, 50*(7), 1969A.
Research conducted through interviews, observations, and examination of written products of four Thai ESL students shows four phases in their composing process. Results indicate the need for teachers of English in Thailand to re-evaluate the traditional materials and methods used to teach writing.
Thai.

114. Austin, J. S. (1992, March). *Collaborative writing: Language development in the L2 writing classroom*. Paper presented at the 26th Annual TESOL Convention, Vancouver, BC.
Discusses how communicative language pedagogy meshes with academic collaborative learning.
Collaboration/Communicative Writing.

115. Austin, J. S. (1988, March). *A literature-based composition class: Problems and solutions*. Paper presented at the 39th Annual CCCC Meeting, St. Louis, MO.
Literature.

116. Austin, J. S., Eisterhold, J. C., & Hagemann, J. A. (1988, March). *A critical reading and writing course: Problems and solutions*. Paper presented at the 22nd Annual

TESOL Convention, Chicago, IL.
Workshop discusses problems in teaching critical reading and writing courses.
Reading-Writing Relations/Advanced.

117. Autonomous Metropolitan University. (1979). *On some conjuncts signalling dissonance in written expository English Mexico City, Mexico* . Washington, DC: ERIC/FLL. [ERIC ED 198 732].
Claims that contrastive connectives (yet, in contrast, however, nevertheless, on the other hand) not only express a logical relationship between texts they connect but also in some cases mark a particular kind of contrast called "dissonance." States that this type of use of connectives must be taught to ESL students within the framework of discourse contexts.
Cohesion.

118. Ayari, S. (1993, April). *The role of NL in L2 writing: Arabic learners of English.* Paper presented at the 27th Annual TESOL Convention, Atlanta, GA.
Discusses the influence of native rhetorical conventions on writing in Arabic and English and the extent to which L1 is a positive resource.
Arabic/L1 Influence.

119. Azabdaftari, B. (1981). A quantitative versus a qualitative approach to teaching English composition. *English Language Teaching Journal, 35*(4), 411-415.
Reviews arguments concerning the optimal amount of writing and the extent of control in ESL composition. Concludes that a qualitative approach that engenders a positive learner attitude is best.
Fluency/Control.

120. Azabdaftari, B. (1976). A study of the problems of teaching English composition to Iranian senior high school students and suggestions for improving current practices. *Dissertation Abstracts International, 37*(5), 2766A.
Discusses techniques in learning how to write, such as sentence-combining, the use of grammar, and the relationships between oral language, reading, and the ability to write well in relation to the problems encountered by Iranian students learning to write acceptable English. Recommendations are designed for secondary school teacher in Iran.
Iran/Secondary School.

B

121. Babayan, D., & Mallony, L. (1987, April). *Writing as thinking: A four-step approach.* Paper presented at the 21st Annual TESOL Convention, Miami Beach, FL.
Offers a workshop on teaching of writing as a thinking process.
Cognition.

122. Bacha, N. S., & Hanania, E. A. S. (1980). Difficulty in learning and effectiveness of teaching transitional words: A study on Arabic-speaking university students. *TESOL Quarterly, 14*, 251-254.
Claims that the difficulty Arabic students have with transitional words in

English is developmental rather than due to interference from native rhetorical pattern. Suggests suitable teaching material.
Cohesion/Arabic.

123. Bacheller, F. I. (1991, March). *Teaching ESL graduate students to summarize research articles*. Paper presented at the 25th Annual TESOL Convention, New York, NY.
Discusses techniques that help ESL graduate students learn to summarize research articles in their own words.
Summary Writing/Research Writing.

124. Bacheller, F. I. (1988). *Start writing*. Englewood Cliffs, NJ: Prentice Hall.
Leads novice writers learning academic writing skills from structured listening practice to the writing of simple paragraphs. Model compositions are read and discussed; dictation and exercises on the conventions of writing included.
Beginners/Textbook.

125. Bacheller, F. I., & Harter, C. (1980, May). *An integrated approach to ESL classroom teaching and learning*. Paper presented at the Annual NAFSA Meeting, St. Louis, MO.
Curriculum.

126. Badawi, M., Iskander, M., & Hozayin, R. (1993, April). *IEP composition raters: Hidden agendas and consciousness-raising*. Paper presented at the 27th Annual TESOL Convention, Atlanta, GA.
Discusses the influence of characteristic rating styles on the scoring of ESL compositions by IEP teachers.
IEP/Raters.

127. Badger, R. (1989, April). *Referential cohesion in law cases*. Paper presented at the IATEFL Meeting, Coventry, ENG. [ERIC ED 321 886].
Analyzes referential cohesion in text reporting a law case for use in ESL materials.
Cohesion/Law.

128. Bahtia, A. T. (1974). An error analysis of students' compositions. *IRAL, 12*(4), 337-350.
The most frequent errors in the compositions of ten American Indians were predominantly with verb forms and article usage.
Error Analysis/Amer-Indian.

129. Bailey, L. (1993, April). *How ESL writers use commonly taught prewriting techniques*. Paper presented at the 27th Annual TESOL Convention, Atlanta, GA.
Discusses how ESL students incorporate invention techniques into their own writing processes.
Invention.

130. Bailey, N. H., & Flahive, D. E. (1992, March). *Integrating social and cognitive approaches in reading/writing curricula*. Paper presented at the 26th Annual TESOL Convention, Vancouver, BC.
Argues for a holistic, theoretical approach to the reading-writing curriculum. Shows how social interaction and reader response can be integrated with content-

based instruction and formalism.
Reading-Writing Relations/Curriculum.

131. Bajek, M. M., & Bratt, T. D. (1984, March). *A structured approach to freeing ESL students to write*. Paper presented at the 18th Annual TESOL Convention, Houston, TX.
Proposes a five-step writing process to bring out the best in high school ESL students.
Secondary School/Control.

132. Ball, W. E. (1986). Writing English script: An overlooked skill. *ELT Journal, 40*, 291-298.
Identifies common English handwriting problems of writers whose native script is Arabic and recommends ways to improve.
Handwriting/Arabic.

133. Ballajthy, E. (1989, November). *Computers in curricula program for networked college-level writing process instruction: A first-year report*. Paper presented at the College Reading Association, Philadelphia, PA. [ERIC ED 309 455].
Describes applications of local area computer networks for ESL and developmental writing.
Computers/Networking/NS-NNS Comparisons.

134. Ballard, B. (1984). Improving student writing: An integrated approach to cultural adjustment. In R. Williams, J. M. Swales, & J. Kirkman (Eds.), *Common ground: Shared interests in ESP and communication studies* (pp. 43-53). Oxford: Pergamon.
Describes the double cultural shift in styles of thinking and learning encountered by second language students entering the university discourse community in Australia.
Discourse Communities/Culture.

135. Ballard, B., & Clanchy, J. (1991). Assessment by misconception: Cultural influences and intellectual traditions. In L. Hamp-Lyons (Ed.), *Assessing second language writing in academic contexts* (pp. 19-35). Norwood, NJ: Ablex.
Discusses ways in which second language students in the Australian context are actually assessed in their university courses across the curriculum.
Assessment/University/WAC.

136. Ballwey, L. W., Muhlhousen, K. E., de Quincey, P., & Reid, J. M. (1987, April). *A farewell to typewriters: Computer-associated writing*. Paper presented at the 21st Annual TESOL Convention, Miami Beach, FL.
Colloquium on theoretical and practical aspects of using computer technology in writing class.
Computers/Word Processing.

137. Bander, R. G. (1985). *American English rhetoric: A writing program for English as a second language*. (Third Ed.) NY: Harcourt Brace Jovanovich.
Classic text on expository writing contains examples with commentary so that students will become more aware of significant aspects of writing organization from the paragraph to complete composition. Covers topic sentences, coherence, outlining, subordination, run-on sentences, and transitions.

Advanced/University/Textbook.

138. Bander, R. G. (1982). *Sentence making: A writing workbook in English as a second language*. NY: Harcourt Brace Jovanovich.

   Aims to lead students to write complex sentences.
   Intermediate/Textbook.

139. Bang, H. P. (1986). The effect of using class discussion as a pre-writing activity in teaching composition to ESL students (Texas). *Dissertation Abstracts International, 47*(11), 4005A.

   Examines the effect of class discussion as a pre-writing activity on writing performance of two levels of ESL students in an intensive English program. Results indicate no significant differences, although verbally active students wrote better compositions than non-verbally active students. Quality of discussion also affected writing.
   Invention/Speaking-Writing Relations.

140. Bannai, H., & Wulf, K. M. (1986, March). *The USC-ESL secondary writing project: A preliminary report*. Paper presented at the 20th Annual TESOL Convention, Anaheim, CA.

   Discusses a four-week program based on the Bay Area Writing Project.
   Secondary School/Programs.

141. Bannai, H., & Wulf, K. M. (1987, April). *Teaching writing to secondary ESL students: A checklist*. Paper presented at the 21st Annual TESOL Convention, Miami Beach, FL.

   Discusses a checklist designed for teachers to coach each other on techniques learned.
   Secondary School/Teacher Preparation.

142. Bardovi-Harlig, K. (1992). A second look at T-unit analysis: Reconsidering the sentence. *TESOL Quarterly, 26*, 390-395.

   Proposes a coordination measure of sentences as an alternative to T-unit analysis which has several disadvantages in assessing syntactic complexity. Results of a study of eighty-six compositions by ESL students at seven proficiency levels in an intensive program indicate that the number of combinations from coordination decreases with proficiency.
   Objective Measures/Syntactic Structures.

143. Bardovi-Harlig, K. (1990). Pragmatic word order in English composition. In U. M. Connor, & A. M. Johns (Ed.), *Coherence in writing: Research and pedagogical perspectives* (pp. 43-65). Alexandria, VA: TESOL.

   Discusses the pragmatic function of word order in English, using five syntactic structures to illustrate how the English sentence is sensitive to pragmatic organization. Shows five ways to introduce the concepts of topic and focus in the teaching of composition.
   Coherence.

144. Bardovi-Harlig, K., & Bofman, T. (1989). Attainment of syntactic and morphological accuracy by advanced language learners. *Studies in Second Language Acquisition, 11*(1), 17-34.

Examines relationship between syntactic development and overall accuracy in written compositions of advanced EFL students. Finds similar acquisition profiles among thirty learners across five language groups: Arabic, Chinese, Korean, Spanish, and Malay. Learners are relatively weak in morphological accuracy but strong in syntactic patterning.
Language Development/Arabic/Chinese/Korean/Hispanic/Malay.

145. Bardovi-Harlig, K., & Bofman, T. (1988, March). *A second look at T-unit analysis.* Paper presented at the 22nd Annual TESOL Convention, Chicago, IL.
Shows that a sentence-based analysis with a coordination index is superior to that T-unit in measuring syntactic complexity.
Objective Measures/Syntactic Development.

146. Barker, D., & Morrisroe, S. (1983, March). *Independent and instructional levels of writing: A dual approach.* Paper presented at the 17th Annual TESOL Convention, Toronto, BC.
Offers a two-level approach to problems ESL high school students have writing in class.
Secondary School/Curriculum.

147. Barkho, L. Y. (1987). Interlanguage across academic contexts. *English for Specific Purposes, 6,* 157-161.
Attributes variation in essay examination products by Iraqi university students to motivation and preparation for an ESP course.
Interlanguage/Evaluation/Arabic.

148. Bar-Lev, Z. (1986). Discourse theory and "Contrastive Rhetoric". *Discourse Processes, 9*(2), 235-246.
Appraises Kaplan's notion in light of a multilingual research project on discourse structure but concludes that contrastive rhetoric needs revision.
Contrastive Rhetoric.

149. Barnes, G. A. (1983). Comments on Vivian Zamel's "Writing: The process of discovering meaning" . . . [In The Forum]. *TESOL Quarterly, 17,* 137-139.
Questions the absence of a definition of the written product in Zamel's approach, especially for ESP.
Process Instruction/ESP.

150. Barnes, L. L. (1990, March). *Training ESL writing instructors: The ignored curriculum.* Paper presented at the 24th Annual TESOL Convention, San Francisco, CA.
Offers guidance to writing teachers and administrators in differentiating basic ESL writers from proficient ESL writers. Examines ESL writing samples in order to compare the characteristic rhetorical and stylistic features of proficient ESL writing to those of basic writing.
Evaluation/NS-NNS Comparisons.

151. Barnes, L. L. (1984). Communicative competence in the composition classroom: A discourse analysis. *Dissertation Abstracts International, 45*(9), 2856A.
Examines the written interchange between teacher and student in the composition class. Findings reveal that teachers' comments vary according to

proficiency of student and that teachers' comments are often misunderstood by unskilled students, therefore, affecting revision. Suggests skills required for communicative competence in composition class.
Interaction/Feedback/Revision.

152. Barnes, M. E., Medina, S. L., Plaskoff, J., & Robertson, M. M. (1990, March). *A metacognitive strategy for teaching essay planning to ESL students: A computer-based instructional design*. Paper presented at the 24th Annual TESOL Convention, San Francisco, CA. [ERIC ED 359 807].
Describes a lesson that aims to help ESL college and graduate students develop the metacognitive skills for planning well-organized essays.
Metacognition/Computers/Planning.

153. Barnwell, D. (1988). Some comments on T-unit research. *System, 16*, 187-192.
Shows how the T-unit is not symptomatic of greater maturity.
Objective Measures/T-Unit.

154. Barrett, M. E. (1992, March). *Learner perceptions about word processing and improved language skills*. Paper presented at the 26th Annual TESOL Convention, Vancouver, BC.
Reports the results of a survey of 74 students about using word processing in writing classes. Results indicate a self-reported decrease in anxiety and belief in its effectiveness in improving writing skills.
Computers/Word Processing.

155. Barrett. M. E. (1987). Two critical elements in teaching composition. In C. Cargill (Ed.), *A TESOL professional anthology: Grammar and composition* (pp. 67-75). Littlewood, IL: National Textbook Co.
Offers practical suggestions and examples for getting university ESL students started composing by presenting several sources for topic assignments and by teaching them how to plan an introduction to an academic composition.
Academic Writing/Topic/Introductions.

156. Bartelo, D. M. (1984). *Getting the picture of reading and writing: A look at drawings, composing and oral language of limited English proficient children*. Alexandria, VA: United States Department of Education. [ERIC ED 245 533].
Reports research from a descriptive study of first-grade LEP children writing after a natural reading experience.
Reading-Writing Relations/Children.

157. Bartelo, D. M. (1983). *Bridging the gap to literacy: Functional writing instruction for ESOL students* . Washington, DC: ERIC/FLL. [ERIC ED 230 029].
Proposes an introductory lesson plan to help ESL writers put into words what they want to say. Reviews basic capitalization rules on how to write sentences expressing name, address, and employment.
Literacy.

158. Bartelo, D. M. (1982). Functional lessons for ESL students. In C. Carter (Ed.), *Non-native and non-standard dialect students* (pp. 3-5). Urbana, IL: NCTE.
Describes lessons for integrating language skills.
Classroom Activities/Secondary School.

159. Bartelt, H. G. (1983). Transfer and variability of rhetorical redundancy in Apachean English. In S. M. Gass, & L. Selinker (Eds.), *Language transfer in language learning* (pp. 297-305). Rowley, MA: Newbury House.
    Studies the transfer of oral discourse style of Navajo and Apache to written English.
    Amer-Indian/L1 Influence/Speaking-Writing Relations.

160. Bartelt, H. G. (1982a). Rhetorical redundancy in Apachean English inter-language. In H. G. Bartelt, S. Penfield-Jasper, & B. Hoffner (Eds.), *Essays in native American English* (pp. 157-172). San Antonio, TX: Trinity University Press.
    The writing of English by Navaho and Apache-speaking college students shows use of lexical and phrasal redundancy to emphasize emotional concerns, exemplifying transfer of a spoken language rule.
    Amer-Indian/L1 Influence.

161. Bartelt, H. G. (1982b). Tense switching in narrative English discourse of Navajo & Western Apache speakers. *Studies in Second Language Acquisition*, *4*(2), 201-204.
    Native American ESL writers make transfer errors in the English tense-aspect system.
    Amer-Indian/Narrative.

162. Bartelt, H. G. (1980a). Creative ESL composition for the bilingual Indian student. *Journal of American Indian Education*, *19*(3), 8-10.
    A case is made for using a cognitive-based model in English as a second language (ESL) composition courses for bilingual Indian students. A cognitive teaching method, such as the generative rhetoric approach, can capitalize on the innate language competence of the bilingual Indian student. In this approach, the bilingual Indian student is allowed to be creative with maximum control of his own learning efforts.
    Amer-Indian/Generative Rhetoric.

163. Bartelt, H. G. (1980b). Exercises for writing problems of Navajo and Spanish speakers. *Teaching English in the Two-Year College*, *7*, 45-53.
    Provides the rationale, goals, and procedures for three levels of writing instruction for non-native students attending U.S. junior colleges.
    Hispanic/Amer-Indian/University.

164. Barton, E. L., & Yontz, R. A. (1986, March). *The conventions of argumentative essays: What ESL writers need to know.* Paper presented at the 37th Annual CCCC Meeting, New Orleans, LA.
    Argumentation/Conventions.

165. Basham, C. S. (1987, April). *Summary writing in cross-cultural perspective.* Paper presented at the 21st Annual TESOL Convention, Miami Beach, FL.
    Compares summary protocols of Alaskan native students, remedial English students, and experienced writers. Shows influence of cultural schemata on task.
    Summary Writing/Culture.

166. Basham, C. S. (1983, March). *Talking about writing.* Paper presented at the 17th Annual TESOL Convention, Toronto, BC.

Discusses research on the effect of question types on ESL writing in the context of peer reading and editing in advanced intensive English.
Speaking-Writing Relations/Peer Response.

167. Basham, C. S., & Kwachka, P. E. (1991). Reading the world differently: A cross-cultural approach to writing assessment. In L. Hamp-Lyons (Ed.), *Assessing second language writing in academic contexts* (pp. 37-49). Norwood, NJ: Ablex.
Finds two major trends: personalization of knowledge and excessive qualification -- in a limited sample of Alaskan Native student writers.
Assessment/Culture/Alaskan.

168. Basham, C. S., & Kwachka, P. E. (1989a, March). *Reading the world differently: Cross-cultural writing assessment*. Paper presented at the 23rd Annual TESOL Convention, San Antonio, TX.
Discusses cultural sensitivity in testing writing for native American Alaskan students because they interpret test prompts in a culturally related way.
Prompts/Culture/Alaskan.

169. Basham, C. S., & Kwachka, P. E. (1989b). Variations in modal use by Alaskan Eskimo student writers. In S. M. Gass, C. Madden, D. Preston, & L. Selinker (Eds.), *Variations in second language acquisition: Discourse and pragmatics* (pp. 129-143). Clevedon, UK: Multilingual Matters.
Discusses several ways in which Eskimo students have extended the standard functions of models to encode their own cultural values.
Variation/Alaskan/Culture.

170. Basham, C. S., Ray, R. E., & Whalley, E. (1993). Cross-cultural perspectives on task representation in reading to write. In J. G. Carson, & I. Leki (Eds.), *Reading in the composition classroom: Second language perspectives* (pp. 299-314). Boston: Heinle & Heinle.
Reports research investigating cultural assumptions about reading, authorship, and task representation and how differences among students influence the "reading-when-you-intend-to-write" and their resulting texts.
Reading-Writing Relations/Culture.

171. Basham, C. S., & Rounds, P. L. (1984a). A discourse analysis approach to summary writing. *TESOL Quarterly, 18*, 527.
A study of reporting and evaluating writing done by advanced ESL students in an academic entry English program finds that students tend to use author's exact words.
Summary Writing/Advanced.

172. Basham, C. S., & Rounds, P. L. (1984b, March). *A discourse analysis approach to summary writing*. Paper presented at the 18th Annual TESOL Convention, Houston, TX.
Analyzes the typical strategies and discourse level errors in post-reading summaries written by advanced ESL students.
Summary Writing/Strategies/Errors.

173. Baskoff, F. S. (1990a). *New worlds: A course in guided composition, with reading and conversation*. Boston: Heinle & Heinle.

Text uses readings and conversation activities to generate discussion, provide an overview of American culture, and create a context for students' written work. Each chapter includes a model composition, grammar, review, adapted readings from books, newspapers, and magazines, as well as oral and written exercises aimed at helping students in everyday situations.

Intermediate/Textbook.

174. Baskoff, F. S. (1990b, March). *Overcoming writing anxiety*. Paper presented at the 24th Annual TESOL Convention, San Francisco, CA.

Claims that the use of topical readings and discussions, pre-writing interactive group exercises, and carefully chosen models and outlines enable students to start writing compositions with a minimum of errors and reluctance at a very early stage of second language learning.

Affect/Beginners.

175. Baskoff, F. S. (1981). A new look at guided writing. *English Teaching Forum*, *19*(3), 2-6.

Reviews the basic procedures for teaching students to follow a model when writing their own paragraphs.

Control/Paragraph.

176. Baskoff, F. S. (1979, May). *A new look at guided writing or overcoming the "I hate to write" syndrome*. Paper presented at the ESL section of the Annual Conference of the Canadian Council of Teachers of English, Ottawa, Ontario. [ERIC ED 193 957].

Describes a technique that uses guided writing after model paragraphs to teach writing to beginning and intermediate ESL students. Claims that this method makes writing a more pleasurable activity.

Control/Models/Beginners.

177. Bassett, L. (1991, March). *The politics of teaching writing in adult ESL*. Paper presented at the 25th Annual TESOL Convention, New York, NY.

Examines one teacher's goals, assignments, interventions, and responses in order to identify the underlying ideology in the teaching of writing in community-based adult ESL.

Adult Education.

178. Bassett, L. (1990, March). *Empowerment or silencing: Teaching writing in adult ESL*. Paper presented at the 24th Annual TESOL Convention, San Francisco, CA.

Presents a model for assessing factors that empower and silence writers in community-based adult ESL classes. Using results of a four-month ethnographic study of writing in one classroom, it discusses how writing assignments, teaching processes, and teacher responses empower or silence these writers.

Adult Education/Ethnographic Research.

179. Bataineh, R. F. (1993). English syntax: Problems of acquisition. A cross-sectional study of the written compositions of Jordanian learners of English as a second language. *Dissertation Abstracts International*, *54*(1), 113A.

Conducts a cross-sectional study of the major syntactic errors in compositions by sixty Jordanian ESL students at three proficiency levels. The five major syntactic errors tabulated are the use of articles, prepositions, verbs, tense, and concord.

Offers a variety of explanations as to the cause of these errors.
Error Analysis.

180. Batchelor, K., & Slaughter, R. (1993). *The writing challenge*. Boston: Heinle & Heinle.
Text addresses the adult ESL learner's writing skills in a variety of areas: academic, vocational, survival, and personal. Features learning by doing, examples, and exercises and contains a section on new vocabulary in each lesson.
Adult Education/Intermediate/Textbook.

181. Bates, L. N. (1993a, April). *Teaching coherence in the ESL technical writing classroom*. Paper presented at the 27th Annual TESOL Convention, Atlanta, GA.
Shows how to assist technical writers with coherence by improving a number of discourse factors.
Technical Writing.

182. Bates, L. N. (1993b). *Transitions: An interactive reading, writing, and grammar text*. NY: St. Martin's Press.
Designed for students moving from writing paragraghs to essays, from concrete to abstract topics, and from personal to academic writing.
Textbook/Advanced.

183. Bates, L. N. (1988, March). *Application: Helping the non-ESL teacher work with the ESL basic writer*. Paper presented at the 39th Annual CCCC Meeting, St. Louis, MO.
NS-NNS Comparisons.

184. Bates, L. N., Lane, J., & Lange, E. (1993). *Writing clearly: Responding to ESL compositions*. Boston: Heinle & Heinle.
A practical teaching resource for writing instructors at all levels that provides a step-by-step system dealing with aspects of responding, correcting, and grading ESL writing. Addresses the questions of stance and of content and offers sample student papers.
Responding/Teacher Preparation.

185. Bates, L. N., Lane, J., & Lange, E. (1989, March). *Training mainstream composition teachers to work with ESL students*. Paper presented at the 23rd Annual TESOL Convention, San Antonio, TX.
Presents error analysis charts for training instructors without ESL experience.
NS-NNS Comparisons/Error Analysis.

186. Bauder, T. (1981). *Write English!: Books 1,2, 3*. Glenview, IL: NTC Publishing Group.
Provides practice in writing tasks needed to function in school and everyday life.
Secondary School/Textbook.

187. Bauer, W. J. (1979). *A guide to teaching writing and composition skills to students of ESL*. Unpublished master's thesis, Hunter College, CUNY, New York, NY.
Pedagogy/Teacher Preparation.

188. Baumhover, M. J. (1984). The intercultural class: A challenge for English composition teachers. *Dissertation Abstracts International, 44*(8), 2594A.

Discusses teaching experience with several ESL students in a composition class for native students. Finds that ESL students are the strongest writers in one class. Argues that motivation, especially desire to communicate, can lead to effective writing.

Culture/University/NS-NNS Comparisons.

189. Bayley, R. J. (1990, March). *Some contexts of composing: Case studies of Bolivian teachers*. Paper presented at the 24th Annual TESOL Convention, San Francisco, CA.

Examines the composing processes of EFL teachers responding in English and Spanish to prompts containing graphically represented information. Think-aloud protocol analysis suggests that writers familiar with graphic representation conventions engage in different composing behaviors than those unfamiliar with such conventions, regardless of the language of the task.

Hispanic/Process Research.

190. Bean, M., & Hedgcock, J. (1991, March). *Metaphors and mental imagery: Self-correction aids for novice writers*. Paper presented at the 25th Annual TESOL Convention, New York, NY.

Suggests ways to induce independent editing skills among novice writers.

Beginners/Editing.

191. Bear, J. M. (1986). Development segments in discourse: The interaction of topic and cohesion with implications for native and non-native speakers of English. *Dissertation Abstracts International*, 47(12), 4373A.

Claims that "development segments," i.e., topic plus comment parts that appear as clauses and verbal phrases, can be viewed as the organizing structures of a text. Highlights implication for teaching composition to native and non-native speakers.

Discourse Analysis/Topic.

192. Bear, J. M. (1979). *Topic units in planned English discourse*. Unpublished master's thesis, University of Hawaii, Honolulu, HI. [ERIC ED212 174].

Develops a semantic measure to analyze stylistic variations within texts, which may be effective in teaching composition to non-native students.

Topic/Style/Objective Measures.

193. Beazley, M. R. (1989). The Australaskan writing project: A computer-based intercultural exchange program. In *A Forum anthology, Volume IV: Selected articles from the English Teaching Forum, 1984-1988* (pp. 291-295). Washington, DC: USIA, Bureau of Educational and Cultural Affairs.

Reports the first National Electronic Writing Project in Australia, which networks Australian schools, including Aborigines, exchanging with Inupiat Eskimos in an Alaskan village school. The exchange, incorporating all aspects of English language arts, enables students to build profiles of the respective cultures.

Computers/Secondary School.

194. Bebout, L. J. (1985). An error analysis of misspellings made by learners of English as a first and a second language. *Journal of Psycholinguistic Research*, 14, 569-593.

Three major differences found in a corpus of 700 misspellings by English-

speaking children (9-11 yr. olds) and Spanish adults writing in English attributed to language background and spelling strategies of the two groups.
Spelling/Errors/Hispanic/NS-NNS Comparisons.

195. Beck, R. D. (1977, April). *An error and style analysis of free composition.* Paper presented at the 11th Annual TESOL Convention, Miami Beach, FLA.
Describes written errors by Arabic-speaking university students in Saudi Arabia. Recommends weaker students imitate the sentence style of better students.
Errors/Arabic.

196. Beene, L., Hall, C., & Sunde, K. (1985). *Text linguistics and composition: Research and practical connections.* Urbana, IL: RIE/ERIC. [ERIC ED 272 863].
Presents two studies derived from text linguistics. One uses Grice's Cooperative Principle to analyze instructors' comments on students' writing and to correlate these with freshman writers' evaluation of those comments. The second investigates the use of schema theory to teach rhetorical principles to ESL students.
Pragmatics/Schema.

197. Begay, V., Alarmy, V., Grant, S., & Murphy, B. (1988, March). *Dialogue journals: Teachers and kids learning together.* Paper presented at the 22nd Annual TESOL Convention, Chicago, IL.
Developing writing skills afford teachers insight into communication.
Dialogue Journals/Elementary.

198. Behrens, L., & Rosen, L. J. (1990). *Writing & reading across the curriculum.* (Fourth Ed.). Glenview, IL: Scott Foresman.
A selection of essays from disciplines across the curriculum.
University/Textbook.

199. Beker, C. (1987, April). *The writing process: What's it all about?* Paper presented at the 21st Annual TESOL Convention, Miami Beach, FL.
Advocates exposure to print environment in a non-threatening atmosphere.
Process Instruction/Literacy.

200. Belcher, C. (1990). The case for teacher-student/author conferencing in field-specific writing by graduate students. *TESOL Newsletter, 24*(4), 11-12.
Claims the needs of graduate students call for a field-specific approach to writing and advocates critical awareness of discourse conventions, disciplinary peer pairing, and, especially, conferencing.
Conferencing/ESP.

201. Belcher, D. D. (1992, March). *Writing in multi-paradigm disciplines: The social sciences and humanities.* Paper presented at the 26th Annual TESOL Convention, Vancouver, BC.
Discusses the variability of paradigms and paradigm characteristics in the humanities and social sciences as a problem source for ESL students with high linguistic proficiency who nonetheless have difficulty writing in their fields.
WAC/Research Writing.

202. Belcher, D. D. (1991a). Nonnative writing in a corporate setting. *Technical Writing Teacher, 18*(2), 104-115.
Uses contrastive analysis of semi-technical documents by novice nonnative

speakers and experienced native and nonnative writers to teach advanced learners in a research and development unit of a corporation.
Technical Writing/Advanced.

203. Belcher, D. D. (1991b, March). *Teaching the rhetoric of critical writing.* Paper presented at the 25th Annual TESOL Convention, New York, NY.
Argues for existence of common organizational strategies and evaluative or critical language and the use of critical rhetoric as a heuristic enabling non-native speakers to enter their academic discourse communities.
Discourse Communities/Invention/WAC.

204. Belcher, D. D. (1990). Peer versus teacher response in the advanced composition class. *Issues, 2,* 128-150.
Discusses the problem of response as it relates to discipline-specific writing in either WAC or ESP contexts.
Peer Response/ESP.

205. Belcher, D. D. (1989a, March). *Critical writing and the Chinese ESL student.* Paper presented at the 23rd Annual TESOL Convention, San Antonio, TX.
Compares critical reviews written by advanced ESL students from China, Europe and Latin America.
Academic Writing/Chinese/Hispanic.

206. Belcher, D. D. (1989b, March). *How professors initiate nonnative speakers into the academic discourse community.* Paper presented at the 40th Annual CCCC Meeting, Seattle, WA.
Reports the results of a survey of graduate students about how their content-area professors respond to their writing in the disciplines.
Discourse Communities.

207. Belcher, D. D. (1989c). How professors initiate NNS students into their disciplinary discourse communities. *Texas Papers in Foreign Language Education, 1,* 207-225.
Graduate students attending ESL classes, according to a survey at a major American research institution, perceive content-area professors as more likely to respond to students' ideas and reasoning than to their language, have great faith in the advisor/student relationship, recognize the importance of the reading-writing connection, but do not highly value peer feedback.
Academic Writing/Discourse Communities.

208. Belcher, D. D. (1989d). *Is there an audience in the advanced EAP composition class?* Urbana, IL: ERIC/RCS. [ERIC ED 316 028].
Discusses how EAP students can collaborate as peer reviewers for content-area student writers.
Academic Writing/Audience.

209. Belcher, D. D. (1988, March). *Using peer review in the advanced ESP composition classroom.* Paper presented at the 22nd Annual TESOL Convention, Chicago, IL. [ERIC ED 316 028].
Argues that EAP students should act as peer reviewers for papers in their disciplines.
Peer Response/WAC.

210. Belcher, D. D., & Braine, G. (Eds.). (1994). *Academic writing in a second language: Essays on research and pedagogy* Norwood, NJ: Ablex.

    This collection of 16 original essays by researchers focuses on the issues, research, management, and pedagogy of teaching writing for academic disciplines. It concerns the preparation of ESL students, both graduates and undergraduates, to write for in specific academic discourse communities in ways that are shaped by the genres, tasks, and conventions of the academic cultures to which they seek assimilation and the responses, evaluation, and interaction of courses across the curriculum to writing by ESL students.
    Academic Writing/Graduate Students.

211. Belcher, D. D., Braine, G., Carson, J. E., Johns, A. M., Prior, P. A., & Snow, M. A. (1993, April). *The nature of academic literacy: Approaches to research and pedagogy*. Colloquium presented at the 27th Annual TESOL Convention, Atlanta GA.

    Individual presenters discuss topics on university academic literacy, such as task complexity, cognitive apprenticeship, literacy collaborations, literacy views among others.
    Academic Writing/Literacy.

212. Belcher, D. D., Braine, G., Dudley-Evans, T., Huckin, T. N., Leki, I., Swales, J. M., & Weissberg, R. C. (1992, March). *Teaching research writing to nonnative speakers: Possibilities and proposals*. Colloquium presented at the 26th Annual TESOL Convention, Vancouver, BC.
    Colloquium focuses on how ESL teachers facilitate the research writing process of NNS undergraduates, graduates, and practicing professionals.
    Research Writing.

213. Belcher, L. R. (1989). ESL composition: Analyzing revision. *Dissertation Abstracts International*, 50(5), 1237A.

    Describes a case study of textual changes between the first and final drafts by 22 subjects subdivided into educational levels and language groups (Chinese, Japanese, Korean, Spanish). Finds that most ESL students, despite being unskilled writers, make more meaning changes than surface corrections when they rewrite. However, students from different language backgrounds revise differently. In many ways their revision differences are greater than their similarities.
    Revision/Spanish/Korean/Chinese/Japanese.

214. Belcher, L. R. (1988, March). *Native and non-native composing processes: Analyzing revision*. Paper presented at the 39th Annual CCCC Meeting, St. Louis, MO.
    See previous item.
    Revision/NS-NNS Comparisons.

215. Bell, J. H. (1991). Using peer response groups in ESL writing classes. *TESL Canada Journal*, 8(2), 65-71.
    Describes a structured method for making the transition from traditional class structure to one which uses peer groups, a form of class organization that facilitates audience awareness, at the intermediate-advanced college level.
    Peer Response/University.

216. Bell, J. H., & Burnaby, B. (1984). *A handbook for ESL literacy*. Toronto, Canada: Ontario Institute for Studies in Education.

    A practical guide to teaching initial reading and writing skills to adult students. Chapter on writing advises use of LEA approach, writing whole words, puzzles and games.

    Adult Education/Beginners/LEA.

217. Beller, S. V., Bradin, C., & Hanson-Smith, E. (1992, March). *Computer assisted language learning for reading and writing*. Paper presented at the 26th Annual TESOL Convention, Vancouver, BC.

    Workshop examines ways to match reading and writing objectives with appropriate computer-assisted language learning activities.

    Computers/Reading-Writing Relations.

218. Belnar, J. (1988, March). *From informal to formal: Syntactic variation in written English*. Paper presented at the 22nd Annual TESOL Convention, Chicago, IL.

    Discusses syntactic changes in one writer's use of a variety of registers.

    Register/Syntactic Structures.

219. Benander, R. (1989, March). *An ESL program yearbook as writing and interactional inspiration*. Paper presented at the 23rd Annual TESOL Convention, San Antonio, TX.

    Describes how to use a yearbook as a writing project to give purpose to classroom essays.

    Project Work.

220. Benesch, S. (1993). ESL authors: Reading and publishing autobiographies in a college composition classroom. In J. G. Carson, & I. Leki (Eds.), *Reading in the composition classroom: Second language perspectives* (pp. 247-257). Boston: Heinle & Heinle.

    Describes a class in which students read stories, essays, or poems and write full-length autobiographies in order to demystify the authoring cycle.

    Reading-Writing Relations/Courses.

221. Benesch, S. (1992). Sharing responsibilities: An alternative to the adjunct model. *College ESL*, 2(1), 1-10.

    Critiques the adjunct model of ESL instruction and proposes an approach in which ESL and content area teachers codevelop paired courses.

    Curriculum/University.

222. Benesch, S. (1991). ESL on campus: Questioning testing and tracking policies. In S. Benesch (Ed.), *ESL in America: Myths and possibilities* (pp. 59-74). Portsmouth, NH: Boynton/Cook.

    Discusses the practices and effects of testing and tracking ESL students in the university context. Suggests informal diagnostic interviewing and the linking of language and content instruction as alternative in place of placement testing and remedial coursework.

    University/Assessment.

223. Benesch, S. (1989, March). *Writing chapters: A way to coherence*. Paper presented at the 23rd Annual TESOL Convention, San Antonio, TX.

The drafts and revisions of an ESL class project in which each student wrote a text of several chapters show that project work focuses attention on connections between ideas.
Coherence/Project Work.

224. Benesch, S. (Ed.). (1988a). *Ending remediation: Linking ESL and content in higher education* Washington, DC: TESOL.
Contains six essays which describe efforts to link ESL courses with the content of academic courses in the university, thereby giving ESL courses validity beyond remediation.
University/WAC.

225. Benesch, S. (1988b). Introduction. In S. Benesch (Ed.), *Ending remediation: Linking and content in higher education* (pp. 1-5). Washington, DC: TESOL.
Claims that ESL courses in institutes of higher education should be awarded academic credit and should be equated to foreign language instruction rather than being considered as remedial, since students have demonstrated linguistic ability and skill in a first language. Suggests linking content and instruction as a first step in making ESL students full members of the academic community.
University/NS-NNS Comparisons.

226. Benesch, S. (1988c). Linking content and language teachers: Collaboration across the curriculum. In S. Benesch (Ed.), *Ending remediation: Linking ESL and content in higher education* (pp. 53-66). Washington, DC: TESOL.
Describes an interdisciplinary collaborative project for ESL students that linked together content and language, thereby facilitating learning.
Curriculum/University.

227. Benesch, S. (1987a, March). *Word processing in English as a second language: A case study of three non-native college students*. Paper presented at the 38th Annual CCCC Meeting, Atlanta, GA. [ERIC ED 281 383].
A case study of three non-native speakers of English using a computer reports no effect either upon attitude toward writing or upon composing processes.
Computers/Word Processing.

228. Benesch, S. (1987b, April). *Writing with a computer: The benefits and pitfalls for ESL college students*. Paper presented at the 21st Annual TESOL Convention, Miami Beach, FL.
Reports a case study of how an ESL student used a computer in conjunction with pen and paper to revise and edit.
Computers/Word Processing/Editing.

229. Benesch, S., Rakijas, M., & Rorschach, E. G. (1986). *Academic writing workshop*. Boston: Heinle & Heinle.
Text uses on a process approach and helps students learn to write for college courses. It features exercises involving pair and small-group work, giving and receiving feedback, examples of ESL students' writing and three types of writing assignments per chapter: journal writing, in-class practice, and out-of-class practice.
University/Beginners/Textbook.

230. Benesch, S., & Rorschach, E. G. (1988). *Academic writing workshop II*. Boston:

Heinle & Heinle.

This composition text promotes the fundamentals of fluency, clarity, and correctness of written expression. It encourages peer collaboration, offers strategies for breaking the writing block, and uses writing as a tool for learning. It is organized around a variety of themes and uses samples of student writing.

University/Intermediate/Textbook.

231. Benitez, R. (1990). Using a learning log in an EFL writing class. *English Teaching Forum*, *28*(3), 40-41.

Describes experiences with learning logs in the teaching of writing.

Logs.

232. Benson, B. A. (1980). Quantitative analysis of language structures in compositions written by first and second language learners. *Dissertation Abstracts International*, *41*(5), 1984A.

Describes and compares sentence-level writing abilities of five English-speaking students and six ESL students. Findings show that although there were differences between the groups, they were quantitative rather than qualitative and that groups were similar in syntactic maturity indices and in types of sentence-level difficulties.

Syntactic Structures/NS-NNS Comparisons.

233. Benson, B. A., Deming, M., Denzer, D., & Valeri-Gold, M. (1992). A combined Basic Writing/English as a second language class: Melting pot or mishmash? *Journal of Basic Writing*, *11*(1), 58-74.

A textual comparison of 56 NS and 56 NNS descriptive essays finds many differences among these community college students; advises separate but equal treatments.

Curriculum/NS-NNS Comparisons.

234. Benton, K. H. (1984). Writing without pain (or at least less of it). *Writing Lab Newsletter*, *8*, 8-9.

Describes use of free writing, personal topics, and oral reading to alleviate writer's block.

Affect.

235. Benz, C. (1992, March). *Haitian-Creole discourse in English*. Paper presented at the 43rd Annual CCCC Meeting, Cincinnati, OH.

Haitian.

236. Berens, G. L. (1986a). Using word processors in the ESL composition class. *TESOL Newsletter*, *20*(5), 13.

Suggests why using word processors to teach ESOL composition is appropriate in many EFL programs.

Computers/Word Processing.

237. Berens, G. L. (1986b). Using word processors in the ESL composition class II. *TESOL Newsletter*, *20*(6), 13.

Discusses the disadvantages of word-processing in ESL.

Computers/Word Processing.

238. Berg, C. (1991, March). *Peer analysis in ESL writing classrooms: A preliminary*

inquiry. Paper presented at the 25th Annual TESOL Convention, New York, NY.
Reports a descriptive study of the effect of peer analysis on revision.
Revision/Peer Response.

239. Berg, C., & Meyer, T. (1993, April). *Peer versus teacher response to writing*. Paper presented at the 27th Annual TESOL Convention, Atlanta, GA.
Compares and contrasts the benefits and drawbacks of two types of response to student writing.
Peer Response/Feedback.

240. Berger, D. M. (1988). *Combinations: Beginning strategies in thinking and writing*. Boston: Heinle & Heinle.
Text uses sentence-combining techniques to help students achieve syntactically and idiomatically correct work. Students are expected to progress from grammatical structures to composing short, rhetorical essays. It offers sections on generating ideas, rewriting, writing under pressure, grammatical terms, punctuation, and common writing errors.
Beginners/Textbook.

241. Berk, V. B., & Nevarez, H. O. (1978). The role of handwriting in TESOL. *TESOL Newsletter*, *12*(1), 17.
Points to the need to teach handwriting to Middle Eastern students whose orthography differs from English.
Handwriting.

242. Berk, V. B., Nevarez, H. O., & Hayes, C. W. (1978, April). *The role of handwriting in TESOL*. Paper presented at the 12th Annual TESOL Convention, Mexico City, Mexico.
Discusses the need to teach handwriting to Middle Eastern students whose orthography differs from that of English.
Handwriting/Arabic.

243. Berkman, M., & Bottoms, L. (1990). *Writing and speaking across cultures*. Paper presented at the 24th Annual TESOL Convention, San Francisco, CA.
Describes a writing program that pairs refugee students at one high school with native students at a college preschool. Through the writing of autobiographies, students learn about each others' cultures.
Culture/Secondary School.

244. Berkovitch, M. M. (1983). Tutorials in ESL: A qualitative study of the tutorial component of a writing program for English as a second language (ESL) students at the university level: Teacher and student perceptions, teacher differences, student-teacher interaction, and the role of the tutorial in a writing program. *Dissertation Abstracts International*, *43*(8), 2579A.
Studies the tutorial component of a writing program for ESL students. Examines teacher and student perceptions of the tutorial, benefits and shortcomings of tutorials, similarities and differences in different tutorials by different teachers or involving different students. Results show tutorials conceived of favorably and that the ways that different teachers used tutorials varied considerably.
Tutoring/Research.

245. Berkowitz, D., & Watkins-Goffman, L. (1988, March). *Putting grammar in its place in the writing curriculum*. Paper presented at the 22nd Annual TESOL Convention, Chicago, IL.

>Proposes integrating grammar instruction with the editing stage of composing.
Curriculum/Grammar.

246. Berman, M. (1979). Note-taking practice. *English Language Teaching Journal*, *34*(1), 39-40.

>Explains how to teach note-taking. Procedure involves selecting a passage with paragraphs that contain "clear-cut points" and reading or playing pre-recorded passage without pause. After a passage is read a second time, the reader should stop after each main point to give the students time to take the notes in their own words.
Note-Taking.

247. Berman, R. (1992). Effects of teachers' written comments on the learning by advanced ESL students of discourse in second language writing. *Masters Abstracts International*, *30*(04), 980.

>A teacher's experiment with two of his own classes supports the view that text-specific discourse-oriented comments are more effective in improving advanced ESL students' writing than no marginal or terminal comments at all.
Feedback/Advanced.

248. Bermudez, A. B., & Padron, Y. N. (1987, March). Teachers' perceptions of errors in second language learning and acquisition. In *Theory, research, and applications: Selected papers from the 16th annual meeting of the National Association for Bilingual Education, Denver, CO, March 1987*. Denver, CO: NABE. [ERIC ED 336 964].

>A study examines prevailing views of the role of errors and error correction among a group of school personnel (69 teachers and 18 other personnel). Neither ESL nor bilingual teachers demonstrated greater awareness than did traditional classroom teachers.
Errors/Error Treatment.

249. Bermudez, A. B., & Prater, D. L. (1992, March). *Using group talk in writing instruction for LEP writers*. Poster presented at the 26th Annual TESOL Convention, Vancouver, BC.

>Shows the quantitative and qualitative effects of group talk in all stages of writing.
Speaking-Writing Relations/Group Work.

250. Bermudez, A. B., & Prater, D. L. (1990a). Using brainstorming and clustering with LEP writers to develop elaboration skills. *TESOL Quarterly*, *24*, 523-528.

>Third and fourth-grade Spanish-speaking students who used a metacognitive strategy and then wrote a paragraph produced significantly more elaborations than those who read silently and discussed.
Hispanic/Strategies/Children.

251. Bermudez, A. B., & Prater, D. L. (1990b, April). *Examining the effects of peer versus teacher editing on limited-English proficient writers*. Paper presented at the Annual AERA Meeting, Boston.

Responding/Editing.
252. Berns, M. (1989, March). *Testing programs for ESL writing students: One university's response*. Paper presented at the 40th Annual CCCC Meeting, Seattle, WA.
Programs/Evaluation.
253. Berns, M. (1988, March). *Sociolinguistics and ESL writing: An aspect of a relationship*. Paper presented at the 39th Annual CCCC Meeting, St. Louis, MO.
Sociolinguistics.
254. Berns, M., Silva, T., McNamara, M. J., Moragné e Silva, M., Leki, I., & Deane, D. (1988, March). *ESL composition: Other voices, other views*. Paper presented at the 22nd Annual TESOL Convention, Chicago, IL.
Colloquium proposes an alternative, coherent perspective on the interrelationship of elements of ESL writing.
Approaches.
255. Berry, T. (1989). *Error analysis through oral reconstruction in ESL composition*. Unpublished master's thesis, University of Idaho, Moscow, ID.
Error Analysis/Speaking-Writing Relations.
256. BESL Center. (1978). Gimmicks for teaching composition. In D. Ilyin, & T. Tragardh (Eds.), *Classroom practices in adult ESL* (pp. 178-180). Washington, DC: TESOL.
Suggests copying, comic strip reformulation, rewriting, and letter writing as stimulating activities.
Classroom Activities/Adult Education.
257. Best, L. (1991). Student-centered college level ESL instruction. *Research & Teaching in Developmental Education*, 7(2), 57-66.
Suggests thematic units to elicit authentic language experiences in the college-level ESL program.
University/Instruction.
258. Best, L. (1987a, March). *ESL students as active learners*. Paper presented at 38th Annual CCCC Meeting, Atlanta, GA.
259. Best, L. (1987b, March). *Sociolinguistic theories as means to understand and meet the needs of ESL college writers*. Paper presented at the 38th Annual CCCC Meeting, Atlanta, GA. [ERIC ED 285 389].
Describes four ESL theories of second language learning that help explain the way advanced ESL learners are active learners.
University/Sociolinguistics.
260. Betancourt, F., & Phinney, M. (1988). Sources of writing block in bilingual writers. *Written Communication*, 5, 461-78.
Presents findings of a descriptive study designed to compare instances of writer's block in English and Spanish among and within three groups of bilingual writers. Tries to determine if the same writing factors stymy both the novice bilingual writer and the practiced bilingual writer. Suggests ways to lessen writing apprehension.
Hispanic/Anxiety.

261. Beyers, J., Carrier, M., McNerney, M., Mendelsohn, D. J., & Tyacke, M. (1988). *Real writing*. San Diego, CA: Dominie.

    A competency-based writing course in twenty units which integrates oral and written skills with relevant language functions. Also addresses inferential reasoning and analytic processes. Reading for content is aided by the glossing of difficult words.

    Intermediate/Advanced/Textbook.

262. Bhatia, A. T. (1977). Theory of discourse and the teaching of English composition to undergraduate students. *CIEFL Bulletin (Central Institute of English and Foreign Languages)*, *13*(2), 59-70. [ERIC ED 185 868].

    Describes an integrated approach for teaching composition to university students in India where in the initial stage a "meristic" approach is used to teach students elements of the sentence and at more advanced levels a holistic approach is adopted to teach students the nature and organization of paragraphs.

    Discourse Analysis/University/India.

263. Bhatia, V. K. (1989). Legislative writing: A case of neglect in EA/OLP courses. *English for Specific Purposes*, *8*, 223-238.

    Argues need to link English for Academic/Occupational Legal Purposes with the study of cases and legislative writing.

    ESP.

264. Biaggi, L., & Youngquist, J. A. (1978, April). *Paragraph writing in ESL composition*. Paper presented at the 12th Annual TESOL Convention, Mexico City, Mexico.

    Questions the traditional textbook idea of the paragraph and analyzes organizational problems in ESL compositions according to the concept of stadia.

    Paragraph/Organization.

265. Bickner, R., & Peyasantiwong, P. (1988). Cultural variation in reflective writing. In A. C. Purves (Ed.), *Writing across languages and cultures: Issues in contrastive rhetoric* (pp. 160-176). Newbury Park, CA: Sage.

    Compares reflective essays written in English and Thai by American and Thai students. Concludes that both groups use language in different ways, have different ways of analysis, and have different concepts of essay structure.

    Contrastive Rhetoric/Thai.

266. Bills, B. F., & Dillon, J. (1987, April). *Grappling with Garrison: Closing gaps in the Garrison composition method*. Paper presented at the 21st Annual TESOL Convention, Miami Beach, FL.

    Videotapes, writing modules, and numbered correction key increase the value of the Garrison (1974) method in the ESL environment.

    Conferencing.

267. Birch, B. (1992, March). *Integrating reading/writing in a content area: Peace education*. Paper presented at the 26th Annual TESOL Convention, Vancouver, BC.

    Describes how to use peace education materials in theme-based instruction for advanced learners.

    Reading-Writing Relations/Peace.

268. Birdsong, D., & Kassen, M. A. (1988). Teachers' and students' evaluations of foreign language errors: A meeting of minds? *Modern Language Journal, 72*, 1-12.

    Second language teachers agree with their students about the seriousness of errors even though the degree of severity of their judgments can differ.

    Responding/Errors.

269. Bitterman, E., & Stewart, D. (1988, March). *Word processing and composition: A stimulating blend.* Paper presented at the 22nd Annual TESOL Convention, Chicago, IL.

    Suggests students can learn through self-discovery from peers and with limited instructional guidance.

    Word Processing.

270. Bjork, L. (1985). TUAP and the teaching of writing in Sweden. In N. E. Enkvist (Ed.), *Coherence and composition: A symposium* (pp. 27-37). Abo, Finland: Research Institute of the Abo Akademic Foundation.

    The low quality of student writing in Sweden is attributed to inadequate teacher training, low priority of writing in the secondary curriculum, and inefficiency of "product" oriented methods of teaching. Suggests improving writing by means of teaching writing as a process.

    University/Swedish.

271. Blair, L. (1983). *ESL students and writing acquisition theory.* Washington, DC: ERIC/FLL. [ERIC ED 242 196].).

    Claims that ESL students are often anxious about writing because emphasis on form leads to overactive monitoring. Describes a developmental writing program where less emphasis on form led to greater fluidity and correctness in writing.

    Affect.

272. Blair, T. E. (1980). *A profile of variation in reader paragraphing among native and non-native speakers of English.* Unpublished master's thesis, University of Hawaii, Honolulu, HI. [ERIC ED 210 929].

    Claims that problems of some second language learners may be due to lack of literacy in their first language. Finds differences in accurate reading between (1) native literate and semiliterate and (2) native literate and non-native literate. In paragraphing, native literate readers tended to paragraph at significant rhetorical boundaries while others paragraphed at lower rhetorical breaks, at rhetorical units which begin narrative illustration, and after rhetorical units marked as opening by native literate readers.

    Literacy/Paragraph.

273. Blake, R. W. (1982). Starting off a non-native student in a college basic skills. In C. Carter (Ed.), *Non-native and nonstandard dialect students: Classroom practices in teaching English, 1982-1983* (pp. 19-27). Urbana, IL: NCTE.

    Shows written response of a Spanish-speaking student assigned to write a job recommendation for a friend.

    Hispanic/University.

274. Blanchard, K., & Root, C. (1990). *Ready to write: A first composition text.* Reading, MA: Addison Wesley/Longman.

A textbook for beginners focuses on common functional ways of organizing paragraphs based on purpose. It shows students how to organize ideas by time and space, how to give information, how to express ideas, describe, and compare and contrast.

Beginners/Textbook.

275. Blanton, L. L. (1993a). *Composition practice, book 3: A text for English language learners*. (Second Ed.). Boston: Heinle & Heinle.

Third in a four-part series for adults who learn English for academic, professional or business purposes. Reading and writing exercises illustrate particular modes and organizational frameworks and detailed instruction for students to write their own compositions.

Textbook/Intermediate.

276. Blanton, L. L. (1993b). *Composition practice, book 4: A text for English language learners*. (Second Ed.). Boston: Heinle & Heinle.

Fourth in a four-part writing program for adult learners who learn English for academic, professional or business purposes. Focuses on linguistic and rhetorical conventions special to expository discourse.

Textbook/Advanced.

277. Blanton, L. L. (1993c). Reading as performance: Reframing the function of reading. In J. G. Carson, & I. Leki (Eds.), *Reading in the composition classroom: Second language perspectives* (pp. 234-246). Boston: Heinle & Heinle.

Argues for the importance of student social interaction with texts as a means of transforming second language readers into academically and cognitively proficient readers and writers.

Reading-Writing Relations/Social.

278. Blanton, L. L. (1993d, April). *Academic literacy: Reading and writing like a college student*. Paper presented at the 27th Annual TESOL Convention, Atlanta, GA.

Describes the behavior required for academic literacy in colleges.

Literacy/University.

279. Blanton, L. L., Carson, J. E., Hudelson, S., Hamayan, E. V., Ruetten, M. K., & Pease-Alvarez, L. (1993e, April). *Reading and writing connections: designing a literate world*. Paper presented at the 27th Annual TESOL Convention, Atlanta, GA.

Discusses cognitive, social, and pedagogical aspects of the literate world students need to construct and enter.

Reading-Writing Relations.

280. Blanton, L. L. (1992a). A holistic approach to college ESL: Integrating language and content. *ELT Journal, 46*, 285-293.

Argues that the traditional skills model of college ESL is inadequate -- especially for refugee and immigrant ESL students. A context-oriented curriculum with a text-based, student-centered approach is suggested as a viable alternative.

Curriculum/University.

281. Blanton, L. L. (1992b). Reading, writing, and authority: Issues in developmental ESL. *College ESL, 2*(1), 11-17.

Developmental (i.e., immigrant and refugee) ESL college students need to adopt the posture of authority when reading texts and then use those experiences when writing in order to develop their academic language proficiency.
Reading-Writing Relations.

282. Blanton, L. L. (1992c, March). *Text and context: Changing roles of readings for writers*. Paper presented at the 26th Annual TESOL Convention, Vancouver, BC.

Reformulates the role of printed texts in the classroom from "models" to "contexts" and advocates combining reading journals, freewriting, critical questioning, and collaboration.
Reading-Writing Relations.

283. Blanton, L. L. (1988a). *Composition practice, book 1: A text for English language learners*. (Second Ed.). Boston: Heinle & Heinle.

First of a four-part writing program for adult learners who learn English for academic, professional or business purposes. Textbook creates awareness of different methods of organization in ten units, each illustrating a type of communication with a disinct grammatical, rhetorical, and organizational focus. Reading selection and model composition serves as a models for students' own compositions.
Beginners/Textbook.

284. Blanton, L. L. (1988b). *Composition practice, book 2: A text for English language learners*. (Second Ed.). NY: Heinle & Heinle.

Second in a four-part writing program for adults who learn English for academic, professional or business purposes. Reading and writing exercises illustrate particular modes and organizational frameworks and detailed instruction for students to write their own compositions.
Intermediate/Textbook.

285. Blanton, L. L. (1988c). *Idea exchange 1: Writing what you mean*. Boston: Heinle & Heinle.

First in a series of textbooks intended to help students generate several pages of accurately written English. It uses authentic student essays as models, includes a learning log, grammar reviews, pre-writing, pre-reading, and post-writing activities.
Beginners/Textbook.

286. Blanton, L. L. (1988d). *Idea exchange 2: Writing what you mean*. Boston: Heinle & Heinle.

Second in a series for intermediate level students to generate a quantity of written English. Each of ten lesson focuses on a different rhetorical, organizational and grammatical element of writing competency. The content of the text deals with day-to-day life of students, their friends, and relatives. Contains student essays, learning log, and line drawings.
Intermediate/Textbook.

287. Blanton, L. L. (1987). Reshaping ESL students' perceptions of writing. *ELT Journal*, *41*, 112-118.

Proposes a multi-step writing program centered around journal writing and learning logs to involve students in the gradual process of writing skills development. Discusses activities which let students participate in writing and relate to the teacher

and classmates, lower the anxiety level, and change their perceptions about writing.
Classroom Activities.

288. Blanton, L. L. (1986, March). *Reshaping ESL students' perceptions about writing: Payoffs in language acquisition.* Paper presented at the 37th Annual CCCC Meeting, New Orleans, LA.
See previous item.
Perceptions.

289. Blasky, A., & Gaer, S. (1988, March). *Creative visualization and the writing process.* Paper presented at the 22nd Annual TESOL Convention, Chicago, IL.
Visualization -- imagining scenes that can be turned into personal essays -- reduces writing anxiety.
Expressive Writing.

290. Blass, L. J., & Durighello, J. (1985). *From concept to composition: Reading & writing for ESL students.* Englewood Cliffs, NJ: Prentice Hall/Regents.
Intended for students who need to refine their writing skills in preparation for university academic work. Uses extensive, unadapted reading materials and exercises as a basis for journal and essay writing. Content primarily covers issues of life and learning.
Advanced/Textbook.

291. Blass, L. J., & Pike-Bakey, M. (1993). *Reflection and beyond: Expanding written communication.* Boston: Heinle & Heinle.
A low-intermediate component of the Tapestry series, offering theme-based learning linked to reflective and personal writing.
Textbook/Intermediate.

292. Blass, L. J., & Pike-Bakey, M. (1985a). *Mosaic I: A content-based writing book, Level III.* (Second Ed.). St. Louis, MO: McGraw-Hill.
Third writing text in a four-level, integrated notional-functional textbook series, which helps students formulate ideas through revising on general life themes.
Intermediate/Textbook.

293. Blass, L. J., & Pike-Bakey, M. (1985b). *Mosaic II: A content-based writing book, Level IV.* (Second Ed.). St. Louis, MO: McGraw-Hill.
Fourth writing text in a notional-functional four-level, integrated textbook series with content-based themes for students of the writing process.
Advanced/Textbook.

294. Blau, E. K., Galantai, F. L., & Sherwin, A. T. (1989). Employment interviewers' judgments of business and technical writing of non-native speakers of English. *The Technical Writing Teacher, 16,* 136-146.
An experiment finds that employment interviewers judge local syntactic errors as more serious than lexical errors.
Technical Writing/Error Gravity.

295. Bloch, J. (1993, April). *The social and historical context of the use of source texts: A comparison of Chinese and English language academic texts.* Paper presented at 44th Annual Convention of CCCC, San Diego, CA.
Chinese//Academic Writing.

296. Bloch, J. (1992a, March). *Contrastive rhetoric today*. Paper presented at the 43rd Annual CCCC Meeting, Cincinnati, OH.
Discusses the history, importance, challenges to, and new directions in contrastive rhetoric. Stresses limitations of our knowledge about non-western rhetorics.
Contrastive Rhetoric.

297. Bloch, J. (1992b, March). *The tradition of Chinese rhetoric: Its implications for the Chinese ESL student*. Paper presented at the 43rd Annual CCCC Meeting, Cincinnati, OH.
Indicates possible implications for Chinese ESL writers of the history of Chinese rhetoric since Confucius.
Contrastive Rhetoric/Chinese.

298. Bloch, J. (1990, March). *Universalism versus particularism: The relationship between Chinese and English rhetoric*. Paper presented at the 41st Annual CCCC Meeting, Chicago, IL.
Explores similarities and differences between Chinese and Western rhetoric.
Contrastive Rhetoric/Chinese.

299. Bloch, J. (1988a, March). *Academic writing in Chinese and English: Is there a difference?* Paper presented at the 39th Annual CCCC Meeting, St. Louis, MO.
Compares the introduction to academic articles written in Chinese and English. Results of analysis using Swales' categorization of introductory moves indicate that texts in both languages use similar patterns of introductory moves except for citation of previous research (far fewer in English).
Introductions/Text Analysis/Chinese.

300. Bloch, J. (1988b, March). *The effects of teacher comments on revision strategies*. Paper presented at the 22nd Annual TESOL Convention, Chicago, IL.
Think aloud protocols of advanced ESL writers responding to teachers show students are able to make meaning-changing revisions.
Revision/Responding/Advanced.

301. Bloch, J. (1991a, March). *Chinese writer's perceptions of academic writing tasks*. Paper presented at the 42nd Annual CCCC Meeting, Boston.
Interviews suggest how Chinese graduate students view the relationship between Chinese and English rhetoric.
Task/Chinese/University.

302. Bloch, J. (1991b). The historical dimension of comparative rhetoric: The relationship between English and Chinese rhetoric. In Y. J. Vitanza, & M. Ballif (Eds.), *Realms of rhetoric: Phonic, graphic, electronic* (pp. 97-105). Arlington, TX: Rhetoric Society of America.
Discusses the historical dimension of Chinese rhetoric.
Chinese/Contrastive Rhetoric.

303. Bloch, J. (1991c, March). *Twenty-five years of contrastive rhetoric: Where we are now*. Paper presented at the 25th Annual TESOL Convention, New York, NY.
Discusses the evolution of contrastive rhetoric, especially responses to criticisms of Kaplan (1966) and new challenges.

Contrastive Rhetoric.

304. Bloch, J. (1986). Prewriting and composing on the computer. *TESOL Newsletter, Supplement on computer-assisted language learning, no. 3, 20*(1), 4.

Reviews some computer aids to pre-writing, such as <u>TOPOI</u> and <u>Wordsmith II</u>, for native writers and suggests other ideas to help students get ideas flowing on the computer.

Computers/Invention.

305. Bloor, M., & St. John, M. J. (1988). Project writing: The marriage of process and product. In P. C. Robinson (Ed.), *Academic writing: Process and product* (pp. 85-94). London: Modern English Publications/British Council.

Argues that project writing provides opportunities for process-oriented instruction yet is directly relevant to target needs of ESP students which are usually product specific. Presents a course design for an intensive class that provides ESP students a choice of project types, discipline specific topics, as well as related activities and skills.

ESP/Academic Writing/Project Work.

306. Blot, D. (1993). Testimonials: Empowering ESL students to write. *College ESL, 3*(1), 15-24.

Recommends using testimonials, i.e, oral narratives by Third World people, to validate students' experience and culture. Response to such reading may be point of view writing and personal narrative.

Narration/Reading-Writing Relations.

307. Blot, D., & Davidson, D. M. (1988). *Put it in writing: Writing activities for ESL students*. (Second Ed.). Boston: Heinle & Heinle.

Based on the counseling-learning approach to language teaching, text covers both creative and expository writing skills and uses exercises and materials designed to interest students.

Intermediate/Textbook.

308. Blue, G. M. (1988). Individualizing academic writing tuition. In P. C. Robinson (Ed.), *Academic writing: Process and product* (pp. 95-99). London: Modern English Publications/British Council.

Discusses how essay writing is taught to ESP students on an individualized basis prior to the start of an academic year by assigning them topics in their subject area. Topics are solicited from cooperating subject matter departments which eventually receive a copy of the student essays.

Academic Writing/Conferencing/Topic.

309. Blumenthal, A., & Hildenbrand, J. L. (1993, April). *Oral and written strategies among inexperienced writers*. Paper presented at the 27th Annual TESOL Convention, Atlanta, GA.

Discusses the oral and written strategies of experienced and inexperienced developmental writing students from a traditional Afro-American college.

Speaking-Writing Relations/Sociolinguistics.

310. Boardman, C. A. (1981). *The copying mistake*. Unpublished master's thesis, University of Illinois, Urbana, IL.

311. Bodnar, B., & Kuehn, P. A. (1991, March). *Relationships between direct and multiple choice measures of writing.* Paper presented at the 25th Annual TESOL Convention, New York, NY.

   Reports sufficient discrepancy between ESL students' ability to locate errors in a multiple choice item-type test (e.g., TOEFL Written Expression section), to correct them, and to write. Questions the validity of inferences about writing ability made from such tests.
   Assessment/Objective Measures/Errors.

312. Boehm, P. W. (1992, March). *Peer editing for low level writing students.* Paper presented at the 26th Annual TESOL Convention, Vancouver, BC.

   Discusses and simulates a peer editing session for secondary school students.
   Beginners/Peer Response/Secondary School.

313. Bolman, D. L. (1989). Preposition errors in the compositions of Mexican-American basic writing students. *Dissertation Abstracts International, 50*(6), 1583A.

   Seeks to identify factors contribution to preposition errors by examining 370 themes written by Anglo, African-American, and Mexican-American college students.
   Error Analysis/Hispanic/NS-NNS Comparisons.

314. Bonheim, H. (1981, September). *The style test.* Paper presented at the Practice and Problems in Language Testing Conference, Essex, England. [ERIC ED 217 725].

   Describes several formats for testing style in English. Claims that style is more difficult to acquire and test, and that style tests have special features that distinguish them from other tests since they test suitability not correctness.
   Evaluation/Style.

315. Bonner, M. (1990). *Step into writing: A basic writing text.* White Plains, NY: Addison-Wesley/Longman.

   A textbook for beginners who wish to write paragraphs in controlled, contextualized tasks for all rhetorical modes.
   Beginners/Textbook.

316. Borkin, A. (1978a). On the role of contrastive connectives in expository discourse. *TESOL Newsletter, 12*(1), 17.

   Points out that contrast connectives (e.g., yet, however, etc.) typically function in scientific discourse as part of a complex conventionalized rhetorical pattern.
   Cohesion/Conventions.

317. Borkin, A. (1978b, April). *On the role of contrastive connectives in expository discourse.* Paper presented at the 12th Annual TESOL Convention, Mexico City, Mexico.

   Discusses the rhetorical functions of contrastive connectives in linking complex chains of reasoning and argumentation.
   Contrastive Rhetoric/Cohesion/Argumentation.

318. Borodkin, T. (1979, March). *Teaching freshman composition: Why separate but equal isn't equal.* Paper presented at the 13th Annual TESOL Convention, Boston.

   Argues that some remedial and ESL students need the same kind of program.
   Curriculum/University.

319. Bosher, S. (1992, March). *Interrupted educational background and its impact on the acquisition of academic writing skills: Case studies of Southeast Asian writers*. Paper presented at the 43rd Annual CCCC Meeting, Cincinnati, OH. [ERIC ED 357 659].

    An investigation of three Southeast Asian students with and without interrupted education shows that they differ in their degree of metacognitive awareness, their abilty to integrate information from reading into writing, the attention they pay to different aspects of writing, and problem-solving strategies used.
    Academic Writing/Asian/Metacognition.

320. Bosher, S. (1990). The role of error correction in the process-oriented ESL composition classroom. *MinneTESOL Journal, 8*, 89-101. [ERIC ED 336 987].

    Gives a correction code, error analysis chart, and procedures for students to practice gaining control over language in their writing.
    Error Treatment.

321. Bosher, S. (1988, March). *The role of error correction in the process-oriented ESL composition class*. Paper presented at the 39th Annual CCCC Meeting, St. Louis, MO.

    See previous item.
    Error Treatment/Process Instruction.

322. Boswood, T., & Dwyer, R. (1993, April). *Audiotaped feedback on writing: A personal and substantive approach*. Paper presented at the 27th Annual TESOL Convention, Atlanta, GA.

    Research on the use of audiotaped feedback to develop writing skills of university sci-tech students is reported.
    Feedback/ESP.

323. Bott, D. E. (1980). A method of teaching writing. In D. L. Bouchard, & L. J. Spaventa (Comps.), *A TEFL anthology: Selected articles from the English Teaching Forum, 1973-78* (pp. 181-184). Washington, DC: International Communication Agency.

    Provides a procedure for assigning and grading composition papers, which focuses on error correction.
    Errors/Feedback/Evaluation.

324. Boucher, H. W., & Singley, C. J. (1987, April). *Writing: The essential ingredient in ESL*. Paper presented at the 21st Annual TESOL Convention, Miami Beach, FL.

    Advocates teaching writing as a social act involving purpose, audience, and stance.
    Social.

325. Bowen, J. D., Madsen, H., & Hilferty, A. (1985). Writing. In J. D. Bowen, H. Madsen, & A. Hilferty, *TESOL: Techniques and procedures* (pp. 252-278). Rowley, MA: Newbury House.

    Describes a developmental approach to the teaching of writing, from mechanical to communicative.
    Teacher Preparation.

326. Bowie, D. G. (1987). Converting thought to oral narrative composition in a second language. *Dissertation Abstracts International, 48*(5), 1135A.

Investigates the spoken language ability of twelve Brazilian adult ESL speakers who produced two oral narratives from wordless stories, first in Portugese and then in English. Think-aloud protocols of the speakers when viewing their storytelling videotape provides evidence for several psycholinguistic premises.
Speaking-Writing Relations/Brazil/Narration.

327. Boyd, J. A. (1988). Evaluating the active communication skills: Writing. In G. H. Irons (Ed.), *Second language acquisition: Selected readings in theory and practice* (pp. 133-143). Ontario, Canada: The Canadian Modern Language Review.
Discusses how to structure teaching and testing programs to enable students to gradually but systematically progress from copying to free composition.
Approaches/Beginners.

328. Boyd, J. R., & Boyd, M. A. (1993, April). *Increasing student self-reliance through Self-correcting compositions*. Paper presented at the 27th Annual TESOL Convention, Atlanta, GA.
Offer a text that gives a variety of ways for students to edit their own work.
Beginners/Editing.

329. Boyd, Z., & Buchanan, H. C. (1979, March). *English as a second language techniques in developmental writing*. Paper presented at the meeting of College English Association, Savannah, GA. [ERIC ED 176 324].
Suggests that writing teachers can lower student anxiety in their initial writing assignments, show more patience with mistakes, and recognize that students might use interlanguage. ESL techniques can also be used in teaching grammar through drills and in helping students transfer the drills to actual compositions.
Teacher Preparation.

330. Bracey, M. (1973, May). *The cassette tape recorder: A bonus or bother in ESL composition correction*. Paper presented at the 7th Annual TESOL Convention, San Juan, Puerto Rico.
Explores advantages and disadvantages in giving feedback on audiotape.
Feedback.

331. Bracey, M. (1971a). Controlled writing vs. free writing. *TESOL Quarterly*, 5, 239-246.
Proposes curriculum revision in intermediate ESL, especially that of substituting free composition for advanced controlled writing.
Intermediate/Control/Curriculum.

332. Bracey, M. (1971b, March). *Controlled writing vs. free composition or "write 300 words on 'Problems of a foreign student at UCLA'"*. Paper presented at the 5th Annual TESOL Convention, New Orleans, LA.
Suggests using discussion methods, current publications as models, revising, and student-oriented topics in a course on free writing.
Control/Speaking-Writing Relations.

333. Bradford, P. P. (1988). *Invented spelling in Mexican-American Spanish speaking students who make a transition to English writing*. Unpublished master's thesis, Arizona State University, Tempe, AZ.
Spelling/Hispanic.

334. Braine, G. (1993). *ESL students in Freshman English: An evaluation of the placement options*. Washington, DC: ERIC/FLL. [ERIC ED 359 559].

Argues that ESL students are best served in classes specially designed for their needs, although mainstreaming continues to be the most common placement option despite research to the contrary.

Freshman Composition/Placement.

335. Braine, G. (1992a, March). *Starting freshman writing courses for foreign students*. Paper presented at the 43rd Annual CCCC Meeting, Cincinnati, OH.

Describes a two-day program to inform English department faculty about ESL students and their writing.

Teacher Preparation.

336. Braine, G. (1992b, March). *Teaching research writing to nonnative speakers: Experimental reports in undergraduate engineering courses*. Paper presented at the 26th Annual TESOL Convention, Vancouver, BC.

Discusses the structure of the lab report as one genre in Engineering writing.

ESP/Lab Report Writing.

337. Brainer, C. (1990a, March). *Uses retrospective methodology in analyzing L2 writing conference interaction*. Paper presented at the 24th Annual TESOL Convention, San Francisco, CA.

Presents the results of a study of L2 writing conference interaction utilizing videotaped sessions and retrospective methodology. The effect that cross-cultural differences in verbal and nonverbal communication, pedagogical expectations, and rhetorical strategies have on conference interaction and student revision are examined.

Conferencing/Research.

338. Braine, G. (1990b, March). *The laboratory report: Rhetorical analysis and pedagogical implications*. Paper presented at the 24th Annual TESOL Convention, San Francisco, CA.

Claims that nearly 75% of writing in the natural sciences and engineering consists of laboratory reports. Gives a rhetorical analysis of laboratory reports from subject areas with pedagogical implications for foreign students in American universities.

ESP/University/Lab Report Writing.

339. Braine, G. (1989a). Writing in science and technology: An analysis of assignments from ten undergraduate courses. *English for Specific Purposes*, 8, 3-15.

Classifies 61 assignments from ten courses according to task and audience specification. All assignments were highly controlled and at least one-fourth did not specify audience.

ESP/Task/Audience.

340. Braine, G. (1989b, March). *Writing in science and technology: Implications for ESL*. Paper presented at the 23rd Annual TESOL Convention, San Antonio, TX. [ERIC ED 304 881].

Classifies writing assignments from 30 undergraduate courses in science and technology.

ESP/Assignments.

341. Braine, G. (1988). Two commentaries on Ruth Spack's "Initiating ESL students into the academic discourse community: How far should we go?": A reader responds ... [In The Forum]. *TESOL Quarterly, 22*, 700-702.

   Contends that integrating academic assignments into ESL writing can help students succeed.

   Academic Writing.

342. Braun, S. (1992). United Nations resources for an ESL writing class. *TESOL Matters, 2*(2), 8.

   Discusses materials and how an advanced ESL class studied the problems and goals of a UN conference on environment and development.

   Project Work/Advanced.

343. Breland, H. M., Camp, R., Jones, R. J., Morris, M. M., & Rock, D. A. (1987). *Assessing writing skill* NY: College Entrance Examination Board.

   Finds that syntax and lexis scores are relatively more important for ESL than NES groups, although discourse level characteristics are the best predictors of holistic essay scores for both first and second language writers.

   Assessment/NS-NNS Comparisons/Syntactic Structures/Lexis.

344. Brenner, C. A. (1989). *Teaching the research paper to ESL students in American colleges and universities*. Unpublished master's thesis, School for International Training, Brattleboro, VT. [ERIC ED 311 714].

   Offers a six-step classroom approach to teaching the research writing process in order to address the linguistic, cultural, educational, and discourse community problems faced by the ESL student.

   Research Writing/University.

345. Brickman, B. (1993, April). *From portfolio to publication: Publishing student writing*. Paper presented at the 27th Annual TESOL Convention, Atlanta, GA.

   Discusses producing and funding publications by ESL college students.

346. Brickman, B. (1992, March). *Using print and electronic ads in the writing class*. Paper presented at the 26th Annual TESOL Convention, Vancouver, BC.
   Portfolios/Student Publications.

   Computers.

347. Bridgeman, B., & Carlson, S. B. (1984). Survey of academic writing tasks. *Written Communication, 1*(2), 247-280.

   Reports responses from 190 academic departments at 34 universities to a survey seeking to determine the writing tasks faced by beginning undergraduate and graduate students. Results suggest considerable variability across fields.

   Evaluation/Task/University.

348. Bridgeman, B., & Carlson, S. B. (1983). *Survey of academic writing tasks required of graduate and undergraduate foreign students*. (TOEFL Research Report 15). Princeton, NJ: Educational Testing Service.

   See previous item.

   Task.

349. Briére, E. J. (1964). Testing the control of parts of speech in foreign language composition. *Language Learning, 14*, 1-10.

Reports an experiment showing that a topic assignment in itself does not control the frequency of use of specific parts of speech, as hypothesized by Lado (1957).
Topic/Syntactic Structures.

350. Briére, E. J. (1966). Quality versus quantity in second language composition. *Language Learning*, *16*, 141-151.
Found improvement in fluency and grammatical accuracy at the sentence level in the writing of university level ESL students when quantity of writing is emphasized.
Fluency/University.

351. Briggs, S., Hayer, J., & Spaan, M. (1984, March). *Writing as an indicator of language proficiency: A workshop for training evaluators*. Paper presented at the 17th Annual TESOL Convention, Houston, TX.
Argues that holistic grading by trained evaluators can indicate overall language proficiency at all levels.
Evaluation/Proficiency.

352. Brinton, D. M. (1986, March). *Adjunct instruction: Linking ESL courses with university content courses*. Paper presented at the 37th Annual CCCC Meeting, New Orleans, LA.
Adjunct/Content.

353. Brinton, D. M., Goodwin, J. M., & Holten, C. A. (1989, March). *Responding to dialog journals in teacher training: What's effective?* Paper presented at the 23rd Annual TESOL Convention, San Antonio, TX.
Reports a study of teacher commenting strategies in dialogue journals used in teacher training. Student input apparently affects the quality of teacher response.
Dialogue Journals/Teacher Preparation.

354. Brinton, D. M., Holten, C. A., & Goodwin, J. M. (1993). Responding to dialogue journals in teacher preparation: What's effective? *TESOL Journal*, *2*(4), 15-19.
Novice teachers can engage in reflective practice by using dialogue journals.
Dialogue Journals/Teacher Education.

355. British Council (1973). *The teaching of composition writing with reference to EFL: Specialized Bibliography B28*. London: English Teaching Information Center. [ERIC ED 115 099].
Gives a list of books and articles published from 1965 to 1972, related to the teaching of composition to ESL students.
Bibliography.

356. Britton, R. T., & Youngkin, B. N. (1984, March). *Debate: A natural heuristic for writing and composition*. Paper presented at the 18th Annual TESOL Convention, Houston, TX.
Advocates a model based on Ong's rhetorical ideas in which preparation and presentation of a debate on a controversial subject leads to satisfactory experience with writing.
Speaking-Writing Relations.

357. Brock, M. N. (1993a). A comparative study of computerized text analysis and peer

tutoring as revision aids for ESL writers. *Dissertation Abstracts International, 54*(3), 912A.

Reports that text analysis limited the number of words written and revisions made across drafts compared to peer tutoring in a quasi-experimental study of two groups of Hong Kong college students, although both groups showed significant growth in writing performance as measured.

Computers/Peer Response/Chinese.

358. Brock, M. N. (1993b, April). *Computerized text analysis and peer feedback: A comparative study.* Paper presented at the 27th Annual TESOL Convention, Atlanta, GA.

See previous item.
Peer Response/Computers.

359. Brock, M. N. (1993c). Made in Hong Kong: An imperialist rhetoric and the teaching of composition. In M. N. Brock, & L. W. Walters (Eds.), *Teaching composition around the Pacific Rim: Politics and pedagogy* (pp. 28-34). Clevedon, ENG: Multilingual Matters.

The use of western rhetoric in Hong Kong English-medium education is claimed to impair the development of students' authentic voices. Suggests the need for developing a Hong Kong-centric rhetoric in these schools.

Chinese/Politics/Rhetoric.

360. Brock, M. N. (1993d). Three disk-based text analyzers and the ESL writer. *Journal of Second Language Writing, 2*, 19-40.

Reviews three programs -- RightWriter, Grammatik, Correct Grammar -- finding their value questionable as stand-alone aids to ESL writing.

Computers.

361. Brock, M. N. (1990a). Can the computer tutor? An analysis of a disk-based text analyzer. *System, 18*, 351-359.

Argues that the Grammatik III computerized text analysis is unsuitable for ESL composition pedagogy.

Computers/Programs.

362. Brock, M. N. (1990b). Customizing a computerized text analyzer for ESL writers: Cost versus gain. *CALICO Journal, 8*(2), 51-60.

Although text-analysers like Grammatik IV permit customization for specific populations, a test of Cantonese-speaking ESL students found that time, effort, and accuracy in creating parsing rules makes the worth of the endeavor questionable.

Computers/Chinese.

363. Brock, M. N. (1988). *The computer as writing tutor: Is there a place in the process for computer-based text analysis?* Washington, DC: ERIC/FLL. [ERIC ED 318 429].).

A study of four writers compares product- and process-oriented computer feedback, finding the former resulted in shorter drafts with fewer meaningful revisions.

Computers.

364. Brock, M. N., & Walters, L. W. (Eds.). (1993). *Teaching composition around the*

Pacific Rim: Politics and pedagogy Clevedon, ENG: Multilingual Matters.

A collection of original essays devoted to the theme of composition in the situation of Pacific rim contexts.

Asian/Culture.

365. Brodkey, D. G. (1983a). An expectancy exercise in cohesion. *TESL Reporter*, *16*(3), 43-45.

Students attempt to predict the sequence of a written passage one sentence at a time when peers read aloud their papers.

Cohesion.

366. Brodkey, D. G. (1983b, March). *Getting cohesion into ESL writing*. Paper presented at the 17th Annual TESOL Convention, Toronto, BC.

Shows three ways to teach cohesion: using a computer-generated story, an expectancy exercise, and verbatim repetition of a key element.

Cohesion.

367. Brodkey, D. G., & Young, R. K. (1981). Composition correctness scores. *TESOL Quarterly*, *15*, 159-167.

Describes a teacher-scored method useful in determining the proportion of correct usage in freshman ESL composition. Concludes correctness scores provide a tool for investigation of the hierarchy of significant errors in English.

Evaluation/Assessment/Accuracy.

368. Bromage, M. C. (1980). *Writing for business*. (Second Ed.). Ann Arbor, MI: University of Michigan Press.

Seeks to prepare the ESL student for business communication. Focuses on the problems encountered by the business writer -- from word choice to organizing a long report. Shows basic principles of effective communication which are vital to the student preparing for the business world.

University/Business Writing/Textbook.

369. Brookes, A., & Grundy, P. (1990). *Writing for study purposes: A teacher's guide to developing individual writing skills*. New York: Cambridge University Press.

Describes a humanistic approach to the communicative teaching of academic writing. It emphasizes the processes by which learners can write free from the constraints of others' ideas and the need to conform to prescriptions.

Approaches.

370. Brookes, A., & Grundy, P. (1988). Activating the learner's contribution in the development of academic writing skills. In P. C. Robinson (Ed.), *Academic writing: Process and product* (pp. 100-108). London: Modern English Publications/British Council.

Argues that a more humanistic perspective which places the learner before the subject matter can effectively motivate students of academic writing. Also presents four academic writing exercises to help students with macro and microskills to accomplish this goal.

Academic Writing/Approaches.

371. Brookes, G. (1992, March). *In the writing classroom: Approaches to teaching beginning writers*. Colloquium presented at the 26th Annual TESOL Convention,

Vancouver, BC.

Compares and contrasts what is done now and what was done 15 years ago in teaching beginners to write.

Beginners.

372. Brookes, G. (1988a). Promising sets of practices in the teaching of writing to ESL and native speaker students. *Dissertation Abstracts International, 48*(1), 1679A.

Reports the results of a classroom observation study of teaching practices by seven ESL composition instructors teaching writing to ESL writers and NES basic writers at the college level. Successful teachers use classrooms as places of social interaction where students can work on writing tasks in class, choose from a variety of topics, and get feedback from peers.

Classroom Research/Teacher Preparation/NS-NNS Comparisons.

373. Brookes, G. (1988b, March). *Inside the black box: Classroom practices for teaching writing*. Paper presented at the 22nd Annual TESOL Convention, Chicago, IL.

Observations of college level writing courses suggest promising classroom practices.

Teacher Preparation.

374. Brookes, G., Cummings, M. C., & Withrow, J. (1987). Reading, an essential part of the writing process. In G. Brookes, & J. Gantzer (Eds.), *Students, texts, contexts. Research and practice in ESL instruction: Selected papers from the CUNY ESL Council Conference, New York, NY.* NY: CUNY Instructional Resource Center. [ERIC ED 328 068].

Describes ways to integrate reading into the college ESL writing course. The aim is to learn to read like writers.

Reading-Writing Relations/Process Instruction.

375. Brookes, G., Cummings, M. C., & Withrow, J. (1985, April). *Can we teach writing as a process to low-level students?* Paper presented at the 19th Annual TESOL Convention, New York, NY.

Classroom research shows that low-level students can acquire language and develop writing through writing-as-process activities.

Process Instruction/Beginners.

376. Brookes, G., & Fanselow, J. F. (1991, March). *Nothing new, just rare.* Paper presented at the 25th Annual TESOL Convention, New York, NY.

Workshop demonstrates how reading and writing are connected and how to teach writing as a process and reading as a social activity.

Reading-Writing Relations.

377. Brookes, G., & Withrow, J. (1988). *10 steps: Controlled composition for beginning and intermediate language development.* (Second Ed.) Hayward, CA: Alemany Press.

Textbook guides students through conventions of written English by means of copy and rewrite activities associated with short, readable passages on various topics.

Beginners/Textbook.

378. Brookes, G., & Withrow, J. (1985). *26 steps: Controlled composition for beginning and intermediate ESL students.* Old Tappan, NJ: Prentice Hall Regents.

Textbook guides students through conventions of written English with short, readable passages on various topics.
Intermediate/Textbook.

379. Brooks, E. B. (1989). Interview with students and colleagues: What can we learn? In J. D. Macero, B. J. Agor, & N. Tumposley (Eds.), *Realizing the dream: Selected conference proceedings of the annual meeting of the New York State TESOL* (pp. 100-113). NY: NY TESOL. [ERIC ED 314 958].
A follow-up study of six of 14 unskilled college ESL writers examines two writing samples, one elicited for the study and another for an outside class, as well as interviews. Finds dramatic change in fluency, vocabulary, and idiomaticity of written products, although there were some unresolved problems of form. Teachers regarded ESL writers highly.
Assessment.

380. Brooks, E. B. (1988). When there are no links between ESL and content courses. In S. Benesch (Ed.), *Ending remediation: Linking ESL and content in higher education* (pp. 20-32). Washington, DC: TESOL.
Discusses efforts of ESL faculty to structure their programs for preparing students for requirements of core courses. Expresses need for more interaction between ESL courses and courses in other disciplines.
Curriculum/University.

381. Brooks, E. B. (1987, March). *Follow-through: An update of case studies of ESL writers*. Paper presented at the 38th Annual CCCC Meeting, Atlanta, GA.
See previous item.
Process Research.

382. Brooks, E. B. (1986a). Case studies of the composing processes of five "unskilled" English as-a-second-language college writers. *Dissertation Abstracts International, 47*(1), 164-165A.
The composing processes of "unskilled" ESL writers develop in three stages based on the writer's personal characteristics, L2 proficiency, abilities, and needs. The stages range from less experienced to more experienced to experienced and confident.
Process Research.

383. Brooks, E. B. (1986b, March). *Writers of any language: Case studies of the composing processes of "unskilled" ESL college writers*. Paper presented at the 37th Annual CCCC Meeting, New Orleans, LA. [ERIC ED 314 958].
A follow-up study with six of 14 participants in Brooks (1985) finds that the skilled writers continue to use many constructive composing strategies while differences between writers diminished.
Process Research/Beginners.

384. Brooks, P. (1981). Working with ESL students. In T. Hawkins, & P. Brooks (Eds.), *New directions for college learning assistance: Improving writing skills* (pp. 45-52). San Francisco: Jossey-Bass.
Writing Center.

385. Broom, M. J. (1984). Something to carry along: A student-produced writing

handbook. *Utah English Journal*, 27-31.
   Describes a reading and writing curriculum for junior high ESL students.
   Project Work/Middle School.

386. Brosnahan, I. (1988, March). *Grammar vs. intuition: A comparison of native and non-native writers*. Paper presented at the 39th Annual CCCC Meeting, St. Louis, MO.
   Grammar/NS-NNS Comparisons.

387. Brosnahan, I., Coe, R. M., & Johns, A. M. (1987). Discourse analysis of written texts in an overseas teacher training program. *English Quarterly*, 20(1), 16-25.
   Describes a teacher-training research project for Chinese students in a Fulbright program in Shanghai.
   Teacher Preparation/Text Analysis.

388. Broukal, M. (1993). *Weaving it together, Books 1-3*. Boston: Heinle & Heinle.
   A three-book series that seeks to comprehensively integrate reading with writing.
   Textbook/Beginners.

389. Brown, H. D. (1970). Categories of spelling difficulty in speakers of English as a first and second language. *Journal of Verbal Learning and Verbal Behavior*, 9(2), 232-242.
   Provides supporting tests for the hypothesis that word frequency rather than spelling regularity is the key factor in the ability to spell of both native and nonative speakers.
   Spelling/NS-NNS Comparisons.

390. Brown, H. D., Cohen, D. S., & O'Day, J. (1991). *Challenges: A process writing course in English*. Englewood Cliffs, NJ: Prentice Hall.
   Text shows students how to develop successful reading and writing strategies, to extract information from text, and how the act of writing helps develop thinking process. Also contains a process writing approach and demonstrates how to integrate both reading and writing. Offers activities and readings in each unit.
   University/Advanced/Textbook.

391. Brown, J. D. (1992). Do English and ESL faculties rate writing samples differently? *TESOL Quarterly*, 25, 587-603.
   Investigates the degree of difference in the holistic rating assigned to native and nonnative writers at the end of parallel courses by an equal number of EASL and English Department faculty. Finds no significant mean difference between compositions of two student types but some evidence that the respective faculties may arrive at the same outcome by different means.
   Raters/NS-NNS Comparisons/Assessment

392. Brown, J. D. (1990). Placement of ESL students in writing-across-the-curriculum programs. *University of Hawaii Working Papers in ESL*, 9(1), 35-58.
   Finds that ESL students in a large-scale testing program (writing and revising 2 topics) form a separate population which ranks relatively low compared with the NS population on a five-hour placement test.
   Placement/NS-NNS Comparisons.

393. Brown, J. D. (1989). Rating writing samples: An interdepartmental perspective. *University of Hawaii Working Papers in ESL, 8*(2), 119-141.

> Found only chance differences between the mean holistic scores of essays written by NSs and international students after comparable composition courses. Furthermore, there was no significant variation between ratings within or between the ESL and English departments.
> Rating/Holistic/NS-NNS Comparisons.

394. Brown, J. D., & Bailey, K. M. (1984). A categorical instrument for scoring second language writing skills. *Language Learning, 34*, 21-42.

> Finds that an evaluation instrument is moderately reliable in measuring the organization, development, as well as grammar, style and mechanics of high intermediate ESL compositions.
> Evaluation.

395. Brown, J., & Paiva, J. L. (1984b, March). *Teaching a writing lab*. Paper presented at the 18th Annual TESOL Convention, Houston, TX.

> Demonstrates stage process model of composing.
> Process Instruction/Laboratory.

396. Brown, L. C. (1993, April). *An integrated writing program for nonnative speakers of English*. Paper presented at the 27th Annual TESOL Convention, Atlanta, GA.

> Discusses the design and implementation of one univeristy's writing program.
> Curriculum.

397. Brown, Y. D., & Bailey, K. M. (1984). A categorical instrument for scoring second language writing skills. *Language Learning, 34*, 21-42.

> Reviews research on evaluating writing skills of ESL learners and discusses the results of a study of the reliability of a categorical instrument which tests organization, development of ideas, grammar, mechanics, and style in compositions written by intermediate ESL students.
> Evaluation/Assessment.

398. Browne, S. R. (1990). Social cognition as a predictor of the writing quality of students using English as a second language in freshman English composition. *Dissertation Abstracts International, 51*(10), 3348A.

> Analyzes three social cognitive variables and two essay topics by 43 students from six freshman composition classes in order to determine whether there is any correlation between the social cognitive skills of ESL students and their proficiency levels in written expository and persuasive writing. Positive correlations were found between writing quality in both modes and social cognition. Impression organization and length of essays were the most significant predictors of writing quality.
> Social/NS-NNS Comparisons.

399. Bruder, M. N., & Furey, P. R. (1979). The writing segment of an intensive program for students of English as a second language. *Journal of Basic Writing, 2*(2), 67-84.

> Describes goals and procedures of the writing segment of an intensive program for learners of ESL at three levels: basic, intermediate, and advanced.
> Curriculum/IEP.

400. Bruder, M. N., & Williams, E. (1986). *Cracking the code: Learning to read and

write in English. Ann Arbor, MI: University of Michigan Press.

Textbook presents a variety of exercises for students who do not know the Roman alphabet or who need to know the sound-letter relationship in English.

Beginners/Textbook.

401. Bruton, A. S. (1982, May). *Teacher decisions in the secondary ESL extended writing lesson*. Paper presented at the 16th Annual TESOL Convention, Honolulu, HI.

Presents a framework to show various options a teacher has in making decisions when preparing a writing lesson.

Teacher Preparation/Secondary School.

402. Bruton, A. S. (1981). A decision-making approach to the extended writing lesson. *English Language Teaching Journal*, 35(2), 141-146.

Outlines the basic decisions the ESL teacher should make in planning the extended writing lesson. Decisions regarding objectives, teacher input, oral build-up procedures, types of writing exercises, correctness and markings are discussed.

Instruction/Teacher Preparation.

403. Bryant, W. H. (1984). Typical errors in English made by Japanese ESL students. *JALT Journal*, 6(1), 1-18.

A study based on a survey of L1 and L2 errors in English compositions by Japanese ESL students identifies various kinds of errors in order to describe those which present special difficulties for Japanese students. The analysis of errors shows that of the two basic types of errors -- interlingual or L1 and intralingual or L2 -- the interlingual errors, even though fewer than intralingual, most hinder communication.

Errors/Japanese.

404. Buchanan, L. M. (1990, March). *Teaching proofreading and editing to advanced students*. Paper presented at the 24th Annual TESOL Convention, San Francisco, CA.

Demonstrates various methods of teaching proofreading and editing to advanced students. The final stage of the composing process has not been stressed as greatly as the earlier stages. The object for teachers is to help students become more independent editors of their final copy.

Advanced/Editing.

405. Buchanan, L. M. (1986, March). *Using the case method for teaching advanced composition*. Paper presented at the 20th Annual TESOL Convention, Anaheim, CA.

The realistic materials of a case method enable composition to be relevant.

Advanced/Materials.

406. Buchanan, L. M. (1982, May). *Research on native-speaker composing: Implications for ESL*. Paper presented at the 16th Annual TESOL Convention, Honolulu, HI.

Points out that some native subject research on the composing process has implications for ESL composition.

NS-NNS Comparisons.

407. Buchanan, L. M. (1976). ESL composition texts: An annotated bibliography. *TESL Talk*, 7, 6-8.

Reviews the most commonly used textbooks for ESL composition in mid 70's.

Bibliography.

408. Buckingham, T. (1979). The goals of advanced composition. *TESOL Quarterly, 13,* 241-254.

Suggests three levels of composition instruction, each with clearly defined goals. Sets goals for advanced students, which involve training students to monitor their own work.

Contrastive Rhetoric/Advanced.

409. Buckingham, T. (1977, April). *The effects of transformational sentence-combining practice on the writing ability of non-native speakers of English.* Paper presented at the 11th Annual TESOL Convention, Miami Beach, FL.

Reports results of an experiemental test of non-native students using sentence-combining.

Sentence Combining.

410. Buckingham, T., & McGough, J. (1975, March). *A language experience approach to teaching composition.* Paper presented at the 9th Annual TESOL Convention, Los Angeles, CA.

Analyzes problems of controlled composition and the imitation of models. Describes use of students' own interests and encouragement to communicate through the language experience approach used in native language education.

LEA.

411. Buckingham, T., & Pech, W. C. (1976). An experience approach to teaching composition. *TESOL Quarterly, 10,* 55-65.

Students trained in controlled writing are usually unprepared to deal with the problems of free writing when they reach the intermediate stage. An experience-based instruction program can be more effective. The student bases his writing on such things as pictures and answers to questions and develops paragraphs on his own before shifting toward development of a complete composition

Approaches/Intermediate.

412. Buell, F., & Kelly, W. (1988). *ESL students and the study of American culture.* Washington, DC: ERIC/FLL. [ERIC ED 306 850].

ESL students at Queens College (NYC) were found to lack sufficient acculturation to succeed in humanities courses. Faculty redesigned the curriculum, assuming student unfamiliarity with the assumptions of American culture. It was found that teaching required a density of culturally and historically significant materials.

Curriculum/University.

413. Buker, S. (1984, March). *Initiating writing: A process approach to teaching prewriting and drafting.* Demonstration at the 18th Annual TESOL Convention, Houston, TX.

Offers specific pre-writing techniques and a drafting strategy using the given/new contract.

Invention/Drafting.

414. Buley-Meissner, M. L. C. (1985). Understanding how native and non-native students learn to write. *Dissertation Abstracts International, 46*(7), 1917A.

Documents personal case histories of 12 basic writers and reports on their

development in terms of overcoming anxiety and inefficiency and in developing personal and rhetorical control of composing. Proposes a six-stage model of development for basic writers, based on students' perception of their progress.
Anxiety/NS-NNS Comparisons.

415. Bull, W. E. (1986). Writing English script: An overlooked skill. *ESL Journal, 40*, 291-298.

Discusses the handwriting skills of Arabic-script writers composing in English. Symptoms of the lack of handwriting skills in a foreign language, such as the right-left orientation transferred from L1, are discussed. Claims that, while handwriting skills are non-linguistic, perceptual and motor skills are interrelated, and both linguistic and non-linguistic skills are necessary in reading and writing.
Handwriting/Arabic.

416. Bulos, A. (1982). Teaching a few ESL students in a regular English class. In C. Carter (Ed.), *Non-native and nonstandard dialect students* (pp. 6-10). Urbana, IL: NCTE.

Offers some specific suggestions for coping with the needs of the few.
Middle School/Classroom Activities.

417. Buras, K. M. (1987). The effect of free composition and controlled composition on the performance of twelfth-grade students in the Libyan secondary schools. *Dissertation Abstracts International, 47*(9), 3339-3340A.

An experimental evaluation of sixteen themes by twenty-four Libyan third and fourth year secondary students suggests that free composition is more effective in improving writing proficiency than is controlled composition.
Arabic/Fluency/Control.

418. Burger, S. (1989). Content based ESL in a sheltered psychology course: Input, output, and outcomes. *TESL Canada Journal, 6*(2), 45-59.

Finds that focused reading rather than actual writing may have accounted for gains made in writing skills by ESL psychology students enrolled in a sheltered content area ESL writing course compared with similar students enrolled in a course with more traditional instruction.
Courses/WAC.

419. Burkhalter, N. (1990a). Second language writing mistakes: Are they cognitively or developmentally based? In H. Burmeister, & P. L. Rounds (Eds.), *Proceedings of the tenth meeting of the Second Language Research Forum: Variability in second language acquisition* (pp. 233-250). Eugene, OR: University of Oregon, Department of Linguistics.

Attributes rhetoric errors in English L2 to underdevelopment of NL writing skills. Argues that ESL students need to be trained to go beyond the inner speech of their first language and to learn metaskills to facilitate writing in their second language.
L1 Influence/Errors.

420. Burkhalter, N. (1990b, March). *Second language writing mistakes: Are they cognitively or developmentally based?* Paper presented at the Second Language Research Forum, Eugene, OR. [ERIC ED 322 728].

See previous item.
Errors/L1 Influence.

421. Burns, A. (1990). Genre-based approaches to writing and beginning adult ESL learners. *Prospect: A Journal of Australian TESOL, 5*(3), 62-71.
Genre/Beginners.

422. Burns, A., Hood, S., & Winser, B. (1993, April). *Genre theory and literacy development in ESL.* Paper presented at the 27th Annual TESOL Convention, Atlanta, GA.
Findings from classroom-based research in the Australian context suggest the utility of genre theory for connecting language and context and moving from speaking to writing.
Genre/Speaking-Writing Relations.

423. Burns, W. T. (1993, April). *From dialog journals to authentic correspondence.* Paper presented at the 27th Annual TESOL Convention, Atlanta, GA.
Compares an exchange of weekly letters with students at a Korean university to dialog journaling and E-mail.
Letter Writing/Dialogue Journals.

424. Burruel, J. M., & Ney, J. W. (1974, March). *Transformational sentence combining in a barrio school.* Paper presented at the 8th Annual TESOL Convention, Denver, CO.
Finds that barrio children started behind Anglos but made similar progress toward improvement.
Hispanic/Elementary.

425. Burtoff, M. J. (1984, March). *Where coherence breaks down: Identifying problems of logical structure in student writing.* Paper presented at the 18th Annual TESOL Convention, Houston, TX.
Presents a system for analyzing the underlying logical structure of student essays for teaching and evaluating coherence.
Coherence.

426. Burtoff, M. J. (1983). The logical organization of written expository discourse in English: A comparative study of Japanese, Arabic, and native speaker strategies (ESL). *Dissertation Abstracts International, 45*(9), 2857A.
Examines the validity of Kaplan's notion of contrastive rhetoric by studying essays written in English by Arabic, Japanese, and native speakers, on "culturally-loaded" topics and on "universal topics." Results indicate: (1) that there are culturally preferred strategies not culturally-specific strategies of organization; (2) strategies differ according to discourse topics.
Japanese/Arabic/Organization.

427. Butler, J. (1990). Concordancing, teaching and error analysis: Some applications and a case study. *System, 18,* 343-349.
A case study of an ESL student shows that a software package, such as Microconcord, may be used for basic error analysis as a help to language teachers seeking to identify transfer.
Computers/Errors/Korean.

428. Butler, J. (1980). Teaching editing skills through student monitoring. *TESL Reporter, 13*(3), 58-60.

    Discusses "phased monitoring" in which students meet in small groups with teacher to read and edit their finished papers. The group process goes through three stages: self-monitoring, group monitoring, and teacher monitoring.

    Responding.

429. Butler, S., & Butler, A. J. (Comps.). (1990). *Stories from Prague: Oral and written lifestorying by students at the Prague Institute of Chemical Technology in the process of learning English* . Vancouver, BC: Language Education Department, University of British Columbia.

    Stories by upper-level post-secondary students sample the results of classroom activities in which students shared personal or anecdotal experiences.

    Narration/Secondary School.

430. Butler-Nalin, K. (1984). Revising patterns in students' writing. In A. Applebee (Ed.), *Contexts for learning to write* (pp. 121-133). Norwood, NJ: Albex.

    Reports that ESL high school students revise very little and when they do mostly at the word and phrase levels to a far greater extent than their native speaking peers.

    Revision/NS-NNS Comparisons/Secondary School.

431. Butler-Pascoe, M. E. (1991). Effective uses of computer technology in the development of writing skills of students in a college level English as a second language program. *Dissertation Abstracts International, 51*(7), 2295A.

    A computer-based communicative group learning environment was found to be better than individualized drill and practice grammar classes when twenty-four intermediate ESL students were compared on both quantitative and qualitative measures.

    Computers/Grammar.

432. Byrd, D. R. H., & Gallingane, G. (1992). *Write away 2: A course for writing English*. Boston: Heinle & Heinle.

    Second in a series of texts designed to provide extensive writing practice for the classroom or self-study. See previous item.

    Beginners/Textbook.

433. Byrd, D. R. H., & Gallingane, G. (1991a). *Write away 1: A course for writing English*. Boston: Heinle & Heinle.

    First in a series of texts designed to provide extensive writing practice for the classroom or self-study. Each book presents grammar in paragraphs that begin with receptive tasks and lead to production tasks. A variety of exercises in rewriting and sentence combining allow students to create well-written work. The exercises center around real-life situations such as writing reports, letters, and articles.

    Beginners/Intermediate/Textbook.

434. Byrd, D. R. H., & Gallingane, G. (1991b). *Write away 3: A course for writing English*. NY: Heinle & Heinle/HarperCollins.

    Third of a three-volume series designed to provide extensive writing practice for the classroom or self-study. See previous items.

Intermediate/Textbook.

435. Byrd, D. R. H., & Gallingane, G. (1990). *Write away 3: A course for writing English*. Boston: Heinle & Heinle.

Third of a three-volume series designed to provide extensive writing practice for the classroom or self-study. See previous items.

Intermediate/Textbook.

436. Byrd, P. (1993, April). *Punctuation in ESL writing: Sentences sense and academic style*. Paper presented at the 27th Annual TESOL Convention, Atlanta, GA.

Discusses how punctuation reflects student misconceptions about sentences and academic writing, based on a corpus of ESL essays written for a required essay test.

Punctuation.

437. Byrd, P. (1985). *Write on: A student's guide to handwriting*. Boston: Heinle & Heinle.

A textbook, especially for students unfamiliar with the Roman alphabet, with writing tasks designed to produce the kind of handwriting most commonly used in the American classroom.

Handwriting/Textbook.

438. Byrd, P., & Benson, B. A. (1993). *Problem/solution: A reference for ESL writers*. Boston, MA: Heinle & Heinle.

A handbook for student writers who need to develop accuracy during revision and editing. Follows a problem/solution format, covering the most troublesome aspects of grammar and punctuation.

Textbook/Advanced.

439. Byrd, P., & Benson, B. A. (1989). *Improving the grammar of written English: The handbook*. Boston: Heinle & Heinle.

A combined grammar and writing program designed to enhance the ability of ESL students to write more sophisticated and accurate English. It presents information about the grammar of written English, focusing step-by-step on aspects of the written sentence. Includes exercises and passages illustrating use in texts.

Grammar/Intermediate/Textbook.

440. Byrd, P., & Benson, B. A. (1988). *Improving the grammar of written English: The editing process*. Boston: Heinle & Heinle.

A comprehensive workbook to accompany Byrd & Benson (1989) that seeks to train students to accurately edit their own writing.

University/Textbook.

441. Byrd, P., & Benson, B. A. (1987, April). *Learning to edit: Self-monitoring for advanced ESL writers*. Paper presented at the 21st Annual TESOL Convention, Miami Beach, FL.

Claims ESL students in university academic courses need to become independent learners of grammar as part of the editing process.

University/Editing.

442. Byrd, P., & Canseco, G. (1989, March). *Writing required in graduate courses in business administration*. Paper presented at the 23rd Annual TESOL Convention, San Antonio, TX.

Syllabi from 55 graduate business administration courses are analyzed in order to determine the type of writing assignments required.
Business Writing/Assignments.

443. Byrd, P., Denick, M., Blau, E. K., & McKinley, S. (1978). Memo writing and silence in the ESL composition class. In D. Ilyin, & T. Tragardh (Eds.), *Classroom practices in adult ESL* (pp. 171-175). Washington, DC: TESOL.
Students write to survive by writing each other memos.
Adult Education.

444. Byrd, P., & West, G. K. (1981). The purposes of technical writing courses for foreign students in U.S.colleges and universities. *TESOL Newsletter*, 15(2), 19- 20.
Claims that special courses in technical or scientific fields in the U.S. for ESL students should be EAP since it will also help students in their immediate writing needs.
Technical Writing/University.

445. Byrne, D. (1979). *Teaching writing skills*. NY: Longman.
Offers traditional advice about the methodology and content of teaching writing as a skill.
Teacher Preparation.

446. Byrne, R. (1974). Developing writing skills. *English Teachers Journal (Israel)*, 24-32.
Discusses some difficulties in learning to write in a foreign language. Suggests ways of teaching the skill.
Methods.

C

447. Cabello, B., & Raupp, M. (1984, March). *Strategies for writing*. Paper presented at the 18th Annual TESOL Convention, Houston, TX.
Presents instructional strategies based on recent research in teaching writing.
Process Instruction.

448. Cadet, N. E. (1987). Class writing projects with computers: Student collaboration and autonomy. *TESL Reporter*, 20(1), 3-5.
Describes a group writing project that involves word-processors and claims that it makes students use all language skills, fosters independence and collaboration and, on the whole, leads to more effective writing.
Project Work/Computers/Collaboration.

449. Cadiz, Y. (1987). Teaching intermediate composition to the adult learning English as a second language. In C. Cargill (Ed.), *A TESOL professional anthology: Grammar and composition* (pp. 77-89). Littlewood, IL: National Textbook Co.
Discusses traditional goals, plans, exercises, and techniques for teaching intermediate ESL composition in an intensive program.
Intermediate/IEP.

450. Cai, G. (1993, April). *Don't label them as "poor writers!" Look at what is behind their writing: Teaching Chinese ESL students English composition*. Paper presented at 44th Annual Convention of CCCC, San Diego, CA.

Chinese.

451. Calkins, L. M., Cummings, M. C., & Montera, A. (1985, April). *Teaching the writing process*. Paper presented at the 19th Annual TESOL Convention, New York, NY.

Describes how to convert classrooms into writing workshops by using response groups, writing as discovery, revision, and conferencing.

Process Instruction.

452. Calkins, L. M., Finn, P., Maher, M., Rigg, P., & Hu, Y. (1991, March). *Our newest frontiers in the teaching of writing*. Paper presented at the 25th Annual TESOL Convention, New York, NY.

Discusses new directions and how students' habits of thought, classroom observations, and family stories help in the learning and teaching of writing.

Teacher Preparation.

453. Campbell, C. C. (1990). Writing with others' words: Using background reading text in academic compositions. In B. Kroll (Ed.), *Second language writing: Research insights for the classroom* (pp. 221-230). Cambridge: Cambridge University Press.

Study documents how native and nonnative university students use information from a background reading text in their own writing. It describes their use of direct quotations, paraphrases, summaries, and other textual information.

Reading-Writing Relations/Research Writing/University.

454. Campbell, C. C. (1988a). Writing with others' words: The use of information from a background reading text in the writing of native and non-native university composition students. *Dissertation Abstract International, 48*(7), 1679A.

Examines the differences in the use of information from an extended reading source in the academic writing of native and non-native university students. Text analysis of 30 compositions shows that native speakers include more information copied from the background text and more text information that was backgrounded rather than foregrounded. Think-aloud protocols indicate that the non-native speakers rely on the background text (copying, simplifying, rereading) more than the native speakers because of the lack of authority over the background text and the emerging text.

Reading-Writing Relations/NS-NNS Comparisons.

455. Campbell, C. C. (1988b, March). *Writing with others' words: The need for authority*. Paper presented at the 39th Annual CCCC Meeting, St. Louis, MO.

See previous item.

Research Writing.

456. Campbell, C. C. (1987). *Writing with others' words: Native and non-native university students' use of information from a background reading text in academic compositions*. (Technical Report 4). Los Angeles, CA: Center for Language Education and Research, University of California.

Examines use of background information by native and non-native English-speaking university students in their academic compositions. Findings show that: (1) use of background information predominates in final paragraphs, (2) in opening paragraphs, non-native speakers used more information from source text, often with

little variations, (3) many of this copied information formed foreground rather than background, and (4) native language writers received consistently higher holistic scores.
Background Knowledge/Research Writing/NS-NNS Comparisons.

457. Campbell, D., Clark, C., & Rowoth, J. D. (1984). *The research paper for advanced ESL students*. Urbana,IL: ERIC/RCS. [ERIC ED 238 263].
A teaching guide to preparing students for college research writing.
Research Writing.

458. Canagarajah, A. S. (1993). Up the garden path: Second language writing approaches, local knowledge, and pluralism. Comments on Ann Raimes's "Out of the woods: Emerging traditions in the teaching of writing" . . .[In The Forum]. *TESOL Quarterly, 27*, 301-306.
Criticizes Raimes's pluralism for not unequivocably supporting a social criticism approach to academic writing. Suggests that ESL students should be taught to "negotiate with the dominant discourses for expression of local knowledge".
Instruction.

459. Canale, M. (1982). *Evaluating the coherence of student writing in L1 and L2*. Paper presented at the 16th Annual TESOL Convention, Honolulu, HI.
Coherence/Evaluation.

460. Canale, M., Frenette, N., & Belanger, M. (1988). Evaluation of minority student writing in first and second languages. In J. Fine (Ed.), *Second language discourse: A textbook of research* (pp. 147-165). Norwood, NJ: Ablex.
Examines the relationship between writing performance in French as a first language and English as a second language at the grade 9 and 10 levels in Ontario (N=1407), based on Cummins' Language Interdependence Hypothesis. Results indicate a significant relationship whose strength, however, varies with method of scoring.
French/L1 Influence/Children.

461. Cannilao, P. N. D. (1991). Audience awareness: An inquiry into its impact in ESL composition. *Dissertation Abstracts International, 52*(1), 147A.
Based on data from textual analysis, interviews, and questionnaires, this study concludes that the thirteen ESL students possess a current-traditional sense of audience. Specification of audience had little effect on student writing, yet audience was an important factor in effective writing.
Audience.

462. Cannon, B., & Polio, L. (1987, April). *Analyzing written interaction in dialogue journals*. Paper presented at the 21st Annual TESOL Convention, Miami Beach, FL.
Examines modification of teacher's response and interactional features in student writing.
Dialogue Journals/interaction.

463. Canseco, G., & Byrd, P. (1989). Writing required in graduate courses in business administration. *TESOL Quarterly, 23*, 305-316.
Reports on characteristics of writing assignments in graduate courses in busines -- the types, the prompts, and the vocabulary.

Academic Writing/Business Writing.

464. Card, P., & Simanu-Klutz, L. (1992, March). *Collaborative writing and math: An interactive model.* Workshop presented at the 26th Annual TESOL Convention, Vancouver, BC.

A workshop for teachers of grades 4 through 8 demonstrates how collaborative writing happens in a math class.

Elementary/Collaboration.

465. Cardelle, M., & Corno, L. (1981). Effects on second language learning of variations in written feedback on homework assignments. *TESOL Quarterly, 15,* 251-261.

Assesses the effects on second language learning of two kinds of written feedback: those that focus on errors or those that suppress them. Results indicate that the second language improves with a constructive focus on errors.

Error Treatment/Assignments.

466. Cargill, C. (Ed.). (1987). *A TESOL professional anthology: Grammar and composition* Lincolnwood, IL: National Textbook Co.

Papers by Barrett, Cadiz, Strei and Sunderman in this anthology for teachers and teacher-trainers concern the teaching of composition.

Teacher Preparation.

467. Carlisle, R. S. (1987). The writing of Anglo and Hispanic fourth- and sixth-graders in regular, submersion, and bilingual programs. *Dissertation Abstracts International, 47*(9), 3340A.

A descriptive cross-sectional study designed to compare the writing of Hispanic students in a bilingual program with that of Hispanic students in a submersion program and with native speakers shows that the regular program students had higher scores on rhetorical effectiveness and writing quality than the submersion and bilingual students, while the bilingual program students scored higher on syntactic maturity, productivity, and rhetorical effectiveness than the submersion program students.

Hispanic/Elementary.

468. Carlisle, R. S. (1989). The writing of Anglo and Hispanic elementary school students in bilingual, submersion, and regular programs. *Studies in Second Language Acquisition, 11*(3), 257-280.

Compares three groups of fourth- and sixth-grade students (N=64): Hispanic students in a bilingual program, those in a submersion program, and NES students. Results indicate that learning to write in L1 prior to L2 enables students to write as efectively in L2 as those learning to write only in L2.

Hispanic/Elementary.

469. Carlisle, R. S., & McKenna, E. (1991). Placement of ESL/EFL undergraduate writers in college-level writing programs. In L. Hamp-Lyons (Ed.), *Assessing second language writing in academic contexts* (pp. 197-211). Norwood, NJ: Ablex.

Reports a study of the readers of ESL essays on a 50-minute assessment test at the University of Michigan. Readers paid more attention to content and structure than to surface errors in their assesments.

Evaluation/Placement.

470. Carlisle, R. S., Hudelson, S., Samway, K. D., Serna, I. A., Taylor, D., & Urzua, C. (1991, March). *The writing development of language minority children* Colloquium presented at the 25th Annual TESOL Convention, New York, NY.

   Six presentations explore research on and development of children's writing. Topics include writing in bilingual and submersion programs, peer tutoring, letter writing, and the development of writing in the primary language.

   Children/Development.

471. Carlson, S. B. (1991). Program evaluation procedures: Reporting the program publically within the political context. In L. Hamp-Lyons (Ed.), *Assessing second language writing in academic contexts* (pp. 293-320). Norwood, NJ: Ablex.

   Suggests how to advise the public about writing assessment programs and presents responses to seven frequently asked questions.

   Evaluation/Programs.

472. Carlson, S. B. (1988). Cultural differences in writing and reasoning skills. In A. C. Purves (Ed.), *Writing across languages and cultures: Issues in contrastive rhetoric* (pp. 227-260). Newbury Park, CA: Sage.

   Presents a study that examines the interrelation of the features of written discourse to thinking and writing skills of non-native speakers of English.

   Variation/Culture.

473. Carlson, S. B., & Bridgeman, B. (1986). Testing ESL student writers. In K. L. Greenberg, H. S. Wiener, & R. A. Donovan (Eds.), *Writing assessment: Issues and strategies* (pp. 126-152). NY: Longman.

   Discusses research on measurement issues, the assessment of academic writing skills, as well as designing measures to assess ESL writing performance.

   Evaluation.

474. Carlson, S. B., Bridgeman, B., Camp, R., & Waanders, J. (1985). *Relationship of admission test scores to writing performance of native and nonnative speakers of English* TOEFL Research Report, 19. Princeton, NJ: Educational Testing Service.

   Finds that (1) writing samples provide additional information regarding English proficiency and are an indicator of English language skills, and (2) holistic scores consistently correlate with GRE General test.

   Assessment/Academic Writing.

475. Carlson, S. B., & Camp, R. (1985, April). *Relationships between direct and indirect measures of writing ability*. Paper given at the National Council of Measurement in Education Meeting, Chicago, IL. [ERIC ED 255 543].

   Summarizes ETS studies on native and non-native writers.

   Assessment/Objective Measures.

476. Carney, H. L. (1973). An inquiry into criteria for composition evaluation in English as a foreign language. *Dissertation Abstracts International, 34*(8), 5139-5140A.

   Studies experienced and inexperienced ESL evaluators. Finds that the former stress organization and meaning in communication, while the latter emphasized mechanical features of writing. Also compiles and assesses a set of rating criteria drawn from both groups of teachers.

   Assessment/Responding.

477. Carpenter, C., & Hunter, J. (1981a). Functional exercises: Improving overall coherence in ESL writing. *TESOL Quarterly*, *15*, 425-434.
    Presents writing exercises for advanced ESL students which consist of different organizational patterns.
    Coherence/Classroom Activities.

478. Carpenter, C., & Hunter, J. (1981b, March). *Writing signals: Improving overall organization of ESL writing*. Paper presented at the 15th Annual TESOL Convention, Detroit, MI.
    Presents a semi-programmed design for paragraph writing exercises that familiarize advanced students with the rhetoric of English passages.
    Paragraph/Advanced.

479. Carr, D. H. (1967). A second look at teaching reading and composition. *TESOL Quarterly*, *1*, 30-34.
    Claims that analytical reading should precede writing since the former provides organizational principles on which to base writing.
    Reading-Writing Relations.

480. Carr, M. (1983, July). *A five-step evaluation of a holistic essay-evaluation process*. Paper presented at the summer TESOL meeting, Toronto, BC. [ERIC ED 238 263].
    Describes how an intensive ESL program developed new criteria for evaluating essays.
    Evaluation/Holistic/IEP.

481. Carr, R., Price, P., & Athey, S. (1990). *Conference groups in the writing center: Shared resources*. Urbana, IL: ERIC/RCS. [ERIC ED 328 070].
    Designs a new writing course for ESL students at a major university. Course offers unit topics on ideal careers, career-related communication-needs, and narratives based on students' home cultures which are discussed in weekly conference group meetings and weekly individual conferences with teachers. Improvements found in student confidence, productivity, and skills in a pilot evaluation.
    Courses/Conferencing/Writing Center.

482. Carrell, P. L. (1991, March). *Research on reading-writing relationships*. Paper presented at the 26th Annual TESOL Convention, Vancouver, BC.
    Reviews research on the state of the art in this field in Symposium "Towards a Holistic Model of ESL Reading and Writing".
    Review.

483. Carrell, P. L. (1989, March). *The reading-writing connection*. Paper presented at the 40th Annual CCCC Meeting, Seattle, WA.
    Position paper on the current "state of the art" of L2 reading-writing research.
    Reading-Writing Relations.

484. Carrell, P. L. (1987). Text as interaction: Some implications of text analysis and reading research for ESL composition. In U. M. Connor, & R. B. Kaplan (Ed.), *Writing across languages: Analysis of L2 text* (pp. 47-56). Reading, MA: Addison-Wesley.
    Discusses theoretical advances in text analysis and reading comprehension research and suggests implications of these findings for ESL composition.

Reading-Writing Relations/Text Analysis/Interaction.

485. Carrell, P. L. (1984a). The author responds reply to Rankin . . . [In The Forum]. *TESOL Quarterly, 18,* 161-168.

Responds to Rankin's criticism of "Cohesion is not coherence." Claims that Rankin's assertions are not empirically based and reiterates that, while both cohesion and coherence can occur together, they are nonetheless mutually exclusive.

Cohesion/Coherence.

486. Carrell, P. L. (1984b, March). *Text as interaction: Some implications of text analysis and reading research for ESL composition.* Paper presented at the 18th Annual TESOL Convention, Houston, TX. [ERIC ED 243 313].

Claims that research in text analysis and reading comprehension, which view the written text as communicative interaction, has implications for ESL composition instruction. Suggests teaching the top-level rhetorical organization of expository texts, the way to achieve specific communication goals, and the use of linguistic devices to achieve textual organization.

Reading-Writing Relations/Text Analysis/Interaction.

487. Carrell, P. L. (1983). The author responds to Ghadessy . . . [In The Forum]. *TESOL Quarterly, 17,* 687-691.

Responds to Ghadessy by clarifying perspectives and reiterating claim that coherence and cohesion are not the same thing -- coherence logically precedes cohesion.

Cohesion/Coherence.

488. Carrell, P. L. (1982). Cohesion is not coherence. *TESOL Quarterly, 16,* 479-488.

The concept of cohesion as a measure of a text's coherence is criticized in the light of theoretical and empirical research on schema theory. Second language teachers are cautioned not to expect cohesion theory to be the solution to ESL reading and writing coherence problems at the text level.

Cohesion/Coherence.

489. Carrell, P. L., & Connor, U. M. (1991a). Reading and writing descriptive and persuasive texts. *Modern Language Journal, 75,* 314-324.

With multiple measures, this study examines relationships between reading and writing by intermediate proficiency students. Results suggest that the reading-writing relationship varies, that genre complexly effects the relationship, and that educational level as distinct from language proficiency plays a role.

Reading-Writing Relations/Persuasion/Description.

490. Carrell, P. L., & Connor, U. M. (1991a, March). *Reading and writing different genres.* Paper presented at the 25th Annual TESOL Convention, New York, NY.

Uses multiple measures to investigate the reading and writing of narrative, descriptive/expository, and persuasive/ argumentative genres by intermediate ESL students.

Genre/Reading-Writing Relations/Intermediate.

491. Carrell, P. L., & Connor, U. M. (1991c, March). *Second language and writing in different genres.* Paper presented at the 42nd Annual CCCC Meeting, Boston.

See previous item.

492. Carrell, P. L., & Eisterhold, J. C. (1987, April). *Training formal schemata for reading and writing ESL*. Paper presented at the 21st Annual TESOL Convention, Miami, FL.

Reports an empirical study of training formal schemata for reading or for writing with effects on writing or reading, respectively.

Schema/Reading-Writing Relations.

493. Carrell, P. L., & Monroe, L. B. (1993). Learning styles and composition. *Modern Language Journal, 77*, 148-162.

Discusses relative value for NNS writers of learning style measures, such as the Group Embedded Figures Test, Oxford's Strategy Inventory for Language Learning, Schmeck's Inventory for Learning Processes, and the Meyer-Briggs Type Indicator. Finds a number of significant correlations between Meyers Briggs Type Indicator of learning style and both objective and holistic measures of writing among essays by basic, freshman composition, and ESL composition writers.

Learning Styles.

494. Carrell, P. L., & Monroe, L. B. (1992a, March). *Learning styles and composition*. Paper presented at the 26th Annual TESOL Convention, Vancouver, BC.

See Carrell & Monroe, 1993.

Learning Styles/Assessment.

495. Carrell, P. L., & Monroe, L. B. (1992b, March). *Learning styles and composition*. Paper presented at the 43rd Annual CCCC Meeting, Cincinnati, OH.

See Carrell & Monroe, 1993.

Learning Styles/Assessment.

496. Carrell, P. L., & Monroe, L. B. (1991, March). *Investigating ESL students' learning styles*. Paper presented at the 25th Annual TESOL Convention, New York, NY.

See Carrell & Monroe 1993.

Learning Styles/Assessment.

497. Carroll, J. (1992, March). *Heart and hand: Conceptualizing Asian rhetorics*. Paper presented at the 43rd Annual CCCC Meeting, Cincinnati, OH.

Asian/Rhetoric.

498. Carson, J. E. (1990a, March). *Evidence of transfer and loss in developing second language writers*. Paper presented at the Second Language Research Forum, Eugene, OR.

Investigates the role that transfer and/or loss of L1 writing abilities plays in the development of L2 proficiency. Data from Chinese ESL writers indicate that academic writing skills develop as a function of educational experience. While good L1 writers tend to be good L2 writers, a tradeoff in L1-L2 proficiency as well as a ceiling effect are also in evidence.

L1 Influence/Transfer/Chinese.

499. Carson, J. E. (1990b). Reading-writing connections: Toward a description for second language learners. In B. Kroll (Ed.), *Second language writing: Research insights for the classroom* (pp. 88-101). Cambridge: Cambridge University Press.

Reports three hypotheses (directional, nondirectional, and bidirectional) concerned with the way reading may influence writing in a second language. Unlike in L1, L2 literacy seeks support from a language system not yet fully developed. Acquiring literacy seems to result from both L2 input and the transfer of L1 literacy skills.

Reading-Writing Relations/Literacy/L1 Influence.Meeting,

500. Carson, J. G. (1993a). Reading for writing: Cognitive dimensions. In J. G. Carson, & I. Leki (Eds.), *Reading in the composition classroom: Second language perspectives* (pp. 85-104). Boston: Heinle & Heinle.

Presents a theoretical overview of the cognitive aspects of literacy development, especially of meaning construction in reading and writing and the influence of first language literacy.

Reading-Writing Relations/Cognition.

501. Carson, J. G. (1993b, April). *The relationship between ESL writing instruction and content courses*. Paper presented at 44th Annual Convention of CCCC, San Diego CA.

Instruction/Content.

502. Carson, J. G. (1992a). Becoming biliterate: First language influences. *Journal of Second Language Writing*, 1(1), 37-60.

Explores three aspects of literacy development for Japanese and Chinese elementary and secondary students: social context of schooling, cognitive considerations of the written code, and the pedagogical practices used to teach reading and writing.

Literacy/Chinese/Japanese.

503. Carson, J. G. (1992b, March). *Collaborative writing: A cross-cultural issue*. Paper presented at the 43rd Annual CCCC Meeting, Cincinnati, OH.

Demonstrates that group work is not necessarily collaborative work with reference to Japanese and Chinese cultural values.

Collaboration/Culture.

504. Carson, J. G. (1991a, April). *The influence of L1 education on L2 literacy*. Paper presented at the 25th Annual TESOL Convention, New York, NY.

505. Carson, J. G. (1991b, October). *Writing in academic discourse communities: Student perceptions*. Paper presented at the Southeast Regional TESOL Conference, Atlanta, GA.

Presents data from interviews with professors and ESL students in four academic disciplines about the literacy demands of their courses. Suggests that students are not always able to translate instructor's goals for a course into effective writing and study strategies. How writing varies across disciplines appears to be a major source of this problem.

Discourse Communities/WAC.

506. Carson, J. E., Carrell, P. L., Silberstein, S., Kroll, B., & Kuehn, P. A. (1990a). Reading-writing relationships in first and second language. *TESOL Quarterly, 24*, 245-266.

Investigates relationships across languages (LI and L2) and modalities (reading and writing) in the acquisition of L2 literacy. Japanese and Chinese students in academic settings wrote essays and completed closed exams in two languages. Results suggest that literacy can transfer across languages. However, the pattern of transfer varies for each language group. Reading transfers more easily than writing ability. A number of background factors are related to L2 literacy acquisition.

Literacy/Reading-Writing Relations/L1 Influence.

507. Carson, J. E., Carrell, P. L., Silberstein, S., Kroll, B., & Kuehn, P. A. (1990b, March). *The transfer of literacy skills across and within languages.* Paper presented at the 24th Annual TESOL Convention, San Francisco, CA.

Reports on a study of Japanese and Chinese ESL students in academic settings, focusing on the nature of reading-writing relationships in L1 and L2. Examines the ways in which L1 literacy skills affect L2 literacy development and also the ways in which reading and writing skills are related in L1 and/or L2.

Reading-Writing Relations/L1 Influence/Japanese/Chinese.

508. Carson, J. G., & Kuehn, P. A. (1992). Evidence of transfer and loss in developing second language writers. *Language Learning*, 42, 157-182.

Investigates the role that transfer and/or loss of L1 writing abilities plays in the development of L2 proficiency. Data from Chinese ESL writers indicate that academic writing skills develop as a function of educational experience. While good L1 writers tend to be good L2 writers, a tradeoff in L1-L2 proficiency as well as a ceiling effect are also in evidence.

Transfer/Literacy/Chinese.

509. Carson, J. G., & Leki, I. (1993a). Introduction. In J. G. Carson, & I. Leki (Eds.), *Reading in the composition classroom: Second language perspectives* (pp. 1-7). NY: Heinle & Heinle.

Describes how the interrelatedness of reading and writing in one specific context-- the classroom-- is presented in this volume of original research papers. The first section gives relevant background knowledge; the second, presents studies of individual cognitive L2 development, and the third, offers examinations of meaning-making acts in a social context.

Reading-Writing Relations.

510. Carson, J. G., & Leki, I. (Eds.). (1993b). *Reading in the composition classroom: Second language perspectives* (pp. 1-7). Boston: Heinle & Heinle.

A collection of nineteen original essays examines the importance and potential impact of second language reading on second language writing. Embraces both social and cognitive dimensions of literacy development and presents theoretical and practical perspectives on integrating reading in the writing curriculum.

Reading-Writing Relations.

511. Carter, M. E. (1976). Error analysis in the free compositions of Spanish speakers. *Dissertation Abstracts International*, 36(9), 6061A.

Examines the errors in free-writing composition in English by Spanish speakers in order to: (1) develop a taxonomy of errors; (2) to test the validity of error analysis in deducing pedagogical implications; (3) and to test if contrastive

analysis should be a part of error analysis. Finds a relationship between errors and methodology, and that contrastive analysis can only predict interlingual not intralingual errors.
Hispanic/Error Analysis.

512. Carter, R. D. (1986, March). *Teaching the process approach in Poland*. Paper presented at the 37th Annual CCCC Meeting, New Orleans, LA. [ERIC ED 268 531].
Finds that a process approach to writing does not eliminate the Slavic discourse patterns in writing by Polish EFL students of moderate proficiency.
Contrastive Rhetoric/Process Instruction/Polish.

513. Carthy, V. (1978). *An analysis of transitional devices in descriptive compositions of native and non-native speakers of English*. Unpublished master's thesis, American University, Cairo, Egypt.
Arabic/Cohesion.

514. Carver, T., Fotinis, S. D., & Olson, C. K. (1982). *A writing book: English in everyday life*. NY: Prentice Hall Regents.
Textbook for students without the oral proficiency needed to perform necessary writing tasks in exercises that simulate life situations.
Beginners/Textbook.

515. Casey, B. I. (1981, March). *Message design -- Blueprints for oral and written communication*. Paper presented at the 15th Annual TESOL Convention, Detroit, MI.

Discusses "attribute cards" as a teaching aid that leads to four types of "message design": description, process, definition, and comparison/ contrast.
Elementary/Materials.

516. Castellano, M. (1989, March). *The literacy experiences of a Chicano student: A case study of Ernesto*. Paper presented at the 40th Conference on College Composition and Communication, Seattle, WA. [ERIC ED 320 457].
A case study of a bilingual Chicano basic writer reveals that inabilities are linked with unsuccessful and negative early literacy experiences in English- medium immersion classes.
Spanish/Literacy.

517. Castille, P. (1984, March). *Teaching technical writing to international students through case-study methods*. Paper presented at the 18th Annual TESOL Convention, Houston, TX.
Describes a case study approach to teaching the conventions of technical reporting and formating in business and industrial writing situations.
Technical Writing.

518. Cave, G. (1972). From controlled to free composition. *English Language Teaching*, 26, 262-269.
Advocates a mixture of quantity and quality in teaching extended writing.
Control/Fluency.

519. Cech, E. (1984, March). *A fusion of traditions: Family folklore as a new method for teaching composition*. Paper presented at the 18th Annual TESOL Convention,

Houston, TX.

By creating a family folklore book, students are motivated to write meaningfully and in a sustained way.

Student Publications/Motivation.

520. Celce-Murcia, M. (1985). Making informed decisions about the role of grammar in language teaching. *TESOL Newsletter*, *19*, 1, 4-5.

Claims that ESL teachers should consider learner and instructional variables before deciding the role of grammar in the classroom. Suggests using grammatical rules in error correction.

Grammar/Error Treatment.

521. Celce-Murcia, M. (1988, March). *Integrating grammar into the ESL composition class*. Paper presented at the 22nd Annual TESOL Convention, Chicago, IL.

Suggests a variety of ways to include grammar practice in prewriting, writing, revision, and editing phases of composition.

Curriculum/Grammar.

522. Celce-Murcia, M., Connor-Linton, J., Holliday, C. W., Holten, C. A., Tribble, C., & Widdowson, H. G. (1991, March). *Discourse analysis and the teaching of writing*. Paper presented at the 25th Annual TESOL Convention, New York, NY.

Colloquium presents a theoretical framework, four instructional activities; and discussion of the use of discourse analysis as a learning tool in the writing classroom.

Discourse Analysis.

523. Cerniglia, C., Medsker, K., & Connor, U. M. (1990). Improving coherence by using computer-assisted instruction. In U. M. Connor, & A. M. Johns (Eds.), *Coherence in writing: Research and pedagogical perspectives* (pp. 227-241). Alexandria, VA: TESOL.

Describes the development and implementation of Studying Topical Analysis to Revise (STAR), a computer-assisted instructional program for helping students analyze and revise their writing for coherence.

TSA/Revision/Computers.

524. Chalaysap, A. (1981). Syntactic variables in the written English of Thai university students from three proficiency levels. *Dissertation Abstracts International*, *41*(7), 2976A.

Examines the syntactic maturity of EFL Thai students at three proficiency levels. Clause length, T-unit length, sentence length, and average number of less-than-a-predicate and less-than-a-clause structures were found efficient variables in measuring EFL development. Error-free data were found more valid. Claims that trend in development of Thai students paralleled that of native speakers.

Syntactic Development/Thai.

525. Chambers, F., & Brigham, A. (1989). Summary writing: A short cut to success. *English Teaching Forum*, *27*(1), 43-44.

Describes a "deletion approach" to summary writing.

Summary Writing.

526. Chamot, A. U. (1981, March). *ESL writing skills in the elementary bilingual classroom*. Paper presented at the 15th Annual TESOL Convention, Detroit, MI.

Presents a cognitive ESL writing model and demonstrates mechanical, meaningful and communicative writing activities for each level of written production.
Elementary/Instruction.

527. Chamot, A. U., & O'Malley, J. M. (1989, March). *Teaching learning strategies for literature and composition*. Demonstration presented at the 23rd Annual TESOL Convention, San Antonio, TX.
Shows how academic language development and learning strategy instruction are incorporated into children's literature and composition lessons.
Strategies/Literature/Children.

528. Chan, M. M. (1990a). *Process and practice: Activities for composing English*. Boston: Heinle & Heinle.
Demonstrates how a process approach is applied to actual student writing. Common problems of second language learners are highlighted and useful steps on how to avoid these problems are offered. Uses actual ESL students' writing samples as illustrations of these problems. Various exercises include practice assignments, process activities, and feedback questions.
University/Advanced/Textbook.

529. Chan, M. M. (1990b, March). *Ethnography and the study of writing in academic contexts*. Paper presented at the 24th TESOL Annual Convention, San Francisco, CA.
Describes an ethnographic study of writing in a university business course.
University/ESP/Ethnographic Research.

530. Chan, M. M. (1988a). What we already know about teaching ESL writers. *English Journal, 77*(6), 84-85.
A review of research suggests teaching strategies for elementary and secondary school ESL writers.
Elementary/Secondary School.

531. Chan, M. M. (1988b, March). *Learning by doing, discussing, and questioning: A collaborative writing course*. Paper presented at the CCCC Meeting, St. Louis, MO. [ERIC ED 296 336].
Describes a collaborative writing course at Chinese University of Hong Kong.
Courses/Collaboration/Chinese.

532. Chance, L. L. (1974). The development of an objective composition test for non-native speakers of English. *Dissertation Abstracts International, 34*(12), 7511A.
Develops and administers an objective composition test and examines if it correlates with grades on written compositions. Results show that there is a correlation between the two. Concludes that skill in composition is a function of total language proficiency, that objective composition tests are useful time-savers and can be used diagnostically.
Evaluation/Assessment.

533. Chandrasegeran, A. (1986). An exploratory study of EFL student revision and self-correction skills. *RELC Journal, 17*(2), 26-40.
Finds students capable of detecting and correcting 25% of their errors and defects.

Error Treatment/Revision.

534. Chang, S. J. (1982). Linguistics and written discourse in particular languages: Contrastive studies: English and Korean. *Annual Review of Applied Linguistics, 3,* 85-98.

   Offers a review of some grammatical, sociocultural, and pedagogical contrasts between Korean and English, with bibliographies.

   Contrastive Rhetoric/Korean.

535. Chang, W. L. (1971). *A comparison of certain structures written in English by monolingual and bilingual sixth graders.* Unpublished doctoral dissertation, Boston University, Boston.

   Conducts a correlation study of textual features in writing samples by monolingual and bilingual twelfth-graders and their language proficiency, intelligence, and socio-economic status. Finds that monolinguals and bilinguals are more homogenous in one SES community than another. The amount and type of subordination in the non-homogenous sample correlated significantly with SES status and test scores.

   Children/NS-NNS Comparisons.

536. Chapin, R., & Kirk, A. (1989, March). *Evaluating effective responses to ESL student writing.* Paper presented at the 23rd Annual TESOL Convention, San Antonio, TX.

   Discusses selected responding strategies which promote learning and effective revision.

   Responding/Revision.

537. Chapman, J. B. (1980). *Composition materials for adult ESL students: Adapting English as a foreign language.* Unpublished master's thesis, University of Illinois, Chicago Circle, Chicago, IL.

   Presents advanced composition materials for university students for use with adult education English-as-a-second language students.

   Programs/Materials/Advanced.

538. Chappell, V. A. (1988). Fitting texts to context: Student writers and the construction of audience. *Dissertation Abstracts International, 49*(9), 2567A.

   Investigates how native and non-native student writers interpret, accomodate, and construct the contexts for which they were assigned to write in an advanced technical report writing class. Data from writing conferences in which students discussed their drafts suggests that writing problems relate to situation and convention. A disregard for audience is attributed to misinterpretation of audience needs and the writer's role which in turn stems from inexperience with rhetorical authority. A follow-up of three students finds some learning to shape text into context.

   Conferencing/NS-NNS Comparisons.

539. Chappell, V. A., & Rodby, J. (1983). Verb tense and ESL composition: A discourse level approach. In M. A. Clarke, & M. Handscombe (Eds.), *On TESOL '82: Pacific perspectives on language learning and teaching* (pp. 309-320). Washington, DC: TESOL.

   Examines ESL students' perceptions of their verb tense errors. States that their

difficulty lies in relating tense to context and rhetorical stance. Lack of temporal adverbials is often responsible for apparent arbitrariness of tense shifts in the writing of ESL students. Claims that exercises in verb tense should be within a context and provides guidelines for materials development.
Syntactic Structures.

540. Chappell, V. A., & Rodby, J. (1982, May). *Verb tense and ESL composition: A discourse level approach.* Paper presented at the 16th Annual TESOL Convention, Honolulu, HI. [ERIC ED 219 964].
See previous item.
Errors/Materials.

541. Chargvis, G. V. (1985). A plan to make correcting writing errors enjoyable: Implementing peer revision. *TECFORS, 8*(2), 6-8. [ERIC ED 267 650].
Suggests using peer work in pairs to correct errors in student papers compiled (one imperfect sentence from each paper) by the teacher.
Error Treatment/Peer Response/Editing.

542. Charles, A. H. (1991). Guiding second-language students in beginning to speak and write freely. *English Teaching Forum, 29*(3), 48-49.
Describes a "guided speech and writing" method for beginners.
Secondary School/Beginners/Speaking-Writing Relations.

543. Charles, M. (1990). Responding to problems in written English using a student self-monitoring technique. *ELT Journal, 44*, 286-293.
Presents a technique of self-monitoring whereby students annotate their written drafts with comments and queries about their problem areas prior to submission of text to teacher who responds in writing to these notes.
Feedback/Interaction.

544. Charoenrath, P. (1976). *Teaching college composition in English as a foreign language.* Unpublished master's thesis, University of Texas, Austin, TX.
Thai/University.

545. Charry, M. B. (1988). *Teaching ESL students to paraphrase what they read.* Paper presented at the New York College Learning Skills Association, New York, NY. [ERIC ED 299 537].
Suggests that paraphrasing is an assessment as well as instructional technique.
Paraphrase Writing/Assessment.

546. Chaudron, C. (1987). Introduction -- analysis of products and instructional approaches in writing: Two articles on the state of the art. *TESOL Quarterly, 21*, 673-675.
Introduces articles by Connor (1987) and Zamel (1987), by highlighting the fact that the provision of explicit knowledge about the target language and of structure for learners is not incompatible with a process view of L2 writing.
Instruction.

547. Chaudron, C. (1984). The effects of feedback on students' composition revisions. *RELC Journal, 15*(2), 1-14.
Finds neither teacher nor peer evaluation superior in promoting improvements on revisions in an advanced ESL writing course.

Feedback/Revision/Advanced.

548. Chaudron, C. (1983, March). *Evaluating writing: Effects of feedback on revision.* Revised version of a paper presented at the 17th Annual TESOL Convention, Toronto, Ontario. [ERIC ED 227 706].

   Compares different methods of evaluating compositions for their influences on learners revisions of their own compositions.

   Evaluation/Revision.

549. Chaudron, C., Connor, U. M., Gaskill, W. H., & Zamel, V. (1986, March). *State of the art in writing: Process, product, and pedagogy.* Colloquium presented at the 20th Annual TESOL Convention, Anaheim, CA.

   Panel reviews studies of the writing process, of products, and their evaluations.

   Review.

550. Chelala, S. I. (1982). The composing process of two Spanish-speakers and the coherence of their texts: A case study. *Dissertation Abstracts International, 42*(12), 5045A.

   Examines coherence in the composing process of two Argentinian women using a talk-aloud protocol. Devises a scheme to analyze successful and unsuccessful strategies in composing.

   Process Research/Spanish/Coherence.

551. Chen, D. W. (1993). A study of the relationship of ESL students' English language proficiency and writing expertise and its implications to the curriculum of teaching ESL writing. *Dissertation Abstracts International, 53*(11), 3826A-3827A.

   An investigation of the pauses made by five Chinese graduate students when writing on two topics in Chinese and English as well as qualitative data suggest that attitude and methods of writing (similar in English and Chinese) are more effective strategies than language-focused factors.

   Expertise/Curriculum.

552. Chen, E. S. H. (1989). Teaching research paper writing in EST: Content, language and communication. In *A Forum anthology, Volume IV: Selected articles from the English Teaching Forum, 1984-1988* (pp. 141-146). Washington, DC: USIA, Bureau of Educational and Cultural Affairs.

   Describes a research paper writing course in Taiwan for engineering students.

   Research Writing/Chinese.

553. Chen, S. I. (1986). *Argumentative discourse structure in Chinese and English writing: A comparative analysis.* Unpublished master's thesis, Simon Fraser University, Vancouver, BC. [ERIC Discovers that language (Chinese vs. English) and political stance (communist vs. capitalist) influenced discrepant discourse structures in newspaper editorials from the People's Republic of China and Taiwan.

   Chinese/Argumentation/Contrastive Rhetoric.

554. Chen, Y. F. (1982). *Teaching advanced English composition to Chinese college students.* Unpublished master's thesis, California State University, Fresno, CA.

   Advanced/Chinese.

555. Chen, Y. M. (1993). The writing development of college students and effective

instruction. *Dissertation Abstracts International, 53*(10), 3463A-3464A.

    Attempts to identify factors affecting the comparative writing development of NES and NNS college students in required composition courses through a qualitative approach. Classrom observations and interviews with four NSs and 8 NNSs (Koreans and Mexicans), their instructors, and program administrators reveal relevant contextual, cultural, and individual factors. Describes effective writing instruction in light of these factors.

    NS-NNS Comparisons/University.

556. Cheng, P. G. P. (1985). An analysis of contrastive rhetoric: English and Chinese expository prose, pedagogical implications, and strategies for the ESL teacher in a ninth grade curriculum. *Dissertation Abstracts International, 46*(9), 2539A.

    Analysis of a sample of sixty ESL compositions finds influence of Chinese rhetorical style and organization.

    Chinese/Contrastive Rhetoric/Exposition/Secondary School.

557. Chenoweth, A. (1987). The need to teach rewriting. *ELT Journal, 1*, 25-29.

    Recent research shows that there is a difference in how unskilled and skilled writers write and in how they rewrite. Better writers have strategies for correcting local problems such as word choice, grammar, and punctuation and also to deal with the overall content and meaning of their writing by adding, deleting, or reorganizing large chunks of discourse.

    Revision.

558. Chen-yu, F. (1981). *Teaching advanced English composition to Chinese college students*. Unpublished master's thesis, California State University, Fresno

    Advanced/Chinese/University.

559. Chessin, L., & Auerbach, E. R. (1982). Teaching composition to Northwest American Indians. In H. G. Bartelt, S. Penfield-Jasper, & B. Hoffer (Eds.), *Essays in native American English* (pp. 173-186). San Antonio, TX: Trinity University Press.

    Errors in English composition by Northwest American Indian college students are similar to those made by students of other language backgrounds, but frequency and causal factors are not always the same.

    Amer-Indian/Error Analysis.

560. Cheung, K. K. (1984). Drawing out the silent majority. *College Composition and Communication, 35*, 452-454.

    Claims that there is a correlation between oral participation and writing progress. Suggests ways of making silent ESL students participate in discussions.

    Responding.

561. Chi, M. M. Y. (1987, November). *The development of early literacy in Chinese-speaking children*. Paper presented at the 77th Annual NCTE Convention, Los Angeles, CA.

    Chinese/Literacy.

562. Chiang, Y. S. D. (1993). The process-oriented writing workshop and "non-native" speakers of English: A teacher-researcher study. *Dissertation Abstracts International, 53*(9), 3090-91A.

Describes the development of sixteen NNS student writers in a process-oriented writing workshop. Multiple data, collected over a sixteen-week period and analyzed using a constant comparative method (Glaser & Strauss, 1967), suggest student development, teacher growth, and the creation of sense of community between teacher and students. Th study claims to challenge current views of needs and pedagogy for NNS writers.

Workshop.

563. Chiang, Y. S. D. (1991). *A voice of own's own: Reconsidering the needs of non-native speakers of English*. Paper presented at the 42nd Annual Meeting of the CCCC, Boston, MA. [ERIC ED 340 014].

Reflects experience of a teacher-researcher who illustrates the value of inviting students to write by showing how a Malaysian-American student progressed from a translation mode to writing meaningfully.

Voice/Malay.

564. Chimombo, M. (1987). Towards reality in the writing class. *ELT Journal, 52*, 204-210.

Using the editor of a local newspaper provides a genuine purpose and audience for writing, stimulates argumentative discussion based on identifying opinions and constructing a balanced argument, and introduces reality in a writing class.

Malawi/Argumentation.

565. Chimombo, M. (1986). Evaluating compositions with large classes. *ELT Journal, 40*, 20-26.

Suggests alternative techniques for marking errors and evaluating compositions in large classes ranging from sentence-level, paragraph-level, to composition-level techniques, based on a longitudinal research project exploring students' progress in writing in secondary schools in Malawi.

Evaluation/Secondary School/Malawi.

566. Ching, L. P., & Ngooi, A. C. (1991). How journal writing improved our classes. *English Teaching Forum, 29*(3), 43-44.

Journal Writing.

567. Ching, R. J., McKee, S., & Tooker, N. (1990, March). *Making connections: Computers, tutors, and ESL students*. Paper presented at the 24th Annual TESOL Convention, San Francisco, CA. [ERIC ED 324 978].

Discusses a four-semester individualized program to promote the use of computers for writing by ESL students.

Computers/Word Processing.

568. Chirinos, S. L. (1982). Adaptations in the teaching of composition to non-native speakers of English. *Alternative Higher Education: The Journal of Non-Traditional Studies, 6*, 184-192.

Two composition courses were modified to meet the needs of students who were beyond English as a second language composition but not yet ready for mainstream study. It is suggested that adaptations in approach and content are necessary in order to fulfill the needs of these special students.

Curriculum.

569. Chisholm, J., & Al-Batal, K. (1992, March). *Is "furthermore" going far enough? Moving beyond connectors in cohesion*. Paper presented at the 26th Annual TESOL Convention, Vancouver, BC.

　　Presents tasks that give university ESL students in business and science opportunities to use topic-chaining and complex grammatical structures to achieve cohesion.
　　Cohesion/ESP.

570. Chiste, K. B., & O'Shea, J. (1988). Patterns of question selection and writing performance of ESL students. *TESOL Quarterly, 22*, 681-684.

　　Finds that ESL writers prefer shorter, earlier positioned questions when options are offered on an essay-type entrance essay test.
　　Assessment/Prompts.

571. Choi, Y. H. (1991, March). *Discourse references in Korean students' writing in English*. Paper presented at the 25th Annual TESOL Convention, New York, NY.

　　Compares discourse references in ESL writing of Korean students and of professional American and Korean writers. Discusses strategies, domain of reference, factors affecting choices, and the proportion of referential devices used.
　　Korean/Cohesion/NS-NNS Comparisons.

572. Choi, Y. H. (1989). Textual coherence in English and Korean: Analysis of argumentative writing by American and Korean students. *Dissertation Abstracts International, 50*(2), 429A.

　　Analyzes the holistic and analytic assessments by Korean and American evaluators of 76 English and 49 Korean ESL/EFL essays. Finds different notions of text coherence among native English and Korean judges, related to cultural conventions.
　　Korean/Argumentation/Coherence.

573. Choi, Y. H. (1988a). Text structure of Korean speakers' argumentative essays in English. *World Englishes, 7*(2), 129-142.

　　A text structure analysis using an interactional approach shows relative differences in the structure of argumentative essays by Korean speakers writing in Korean and English and native speakers of English. Korean essays are nonlinear while English essays are based on the claim+justification+conclusion structure. Similarities in these three basic components, however, indicate that there are some universal characteristics of argumentative texts common to both Korean and English writing.
　　Contrastive Rhetoric/Argumentation/Korean.

574. Choi, Y. H. (1988b, March). *Coherence problems in Korean ESL/EFL students' argumentative writing*. Paper presented at the 22nd Annual TESOL Convention, Chicago, IL.

　　Classifies and discusses frequent coherence problems.
　　Coherence/Korean/Argumentation.

575. Choi, Y. H. (1986). A study of coherence in Korean students' argumentative writing in English. *Studies in Linguistic Science, 16*(2), 67-94.

Examines two aspects of coherence -- text structure and coherence breaks -- in Korean speakers' argumentative writing in English. Eleven essays on three argumentative tasks were analyzed according to Aston (1977), Tirkkonen-Condit (1985), and Wikborg (1985). A pattern of claim+justification+conclusion dominates native English speaker essays but no single pattern is evident in either the English or Korean essays by Korean speakers. Coherence breaks among the Korean speaker essays far outnumber those in native speaker essays, suggesting higher toleration in former.
Contrastive Rhetoric/Coherence/Korean/Argumentation.

576. Christensen, J. P. (1993). Writing by example: The prose models approach revisited. *TESL Reporter*, 26(2), 65-67.

Contends that ESL students need to read, analyze, and mimick essys similar to those they are expected to produce in order to acquire the ability to write.
Models.

577. Christensen, T. (1986). An approach to English composition for college freshmen in an EFL situation. *Hokusei Women's Junior College Kiyo*, 23, 79-86. [ERIC ED 281 351].

Describes a teaching technique which stresses frequency and volume of writing, but does not require complexity. Simple writing tasks involve rewriting sentences to change certain conditions such as time or voice. This approach is recommended for competent students of English with little training experience.
Fluency/Assignments/Revision.

578. Christopher, V. (1993, April). *Writing tests versus objective tests as placement measures*. Paper presented at the 27th Annual TESOL Convention, Atlanta, GA.

Compares two measures: a holistically-rated essay and the MTELP, to decide which is a better placement instrument.
Placement/Evaluation.

579. CILT (1968). *A language teaching bibliography*. Cambridge: University Press.
Only two of 518 items about ESL writing.
Bibliography.

580. Clair, E. (1982). *A writing program for elementary-age children who have English as a second language*. Unpublished master's thesis, Washington State University, Pullman, WA. [ERIC ED 229 771].

Designs an experimental writing project for three elementary school ESL students: a third grader from Japan, a fourth grader from Costa Rica, and a fifth grader from Indonesia, based on fluency activities as defined by Mina Shaughnessy. Children showed marked gains in syntactic fluency, verbal fluency, and ability to express a specific purpose in writing after a semester.
Curriculum/Elementary.

581. Clark, B. L. (1984). *Talking about writing: A guide for tutor and teacher conferences*. Ann Arbor, MI: University of Michigan Press.

Provides guidelines for teachers and tutors teaching writing through conference with individuals. Uses excerpts from journals of experienced tutors to deal with important issues.

Tutoring.

582. Clark, G. (1982). Making the need to write seem real. *TECFORS*, *5*(4), 1-3. [ERIC ED 267 648].

Claims that writing tasks in a compositon class can be made more realistic if assignments that pose real rhetorical problems are given and if students are taught how to plan their responses in accordance to it.

Assignments/Rhetoric.

583. Clark, J. A. R. (1980). A comparative analysis of selected writing errors of Oklahoma State University students learning English as a second language. *Dissertation Abstracts International*, *40*(12), 6256A.

Examines errors related to articles, prepositions, word order, concord, and formation of plurals in the written compositions of Persian, Hindi, Chinese and Spanish speaking ESL students. Findings show some interference from individual native languages.

Error Analysis/University/Persian/Hindi/Chinese/Spanish.

584. Clark, W. G. (1986). The ESL student in the freshman composition class. *Teaching English in the Two-Year College*, *13*(1), 13-19.

To help ESL students immersed in the freshman composition class, suggests the importance of understanding the second language acqusition process, of going beyond attention to surface error, and of creating a secure environment in which to use language.

Freshman Composition.

585. Clarke, D. L. (1976). *A survey of the writing needs and problems of foreign graduate students in Engineering as a basis for the development of an ESL technical writing course.* Unpublished master's thesis, UCLA, Los Angeles, CA.

Finds theses and dissertations are the most important forms of writing and paragraph organization, the most important skill needed.

Needs/Technical Writing.

586. Clarke, D. L., & Walker, D. (1980). Speedwriting: A technique for improving writing fluency. *English Teaching Forum*, *18*(3), 20-21.

Discusses use of variations on an idea first observed by Celce-Murcia (1974) of having students write non-stop for a definite, limited time period.

Fluency.

587. Clarke, M. A. (1984). On the nature of technique: What do we owe the gurus? *TESOL Quarterly*, *18*, 577-594.

Examines relationship between theoretical insights gained from gurus and actual classroom practice. Demonstrates with the use of "blackboard composition" that, though theoretical insights may form the framework for classroom activity, its success depends on teachers' innovations.

Classroom Activities.

588. Clarke, M. A. (1973, May). *Five steps to freedom: Theory and practice in composition teaching.* Paper presented at the 7th Annual TESOL Convention, San Juan, Puerto Rico.

Details a proposal for a composition program that leads students to express

themselves fluently. Stresses motivating students and providing them guidelines for improvement.
Fluency/Programs.

589. Clarke, W. G. (1986). The ESL student in the freshman composition class. *Teaching English in the Two-Year College*, *13*(1), 12-19.
Offers suggestions to the freshman composition teacher, stemming from ESL theory and research.
NS-NNS Comparisons/Teacher Preparation.

590. Clasen, M. P., & Rutkowski-Weber, R. K. (1989, March). *A collaborative approach to research paper writing*. Paper presented at the 23rd Annual TESOL Convention, San Antonio, TX.
Approaches the research paper in a step-by-step procedure which uses group work to overcome anxiety.
Affect/Research Writing/Group Work.

591. Clayton, T. (1993). Using background knowledge to stimulate composition in Malay students. In M. N. Brock, & L. W. Walters (Eds.), *Teaching composition around the Pacific Rim: Politics and pedagogy* (pp. 48-60). Clevedon, Eng: Multilingual Matters.
Presents a culturally sensitive course that uses students' background knowledge in composing.

592. Cleary, C. (1988). Testing lower intermediate writing: A comparison of two scoring methods. *British Journal of Language Teaching*, *26*(2), 75-80.
A pilot study of essays by Arabic EFL students compares holistic, error count, and categorical methods of evaluation. Results suggest greater validity of error-count procedure.
Assessment/Errors/Arabic.

593. Cleary, L. M. (1991a). Carlos: Dismantling the cage of the unsuccessful writer. *From the other side of the desk: Students speak out about writing* (pp. 27-52). Portsmouth, NH: Boynton/Cook.
Describes the unsuccessful, problem-ridden experiences of a high school basic writer from a Puerto Rican cultural background who speaks a complex non-standard English dialect and who attended school in the U.S. since kindergarden. His unsuccessful efforts show that greater attention and advocacy are needed for such basic writers.
Hispanic/Secondary School.

594. Cleary, L. M. (1991b). Jenny: Second language blues. *From the other side of the desk: Students speak out about writing* (pp. 118-144). Portsmouth, NH: Boynton/Cook.
Describes the writing experiences of a Korean immigrant high school student mainstreamed in English in order to illustrate the problems of similar ESL students with literate backgrounds. Cites their lack of experience in coping successfully with the cognitive overload caused by their manifold English language and writing problems. Also considers new life experiences, sensitivity to new peers, the threat a teacher represents, and motivation to write of these immigrating ESL students.

Korean/Secondary School.

595. Clifford, M. (1991). Developing writing skills in basic ESL for adults. *English Teaching Forum*, *29*(2), 41-42.

Identifies some key principles in teaching writing to adults.

Adult Education.

596. Clintron, R. E. (1990). The use of oral and written language in the homes of three Mexican families. *Dissertation Abstracts International*, *51*(9), 3055A.

Documents the use of oral and written language in working-class <u>mexicano</u> homes of migrant workers near Chicago. Ethnography finds unexpected levels of literacy in English both historically and in the present, suggesting the view of individuals as adaptable learners who use a variety of oral and occasionally literary settings to make knowledge.

Hispanic/Literacy/Speaking-Writing Relations.

597. Cloud, N. (1992, March). *Assessing the writing abilities of elementary ESL students*. Workshop presented at the 26th Annual TESOL Convention, Vancouver, BC.

Explores the assessment procedures for analyzing the early writing behavior and abilities of young ESL writers.

Elementary/Assessment.

598. Clough, M. (1986, March). *Adapting a process approach to beginning ESL writing classes*. Paper presented at the 20th Annual TESOL Convention, Anaheim, CA.

Advocates a traditional approach as preparation for teaching writing process.

Beginners/Process Instruction.

599. Clouse, B. F. (1990). *Progressions*. NY: Macmillan.

Text presents well-defined procedures and protocols for more effective writing, with revision checklists, problem-solving guides, and other helpful features. It also includes tips on handling essay exams, writing assignments, and other academic tasks. Various styles and methods are illustrated through examples of student writing and professional essays.

University/Advanced.

600. Clyne, M. G. (1991). The sociocultural dimension: The dilemma of the German-speaking scholar. In H. Schroder (Ed.), *Subject-oriented texts: Language for special purposes and text theory* (pp. 49-67). Berlin: deGruyter.

Presents results of a case study the culturally-determined arguments in texts produced by English and German-speaking scholars. An examination of German-language, German-English and English texts in Linguistics and Sociology shows quantifiable differences in discourse structures. Tendency for German texts to be asymmetrical and to involve greater hedging is reported among other findings.

Contrastive Rhetoric/German/Culture.

601. Clyne, M. G. (1987). Cultural differences in ther organization of academic texts: English and German. *Journal of Pragmatics*, *11*(2), 211-247.

Discusses cultural differences in the organization and style of texts in English and German. Analysis of position of definitions, advance organizers, and the integration of data in 52 texts suggests the influence of native educational systems as well as intellectual styles and attitudes toward content.

German/Culture/Contrastive Rhetoric.

602. Clyne, M. G. (1985). Development of writing skills in young second language learners. *ITL Review of Applied Linguistics, 67-68*, 9-24.

Approaches to the teaching of writing in second-language courses in Australia are examined. A primary level English-German bilingual program is evaluated. The program uses written language as a reinforcement for oral language skills. Results on acquisition of German orthography and three writing samples and dictation from second and fourth grades are evaluated. While the children all experience difficulties in acquiring German orthography, some positive transfer from the first language (English) is evident.

Children/German.

603. Clyne, M. G. (1983). Linguistics and written discourse in particular languages: Contrastive studies: English and German. *Annual Review of Applied Linguistics, 3*, 38-49.

Reviews studies that contrast English and German linguistically, communicatively, and rhetorically in Germany. Includes bibliographies.

Contrastive Rhetoric/German/Bibliography.

604. Clyne, M. G. (1981). Culture and discourse structure. *Journal of Pragmatics, 5*, 61-66.

Examines four aspects of German and English discourse: degree of linearity, verbality, formality, and rhythm of discourse. Finds greater emphasis on formal discourse rules in English than in German. Claims that culture-specific discourse structures should occupy an important place in second and foreign language teaching.

Academic Writing/German/Culture.

605. Clyne, M. G., & Kreutz, H. J. (1987). The nature and function of disaggression and other discourse structure phenomena in Academic German. *Working Papers in Migrant and Intercultural Studies, 8*, 1-22.

A correlation analysis of 26 texts by English speakers and 26 texts by German speakers shows that in English (but absent in German) there is a bundle of features correlating significantly with linear organization which may be seen as properties of a "well-organized" text: early advance organizers, data integration, as well as propositional and textual symmetry.

German/Culture/Academic Writing.

606. Cobb, C. M. (1984). *Process and pattern: Controlled composition practice for ESL students*. Boston: Heinle & Heinle.

Three-part textbook focuses on writing individual paragraphs, paragraph combinations, and summary writing and evaluation.

Intermediate/Textbook.

607. Coe, R. M. (1988). *Toward a grammar of passages*. Carbondale, IL: Southern Illinois University Press.

Expands on the rhetorical analysis of Francis Christensen, Ellen Nold, and Brent Davis by creating a two-dimensional graphic matrix for textual analysis of passages. Uses this instrument to identify rhetorical pattern in writing by Chinese learners. Presents broad applications as well as implications for researchers, teachers,

and writers.
Coherence/Text Analysis/Chinese.

608. Coe, R. M. (1983, March). *Chinese and American discourse: Some contrasts and their implications*. Paper presented at the 34th Annual CCCC Meeting, Detroit, MI.
See previous item.
Text Analysis/Culture/Chinese.

609. Coffey, M. P. (1987). *Communication through writing*. Englewood Cliffs, NJ: Prentice Hall Regents.
Presents a step-by-step guide to basic writing patterns and short essays. It offers details on writing strategies used to gather information and provides sequences involved in creating compositions.
University/Advanced/Textbook.

610. Cohen, A. D. (1994). *Assessing language ability in the classroom*. (Second Ed.). Boston: Heinle & Heinle.
Devotes one chapter to a variety of ways to assess writing in the classroom, from primary trait scoring to portfolios. Research notes, sample essays, scoring guides, and an interpretation of relevant research provide useful additional dimensions to this introduction to assessment.
Assessment.

611. Cohen, A. D. (1991). Feedback on writing: The use of verbal report. *Studies in Second Language Acquisition*, *13*, 133-159.
Describes a study of the strategies teachers use in giving feedback on compositions and those learners employ in handling this feedback in English foreign language and Portugese native language classrooms in Brazil. Study uses a variety of verbal report measures. Points out the limited nature of the learners' repertoire for handling feedback and methodological problems.
Feedback/Portugese.

612. Cohen, A. D. (1990). Writing as process and product. *Language learning: Insights for learners, teachers, and researchers* (pp. 103-131). NY: Newbury.
Reviews some ideas about providing feedback on written work, including his notion of reformulation.
Revision.

613. Cohen, A. D. (1987a). Student processing of feedback on their compositions. In A. L. Wenden, & J. Rubin (Eds.), *Learner strategies in language learning* (pp. 57-69). Englewood Cliff, NJ: Prentice-Hall.
Reports results of a questionnaire administered to native and non-native US college students about how they relate to teacher comments on papers they wrote. Most read them, making a mental note of the comment for later reference, except the (self-judged) poorer students.
Revision/Feedback/Style.

614. Cohen, A. D. (1987b). Viewing feedback on compositions from the teacher's and student's perspective. *The ESPecialist*, 13-29.
Examines the relationship between the teacher's feedback on compositions in ESL and students' appreciation and utlization of this feedback. A good correlation

was found between what the teacher reported and her actual feedback and students' preferences.
Revision/Feedback/Style.

615. Cohen, A. D. (1985). Reformulation: Another way to get feedback. *Writing Lab Newsletter*, *10*, 6-10.

Having a native speaker rewrite a student's work can help the nonnative improve his/her style.
Revision/Feedback/Style.

616. Cohen, A. D. (1984). Written reformulation as a source of input for learners. *English Teachers' Journal (Israel)*, *30*, 62-67.

Advocates using reformulation, a technique for revising compositions, which involves a native speaker who rewrites an ESL composition in a more native-like way without changing the content. Such reformulation may involve several stages, each focusing on a different aspect of the essay (vocabulary choice, cohesion, grammar). Claims this method prevents fossilization of written errors in ESL students' essays.
Revision/Feedback/Style.

617. Cohen, A. D. (1983a). Reformulating compositions. *TESOL Newsletter*, *6*(12), 1, 4-5.

Suggests that we can bring students closer to native-like mastery of written English by using a technique originated by Levenston (1978). The technique involves having non-native students give a short composition to a native speaker for reformulation. Suggests this peer revision may be reserved for some ESL students some of the time (advanced do best). Benefit allegedly derives from exposure and comparative analysis.
Feedback/Revision/Style.

618. Cohen, A. D. (1983b, March). *Reformulating second language compositions: A potential source of input for the learner*. Revised version of paper presented at the 17th Annual TESOL Convention, Toronto, Ontario. [ERIC ED 228 866].

Describes reformulation as a feedback technique for L2 compostitions. A native speaker rewrites a student's teacher-corrected essay, preserving the ideas. The learner then compares the two essays to see how it could have been written diffferently. Findings indicate the rewritten essays were more appreciated.
Revision.

619. Cohen, A. D. (1982, May). *Writing like a native: The process of reformulation*. Paper presented at the 17th Annual TESOL Convention, Honolulu, HI. [ERIC ED 224 338].

Examines the use of reformulation, whereby a native speaker rewrites second language learner's essay, as a form of feedback. Claims reformulation provides more extensive feedback on cohesion and appropriate rhetorical devices.
Revision/Feedback.

620. Cohen, A. D., & Cavalcanti, M. C. (1990). Feedback on compositions: Teacher and student verbal reports. In B. Kroll, *Second language writing: Research insights for the classroom* (pp. 155-177). Cambridge: Cambridge University Press.

Results from three studies suggest both matches and mismatches between

student preference for feedback and what they received.
Revision/Feedback/Style.

621. Cohen, A. D., & Cavalcanti, M. C. (1987). Giving and getting feedback on composition: A comparison of teacher and student verbal report. *Evaluation in Research in Education, 1*(2), 63-73.

A study of feedback on Portuguese (L1) and ESL compositions at a university in Brazil reveals that teachers' feedback often does not match students' expectations. EFL students are more receptive to the comments about syntax, organization, and sentence structure than native students. The authors warn that EFL teachers' preconceptions about the type of feedback required by low-ability students may deprive such students of other types of feedback.
Revision/Feedback.

622. Cohen, L. J. (1950). Composition through precis-writing. *Modern Language Journal, 34*, 389-391.

Views precis writing as a preparation for free composition because it leads to mastery of vocabulary, structure, and style.
Summary Writing/Control.

623. Colby, J. (1983, March). *Individual writing instruction: Instruction commentary and the growth of editorial skills*. Paper presented at the 17th Annual TESOL Convention, Toronto, Ontario.

Written commentaries on revisions of an ESL assignment should introduce students to internalizing the editorial perspective.
Revision/Feedback.

624. Collignon, F. F. (1993). Writing for the helping professions. In J. G. Carson, & I. Leki (Eds.), *Reading for composing: Connecting processes to advancing ESL literacy* (pp. 258-273). Boston: Heinle & Heinle.

Describes a course for Southeast Asian refugees employed as workers in a bicultural/bilingual context. Student-teacher collaboration is viewed from Vygotskyean and Freireian perspectives.
Reading-Writing Relations/Courses/Collaboration.

625. Collins, T. G. (1991, March). *Teaching process-based writing in large classes*. Paper presented at the 25th Annual TESOL Convention, New York, NY.

Discusses EFL experiences teaching process to classes as large as 300 students.
Large Classes/Process Instruction.

626. Colman, L. R. M. (1990, March). *Teaching informal writing: From the simple to the sublime*. Paper presented at the 24th Annual TESOL Convention, San Francisco, CA.

Suggests progressing from basic informal writing to formal composition through the practice of fulfilling students' everyday writing needs.
Register.

627. Colton-Montalto, B. (1991, March). *Writing the research paper: Designing relevant and practical exercises*. Paper presented at the 25th Annual TESOL Convention, New York, NY.

Presents practical exercises for ESL students in how to paraphrase, summarize, and avoid plagiarism in writing the research paper.
Research Writing.

628. Concepcion, B. E. (1993). The effects of grammar knowledge on the writing skills of business English students in Puerto Rico. *Dissertation Abstracts International*, *53*(11), 3780A.

A quasi-experiment rejects the null hypothesis that no significant differences exist in the writing of Business English students in Puerto Rico between those who received traditional instruction plus a module of grammar instruction as opposed to those getting traditional instruction alone.
Grammar/Spanish/Business Writing.

629. Condon, W., & Hamp-Lyons, L. (1991). Introducing a portfolio-based writing assessment: Progress through problems. In P. Belanoff, & M. Dickson (Eds.), *Portfolio assessment: process and product*. Portsmouth, NH: Boynton/Cook.
Assessment/Portfolios.

630. Cone, D. (1985, March). EFL plagiarism: A pound of prevention. *Indiana English*, 23-30.

Advises that instruction in paraphrasing preempts inadvertent plagiarism.
Conventions/Standards.

631. Conklin, A. (1990, March). *Beyond the "intelligent typewriter": Computer revision for basic writers*. Paper presented at the 24th Annual TESOL Convention, San Francisco, CA.

Claims word processing alone does not teach the basic writer how to revise successfully. Without help, most continue editing at word level. Uses examples from an ESL computer writing lab that focus on effective revision techniques.
Computers/Word Processing/Revision/Beginners.

632. Connor, U. M. (1994). Second-language processing: Writing. In D. Wilkins (Ed.), *Encyclopedia of linguistics*. London: Pergamon Press.

Reviews current theories of writing in L1 and L2 with emphasis on writing as a cultural activity and on cross-cultural differences in text coherence.
Review.

633. Connor, U. M. (1992a). A reader reacts to Raimes's "The TOEFL Test of Written English: Causes for Concern" . . . [In The Forum]. *TESOL Quarterly*, *26*, 177-179.

Relates her experience of finding no obstacles in using data from ETS in her own research studies.
TWE.

634. Connor, U. M. (1992b, March). *Paradigm shifts in contrastive rhetoric: Implications for ESL*. Paper presented at the 26th Annual TESOL Convention, Vancouver, BC.

Discusses traditional and new directions in the study of contrastive and comparative rhetorics.
Contrastive Rhetoric.

635. Connor, U. M. (1992c, March). *Paradigm shifts in contrastive rhetoric*. Paper presented at the 43rd CCCC Meeting, Cincinnati, OH.

See previous item.

Contrastive Rhetoric.

636. Connor, U. M. (1992d, March). *Writing from sources: A study of ESL writers in a graduate business class*. Paper presented at the 26th Annual TESOL Convention, Vancouver, BC.

Examines the effects of writing experience and language proficiency on the quality of reading and writing processes and products of five graduate business students.
Business Writing/Research Writing.

637. Connor, U. M. (1991). Linguistic/rhetorical measures for evaluating ESL writing. In L. Hamp-Lyons (Ed.), *Assessing second language writing in academic contexts* (pp. 215-225). Norwood, NJ: Ablex.

Reports a small-scale study indicating correlations between holistic scores on a TWE-type essay and a measure of argumentation based on Toulmin's analysis of reasoning (1958). Highest reported correlations (r = .72) are between the claims of essays and holistic scores. Results are interpreted to suggest that the criteria of "addressing the task" on the TWE scoring guidelines may not reflect what raters consider important.
Assessment/Argumentation/Objective Measures.

638. Connor, U. M. (1990a). Discourse analysis and writing/reading instruction. *Annual Review of Applied Linguistics*, *11*, 164-180.

Reviews research in discourse analysis which can be applied to writing and reading instruction. Also reviews research conducted in the International Association for the Evaluation of Educational Achievement (IEA) and the NORDTEXT and NORDWRITE projects in Scandinavia.
Review.

639. Connor, U. M. (1990b). Linguistic/rhetorical measures for international persuasive student writing. *Research in the Teaching of English*, *24*(1), 67-87.

Finds that three linguistic/rhetorical measures (a Toulmin measure, a credibility appeal, and a syntactic style measure) developed to analyze and evaluate argumentative/persuasive student writing were the best predictors of writing quality among 150 essays from three native English speaking countries.
Argumentation/Objective Measures.

640. Connor, U. M. (1990c, March). *Application of contrastive rhetoric in advanced ESL writing*. Paper presented at the 24th Annual TESOL Convention, San Francisco, CA.

Discusses how contrastive rhetoric research applies to advanced ESL learners writing for specific discourse communities, in particular, business and management communications. Emphasizes teacher awareness of differences and similarities in building effective arguments in L1 and L2 discourse communities.
Contrastive Rhetoric/Business Writing/Discourse Communities.

641. Connor, U. M. (1988). A contrastive study of persuasive business correspondence: American and Japanese. In S. J. Bruno (Ed.), *Global implications for business communications: Theory, technology, and practice* (pp. 57-72). Houston, TX: University of Houston-Clear Lake.

A case study compares the written correspondence by an American and a

Japanese corporate manager of marketing. Attitudes toward directness, concern for harmony, and sense of time and rhythm of interaction, as expected, were found to be general cross-cultural differences. Also finds distinct rhetorical differences in use of claim, data, and warrant in persuasive reports.
Persuasion/Japanese/Business Writing.

642. Connor, U. M. (1988, March). *Analytic and holistic measures for understanding ESL persuasive writing*. Paper presented at the 39th Annual CCCC Meeting, St. Louis, MO.
Persuasion/Evaluation.

643. Connor, U. M. (1987a). Argumentative patterns in student essays: Cross-cultural differences. In U. M. Connor, & R. B. Kaplan (Eds.), *Writing across languages: Analysis of L2 text* (pp. 57-72). Reading, MA: Addison-Wesley.
Presents a system for analyzing argumentative patterns in writing by students of different cultural and linguistic backgrounds in their native languages.
Culture/Argumentation.

644. Connor, U. M. (1987b, April). *Analytic vs. holistic essay rating: A place for both in ESL*. Paper presented at the Fifth Annual Conference on Writing Assessment, Atlantic City, NJ.
Assessment.

645. Connor, U. M. (1987c, June). *Examining and teaching coherence in ESL: Use of topical structure analysis*. Paper presented at the Nordtext Conference, Turku, Finland.
See Connor & Farmer (1990).
Coherence/TSA.

646. Connor, U. M. (1987d, March). *Examining and teaching coherence in ESL*. Paper presented at the 38th Annual CCCC Meeting, Atlanta, GA.
See Connor & Farmer (1990).
Coherence/TSA.

647. Connor, U. M. (1987e). Research frontiers in writing analysis. *TESOL Quarterly, 21*, 677-696.
Describes recent developments in writing analysis and their contributions to process-oriented research and the paradigm shift in writing from the product-based to process-based writing. Presents a literature review including some empirical studies and their implications for ESL writing.
Review.

648. Connor, U. M. (1986, March). *Student arguments from three countries*. Paper presented at the 37th Annual CCCC Meeting, New Orleans, LA.
Argumentation/Contrastive Rhetoric.

649. Connor, U. M. (1984). A study of cohesion and coherence in English as a second language students' writing. *Papers in Linguistics: International Journal of Human Communications, 17*(3), 301-316.
Compares cohesion and coherence in writing by ESL learners with that of native English writers. Six essays on an argumentative task were analyzed using Halliday and Hasan's (1976) cohesion taxonomy. Results show that to be cohesive

an ESL essay did not have to be coherent.
Cohesion/Coherence/Argumentation.

650. Connor, U. M., Belcher, D. D., Blot, R., Carrell, P. L., Chaudron, C., Enright, D. S., Watson, N., & Zamel, V. (1992, March). *Classroom-centered research: Perspectives from teachers, teacher-researchers, and researchers.* Colloquium presented at the 26th Annual TESOL Convention, Vancouver, BC.

Panel surveys different types of classroom-centered research: teacher, ethnographic, action, experimental, and teacher-researcher collaboration. Panel discusses generation of research questions, methods, and interactions.
Classroom Research.

651. Connor, U. M., & Carrell, P. L. (1991, March). *Interpretation of writers'/readers' prompts in holistic direct assessment.* Paper presented at the 25th Annual TESOL Convention, New York, NY.

Explores the perspectives of ESL writers and essay raters who used the TWE scoring guide about the essay task and the final product.
Prompts/Holistic/Reading-Writing Relations.

652. Connor, U. M., & Carrell, P. L. (1993). The interpretation of tasks by writers and readers in holistically rated direct assessment of writing. J. G. Carson, & I. Leki (Eds.), *Reading in the composition classroom: Second language perspectives* (pp. 141-160). Boston: Heinle & Heinle.

Examines how ESL writers perceive an essay writing task and how reader-raters interpret the same task and rate the essay, using the TWE scoring guide.
Reading-Writing Relations/Assessment/Holistic.

653. Connor, U. M., & Cerniglia, C. (1988, March). *Using CAI in the process-based ESL writing class.* Paper presented at the 22nd Annual TESOL Convention, Chicago, IL.

Suggests ways to integrate current ESL writing theory into CAI
Computers/Process Instruction.

654. Connor, U. M., & Farmer, M. (1990). The teaching of topical structure analysis as a revision strategy for ESL writers. In B. Kroll (Ed.), *Second language writing: Research insights for the classroom* (pp. 126-139). NY: Cambridge.

Describes and illustrates how to use topical structure analysis (Lautamatti, 1978) for the purpose of showing coherence in texts. The semantic meaning of sentences have three types of possible progression: parallel, sequential, and extended parallel. Recommends analysis as a heuristic for the improvement of revised drafts.
Coherence/Revision/TSA.

655. Connor, U. M., Grabe, W., & Johns, A. M. (1986, March). *Coherence: Theory and practice.* Colloquium presented at the 20th Annual TESOL Convention, Anaheim, CA.

Addresses how to define coherence and whether it can be taught.
Coherence.

656. Connor, U. M., Harris, D. P., & Kaplan, R. B. (1983, March). *Contrastive rhetoric colloquium.* Colloquium presented at the 17th Annual TESOL Convention, Toronto, Ontario.

Panel features six papers, including English to L1 comparisons and rhetorical

structure analysis (both synchronic and diachronic) of selected languages.
Contrastive Rhetoric.

657. Connor, U. M., & Johns, A. M. (1989, March). *Introducing ESL students into academic discourse communities: Differences do exist*. Paper presented at the 23rd Annual TESOL Convention, San Antonio, TX.

The similarities and differences in development of basic argument and problem-solution structure among different discourse communities leads to the conclusion that ESL teachers need to go beyond the teaching of general academic writing (Spack, 1988) to be effective.
Academic Writing/Discourse Communities.

658. Connor, U. M., & Johns, A. M. (Eds.). (1990). *Coherence in writing: Research and pedagogical perspectives*. Washington, DC: TESOL.

A collection of twelve original essays which treat a variety of models and interpretations of the concept of coherence. Covers both the processes of making and understanding coherence and the products, theory and practice. In addition to an introduction, the editors provide discussion questions and activities for each chapter.
Coherence/Text Analysis.

659. Connor, U. M., & Kaplan, R. B. (1984, March). *Problems and techniques of text analysis*. Colloquium presented at the 18th Annual TESOL Convention, Houston, TX.

Presents theoretical views of texts as creative and interpretive processes as well as products.
Text Analysis.

660. Connor, U. M., Kaplan, R. B., Canale, M., Grabe, W., Jones, C. S., Scarcella, R. C., Blum-Kulka, S., & Ostler, S. E. (1985, April). *Contrastive rhetoric: Writing across cultures*. Colloquium presented at the 19th Annual TESOL Convention, New York, NY.

Reports recent advances in the field of contrastive rhetoric, including comparisons with NES writing and rhetorical-structure analyses (both synchronic and diachronic) of selected languages.
Contrastive Rhetoric.

661. Connor, U. M., & Kaplan, R. B. (Eds.). (1987). *Writing across languages: Analysis of L_2 text* Reading, MA: Addison-Wesley.

An important collection of original essays covering theory (Kaplan; Enkvist), models of exposition and argument (Carrell; Connor; Connor & McCagg) and interlanguage studies (Lautimatti; Hinds; Eggington; Ostler).Essays elucidate the nature of written language in discourse on the assumption, as Widdowson says in the "Preface," that "texts have schematic structure which are culturally variable".
Text Analysis.

662. Connor, U. M., Kaplan, R. B., Carlson, S. B., Eveersen, L. S., Friedlander, A. C., Huckin, T. N., Johns, A. M., & Zellermayer, M. (1987, April). *Contrastive Rhetoric*. Colloquium presented at the 21st Annual TESOL Convention, Miami Beach, FL.

Annual review of work done in contrastive rhetoric.

Contrastive Rhetoric.

663. Connor, U. M., & Kramer, M. G. (1993). *Writing from sources: Case studies of graduate students in business management.* Unpublished manuscript, Indiana University at Indianapoilis, IN.

Investigates native and nonnative writers' task representations (Flower 1987) when reading a business management case report and writing a subsequent policy report. The task representation of ESL students, differed but not uniformly, from native speakers. Two of the five cases (including one ESL writer) understood the intended rhetorical task. Differences are attributable to cultural, educational as well as linguistic factors.

Task/Business Writing/Reading-Writing Relations.

664. Connor, U. M., & Lauer, J. (1985). Understanding persuasive essay writing: Linguistic/rhetorical approach. *Text, 5,* 309-326.

Studies reliable and valid indicators of writing quality in persuasive essays. Results show that adequate assessment of linguistic and rhetorical features requires a multidimensional methodology.

Persuasion/Rhetoric.

665. Connor, U. M., & Lauer, J. (1986, April). *Understanding persuasive essay writing.* Paper presented at the Annual AERA Meeting, San Francisco, CA.

See next item.

Persuasion/Academic Writing.

666. Connor, U. M., & Lauer, J. (1988). Cross-cultural variation in persuasive student writing. In A. C. Purves (Ed.), *Writing across languages and cultures: Issues in contrastive rhetoric* (pp. 138-159). Newbury Park, CA: Sage.

Examines the identification of reliable and valid indicators of writing quality in persuasive composition. Describes three theories related to persuasive writing: (1) problem-solution superstructure; (2) Toulmin analysis of informal meaning; (3) persuasive appeals analysis. Discusses use of these measures to detect cultural differences.

Culture/Persuasion.

667. Connor, U. M., & McCagg, P. (1987). A contrastive study of English expository prose paraphrases. In U. M. Connor, & R. B. Kaplan (Eds.), *Writing across languages: Analysis of L2 text* (pp. 73-86). Reading, MA: Addison-Wesley.

Compares sequencing of information in paraphrases of an English expository prose passage written by native and non-native speakers of English. Finds no indication of Kaplan's notion of culture-specific rhetorical patterns in paraphrases.

Exposition/NS-NNS Comparisons/Contrastive Rhetoric.

668. Connor, U. M., & McCagg, P. (1983). Cross-cultural differences and perceived quality in written paraphrases of English expository prose. *Applied Linguistics, 4,* 259-268.

Examines the written recall paraphrases of native and non-native speakers of English. Finds that there is no transfer of culture-specific rhetorical patterns, but differences in paraphrases can be attributed to differences in linguistic proficiency.

Contrastive Rhetoric/Paraphrase Writing/Exposition.

669. Connor, U. M., & McCagg, P. (1982, May). *Cross-cultural differences in written paraphrases of English expository prose*. Paper presented at the 16th Annual TESOL Convention, Honolulu, HI.

    Compares a propositional analysis of a "typical" expository English prose passage with written paraphrases by Japanese, Spanish, and English native-speakers.
    Exposition/Japanese/Hispanic.

670. Connor, U. M., & Schneider, M. L. (1988, April). *Topical structure and writing quality: Results of an ESL study*. Paper presented at the 22nd Annual TESOL Convention, Chicago, IL.

    Finds that the proportion of sequential and parallel topics in essays seems to differentiate the highest from lower quality ESL essays but with different results than those found for NES students.
    Coherence/TSA.

671. Connor-Linton, J. (1993, April). *Comparing Japanese EFL and American ESL instructors' writing standards*. Paper presented at the 27th Annual TESOL Convention, Atlanta, GA.

    Compares the evaluative criteria used by Japanese EFL and American ESL teachers when rating and correcting the same ten essays by Japanese learners of English.
    Standards/Japanese.

672. Conrad, S. M. (1991, March). *Teaching grammar through writing conferences: Form and meaning meet*. Paper presented at the 25th Annual TESOL Convention, New York, NY.

    Hypothesizes that conferences about students' own drafts can provide meaningful contexts for the teaching of grammar.
    Conferencing/Grammar.

673. Constantinides, J. C. (1984). Technical writing for ESL students. *Technical Writing Teacher, 11*, 136-144.

    Presents a model for a technical writing course with special emphasis on the needs of English as a second language students. Explanations of assignments focus on the rhetorical, syntactical, and grammatical features to be stressed. Also considers problems resulting from cultural differences, and the advantages and disadvantages of the sequence.
    Curriculum/Technical Writing.

674. Constantinides, J. C. (1983, May). *International students in the scientific and technical writing class*. Paper presented at the Annual Conference of NAFSA, Cincinnati, OH. [ERIC ED 232 439].

    Describess a sequence of assignments for teaching scientific and technical writing to undergraduate ESL students. Writing tasks are made realistic by making students create an audience and practice real forms and formats.
    Technical Writing/University.

675. Constantinides, J. C., & Hall, C. (1982). Advanced composition: Beginning at the top. In M. Hines, & W. Rutherford (Eds.), *On TESOL '81* (pp. 79-87). Washington, DC: TESOL.

Proposes a method of teaching composition to advanced ESL students, which instead of proceeding from sentence to paragraph moves from overall organization to paragraph and sentence models.

Advanced.

676. Constantinides, J. C., & Hall, C. (1981). Advanced composition: Beginning at the top. Paper presented at the 15th Annual TESOL Convention, Detroit, MI.

See previous item.

Advanced/Speaking-Writinbg Relations.

677. Cook, J. (1992, March). *When classroom cultures collide: ESL students in the composition classroom.* Paper presented at the 43rd Annual CCCC Meeting, Cincinnati, OH.

NS-NNS Comparisons/Culture.

678. Cook, M. L. (1989, March). *The contrastive rhetoric hypothesis and Spanish-speaking ESL students.* Paper presented at the 23rd Annual TESOL Convention, San Antonio, TX.

Reports results of a study that does not uphold Kaplan's thesis with respect to the transfer of a digressive pattern of rhetorical organization by Spanish-speaking students.

Hispanic/Contrastive Rhetoric.

679. Cook, M. L. (1988). The validity of the contrastive rhetoric hypothesis as it relates to Spanish-speaking advanced ESL students. *Dissertation Abstracts International, 49*(9), 2567A.

Examines Kaplan's hypothesis that Spanish-speaking ESL learners transfer rhetorical patterns of Spanish to their writing in English as well as the relationship between L1 and L2 writing proficiency. Results do not validate Kaplan's hypothesis but show correlation between L1 and L2 writing proficiency.

Hispanic/Contrastive Rhetoric.

680. Cook, M. L. (1985, April). *The relation of first and second language writing: A study of essays written in Spanish and English by Hispanic foreign graduate students.* Paper presented at the 19th Annual TESOL Convention, New York, NY. [ERIC ED 232 439].

Describes a study investigating the validity of the contrastive rhetoric hypothesis as well as the correspondence of L1 and L2 writing proficiency.

Hispanic/Contrastive Rhetoric/University.

681. Cooper, R. (1990). *ESL students and process-writing approaches: Necessary adaptations to insure language proficiency.* Unpublished master's thesis, University of Idaho, Moscow, ID.

Process Instruction.

682. Cooper, T. C. (1977). A strategy for teaching writing. *The Modern Language Journal, 61*, 251-256.

Based on findings that longer T-units are signs of syntactic "maturity," suggests sentence-combining exercises for teaching writing to ESL students. Exercises are arranged in order of difficulty and use other skills as well.

Sentence Combining.

683. Cooper, T. C., Morain, G., & Kalivoda, T. (1980). *Sentence combining in second language instruction.* Washington, DC: ERIC/CLL. [ERIC ED 195 167].
   An experiment shows that consistent use of sentence-combining exercises with intermediate proficiency college students learning three different languages accelerates acquisition of writing skills and the use of more advanced syntactic structures.
   Sentence Combining/Syntactic Development/Intermediate.

684. Corbett, J. (1992, March). *Academic reading and writing: Appropriating arguments.* Paper presented at the 26th Annual TESOL Convention, Vancouver, BC.
   Describes a university course that teaches students to "appropriate" through paraphrase, synthesis, and evaluation instead of plagiarism.
   Reading-Writing Relations/Argumentation.

685. Corio, R. (1992, March). *Word processing techniques for teaching composition.* Paper presented at the 26th Annual TESOL Convention, Vancouver, BC.
   Describes techniques for teaching composition with word processing.
   Computers/Word Processing.

686. Cortese, G. (1985). From receptive to productive in post intermediate EFL classes. *TESOL Quarterly, 19,* 7-25.
   Describes a class project that uses reading to improve speaking and writing.
   Project Work/Reading-Writing Relations.

687. Costello, J. (1990a). "Because it is suitable to me": Eliciting support and specificity in ESL writing. *The Language Quarterly, 28,* 68-74.
   Shows the techniques and results of guiding a Chinese student -- whose writing tended to rely on generalization -- to use concrete examples and specific details.
   Chinese/Contrastive Rhetoric.

688. Costello, J. (1990b). Promoting literacy through literature: Reading and writing in ESL composition. *Journal of Basic Writing, 9*(1), 20-30.
   Argues for combining reading, writing, grammar, and American culture in literature courses for nonnative students.
   Literature/Reading-Writing Relations.

689. Costello, J., & Tucker, A. (1984, March). *"I will not be refined in specific details...": Teaching exemplification in ESL composition.* Paper presented at the 18th Annual TESOL Convention, Houston, TX.
   Offers suggestions for the use of exemplification and the movement back and forth between abstract and concrete writing.
   Process Instruction.

690. Couch, P., & Oppenheim, C. (1993, April). *Literature response journals.* Paper presented at the 27th Annual TESOL Convention, Atlanta, GA.
   Students learn to respond to literature by writing journals while the teacher's replies help students refine their understanding of literature.
   Journal Writing/Literature.

691. Coulibaly, Y. (1992). A descriptive study of errors in Senegalese students' composition writing. *Dissertation Abstracts International, 52*(7), 2526A.
   Describes microlinguistic errors in compositions by 40 adult students with

English as their L3. Finds that transfer errors, mostly from French (L2), predominate over intralingual errors. Argues that in the Seneghalese situation, prestige, native language, and culture may be causes along with proximity of L2 and L3.
Errors/Senegal/Transfer.

692. Cox, P. (1993, April). *Environmental issues in advanced composition.* Paper presented at the 27th Annual TESOL Convention, Atlanta, GA.
Shows how to find and use information sources on environmental topics.
Research Writing/Argumentation.

693. Cramer, N. A. (1985). *The writing process: 20 projects for group work.* Boston: Heinle & Heinle.
Based on the importance of practice, group work, and attention to process, textbook provides twenty interesting writing projects for advanced learners.
Advanced/Textbook.

694. Crawford, J., & Gregor, L. (1982, May). *Making and using a student written mini-newspaper.* Paper presented at the 16th Annual TESOL Convention, Honolulu, HI.
Suggests an opportunity to motivate real writing.
Student Publications.

695. Crerand, M. E. L. (1993, April). *From first language literacy to second language literacy: The act of writing in a foreign language context.* Paper presented at the Annual Meeting of the American Educational Research Association, Atlanta, GA.
Literacy.

696. Crew, L. (1987). A comment on "Contrastive Rhetoric: An American writing teacher in China". *College English, 49,* 827-830.
Argues that Matalene (1987) ignores much of the rhetoric of revolution which shapes cultural discourse in China.
Rhetoric/Chinese.

697. Crewe, W. J. (1990). The illogic of logical connectives. *ELT Journal, 44,* 316-325.
Finds that ESL undergraduate students use a small subset of relatively comprehensible connectives, employ connectives for phrasal expansion, and view logical progression as integral to writing.
Cohesion.

698. Crewe, W. J. (1978a). Singapore English in perspective: A reply to Yap. *RELC Journal, 9*(2), 97-104.
Claims Yap (1978) misinterpreted his article.
Singapore/Standards.

699. Crewe, W. J. (1978b). The Singapore writer and the English language. *RELC Journal, 9*(1), 77-86.
Argues that the Singapore writer needs to use the standard dialect and look beyond the local community for norms of usage.
Singapore/Standards/Audience.

700. Crismore, A., Markkanen, R., & Steffensen, M. S. (1993). Metadiscourse in persuasive writing: A study of texts written by American and Finnish university students. *Written Communication, 10*(1), 39-71.

Investigates the culture and gender variation in the use of metadiscourse -- writer's directions for how readers should read and react -- by ten male and ten female students. Finds some quantitative differences, especially that Finnish students and male students used more metadiscourse than US and female students.

Finnish/Variation.

701. Cronnell, B. (1985). Language influences in the English writing of third- and sixth-grade Mexican-American students. *Journal of Educational Research, 8*(3), 168-173.

Analyzes errors found in a set of writing samples produced by Mexican-American children attending a city school. The types of errors found may have been influenced by native language usage from Spanish.

Hispanic/Children/Error Analysis/L1 Influence.

702. Cronnell, B. (Ed.). (1981). *The writing needs of linguistically different students. Proceedings of a research practice conference.* Los Alamitos, CA: Southwest Regional Laboratory for Educational Research and Development.). [ERIC ED 210 932].

Reports the proceedings of a conference on differences in learning writing among students who do not speak standard American English, including Mexican-Americans and Native American Indians.

Hispanic/Amer-Indian/Needs.

703. Cronnell, B. (1979, March). *Spelling English as a second language.* Paper presented at the 13th Annual TESOL Convention, Boston.

Offers suggestions for helping learners with the English spelling system.

Spelling.

704. Crookall, D. (1986). Writing short stories for the BBC World Service. *System, 14,* 295-300.

Authentic writing requires an authentic reader or listener. By writing for the BBC World Service "Short Story" program, students compose for an authentic audience, produce authentic and communicative texts, improve all language skills, and use writing in the second context.

Student Publications.

705. Crookes, G. (1986). Towards a validated analysis of scientific text structure. *Applied Linguistics, 7,* 57-70.

Studies the validity of Swales' analyses of the structure of the experimental scientific research paper. Results show consistency with Swales basic units, yet do not rule out other possibilities. Highlights importance of validity of structure types in materials development.

Scientific Writing.

706. Cross, J. C. (1978). *Discourse analysis, unity, and ESL composition.* Unpublished master's thesis, University of Florida, Gainesville, FL.

Discourse Analysis.

707. Crowe, C. (1992, March). *Asian students and research papers.* Paper presented at the 43rd Annual CCCC Meeting, Cincinnati, OH.

Asian/Research Writing.

708. Cruickshank, D., Hamp-Lyons, L., Hutton-Yoshihara, S., & Silva, T. (1992,

March). *Perspectives on ESL college composition: Teacher training, assessment, and program types*. Academic session presented at the 26th Annual TESOL Convention, Vancouver, BC.

    Discusses a range of issues at two- and four-year colleges, including diverse populations, assessment, teacher training, and program types.

    Programs/Assessment/Teacher Preparation.

709. Cruickshank, D., Perkins, K., Purves, A. C., Hawisher, G. E., Connor, U. M., Soter, A. O., & Schneider, M. L. (1988, March). *Approaches to composition assessment: Research, theory, and practice*. Colloquium presented at the 22nd Annual TESOL Convention, Chicago, IL.

    Examines the relationship between writing assessment and contrastive rhetoric.

    Assessment/Contrastive Rhetoric.

710. Cruickshank, D., & Sullivan-Tuncan, S. (1987, April). *The assessment of critical thinking skills in ESL composition*. Paper presented at the 21st Annual TESOL Convention, Miami Beach, FL.

    Discusses use of a scale that measures critical thinking skills along with the ESL Composition Profile (Jacobs et. al, 1981) for placement purposes.

    Assessment.

711. Cruickshank, D., & Vande Berg, M. (1984, March). *Training basic writing teachers through ESL methodology: An innovative approach*. Paper presented at the 18th Annual TESOL Convention, Houston, TX.

    Offers alternative training approach for basic writing teachers, based on ESL theory and practice.

    Teacher Preparation.

712. Cruickshank, D., & Yates, R. (1990, March). *Academic writing problems of L1-L2 students: Same or different?* Paper presented at the 24th Annual TESOL Convention, San Francisco, CA.

    Discusses research to test whether the sources of rhetorical writing problems of international students are due to interference from L1 or learning new conventions for academic writing. Papers written by American and international students are compared for patterning of concrete and abstract statements and use of transitions.

    NS-NNS Comparisons.

713. Cruz, J. (1988, March). *I know the writing process: Now what?* Paper presented at the 22nd Annual TESOL Convention, Chicago, IL.

    Discusses techniques covering conflict resolution, autobiographical information, and proverb illustration.

    Instruction.

714. Cruz, M. C. E. (1988, November). *From experience to essay: Success stories*. Paper presented at the 78th Annual NCTE Convention, St. Louis, MO.

    Approaches.

715. Cukor-Avila, P., & Swales, J. M. (1989, March). *Investigating the writing needs of research students*. Paper presented at the 23rd Annual TESOL Convention, San Antonio, TX.

    Uses case study approach for planning a course on dissertation writing.

Research Writing.

716. Culbertson, P. (1992, March). *The invented spelling of Spanish-English bilingual children*. Paper presented at the 26th Annual TESOL Convention, Vancouver, BC.

Presents evidence to suggest patterns and development in the invented spelling of bilingual children in both languages.

Hispanic/Children/Spelling.

717. Cullup, M., Pavlik, C., & Wolff, L. (1983). *Write about: Intermediate writing activities*. Boston: Heinle & Heinle.

A short, practical text with forty-two graded chapters, progressing from structured to free composition.

Intermediate/Textbook.

718. Cumming, A. H. (Ed.). (1994a). *Bilingual performance in reading and writing*. Ann Arbor, MI: Language Learning/John Benjamins.

Reprints 11 research articles that appeared in recent years in Language Learning on the theme of bilingual literacy with an introduction by the editor. Separate sections on bilingual reading, writing, and assessing innovative approaches to biliteracy instruction.

Literacy/Bilingual/Reading-Writing Relations.

719. Cumming, A. H. (1994b). Fostering writing expertise in ESL composition instruction: Modeling and evaluation. In D. D. Belcher, & G. Braine (Eds.), *Academic writing in a second language: Essays on research and pedagogy*. Norwood, NJ: Ablex.

Provides two vignettes that portray experiences characteristic of adult ESL learners. The contrast shows distinct approaches (Bereiter & Scardamalia, 1987) to thinking while composing -- knowledge telling and knowledge transforming. Argues that ESL teachers need to know how to use instructional strategies that foster writing expertise and also how to vary these functions for more or less expert writers.

Expertise/Cognition/Teacher Preparation.

720. Cumming, A. H. (1992). Instructional routines in ESL composition teaching: A case study of three teachers. *Journal of Second Language Writing*, *1*(1), 17-35.

Reports findings from a naturalistic case study of three experienced ESL composition instructors. Six routines, frequently alternated and consistently proportionate in class time, accounted for all of the teaching practices of the instructors.

Teacher Preparation/Instruction.

721. Cumming, A. H. (1991). Uses of biliteracy among Indo-Canadian women learning language and literacy. *Canadian Modern Language Review*, *47*, 697-707.

An analysis of the needs of Punjabi-speaking immigrant women in Canada suggests that there are multiple factors of relevance in deciding the language (whether native or majority) of literacy instruction.

Punjabi/Literacy.

722. Cumming, A. H. (1990a). Expertise in evaluating second language compositions. *Language Testing*, *7*(1), 31-51.

A novice-expert study contrasts the thinking processes used by student teachers in pre-service education programs and experienced ESL composition instructors while evaluating the organization, content, and language use in 12 ESL compositions written by students with different levels of ESL proficiency and literacy in their mother tongue.

Evaluation/Expertise.

723. Cumming, A. H. (1990b). An interview with Joy Kreeft Peyton about <u>Students and teachers writing together: Perspectives on journal writing</u>. *TESOL Newsletter*, *24*(3), 26-29.

An interview with Joy Peyton who says her book links personal journal writing with academic writing, deaf education with second language education, and theory with practice.

Review.

724. Cumming, A. H. (1990c). Metalinguistic and ideational thinking in second language composing. *Written Communication*, *7*(4), 482-511.

Describes episodes of concurrent metalinguistic and ideational thinking in the verbal reports of 23 adult ESL learners composing on two tasks. Three kinds of thinking episodes, appearing in about 30% of the decisions learners reported while composing, show potential value for incidental learning of the second language: (1) searching out and assessing appropriate wording, (2) comparing cross-linguistic equivalents, and, much less frequently, (3) reasoning about linguistic choices in the second language. Multivariate analyses indicated the frequency of these thinking episodes is significantly related to learners' writing expertise in their mother tongue.

Cognition/L1 Influence.

725. Cumming, A. H. (1990d). The thinking, interactions, and participation to foster in adult ESL literacy instruction. *TESL Talk*, *20*, 34-51.

Describes three instructional approaches to adult ESL literacy in the context of our knowledge of literacy and shows how these approaches are applied in a project for Indo-Canadian women in Vancouver.

Adult Education/Literacy/Punjabi.

726. Cumming, A. H. (1990e, March). *Expertise in evaluating ESL compositions*. Paper presented at the 24th Annual TESOL Convention, San Francisco, CA.

See Cummings, 1990a.

Teacher Preparation.

727. Cumming, A. H. (1990f, April). *Second language learning through second language writing*. Paper presented at the Annual AERA Meeting, Boston.

Describes episodes of concurrent metalinguistic and ideational thinking in the verbal reports of 23 adult ESL learners composing on two tasks.

Strategies/L1 Influence.

728. Cumming, A. H. (1989). Writing expertise and second language proficiency. *Language Learning*, *39*, 81-141.

Examines the relationship between writing expertise and second language proficiency. Concludes both are psychologically distinct and therefore should be taken into account in assessing students' abilities.

Expertise/Proficiency.

729. Cumming, A. H. (1988). *Writing expertise and second language proficiency in ESL writing performance*. Unpublished doctoral dissertation, University of Toronto, Toronto, Ontario.

    Assesses the relations of writing expertise and second language proficiency to adults' writing performance in ESL. Both expertise and proficiency accounted for large proportions of variance in the qualities of ESL texts and composing behaviors.

    Expertise/Proficiency.

730. Cumming, A. H. (1987, April). *Decision making and text representation in ESL writing performance*. Paper presented at the 21st Annual TESOL Convention, Miami Beach, FL.

    Protocols of adult francophones writing three compositions indicate the decisions made during writing as well as the level of expertise of writers.

    Cognition/Expertise.

731. Cumming, A. H. (1986). Intentional learning as a principle in ESL writing instruction: A case study. *TESL Canada Journal, [Special Issue 1]*, 69-83.

    According to analysis of the achievement in composition writing and the think-aloud protocols of 20 young adult ESL students, most learners were able to use learning strategies to make discernable achievements in their writing proficiency.

    Strategies.

732. Cumming, A. H. (1985). Responding to the writing of ESL students. In M. H. Maguire, & A. Pare (Eds.), *Patterns of development* (pp. 58-75). Ottawa: Canadian Council of Teachers of English.

    Finds as a result of a study of ten experienced teachers that they continued to mark an ESL essay only for surface errors.

    Responding/Error Treatment.

733. Cumming, A. H. (1984). Simulation or reality? A group project in writing. *Carleton Papers on Applied Language Studies*, *1*, 147-154. [ERIC ED 264 724].

    Reports on a group project in an ESL composition class, which required both individual and group work and involved collection of data, preparation of oral reports, group communication, revision of drafts, documentation, and peer editing. The joint assignment provided students with an opportunity to work together as well as to focus on their individual writing progress.

    Project Work/Assignments/Collaboration.

734. Cumming, A. H. (1983, May). *Teachers' procedures for responding to the writing of students of English as a second language*. Paper presented at the 16th Annual Canadian Council of Teachers of English Convention, Montreal, Quebec.

    Finds, as a result of a study of ten experienced teachers, that they continued to mark an ESL essay only for surface errors.

    Error Gravity/Evaluation.

735. Cumming, A. H., Cummins, J., Gunderson, L., Christopher, V., Davidson, L., Angerilli, M., Mellow, D., Voth, C., Carrell, P. L., Ostler-Howlett, C., & Folman, S. (1992, March). *Toward a holistic model of ESL reading and writing instruction*. Symposium presented at the 26th Annual TESOL Convention, Vancouver, BC.

    Symposium presents viewpoints in the development of a holistic model of ESL

reading and writing instruction. Discussion includes identification of issues, assessment of instructional needs, and the formulation of an outline for integrating instruction.
    Models/Reading-Writing Relations.

736. Cumming, A. H., & Gill, J. (1991). *Learning literacy and language among Indo-Canadian women*. Paper presented at the Annual AERA Meeting, Chicago, IL.
    Reports findings from an action research project for Punjabi-speaking immigrant women in Canada. Focused on five aspects of their literacy acquisition in the classroom and at home : language code, personal knowledge, self-control strategies and schematic representations of reading and writing, social knowledge, and social experience.

737. Cumming, A. H., & Mackay, R. (1982, May). *Involving students in the evaluation of writing tasks in academic English*. Paper presented at the 16th Annual TESOL Convention, Honolulu, HI.
    Shows how students can use a hierarchically ordered set of thirty questions to evaluate drafts.
    Responding.

738. Cumming, A. H., Rebuffot, J., & Ledwell, M. (1989a). Reading and summarizing challenging texts in first and second languages. *Reading and Writing: An Interdisciplinary Journal, 2*, 201-219.
    Analyses of the L1 and L2 verbal reports of fourteen adult Anglophone students of French reveal thinking processes which are common to reading and summary writing in first and second languages. However, these appear to vary with literate expertise and relevant knowledge. Subjects' use of equivalent proportions of higher-order problem solving strategies while writing and reading in both languages seems unrelated to participants' second language proficiency level (beginning and intermediate). Rather, literate expertise in the mother tongue correlates with the qualitites of the written summaries produced in both languages.
    Literacy/Strategies/Reading-Writing Relations.

739. Cumming, A. H., Rebuffot, J., & Ledwell, M. (1989b, April). *Problem solving strategies in writing and reading in first and second languages*. Paper presented at the Annual AERA Meeting, San Francisco, CA.
    See previous item.
    Strategies/Reading-Writing Relations.

740. Cummings, M. C. (1989). What we talk about when we talk about writing. *Dissertation Abstracts International, 49*(9), 2567A.
    Studies conferences with four students learning to compose, the weaker of whom were treated differently than the stronger writers.
    University/Conferencing.

741. Cummings, M. C. (1989, March). *What we talk about when we talk about writing*. Paper presented at the 23rd Annual TESOL Convention, San Antonio, TX.
    Analyzes the questions and answers, face-work, and negotiation of L2 identity of a successful ESL teacher and four students in one-to-one writing conferences.
    Conferencing/interaction/Speaking-Writing Relations.

742. Cummings, M. C., & Genzel, R. B. (1989). *Writing your way: A writing workshop for advanced learners*. Boston: Heinle & Heinle.

  A series of interactive activities in this text aims to help students effectively express their ideas and achieve proficiency skills in writing for an academic environment. It offers a wide range of activities that enable the student to write in different rhetorical modes, to effectively respond to essay questions, to organize information for a resume, and to write a business letter.

  Advanced.

743. Cummings, V. (1992, March). *Spoken and written style-shifting by ESL students*. Paper presented at the 26th Annual TESOL Convention, Vancouver, BC.

  Presents results of a study contrasting the speech and writing of L1 and L2 college freshmen.

  Speaking-Writing Relations/Style.

744. Cummings, V. (1990). Speech and writing: An analysis of expository texts composed by native and non-native speakers of English at the City University of New York. *Dissertation Abstracts International, 51*(7), 2296A.

  Presents a textual analysis of expository essays and spoken discourse in English by American and native Spanish-speaking college freshmen. Examines local and global features of text and discourse which were successful and unsuccessful. Successful written texts were thoroughly framed and contained well-developed mid-level generalizations. Unsuccessful written texts were briefly framed, contained more generalizations, and lacked support for these generalizations. Non-native students varied between narrative and hyper-literate approaches to exposition whereas native students maintained an informal expository style.

  Hispanic/Speaking-Writing Relations/NS-NNS Comparisons.

745. Cummings, V. (1989, March). *Orality and L2 writing*. Paper presented at the 23rd Annual TESOL Convention, San Antonio, TX.

  Examines stylistic, syntactic, and rhetorical characteristics of "orality" in successful and unsuccessul L2 writers.

  Speaking-Writing Relations.

746. Cummings, V. (1988, March). *The inequities of assessing L2 writing*. Paper presented at the 22nd Annual TESOL Convention, Chicago, IL.

  Discusses inequity in judging ESL writing in terms of native speaker texts and standards.

  Assessment/Standards.

747. Cummings, V., & Watkins-Goffman, L. (1992, March). *Conducting a contrastive analysis of argumentation in English and Spanish*. Paper presented at the 26th Annual TESOL Convention, Vancouver, BC.

  Describes a study of successful and unsuccessful argumentative essays written in English and Spanish. Texts are analyzed into multi-sentential argumentative sequences.

  Hispanic/L1-L2 Comparison/Argumentation.

748. Cummins, J. (1989). The sanitized curriculum: Educational disempowerment in a nation at risk. In D. M. Johnson, & D. H. Roen (Eds.), *Richness in writing:*

Empowering ESL students (pp. 19-38). NY: Longman.

Claims that educational reforms initiated as a result of the publication of <u>A Nation at Risk</u> have led to the disempowerment of teachers and students, especially minority students. Suggests ways of empowering teachers and students through interactive teacher-student relationships, enriching linguistic and cultural resources, and through change in certain attitudes.

Curriculum/Politics.

749. Cummins, M. Z. (1982). Group activities for non-native students in regular freshman English. In C. Carter (Ed.), *Non-native and nonstandard dialect students: Classroom practices in teaching English, 1982-1983* (pp. 44-45). Urbana, IL: NCTE.

Discusses how to get a group to write a summary following discussions.

Collaboration.

750. Currie, P. (1993). Entering a disciplinary community: Conceptual activities required to write for one introductory university course. *Journal of Second Language Writing, 2*, 101-117.

Describes eight categories of conceptual activities called for in nine written assignments in an undergraduate business course. Argues that these activities can and should be taught in EAP.

Discourse Communities/EAP/Assignments.

751. Currie, P. (1991). *Basically academic: An introduction to EAP*. NY: Heinle & Heinle.

For ESL students preparing for full-time academic study, this textbook offers eight chapters on current themes (e.g., "Endangered Species," "Child Labor," etc.) in which the reading selections are integrated with writing assignments. Such content is related to writing essays, research papers, essay tests, articles, letters, and oral summaries.

Advanced/Textbook.

752. Currie, P., & Cray, E. (1987). *Strictly academic: A reading and writing text*. Boston: Heinle & Heinle.

Incorporates authentic texts used to help students become prepared for what they will encounter in college. Includes skills such as note taking, participating in group discussions, writing exams and essays. The text is broken down into segments and manageable steps for student mastery.

University/Intermediate/Textbook.

753. Curry, D. (1988). *Eyewitness: A picto-comp for students of English as a foreign language*. Washington, DC: USIA, Bureau of Educational and Cultural Affairs.

An exercise book useful for oral and written composition practice by high beginners.

Beginners/Textbook.

D

754. Dagenais, D. (1989). Perceptions and processes of French and English writing in a French immersion program. *Carleton Papers in Applied Language Studies, 6*, 64-83.

Finds that the instructional focuses and teachers' roles in fifth and sixth grade

French and English writing classrooms were more similar than different in that linguistic form is emphasized over content and process.
French.

755. Dahbi, M. (1984). The development of English writing skills by Moroccan university students. *Dissertation Abstracts International, 46*(5), 1264A.
Investigates the development of sentence-level and rhetorical aspects of composition writing in a four-year English program at a Moroccan university. Concludes that the communicative context of the class leads to focus on form rather than content and suggests content-oriented teaching.
Arabic/Form/University.

756. Dahnke, D. (1986, March). *The process approach: Redefining the role of grammar.* Paper presented at the 20th Annual TESOL Convention, Anaheim, CA.
Offers a developmental methodology for implementing grammar into the process approach to ESL writing.
Grammar.

757. Dailey, B., Downing, B., Leake, A., Tarone, E., & Townsend, K. T. (1991, March). *Assessing the writing skills of Southeast Asian learners.* Paper presented at the 25th Annual TESOL Convention, New York, NY.
Reports results of a study comparing the writing ability of eighth, tenth, and twelfth grade Southeast Asian students and college freshman.
Assessment/Southeast Asian/Secondary School.

758. Dalgish, G. M. (1991a). Computer-assisted error analysis and courseware design: Applications for ESL in the Swedish context. *CALICO Journal, 2*, 39-56.
Compares the common written errors of first-year Swedish-speaking university students with those of a heterogenous ESL college population (drawn from a database of failing essays) in order to develop ESL CALL courseware for Swedish learners.
Computers/Error Analysis/Swedish.

759. Dalgish, G. M. (1991b). An ESL writer's query system: Theory and practice. *Collegiate Microcomputer, 9*, 205-209.
Introduces a computer-assisted program for ESL writers.
Computers.

760. Dalle, T. (1988). Reading journals: Solving the problem of input in the ESL composition class. *TESL Reporter, 21*(2), 23-26.
Proposes using reading journals as a means of providing ESL students with extensive reading experience outside of class. Discusses advantages of reading journals and makes suggestions for the choice of reading materials and procedures.
Classroom Activities/Reading-Writing Relations.

761. Dalle, T., & Hall, C. (1988, March). *Product to process didn't do a thing for cheese!* Paper presented at the 22nd Annual TESOL Convention, Chicago, IL.
Argues need of ESL students without extensive reading practice in English to learn the common modes of development in English.
Rhetoric.

762. Dalle, T., & Hall, C. (1987, April). *Dialogue journals for cross-cultural communication.* Paper presented at the 21st Annual TESOL Convention, Miami

Beach, FL.
   Reports positive outcomes of a university project in which journals were used to communicate between international and American students.
   Dialogue Journals/Culture.

763. Dally, P. (1981). *Contrastive analysis of Chinese letter writing in English as a second language, with special attention to discourse function.* Unpublished manuscript, ESL Department, University of California, Los Angeles.
   Contrastive Rhetoric/Chinese/Letter Writing.

764. Damen, L. (1982, March). *Reading, writing, and culture shock.* Paper presented at the Annual Conference of the Society for Intercultural Education, Training and Research, Long Beach, CA. [ERIC ED 228 876].
   Claims that culture shock is a common experience for anyone learning a second language in a second culture. Suggests ways that teachers can use reading and writing to help students become aware of their ethnocentrism, to understand characteristics of the target culture, and to develop ways of building a personal cultural bridge across that chasm.
   Literacy/Culture.

765. Danielson, D. W. (1965). Teaching composition at the intermediate level. In V. F. Allen (Ed.), *On Teaching English to Speakers of Other Languages: Papers read at the TESOL Conference, Tuccson, AZ, May 8-9, 1964. Series.* (pp. 143-145). Champaign, IL: NCTE.
   Discusses the need for systematic presentation of writing activities at the intermediate level and the need for control in the instruction.
   Intermediate/Control.

766. Danish, B. (1981). *Writing as a second language: A workbook for writing and teaching writing.* NY: Teachers & Writers.
   Book is divided into two parts: the first half introducing a number of writing techniques to challenge and interest the learner and the second half addressing the teacher as authority, critic, and evaluator.
   Classroom Activities/Advanced/Textbook.

767. D'Annunzio, A. (1990). A non-directive combinatory model in an adult ESL program. *Journal of Reading, 34,* 198.
   Claims bilingual tutors using LEA approach can be used to teach reading and writing to adult students.
   Tutoring/LEA/Adult Education.

768. Dantas-Whitney, M., & Grabe, W. (1989, March). *A comparison of Portugese and English newspaper editorials.* Paper presented at the 23rd Annual TESOL Convention, San Antonio, TX.
   Contrastive Rhetoric/Portugese.

769. Das, B. (1985, April). *Comparing rhetorical strategies in expository writing in first and second language.* Paper presented at the 20th Regional Seminar SEAMEO RELC, Singapore.
   Reports that a panel of judges found the writing of bilingual students equally deficient in L1 and L2.

Rhetoric/Exposition/NS-NNS Comparisons.

770. Date, M. (1980). *Rhetorical patterns in American and Japanese college students' compositions: Truth or myth?* Unpublished master's thesis, Illinois State University, Normal, IL.

771. Daubney-Davis, A. E. (1982a). Using invention heuristics to teach writing, Part I: An introduction to heuristics. *TECFORS*, 5(2), 1-3. [ERIC ED 267 648].

   Claims that though there are differences in knowledge and experiences that native and non-native speakers bring to the writing task, some models of the composing process and certain heuristics used in a first language writing class are relevant for an ESL composition class as well.
   Invention.

772. Daubney-Davis, A. E. (1982b). Using invention heuristics to teach writing, Part II: A look at methods. *TECFORS*, 5(3), 1-3. [ERIC ED 267 648].

   Reviews group brainstorming, looping, and a modified tagmemic method of invention for ESL students.
   Invention.

773. Daubney-Davis, A. E. (1982c). Using invention heuristics to teach writing, Part III: More methods to try. *TECFORS*, 5(4), 5-7. [ERIC ED 267 648].

   Describes applications of three invention heuristics: Larson's (1968) model which involves a needs analysis and consists of a series of questions, Cowan & Cowan's (1980) 'Bare-Bones Outlines' and Cowan & Cowan's (1980) 'cubing'.
   Invention.

774. Daubney-Davis, A. E. (1981, March). *Invention techniques: What we can learn from freshman composition.* Paper presented at the 15th Annual TESOL Convention, Detroit, MI.

   Advises use of models of the composing process and pre-writing heuristics in ESL at the intermediate level and above.
   Invention/Intermediate.

775. Davidson, D. M. (1978a). *Test of ability to subordinate.* NY: Language Innovations.
   A test of sentence subordination.
   Evaluation/Objective Measures/TAS.

776. Davidson, D. M. (1978b, April). *A test of ability to subordinate in writing.* Paper presented at the 12th Annual TESOL Convention, Mexico City, Mexico.

   Describes an instrument to diagnose ability to subordinate among college-ready ESL students.
   Assessment/University/TAS.

777. Davidson, D. M. (1977). Sentence-combining in an ESL writing program. *Journal of Basic Writing*, 1(3), 49-62.

   Claims that sentence-combining improves the quality of ESL writing. Suggests methodology and materials to make this exercise most effective.
   Sentence Combining.

778. Davidson, D. M. (1976a). Development and validation of a diagnostic examination of ability to subordinate in writing for ESL college students. *Dissertation Abstracts International*, 37(9), 5790-5791A.

Develops and validates a diagnostic and screening instrument that measures non-native college students' ability to control certain structures of subordination in written composition. Nine structures: prenominal adjectives, adverbs of manner, degree, time, and frequency, prepositional phrases, relative clauses, participial phrases, gerundive phrases, and infinitive phrases -- were identified and tested. The Test of Ability to Subordinate correlated favorably with writing ability and the Michigan Test of English Language Proficiency.
Assessment/Objective Measures/TAS.

779. Davidson, D. M. (1976b, October). *Assessing writing ability of ESL college freshmen*. Paper presented at Meeting of New York State TESOL, New York, NY. [ERIC ED 135247].

Develops a diagnostic instrument, the Test of Ability to Subordinate to test student control of those structures of subordination associated with writing maturity. Tests validity of this objective measure against the Michigan Test of English Language Proficiency.
Assessment/Objective Measures/TAS.

780. Davidson, D. M., & Blot, D. (1984). *Write from the start*. Boston: Heinle & Heinle.

Provides activities, based on the Counseling-Learning/Community Language Learning approach to teaching, that engage students in controlled speaking and writing which encourages interaction.
Beginners/Textbook.

781. Davidson, F. (1991). Statistical support for training in ESL composition rating. In L. Hamp-Lyons (Ed.), *Assessing second language writing in academic contexts* (pp. 155-164). Norwood, NJ: Ablex.

Proposes two solutions based on a Rasch (partial scoring) scalar model to differences in choosing scale steps in ESL composition rating, namely, rater training and scale revision.
Assessment.

782. Davidson, F. (1984, March). *Teaching and testing ESL composition through contract learning*. Paper presented at the 18th Annual TESOL Convention, Houston, TX. [ERIC ED 245 560].

Discusses how to use contracts to reduce persistent errors in student papers.
Error Treatment.

783. Davidson, F., & Henning, G. H. (1985). A self-rating scale of English difficulty: Rasch scalar analysis of items and rating categories. *Language Testing*, 2(2), 164-179.

Demonstrates that a scalar analysis based on the Rasch model of partial credit can be applied to student self-ratings of ability to write (among other skill components).
Assessment.

784. Davidson, J. O. (1985a). An indirect measure of writing skills for student placement in freshman and pre-freshman ESL courses: Part I. *TECFORS*, 8(3), 1-7. [ERIC ED 267 650].

Discusses and illustrates eight item types used as an experimental, indirect measure of writing skill for university level placement.
Evaluation.

785. Davidson, J. O. (1985b). An indirect measure of writing skills for student placement in freshman and pre-freshman ESL courses: Part II. *TECFORS*, *8*(4), 7-9.[ERIC ED 267 650].
Discusses the validity and reliability of an experimental indirect measure of writing ability.
Evaluation/Placement.

786. Davidson, J. O. (1984, March). *A proficiency examination of writing skills used for student placement in freshman-level courses*. Paper presented at the 18th Annual TESOL Convention, Houston, TX.
Reports a multiple-choice exam containing forty items that test specific writing skills basic to any freshman rhetoric and composition course. Psychometric information given for placement instrument.
Assessment/Placement.

787. Davies, E. E. (1985). Looking at style with advanced EFL learners. *ELT Journal*, *39*, 13-19.
Claims that English involves a large number of styles shaped by the context in which they occur. Advocates developing courses that would increase advanced students' awareness and understanding of stylistic variation and improve their receptive and productive skills.
Advanced/Style.

788. Davies, E. E. (1983). Error evaluation: The importance of viewpoint. *ELT Journal*, *37*, 304-311.
A study of 43 Moroccan and 43 English EFL teachers finds that judgments of error gravity are a function of the teachers' experience.
Error Gravity/NS-NNS Comparisons.

789. Davies, F. (1988). Designing a writing syllabus in English for academic purposes: Process and product. In P. C. Robinson (Ed.), *Academic writing: Process and product* (pp. 130-142). London: Modern English Publications/British Council.
Suggests the potential of a genre-based syllabus in which writing is integrated with reading.
Syllabus Design/Reading-Writing Relations.

790. Davies, N. F., & Omberg, M. (1987). Peer group teaching and the composition class. *System*, *15*, 313-323.
Discusses the writing program at Linkoping University which uses peer-group activities at the prewriting and responding stages of the writing process. Points out the advantages of peer-group response in the teaching of composition in the EFL class.
Instruction/Peer Response.

791. Davis, B. J. (1987). Fanciful spellings as a reflection of pronunciation in advanced EFL composition students. *Geolinguistics*, *13*, 107-123.
Collects spelling errors in written essays by advanced ESL writers. Errors are

categorized as those reflecting (1) correct pronunciation/incorrect spelling and (2) incorrect pronunciation.
Spelling/Speaking-Writing Relations.

792. Day, M. (1992, March). *The Japanese model: Outline for a rhetoric of consensus*. Paper presented at the 43rd Annual CCCC Meeting, Cincinnati, OH.
Japanese/Rhetoric.

793. de Alvarado, C. S. (1984). From topic to final paper: A rhetorical approach. *TESOL Newsletter (Supplement No. 1: Writing and Composition)*, 18(1), 9-10.
Offers a step-by-step class procedure for leading students to consider audience and situation in writing expository papers.
Instruction/University/Intermediate.

794. de Andres, R. (1988, March). *Creative writing activities for beginning ESL students*. Paper presented at the 22nd Annual TESOL Convention, Chicago, IL.
Demonstrates various activities suitable for the elementary classroom.
Creative Writing/Elementary.

795. De Jesus, S. (1984, March). *Predictions of English writing performance of native Spanish-speaking college freshmen*. Paper presented at 35th Annual CCCC Meeting, New York, NY. [ERIC ED 256 184].
Spanish-speaking college writers with integrative motivation outperform instrumentally motivated students.
Hispanic/University/Motivation.

796. De Jesus, S. (1983). The relationship between Spanish and English writing proficiency among college freshmen in Puerto Rico. *Dissertation Abstracts International*, 44(3), 692A.
Investigates the relationship between the Spanish and English writing proficiency of college freshmen in Puerto Rico by means of a questionnaire and performance on four writing tasks. Reports a moderate correlation between Spanish and English writing ability, concluding that Spanish writing proficiency is a fair predictor of English writing proficiency.
Hispanic/University/L1-L2 Comparison.

797. De Miller, I. K., Cunha, M. I. A., Becher-Costa, S., de Oliveira, L. P., & Fortes, M. B. (1992, March). *Foreign language performance analyzed through writing*. Poster presented at the 26th Annual TESOL Convention, Vancouver, BC.
Poster displays analysis of Minimal Competency Exam essays by Puerto Rican students.
Hispanic.

798. Deakins, A. H., & Mlynarczyk, R. K. (1993, April). *Reflections on academic discourse: The role of comparison*. Paper presented at the 27th Annual TESOL Convention, Atlanta, GA.
Discusses the pivotal role of the comparison paper in learning to write academically.
Academic Writing.

799. Deakins, A. H., & Mlynarczyk, R. K. (1991, March). *From personal to academic writing: Building bridges*. Paper presented at the 25th Annual TESOL Convention,

New York, NY.

Integration of reading and writing and peer collaboration help ESL students move from personal to academic writing.

Academic Writing/Collaboration/Reading-Writing Relations.

800. Dean, M. (1990). *Write it: Writing for intermediate learners of English*. NY: Cambridge University Press.

Textbook uses an interactive approach to teach writing. It presents a variety of models by using enjoyable tasks which promote natural written communication between learners.

Intermediate/Textbook.

801. Dean, T. (1988, March). *Cultural synthesis: ESL basic writers and academic discourse*. Paper presented at the 39th Annual CCCC Meeting, St. Louis, MO.

Culture/Academic Writing.

802. Decker, D. M. (1978). Assessing writing ability of ESL college freshmen. In R. L. Light, & A. H. Osman (Eds.), *Collected papers in teaching English as a second language and bilingual education* (pp. 86-101). NY: Teachers College, Columbia University. [ERIC ED 135 247].

Results of the Test of Ability to Subordinate and the Michigan Test indicate correlation of writing maturity of ESL students with mastery of particular structures of subordination.

Evaluation/Assessment.

803. Decker, D. M. (1975). Teaching ESL writing skills: The correction sheet and testing technique. *CATESOL Occasional Papers*, 2, 5. [ERIC ED 126 701].

Describes the use of correction sheets and testing techniques geared toward the individual student to enhance effectiveness of teaching skills in intermediate and advanced English as a second language class.

Intermediate/Error Treatment.

804. Deckert, G. D. (1993). Perspectives on plagiarism from ESL students in Hong Kong. *Journal of Second Language Writing*, 2, 131-148.

Results of a questionnaire find that third-year Hong Kong Chinese university students were able to recognize plagiarism and show greater concern for the issue of honesty and the rights of the writer than their first-year peers. The difference is attributed to the younger students' lack of familiarity with the Western concept of plagiarism.

Plagiarism/Chinese.

805. Deckert, G. D. (1992, March). *Perspectives on plagiarism from Hong Kong ESL students*. Paper presented at the 26th Annual TESOL Convention, Vancouver, BC.

Reports the responses of 170 Hong Kong ESL college students, indicating unfamiliarity with the documentation conventions of academic discourse.

Plagiarism.

806. Dedo, D. R. (1992, March). *Profile of an ESL freshman writer: Predicting success*. Paper presented at the 43rd Annual CCCC Meeting, Cincinnati, OH.

See next item.

Assessment/University/Gender.

807. Dedo, D. R. (1991). Profile of the ESL freshman writer: Predicting success in the academic setting. *Dissertation Abstracts International, 52*(3), 889.

   A regression analysis shows that four variables: attained EFL instructional level, a direct measure of writing, an indirect measure of writing, and gender, predict ESL composition course grades and grade point average (but not gender). Some sets of variables better predicted performance by population subgroups (e.g., Puerto Rican, Asian, etc.) than other sets.
   Assessment/University/Gender.

808. Degenhart, R. E., Lehmann, R., & Purves, A. C. (Eds.). (1992). *The IEA study of written composition: Vol. 2* Oxford: Pergamon Press.

   Reports a ten-year study of achievement in native written composition undertaken in fourteen countries (Chile, England, Hamburg, Germany, Finland, Hungary, Indonesia, Italy, the Netherlands, New Zealand, Nigeria, Sweden, Thailand, the United States, and Wales). Study includes curriculum analysis, pilot testing, a main testing of multiple tasks, and data   analysis.
   Assessment/IEA.

809. Degenhart, R. E., & Takala, S. (1988). Developing a rating method for stylistic preference: A cross-cultural pilot study. In A. C. Purves (Ed.), *Writing across languages and cultures: Issues in contrastive rhetoric* (pp. 79-108). Newbury Park, CA: Sage.

   Describes a pilot study to determine validity of rating scales in assessing national, cultural, and stylistic preferences. Results indicate method not adequate. Suggests a more comprehensive system for coding students' responses.
   Assessment/Style.

810. Dehghanpisheh, R. E. (1979). Bridging the gap between controlled and free composition: Controlled rhetoric at the upper-intermediate level. *TESOL Quarterly, 13*, 509-519.

   Argues for moving the intermediate student from controlled writing to free writing, focusing on the expository paragraph rather than description or narration, and aiming for proficiency as a goal.
   Academic Writing/Rhetoric.

811. Dehghanpisheh, R. E. (1973). Contrastive analysis of Persian and English paragraphs. In *Proceedings of the Second Annual Seminar of the Association of Professors of English in Iran* (pp. 106-123). Tehran: APEI.
   Contrastive Rhetoric/Farsi.

812. Delaney, S. S. J. (1986). An analysis of the structure of English narrative discourse of Japanese children. *Dissertation Abstracts International, 46*(12), 3635A.

   Identifies how ten children organized their ideas when telling stories.
   Japanese/Narration/Speaking-Writing Relations.

813. Deligiorgis, I. (1988, March). *Writing for graduates: Learn to write in one semester.* Paper presented at the 22nd Annual TESOL Convention, Chicago, IL.

   Describes a course for graduate students.
   Graduate Students.

814. Dennett, J. T. (1990, March). *ESL technical writing: Process and rhetorical*

differences. Paper presented at the 41st Annual CCCC Meeting, Chicago, IL. [ERIC ED 322 713].

Discusses a study on composing processes by Japanese, Japanese-Americans, and native-speaking Americans writing technical or business English. Finds a major rhetorical difference in the products, one which seems to be culturally defined. Also finds that preference for stage of composing correlates across cultural backgrounds with different measures of product quality.

Technical Writing/NS-NNS Comparisons/Japanese.

815. Dennett, J. T. (1985). Writing technical English: A comparison of the process of native English and native Japanese speakers. *Dissertation Abstracts International*, *46*(11), 3275A.

Examines the composing processes of skilled technical writers in English, who were native English speakers or native Japanese speakers, and categorizes subjects as prewriters, writers or rewriters. Classification did not relate to native language. Nonetheless, suggests the need for process-based approach in technical writing class whatever the first language may be.

NS-NNS Comparisons/Japanese/Technical Writing.

816. DePourbaix, R., & Young, L. (1989). Can students learn what to expect in acdemia: An interview.

Carleton Papers in Applied Language Study, 6, 31-39.

ESL students learned about academic expectations as well as linguistic and academic skills needed in content courses through research interviews.

Discourse Communities/Research Writing.

817. Derrick-Mescua, M., & Gmuca, J. L. (1985, March). *Concepts of writing and sentence structure in Arabic, Spanish, and Malay*. Paper presented at the 36th Annual CCCC Meeting, Minneapolis, MN. [ERIC ED 260 590].

A year-long study investigates the use of a thesis as an organizing principle as well sentence structure in the L2 writing of Arabic, Spanish, and Malay college students. Finds some first language rhetorical influence on Arabic students who have difficulty with the thesis principle, first language linguistic influence on Spanish students who write conjoined independent clauses, but little difference for Malay students in these respects.

Arabic/Hispanic/Malay.

818. Desbonnet, K., Leibman, S., & Van Slyke, A. (1987, April). *For these reasons: Composition development for ESL students*. Paper presented at the 21st Annual TESOL Convention, Miami Beach, FL.

Shares example exercises for composition development aimed at a competency exam.

Instruction/Evaluation.

819. DeSilva, R., & Marenghi, E. (1983, March). *Contrastive rhetoric and ESL composition*. Paper presented at the 17th Annual TESOL Convention, Toronto, Canada.

Finds a variety of rhetorical patterns across five language groups when written descriptions of a process are elicited from advanced ESL learners who viewed a

video tape about setting up technical equipment.
Contrastive Rhetoric/Advanced.

820. Dessner, L. E. (1991). English as a second language college writers' revision responses to teacher-written comments. *Dissertation Abstracts International, 52*(3), 827A.

Examines written comments by ten teachers who provided corrections, direction, questioning hints and the revision changes made by ten ESL college writers. Two-thirds of the teacher comments provided advice and suggestions. Students responded to this comment type by using their own language instead of copying the teacher's model. Teacher comments provided acquisition-oriented features of language development.
Revision/Interaction/Responding.

821. Devenney, R. (1989). How ESL teachers and peers evaluate and respond to student writing. *RELC Journal, 20*(1), 77-90.

This replication of a study by Newkirk finds that the role and function of the teacher evaluator differs from that of the peer evaluator. Subjects were thirty-nine fully matriculated ESL university students and thirteen experienced ESL teachers at the University of Hawaii.
Feedback/Responding.

822. Devine, J. (1993). The role of metacognition in second language reading and writing. In J. G. Carson, & I. Leki (Eds.), *Reading in the composition classroom: Second language perspectives* (pp. 105-127). Boston: Heinle & Heinle.

Reviews recent research on metacognition, especially as it bears on the relationship between reading and writing.
Reading-Writing Relations/Metacognition.

823. Devine, J., & Boshoff, P. P. (1992, March). *The implications of cognitive models in L1 and L2 writing*. Paper presented at the 26th Annual TESOL Convention, Vancouver, BC.

Reports a study comparing NES and ESL writers' mental models, an aspect of metacognition, as it effects their writing performance. Finds that ESL writers have models that are often at odds with expectations of their writing.
Metacognition/NS-NNS Comparisons.

824. Devine, J., Fries, P. H., Eskey, D. E., Zamel, V., Samway, K. D., Carrell, P. L., & Carson, J. E. (1988, March). *The reading/writing connection*. Paper presented at the 22nd Annual TESOL Convention, Chicago, IL.

Colloquium explores various topics that link reading and writing by ESL students.
Reading-Writing Relations.

825. Devine, J., Railey, K., & Boshoff, P. P. (1993). The implications of cognitive models in L1 and L2 writing. *Journal of Second Language Writing, 2*, 203-225.

Reports on the role of cognitive models in the L1 and L2 writing of 21 freshmen -- 10 basic writers and 10 L2 writers. The analysis found that these groups hold different cognitive models and perform differently on writing tasks.
Cognition/L1-L2 Comparison.

826. Deyoe, R. M. (1980). Objective evaluation and self-evaluation of English composition skills. *English Language Teaching Journal, 34*, 148-151.

　　Outlines method for teaching writing that encourages self-improvement while downplaying competition. Scoring grid evaluates and categorizes individual errors relative to group performance which facilitates individual and group evaluation.
　　Evaluation/Error Treatment.

827. Diaz, D. M. (1991). Writing, collaborative learning, and community. *College ESL, 1*(1), 19-24.

　　Discusses how collaborative learning helps language acquisition and entry into academic community.
　　Collaboration.

828. Diaz, D. M. (1989, November). *Language across the curriculum and ESL students: Composition research and "sheltered courses"*. Paper presented at the 79th Annual NCTE Convention, Baltimore, MD. [ERIC ED 326 057].

　　Argues for a writing across the curriculum model instead of a sheltered course model for college ESL writing instruction.
　　WAC.

829. Diaz, D. M. (1988). ESL college writers: Process and community. *Journal of Developmental Education, 12*(2), 6-12.

　　Discusses theoretical framework for analyzing academic and linguistic needs of ESL college writers with suggestions for teaching.
　　Curriculum.

830. Diaz, D. M. (1986a). The writing process and the ESL writer: Reinforcement from second language research. *The Writing Instructor, 5*, 167-175.

　　Argues that research in second language learning provides supporting evidence for the value of a communicatively-based approach to acquisition which is compatible with the teaching of process strategies and techniques.
　　Process Instruction.

831. Diaz, D. M. (1986b, November). *The adult ESL writer: The process and the context*. Paper presented at the 76th Annual NCTE Convention, San Antonio, TX. [ERIC ED 281 235].

　　A classroom-based ethnographic study of process writing techniques of ESL students indicates that process-oriented classroom has positive effects on writers' audience awareness, self-esteem, metacognitive awareness of the writing process, and revising strategies.
　　Adult Education/Ethnographic Research.

832. Diaz, D. M. (1985). The process classroom and the adult L2 writer. *Dissertation Abstracts International, 46*(9), 2601A.

　　Examines the effect of the "process" classroom on the writing ability of Spanish-speaking adult ESL students. Findings show that process-approach can promote L2 writing development of adult first language literate L2 students, since in this approach: (1) errors are viewed as developmental; (2) there is awareness of audience; and (3) there is encouragement for revising and experimenting with language.

Hispanic/Process Research.

833. DiCamilla, F. (1992a, March). *Private writing in the writing of advanced ESL students*. Paper presented at the 43rd Annual CCCC Meeting, Cincinnati, OH.

Argues that inner dialogue, as Vygotsky maintained, appears in written language which is demonstrated by an analysis of gramamtical forms.

Speaking-Writing Relations.

834. DiCamilla, F. (1992b, March). *A study of peer collaboration in the ESL writing classroom*. Paper presented at the 26th Annual TESOL Convention, Vancouver, BC.

Reports whether the comments of advanced students in writing groups were restricted to the teacher's instructions and whether culture interfered with the collaborative process.

Collaboration/Advanced.

835. Dicker, S. J. (1992). *Personal expressions: Writing your way into English*. (Revised Ed.). NY: D. Blot.

Textbook uses student compositions to generate questions for discussion about the process of writing. Each lesson also highlights a grammar section on a typical problem area.

Intermediate/Textbook.

836. Dicker, S. J. (1987). Abstracting in writing: A study of four ESL college students. *Dissertation Abstracts International, 47*(11), 4007A.

Examines the abstracting processes of four college ESL students -- two Dominican and two Chinese. Interviews and observations of students' writing and drawing and an analysis of students' journals show some common abstracting characteristics, such as disregard for planning. However, both cultural and individual factors may play a crucial role in determining the abstracting characteristics in writing.

Hispanic/University/ Chinese.

837. Dicker, S. J. (1981, March). *Applying the monitor model to the editing of compositions*. Paper presented at the 25th Annual TESOL Convention, New York, NY. [ERIC ED 209 925].

Suggests that by monitoring morphemes when they are editing compositions at the end of a writing session intermediate ESL students may give their message a more native-like quality. Before teachers can expect students to apply a rule to their writing, they must discover if the students know how to apply it correctly in a discrete-point task.

Editing/Monitoring/Intermediate.

838. Dicker, S. J., & Sheppard, K. (1985). The effect of multiple drafts on structural accuracy in writing. *TESOL Quarterly, 19*, 168-170.

Reports research showing multiple drafts do not improve surface connections, implying process approach does not influence structural accuracy.

Drafting/Accuracy.

839. Dieckman, E. A. (1993). Secondary limited English proficient Hispanics "doing writing" for teachers and competency tests: A critical ethnography. *Dissertation Abstracts International, 54*(1), 71A.

Provides an ethnography of the activities and interaction of Hispanic high school students receiving writing instruction for the purpose of passing the writing section of a state competency exam. Finds, among other things, that the test limits the number of diplomas non-natives receive.
Ethnographic Research/Spanish/Secondary School.

840. Dimond, E. d. (1986, March). *Using writing as subject matter in teaching advanced English*. Paper presented at the 20th Annual TESOL Convention, Anaheim, CA.
Presents a comprehension-based writing syllabus that involves the other skills as well.
Advanced/Content.

841. Dimond, E. d. (1984). *The effectiveness of productive writing as subject matter in teaching advanced level English*. Unpublished master's thesis, American University, Cairo, Egypt. [ERIC ED 276 252].
Classes of EFL students treated with a "productive writing approach" which emphasized comprehension before production improved their English usage and listening comprehension more than those who were taught by the traditional grammar-based syllabus method.
Methods.

842. Dissayanake, A. S., Basil, A. A., & Nayar, U. (1990). English proficiency in multiple-choice questions. *Academic Medicine*, *65*, 101.
Claims that clear, simple English on objective tests prevents English proficiency from being a determinant in responses.
Proficiency/Assessment/Medicine.

843. Divine, B., & Hurt, P. (1984, March). *Accurate use of transition words in academic discourse: Problems and solutions for the ESL writing teacher*. Paper presented at the 18th Annual TESOL Convention, Houston, TX.
Presents three common problems with student use of conjunctive adverbs in writing: imprecise usage, grammatical placement, and overapplication. Suggests strategies to overcome them.
Cohesion/Instruction.

844. Dixon, D. (1986). Teaching composition to large classes. *English Teaching Forum*, *24*(3), 2-5.
Discusses techniques appropriate for large classes such as how to choose assignments, prewriting activities, journal writing, peer editing, and limited marking.
Assignments/Large Classes.

845. Dobra, S. (1992, March). *Reassessing cultural assumptions about argumentative reasoning*. Paper presented at the 43rd Annual CCCC Meeting, Cincinnati, OH.
Argumentation/Culture.

846. Dole, R. (1989). On teaching the neglected fourth skill. *Bulletin de L'ACLA (Bulletin of the CAAL)*, *11*(1), 49-35.
In a study of 50 ESL students, the experimental goals were to make students feel as anxious as possible when writing in English, to have them write as much as possible, and to make them concentrate on accuracy and fluency. Results show the varying effects of these factors on the quality of their ESL compositions.

Anxiety.

847. Dolly, M. R. (1990a). Adult ESL students' management of dialogue journal conversation. *TESOL Quarterly, 24*, 317-321.
    Reports a study which analyzes patterns of student moves in dialogue journal writing, finding that nonnatives assume substantial responsibility for topic initiation whether giving or soliciting information.
    Dialogue Journals/Responding.

848. Dolly, M. R. (1990b). Integrating ESL reading and writing through authentic discourse. *Journal of Reading, 33*(5), 360-365.
    Discusses how reciprocal discourse and dialogue journals are useful in assisting non-native writers with the conventions of reading and writing.
    Reading-Writing Relations/Dialogue Journals.

849. Dolly, M. R. (1989, August). *Conversation management in the dialogue journals of adult ESL students*. Washington, DC: ERIC/FLL. [ERIC ED 311 711].
    Reports on a study of the patterns of "giving" and "soliciting" in dialogue journals of 12 college ESL students and their native English-speaking teacher
    Dialogue Journals/Interaction.

850. Dolly, M. R. (1987). A study of solicit and give moves in the management of dialogue journal conversation by adult ESL students. *Dissertation Abstracts International, 48*(12), 3099-3100A.
    Examines 260 dialogue journal entries by twelve adult ESL college students. Finds a pattern of "giving" and "soliciting" on both sides of the ledger, indicating reciprocity between students and teacher in sharing responsibility for communication by means of writing.
    Dialogue Journals/Interaction.

851. Donaldson, J. K. (1990, March). *EFL and the "Writing Across the Curriculum Movement"*. Paper presented at the 41st Annual CCCC Meeting, Chicago, IL.
    WAC.

852. Donaldson, J. K. (1984, March). *Discourse cohesion in technical writing: The pedagogical implications of research into its nature*. Paper presented at the 18th Annual TESOL Convention, Houston, TX.
    Presents an inventory of cohesion devices specific to different varieties of technical and sub-technical writing in context of materials development.
    Cohesion/Technical Writing.

853. Donaldson, J. K. (1983, March). *Editing and revision as a method for teaching discourse cohesion in business English*. Paper presented at the 17th Annual TESOL Convention, Toronto, BC.
    Presents a series of graded editing exercises for use in EFL business courses to assist the achievement of cohesion in business writing.
    Cohesion/Revision/Business Writing.

854. Donley, M. (1976). The paragraph in advanced composition: A heuristic approach. *English Language Teaching Journal, 30*(3), 225-235.
    The essay discusses methods to be used in teaching the paragraph as a basic unit in writing, such as asking the student to predict words in a given topic sentence

that they would expect to find in a paragraph. Guessing ahead "should enable students to see that inner cohesion" that helps to create fluidity in writing. Other writing exercises suggested include the jumbled paragraph and the development for support of statements.
Advanced/Paragraph/Classroom Activities.

855. Donley, M. (1975). Precis writing: A rehabilitation. *English Language Teaching Journal, 29*(3), 213-220.
Offers suggestions for teaching precis writing. Advocates stressing the value of language manipulation activitiy, its meaningfulness, the language techniques required, its link with composition, and its appropriateness to the advanced level.
Summary Writing.

856. Donnelly, R. (1993, April). *Essay competence tests and ESL students: A critical evaluation.* Paper presented at the 27th Annual TESOL Convention, Atlanta, GA.
Workshop discusses university-wide essay tests of writing competence.
Evaluation.

857. Dooley, M. S. (1989). *Dialogue journals: Facilitating the reading-writing connection with Native American students.* Washington, DC: ERIC/FLL. [ERIC ED 292 118]).
Dialogue journals proved successful culturally, emotionally, and linguistically with third-grade Native American students on a reservation.
Amer-Indian/Reading-Writing Relations/Dialogue Journals.

858. Doorn, D. (1991, March). *Home-school journals: New discoveries in literacy values.* Paper presented at the 25th Annual TESOL Convention, New York, NY.
Shows ways to use home-school journals to increase language interactions beyond the classroom, identify new curricular-content issues, and promote varied literacy development functions.
Journal Writing/Elementary.

859. Dorrill, G. T. (1988, November). *A journal project: Extending the ESL classroom.* Paper presented at the 78th Annual NCTE Convention, St. Louis, MO.
Journal Writing.

860. Dotson, K. (1988). *Process and evaluation in the ESL classroom: ESL teacher evaluations vs. English teacher evaluations.* Unpublished master's thesis, Eastern Michigan University, Ypsilanti, MI.
Investigates whether native-speaking ESL teachers, non-native English speaking ESL teachers and English-speaking native English teachers differ in their type of evaluation of student work and whether ESL teachers expect less from students' compositions than do English-speaking native English teachers.
NS-NNS Comparisons/Evaluation.

861. Douglas, D., Ray, R. E., & Webb, S. (1984, May). *Foreign student writing in ESL and "freshman composition": What's the difference?* Paper presented at the Annual NAFSA Meeting, Snowmass, CO.
NS-NNS Comparisons.

862. Douglas, F., & Myers, C. (1988, March). *Nonnative writing problems in freshman composition.* Paper presented at the 22nd Annual TESOL Convention, Chicago, IL.
Reports research on the common ESL writing problems reported by teachers

of freshman composition and how these related to the teachers' perceptions and backgrounds.
Freshman Composition/Teacher Preparation.

863. Doushaq, M. H. (1986). An investigation into stylistic errors of Arab students learning English for academic purposes. *English for Specific Purposes*, 5(1), 27-39.
Finds that the most important problem in the writing of university level Jordanian students is the failure to fulfill intentions rhetorically and stylistically. Concludes that educational and cultural factors may be more responsible than linguistic ones.
Errors/Style/Arabic.

864. Dowling, J. (1992). *The Little, Brown ESL workbook*. NY: HarperCollins.
A full-length grammar workbook featuring brief descriptions, illustrations, and exercises on both simple and complex sentence structures. Chapters also on punctuation and pronunciation.
Grammar/Textbook.

865. Doxey, C. (1990). Tutors' column. *Writing Lab Newsletter*, 15, 9.
Unexpectedly finds ESL students eager and interesting writers.
Tutoring.

866. Dreyer, D. Y. (1992). Responding to peers: The language of native and non-native speakers in writing groups. *Dissertation Abstracts International*, 53(12), 4237A.
Examines the quality and quantity of talk about writing shared in small groups (only NS, only NNS, mixed) in two college composition courses. The teacher/researcher applied qualitative research methodology at three levels: whole class, group, and individual. Finds that, regardless of group composition, participants addressed writing concerns and usually focused on content.
Peer Response/NS-NNS Comparisons.

867. Drunagly, J. (1986, March). *ESL students write . . . and publish!* Paper presented at the 20th Annual TESOL Convention, Anaheim, CA.
Points out that students can integrate writing with subject matter by making books that can be used as teaching tools.
Student Publications.

868. Druny, H., & Gollin, S. (1986). The use of systemic functional linguistics in the analysis of ESL student writing and recommendations for the teaching situation. *Occasional Papers -- Applied Linguistics Association of Australia*, 9, 209-236.
Outlines a systemic model of expository genres and discusses its applications in error identification and analysis. Advocates the use of metalanguage and linguistic exploration in the advanced writing class.
Advanced/Exposition/Error Analysis.

869. Dubin, F. (1988, March). *Selecting textbooks for ESL writing courses*. Paper presented at the 39th Annual CCCC Meeting, St. Louis, MO.
Materials.

870. Dubin, F., & Kuhlman, N. A. (1984, March). *Cross-cultural modes of acquiring literacy in L1*. Paper presented at the 18th Annual TESOL Convention, Houston, TX.

Culturally variable learning styles may affect how L1 writing skills will transfer to L2 literacy.
Literacy/Culture/Learning Styles.

871. Dubin, F., Kuhlman, N. A., Isserlis, J., Lewis, M., Ulichny, P., & Kohn James. (1989, March). *Cross-cultural modes of acquiring literacy skills*. Paper presented at the 23rd Annual TESOL Convention, San Antonio, TX.
Literacy/Culture.

872. Dubin, F., & Olshtain, E. (1980). The interface of writing and reading. *TESOL Quarterly, 14,* 353-363.
Claims that reading has guided writing traditionally in ESOL and also that prescriptions given to writers in handbooks can help learners improve their reading strategies.
Reading-Writing Relations/Materials.

873. Dubois, B. L. (1975, March). *The use of newspapers to teach topic-sentence writing*. Paper presented at the 9th Annual TESOL Convention, Los Angeles, CA.
Advocates using newspapers as textbooks for intermediate and advanced students, which allows for reading, grammar, and writing tasks.
Materials/Intermediate/Advanced.

874. Dubois, B. L., & Buker, S. (1979). Micro self-pacing in the university ESL composition course. *System, 7,* 145-157.
Describes a self-pacing procedure for helping students of diverse backgrounds handle the materials of a composition course in English as a second language. Sample instruction materials are appended.
University.

875. Dudley-Evans, T. (1992). *Teaching research writing to nonnative speakers: Genre consciousness-raising for science and engineering thesis writers*. Paper presented at the 26th Annual TESOL Convention, Vancouver, BC.
Experience at one univiersity in England suggests combining a general approach and a specialized strand in the teaching of research writing in order to help student adapt to the discourse communities of plant biology and highway engineering.

876. Dudley-Evans, T. (1989). An outline of the value of genre analysis in LSP work. In C. Laurén, & M. Nordman (Eds.), *Special language: From humans thinking to thinking machines* (pp. 72-79). Clevedon: Multilingual Matters.
Discusses the meaning of genre analysis as a means of indicating to students how texts differ in type.
ESP/Genre.

877. Dudley-Evans, T. (1988). A consideration of the meaning of "discuss" in examination questions. In P. C. Robinson (Ed.), *Academic writing: Process and product* (pp. 47-52). London: Modern English Publications/British Council.
Makes the case against a "common core" approach to ESP (or academic writing courses generally), that is, a focus on particular skills related to subject matter courses but developed in a variety of contexts common to all disciplines and not specific to individual disciplines. This is supported by a contrastive analysis of the general meaning of "discuss" in examination questions and the meaning specific

to the field of Plant Biology to illustrate the much wider range of meanings in the latter.
ESP/Academic Writing.

878. Dudley-Evans, T. (1984). The team teaching of writing skills. In R. Williams, J. M. Swales, & J. Kirkman (Eds.), *Common ground: Shared interests in ESP and communications studies.* (pp. 127-143). Oxford: Pergamon.
Describes collaboration between a language and a subject teacher in an occupational course for ESL students in Singapore that involves report writing.
Collaboration/ESP.

879. Dudley-Evans, T., & Swales, J. M. (1980). Study modes and students from the Middle East. *ELT Documents 109* London: British Council.
Contrasts a translation of an article from an Arabic newspaper with the same article written in English to show different approaches to the development of an argument.
Contrastive Rhetoric/Argumentation.

880. Duffin, B. (1977). *A study of writing problems in a remedial writing program for EOP students* . Washington, DC: ERIC/FLL. [ERIC ED 153 473].
Describes a college writing program in one university English Department for Educational Opportunity Program (EOP) students, seventy-five percent of whom spoke English as a second language. Discusses first language interference, the identification of writing problems, and a comparison of their performance with that of a NES students.
University/Courses/NS-NNS Comparisons.

881. Dulmage, J. K., & Kopec, J. (1984, March). *"Dear diary": Use of the journal as a humanistic and pedagogic tool.* Paper presented at the 18th Annual TESOL Convention, Houston, TX.
Describes use of a personal journal in a secondary school course and an intensive program.
Journal Writing/Secondary School.

882. Dunbar, S. (1985, October). *CAI and English composition for the multi-cultural/lingual student.* Paper presented at the 20th Annual Meeting of the Northeast Regional Conference on English in the Two-Year College, Portland, ME. [ERIC ED 268 525].
Discusses computer-assisted instruction and word processing in a community college ESL program to improve language skills and writing ability.
Computers/Programs.

883. Dungey, J. M. (1984). Book-making for beginning ESL students. *TESOL Newsletter (Supplement No. 1: Writing and Composition), 18*(1), 3.
The whole language activity of making books gives students reading and writing opportunities of personal interest.
Whole Language/Beginners/Children.

884. Dunkelblau, H. S. (1992). *Chinese and English expository writing: A comparative study.* Paper presented at the 26th Annual TESOL Convention, Vancouver, BC.
Examines the use of eleven Chinese rhetorical devices in the Chinese and

English writing of emigre high school students. Findings indicate support for the Contrastive Rhetoric hypothesis.

    Chinese/Exposition.

885. Dunkelblau, H. S. (1990). A contrastive study of the organizational structure and stylistic elements of Chinese and English expository writing by Chinese high school students. *Dissertation Abstracts International*, *51*(4), 1143A.

Compares essays written in Chinese and in English by thirty-nine Chinese emigre high school students. Tentative support for the existence of culturally preferred rhetorical styles but not for rhetorical transfer results from an analysis of essay organization by means of Coe's discourse matrix (1988) and devices commonly found in Chinese rhetoric. In particular, the macro and micro-structures of both essays were similar and contained a common pattern of sub-topic modified by subordinate support. However, essays written in Chinese contained a greater number of rhetorical devices as well as greater usage of set phrases, ornate language, and analogy than were contained in English essays.

    Contrastive Rhetoric/Chinese/Secondary School.

886. Dunlop, I. (1969). Test of writing ability in English as a foreign language. *English Language Teaching*, *24*(1), 54-59.

Introduces report writing test in Sweden.

    Evaluation.

887. Duran, R. P. (1987). Factors affecting development of second language literacy. In S. R. Goldman, & H. T. Treuba (Eds.), *Becoming literate in English as a second language* (pp. 33-55). Norwood, NJ: Ablex.

National surveys show that self-judgments of proficiency in English and the non-English language contribute positively to predicting school outcomes among Hispanic and white high school seniors and college freshman.

    Hispanic/Literacy.

888. Dyck, P. B. (1980). *Written usage of American Indian and Anglo college students*. Unpublished master's thesis, Brigham Young University, Provo, UT.

    Amer-Indian/NS-NNS Comparisons/Usage.

889. Dyer, P. M. (1990). What composition theory offers the writing teacher. In L. A. Arena (Ed.), *Language proficiency: Defining, teaching, and testing* (pp. 99-106). NY: Plenum.

Argues that three elements: process approach, rhetorical strategies, and audience orientation, provide a workable foundation in composition theory for instructing college students in composition.

    Theory.

890. Dykstra, G. (1977). Toward interactive modes in guided compositions. *TESL Reporter*, *10*(3), 1-4, 18-19. [ERIC ED 198 742].

Discusses the origin and rationale for controlled composition and suggests interaction among students and with teachers to enable the production and editing of compositions.

    Control/Speaking-Writing Relations.

891. Dykstra, G. (1975). Breaking down your writing goals. In E. Bauer (Ed.), *English*

for American Indians (pp. 47-56). Albuquerque, NM: Bureau of Indian Affairs. [ERIC ED 125 800].

Suggests that teachers of ESL composition should proceed from immediate to long-term goals in their writing curriculum.

Curriculum.

892. Dykstra, G. (1964). Eliciting language practice in writing. *English Language Teaching, 19*(1), 23-26.

Advocates copying, completing, and substituting model paragraphs drawn from most capable students, graded readers, and other sources.

Classroom Activities.

893. Dykstra, G., & Paulston, C. B. (1967). Guided composition. *English Language Teaching, 21*(2), 136-141.

Proposes application of graded and structured language manipulations to model passages which students rewrite, focusing on targeted forms.

Control.

894. Dziombak, C. E. (1990). Searching for collaboration in the ESL computer lab and the ESL classroom. *Dissertation Abstracts International, 51*(7), 2296A.

Observes the teaching of two ESL writing classes both in the classroom and the computer lab to determine the characteristics of collaboration in the two settings. The results showed little student-student collaboration in either instructional setting. The lab, especially, seldom exploited the communicative potential of the situation. Little thematic connection between classroom and lab existed. Tension existed between teacher's desire to implement process writing and student perception of need to pass writing tests.

Collaboration/Computers/Laboratory.

E

895. Early, M. (1990). From task to text: A case study of ESL students' development of expository discourse. *TESL Talk, 20*(1), 111-125.

A study of ten fifth grade beginning ESL students finds support for the children's ability to cope with the linguistic and cognitive demands of a nonnarrative writing task.

Elementary/Exposition.

896. Easton, B. J. (1983). Blended beginnings: Connections and the effects of editing in a case of academic "Japanese English". *Dissertation Abstracts International, 43*(9), 2983A.

Examines writing of a Japanese student and the comments made by American university professors. Findings show different rhetorical patterns of organization. Japanese student uses indirectness and initial connectives to provide coherence. Claims that this pattern represents the students' "Japanese English," which American readers do not always understand.

Japanese /Contrastive Rhetoric.

897. Ebaru, O. O. (1989). On the reliability and validity of holistic scoring on compositions in Nigeria. *British Journal of Language Teaching, 27*(3), 152-158.

Holistic scoring lacked concurrent validity with the subject pool in a correlational study of 120 student essays and a standardized proficiency test (SLEP) despite high inter and intra-rater reliability.

Assessment/Nigerian.

898. Ebel, C. (1984, March). *Total participation approach to writing: Natural language activities for teaching reading and writing to elementary and secondary students.* Workshop presented at the 18th Annual TESOL Convention, Houston, TX.

Outlines Deweyan principles in using ideas from SPECTRA experiential learning in mainstream reading and writing classes.

Elementary/Secondary School.

899. Echeverria, E. W., & Moreland, K. (1990, March). *Writing centers and the foreign student.* Paper presented at the 24th Annual TESOL Convention, San Francisco, CA.

Discusses writing centers in general, their history, identity, and theory, as well as the way one university center, in particular, tries to help ESL students cope with the clash of cultures and discourse expectations.

Writing Center.

900. Edalat, H. (1981). *Some sources of errors in the English compositions of Iranian students.* Unpublished master's thesis, Eastern Washington University, Cheney, WA.

Errors/Persian.

901. Edelsky, C. (1989a). Bilingual children's writing: Fact and fiction. In D. M. Johnson, & D. H. Roen (Eds.), *Richness in writing: Empowering ESL students* (pp. 165-176). NY: Longman.

Presents several myths associated with writing: (1) that any graphic display is writing; (2) that bilingualism limits learning to write; (3) that young children are insensitive to audience. Counters these myths with evidence from a bilingual program. Claims much writing in classrooms is only a simulation of writing and that confusion in writing is not due to bilingualism. Children show definite signs of audience awareness.

Hispanic/Bilingual/Children.

902. Edelsky, C. (1989b). Putting language variation to work. In P. Rigg, & V. F. Allen (Eds.), *When they all don't speak English: Integrating the ESL student into the regular classroom* (pp. 96-107). Urbana, IL: NCTE.

Suggests use of dialogue journals, parody of fiction, and writing about a community's language usage as ways to develop writing ability in the multi-speech community elementary classroom.

Classroom Activities/Curriculum.

903. Edelsky, C. (1986). *Writing in a bilingual program: Habia una vez.* Norwood, NJ: Ablex.

Studies, primarily, the change that occurs during one year of writing by elementary school children in a bilingual program. Results indicate a number of specific changes in the writing of children in the first three grades. These "changes in purposes and their means of accomplishment," or developmental growth, is postulated for all grades. The children formulated various specific hypotheses about writing and modified or abandoned some through specific interactions with various

contexts.
Elementary/Hispanic/Development.

904. Edelsky, C. (1983). SEGMENTATIONANDPUNC.TU.A.TION: Developmental data from young writers in a bilingual program. *Reseach in the Teaching of English*, 17, 135-156.

Provides a descriptive study of the writing development of migrant farm workers' children in grades 1 through 3. Finds emergence of invented patterns in word segmentation and development of conventionality in their punctuation of text.
Hispanic/Children.

905. Edelsky, C. (1982a). Three myths about literacy and some counter-evidence. *Journal of the Linguistic Association of the Southwest*, 5(2), 66-84.

Reports, contrary to widespread assumptions, that children acquiring a second literacy adjust register, language, and the amount of contextualization according to their intended audience.
Literacy/Children.

906. Edelsky, C. (1982b). Writing in a bilingual program: The relation of L1 and L2 texts. *TESOL Quarterly*, 16, 211-228.

Compares the writing in Spanish and English of nine bilingual children. Concludes that a child's knowledge of writing in a first language forms a basis of a new hypothesis about writing in the second language.
Children/Hispanic.

907. Edelsky, C. (1981). From "Jimosal(c)sco to "7 narangas se calleron y el-arbol-est-triste en lagrymas": Writing development in a bilingual program. In B. Cronnell (Ed.), *The writing needs of linguistically different students: Proceedings of a research practice conference* (pp. 63-98). Los Alamitos, CA: Southwest Regional Laboratory for Educational Research and Development. [ERIC ED 210 932].

Investigates the writing of twenty-seven first through third grade students in a bilingual program in the southwest.
Hispanic/Children.

908. Edelsky, C., & Hudelson, S. (1991). Contextual complexities: Written language policies for bilingual progams. In S. Benesch (Ed.), *ESL in America: Myths and possibilities* (pp. 75-90). Portsmouth, NH: Boynton/Cook.

Offers a general position concerning written language policies to be adopted by urban school districts in the U.S., emphasizing that contextual variation in learning to write in school precludes uniform policy making. Advocates local autonomy for teachers and students.
Administration/Bilingual.

909. Edelsky, C., & Hudelson, S. (1987). *Contextual complexities: Written language politics for bilingual programs* . Berkeley, CA: Center for the Study of Writing.
[See next item].
Bilingual/Elementary.

910. Edelsky, C., & Jilbert, C. (1985). Bilingual children and writing: Lessons for all of us. *Volta Review*, 87, 57-72.

Reviews issues in the writing development of bilingual children.

Children/Hispanic.

911. Edge, J. (1989). *Mistakes and correction*. NY: Longman.

A practical guide for teachers concerned about when to correct mistakes and how to do it. One chapter is devoted to correction and writing.

Error Treatment.

912. Edge, J. (1984). Structuring the information gap. *ELT Journal, 38*, 256-261.

Describes a communication procedure for searching for information through writing.

Classroom Activities.

913. Edge, J. (1980). Teaching writing in large classes. *English Language Teaching Journal, 34*(2), 146-151.

Describes experience of forming groups in an EFL composition class, based on the kind of writing the students were called on to do and based on the kinds of errors made in their papers. Finds that peer correction reduced the occurrences of careless mistakes without sacrificing coverage of type of writing.

Group Work/Large Classes.

914. Edlund, J. R. (1986). Composition and the non-native speaker: Issues and solutions. *The Writing Instructor, 5*, 149-151.

Raises the question of communication between TESOL and the writing community as a preface to special journal issue on ESL.

Instruction.

915. Edlund, J. R. (1988). Bakhtin and the social reality of language acquisition. *Writing Instructor, 2*, 56-67.

Illustrates the assimilation and restructuring of an individual's belief system in the writing of non-native students.

Social.

916. Edmondson, M., Edmondson, P., & Thompson, S. (1986, March). *Advanced composition: An integrative approach*. Paper presented at the 20th Annual TESOL Convention, Anaheim, CA.

Views a rhetorical approach as inadequate to teach skills needed in academic courses.

Advanced/Rhetoric.

917. Edmondson, P., & Thompson, S. (1988, March). *Evaluating student writing and the process approach*. Paper presented at the 22nd Annual TESOL Convention, Chicago, IL.

Discusses several methods of evaluating compositions in a process approach.

Process Instruction/Assessment.

918. Edwards, B. H. (1988). *The broad nature of intermediate EFL writing: Difficulties and challenges for the EFL instructor*. Paper presented at the Eighth Annual University of Southern Florida Linguistics Club Conference on Second Language Acquisition and Second Language Teaching, Tampa, FL.

Reports a pilot study of writing skills of intermediate ESL students. The study identified the clause structures and relative low-order linguistic skills in the writing samples of 25 college students which were evaluated of writing using criteria of

conformity to correct word form, word order, and word choice.
Intermediate/Error Analysis.

919. Egbert, J., Tebbets, D., & Barclay, G. (1993, April). *Computer-supported writing projects*. Paper presented at the 27th Annual TESOL Convention, Atlanta, GA.
Finds that pre-literate beginning level adults can participate in computer-supported writing projects.
Computers/Beginners.

920. Eggington, W. G. (1987). Written academic discourse in Korean: Implications for effective communication. In U. M. Connor, & R. B. Kaplan (Eds.), *Writing across languages: Analysis of L2 text* (pp. 153-168). Reading, MA: Addison-Wesley.
Describes features of Korean academic written discourse and claims that they support Kaplan's description of Korean discourse structure. Examines implications for effective communication.
Academic Writing/Korean.

921. Eggington, W. G., & Ricento, T. (1983). Discourse analysis as a pedagogical tool. *CATESOL Occasional Papers*, 9, 75-85. [ERIC ED 236 938].
Advocates using discourse bloc analysis (i.e., graphic depictions of errors in units of meaning) to overcome transfer of culturally-based rhetorical norms.
Discourse Analysis/Contrastive Rhetoric.

922. Eison, D. M. (1984). *Process oriented composition: A pedagogy for both native and second language learners of English*. Unpublished master's thesis, Western Kentucky University, Bowling Green, KY.
Process Instruction.

923. Eisterhold, J. C. (1989, March). *Reading and writing relationships in first and second language: The transfer of writing skills across language*. Paper presented at the 40th Annual CCCC Meeting, Seattle, WA.
Examines student writing in Arabic, Chinese, Japanese, and Spanish as well as ESL to determine the contribution of first language writing ability to L2 writing skills.
L1 Influence/Chinese/Arabic/Spanish.

924. Eisterhold, J. C. (1988, March). *Reading/writing connections: What the research suggests*. Paper presented at the 39th Annual CCCC Meeting, St. Louis, MO.
Argues from several different research areas that reading must be viewed as an essential component of the ESL composition class.
Reading-Writing Relations.

925. Ekmeçi, F. O. (1991, March). *Validity of translation and composition in assessing written performance*. Paper presented at the 25th Annual TESOL Convention, New York, NY.
Uses a quantitative analysis (Reid, 1986) to compare translation and composition as methods of assessment.
Assessment/Translation.

926. Ekmeçi, F. O. (1971). *Teaching composition through comprehension: A survey of teaching English composition to foreign students and its application to the English Program at the Middle East Technical University*. Unpublished master's thesis,

University of Texas, Austin, TX. [ERIC ED 060 739].

Surveys techniques for teaching composition and methods for each kind of communication with some lesson plans.

Classroom Activities.

927. El Gamil Abdel Fattah, A. (1993). *The influence of dialogue journals and other practicum activities on the writing proficiency and pedagogical knowledge of EFL student teachers*. Unpublished doctoral dissertation, IUP, Indiana, PA.

Claims that dialogue journals improved the written fluency but not the accuracy of student teachers in a teacher education practicum at a community college in the United Arab Emirates.

Dialogue Journals/Teacher Preparation.

928. El-Badri, L. (1991, March). *Grammar clinic to the rescue: For freshman writing students*. Paper presented at the 25th Annual TESOL Convention, New York, NY.

Shows how to set up a grammar clinic for EFL students.

Grammar.

929. El-Daly, H. M. (1991). A contrastive analysis of the writing proficiency of Arabic and Spanish speakers: Linguistic, cognitive, and cultural perspectives. *Dissertation Abstracts International*, 52(5), 1624A.

Investigates the role of grammar in the written productions of four Arabic and four Spanish college students by means of questionnaires, interviews and an examination of two writing tasks and two error correction tasks. Finds that these L2 learners' proficiency is not unitary nor systematic, varying from task to task and person to person. Students could correct errors when they were pointed out to them. All subjects reported "translating" but only two engaged in "reviewing" and "monitoring" when writing.

Arabic/Hispanic/Grammar/Error Analysis.

930. El-Ezabi, Y. A. (1968). A sector analysis of modern written Arabic with implications for teaching English to Arab students. *Dissertation Abstracts International*, 28(9), 3657A.

Analyzes the syntax of written Arabic using Robert Allen's sector analysis and compares sectors of Arabic and English. Finds correspondences and differences between sectors on every level.

L1-L2 Comparison/Arabic/Syntactic Structures.

931. El-Hibir, B. I., & Altaha, F. M. (1993). Tips for dealing with spelling errors. *English Teaching Forum*, 31(1), 41-42.

Outlines a series of steps in teaching standard English spelling.

Spelling.

932. El-Khatib, A. S. A. (1984a). Case studies of four Egyptian college freshman writers majoring in English. *Dissertation Abstracts International*, 46(4), 969A.

Analyzes the rhetorical patterns of Arabic students writing in English, classifies their lexical problems, and describes students' apprehension about the writing process. Suggests ways for teaching rhetorical patterns, developing vocabulary, and reducing apprehension.

Arabic/University/Rhetoric/Affect.

933. El-Khatib, A. S. A. (1984b). *A classification of the lexical problems of EFL/ESL students* . Washington, DC: ERIC/FLL. [ERIC ED 246 691].

Finds eight types of lexical problems in the writing samples of four Arab ESL freshman. These types include: overgeneralization, literal translation, divergence, word form confusions, word meaning confusions, unfamiliarity with word collocations, and overuse of a few items.

Arabic/Lexis/Exposition.

934. El-Khatib, A. S. A. (1983). *Toward a descriptive rhetoric of the ESL paragraph* . Washington, DC: ERIC/FLL. [ERIC ED 234 622].

Analyzes expository compositions written by Arab freshman English majors in order to describe inter-sentence relationships. Shows that ESL students do not know how to subordinate sentences. Suggests that in order to produce acceptable writing, ESL Arab students should study paragraphs containing inter-sentence structural relationships.

Contrastive Rhetoric/Paragraph/Arabic.

935. Elliot, L. G., Sampaio de Moraes, M., & da Rocha Bastos, L. (1991, April). *Relationships between language teaching methods and writing quality*. Paper presented at the Annual Meeting of the AERA, Chicago, IL.

Methods.

936. Elliott, M. (1986). Nasr's development as a writer in his second language: The first six months. *Australian Review of Applied Linguistics*, 2, 120-153.

Discusses the development of writing skills in ESL in an adolescent native speaker of Arabic over a six-month period. The most significant change observed was acquisition of an appreciation of the way in which English as a written language differs from the spoken language. Changes were manifested not only in the subject's texts, but also in the processes by which they were produced. Traces the acquisition of various discourse cohesion devices and identifies Intermediate forms of writing development process.

Development/Arabic.

937. Elliott, N., Paris, J., & Bodner, J. (1990). *The teacher of writing in the ESL Curriculum*. Urbana, IL: ERIC/RCS [ED323762]).

Finds several common instructional practices in the teaching of writing and ESL. Greater validity is achieved by distinguishing levels of literacy (basic, intermediate, academic, and disciplinary) and levels of writing ability. Suggests better instruction can be achieved by using teachers of ESL writing, not merely at the lowest levels, but at the academic and disciplinary levels as well.

NS-NNS Comparisons/Literacy/University.

938. Elsasser, N. (1978, April). *Literacy: The writing on the wall*. Paper presented at the 12th Annual TESOL Convention, Mexico City, Mexico.

A panel reports on the development of a theory of literacy, drawing on Vygotsky and Freire, for students who have oral competence but write incoherently.

Literacy/Speaking-Writing Relations.

939. El-Sayed, A. (1983). An investigation into the syntactic errors of Saudi freshmen's

compositions. *Dissertation Abstracts International, 43*(10), 3306A.

    Examines syntactic errors in compositions by sixty male Saudi students by means of contrastive analysis. Studies interlingual errors which are the result of L1 interference. Claims that L1 interference is the primary cause of syntactic errors in writing.

    Error Analysis/Arabic/University.

940. El-Shafie, A. S. (1990). English writing development of Arab twelfth grade students: Case studies of six EFL writers. *Dissertation Abstracts International, 51*(11), 3653-3654A.

    Presents case studies of six female United Arab Emirates twelfth-graders with intermediate English language proficiency who were learning to write in a process-oriented classroom. Results identify consistent progress in writing development, both in quantity and quality of writing over the span of ten compositions written at intervals during one full academic year. Revision (Bridwell,1980; Faigley & Witte, 1981;1984) is similar among students, but there is wide variation in the amount from student to student and topic to topic. Within-subject variation in quantity of revisions, however, does not correspond to improvement in writing quality.

    Revision/Arabic/Secondary School.

941. El-Shushabi, M. A. H. (1988). Substitution and lexical cohesion in the editorial argumentative discourse of Arabic and American English. *Dissertation Abstracts International, 49*(7), 1786A.

    Finds that the cohesive devices of synonymy and pronominalization occur with a higher frequency in Arabic than in American English whereas contrastives and semantic domains occur with a greater frequency in American English.

    Arabic/Cohesion.

942. Emel, L. J., Goodrum, R., Young, R. K., & Laothamatas, J. (1985, April). *Extra! Read all about it! Publishing ESL student newspapers*. Poster presented at the 19th Annual TESOL Convention, New York, NY.

    Posters show an ESL student published newspaper.

    Student Publications.

943. Engber, C. A. (1993, April). *The relationship of lexis to quality in L2 compositions*. Paper presented at the 27th Annual TESOL Convention, Atlanta, GA.

    Shows that continuous progress toward precise use of language, judged holistically, in the compositions by ESL learners is associated with a variety of lexical forms and resources.

    Lexis.

944. Engelbrecht, G. (1987, November). *Literacy in the bilingual classroom: Some observations*. Paper presented at the 77th Annual NCTE Convention, Los Angeles, CA.

    Bilingual/Hispanic.

945. Enginarlar, H. (1993). Student response to teacher feedback in EFL writing. *System, 21*, 193-204.

    Surveys attitudes of 47 freshmen students at a Turkish university to feedback procedures in EFL composition. Findings corroborate Radecki & Swales (1988).

Feedback/Turkish.

946. England, L. (1984). *The use of basic writing materials in ESL writing classes*. Paper presented at the 35th Annual CCCC Meeting, New York, NY. [ERIC ED 245 418].

Advocates appropriateness in ESL classes of materials for basic writers in ESL classes.

Materials/NS-NNS Comparisons.

947. Enkvist, N. E. (1990). Seven problems in the study of coherence and interpretability. In U. M. Connor, & A. M. Johns (Ed.), *Coherence in writing: Research and pedagogical perspective* (pp. 9-28). Alexandria, VA: TESOL.

Discusses seven problems that arise in the study of coherence: (1) distinction between cohesion and coherence, (2) metamessages that accompany any message, (3) inference involved in interpretation, (4) importance of situation in meaning, (5) the knowledge of the interpreter, (6) discourse function and text types, (7) use of strategy, structure and process. Concludes saying that knowledge of language and culture go hand in hand and that advanced ESL students who are not proficient in coherence should be treated with tolerance and teachers should see their achievements rather than deficiencies.

Review.

948. Enkvist, N. E. (1987). Text linguistics for the applier: An orientation. In U. M. Connor, & R. B. Kaplan (Eds.), *Writing across languages: Analysis of L2 text* (pp. 23-43). Reading, MA: Addison-Wesley.

Discusses four different types of models operating in text linguistics -- sentence-based, prediction-based, cognitive, and interactional. Justifies them on grounds that they are objective and process-oriented.

Text Analysis/Approaches.

949. Enkvist, N. E. (Ed.). (1985a). *Coherence and composition: A symposium*. Abo, Finland: Research Institute of the Abo Akademi Foundation.

A volume consisting of five papers presented at a symposium in March 1984. Contains chapters on discourse analysis and text linguistics, teaching of writing to university students in Sweden, interlanguage studies and their role in ESL/EFL composition, and cohesion,coherence in EFL compositions.

Text Analysis/Coherence/University.

950. Enkvist, N. E. (1985b). Introduction: Coherence, composition, and text linguistics. In N. E. Enkvist (Ed.), *Coherence and composition: A symposium* (pp. 11-26). Abo, Finland: Research Institute of the Abo Akademi Foundation.

Surveys recent developments in linguistics of relevance to the teacher of composition.

Review.

951. Epes, M., & Kirkpatrick, C. (1988). *Editing your writing: The comp-lab exercises level 2*. Englewood Cliffs, NJ: Prentice Hall Regent.

The second in a series provides self-instruction exercises in improving correctness of written English.

Advanced/University/Textbook.

952. Epes, M., Kirkpatrick, C., & Southwell, M. G. (1990). *Mastery written English:*

Comp-lab exercises level 1. (Third Ed.). Englewood Cliffs, NJ: Prentice Hall Regent.

    A self-teaching book for underprepared college writers which offers a dozen chapters of exercises devoted to grammar, sentence structure, and usage.
    Intermediate/University.

953. Era, K., Chenoweth, A., & Kocher, S. (1992, March). *Returnees: Are they better writers?* Paper presented at the 26th Annual TESOL Convention, Vancouver, BC.
    Study reports a comparsion of the quality and errors from in-class essays written by Japanese students who have studied abroad and those who have not.
    Japanese/University.

954. Erazmus, E. T. (1960). Second language composition teaching at the intermediate level. *Language Learning*, *10*, 25-31.
    Advocates extensive amount of free composition practice for intermediate learners who exhibit "interference of the stylistic and cultural literary expression patterns of native language".
    Intermediate/Fluency.

955. Erazo, E. (1986, March). *ESL meets freshman English: A collaborative enterprise.* Paper presented at the 37th Annual CCCC Meeting, New Orleans, LA.
    NS-NNS Comparisons.

956. Erbaugh, M. S. (1990). Taking advantage of China's literacy tradition in teaching Chinese students. *Modern Language Journal*, *74*, 15-27.
    Summarizes Chinese literary tradition which Chinese students presumedly draw upon when they read and write in English.
    Chinese/Literacy.

957. Eskey, D. E. (1993). Reading and writing as both cognitive processes and social behavior. In J. G. Carson, & I. Leki (Eds.), *Reading in the composition classroom: Second language perspectives* (pp. 221-233). Boston: Heinle & Heinle.
    Argues that second language literacy is a social as well as cognitive process. Stresses the importance for learners to participate in the universe of English texts, or literacy club (Smith, 1988).
    Reading-Writing Relations/Literacy.

958. Eskey, D. E. (1980, March). *Second-language writing: A cognitive skills model.* Paper presented at the 14th Annual TESOL Convention, San Francisco, CA.
    Infers an intensive/extensive program for learning to write in a second language from a cognitive skills model of how information is processed.
    Programs/Cognition.

959. Etheridge, J. (1993, April). *Alhamdelelah: Language teaching through international letter writing.* Paper presented at the 27th Annual TESOL Convention, Atlanta, GA.
    Claims that letter writing across cultures enhances learner self-esteem and language proficiency.
    Letter Writing.

960. Evans, L. S. (1987). Purpose produces proficiency: Writing-based projects for an integrated curriculum. In *Planning for proficiency. Dimension: Language '86. Report of the Southern Conference on Language Teaching*. n.p. (pp. 75-82. [ERIC ED 337

014]
Writing projects on culture shock, personalities in the news, and simulating a job-hunt are designed to improve the value of writing to college ESL students.
Project Work/Proficiency.

961. Evans, M., Chernick, S. D., & Savage, S. (1978, April). *Teaching principles of writing to economists and engineers*. Paper presented at the 12th Annual TESOL Convention, Mexico City, Mexico.
Presents a communicative, meaning-oriented writing course designed for the needs of non-native professionals who prepare reports in areas such as economics, engineering, agriculture, and education.
Courses/ESP.

962. Evans, N. W. (1990, March). *Writing centers: Meeting ESL needs*. Paper presented at the 24th Annual TESOL Convention, San Francisco, CA.
Paper discusses techniques used to meet ESL students' needs at Writing Centers which are usually established for students whose first language is English.
Writing Center.

963. Evans, N. W., & Whittaker, P. F. (1984a). Will publishing ESL student writing keep them from perishing? *TESL Reporter, 17*(4), 76-78.
Second part of a two-part article suggests that the activity is motivating and a useful source of relatively good prose students find unintimidating.
Student Publications.

964. Evans, N. W., & Whittaker, P. F. (1984b, March). *Publishing ESL students writing: Will it keep them from perishing?* Paper presented at the 18th Annual TESOL Convention, Houston, TX.
Publishing the best of student writing is a means of motivating ESL writers.
Student Publications.

965. Evensen, L. S. (1990). Pointers to superstructure in student writing. In U. M. Connor, & A. M. Johns (Eds.), *Coherence in writing: Research and pedagogical perspectives* (pp. 169-183). Alexandria, VA: TESOL.
Presents a justification for and a tentative taxonomy of linguistic items that signal global coherence. Classification includes metatextual deixis, internal logical structure, topic markers, temporal pointers, and connectors used as pointers. Illustrates validity of taxonomy for analysis of EFL writing by including it in a small exploratory study.
Coherence/University.

966. Evensen, L. S. (1985). Discourse-level interlanguage studies. In N. E. Enkvist (Ed.), *Cohesion and composition: A symposium* Abo, Finland: Research Institute of the Abo Akademic Foundation.
Introduces the methodology of the Trondheim Corpus of Applied Linguistics, a stratified sample of compositions by EFL students in grades 8-11 in Norway. Reports frequencies for use of connectors, finding that non-use of connectors correlates with age and skill development. Concludes that certain discourse-level connectors are acquired late.
Coherence/Development/Norwegian.

967. Everson, P., Berezovsky, H., & Semen, K. P. (1992, March). *Pretesting and the Test of Written English*. Paper presented at the 26th Annual TESOL Convention, Vancouver, BC.

    Describes how the TOEFL writing test pretests essay prompts to establish their validity and reliability.

    Assessment/TWE.

968. Evolva, J., Mamer, E., & Lenz, B. (1980). Discrete point versus global scoring for cohesive devices. In C. Yorio, K. Perkins, & J. Schachter (Eds.), *Research in language testing* (pp. 177-181). Rowley, MA: Newbury.

    Argues that totalling the correct usages of conjunctions, pronouns, and articles that function cohesively in ESL essays is a better indicator of language development than counting words, errors, or obligatory contexts.

    Evaluation/Cohesion.

969. Ewoldt, C., & Hallau, M. (1985, April). *Developing a writing-evaluation instrument for young deaf students*. Paper presented at the 19th Annual TESOL Convention, New York, NY.

    Reports the development of proficiency levels, based on a three-year sampling of deaf elementary children, for placement.

    Hearing-Impaired/Assessment.

970. Eyring, J. (1989, March). *Mini-projects in ESL composition instruction*. Paper presented at the 23rd Annual TESOL Convention, San Antonio, TX.

    Shows teachers how to motivate university ESL students by integrating three-week mini-reports into coursework.

    Project Work.

971. Ezer, H. (1990). Writing development in a bilingual first-grader: A case study. *Dissertation Abstracts International, 51*(4), 1143A.

    Study documents a native Hebrew-speaking child's literacy development in English. The written development of both languages was viewed in natural, spontaneous writing of four environments: at home, in the homeroom and ESL classes at school, and in an Israeli after-school program. Finds that the subject wrote mostly in English and mostly at home or in the homeroom class. Learner appears to have undergone the same stages as do L1 emergent writers but did progress more quickly through stages of L2 textual development.

    Children/Hebrew.

F

972. Fagan, E. R., & Cheong, P. (1987). Contrastive rhetoric: Pedagogical implications for the ESL teacher in Singapore. *RELC Journal, 18*(1), 19-30.

    Study of sixty ninth-grade compositions in Singapore. Students have problems with English three-part organization style, use digression and repetition, and an excess of stylized language which are regarded as characteristics of Chinese rhetoric.

    Contrastive Rhetoric/Chinese/Secondary School.

973. Fagan, W. T., & Hayden, H. M. (1988). Writing processes in French and English

of fifth grade French immersion students. *Canadian Modern Language Review, 44*, 653-668.

    Ten high-ability grade five French immersion children display a wide range of writing processing behaviors within a unitary writing process for both languages.

    Process Research/Children/French.

974. Faigan, S. B. (1985). *Basic ESL literacy from a Freirean perspective: A curriculum unit for farmworker education.* Unpublished master's thesis, University of British Columbia, BC. [ERIC ED 274 196].

    Produces a curriculum unit, a videotaped drama concerning the rights of Canadian workers, intended for Punjabi migrant workers as a meaningful context for oral and written language instruction. Literacy is viewed as a vehicle for personal, social, and political empowerment.

    Punjabi/Adult Education.

975. Falk, B. (1984). Can correctness and communication be tested simultaneously? *Occasional Papers -- University of Essex, Department of Language and Linguistics, 29*, 90-96.

    Discusses problems with traditional testing of written and oral proficiency of ESL speakers. Suggests that the discrepancy between oral and written test results may be much smaller than traditionally perceived and proposes more flexible testing procedures.

    Evaluation/Speaking-Writing Relations.

976. Fan, W. J. (1992, March). *Can limited-English proficient children write in English?* Paper presented at the 43rd Annual CCCC Meeting, Cincinnati, OH.

    Describes an ethnographic study of three Asian LEP children in structured and non-structured classrooms. Results show that LEP Asian children can write and more meaningfully in non-structured writing sessions.

    Children/Asian/Ethnographic Research.

977. Fang, X., & Kennedy, G. D. (1992). Expressing causation in written English. *RELC Journal, 23*(1), 62-80.

    Ranks the frequency of 130 causative devices in a large computerized corpus of written British English. Causative conjunctions (e.g., because, for, since, as, so...that, so that) and causative adverbs (e.g., why, so, thus, therefore, then) were the most highly ranked.

    Cohesion.

978. Fanselow, J. F., & Brookes, G. (1987, April). *Readin', writin', and . . . A model of in-service teacher preparation.* Paper presented at the 21st Annual TESOL Convention, Miami Beach, FL.

    Describes a practicum for experienced teachers working in pairs.

    Teacher Preparation.

979. Farghal, M. (1992). Naturalness and the notion of cohesion in EFL writing classes. *IRAL, 30*(1), 45-50.

    maintains the role of cohesion in coherence needs to be rethought since variation in coherence seems to be a function of variation in the cohesive harmony of a text.

Cohesion.

980. Farnsworth, M. B. (1974). The cassette tape recorder: A bonus or a bother in ESL composition correction? *TESOL Quarterly*, *8*, 285-291.

Highlights the advantages in using the cassette tape recorder over the traditional method of marginal notations in the correction of ESL compositions at the intermediate and advanced levels.

Feedback/Accuracy.

981. Farrell, A. (1988, October). *Oral patterns and written composition*. Paper presented at the Conference on the Teaching of Foreign Languages and Literatures, Youngstown, OH. [ERC ED 318 216].

Offers exercises on distinguishing acceptable oral and written patterns.

Speaking-Writing Relations.

982. Fathman, A. K. (1991, March). *Teacher response to error: The writing conference*. Paper presented at the 25th Annual TESOL Convention, New York, NY.

Examines the effectiveness of student-teacher conferences and reports the results of a comparsion of written versus oral feedback.

Feedback/Conferencing.

983. Fathman, A. K. (1977, April). *Some factors influencing learning to read, write and speak English as a second language*. Paper presented at the 11th Annual TESOL Convention, Miami Beach, FLA.

Seeks factors related to successful language learning.

Elementary/Secondary School.

984. Fathman, A. K., & Whalley, E. (1990). Teacher response to student writing: Focus on form versus content. In B. Kroll (Ed.), *Second language writing: Research insights for the classroom* (pp. 178-190). Cambridge: Cambridge University Press.

Compares the kind of feedback teachers provided to 72 intermediate ESL composition students who wrote and revised a composition telling a story about a sequence of eight pictures. Found that, while a focus on grammar in addition to content does not significantly effect the content of rewrites, grammar and content feedback, whether given alone or simultaneously, positively affects rewrites.

Responding.

985. Fathman, A. K., & Whalley, E. (1985, April). *Teacher treatment of error and student writing accuracy*. Paper presented at the 19th Annual TESOL Convention, New York, NY.

Reports two studies of sixteen ESL college students given different kinds of feedback on a variety of tasks. Focuses on the connection between teacher feedback and student ability to monitor and correct.

Error Treatment/Feedback.

986. Fayer, J. (1986, November). *Writing apprehension among Puerto Rican university students*. Paper presented at the Annual Meeting of the Speech Communication Aassociation, Chicago, IL. [ERIC ED 280 283].

Administers the Daley & Miller anxiety measure to L2 students in an ESL writing class (n=96) and English-medium content classes (n=81). Writing apprehension is higher in ESL writing classes than in content-classes but lower for

writing than for speaking in L2.
Hispanic/Affect/Speaking-Writing Relations.

987. Fein, D. (1980). *A comparison of English and ESL compositions.* Unpublished master's thesis, UCLA, Los Angeles, CA.

Finds ESL writers scoring significantly lower on holistic assessment, error count, content analysis, organization, and style than first language writers in equivalent college courses.
Assessment/University/NS-NNS Comparisons.

988. Ferris, D. R. (1993a). The design of an automatic analysis program for L2 text research: Necessity and feasibility. *Journal of Second Language Writing, 2,* 119-129.

Data from a non-automatized analysis of 62 variables in 160 texts suggests that L1 text analyzers are inaccurate when applied to L2 texts. Suggests how to create a better L2 text analysis program
Text Analysis/Computers/L1-L2 Comparison.

989. Ferris, D. R. (1993b, April). *What do students really do with our composition feedback?* Paper presented at the 27th Annual TESOL Convention, Atlanta, GA.

Reports discouraging results when university ESL composition students were surveyed about their understanding and response to instructors' feedback.
Feedback.

990. Ferris, D. R. (1992). Syntactical and lexical characteristics of ESL student writing: A multidimensional study. *Dissertation Abstracts International, 52*(8), 2907A.

Tests elements of a multidimensional model of text analysis by measuring 62 text variables in the compositions (N=160) of four different L1 groups (Arabic, Mandarin, Japanese, and Spanish) at two proficiency levels ("high" and "low"). Finds significant differences among writers across L1 groups and proficiency levels. For example, Arabic and Spanish writers produced longer sentence with more coordination; higher-level writers used more cohesive devices, especially referential, and a wider variety of syntactic and lexical choices.
Contrastive Rhetoric/Arabic/Chinese/Japanese/Spanish.

991. Ferris, D. R. (1990, March). *Rhetorical and linguistic characteristics of ESL students' argumentative writing.* Paper presented at the 24th Annual TESOL Convention, San Francisco, CA.

Contrasts argumentative essays written by both NES and ESL university students, looking at such global discourse features as the propositional structures of the arguments and also specific linguistic elements.
NS-NNS Comparisons/Contrastive Rhetoric/Argumentation.

992. Ferris, M. R., & Politzer, R. L. (1981). Effects of early and delayed second language acquisition: English composition skills of Spanish-speaking junior high school students. *TESOL Quarterly, 15,* 263-274.

Compares the English composition skills of two groups of junior high school Spanish-speaking students from two differing educational and cultural backgrounds: Mexico-born and Spanish-schooled and US-born and schooled. The results show that students with elementary grade instruction in Spanish in Mexico "did not possess demonstrably lower skills than students who had received all of their schooling in

English in the United States." In fact, the former students (Spanish) surpassed the latter in grades, motivation, and interpersonal relations with students
Bilingual/Hispanic/Middle School.

993. Ferris, R. (1989, March). *English argumentative writing by first and second language students*. Paper presented at the 40th Annual CCCC Meeting, Seattle, WA.
Argumentation/NS-NNS Comparisons.

994. Ferris, R., Hared, M., Patthey, G. G., & Lapp, R. E. (1989, March). *The influence of conferencing on student writing and revision*. Paper presented at the 23rd Annual TESOL Convention, San Antonio, TX.

Discusses variation in teacher input and the effect of conferences on students' subsequent revisions.
Conferencing/Revision.

995. Fieg, J. P. (1983). Thai students' written English -- A syntactic analysis. *PASAA, 13*(1-2), 1-40.

Examines writing by four ESL students for possible interference from Thai: problems with although/even though constructions; confusion of have and there; is/are; misuse of almost all/most constructions; problems with comparison omission of copula; overnominalization; failure to distinguish between restrictive and nonrestrictive relative clauses; and incorrect patterns of complementation. Problems analyzed include the overuse or incorrect use of -ing, incorrect use of since, problems with in order to constructions, undernominalization, pronoun omission, confusion of after and afterwards, and omission of -ed. Concludes that most of the common errors are due to interference from Thai and suggests the use of student profiles in lesson planning and devising problem-specific exercises.
Error Analysis/Thai.

996. Fieg, J. P., Boyd, M. A., & Boyd, J. R. (1991). *Self-correcting compositions*. Normal, IL: Abaca Books.

Textbook for beginners contains twelve units for students to internalize the components of successful compositions as they are led to the creation of their own work. A variety of activities enable students to correct compositions in detail. All text material is on audiotape and can be used in either an out-of-class or listening lab setting as well as the classroom.
Beginners/Textbook.

997. Field, Y., & Oi, Y. L. M. (1992). A comparison of internal conjunctive cohesion in the English essay writing of Cantonese speakers and native speakers of English. *RELC Journal, 23*(1), 15-28.

Cantonese writers used internal conjunctive cohesion significantly more often than NSs, although only a small number of essays are compared.
Cohesion/NS-NNS Comparisons.

998. Findley, D. F. (1985). Working with the E.S.L. and the developmental student in the same classroom. *TECFORS, 8*(1), 7-10. [ERIC ED 267 650].

Discusses sentence writing and other exercises for classes involving both types of learners.
NS-NNS Comparisons/Courses.

999. Fink, D. (1988). A descriptive study of teacher and student questioning patterns in university ESL and native writing classes. *Dissertation Abstracts International*, *48*(8), 2007A.

    A study of teacher questioning behavior in non-native and native university-level composition classes indicates that student's proficiency level and teacher training are crucial factors determining teacher questioning patterns. The higher percentage of <u>present queries</u> (Fanselow's <u>FOCUS</u>) of the NSs is attributed to the higher level of proficiency of the NNSs to whom they were addressing.

    Interaction/NS-NNS Comparisons.

1000. Finocchiaro, M. (1967, April). *Writing: Problems and practices*. Paper presented at the 1st TESOL Convention, Miami Beach, FLA.

1001. Fiore, K., & Elsasser, N. (1982). "Strangers no more": A liberatory literacy curriculum. *College English*, *44*, 115-128.

    Describes an experimental preparatory writing course at the University of the Bahamas, based on Vygotsky and Freire, which offered advanced literacy techniques on the generative theme of marriage.

    Literacy.

1002. Fischer-Kohn, E. (1987, April). *Holistic scoring of ESL writing: Post-diagnostic feature analysis scales*. Paper presented at the 21st Annual TESOL Convention, Miami Beach, FL.

    Holistic scoring fails to distinguish different qualities of middle-range ESL writing which makes useful a follow-up feature analytic scale.

    Assessment/Scoring.

1003. Fitzgerald, J. (1993). Literacy and students who are learning English as a second language. *Reading Teacher*, *46*(8), 638-647.

    Argues that learning to read and write is a fundamental right of all language minority students in the U.S.

    Literacy/Children.

1004. Flahive, D. E. (1993, April). *Instructional routines in conventional and computer-assisted writing classes*. Paper presented at the 27th Annual TESOL Convention, Atlanta, GA.

    Reports a study comparing two instructional settings: a conventional process-oriented class and a computer-assisted writing class.

    Computers/Process Instruction.

1005. Flahive, D. E. (1991, March). *Rhetorical reading and ESP writing*. Paper presented at the 25th Annual TESOL Convention, New York, NY.

    Designs materials to assist students in the critical reading and writing of scientific discourse.

    ESP/Reading-Writing Relations/Materials.

1006. Flahive, D. E. (1989, March). *Topic continuity in spoken and written narratives*. Paper presented at the 23rd Annual TESOL Convention, San Antonio, TX.

    Uses Givon's topic continuity hierarchy (1984) to compare oral and written narratives by native and nonnative subjects.

    Topic/NS-NNS Comparisons/Narration.

1007. Flahive, D. E., & Bailey, N. H. (1993). Exploring reading/writing relationships in adult second language learners. In J. G. Carson, & I. Leki (Eds.), *Reading in the composition classroom: Second language perspecitves* (pp. 128-140). NY: Heinle & Heinle.

    A correlational study finds a modest correlation of reading comprehension and writing quality, but no relationship between the quantity of reading by ESL students and the quality of their writing and no increase in grammatical proficiency associated with pleasure reading, although there seems to be a clear relationship between holistic writing and grammar. Krashen's reading input hypothesis, thus, is not supported yet reading more is connected with better reading comprehension.

    Reading-Writing Relations.

1008. Flahive, D. E., & Bailey, N. H. (1990, March). *Relationships between rhetorical reading and written summary strategies*. Paper presented at the 24th Annual TESOL Convention, San Francisco, CA.

    Describes the use of reading and summary writing strategies of skilled and unskilled native and non-native subjects, demonstrating a research approach which employs think-aloud protocols supplemented by traditional measures.

    Reading-Writing Relations/Summary Writing/NS-NNS Comparisons.

1009. Flahive, D. E., & Bailey, N. H. (1989, March). *Investigating reading/writing relationships in L2 learners*. Paper presented at the 23rd Annual TESOL Convention, San Antonio, TX.

    Reports correlation of holistic evaluation and reading time and achievement among non-native university writing students.

    Evaluation/Reading-Writing Relations.

1010. Flahive, D. E., & Snow, B. G. (1980). Measures of syntactic complexity in evaluating ESL compositions. In J. W. Oller, & K. Perkins (Eds.), *Research in language testing* (pp. 171-176). Rowley, MA: Newbury.

    While T-unit length and clause/T-unit ratio correlate only moderately with holistic scores of ESL writing, the same developmental trends are found for non-native writers as in Hunt (1965).

    Evaluation/T-Unit/Objective Measures.

1011. Flanigan, B. O., & Shuman, J. A. (1988, March). *Responding across the curriculum: Evaluations of non-native academic writing*. Paper presented at the 22nd Annual TESOL Convention, Chicago, IL.

    Finds among other things that non-ESL faculty across the curriculum offer little help in improving writing skills of either native or non-native students.

    NS-NNS Comparisons/Teacher Preparation.

1012. Flores, B., & Garcia, E. A. (1984). A collaborative learning and teaching experience using journals. *NABE: The Journal for the National Association for Bilingual Education, 8*(2), 67-83.

    Describes how a bilingual teacher and teacher educator collaborated on the daily use of dialogue journals to promote the development of bilingual first graders.

    Collaboration/Dialogue Journals/Elementary.

1013. Florez Tighe, V., & Hadaway, N. L. (1987a, January). *Relationship of oral language proficiency and writing behaviors of secondary second language learners.* Paper presented at the 15th Southwest Regional Conference of the International Reading Association, Phoenix, AZ. [ERIC ED 283 359].

Examines the effect of oral language proficiency on the writing strategies of secondary ESL students. Comparison of writing in English and Spanish in terms of topic, organization, meaning, sentence construction, and mechanics and quantitative analysis of main independent clauses and total words with oral proficiency test scores indicates that oral language development can have effects on writing, but oral proficiency tests do not necessarily reveal students' writing behavior.

Speaking-Writing Relations/Hispanic.

1014. Florez Tighe, V., & Hadaway, N. L. (1987b, April). *Second language writers: Imagination in story retelling.* Paper presented at the 21st Annual TESOL Convention, Miami Beach, FL.

Shows importance of story segments and imagery for young ESL writers.

Children/Narration.

1015. Flowerdew, J. (1993). An educational, or process, approach to the teaching of professional genres. *ELT Journal, 47,* 305-316.

Argues for an educational approach to teaching genres. Describes the distinctive features of professional genres and some genre analysis activities.

Genre/Professional Writing.

1016. Flowerdew, J. (1992, March). *Computer-based text analysis for teaching rhetorical/organizational lexis.* Paper presented at the 26th Annual TESOL Convention, Vancouver, BC.

Shows how computer text analysis can be used in an EAP program to determine the sub-technical vocabulary occurring in academic discourse.

Academic Writing/Vocabulary/Computers.

1017. Fluitt, J. M. (1987, April). *Evaluating ESL composition: Accuracy versus fluency.* Paper presented at the 21st Annual TESOL Convention, Miami Beach, FL.

Advocates traditional ways of correcting essays.

Evaluation.

1018. Foley, D. (1973). Teaching composition to ESL students. *TESL Reporter, 6*(1), 10. [ERIC ED 077 287].

Describes a method used to teach writing, which proceeds from content to form and suggests some materials that can be used in the ESL classroom.

Methods.

1019. Folman, S. (1989). The benefits of interrelating reading and writing in the EFL classroom. *Interface: Journal of Applied Linguistics, 3*(2), 107-115.

Reading-Writing Relations.

1020. Folman, S. (1992a, March). *Intercultural rhetorical styles differ.* Paper presented at the 26th Annual TESOL Convention, Vancouver, BC.

Analyzes style of synthesizing information in research papers by two cultural groups in order to determine cross-cultural differences.

Style/Rhetoric/Culture.

1021. Folman, S. (1992b, March). *Towards an EFL/ESL reading-writing model of academic learning*. Paper presented at the 26th Annual TESOL Convention, Vancouver, BC.

Offers a theoretical study that extends Mosenthal's (1982) pyramid model of writing to include socio-cognitive, parallelistic-mirror and reciprocally-informative aspects of the reading-writing relationship.

Reading-Writing Relations.

1022. Folman, S., Johns, A. M., Widdowson, H. G., Sarig, G., Horowitz, D. M., & Olshtain, E. (1988, March). *The interactive relationship of reading and writing in EFL*. Colloquium presented at the 22nd Annual TESOL Convention, Chicago, IL.

Colloquium discusses benefits accruing from intergroup reading and writing.

Reading-Writing Relations.

1023. Folman, S., & Sarig, G. (1990). Intercultural rhetorical differences in meaning construction. *Communication and Cognition*, *23*(1), 45-92.

Investigates whether the rhetorical structures preferred by native Hebrew and native English speakers differ when they are constructing meaning in reading and writing in their native language. Results affirm native speaker preferences for NL rhetoric in constructing meaning in writing which may be related to instruction rather than transfer.

Culture/Contrastive Rhetoric/Hebrew.

1024. Folse, K. S. (1993). Advice columns: The writing on the wall. *TESOL Journal*, *3*(2), 37.

Describes a classroom activity in which students read an advice column from a newpaper and write responses.

Reading-Writing Relations/Classroom Activities.

1025. Fontana, N. M., & Caldeira, S. M. A. (1993). Computer-assisted writing: Applications to English as a foreign language. *Computer-Assisted Language Learning*, *6*(2), 145-161.

Describes a software tool, CHUSAURUS, used to help Brazilian students writing in the Amadeus environment to find substitute expressions when writing technical articles.

Computers/Brazil.

1026. Ford, C. K. (1982). Determining the significant errors in foreign student compositions by means of a composition checklist. *Dissertation Abstracts International*, *42*(12), 5050A.

Examines the validity of an objective instrument in assessing the freshman placement exams of ESL students, by comparing these scores to holistic scores. Results show that error-free T-units, noun ratio, preposition ratio, and sentence structure ratio are variables that categorize compositions into groups that correlate to holistic scores.

Errors/Evaluation.

1027. Ford, J. (1993, April). *Getting started writing...comfortably*. Paper presented at the 27th Annual TESOL Convention, Atlanta, GA.

Shows that focused invention techniques result in more and better writing.

Invention.

1028. Forester, J. M. (1984, March). *Using computers in ESL writing instruction*. Paper presented at the 18th Annual TESOL Convention, Houston, TX.

Observations of elementary ESL students suggests that use of a computer for tasks such as text editing helps motivate students.

Computers/Elementary/Editing.

1029. Forster, J. H., & Madden, L. R. (1984, March). *Syntactic blurs: A universal in the acquisiton of writing*. Paper presented at the 18th Annual TESOL Convention, Houston, TX.

Similar blurred constructions in the writing of advanced ESL students and native remedial writers suggest a universal stage in acquisition.

Errors/Advanced/NS-NNS Comparisons.

1030. Forster, J. H., & Madden, L. R. (1983, March). *Helping advanced ESL writers clean up blurred syntax*. Paper presented at the 17th Annual TESOL Convention, Toronto, BC.

Claims syntactic blurs differ from other types of writing errors in that they result from a confusion of several acceptable options.

Error Analysis/Advanced.

1031. Fox, C. J. (1983). Teaching writing. *TESL Talk*, *14*, 73-88.

Discusses the various aspects of writing instruction, especially the newer approaches such as journal writing and sentence combining. These approaches cover the teaching of English script to the teaching of rhetorical patterns in compositions.

Approaches.

1032. Fox, C. J., & Tippetts, R. (1971). A portfolio program for teaching English composition. *TESL Reporter*, *4*(3), 1. [ERIC ED 184 350].

Describes the use of the portfolio system in a writing program which included grading by two faculty. Claims system was successful because it made students motivated and more confident in the grading system since grades of two faculty were fairly consistent, and it led to an emphasis on writing as a work of art.

Evaluation/Portfolios.

1033. Fox, H. (1991). "It's more than just a technique": International graduate students' difficulties with analytic writing. *Dissertation Abstracts International*, *52*(6), 2050-2051A.

An ethnographic investigation of the ability of non-western graduate students (N=16) to produce analytic papers for their graduate courses. Interviews with the students and their professors as well as a consideration of their papers suggest ten issues affecting student writing. These issues include background factors: prior education, knowledge of target culture/language, gender, native communicative style, home country status as well as curent contextual factors: concept of truth, belief about authorities, use of writing and thinking strategies voice, and sense of audience.

Graduate Students/Academic Writing.

1034. Fox, J. (1989). Interactional differences in writing conferences between TAs and students in writing tutorial services. *Carleton Papers in Applied Language Studies*, *6*, 1-30.

An in-depth comparative analysis of the style of conferencing in four representative encounters. Findings suggest that teaching assistants treat native

speaking writers and ESL college students differently-- to the detriment of the ESL students.
Conferencing/Tutoring/NS-NNS Comparisons.

1035. Fox, L. (1991, March). *Focused editing: What's been left out of writing process.* Paper presented at the 25th Annual TESOL Convention, New York, NY.
Discusses an approach to editing for advanced ESL writers.
Grammar.   Intermediate/Advanced/Textbook.

1036. Fox, L. (1990). Planethood: An ESL writing course on globalcommunity. *TESOL Newsletter, 24*(2), 19.
Describes an ESL writing course which used Planethood, a book on nuclear disarmament, and recommends that ESL writing teachers teach thematic writing courses.
Curriculum/Courses.

1037. Fox, L. (1989). *A grammar workbook for advanced writers.* White Plains, NY: Addison Wesley.
Teaches advanced writers how to edit and proofread their own writing.
Textbook/Advanced.

1038. Fox, L. (1983). *Passages: An intermediate/advanced writing book.* NY: Harcourt Brace Jovanovich.
Organized around the writing process, each of fourteen chapters has a unique theme, featuring a reading by authors. Starts with the writing of paragraphs and progresses to the writing of essays in the second part.
Textbook.

1039. Frager, A. M., & Freeman, C. (1985). *A content area writing lab for preservice teachers and second language learners* . Washington, DC: ERIC/FLL. [ERIC ED 258 924].
Describes use of Cohen's technique (1982;1983) of reformulation in a writing lab. Gives a verbatim example of one segment from a student essay, the reformulation, and a re-write by the original ESL author.
Writing Center.

1040. Frank, M. (1990). *Writing as thinking: A guided approach.* Englewood Cliffs, NJ: Prentice Hall.
Workbook offers guided process approach with critical thinking and a focus on writing techniques for different academic disciplines.
Advanced/Textbook.

1041. Frank, M. (1987b, April). *Teaching sentence structure constructively in the advanced composition class.* Paper presented at the 21st Annual TESOL Convention, Miami Beach, FL.
Believes advanced students need to be aware of a range of sentences and their correct use.
Advanced/Usage.

1042. Frank, M. (1983a). *Writer's companion.* Englewood Cliffs, NJ: Prentice-Hall.
An index of standard English usage and rhetoric for guiding students to avoid errors as they write and edit their compositions.

Advanced/Grammar/Textbook.
1043. Frank, M. (1983b). *Writing from experience.* Englewood Cliffs, NJ: Prentice-Hall.

Each of the ten units on various topics in this workbook aids students in learning rhetorical, semantic, grammatical, and communicative control of their compositions.

Intermediate/Advanced/Textbook.
1044. Frank, M. (1981, March). *Sentence combining that integrates logical relationships, usage, style.* Paper presented at the 15th Annual TESOL Convention, Detroit, MI.

Demonstrates a unit on sentence combining for high intermediate proficiency students that promotes an awareness of several factors of choice in writing sentences.

Sentence Combining/Intermediate.
1045. Frank, M. (1980). A new approach to guided composition for intermediate students. D. L. Bouchard, & L. J. Spaventa (Comps.), *A TEFL anthology: Selected articles from the English Teaching Forum, 1973-78* (pp. 185-190). Washington, DC: International Communication Agency.

Contrasts her approach to guided composition which stems from spoken rather than written language with model imitation and precis writing. Two examples of the procedure are discussed.

Approaches/Control/Intermediate.
1046. Frank, M. (1975, March). *A new approach to teaching guided composition to intermediate ESL/EFL university students.* Paper presented at the 9th Annual TESOL Convention, Los Angeles, CA.

Describes an approach to guided composition that is initiated not from text but from a prewriting outlining and discussion process.

Control/Invention.
1047. Franken, M. (1991, March). *The use of collaborative mapping during rehearsal for writing.* Paper presented at the 25th Annual TESOL Convention, New York, NY.

Describes the effects of collaborative mapping on the pre-writing activities of native and nonnative writers. Linguistic refinement occuring in the rehearsal and final production of a text can be traced to talk generated during group sessions.

Collaboration/NS-NNS Comparisons.
1048. Franken, M. (1987a). Self-questioning scales for improving academic writing. *Guidelines (RELC Journal Supplement), 18*(1), 1-8.

Presents a procedure for providing feedback to both NS and NNS writers, which involves the use of self-questioning scales. The scales, consisting of questions about the topic, provides students with guidance in the idea-search and organization of content. The procedure is based on the research in topic types and writing-as-a process.

Feedback/Academic Writing.
1049. Frankenberg-Garcia, A. (1990). Do the similarities between L1 and L2 writng processes conceal important differences? *Edinburgh Working Papers in Applied Linguistics, 1*, 91-102.

L1-L2 Comparison.
1050. Franklin, E. A. (1989). Encouraging and understanding the visual and written works

of second-language children. In P. Rigg, & V. F. Allen (Eds.), *When they all don't speak English: Integrating the ESL students into the regular classroom* (pp. 77-95). Urbana, IL: NCTE.

Exemplifies how much the teacher can learn about ESL children who explore and express meaning when they read and write.

Children.

1051. Franklin, E. A. (1985, February). A naturalistic study of literacy in bilingual classrooms. *Dissertation Abstracts International, 45*(8), 2463A.

Describes literacy instruction in first-grade bilingual classes by an Hispanic and an Anglo teacher. Both bilingual programs emphasized English literacy but the teachers approached the relationships between speaking and reading and writing differently.

Literacy/Children.

1052. Franklin, E. (1988, March). *Collaborative learning: Teaching writing in the refugee classroom*. Paper presented at the 39th Annual CCCC Meeting, St. Louis, MO.

Collaboration/Refugees.

1053. Franklin, S. (1990). Samuels School: Collaborative diversity. *Writing Notebook: Creative Word Processing in the Classroom, 8*(1), 13-15.

Describes a computerized writing lab in a bilingual school in Colorado.

Computers/Word Processing/Elementary.

1054. Fraser, C. (1979, May). *Teaching writing skills: Focus on the process*. Paper presented at the Conference of the Canadian Council of Teachers of English, Ottawa, Ontario. [ERIC ED 200 044].

Teacher input into the writing process is most effective in the pre-writing and re-writing stages, in that the teacher provides input by facilitating student recall of information, specifying the context as clearly as possible, helping the student get the data right in terms of his intentions, correcting student errors, teaching the student to edit, and using controlled exercises.

Process Instruction.

1055. Frawley, W. E., & Lantolf, J. P. (1985). Second language discourse: A Vygotskyean perspective. *Applied Linguistics, 6*, 19-44.

Presents an explanation of second language discourse in terms of the claims of Vygotskyan psycholinguistics. The principle claim is that there is no absolute difference between native and second language discourse.

Psychology/NS-NNS Comparisons.

1056. Freedman, A., Pringle, I., & Yalden, J. (Eds.). (1983). *Learning to write: First language, second language* NY: Longman.

Presents a collection of essays that seek to discern the place of learning to write in learning how to mean. Addresses the issue of product versus process, teaching versus development and examines the distinction between text and discourse. Papers on ESL include those by Widdowson, Kaplan, Kameen, Johnson, and Raimes. Offers editorial introductions to each of the four parts and implications for teaching.

Instruction.

1057. Freeman, Y. S., & Freeman, D. E. (1992a). What are portfolios, and how are they used to assess students [Ask the TJ]. *TESOL Journal, 1*(2), 39.

Describes the advantages of using a system of student selected samples of their own drafts and writing as fulfillment of writing requirements.

Assessment/Portfolios.

1058. Freeman, Y. S., & Freeman, D. E. (1992b). *Whole language for second language learners*. Portsmouth, NH: Heinemann/Boynton Cook.

Offers teachers a view of the methods, acquisition and role of the L1 culture in understanding whole language instruction as well as examples of successul applications with students of all ages and backgrounds.

Whole Language/Approaches.

1059. Freeman, Y. S., & Freeman, D. E. (1989). Whole language approaches to writing with secondary students of English as a second language. In D. M. Johnson, & D. H. Roen (Eds.), *Richness in writing: Empowering ESL students* (pp. 177-192). NY: Longman.

Discusses the theoretical principles of the whole language approach and describes its implementation in an ESL class. Claims that this approach is more effective than traditional practices because students are engaged in meaningful activities that empower them.

Whole Language

1060. French, C. R. (1986). Vivifying the writing class "you are there" style. *TESL Reporter, 19*(1), 13-16.

Describes how a journalistic technique -- 'the you are there' style -- can be used in an ESL composition class to make writing more spontaneous and arresting.

Style.

1061. Frestedt, M., & Sanchez, M. (1980). *Navajo world-view harmony in directives for English texts*. Paper presented at the Annual Meetng of the University of Wisconsin/Milwaukee Linguistics Symposium, Milwakee, WI. [ERIC ED 193 661].

English compositions by Navajo students show the influence of native discourse responsibilities. The fact that writers are required only to show evidence of knowledge about the subject while readers are expected to connect and evaluate that knowledge is attributed to a Navajo world view.

Amer-Indian/Culture.

1062. Friederichs, J., & Pierson, H. D. (1981). What are science students expected to write? *English Language Teaching Journal, 35*, 407-410.

Describes attempt to collect and use data relating to use of English as an instructional medium for Chinese science students at the University of Hong Kong. Gives examples of question pattern exercises with blank content slots into which subject matter can be inserted.

Scientific Writing/Classroom Activities.

1063. Friedlander, A. C. (1992, March). *Constraints on ESL writing: Correct production and text generation*. Paper presented at the 43rd Annual CCCC Meeting, Cincinnati, OH.

1064. Friedlander, A. C. (1990). Composing in English: First language effects. In B. Kroll (Ed.), *Second language writing: Research insights for the classroom* (pp. 109-125).

Cambridge: Cambridge University Press.

An experimental study tests the hypothesis that ESL writers can plan more effectively and produce texts with better content when they are able to plan in the language related to the acquisition of topic knowledge. Results show that subjects did better when planning in the language in which they had acquired their topic knowledge, hence sustaining the hypothesis that the first language exerts an influence on memory for composing in a second language.

LI Influence/Topic/Background Knowledge

1065. Friedlander, A. C. (1989, April). *Composing written sentences in two languages.* Paper presented at the Annual AERA Meeting, San Francisco, CA.

Process Research/L1-L2 Comparisons

1066. Friedlander, A. C. (1988, March). *First-language effects on second language composing: Aid or hindrance.* Paper presented at the 39th Annual CCCC Meeting, St. Louis, MO.

L1 Influence/L1-L2 Comparisons

1067. Friedlander, A. C. (1987a). The writer stumbles: Constraints on composing in English as a second language. *Dissertation Abstracts International, 49*(11), 3291A.

Reports on two studies examining factors -- language and correctness -- that constrain ESL writers' retrieval of topic knowledge from memory. Findings support the hypothesis that ESL writers benefit from generating plans in the language in which topic knowledge is acquired. Moreover, writers have a harder time retrieving information and producing text when focused on form.

L1 Influence/Background Knowledge/L1-L2 Comparisons

1068. Friedlander, A. C. (1987b, March). *Writing in ESL: Notes towards a research-based theory of instruction.* Paper presented at the 38th Annual CCCC Meeting, Atlanta, GA.

Theory.

1069. Friedlander, A. C. (1986a, March). *The influence of correct production on ESL composing.* Paper presented at the 37th Annual CCCC Meeting, New Orleans, LA.

Accuracy.

1070. Friedlander, A. C. (1986b, March). *Surface error: Effects on ESL composition evaluation and pedagogy.* Paper presented at the 20th Annual TESOL Convention, Anaheim, CA.

Finds student grades are unduly influenced by surface corrections yet evaluators can recognize and agree on quality.

Accuracy/Evaluation

1071. Friedlander, A. C. (1984). Meeting the needs of foreign students in the Writing Center. In G. Olson (Ed.), *Writing Centers: Theory and administration* (pp. 206-214). Urbana, IL: NCTE.

Describes an ESL tutorial program in the context of a writing center.

Writing Center/Tutoring.

1072. Friedlander, A. C., & Huckin, T. N. (1987, April). *Composing in ESL: Language acquisition and the retrieval of topic knowledge from memory.* Paper presented at the Annual AERA Meeting, Washington, DC.

Process Research/Psychology.
1073. Friend, J. A. (1970). *A writing program for students of English as a second language, based in a critical examination of relevant research and theories in Linguistics, Psychology, and Composition*. Unpublished doctoral dissertation, Southern Illinois University, Carbondale, IL.

Presents a theory-based writing program for ESL college students consisting of six units working with syntactic structures, paragraphs, and offers exercises and an evaluation method.
Programs.

1074. Friend, J. A. (1969). "It ain't whatcha say". *TESOL Quarterly*, 3, 309-314.

Reports a successful experiment in teaching levels of diction in a college ESL composition course.
Vocabulary.

1075. Frodesen, J. M. (1992, March). *Untangling syntactic snarls: Revision techniques for ESL writers*. Paper presented at the 26th Annual TESOL Convention, Vancouver, BC.

Analyzes some common ESL sentence structure problems and techniques for revision that focus on meaning, rhetoric, and ideas.
Revision/Syntactic Structures.

1076. Frodesen, J. M. (1991a). Aspects of coherence in a writing assessment context: Linguistic and rhetorical features of native and nonnative English essays. *Dissertation Abstracts International*, 52(1), 150A.

Examines the coherence of 100 essays by twelfth-graders, divided between successful and unsucccessful native and non-native speakers. Readers' expectations were analysed by examining essays in terms of rhetorical criteria. Topical structure analysis and error analysis were also employed. The findings indicate that nonpassing essays failed to show expository writing conventions, such as focusing on central points, reporting meaning accurately, and signalling parts of the discourse. Topic structure analysis revealed ineffective paragraph development in nonpassing exams.
Coherence/Chinese/Korean/Hispanic.

1077. Frodesen, J. M. (1991b). Grammar in writing. In M. Celce-Murcia (Ed.), *Teaching English as a second or foreign language* (pp. 264-276). NY: Newbury/HarperCollins.

Argues that grammar is an essential part of written communication and that ESL students should be taught that it is an aid to shaping effective and appropriate messages.
Grammar.

1078. Frodesen, J. M. (1991c, March). *What's off topic? -- Writers' responses to an essay prompt*. Paper presented at the 25th Annual TESOL Convention, New York, NY.

Compares content and rhetorical features in ESL and NES writers' responses to a prompt eliciting summary and evaluation.
Assessment/Prompts/NS-NNS Comparisons.

1079. Frodesen, J. M. (1989a, March). *Effects of editing instruction on ESL writers' grammatical errors*. Paper presented at the 23rd Annual TESOL Convention, San

Antonio, TX.

>Presents quantitative analysis of grammatical errors in compositions and their revisions made during grammar editing sessions before and after instruction.

>Errors/Editing.

1080. Frodesen, J. M. (1989b, March). *Writing conference: Alternatives to written feedback on compositions*. Paper presented at the 23rd Annual TESOL Convention, San Antonio, TX.

>Describes potential problems with conferencing for ESL students.

>Conferencing.

1081. Frodesen, J. M. (1988, March). *Designing peer editing component for ESL composition*. Paper presented at the 22nd Annual TESOL Convention, Chicago, IL.

>Describes techniques for building confidence, designing guidelines, and organizing peer work.

>Error Analysis/Editing.

1082. Frodesen, J. M., & Holten, C. A. (1993, April). *Teacher as learner in the writing conference: A role reversal*. Paper presented at 44th Annual Convention of CCCC, San Diego, CA.

>See next item.

>Conferencing.

1083. Frodesen, J. M., & Holten, C. A. (1991, March). *Teachers as learner in writing conferences: A role reversal*. Paper presented at the 25th Annual TESOL Convention, New York, NY.

>Compares university teachers' written comments on student papers with information from student/teacher dialogs in writing conferences.

>Conferencing/University.

1084. Frolich-Ward, L. (1992). Let them read!--later: Problems of introducing reading and writing to young learners of English as a foreign language. In A. Van Essen, & I. E. Burkart (Eds.), *Homage to W. R. Lee: Essays in English as a foreign or second language*. Berlin: Foris.

>Reading-Writing Relations.

1085. Fruger, A. M., & Freeman, C. F. (1985). Creating a writing lab based on composition reformulation techniques. *TESOL Newsletter, 19*(5), 15, 17.

>Designs a writing lab which addresses concerns raised about the reformulation technique (Cohen 1983). Focuses on the prepararation and execuition of the writing lab, cites student reactions, and provides samples of original and reformulated essays.

>Writing Center/Reformulation.

1086. Frydenberg, G. (1990, March). *Teaching advanced ESL writing: Format and process*. Paper presented at the 24th Annual TESOL Convention, San Francisco, CA.

>Examines what advanced ESL writers can and cannot do in terms of organization and language use, comparing this to proficient native speakers' purposes for and products of writing. Proposes goals, a course outline, methodology, and describes relevant exercises.

>Advanced/Courses/NS-NNS Comparisons.

1087. Frydenberg, G., & Boardman, C. A. (1990). *You're in charge! Writing to *communicate.* Reading, MA: Addison Wesley/Longman.

 A text which moves from the basics of simple paragraph writing to full-length essay writing. Paragraph organization, transition to essays, and rhetorical patterns are featured.

 University/Intermediate/Textbook.

1088. Fuentes, J. (1990). Effect of a writing program on second language skills of Hispanic students. *Dissertation Abstracts International, 50*(11), 5344B.

 An experimental study of 8-13 year olds (N=109) enrolled in an after school "writing-as-process" program found that intensive writing experience with computer assistance enabled students to outperform those taught with traditional methods.

 Hispanic/Computers/Process Instruction.

1089. Fulton, M. (1988, November). *From ESL to mainstream English.* Paper presented at the 78th Annual NCTE Convention, St. Louis, MO.

 Approaches.

1090. Furey, P. R., & Menasche, L. (1990). *Making progress in English: Grammar and composition.* Ann Arbor, MI: University of Michigan Press.

 Information, exercises, and assignments for intermediate-level students who need both grammar, mechanics, and composition in a single course. Chapters review grammar, treat several types of paragraph forms, as well as the basic modes of writing.

 Intermediate/Grammar/Textbook.

G

1091. Gabrielle, S. F. (1985). *Beginning composition, step by step.* Burlingame, CA: Alta.

 A four-step, 22 lesson structured writing program for pre-university learners with accompanying posters.

 Textbook/BEGINNERS.

1092. Gadbow, K. (1992). Foreign students in the writing lab: Some practical and ethical considerations. *Writing Lab Newsletter, 17*(3), 1-5.

 Discusses experiences at one writing center tutoring ESL students who seek help with editing for graduate and other content courses.

 Writing Center.

1093. Gadda, G. (1988, March). *The University of California's subject-A examination: Nonnative papers and the communty of judgment.* Paper presented at the 39th Annual CCCC Meeting, St. Louis, MO.

 Assessment/Discourse Communities.

1094. Gadda, G. (1986, March). *ESL markers: Defining their significance for placement and instruction.* Paper presented at the 37th Annual CCCC Meeting, New Orleans, LA.

 Assessment.

1095. Gadda, G., Goodwin, J. M., & Peitzman, F. (1992, March). *Nonnative writers, mainstream practices and expectations: Mutual influences.* Paper presented at the 26th Annual TESOL Convention, Vancouver, BC.

 Discusses theoretical justification and new practices for engaging students in

the reading and writing of demanding texts.
Reading-Writing Relations/Content.

1096. Gaies, S. J. (1980). T-unit analysis in second language research: Applications, problems and limitations. *TESOL Quarterly, 14*, 53-60.

Reviews criticism of the validity of the T-unit as a measure of syntactic maturity in second language acquisition. Makes suggestions about validity, usefulness, and limitations of this and other measures of overall syntactic complexity.
Objective Measures/Evaluation.

1097. Gaies, S. J. (1976, May). *Sentence-combining: A technique for assessing proficiency in a second language.* Paper presented at the Conference on Perspectives in Language, University of Louisville, Louisville, KY. [ERIC ED 130 512].

Results of a study indicate that the recognition of correct grammatical structure is not always accompanied by proficiency in writing. Attempts to measure the active syntactic proficiency of ESL learners through sentence-combining exercises (O'Donnell's Aluminum Passage), concluding that a definitive judgment cannot be obtained about the effectiveness of the rewriting exercises.
Evaluation/T-Unit.

1098. Gajdusek, L. (1990, March). *Responding to written errors: Respecting process, teaching language.* Paper presented at the 24th Annual TESOL Convention, San Francisco, CA.

Describes procedures for error correction consistent with writing as process and with contextualized teaching of grammar as meaning. After the final draft is evaluated, students analyze and correct selected errors, using procedures to reveal their production rules. Results of a study to evaluate the effectiveness are also reported.
Error Treatment.

1099. Gajdusek, L. (1989). Contextualized grammar teaching in ESL: A study of its effect on the grammar and overall writing proficiency of university students. *Dissertation Abstracts International, 51*(4), 1443A.

Reports on a college ESL course designed to implement contextualized grammar teaching. Analysis of pre-and post-test writing samples of students in an ESL speech class, those who received a grammatically-focused course involving reading short pieces of literature, discussing ideas, and writing purposefully, and a group who took no ESL, the grammar treatment class made more progress in overall writing proficiency but no significant difference in grammatical development.
Grammar/University/Proficiency.

1100. Gajdusek, L., & van Dommelen, D. (1993). Literature and critical thinking in the composition classroom. In J. G. Carson, & I. Leki (Eds.), *Reading in the composition classroom: Second language perspectives* (pp. 197-217). Boston: Heinle & Heinle.

Uses a modern American short story to demonstrate how composition teachers can model critical thinking procedures for students reading literature.
Reading-Writing Relations/Literature.

1101. Galindo, L. R. (1991). Young bilingual children's appropriations of dialogue journals as a literacy event: A study of literacy socialization. *Dissertation Abstracts International, 51*(10), 3325.

A case study focusing on the personal narratives written by four bilinguals in first and second grade urban southwestern classrooms. The social worlds created by the children's interactions in the classroom were analyzed through five phases of a dialogue journal literacy event.

Bilingual/Dialogue Journals/Literacy.

1102. Gallingane, G., & Byrd, D. R. H. (1978). A capsule course in ESL composition for adults. In R. L. Light, & A. H. Osman (Eds.), *Collected papers in teaching English as a second language and bilingual education* (pp. 75-85). New York: Teachers College, Columbia University.

Discusses the organization and rationale for the composition component of an ESL writing course at a community college. An examination of writing grammar needs resulted in four basic operations: inflection, coordination, derivation, and subordination, that were taught to enable students to write with more flexibility. Each operation is explained and examples of each presented. Also included are cartoons (The Purse Snatcher) with a list of statements under the cartoons.

Grammar/University/Courses/Adult Education.

1103. Gallo, R. Q., Sumagaysay, G., & Concepcion, G. (1992, March). *Spelling development: The nonnative speaker.* Paper presented at the 26th Annual TESOL Convention, Vancouver, BC.

Reports an ethnographic study of the evolution of invented spelling of six Vietnamese students.

Spelling/Ethnographic Research/Vietnamese.

1104. Galvan, M. (1986). *The writing processes of Spanish-speaking bilingual/bicultural graduate students* . Washington, DC: ERIC/FLL. [ERIC ED 270 744].

An ethnographic study investigates the writing processes of 10 Spanish-speaking bilingual/bicultural graduate students. Shows that native culture and language control to a great extent the composing processes in English which are recursive and doubt-riddled.

Hispanic/Culture/Ethnographic Research.

1105. Galvan, M. (1985). The writing processes of Spanish-speaking bilingual/bicultural graduate students: An ethnographic perspective. *Dissertation Abstracts International, 47*(2), 481A.

Examines the writing processes of Spanish-speaking bilingual and bicultural graduate students. Results show that writing was controlled both by acquired and native languages. Subjects wrote in three modes: expressive, instrumental, and technical.

Hispanic/Process Research/L1 Influence.

1106. Gantzer, J., & Cadet, N. E. (1987). Student autonomy and group reliance in an ESL reading/writing course. In G. Brookes, & J. Gantzer (Eds.), *Improving the odds: Helping ESL students succeed. Selected papers from the 1987 CUNY ESL Council Conference, New York, NY* (pp. 14-19). NY: CUNY Resource Center. [ERIC ED 328 068].

Shares how to integrate reading and writing in a single college course while emphasizing student generated questionning and writing as a part of the reading done by the whole class.

Reading-Writing Relations/University.

1107. Ganz, D. S. (1986, March). *Peer-response workshops in ESL composition courses*. Paper presented at the 37th Annual CCCC Meeting, New Orleans, LA.

Peer Response/Workshop.

1108. Garcia de Riley, L. (1976). *A resource manual in techniques of teaching composition skills to intermediate and advanced English as a second language students*. NY: Hunter College, CUNY.

Hispanic/Teacher Preparation.

1109. Garcia, de Riley. L. (1975). A linguistic frame of reference for critiquing Chicano compositions. *College English*, 37, 184-188.

Discusses interference in phonology and morphology and its absence in Chicano compositions.

Hispanic/L1 Influence.

1110. Garcia, de Riley. L. (1973). *Identification and comparison of oral English syntactic patterns of Spanish-English speaking adolescent Hispanos*. Unpublished doctoral dissertation, University of Denver, Denver, CO.

Finds no syntactic interference from Spanish in written work of either lower or middle class Chicano students.

Speaking-Writing Relations/L1 Influence.

1111. Garcia Duran, S. S. (1990). A test of a Mastery Learning approach for teaching basic paragraph writing skills to Spanish language background students. *Dissertation Abstracts International*, 52(5), 1624-1625A.

A pre-test/post-test study attempts to determine whether mastery learning improves the writing ability of elementary students from Spanish language background. Results were not conclusive about the effect of mastery learning.

Hispanic/Paragraph/Instruction.

1112. Gargagliano, A., & Capobianco, P. (1993, April). *Intergenerational pen pals: ESL across the ages*. Paper presented at the 27th Annual TESOL Convention, Atlanta, GA.

The advantages of using real audiences in letter writing is illustrated by a comparsion of two programs.

Letter Writing.

1113. Gartz, I. T. (1985). Discourse and fluency features in the English interlanguage structures of Mexican bilingual-curricula college students: A longitudinal study based on data taken from compositions. *Dissertation Abstracts International*, 46(10), 13017A.

Examines the interlanguage patterns in discourse structure and general fluency in the English compositions of Mexican bilingual college students over a period of twenty-two months. Results show progress more evident with "language acquirers" rather than "language learners".

Hispanic/Discourse Analysis/University.

1114. Gaskill, W. H. (1987). Revising in Spanish and English as a second-language: A process-oriented study of composition. *Dissertation Abstracts International, 47*(10), 3747-3748A.

Reports on the revisions and composing processes in Spanish and English of four native speakers of Spanish. Analysis of the revisions according to Faigley and Witte's (1981) revision taxonomy indicates that most revision occurs during actual composing. Composing processes and revisions were similar in both English and Spanish. Composing behaviors of more proficient and less proficient writers differ with respect to planning and reading.

Hispanic/Revision/Process Research.

1115. Gaskill, W. H. (1985, April). *Composing in Spanish and English: Focus on revision.* Paper presented at the 19th Annual TESOL Convention, New York, NY.

Analysis of semantic revisions by four university-level Spanish speakers writing in Spanish and English reveals similar type and number of revisions in both languages.

Hispanic/University/Revision.

1116. Gaskill, W. H. (1984, March). *Revision in L2: A process-oriented study of a Taiwanese student writing in English.* Paper presented at the 18th Annual TESOL Convention, Houston, TX.

Case study of semantic revisions in multiple drafts of a graduate course assignment elaborates the findings of L1 revision research that 60% of revisions involve vocabulary and syntax.

Revision/NS-NNS Comparisons/Chinese.

1117. Gates, R. D. (1978). An analysis of grammatical structures in the compositions written by four groups of students at Southern Technical Institute: Indo-Iranian, Latin-Romance, Sino-Tibetan, and American. *Dissertation Abstracts International, 39*(4), 2026A.

Seeking to create a profile that would objectively measure the writing ability of international students, this study compares a placement essay written by American students with those written by Iranian, Hispanic, and Thai students.

Hispanic/Iran/Thai/NS-NNS Comparisons.

1118. Geisler, C. (1985). WARRANT: A pedagogical environment for critical reading, reasoning, and writing. *CALICO Journal, 2*(4), 43-44.

Discusses the design of an experimental computer program that allows interaction between a syllabus, a writing plan, and advice to a student.

Computers/Reading-Writing Relations.

1119. Geisler, C., Friedlander, A. C., Neuwirth, C., & Kaufer, D. S. (1986). WARRANT: A pedagogical environment for critical reading, reasoning, and writing. *TESOL Newsletter, Supplement on computer-assisted language learning, No. 3, 20*(1), 12.

Describes an experimental system, WARRANT, to assist students in handling the complex interrelationships between reading, writing, and reasoning. Students may draw from sub-programs on Syllabus, Plan, and Advice to receive guidance in performing the reading-writing-reasoning tasks of an experimental curriculum. An authoring system for ESL teachers may be available in the future.

Computers/Reading-Writing Relations.

1120. Genesee, F., & Stanley, M. H. (1976). The development of English writing skills in French immersion programs. *Canadian Journal of Education*, *1*, 1-17.

Found more similarities than differences in written organization, sentence-making, and spelling of French immersion students in grades 4, 6, 7, and 11 and their English instructed counterparts.

Development/Children/French.

1121. Gentry, L. A. (1982). What research says about revision. *CATESOL Occasional Papers*, *8*, 96-108. [ERIC ED 225 413].

Reviews research on the process, content, and effect of revision on the writing process.

Revision/Review.

1122. Genzel, R. B. (1992). *On your way to writing: A writing workshop for intermediate learners*. Boston: Heinle & Heinle.

Discusses audience, speaking-writing differences, and writing sentences before devoting chapters to extended writing practice. Subsequent chapters focus step-by-step on the writing of descriptions, dialogues, folktales, criticism, functional messages, and comparison and contrast. Culminating chapter guides students to use class material generated during the course to produce a class magazine.

Intermediate/Textbook.

1123. Genzel, R. B. (1991, March). *A matrix approach to writing and speaking*. Paper presented at the 25th Annual TESOL Convention, New York, NY.

Introduces the concept of the matrix, a simple device used to organize essays or prepare oral presentations as an aid to developing productive language abilities.

Speaking-Writing Relations/Instruction.

1124. Getkham, K. T. (1988). Reading and writing connections as revealed in synthesis essays of English as a second language students. *Dissertation Abstracts International*, *49*(8), 2130A.

Investigates the reading and writing performance of forty twelfth-grade ESL students in Thailand. Subjects, classified as more reading able or less reading able, read two sources aloud and wrote a synthesis essay using information available in the two source texts. Able readers did more extensive planning and produced better organized texts than less able readers, although both included similar content and both used their own knowledge.

Reading-Writing Relations/Thai/Secondary School.

1125. Ghadessy, M. (1984). Going beyond the sentence: Implications of discourse analysis for the teaching of the writing skill. *IRAL: International Review of Applied Linguistics in Language Teaching*, *22*, 213-218.

Discusses the weaknesses in teaching strategies and attitudes of EFL teachers and points out various problems in the teaching of discourse analysis. Suggests that effective methods of teaching writing should involve such skills as the manipulation of ideas and structures which leads to the development of coherent essays.

Discourse Analysis/Coherence.

1126. Ghadessy, M. (1983). Comments on Patricia Carrell's "Cohesion is not coherence":

A reader reacts . . . [In The Forum]. *TESOL Quarterly, 17,* 685-686.

Responds to Patricia Carrell's "Cohesion is not coherence" and defends Halliday and Hassan (1976). Claims that they are justified in establishing cohesion as a discourse strategy. Adds that they do not equate the two but only claim to provide an explanation for cohesion not coherence.

Cohesion/Coherence.

1127. Ghaleb, M. L. (1993, April). *Computer networking in an ESL writing class.* Paper presented at the 27th Annual TESOL Convention, Atlanta, GA.

Reports results of an ethnographic comparative investigation of two sections of an ESL university freshman writing class.

Computers/Ethnographic Research/University.

1128. Ghani, S. A. (1986). Group writing: A technique that fosters creativity. *English Teaching Forum, 24*(3), 36-37.

Discusses the use of group writing to promote creativity through discussion and peer-learning.

Group Work/Arabic.

1129. Ghazalah, H. (1988). Literary stylistics: Pedagogical perspectives in an EFL context. *Dissertation Abstracts International, 49*(3), 448A.

Argues that literary stylistics is superior to either linguistic or affective stylistics for the analysis and interpretation of short texts. Proposes that non-native students approach English literary composition via this form of stylistics which can be implemented in a student-centered classroom pedagogy.

Style.

1130. Giansanti, S. P. (1992, March). *Using ASL to teach elements of essay writing.* Paper presented at the 26th Annual TESOL Convention, Vancouver, BC.

Describes the use of American Sign Language to assist deaf ESL students with conceptualizing how an essay is structured.

ASL.

1131. Gibson, D. (1985, November). *A student-centered writing curriculum.* Washington, DC: ERIC/FLL. [ERIC ED 266 648].

Presents a non-credit writing course for ESL students which consists of writing assignments whose subject matter and length are determined by students. Individual writing, as well as peer-group critiques, revisions, and error correction exercises are discussed.

Courses/Assignments.

1132. Giesecke, W. B. (1982). A comparative study of English composition errors of Japanese university students with public school English language textbooks. *Dissertation Abstracts International, 43*(3), 706A.

Results show no one-to-one correlation between the grammatical categories in textbooks used to teach ESL in Japan and actual grammatical difficulties of Japanese-speaking ESL learners as stated in second language research literature. States implications for rewriting textbooks.

Error Analysis/Japanese/University/Materials.

1133. Gilbert, J. W. (1976). *A comparison of syntactic development in the writing of university students, foreign and native.* Unpublished master's thesis, UCLA, Los Angeles, CA.

Compares the syntactic complexity of NES (n=18) and NNS writers (three proficiency levels; n=54) on a single college composition. Finds no significant developmental trend but shows that NES writers have significantly longer T-units and more T-units per sentence than their NNS peers.

Syntactic Development/University/NS-NNS Comparisons.

1134. Gilbert, R., & Grabe, W. (1991, March). *Error patterns in fifth grade English L1, L2 writing.* Paper presented at the 25th Annual TESOL Convention, New York, NY.
See next item.
Elementary/Amer-Indian/Hispanic/L1-L2 Comparison.

1135. Gilbert, R., & Grabe, W. (1990, March). *Comparing English L1 and L2 elementary student writing* Paper presented at the 24th Annual TESOL Convention, San Francisco, CA.

Presents comparative results of a holistic and morphosyntactic error analysis of writing on nine topics by native English, Spanish, and Navajo-speaking fifth graders (N=80) in three elementary schools.

Children/Amer-Indian/Hispanic/L1-L2 Comparisons.

1136. Gilbert, R. A. (1993). *From writing to media with literature in EFL.* Washington, DC: ERIC/FLL. [ERIC 353 824].

Discusses an approach that compares print and video versions of a text (Shakespeare's Macbeth) which can lead to a writing experience for video-oriented ESL students.

Media/Literature.

1137. Gilboa, C. C. (1981, March). *ESL and the well-organized, coherent 500 word essay.* Paper presented at the 15th Annual TESOL Convention, Detroit, MI.

A two-year experiment shows how freshman composition is designed to initiate writers into the academic subculture but does not necessarily pay attention to the needs of ESL students.

Freshman Composition/Discourse Communities.

1138. Gilboa, C. C. (1980, March). *Lexical and rhetorical characteristics of non-standard writing.* Paper presented at the 14th Annual TESOL Convention, San Francisco, CA.

Computational analysis of placement essays of non-standard English speakers shows an unnoticed relationship between word choice and rhetoric.

Vocabulary.

1139. Gilman, C. (1993, April). *The dialogue journal theme: Student-student variations.* Poster session presented at the 27th Annual TESOL Convention, Atlanta, GA.

Exhibits samples of student work and pictures of students at work.

Dialogue Journals.

1140. Gilman, C. (1992, March). *Going interactive with reading and writing.* Poster presented at the 26th Annual TESOL Convention, Vancouver, BC.

Recommends three kinds of interaction between reading amd writing: a read-relate-write-review sequence, a reading-questioning via notes production sequence, and a student-student dialogue journal interaction.

Reading-Writing Relations/Secondary School.

1141. Gilman, R. (1993, April). *Meeting the needs of an expanding ESL and bi-lingual university population*. Paper presented at 44th Annual Convention of CCCC, San Diego, CA.
Placement.

1142. Ginn, D. O. (1988). De-pidginization: A rhetoric and writing dilemma in cross-cultural communications. *Focuses, 1,* 41-50.
Describes some cultural problems and offers pedagogical advice.
Culture/Rhetoric.

1143. Gipps, C., & Ewen, E. (1974). Scoring written work in English as a second language: The use of the T-unit. *Educational Research, 16*(2), 121-1125.
Finds, among other things, that Asian but not West Indian children wrote longer T-units the longer they stayed in Britain.
T-Unit/West Indian/LOR.

1144. Giroux, N. S. (1983, March). *Producing a newsletter as an ESP class in a intensive English program: How to do it and why*. Paper presented at the 17th Annual TESOL Convention, Toronto, Ontario.
Publishing their own newsletter gives ESL students practice in all the basic communication skills.
Student Publications/IEP.

1145. Godsen, H. (1992). Research writing and NNSs: From the editors. *Journal of Second Language Writing, 1*(2), 123-139.
Reports results of a survey of journal editors in U.K. and North America about effective international research reporting. Findings suggest the need for varied linguistics and socio-pragmatic skills.
Research Writing.

1146. Godsen, H. (1991a). Academic writing, language awareness and the EFL writer. *The Language Teacher, 15*(5), 3-6.
Academic Writing.

1147. Godsen, H. (1991b). Teaching Research English to ESL researchers: Questions of cost and benefit. *Journal of Asian Pacific Communication, 2*(1), 139-153.
Research Writing.

1148. Goldberg, J. P., Ford, C. K., & Silverman, A. (1982, May). *Deaf students in ESL composition classes: Challenges and strategies*. Paper presented at the 16th Annual TESOL Convention, Honolulu, HI.
Presents difficulties shared by ESL and deaf students in learning to write English.
Hearing-Impaired.

1149. Golder, P. L. (1991). *Sentence combining and the ESL student*. Unpublished master's thesis, California State University, San Bernardino, CA.
Sentence Combining.

1150. Goldman, S. R., & Duran, R. P. (1988). Answering questions from oceanography texts: Learner, task, and text characteristics. *Discourse Processes, 11,* 373-412.
Introspective inquiry discovers different approaches to answering questions by

native and non-native students.
ESP/NS-NNS Comparisons.

1151. Goldman, S. R., & Treuba, H. T. (Eds.). (1987). *Becoming literate in English as a second language* Norwood, NJ: Ablex.
Volume presents ten research-based papers devoted primarily to the acquisition of literacy in bilingual (Mexican and Chinese) classrooms and home contexts.
Literacy/Hispanic/Chinese.

1152. Goldstein, L. M. (1993a). Becoming a member of the "Teaching Foreign Languages" community: Integrating researching and writing through an adjunct/content course. In J. G. Carson, & I. Leki (Eds.), *Reading in the composition classroom: Second language perspectives* (pp. 290-298). Boston: Heinle & Heinle.
Argues for the integration of reading and writing in adjunct courses.
Reading-Writing Relations/Adjunct.

1153. Goldstein, L. M. (1993b, April). *Training ESL composition teachers: Preservice and inservice models.* Paper presented at the 27th Annual TESOL Convention, Atlanta, GA.
Provides guidelines for creating teacher training programs in ESL composition.
Teacher Education.

1154. Goldstein, L. M. (1989, March). *The role of negotiation of meaning in ESL student conferences.* Paper presented at the 40th Annual Convention CCCC, Seattle, WA.
See Goldstein & Conrad, 1990.
Conferencing.

1155. Goldstein, L. M., & Conrad, S. M. (1990a). Student input and negotiation of meaning in ESL writing conferences. *TESOL Quarterly, 24*, 443-460.
This study of conferences between a teacher and three advanced ESL composition students finds large differences in the degree of participation. Also drafts revised after conferences were much improved when the student had negotiated meaning in the conference, but only mechanical, sentence-level changes when they were not active.
Responding/Conferencing.

1156. Goldstein, L. M., & Conrad, S. M. (1990b, March). *Teacher as researcher: Learning from writing conferences.* Paper presented at the 24th Annual TESOL Convention, San Francisco, CA.
Shows teachers how to research their own writing conferences and how to apply the findings to make their conferences more effective.
Conferencing.

1157. Goldstein, W. L. (Comp.). (1975). *Teaching English as a second language: An annotated bibliography* NY: Garland.
A bibliography on ESL, selectively covering all areas, including writing, up to 1974.
Bibliography.

1158. Golson, E. B. (1986, March). *Foreign student writing: Problems, solutions, problems.* Paper presented at the 37th Annual CCCC Meeting, New Orleans, LA.

1159. Golub-Smith, M., Reese, C., & Steinhaus, K. (1993). *Topic and topic type comparability on the Test of Written English*. (TOEFL Research Report 42). Princeton, NJ: Educational Testing Service.

> Finds small differences in scores obtained from eight prompts differing in subject matter and level of explicitness.
> Prompts/Rating.

1160. Gomez, I. (1987, April). *Implementing the writing process in an elementary ESL classroom*. Paper presented at the 21st Annual TESOL Convention, Miami Beach, FL.

> Finds peer conferences contributed to oral and written language development of elementary LEP students.
> Elementary/Conferencing.

1161. Gomez, M. L., & Grant, C. A. (1990). A case for teaching writing -- In the belly of the story. *Writing Instructor*, (29-41),

> Argues for changes in the practice of teaching writing to diverse student populations.
> Culture/Approaches.

1162. Gonshack, S., & McKenzie, J. (1982). *Send me a letter! A basic guide to letter writing*. Englewood Cliffs, NJ: Prentice-Hall.

> A textbook based on a number of day-to-day functional situations and containing model letters and exercises for adult and secondary students.
> Secondary School/Textbook.

1163. Gonzales, R. D. (1987, November). *Developing language through writing theory*. Paper presented at the 77th Annual NCTE Convention, Los Angeles, CA.

> Language Development.

1164. Gonzales, R. D. (1982). Teaching Mexican-American students to write: Capitalizing on culture. *English Journal*, 71(7), 20-24.

> Favors using the student's culture and folklore to stimulate and develop writing ability.
> Hispanic/Instruction.

1165. Gonzalez, A. (1979, March). *Ethnocentrism and teaching writing to foreign students*. Paper presented at the Annual Meeting of the College English Association, n.p. [ERIC ED 198 734].

> Advises teachers to show ESL students how culture influences American readers' reactions, to compare rhetoric cross-culturally, and to require revisions in the light of the resulting audience and cultural awareness.
> Hispanic/Culture/Audience.

1166. Gonzo, S., & Buckingham, T. (1977, April). *The effects of transformational sentence-combining practice on the writing ability of non-native speakers of English*. Paper presented at the 11th Annual TESOL Convention, Miami Beach, FLA.

> Reports that experimental treatment caused students to gain in syntactic fluency and correctness.
> Sentence Combining/Accuracy/Fluency.

1167. Goodfellow, P., Hirokawa, K., Chisholm, J., & Gaylord, W. (1984, March). EST:

Designing a mini-course for non-native speakers of English in a chemistry lab course. Paper presented at the 18th Annual TESOL Convention, Houston, TX. [ERIC ED 274 183].

A variety of data collected over a nine-week period in a university chemistry class is used to compare note-taking, writing reports, and classroom interaction by NNS students and their NES peers.

ESP/Chemistry.

1168. Goodin, G., & Perkins, K. (1982). Discourse analysis and the art of coherence. *College English, 44*, 57-83.

Offers rules and comments for using discourse analysis to teach student writers how to convert incoherent compositions into coherent/cohesive prose.

Discourse Analysis/Coherence.

1169. Goodrum, R. (1988, March). *Building essayist literacy on a foundation of oral culture.* Paper presented at the 39th Annual CCCC Meeting, St. Louis, MO.

Literacy/Speaking-Writing Relations.

1170. Goodwin, A. A. (1992a, March). *Plagiarism in ESL composition: The cultural perspective.* Workshop presented at the 26th Annual TESOL Convention, Vancouver, BC.

Describes plagiarism problems of students from diverse cultures and how to teach skills to avoid them.

Plagiarism/Culture.

1171. Goodwin, J. M. (1992b, March). *Opening texts for ESL writers.* Paper presented at the 26th Annual TESOL Convention, Vancouver, BC.

Presents the into, through, beyond model of reading and writing academic tasks and activities to implement this new approach.

Reading-Writing Relations.

1172. Gordon, H. H. (1985). *From copying to creative: Controlled compositions and other basic writing exercises.* (Second Ed.). San Diego, CA: Harcourt Brace Jovanovich.

Based on the view that imitative writing is a method of learning conventions, textbook combines lessons in controlled writing with grammar lessons and sentence-combining exercises.

Intermediate/Textbook.

1173. Gordon, H. H. (1982). Controlled compositions: More practice for students, less grading for instructors. *CATESOL Occasional Papers, 8*, 88-95. [ERIC ED 225 412].

Describes how controlled composition permits imitation, mechanical manipulation, and reduced teacher-correction time as students receive more practice.

Control.

1174. Gorman, T. P., Purves, A. C., & Degenhart, R. E. (Eds.). (1988). *The IEA study of written compositions I: The international writing tasks and scoring scales* NY: Pergamon Press.

Describes development of topics and scoring scales and gives benchmark essays for the International Study of Written Composition sponsored by the International Association for the Evaluation of Educational Achievement (IEA) begun

in 1980. Examined the teaching and learning of writing in one's native language in schools in 14 countries.
Assessment/IEA.

1175. Gorrell, D. (1987). *Copy/write: Basic writing through controlled composition.* NY: HarperCollins.
Devotes half the textbook to exercises in controlled, imitative writing and original, self-generated composition and the other half to functional grammar lessons.
Beginners/Textbook.

1176. Gosden, H. (1993). Discourse functions of subject in scientific research articles. *Applied Linguistics, 14,* 56-75.
Presents a Hallidayan functional analysis of the role of grammatical subjects in scientific research articles (RA), showing how the changing role in text characterizes the RA genre.
Genre/Research Writing.

1177. Gosden, H. (1992). Discourse functions of marked theme in scientific research articles. *English for Specific Purposes, 11,* 207-224.
Argues that the Hallidayan notion of theme distinguishes genre. Marked theme in research article provides within text structuring in scientific research articles.
Genre/ESP.

1178. Grabe, W. (1989). Literacy in a second language. *Annual Review of Applied Linguistics, 10,* 145-162.
Maintains that first language writing research is a major resource for four research strands: early literacy development, the composing process, text construction and analysis, and rhetoric, which dominate current research on writing in a second language.
Literacy/Review.

1179. Grabe, W. (1987). Contrastive rhetoric and text-type research. In U. M. Connor, & R. B. Kaplan (Eds.), *Writing across languages: Analysis of L2 text* (pp. 115-137). Reading, MA: Addison-Wesley.
Presents a methodology for defining expository prose in English and explores sub-text groupings and relation between the groupings. States implication of such a study for contrastive rhetoric research.
Contrastive Rhetoric/Text Analysis.

1180. Grabe, W. (1985a, April). *Contrastive rhetoric and text type research.* Paper presented at the 19th Annual TESOL Convention, New York, NY.
A factor and discriminant analysis of 33 linguistic variables in fifteen different text types identifies significant textual parameters important for analysis of expository writing.
Contrastive Rhetoric/Objective Measures.

1181. Grabe, W. (1985b, April). *Towards defining expository prose: Implications for research and instruction.* Paper presented at the 19th Annual TESOL Convention, New York, NY.
Factorial and discriminant analysis research of thirty-three variables lead to defining "expository" prose explicitly.

Text Analysis/Exposition.

1182. Grabe, W. (1984). Towards defining expository prose within a theory of text construction. *Dissertation Abstracts International, 45*(8), 2510A.

Presents a statistical model of textual parameters which define the notion "expository prose" as a genre type. Examines 33 variables in a corpus of 150 texts grouped into 15 sub-types, including syntactic categories and constructions, cohesion counts, lexical counts, and attitude measures. Interprets six factors as distinguishing the genre subtypes which are further analyzed by discriminant analysis so as to determine the distinctions between the groups. Overall, model lends some validity to the notion of "expository prose" as an objective category of text.

Exposition/Text Analysis.

1183. Grabe, W., & Biber, D. (1987, April). *Freshman student writing and the contrastive rhetoric hypothesis*. Paper presented at the Seventh Second Language Research Forum, Los Angeles, CA.

Finds no difference between native and non-native essays and small differences between good and bad essays in a multi-factorial, multidimensional analysis of textual relations. All student essays, however, are unlike any of the published genres of English as analyzed in other studies (Biber,1988; Grabe,1984).

Contrastive Rhetoric/NS-NNS Comparisons.

1184. Grabe, W., & Kaplan, R. B. (1989). Writing in a second language: Contrastive rhetoric. In D. M. Johnson, & D. H. Roen (Eds.), *Richness in writing: Empowering ESL students* (pp. 263-283). NY: Longman.

Claims that research in contrastive rhetoric has relevance for both the teacher and learner of ESL composition. States implications of this research and suggests ways of deriving some teaching techniques.

Contrastive Rhetoric.

1185. Grabe, W., Montano-Harmon, M. R., Ricento, T., Kaplan, R. B., Eggington, W. G., & Dantas-Whitney, M. (1989, March). *Contrastive rhetoric: Current research and pedagogical assumption*. Colloquium presented at the 23rd Annual TESOL Convention, San Antonio, TX.

Reports findings of contrastive studies of written discourse from English, Chicano English, Japanese, Brazilian Portugese, Mexican Spanish, and Australian Aboriginal languages and creoles.

Contrastive Rhetoric/Japanese/Portugese/Hispanic/Creole.

1186. Graber-Wilson, G. L. (1990). The extent of the relationship between reading and writing achievement among international students enrolled in a university freshman composition course. *Dissertation Abstracts International, 50*, 2351A.

Finds a strong, positive correlation between reading and writing skills in a study of timed writing samples, especially among low-level students.

Reading-Writing Relations/University.

1187. Graham, J. G. (1987, November). *Helping the ESOL writer: Constructive feedback*. Paper presented at the 77th Annual Meeting of the NCTE, Los Angeles, CA. [ERIC ED 289 376].

Views errors as natural in the writing process and advises a balanced approach

in responding to students' errors. Discusses the influence of cultural factors in student writing.
Error Treatment/Responding.

1188. Graham, S. Y., & Curtis, W. J. (1986). *Harbrace ESL workbook*. San Diego, CA: Harcourt Brace Jovanovich.
A workbook on grammar, spelling, editing, and revising models.
Grammar/Textbook.

1189. Granfors, T., & Palmberg, R. (1976). *Errors made by Finns and Swedish-speaking Finns learning English at a commercial-college level* Washington, DC: ERIC/FLL. [ERIC ED 122 628].
Finnish-speaking students omitted articles and prepositions more frequently and made more agreement errors than Swedish learners of English, supporting th hypothesis that learning English for Swedes is easier than for Finns because Swedish is more similar to English.
Finnish/Swedish/Contrastive Analysis.

1190. Grant, J. (1989, March). *Developing writing and listening skills in the process*. Paper presented at the 23rd Annual TESOL Convention, San Antonio, TX.
Writing improves when teachers process authentic listening input via worksheets and students exploit individual and group abilities.
Listening-Writing Relations.

1191. Grant, M., & Caesar, S. (1991, March). *Journals revisited: Student-centered materials for teaching writing*. Paper presented at the 25th Annual TESOL Convention, New York, NY.
Instructor response letters about student journal entries create student-centered, student-generated teaching materials to explore literary themes, rhetorical forms, and grammatical features.
Journal Writing/Materials.

1192. Graves, M. E. (1986, March). *Using journals in ESL composition classes*. Paper presented at the 20th Annual TESOL Convention, Anaheim, CA.
Discussion of holistic ratings reveals influence of rater familiarity with students' native culture on the evaluations.
Journal Writing/Assessment.

1193. Grayshon, M. C. (1965). Intensive writing and overseas students. *English Language Teaching, 19*(2), 79-91.
Reports on the effectiveness of reading and writing poetry that appeals to student experiences.
Creative Writing.

1194. Green, J. F. (1967). Preparing an advanced composition course. *English Language Teaching Journal, 21*(3), 141-150.
Recognizes need to view writing as a complex activity, deserving systematic treatment in instruction. But focuses on error classification and use of error analysis for remedial exercises.
Advanced/Error Analysis.

1195. Green, J., & Green, C. (1991, March). *"Secret friend" journals, authentic writing, and audience awareness*. Paper presented at the 25th Annual TESOL Convention, New York, NY.

 Suggests how using journal writing among peers is beneficial to writers and teachers.

 Journal Writing.

1196. Green, P. S., & Hecht, K. (1985). Native and non-native evaluation of learners' errors in written discourse. *System, 13*, 77-97.

 Errors made by young German learners with five years of English and those of native British grammar and secondary students on a communicative writing task were compared and evaluated by native and non-native teachers from a number of points of view. Found problems with establishing errors, the categories, causes and gravity of errors, differences between native and non-native errors, and native and non-native assessment.

 Error Analysis/NS-NNS Comparisons/German.

1197. Greenall, G. M. (1980). Code features of examination scripts: A comparison between native speaker and non-native speaker answers. In G. M. Greenall, & J. E. Price (Eds.), *Study modes and academic development of overseas students* (pp. 134-151). London: The British Council.

 Presents a sample of data from written examinations in Clinical Biochemistry and compares native and non-native responses. Reports differences in length, number of grammatical errors, amount of nominalization as well as verbalization, and type of statements made.

 NS-NNS Comparisons/Examination Essays.

1198. Greenberg, K. L. (1986). The development and validation of the TOEFL writing test: A discussion of TOEFL research reports 15 and 19. *TESOL Quarterly, 20*, 531-544.

 Examines the validity and reliability of the TOEFL writing test (TWE) as a measure to test writing achievement. Claims that it is more valid than purely objective measures for testing proficiency. Topic types are most problematic feature of test.

 Evaluation/Assessment.

1199. Greenberg, K. L. (1985). Error analysis and the teaching of developmental writing. *Research & Teaching in Developmental Education, 2*(1), 34-39.

 Argues that the applied linguistics technique of error analysis allows teachers to diagnose the cognitive strategies and processes used by students.

 Error Analysis.

1200. Greenberg, K. L. (1982). Some relationships between writing tasks and students' writing performance. *The Writing Instructor, 2*, 7-14.

 Discusses several of many variables associated with writing assignments.

 Assessment/Task.

1201. Greene, M. (1993). Beyond insularity: Releasing the voices. *College ESL, 3*(1), 1-14.

 Discusses a wide range of multicultural literature in which new immigrants and others give voice to how things are and how they ought to be which helps to break down insularity and separateness.

 Voice/Ideology.

1202. Gregg, J. (1990). *Communication and culture: A reading-writing text.* (Fourth Ed.). Boston: Heinle & Heinle.
    A text for preparing students for academic work by combining reading and writing in the context of cultural themes.
    Textbook.

1203. Gregg, J. (1986). A reader reacts: A comment on Bernard A. Mohan and Winnie Au-yeung Lo's "Academic writing and Chinese students: Transfer and developmental factors". *TESOL Quarterly, 20,* 354-358.
    Claims that Mohan and Lo's analysis of the rhetorical problem of non-native speakers of English, particularly Chinese students, is one-sided since it ignores the culture-specific style of Chinese writers. Presents ways to teach Chinese students rhetorical patterns of American English.
    Contrastive Rhetoric/Development.

1204. Gregory, G. A. (1990, March). *Aristotle and the Navajo.* Paper presented at the 24th Annual TESOL Convention, San Francisco, CA.
    Presents the two philosophical/rhetorical viewpoints represented by academic writing and Athabaskan oral tradition. Looks specifically at differences in perception of audience and the basis for analysis in the two systems.
    Speaking-Writing Relations/Amer-Indian.

1205. Groden, S. (1992, March). *A curriculum for turning boundaries into thresholds.* Paper presented at the 43rd Annual CCCC Meeting, Cincinnati, OH.
    Curriculum.

1206. Groenewald, J. (1989, March). *A model for the infusion of thinking skills into writing.* Paper presented at the 23rd Annual TESOL Convention, San Antonio, TX.
    Reports a method of teaching thinking skills through process writing.
    Cognition/Process Instruction.

1207. Groff, C. E., & Villamizar, C. (1984, March). *Dialogue journals: A bridge between written and oral communication.* Paper presented at the 18th Annual TESOL Convention, Houston, TX.
    Two papers report on classroom research in ESL and Spanish, using dialogue journals.
    Hispanic/Dialogue Journals.

1208. Groot, I. (1991). *Note-taking in English as a second language acquisition.* Unpublished master's thesis, Indiana University-Purdue, IN.
    Note-Taking.

1209. Gross, C. U. (1984, March). *An experiment in elementary composition.* Paper presented at the 18th Annual TESOL Convention, Houston, TX.
    Finds that a process approach to elementary ESL is an effective alternative.
    Beginners/Process Instruction.

1210. Grossman, A. N., Garretson, K., & Kolb, M. M. (1993, April). *Dialogues in writing: Promoting active learning in the ESL classroom.* Paper presented at the 27th Annual TESOL Convention, Atlanta, GA.
    Discusses the use of journals by students to self-talk about their own texts, to discuss texts with other students, and to negotiate the curriculum with the teacher.

Dialogue Journals.

1211. Groves, P. A. L. (1983). *An examination of the composing behaviors and written products of ninth grade students writing in English as a second language.* Unpublished master's thesis, University of West Florida, Pensacola, FL.

See next item.

Secondary School/Micronesia.

1212. Groves, P. A. L. (1980). *The writing of Micronesian ESL students.* Washington, DC: ERIC/FLL. [ERIC ED 247 573].

Explores content and syntax in the writing of 15 ninth-grade Micronesian students to determine the degree to which their writing parallels their contact with Western culture. Questionnaires were used to measure the students' exposure to Western culture. All subjects produced mostly original prose. Two case study subjects, one more exposed and one less exposed to Western culture, however, showed considerable differences in the content and syntax of their compositions.

Micronesia/Culture/Secondary School.

1213. Grubb, M. H. (1983). The writing proficiency of selected ESL and monolingual English writers at three grade levels. *Dissertation Abstracts International, 45*(1), 103A.

Compares writing of monolingual students and LEPs in grades 5, 8, and 9. Findings show that: (1) a correlation between holistic scores and content level and organizational type; and (2) a relationship between content level and organizational type with holistic scores which did not vary with language group

Elementary/NS-NNS Comparisons/Proficiency.

1214. Guenther, B. (1986, May). *Using audience and process: Six strategies for responding effectively to ESL writers.* Paper presented at the Annual NAFSA Meeting, San Antonio, TX.

Audience/Responding.

1215. Guerra, V. A. (1984). Predictions of second language learners' error judgments in written English. *Dissertation Abstracts International, 45*(5), 1381A.

Investigates metalinguistic ability of Hispanic speakers in recognizing and correcting errors in their second language. Better native language skills and years of schooling in L1 predicted ability to recognize global errors (Burt & Kiparsky, 1975), whereas the more years of schooling in L2, the better students were at recognizing local errors. Results interpreted as supporting hypotheses by both Cummins and Krashen.

Hispanic/Errors.

1216. Gueye, M. (1981). A study of errors in the written production of speakers of Bambara, Fulani, and Songay at the first year English at the Ecole Normale Superieure of Bamako, Mali, West Africa. *Dissertation Abstracts International, 41*(8), 3460A.

Analyzes the stylistic, syntactic, and semantic errors made by Bambara, Fulani, and Songay students of first-year English. Findings show that intralingual errors were most predominant, followed by errors caused by interference of French and then by those of students' native oral languages.

Error Analysis/Mali.

1217. Gundel, J. K. (1982, May). *Effect of spoken vs. written input on second language acquisition*. Paper presented at the 16th Annual TESOL Convention, Honolulu, HI.

Attributes overgeneralization of extraposition to written input rather than language background.

Speaking-Writing Relations.

1218. Gungle, B. W., & Taylor, V. (1989). Writing apprehension and second language writers. In D. M. Johnson, & D. H. Roen (Eds.), *Richness in writing: Empowering ESL students* (pp. 235-248). NY: Longman.

Examines the notion of writing apprehension in ESL students, based on studies of writing apprehension in the first language. Claims that a modified version of the Daley-Miller Writing Apprehension Test may not be adequate for assessing ESL students and, therefore, there is the need for developing a new index. Gives suggestions to teachers for lowering writing apprehension of ESL students.

Anxiety.

1219. Gurnee, D., Knowles, M., & Rice, M. K. (1987, April). *Write again! An alternative approach to conferencing*. Paper presented at the 21st Annual TESOL Convention, Miami Beach, FL.

Recommends a peer/volunteer writing lab to augment existing English/ESL programs.

Writing Center.

1220. Gurrey, P. (1955). *The teaching of English as a foreign language*. London: Longmans & Greene.

Based on experiences in West Africa, provides practical ideas for most aspects of classwork of secondary students, including some related to composition.

Secondary School/West Africa.

1221. Gutierrez, C. D. (1991, April). *The effect of whole language/process writing instruction on Latino students*. Paper presented at the Annual Meeting of the AERA, Chicago, IL.

Hispanic/Process Instruction.

1222. Gutierrez, C. D. (1987). The composing process of four college-aged ethnic minority basic writers: A cognitive, sociocultural analysis. *Dissertation Abstracts International*, *49*(3), 449A.

An ethnographic study of four minority students shows that their writing processes are influenced by their prior knowledge, socialization into the academic culture, and their rhetorical knowledge and skill.

Ethnographic Research/Socio-Cultural Factors.

1223. Gutstein, S. P. (1989). Toward the assessment of communicative competence in writing: An analysis of the dialogue journal writing of Japanese adult ESL students. *Dissertation Abstracts International*, *49*(1), 83A.

Uses three measures to assess communicative competence from the dialogue journals of eighteen adult Japanese students. Findings include a baseline for discourse topic management skills in dialogue journals.

Japanese/Dialogue Journals.

1224. Gutstein, S. P. (1983). *Using language functions to measure fluency*. Washington, DC: ERIC/FLL. [ERIC ED 240 871].

Reports results of a pilot study of the functional nature of language (Shuy, 1982) in dialogue journals of adult Japanese ESL students.

Dialogue Journals/University.

1225. Gutstein, S. P., Batterman, H., Harmatz-Levin, C., Kreeft, J. E., & Meloni, C. (1983, March). *Using REAL English: Writing a dialogue journal*. Paper presented at the 17th Annual TESOL Convention, Toronto, Ontario. [ERIC ED 256 155].

Describes benefits of dialogue journal writing, namely an authentic, natural communication practice in the classroom.

Dialogue Journals.

H

1226. Haas, T., & Smoke, T. (1990). Talking to learn: Conversation workshops for ESL students. *Journal of Developmental Education*, *14*(2), 14-16.

Discusses techniques for using talking as a means to improve both oral and written competencies.

Speaking-Writing Relations/Workshop.

1227. Haas, T., Smoke, T., & Hernandez, J. (1991). A collaborative model for empowering nontraditional students. In S. Benesch (Ed.), *ESL in America: Myths and possibilities* (pp. 112-129). Portsmouth, NH: Boynton/Cook.

Describes a collaboration between teachers from two developmental writing courses, a writing laboratory peer tutor, and a social science instructor.

Collaboration.

1228. Haber, S. B. (1992). Multiple perspectives of group interaction in an ESL writing class. *Dissertation Abstracts International*, *52*(7), 2443A.

Uses an ethnographic approach to investigate small group interaction in a pre-freshman writing class. Observation of the participants' performance was systematically varied according to the observer's approach to categorizing participation activity, task negotiation, and the regularity of interaction. This description suggests that participants need to see themselves as competent in group work.

Group Work/Ethnographic Research.

1229. Haber, S. B. (1987, April). *Drawing out the story: Imagery and experience in writing*. Paper presented at the 21st Annual TESOL Convention, Miami Beach, FL.

Demonstrates how integrating imagery and life experience makes self-expression for lower-level students enjoyable.

Classroom Activities.

1230. Haber, S. B., & Mlynarczyk, R. K. (1993, April). *Finding the right stuff: Creating materials from student writing*. Paper presented at the 27th Annual TESOL Convention, Atlanta, GA.

Demonstration shows how to use student writing to create original instructional materials.

Materials.

1231. Hadaway, N. L. (1990). Writing partnerships: Teaching ESL composition through letter exchanges. *Writing Notebook: Creative Word Processing in the Classroom, 8*(1), 10-12.

Describes advantages of a letter exchange program between university students and bilingual and ESL students.

Letter Writing/Collaboration.

1232. Hadaway, N. L. (1988a). Writing apprehension among second language learners. *Dissertation Abstracts International, 49*(4), 712A.

Uses the Daley-Miller writing apprehension scale, questionnaires and writing samples to study the writing anxiety of second language students. Confirms a significant correlation between L1 and L2 writing attitudes.

Anxiety.

1233. Hadaway, N. L. (1988b, March). *Writing apprehension among second language learners*. Paper presented at the 22nd Annual TESOL Convention, Chicago, IL.

Reports results of a study to determine apprehension level in L1 and L2 writing.

Anxiety/NS-NNS Comparisons.

1234. Hadaway, N. L., & Cukor-Avila, P. (1986). *Composing in two languages: A bilingual child's response*. Paper presented at the Annual Meeting of the National Social Science Association, San Antonio, TX. [ERIC ED 280 288].

Finds that interference errors were more common than code-switching among 35 Spanish-English bilingual children in a third-grade bilingual program. Code-switching of a word or phrase was influenced by genre (personal experience and culture specific matters elicited more).

Spanish/Errors.

1235. Hadaway, N. L., & Tish, V. F. (1982). Encouraging process over product: Writing with second language learners. *English in Texas, 18*, 18-20.

Expresses preference for the use of a process approach for LEP students.

Process Instruction.

1236. Hafernik, J. J. (1990). Relationships among English writing experience, contrastive rhetoric, and English expository prose of L1 and L2 college writers. *Dissertation Abstracts International, 51*(12), 4007A.

Attempts to test the contrastive rhetoric hypothesis (Kaplan 1966, 1987). Timed writing samples from 82 college students (representing English, Norwegian, Chinese, and Japanese) were measured for syntactic and semantic features and for rhetorical pattern features (26 variables). Both writing experience as well as discourse and rhetorical pattern variables discriminate L1 and L2 groups. The former contribute more to discriminating between L1 and L2, while the latter discriminate more among the four culture groups.

Contrastive Rhetoric/Japanese/Chinese/Norwegian.

1237. Hafernik, J. J. (1984a). Composition assignments to foster communications. *TESOL Newsletter (Supplement No, 1: Writing and Composition), 18*(1), 13-14.

Discusses four criteria for designing writing assignments, and offers three

examples of assignments for high intermediate to advanced ESL students. Also, topic preferences surveyed show preference for choice of topics, use of outside sources, and reading-based writing.
Assignments/Intermediate/Advanced.

1238. Hafernik, J. J. (1984b). The how and why of peer editing in the ESL writing class. *CATESOL Occasional Papers*, *10*, 48-58. [ERIC ED 253 064].
Peer editing is useful when teachers create a climate of trust, give clear reasons for the process design activities, and otherwise manage the classroom interactions.
Peer Response/Editing.

1239. Hafernik, J. J. (1984c, March). *ESL student writers and individual goal setting*. Paper presented at the 18th Annual TESOL Convention, Houston, TX.
Uses L1 research on high level goal setting in writing to suggest how to help ESL students make operational and flexible goals while planning to write.
Planning.

1240. Hafernik, J. J. (1983, March). *Fostering real communication in the ESL writing class*. Paper presented at the 17th Annual TESOL Convention, Toronto, BC.
Emphasizes techniques for choosing writing topics and role of individual goal setting in fostering student-directed learning.
Topic.

1241. Hafernik, J. J. (1981). Writing to your audience. *TECFORS*, *4*(5), 1-2. [ERIC ED 267 647].
Describes task of writing different letters with the same purpose as effective classroom procedure for developing register awareness.
Audience/Register/Advanced.

1242. Hagemann, J. A. (1988, March). *Critical reading and writing: An ESL composition course in metacognition*. Paper presented at the 39th Annual CCCC Meeting, St. Louis, MO.
Reading-Writing Relations/Metacognition.

1243. Hagen, S., & Ege-Zavala, B. (1991). *The Prentice Hall workbook for ESL writers*. Englewood Cliffs, NJ: Prentice Hall.
Focuses on grammar and writing problems which are troublesome for ESL students. It emphasizes the structural and stylistic features which interfere with the student's ability to develop a natural and fluid writing style.
Intermediate/Textbook.

1244. Haggan, M. (1991). Spelling errors in native Arabic-speaking English majors: A comparison between remedial students and fourth year students. *System*, *19*, 45-61.
Both mispronunciation and lack of awareness of spelling rules and patterns give rise to errors made by students at both levels, although there is a significantly different distribution of errors between the two groups.
Arabic/Spelling.

1245. Haghighat, C. (1990). Literacy problems of Persian speakers. *TESL Talk*, *20*(1), 234-243.
Discusses difficulties of Persian speakers. Suggests solutions to problems in

handwriting, spelling, punctuation, and related matters.
Literacy/Persian.

1246. Hagiwara, A. L. (1984, March). *Preparing advanced ESL students to write research papers*. Paper presented at the 18th Annual TESOL Convention, Houston, TX.
Demonstrates a step-by-step procedure for teaching how to do research and a term paper on a particular subject.
Research Writing/Advanced.

1247. Hahn, C. (1986). Writing in the early stages of language learning. *English Teaching Forum, 24*(3), 34-35.
Sees psychological and practical advantages to uncontrolled writing from the very beginning of language learning.
Beginners/Free Writing.

1248. Hale, G. (1992a). *Effects of amount of time allowed on the Test of Written English*. (TOEFL Research Report 39). Princeton, NJ: Educational Testing Service.
An additional fifteen minutes of time increased mean scores slightly but did not affect the relative student standing on the TWE test.
TWE/Time.

1249. Hale, G. (1992b). *Effects of amount of time allowed on the Test of Written English*. (TOEFL Research Report 39). Princeton, NJ: Educational Testing Service.
An additional fifteen minutes of time increased mean scores slightly but did not affect the relative student standing on the TWE test.
TWE/Time.

1250. Halimah, A. (1992). EST writing: Rhetorically processed and produced. A case study of Kuwaiti learners. *Dissertation Abstracts International, 53*(2), 481A.
An empirical study of the expository writing of Kuwaiti learners seeks to resolve the duality of process and product as well as of EST rhetoric and Arabic rhetoric. Study leads to the development of a "rhetorically-oriented writing profile relevant to the needs of Arab EST learners".
ESP/Arabic/Exposition.

1251. Halio, M. P. (1989). Writing for international readers. *College Teaching, 37*, 131-134.
Describes a pedagogy for rewriting an essay aimed at an American audience for a first-language audience.
Contrastive Rhetoric.

1252. Hall, A., & Jobe, P. (1992, March). *Group approach to research papers: Cracking the academic code*. Paper presented at the 26th Annual TESOL Convention, Vancouver, BC.
Shows how to guide uninitiated students through a common-context formal research writing project.
Research Writing.

1253. Hall, C. (1991). Two types of student correction procedures in ESL composition: Their effects on global errors. *Journal of Intensive English Studies, 8*, 9-33.
Tests two types of student self-correction procedures for global errors: insert correction for discrete errors and rewrite the sentence. An experimental comparison

shows that the rewrite group showed the greatest decrease in global errors over the span of six compositions.
Feedback/Errors.

1254. Hall, C. (1990). Managing the complexity of revising across languages. *TESOL Quarterly*, *24*, 43-60.

A controlled study of four advanced ESL writers with different first languages shows similarities across languages in the specific discourse and linguistic features of their revisions of argumentative essays.
Revision/Polish/French/Norwegian/Chinese.

1255. Hall, C. (1988). Interacting with a reader: Using the strip story to develop reciprocity. *College Composition and Communication*, *39*, 353-356.

A strip story develops reciprocity because the reader negotiates a text and the writer helps with the process.
Reading-Writing Relations.

1256. Hall, C. (1988, March). *Making ESL students assets, not liabilities*. Paper presented at the 39th Annual CCCC Meeting, St. Louis, MO.
NS-NNS Comparisons.

1257. Hall, C. (1987). Revision strategies in L1 and L2 writing tasks: A case study. *Dissertation Abstracts International*, *48*(5), 1187A.

Examines the revising behaviors of L2 writers in controlled L1 and L2 writing tasks. The linguistic analysis of the L1 and L2 revisions according to the cycle, level, type, and purpose of the revision shows that the main linguistic alternations of the text were substitutions and additions, and that many revisions focused on informational and cohesive purposes. A single system is employed by writers to revise across languages and L1 and L2 knowledge interact in the revision process.
Hispanic/Revision.

1258. Hall, C. (1985, March). *The application of schema theory to advanced ESL composition*. Paper presented at the 36th Annual CCCC Meeting, Minneapolis, MN.
Schema/Advanced.

1259. Hall, D., Hawkey, R., Kenny, B., & Storer, G. (1986). Patterns of thought in scientific writing: A course in information structuring for engineering students. *ESP Journal*, *5*, 147-160.

Information-structuring courses offered at the Asian Institute of Technology in Thailand present concepts, patterns, hypotheses, and procedures for discussion which are claimed to contribute to better idea organization, text production, and text interpretation for engineering and other technology students learning English for science and technology.
Scientific Writing/Curriculum/Thai.

1260. Hall, E. (1993, April). *Sharing the mystery: Reducing your marking*. Paper presented at the 27th Annual TESOL Convention, Atlanta, GA.

Shows techniques such as the use of keys, peer response, and selective marking, to produce pro-active input and to reduce amount and adverse effect of teacher comments on papers.
Feedback/Peer Response.

relate to the social context of assessment.
Assessment.

1282. Hamp-Lyons, L. (1990b, March). *Working with assignments*. Paper presented at the 41st Annual CCCC Meeting, Chicago, IL.
Assessment/Assignments.

1283. Hamp-Lyons, L. (1989a). *Newbury House TOEFL preparation kit: Preparing for the Test of Written English*. Philadelphia: Harper Row.

Text designed to help U.S. college-bound students prepare for academic writing tests, primarily the TOEFL Test of Written English. Chapters discuss the nature of academic writing, typical topics, scoring, and encourage substantial practice on writing tasks.
Advanced/Textbook.

1284. Hamp-Lyons, L. (1989b, March). *Beyond holistic assessment: Combine assessment with diagnostic feedback*. Paper presented at the 23rd Annual TESOL Convention, San Antonio, TX.

A workshop shows how to apply and integrate multiple trait instruments and to write them for their own context.
Assessment/Feedback.

1285. Hamp-Lyons, L. (1989c, November). *English as a second dialect, bilingual, and ESL writers' essay test strategies: Pragmatic failure in a key literacy event*. Paper presented at the 79th Annual NCTE Convention, Baltimore, MD.
Assessment/Bilingual.

1286. Hamp-Lyons, L. (1988a). Construct validity. In A. Hughes, D. Porter, & C. Weir (Eds.), *ELTS Validation Project. Proceedings of the invitational Conference on the ELTS. Research Report (ii)* (pp. 10-14). London: British Council/University of Cambridge Local Examinations Syndicate.

Responds to criticism raised in the ELTS Validation Study report (Criper & Davies, 1988). Suggests using profile scoring on ELTS for diagnostic purpose since the test did not achieve validity in all cases. Also defends the writing component (M2) as fulfilling a need perceived by university faculty in Britain.
Assessment/ELTS.

1287. Hamp-Lyons, L. (1988b). The product before: Task-related influences on the writer. In P. C. Robinson (Ed.), *Academic writing: Process and product* (pp. 35-46). London: MacMillan/British Council.

Develops a model for the analysis of the essay test question, i.e. "the product before," which can cause substantial problems for the test-taker.
Assessment/Task.

1288. Hamp-Lyons, L. (1988c, March). *Questioning the validity of ESP ("discipline-specific") writing tests*. Paper presented at the 39th Annual CCCC Meeting, St. Louis, MO.
Evaluation/ESP.

1289. Hamp-Lyons, L. (1987a). *A generalized performance profile for testing specific academic purpose writing*. Paper presented at the Ninth Annual International Colloquium on Language Testing Research, Miami, FL.

1276. Hamp-Lyons, L. (1991d). Pre-text: Task-related influences on the writer. In L. Hamp-Lyons (Ed.), *Assessing second language writing in academic contexts* (pp. 87-107). Norwood, NJ: Ablex.

Describes a study of the construct validity of writing tasks used on the English Language Testing Service (ELTS) writing test. In-depth examination of two responses which challenged the task suggests the critical significance of the selection and wording of prompts in relation to the needs and background knowledge of the anticipated test audience.

Assessment/Responding/Prompts/ELTS.

1277. Hamp-Lyons, L. (1991e). Reconstructing "academic writing proficiency". In L. Hamp-Lyons (Ed.), *Assessing second language writing in academic contexts* (pp. 127-153). Norwood, NJ: Ablex.

Reports a study of the reader variable in discipline-specific academic writing proficiency tests, namely the study modules of the British Council's English Language Testing Service (ELTS). Four "English Language Qualified" readers read and scored 23 ELTS essays, each by a different writer from six different disciplines (i.e., study modules) on five different questions. Results of this small study "could not uphold a claim that writing teachers as reader-judges can respond validly to discipline-based writing and therefore we must question the usefulness of their scores".

Assessment/Responding/ELTS.

1278. Hamp-Lyons, L. (1991f). Scoring procedures for ESL contexts. In L. Hamp-Lyons (Ed.), *Assessing second language writing in academic contexts* (pp. 241-276). Norwood, NJ: Ablex.

Offers a critical analysis of holistic scoring and reviews the advantages of multiple trait scoring and portfolio assessment.

Assessment/Scoring.

1279. Hamp-Lyons, L. (1991g). Second language writing: Product, process, progress. *Papers in Applied Linguistics -- Michigan, 6*(1), 68-77.

Reviews three approaches to second language writing: product, process, and English for Academic Purposes with suggestions for the improvement of programs.

Approaches.

1280. Hamp-Lyons, L. (1991h). The writer's knowledge and our knowledge of the writer. In L. Hamp-Lyons (Ed.), *Assessing second language writing in academic contexts* (pp. 51-68). Norwood, NJ: Ablex.

Reviews issue of how much is known about ESL writers who take large-scale writing tests and how much they know about the special kind of discourse needed for such formal evaluation.

Assessment/Background Knowledge.

1281. Hamp-Lyons, L. (1990a). Second language writing: Assessment issues. In B. Kroll (Ed.), *Second language writing: Research insights for the classroom* (pp. 69-87). Cambridge: Cambridge University Press.

Gives current overview of the key issues in L2 writing assessment, emphasizing that writer, reader, task, and scoring procedure exert effects and that all by Arab students of English. *Dissertation Abstracts International, 50*(9), 2814A.

Presents results of a study of common written errors in the English syntax of Arab students.

Error Analysis/Arabic.

1269. Hamden, A. S. (1988). Coherence and cohesion in texts written in English by Jordanian students. *Dissertation Abstracts International, 51*(9), 2994A.

In the light of research and theories pertaining to textual analysis of learner texts, this study presents data about the coherence and cohesion of texts written by Jordanian university students.

Text Analysis.

1270. Hamilton, I. N., Gates, A., Lombardi, B., & Manus, J. (1989, March). *Writing: Developing language and writing skills simultaneously.* Paper presented at the 23rd Annual TESOL Convention, San Antonio, TX.

Writing by Navajo children (K-7) illustrates two levels of development when the tasks have a variety of meaningful purposes.

Children/Amer-Indian/Language Development.

1271. Hammond, J. (1987). An overview of the genre-based approach to the teaching of writing in Australia. *Australian Journal of Applied Linguistics, 10,* 163-181.

Genre.

1272. Hamp-Lyons, L. (1992, March). *Research agendas for ESL writing: Alternative assessment approaches.* Paper presented at the 26th Annual TESOL Convention, Vancouver, BC.

Discusses alternatives to current approaches in assessment to investigating variables of writer, reader, and scoring procedure.

Assessment.

1273. Hamp-Lyons, L. (Ed.). (1991a). *Assessing second language writing in academic contexts* Norwood, NJ: Ablex.

This major study of writing assessment presents seventeen previously unpublished essays (five of which are authored by the editor) dealing systematically with major variables in second language writing assessment: the writer, the task, the reader, the discourse community, and accountability as well as discussion of basic concepts and future directions. Includes a glossary of technical terms.

Assessment.

1274. Hamp-Lyons, L. (1991b). Basic concepts. In L. Hamp-Lyons (Ed.), *Assessing second language writing in academic contexts* (pp. 5-15). Norwood, NJ: Ablex.

An application of basic definitions in testing to L2 writing assessment.

Assessment.

1275. Hamp-Lyons, L. (1991c). Issues and directions in assessing second language writing in academic contexts. In L. Hamp-Lyons (Ed.), *Assessing second language writing in academic contexts* (pp. 323-329). Norwood, NJ: Ablex.

Points to further specific areas of research needed on the writers, readers, community, prompts, scoring, and accountability of nonnative English writing assessment.

Assessment/Research.

1261. Hall, E. (1992a, March). *Sharing the mystery: Reducing your marking*. Paper presented at the 26th Annual TESOL Convention, Vancouver, BC.

> Discusses techniques and principles for replacing reactive feedback with proactive input in order to help teachers become writing mentors instead of judges.
> Evaluation/Feedback.

1262. Hall, E. (1992b, March). *Situational variations in composing behaviors of academic ESL writers*. Paper presented at the 26th Annual TESOL Convention, Vancouver, BC.

> Reports study comparing behaviors of university ESL writers in test and non-test situations, finding variation resulting from writing on different occasions.
> Examination Essays/Process Research.

1263. Hall, E. (1991). Variations in composing behaviors of academic ESL writers in test and non-test situations. *TESL Canada Journal*, 8(2), 9-33. [ERIC ED 328 062].

> Observes fluctuations in complexity of texts generated, the time allocated, the pausing behavior, and the types of text alterations made by six ESL writers in a study of their processes and products.
> Process Research.

1264. Hallett, B. (1983). Correcting ESL compositions with a cassette recorder: Getting to know the reader, not the proofreader. *TESL Reporter*, 16(2), 19-32.

> Gives the advantages of this technique over marginal notes and interviews.
> Responding.

1265. Halsell, S. W. (1985). An ethnographic account of the composing behaviors of five young bilingual children. *Dissertation Abstracts International*, 46(9), 2555A.

> Investigates and describes the composing behaviors and perceptions of writing of five bilingual children in an ESL class. Claims that teacher practice and teacher sensitivity are important variables in fostering literacy.
> Ethnographic Research/Elementary/Bilingual.

1266. Halsell, S. W. (1986, April). *An ethnographic account of the composing behaviors of five young bilingual children*. Paper presented at the 67th Annual Meeting of the AERA, San Francisco, CA. [ERIC ED 273 967].

> A study of bilingual children's composing behaviors during classroom writing sessions finds that the composing behaviors of talking while writing (in Spanish), reading back, confirming questions, and concealing writing is unique to bilingual students in kindergarten through third grade. The bilinguals talked while they wrote in order to get started writing.
> Hispanic/Children/Speaking-Writing Relations.

1267. Hamayan, E. V.(1989, June).*Teaching writing to potentially English proficient students using whole language approaches*. (Program Information Guide Series Number 11). Washington, DC: Office of Bilingual Education and Minority Affairs. [ERIC ED 337 038].

> Describes innovative methods and strategies for teaching writing to potentially English proficient students (PEP).
> Whole Language.

1268. Hamdallah, R. W. (1990). Syntactic errors in written English: Study of errors made

Assessment/ELTS.

1290. Hamp-Lyons, L. (1987b). No new lamps for old yet, please . . . [In The Forum]. *TESOL Quarterly, 20,* 790-796.

    Disagrees with Horowitz's view (1986) that process approach is unsuited to teaching L2 academic writing in exam-oriented contexts or otherwise. States need for integration of process and product approaches.

    Process Instruction.

1291. Hamp-Lyons, L. (1987c). Performance profiles for academic writing. In K. M. Bailey, R. Clifford, & E. Dale (Eds.), *Language testing research: Selected papers from the 9th Annual International Colloquium on Language Testing Research* (pp. 78-92). Monterey, CA: Defense Language Institute. [ERIC ED 287 289].

    A study examines the scoring procedures of the ELTS modular academic writing test.

    Assessment/ELTS.

1292. Hamp-Lyons, L. (1987d). Raters respond to rhetoric in writing. In H. W. Dechert, & M. Raupach (Eds.), *Interlingual processes* (pp. 229-244). Tubingen: Gunter Narr Verlag.

    A study of the processes that essay raters undergo when responding to ESL papers reveals the influence of cross-cultural rhetorical transfer among readers.

    Assessment/Culture/Responding.

1293. Hamp-Lyons, L. (1987e, April). *The writing teacher/researcher: Using write-aloud protocols.* Paper presented at the 21st Annual TESOL Convention, Miami Beach, FL.

    Explains a research technique for teacher development.

    Research.

1294. Hamp-Lyons, L. (1986a). *Testing second language writing in academic settings.* Unpublished doctoral dissertation, University of Edinburgh, Edinburgh, Scotland.

    A validation study of the British Council's ELTS M2 (writing test) shows no advantage for specific-purpose over general tests of writing.

    Assessment/Academic Writing.

1295. Hamp-Lyons, L. (1986b). Testing writing across the curriculum. *Papers in Applied Linguistics -- Michigan, 2*(1), 16-29.

    Describes the development of four nine-point scales for assessing content, format, linguistic features, and task fulfillment on the British Council's ELTS writing subtest.

    Assessment/ELTS.

1296. Hamp-Lyons, L. (1986c, March). *Writing in a second culture: Forming judgements.* Paper presented at the 20th Annual TESOL Convention, Anaheim, CA.

    Raters' holistic judgments are found to be influenced not only by native culture rhetorical patterns but also by familiarity with student's native culture.

    Assessment/Culture.

1297. Hamp-Lyons, L. (1986d). Writing in a foreign language and rhetorical transfer: Influences on raters' evaluations. In P. Meara (Ed.), *Spoken language: Papers from the Annual Meeting of the British Association for Applied Linguistics, Edinburgh,*

Scotland London, ENG: CILT. [ERIC ED 348 847].

    The written comments by four raters who evaluated 20 academic essays written by NNS graduate students suggest that students may be bringing L1 rhetorical instruction to their L2 writing.

    Raters/Transfer/Evaluation.

1298. Hamp-Lyons, L. (1985, April). *Exploring the reliability of ESP writing tests*. Paper presented at the 19th Annual TESOL Convention, New York, NY.

    Discusses the British Council's ELTS module testing for discipline-specific writing ability, a major example of testing in the ESP paradigm.

    Assessment/ELTS/ESP

1299. Hamp-Lyons, L., Condon, W., & Bamberg, B. (1991, March). *Portfolios: The second stage*. Paper presented at the 42nd Annual CCCC Meeting, Boston.

    Assessment/Portfolios.

1300. Hamp-Lyons, L., & Courter, K. S. (1982, May). *Teaching the research paper to university-bound ESL students*. Mini-course presented at the 16th Annual TESOL Convention, Honolulu, HI.

    Materials and methods for teaching advanced level students the research paper, later published as Research Matters.

    Research Writing/Materials.

1301. Hamp-Lyons, L., & Courter Berry, K. (1984). *Research matters*. Boston: Heinle & Heinle.

    Student textbook to help advanced learners develop language skills necessary for doing research and understanding methods of library research in Western countries.

    Research Writing/Textbook.

1302. Hamp-Lyons, L., Foulkes, J., Urquhart, A., Prochnow, S. B., Taylor, C., Alderson, J. C., Carlson, S. B., Davidson, F., Johns, A. M., & Stansfield, C. W. (1991, March). *Colloquium on assessing academic writing: Four writing tests*. Paper presented at the 25th Annual TESOL Convention, New York, NY.

    Fourth colloquium focuses on four tests: Cambridge First Certificate, ELTS, MELAB, and TWE, giving descriptions and commentary.

    Assessment/Academic Writing.

1303. Hamp-Lyons, L., & Heasley, B. (1987). *Study writing: A course in written English for academic and professional purposes*. NY: Cambridge University Press.

    Textbook focuses on discoursal and cognitive aspects of writing for advanced students who need to write for study purposes. Divided into two parts: the first explores aspects of textual organization and the second the structure of whole texts. Offers guidelines on conventions and models of academic writing in various fields. Each chapter provides a structured approach and a variety of tasks that guide the student in how to write for different disciplines.

    Advanced/Textbook.

1304. Hamp-Lyons, L., & Henning, G. H. (1991). Communicative writing profiles: An investigation of the transferability of a multiple-trait scoring instrument across ESL writing assessment contexts. *Language Learning*, 41, 337-373.

Finds educational but not statistical grounds for using a multiple-trait scoring instrument, namely the New Profile Scale developed by the first author, in contexts other than the British Council's English Language Testing Service (ELTS).
Assessment/Scoring/ELTS.

1305. Hamp-Lyons, L., Henning, G. H., & DeMauro, G. (1988). *Construct validation of communicative writing profiles*. Paper presented at the 10th Annual International Colloquium on Language Testing Research, University of Illinois, Urbana-Champaign, IL.
See previous item.
Assessment.

1306. Hamp-Lyons, L., Horowitz, D. M., Reid, J. M., & Tedick, D. J. (1990, March). *Assessing academic writing: Focus on prompts*. Paper presented at the 24th Annual TESOL Convention, San Francisco, CA.
Third in a series of colloquia reporting on progress in assessing academic writing. Presenters focus on prompts: Tedick (effects of subject matter knowledge); Horowitz (essay examination prompts vs course assignments); Reid (topic types on the TWE); Hamp-Lyons (writers' prompt interpretation and test planning strategies).
Assessment/Topic/Prompts.

1307. Hamp-Lyons, L., Jones, C. S., Purves, A. C., & Connor, U. M. (1988, March). *Assessing academic writing: Focus on scoring*. Paper presented at the 22nd Annual TESOL Convention, Chicago, IL.
Second in a series of colloquia on alternative procedures for rating writing test answers.
Assessment/Academic Writing/Scoring.

1308. Hamp-Lyons, L., Jones, C. S., Stansfield, C. W., & Weir, C. (1987, April). *Assessing academic writing*. Colloquium presented at the 21st Annual TESOL Convention, Miami Beach, FL.
First colloquium in a series focuses on recent developments in writing process and understanding learner needs (Weir), question design (Hamp-Lyons), rater behavior (Jones), and psychometric methods (Stansfield).
Assessment.

1309. Hamp-Lyons, L., & Prochnow, S. B. (1991). The difficulty of difficulty: Prompts in writing assessment. In S. Anivan (Ed.), *Current developments in language testing* (pp. 58-76). Singapore: SEAMO Regional Language Centre.
A study of topic difficulty, prompt type, and writing performance yields results contrary to expectations. For example, mean writing scores decreased as topic difficulty increased. Moreover, students did best on prompts judged hardest by expert judges.
Prompts/Assessment.

1310. Hamp-Lyons, L., & Prochnow, S. B. (1989, March). *Person dimension, person ability, and item difficulty*. Paper presented at the 11th Annual International Language Testing Research Colloquium, San Antonio, TX.
See previous item.
Assessment/Prompts

1311. Hamp-Lyons, L., Voltmer, B., Parry, K., Davison, C., Campbell, D., & Davidson, F. (1992, March). *Portfolios with mainstreamed ESL school students*. Colloquium presented at the 26th Annual TESOL Convention, Vancouver, BC.

Fifth colloquia discusses the use of portfolios and issues of literacy, contract learning, and washback as an alternative form of assessment compatible with process instruction.

Assessment/Portfolios/Secondary School.

1312. Hanania, E. A. S., & Bacha, N. S. (1980, March). *The teaching of linking words to advanced ESL students*. Paper presented at the 14th Annual TESOL Convention, San Francisco, CA.

Argues that Arab-speaking students improve the coherence of their essays with attention to semantically-based instruction in the use of sentence connectors.

Arabic/Cohesion.

1313. Hanania, E. A. S., & Shikhani, M. (1986). Interrelationships among three tests of language proficiency: Standardized ESL, cloze, and writing. *TESOL Quarterly, 20*, 97-109.

Examines the interrelationship among three tests of language proficiency: a standardized ESL test, a cloze test and a written composition test. Regression analysis indicates high correlation between each pair of tests. Results suggest that the cloze test is a valuable supplement as a language proficiency test.

Assessment/Evaluation.

1314. Hansen-Stain, L. (1989). Orality/literacy and group differences in second language acquisition. *Language Learning, 9*, 469-496.

Studies spoken and written English of ESL students from predominantly oral societies (South Pacific and Asian), finding greater personal involvement than in predominantly literate societies.

Speaking-Writing Relations/Tonga/Samoa/Asian.

1315. Hanson-Smith, E. (1993, April). *Word-processed composition ideas*. Paper presented at the 27th Annual TESOL Convention, Atlanta, GA.

Gives techniques and lesson ideas for word processing which are compatible with a process approach to writing.

Word Processing.

1316. Hanson-Smith, E. (1990a). Word-processed compositions. *TESOL Newsletter, 24*(3), 23.

Describes method and effectiveness of ESL word-processed composition classes.

Computers/Word Processing.

1317. Hanson-Smith, E. (1990b). Word-processed compositions, part II. *TESOL Newsletter, 24*(4), 23.

Describes several applications of word processing in support of the teaching of ESOL composition.

Computers/Word Processing.

1318. Hantrakul, C. (1990). English tense and aspect usage in controlled written discourse by nonnative speakers. *Dissertation Abstracts International, 51*(10), 3349A.

Results from two cloze tests of tense/aspect usage in expository discourse suggest that Japanese learners had significant problems with the present perfective form, tending to rely on the local level of linguistic context rather than global context whereas native speakers used both local and global factors.

Usage/Japanese.

1319. Haque, A. R. (1981). *An evaluative study of Pakistani students written English ability*. Unpublished master's thesis, University of Hawaii, Honolulu, HI.

Compares the language proficiency in written products by Pakistani graduate students with twelfth-grade native English speakers, finding the former exhibit ninth-grade level proficiency.

Evaluation/Pakistani.

1320. Harder, B. D. (1984). Cultural attitudes in discourse analysis. *The Canadian Journal of Linguistics*, *29*(2), 115-130.

Analysis of Japanese writing is provided to illustrate the claim that advanced ESL students have to overcome not only the difficulties caused by linguistic differences between their native and target languages but also the complexities of a stylistic, cognitive, and cultural nature. Cultural values and traditions influence the rhetorical devices used by ESL writers.

Advanced/Culture/Japanese.

1321. Hargett, G. R. (1992). An application of transfer theory to the study of English as a Second Language errors of university-level international students. *Dissertation Abstracts International*, *52*(8), 2833A.

Argues that transfer should be considered as a source of error in second language learning, based on an experiment in which partial support was found. Reports that, with respect to writing, errors in the use of the plural -s by Spanish speakers of several proficiency levels conformed to transfer expectations.

Transfer/Error Analysis/Hispanic.

1322. Harley, B. (1989). Transfer in the written compositions of French immersion students. In H. W. Dechert, & M. Raupach (Eds.), *Transfer in language production* (pp. 3-19). NY: Ablex.

Investigates the use of locative and directional expressions in the written compositions of native speakers of French and the written French compositions of English-speaking students in a French immersion program in Montreal. Finds that second language learners show more systematic reliance on prepositions than native speakers and that they distribute semantic information across syntactic.

L1 Influence/French.

1323. Harrell, B. (1986). Communicative writing methods as culture barrier-breakers. *TESOL Newsletter*, *20*(6), 17-18.

Describes several classroom activities, related to all aspects of the composing process, for bridging the culture barrier between students.

Culture.

1324. Harrington, M. (1988, March). *The treatment of paraphrasing skills in EAP writing texts*. Paper presented at the 22nd Annual TESOL Convention, Chicago, IL.

Finds a tendency to confound global with sentential skills in textbook

explanations of paraphrasing.
Paraphrase Writing/Textbook.

1325. Harris, D. P. (1990). The use of "organizing sentences" in the structure of paragraphs in science textbooks. In U. M. Connor, & A. M. Johns (Eds.), *Coherence in writing: Research and pedagogical perspectives* (pp. 67-86). Alexandria, VA: TESOL.

Describes a study of the organizing functions of the opening sentence and of the common tendencies of additional organizing sentences within paragraphs of natural science textbooks for college undergraduates. Findings show five types of opening sentences, three of which account for 85% of the opening sentence types. Opening sentences are generally the organizing sentence in paragraphs.
Coherence/Paragraph.

1326. Harris, D. P. (1983, March). *The organizational patterns of adult EFL student narratives: Report of a pilot study*. Paper presented at the 17th Annual Convention of TESOL, Toronto, Ontario. [ERIC ED 275 150].

Analysis of words in six thematic elements written by college EFL students who viewed a silent cartoon film reveals three basic patterns of well-organized accounts that are unrelated to either holistic ratings, general EFL level, or language background.
Narration.

1327. Harris, M., & Silva, T. (1993). Tutoring ESL students: Issues and options. *College Composition and Communication, 44*, 525-537.

Discusses ten issues that NES tutors and composition teachers are likely to encounter when working with ESL students in one-to-one settings. Focuses on the grammatical and rhetorical differences between NES and NNS writers that may be unexpected by tutor trainees.
Tutoring/Conferencing/Writing Center.

1328. Harshbarger, B. (1993, April). *O minus 1: An output hypothesis*. Paper presented at the 27th Annual TESOL Convention, Atlanta, GA.

offers a corollary to Krashen's input hypothesis, namely that speaking and writing tasks should demand a little less than the learner knows.
Output Hypothesis/Theory.

1329. Harshbarger, B. (1981, March). *Lateral thinking in the writing class*. Paper presented at the 15th Annual TESOL Convention, Detroit, MI.

Addresses the problem of insufficient quantity in ESL writing and proposes techniques based on DeBono's educational ideas.
Invention/Instruction.

1330. Hartfiel, V. F., Hughey, J. B., Wormuth, D. R., & Jacobs, H. L. (1985). *Learning ESL composition*. Boston: Heinle & Heinle.

Contains writing exercises that examine the writing process, audience, reader-expectations, paragraph development, global coherence, revision, and the purposes for writing. Exercises are arranged for students to work independently at their own pace and collaboratively, and allow for diagnosis of writing strengths and weaknesses.
Intermediate/Advanced/Textbook.

1331. Hartford, B. S. (1978, April). *Error analysis and acquisition hierarchies: The written English of Poles*. Paper presented at the 12th Annual TESOL Convention, Mexico City, Mexico.

    Finds identifiable hierarchies of errors as well as predictable error variability in compositions of Polish learners of English.

    Errors/Polish.

1332. Hartmann, P. (1989). *Clues to culture: A cross-cultural reading/writing book*. San Francisco, CA: Random House.

    Elementary writing/grammar skills are practiced after students read detective stories and discuss information about North American culture.

    Beginners/Adult Education/Textbook.

1333. Hartmann, P., & Mentel, J. (1990). *Interactions access: A reading/writing book*. St. Louis, MO: McGraw-Hill.

    Integrated thematically with a basal textbook series, this volume ombines reading and writing in a single text. Reading occupies three-fourths of each chapter while writing practice is used to recycle and reinforce vocabulary and grammar.

    Textbook/Beginners.

1334. Hatch, E. (1992). *Discourse and language education*. Cambridge: Cambridge University Press.

    An introductory textbook in applied linguistics which reviews analytic procedures for observing and describing discourse. Three chapters: "Rhetorical Analysis," Coherence, Cohesion, Deixis, and Discourse," and "Discourse Mode and Syntax" make reference to various analyses of written text produced by ESL learners.

    Discourse Analysis.

1335. Hatch, E. (1984). Theoretical review of discourse and interlanguage. In A. Davies, C. Criper, & A. Howatt (Eds.), *Interlanguage* (pp. 190-203). Edinburgh: Edinburgh University Press.

    Reviews studies of cohesion and coherence in second language discourse.

    Review/Cohesion.

1336. Haugen, E. (1986). Bilinguals have more fun! *Journal of English Linguistics*, *19*, 106-112.

    Points out that even writers isolated for years from L1 culture produce texts in their L2 with noticeable native influences.

    L1 Influence/Bilingual.

1337. Hauptman, P. C. (1988). Teaching writing to beginning adult ESL students: A cognitive view. In G. H. Irons, *Second language acquisition: Selected readings in theory and practice* (pp. 144-162). Ontario, Canada: The Canadian Modern Language Review.

    See next item.

    Beginners/Form.

1338. Hauptman, P. C. (1980). Teaching writing to beginning adult ESL students: A cognitive view. *Canadian Modern Language Review*, *36*, 693-712.

    Provides a plan for teaching students the fundamentals of organization and coherence based on a spiral method of sequencing lessons. The student proceeds from

chronological ordering to spatial development to contrast then to cause end effect. This sequence is repeated several times until student learns the appropriate patterns.
Curriculum/Beginners/Coherence.

1339. Hawkes, L., & Richards, B. (1977). A workshop approach to teaching composition. *TEAL Occasional Papers*, *1*, 16.

Describes use of adapted version of the Garrison approach to teaching composition to ESL students. Claims that this informal and student-centered approach is beneficial for ESL students.
Conferencing.

1340. Hawrani, S. (1974). *Contrastive analysis of meaning relationships and linking devices in English and Arabic*. Unpublished master's thesis, American University, Beirut, Lebanon.
Cohesion/Contrastive Rhetoric/Arabic.

1341. Hayes, C. W. (Ed.). (1993). *Migrating toward literacy* Washington, DC: ERIC/RCS. [ERIC ED 357 634].

Provides a guide to strategies for teaching reading and writing to reluctant and hesitant LEP students, drawn from experiences with six elementary schools in San Antonio in a special project.
Elementary/Hispanic/Reading-Writing Relations.

1342. Hayes, C. W., & Kessler, C. (1982, May). *ON "doing" reading and writing: A second language workshop*. Paper presented at the 16th Annual TESOL Convention, Honolulu, HI.

Presents strategies for teaching literate skills.
Literacy.

1343. Haynes, L. A. (1990a). Variability between the spoken and written narratives of nonnative English speakers. In L. Bouton, & Y. Kachru (Eds.), *Pragmatics and language learning. Vol. 1* (pp. 115-128). Urbana-Champaign: University of Illinois Press.
Speaking-Writing Relations/Narration.

1344. Haynes, L. A. (1990b). *Variability in the spoken and written narratives of nonnative English speakers*. Unpublished master's thesis, Texas A & M University, College Station, TX.
Speaking-Writing Relations.

1345. Hayward, M. (1990). Evaluations of essay prompts by nonnative speakers of English. *TESOL Quarterly*, *24*, 753-758.

Finds that for ESL college composition students prefer longer prompts although the readability of the prompt was found not to be significant factor.
Academic Writing/Prompts.

1346. Hayward, N. M. (1989, March). *An ESL textbook writer's developing sense of audience*. Paper presented at the 23rd Annual TESOL Convention, San Antonio, TX.

A case study of audience awareness and adaptation of one ESL textbook writer's developing sense of audience.
Audience.

1347. Hayward, N. M. (1992a, March). *Conferences with ESL students*. Paper presented at the 43rd Annual CCCC Meeting, Cincinnati, OH.

    Examines three conferences with ESL students, using Fanselow's FOCUS system.

    Conferencing.

1348. Hayward, N. M. (1992b). Conferencing with ESL students. *WATESOL Working Papers*, 37-51.

    Reports two excerpts from a larger study about the interactions between the researcher and students in conferences held routinely during a college writing course. Makes several practical suggestions about conferencing with ESL students.

    Conferencing.

1349. Hayward, N. M. (1991, March). *Training teachers to be better conferencers*. Paper presented at the 25th Annual TESOL Convention, New York, NY.

    Presents a model of conference interaction between instructors and ESL students in order to help teachers analyze and adapt their own speech patterns and behavior.

    Conferencing/Teacher Preparation.

1350. Hayward, N. M. (1991). The reluctant writer: A descriptive study of student behavior and motivation in the composition class. *Dissertation Abstracts International*, *51*(6), 2054A.

    Investigates resistance or reluctance to write among native and non-native college writing students. No single profile of resistant writers was found, although resistant writers tended to either fight or flee from responses by instructors, suggesting a lack of engagement with their written work.

    NS-NNS Comparisons/Conferencing/Motivation.

1351. He, A. W. (1991, March). *Exploring the genre of peer review*. Paper presented at the 25th Annual TESOL Convention, New York, NY.

    Provides a linguistic description of L1 and L2 peer review texts, searching for critical features in order to determine whether peer review is a functionally motivated genre.

    Peer Response/Genre.

1352. He, G. Q. (1989). Let the students write actively. *English Teaching Forum*, *27*(2), 36-37.

    Suggests ways of converting students into active writers.

    Motivation/Chinese.

1353. Healy, D., & Bosher, S. (1992). ESL tutoring: Bridging the gap between curriculum-based and writing center models of peer tutoring. *College ESL*, *2*(2), 25-32.

    Advocates integrating ESL tutors into the subject matter classroom instead of tutoring in the context of a writing center.

    Tutoring/Writing Center.

1354. Heath, R. (1986). Teaching information sequence in scientific writing to primary ESL pupils in Singapore. *Working Papers in Linguistics and Language Teaching*, *9*, 58-68.

    Discusses the difficulties of teaching children how to organize information

before writing. Examines three ways of teaching information sequence: brainstorming and reordering, text analysis and parallel writing, and constructive matrices. Global cohesion and organization of information are emphasized, while spelling and grammar are deemphasized.
Scientific Writing/Singapore/Cohesion.

1355. Heath, R. (1985). *Teaching information sequence in scientific writing to primary ESL students in Singapore.* Paper presented at a regional Seminar of the SEAMEO Regional Language Center, Singapore. [ERIC ED 262 602].

Advocates teaching 10-11 year old ESL students preparatory activities for information sequencing in order to improve their expository writing ability.
Exposition/Children.

1356. Heath, S. B. (1985). Literacy or literate skills? Considerations for ESL/EFL learners. In P. Larson, E. L. Judd, & D. S. Messerschmitt (Eds.), *On TESOL '84: A brave new world for TESOL* (pp. 15-28). Washington, DC: TESOL.

Proposes a radical restructuring of the teaching of writing in ESL/EFL classes to bring skills in written language in line with oral language learning, arguing that becoming literate is not learning to read and write but learning to talk reading and writing.
Literacy/Speaking-Writing Relations.

1357. Heaton, J. B. (1990). *Writing through pictures.* NY: Addison Wesley/Longman.

This text uses exercises to guide students from controlled to free composition writing. Many writing tasks, from informal letter writing to writing reports on scientific process, are practiced.
Intermediate/Textbook.

1358. Hedge, T. (1988). *Writing.* Oxford: Oxford University Press.

Resource book offers the classroom teacher guidance about using writing tasks within the framework of the process of writing. It discusses how classroom activities help learners develop different aspects of writing ability, especially authoring and crafting.
Materials/Process Instruction.

1359. Hedgecock, J., & Atkinson, D. (1993). Differing reading-writing relationships in L1 and L2 literacy development? *TESOL Quarterly, 27,* 329-333.

Describes 2 parallel school-based literacy studies of L1 (university) and L2 (mainly Asian university ESL) students. Whereas the academic expository writing proficiency of NES students was significantly related to many of the reading habits measured, no significant regression results were obtained in the L2 study.
Reading-Writing Relations.

1360. Hedgecock, J., & Lefkowitz, N. (1992). Collaborative oral/aural revision in foreign language writing. *Jounal of Second Language Writing, 1*(3), 255-276.

An experimental study of college-level writers of French as a second language shows higher scores for the products of those who revised collaboratively in comparsion to those who revised based on teacher written comments.
Collaboration.

1361. Hedgecock, J., & Pucci, S. (1993). Whole language applications to ESL in secondary

and higher education. *TESOL Journal, 3*(2), 22-26.
    Focuses mainly on reading rather than writing whole language.
    Whole Language.

1362. Heim, A. L. (1971). *The use of English as a second language techniques in teaching writing in open admissions colleges*. Unpublished doctoral dissertation, University of Illinois, Urbana-Champaign, Urbana, IL.
    Discusses the use of TESL materials and methodology for college freshman who speak a nonstandard dialect and who experience difficulty writing.
    Methods/Materials.

1363. Heiser, P. (1992, March). *Revision: Empowering the beginning writer*. Paper presented at the 26th Annual TESOL Convention, Vancouver, BC.
    Workshop develops activities and materials for different stages of the writing process: learner training, peer response work, and self-revision.
    Process Instruction/Beginners.

1364. Heiser, P. (1991, March). *Revision: Empowering the beginning writer*. Paper presented at the 25th Annual TESOL Convention, New York, NY.
    Shows how peer group work coupled with learner training at the prewriting and initial drafting stages facilitates process for beginner and intermediate writers.
    Revision/Group Work/Beginners.

1365. Heller, M. D. (1983, March). *Writing toward a world*. Paper presented at the 17th Annual TESOL Convention, Toronto, Ontario.
    Explores the meanings of revision as a transpersonal and intentional act with social and political implications for the language learner.
    Revision.

1366. Henderson, K. (1990). *Write to the point!* Reading, MA: Addison-Wesley.
    Text integrates reading, speaking, and grammar while focusing on writing. It enables students to become competent and successful writers of English. It features reading passages, abundant writing activities, and communicative activities in chapters that deal with different types of writing.
    Beginners/Textbook.

1367. Henderson, R. T., & Vernick, J. A. (1980, March). *Problems in learning English as a foreign writing system*. Paper presented at the 14th Annual TESOL Convention, San Francisco, CA.
    Describes way to discover decoding strategies of literate learners new to the Roman alphabet.
    Orthography.

1368. Hendrichsen, L. E. (1981). Ten perfect sentences. *English Language Teaching Journal, 35*(3), 307-310.
    Proposes starting rather than ending with attention to sentence form through an initial assignment to write ten perfect sentences on a given topic.
    Form/Assignments.

1369. Hendrichsen, L. E. (1978). Distinctive features of written English. *TESL Reporter, 11*(4), 1-3, 12-14. [ERIC ED 159 893].
    Reviews design features of written language and characteristic linguistic

structures that are important to learn when shifting from an oral to a written register.
Register/Speaking-Writing Relations.

1370. Hendrichsen, L. E., & Pack, A. C. (1992). *Sentence construction: Writing, combining, and editing standard English sentences*. (Second Ed.). Boston: Heinle & Heinle.

A sentence writing exercise book for elementary proficiency learners.
Beginners/Textbook.

1371. Hendrickson, J. M. (1980). The treatment of error in written work. *Modern Language Journal, 64*, 216-221.

Provides guidelines and suggestions for dealing with written errors in the adult foreign language classroom. Claims that constructive feedback in the form of direct or indirect correction is helpful.
Error Treatment.

1372. Hendrickson, J. M. (1979, March). *Selective correction strategies of written errors*. Paper presented at the 13th Annual TESOL Convention, Boston.

Demonstrates various strategies for correcting L2 written errors.
Error Treatment.

1373. Hendrickson, J. M. (1978). Error correction in foreign language teaching: Recent theory, research, and practice -- An historical perspective of learner errors. *Modern Language Journal, 62*, 387-398.

Discusses the place of error correction in foreign language teaching, not exclusively in written work. Claims that certain kinds of errors should be corrected, error correction should be at intervals, and correction should be by teacher and peers.
Error Treatment.

1374. Hendrickson, J. M. (1977). The effects of error correction treatments upon adequate and accurate communication in the written compositions of adult learners of English as a second language. *Dissertation Abstracts International, 37*(11), 7002A.

Examines, first, the major problems of foreign students writing in English and, secondly, the effects of two types of error correction on communicative adequacy and linguistic accuracy of compositions. Results show major problems were a lack of sufficient knowledge, difficulty in spelling, misuse of prepositions, lack of concord, and incorrect word order. No significant difference was found in effects of two types of error correction studied.
Error Treatment.

1375. Henner-Stanchina, C. (1985). From reading to writing acts. In P. Riley (Ed.), *Discourse and learning* (pp. 91-104). Longman: London.

Suggests methods for intermediate ESL students to learn to read and write academic texts.
Intermediate/Academic Writing/Reading-Writing Relations.

1376. Henning, G. H. (1992). *Scalar analysis of the Test of Written English* . (TOEFL Research Report 38). Princeton, NJ: Educational Testing Service.

Use of Rasch model scalar analysis of the TWE rating scale suggests that the intervals between the TWE scale steps are uniform and interval size appropriate.
TWE/Rating.

1377. Henning, G. H. (1991). Issues in evaluating and maintaining an ESL writing assessment program. In L. Hamp-Lyons (Ed.), *Assessing second language writing in academic contexts* (pp. 279-291). Norwood, NJ: Ablex.

Discusses a variety of issues associated with maintaining a program of writing evaluation, especially concerns for validity and reliability which merit much more careful attention than is usually the case.

Evaluation/Programs.

1378. Henning, G. H. (1985, April). *Latent-trait analysis of holistic ratings of language*. Paper presented at the 19th Annual TESOL Convention, New York, NY.

Reports procedures, results, and advantages of latent-trait analysis of oral or written language production.

Assessment/Objective Measures.

1379. Henning, G. H. (1981). Comprehensive assessment of language proficiency and achievement among learners of English as a foreign language. *TESOL Quarterly, 15*, 157-166.

Study examines optional combination of subtests for predicting proficiency in English at the end of the third year secondary stage in Egypt. Identifies best predictors which include grammar accuracy, reading comprehension, vocabulary and composition subscales.

Evaluation/Arabic/Proficiency.

1380. Henning, G. H., & Davidson, F. (1987). Scalar analysis of composition ratings. In K. M. Bailey (Ed.), *Language testing research: Selected papers from the 1986 colloquium*. Monterey, CA: Defense Language Institute. [ERIC ED 287 285].

Study evaluates the UCLA ESL composition grading scale. Results indicate high measurement accuracy but some misfit of subjects in content and cohesion in mid-range performance.

Evaluation.

1381. Henning, G. H., & Taylor, C. (1991, March). *Current research on the TOEFL, TWE, and TSE*. Paper presented at the 25th Annual TESOL Convention, New York, NY.

Reviews current research on the TWE and other ETS programs for testing English language ability.

Assessment/TWE.

1382. Hepworth, G. R. (1979a). Rhetorical competence and EST discourse. In C. Yorio, K. Perkins, & J. Schachter (Eds.), *On TESOL '79: The learner in focus* (pp. 148-159). Washingtron, DC: TESOL.

Paper presents the results of an analysis of EST discourse using the Pitkin's Discourse Bloc model. Results show that the model predicts the functions in the introductions to experiment reports.

ESP/Discourse Analysis/Academic Writing.

1383. Hepworth, G. R. (1979b, March). *"Rhetorical competence" and EST discourse*. Paper presented at the 13th Annual TESOL Convention, Boston.

Uses Pitkin's Discourse Bloc Analysis (1967) to identify units in the introduction to experiment reports in several science fields.

Discourse Analysis/ESP.

1384. Herendeen, W. (1986). Of tricksters and dilemmas in ESL writing classes: An epistolary account. *Journal of Basic Writing*, 5(2), 49-58.

    Explains how to use trickster and dilemma tales in the ESL classroom to develop and initiate written assignments and discussions.

    Reading-Writing Relations/Assignments.

1385. Hermann, A. W. (1986). Teaching ESL students writing using word processing. *TESOL Newsletter, Supplement on computer-assisted language learning*, 20(1), 5-6.

    Shares experiences about ESL students who learned word processing.

    Computers/Word Processing.

1386. Hermann, A. W. (1985, December). *Word processing in the ESL class: Integrating reading, writing, listening, and speaking skills*. Paper presented at the Annual Meeting of the Modern Language Association, Chicago, IL. [ERIC ED 274 980].

    · Advises using computers in the ESL classroom to improve all language skills in a writing workshop atmosphere.

    Computers/Word Processing.

1387. Herzog, M. (1988). Issues in writing proficiency assessment: The government scale. In P. Lowe, & C. W. Stansfield (Eds.), *Second language proficiency assessment: Current issues* (pp. 149-177). Englewood Cliffs, NJ: Prentice Hall Regents.

    Discusses the development since 1980 of a writing proficiency assessment scale for government language schools and the need to further improve guidelines and measurement instruments through research.

    Assessment.

1388. Heuring, D. L. (1984a). *The revision strategies of skilled and unskilled ESL writers*. Unpublished master's thesis, University of Hawaii, Honolulu, HI.

    See next item.

    Revision.

1389. Heuring, D. L. (1984b, March). *The revision strategies of skilled and unskilled ESL writers: Five case studies*. Paper presented at the 18th Annual TESOL Convention, Houston, TX.

    Identifies and categorizes different revision types derived from case studies and shows how some correspond to better writing.

    Revision.

1390. Hewins, C. (1986). Writing in a foreign language: Motivation and the process approach. *Foreign Language Annals*, 19, 219-223.

    Presents techniques from writing across the curriculum adapted to the foreign language classroom. Describes such strategies as assigning relevant topics, process-approach to writing, prewriting, responding to writing, feedback, and proofreading. The author espouses process-approach to writing and motivating students by creating supportive atmosphere in the classroom as the two major elements of successful foreign language writing class.

    Classroom Activities/Motivation.

1391. Hickey, C. C. (1989, November). *Case study: Error analysis of an adult ESL writer*. Paper presented at the 79th Annual NCTE Convention, Baltimore, MD.

    Error Analysis.

1392. Higa, T. K. (1979). *A teacher's manual of teaching techniques for composition*. Unpublished master's thesis, University of Hawaii, Honolulu, HI.
    Pedagogy/Teacher Preparation.

1393. Hildenbrand, J. L. (1985). Carmen: A case study of an ESL writer. *Dissertation Abstracts International*, 46(12), 3637A.
    Examines the writing processes of a Hispanic woman in two different classrooms, and analyzes the strategies used and the product produced in light of different teachers' orientations and students' own preferred style versus institutional style.
    Hispanic/Process Research.

1394. Hildenbrand, J. L. (1983). *ESL writers revising*. Paper presented at the 17th Annual TESOL Convention, Toronto, Ontario.
    Findings from case studies of two ESL writers show that inexperienced writers make changes in meaning and global structure when conditions are encouraging.
    Revision.

1395. Hill, S. S., Soppelsa, B. F., & West, G. K. (1982). Teaching ESL students to read and write experimental-research reports. *TESOL Quarterly*, 16, 333-347.
    Discusses experimental research paper organization and describes a method for teaching reading and writing of such papers to ESL students.
    Research Writing/Reading-Writing Relations/ESP.

1396. Hinds, J. (1990). Inductive, deductive, quasi-inductive: Expository writing in Japanese, Korean, Chinese, and Thai. In U. M. Connor, & A. M. Johns (Eds.), *Coherence in writing: Research and pedagogical perspectives* (pp. 87-109). Alexandria, VA: TESOL.
    Examines expository writing in Japanese, Korean, Chinese and Thai for organizational principles. Concludes (1) that although the writings differ from expectations of English-speaking audience, they have an internal logic, which is evident to native speakers; and (2) that the inductive-deductive parameter is unsuitable to characterize writings in these language since many of them are quasi-inductive.
    Contrastive Rhetoric/Japanese/Korean/Chinese/Thai.

1397. Hinds, J. (1987). Reader versus writer responsibility: A new typology. In U. M. Connor, & R. B. Kaplan (Eds.), *Writing across languages: Analysis of L$_2$ text* (pp. 141-152). Reading, MA: Addison-Wesley.
    Examines the notion of reader versus writer responsibility in written texts. Claims the writer in English is responsible to give unity and present ideas clearly but in Japanese the reader is responsible for getting the required information. Implications for ESL writing classes for Japanese and other Asian students cited.
    Contrastive Rhetoric/Japanese/Asian.

1398. Hinds, J. (1983). Contrastive rhetoric: Japanese and English. *Text*, 3(2), 183-195.
    An analysis of Japanese rhetorical organization supports the contrastive rhetoric hypothesis. A major rhetorical style in Japanese, termed ki-sho-ten-ketsu, that does not exist in English is explicated. In this style, ki introduces the topic, show develops the topic, ten forms an abrupt transition or a vaguely related point, and

ketsu concludes the topic. Potential problems for English as a second language learners are noted with ten, since it introduces information considered irrelevant by Western audiences, and with ketsu, since "conclusion" is defined differently in Japanese than in English.
Contrastive Rhetoric/Japanese.

1399. Hinds, J. (1982, May). *Contrastive rhetoric -- Japanese and English.* Paper presented at the 16th Annual TESOL Convention, Honolulu, HI.

Explains three rhetorical styles in Japanese. Presents two problems of Japanese ESL students: ten which introduces irrelevant information and ketsu which differs in meaning from the English "conclusion."
Contrastive Rhetoric/Japanese.

1400. Hinds, J. (1980). Japanese expository prose. *Papers in Linguistics, 13,* 77-99.

Discusses one type of popular writing style in Japanese, "return to baseline theme," untypical of English paragraphs.
Contrastive Rhetoric/Japanese.

1401. Hinkel, E. (1992, March). *Insight into ESL writing: What determines text clarity?* Paper presented at the 26th Annual TESOL Convention, Vancouver, BC.

Reports a study in which the majority of ESL college students preferred a NNS learner text, which had been placed at the intermediate level of proficiency on grounds of clarity, persuasiveness, and quality, over a professionally-written NS text.
Text Analysis/NS-NNS Comparisons.

1402. Hirokawa, K. (1986a). An investigation of native/non-native speaker examination essays. *Papers in Applied Linguistics -- Michigan, 1*(2), 105-131.

A comparison of exam essays by native and nonnative students of linguistics which show highly conventionalized linguistic, discoural and pragmatic elements suggests that it is necessary to learn some task-specific skills in order to write good in-class essay exams.
NS-NNS Comparisons/Examination Essays.

1403. Hirokawa, K. (1986b, March). *An investigation of native-speaker and non-native speaker essay examinations.* Paper presented at the 20th Annual TESOL Convention, Anaheim, CA.

Exams written for a linguistics class show need for both linguistic proficiency and task-specific writing skills.
NS-NNS Comparisons/Examination Essays.

1404. Hirokawa, K., & Swales, J. M. (1986). The effects of modifying the formality level of ESL composition questions. *TESOL Quarterly, 20,* 343-345.

When a topic is phrased academically rather than in a more conversational manner, essay test answers by a small sample of nonnative university students exhibit a high proportion of Greco-Latin vocabulary, fewer first person pronouns, and fewer words in response to the topic.
Register/Prompts.

1405. Hirsch, L. M. (1989, November). *Are principles of writing across the curriculum applicable to ESL students in content courses? Research findings.* Paper presented at the 79th Annual NCTE Convention, Baltimore, MD. [ERIC ED 319 264].

Reports results of a study that employed learning talking to write procedures in content course tutorials.
Speaking-Writing Relations/WAC.

1406. Hirsch, L. M. (1988). Language across the curriculum: A model for ESL students in content courses. In S. Benesch (Ed.), *Ending remediation: Linking ESL and content in higher education* (pp. 67-89). Washington, DC: TESOL.
Presents theoretical and practical implications of a tutoring model for advanced ESL students that uses language skills of talking and writing to increase comprehension of course material. Discusses success of model.
Tutoring/Speaking-Writing Relations.

1407. Hirsch, L. M. (1987). The use of expressive function talk and writing as a learning tool with Adult ESL students across the curriculum. *Dissertation Abstracts International, 47*(8), 2927A.
Expressive talk and writing significantly increased comprehension of content in community college courses.
Speaking-Writing Relations/Expressive Writing.

1408. Hirsch, L. M., & Diaz, D. M. (1990, March). *ESL students in content courses: Talking, writing and learning.* Paper presented at the 24th Annual TESOL Convention, San Francisco, CA.
Reports on research findings that demonstrate the value of talk and writing in a student-centered environment with ESL students in content courses. Presenters propose enhancing the success of "sheltered," or specially-designed, linguistically-enhanced content courses by integrating research findings into the pedagogy of these courses.
Speaking-Writing Relations/Content.

1409. Ho, B. (1992). Journal writing as a tool for reflective learning: Why students like it. *English Teaching Forum, 30*(4), 40-42.
Introduces journal writing as a means of reflecting on learning about research paper writing. Reports students found the activity useful and interesting.
Journal Writing.

1410. Ho, W. K. (1973). An investigation of errors in English compositions of some pre-university students in Singapore, with suggestions for the teaching of written English. *RELC Journal, 4*(1), 48-65.
Errors in compositions of Chinese-speaking pre-university students in Singapore are primarily with verbs, noun number, lexical items, and function words.
Error Analysis/Chinese.

1411. Hobelman, P., & Wiriyachitra, A. (1990). A balanced approach to the teaching of intermediate-level writing skills to EFL students. *English Teaching Forum, 28*(4), 37-39.
Offers a compromise between a traditional "read-analyze-write" approach and a communicative/process approach to intermediate level composition.
Intermediate/Thai.

1412. Hochstein, D., & Rounds, P. L. (1993, April). *Streamlining the writing placement procedure.* Paper presented at the 27th Annual TESOL Convention, Atlanta, GA.

Discusses an accurate but more efficient mechanism for placement at one IEP.
Placement/IEP.

1413. Hodor, M. J. (1981, May). *The foreign student's first research paper*. Paper presented at the Annual NAFSA Meeting, Nashville, TN.
Research Writing.

1414. Hodson, J. (1988). Writing fiction: Three case studies of writers of English as a foreign language. *English Teaching Forum, 26*(2), 25-27.
Outlines an approach to teaching EFL composition that uses fiction writing as a way for students to become more personally involved and interested in writing.
Creative Writing.

1415. Hoffer, B. (1975). Towards implicational scales for use in Chicano English composition. In J. D. Brantley (Eds.), *Papers in Southwest English 1: Research techniques and prospects* (pp. 59-71). San Antonio, TX: Trinity University. [ERIC ED 111 209].
Claims a contrastive analysis of Mexican-American dialect and standard English leads to an understanding of error patterns in written English.
Errors/Assessment/Hispanic.

1416. Hoffman, L. (1988). Intercultural writing: A pragmatic analysis of style. In W. van Peer (Ed.), *The taming of the text: Explorations in language, literature and culture* (pp. 152-175). London: Routledge.
Demonstrates textual problems and their stylistic solutions when writer and reader belong to different cultures.
Style/Culture/Text Analysis.

1417. Holdrich, D. L. (1978). *The development of a self-instructional handbook to teach punctuation to ESL students*. Unpublished master's thesis, UCLA, Los Angeles, CA.
Pedagogy/Mechanics/Editing.

1418. Holes, C. (1984). Textual approximation in the teaching of academic writing to Arab students: A contrastive approach. In J. M. Swales, & H. Mustafa (Eds.), *English for Specific Purposes in the Arab world* (pp. 228-242). Birmingham, UK: University of Aston, Language Studies Unit.
Discusses linguistic differences and stylistic preferences in four versions of a sample text by a Yemeni student on the topic of contrasting the British and Yemini educational systems. Concludes that each version is a gradual approximation of the textual cohesion and tone expected of an English academic essay.
Cohesion/Style/Arabic.

1419. Holliday, C. W., Hughey, J. B., & Wormuth, D. R. (1986, March). *ESL composition: Testing and teaching*. Workshop presented at the 20th Annual TESOL Convention, Anaheim, CA.
Part I practices evaluating essays with the Profile (Jacobs, et al. 1981); Part II gives practice in techniques that promote student writing, based on the Profile.
Assessment.

1420. Holm, J. (1985, April). *The Creole core: Grammatical interference in college composition*. Paper presented at the 19th Annual TESOL Convention, New York, NY.

Finds twenty common grammatical features of Caribbean Creole in college English compositions.
Grammar/Creole.

1421. Holmes, D. (1988, November). *A guided poetry project: Developing ESL grammar.* Paper presented at the 78th Annual NCTE Convention, St. Louis, MO.
Literature/Grammar.

1422. Holmes, J., & Ramos, R. G. (1993). Study summaries as an evaluation instrument: Questions of validity. *English for Specific Purposes, 12*, 83-94.
Reports a survey of 20 graduate students writing summaries in the context of an ESP course. An analysis of drafts and products over a semester suggests they lose control over the summarizing strategies when placed in a test-like situation.
Summary Writing/Evaluation.

1423. Holt, S. (1993, April). *Critical thinking skills in ESL students.* Paper presented at 44th Annual Convention of CCCC, San Diego, CA.
Critical Thinking.

1424. Holtzknecht, S., & Smithies, M. S. (1980). *The errors in written English made by students at the Papua New Guinea University of Technology*. (Final Report). Lae: Papua New Guinea University of Technology. [ERIC ED 201 201].
Describes and categorizes errors made by first- and second-year university students. Suggests a methodology for remedying errors.
Error Analysis/Papua New Guinea.

1425. Holwitz, E. K. (1985). Focused writing exercises: Word association, stream of consciousness writing and Friday specials. *TESL Reporter, 18*(4), 67-69.
Gives three examples of communicative writing activities.
Classroom Activities.

1426. Homburg, T. J. (1984). Holistic evaluation of ESL compositions: Can it be evaluated objectively? *TESOL Quarterly, 18*, 87-107.
Uses objective measures of writing proficiency to validate holistic ESL composition grading. Presents a funnel model of the holistic evaluation process which shows that graders categorize ESL compositions by moving from one category to other categories, thus arriving at the final narrowed evaluation. Training of readers is important to reliability and validity of holistic grading.
Holistic/Assessment/Objective Measures.

1427. Homburg, T. J. (1983, March). *The relative discriminatory power of some objective measures of attained ESL writing proficiency at three successive ability levels.* A paper presented at the 17th Annual TESOL Convention, Toronto, Ontario.
Reports results from a study showing that certain objective research measures account for a major portion of the variance in subjectively scored writing component of the Michigan Test Battery.
Assessment/Objective Measures.

1428. Homburg, T. J. (1980). *A syntactic complexity measure of attained ESL writing proficiency.* Unpublished master's thesis, Southern Illinois University, Carbondale, IL.
See Homburg, 1984.

Proficiency/Objective Measures/Syntactic Development.

1429. Homer, M. (1976). University writing: Non-materials. *TESOL Talk*, 7(2), 21-28.

Discusses "non-materials" -- defined as useful resources of various kinds which are not specifically intended for use in teaching writing to the ESL student. An annotated bibliography of nineteen such writing texts is included.

Teacher Preparation.

1430. Hood, M. A. (1967, April). *The ESOL composition course: Its role in the university curriculum.* Paper presented at the 1st TESOL Convention, Miami Beach, FL.

Courses/University.

1431. Hood, S. (1990). Second language literacy: Working with non-literate learners. *Prospect: A Journal of Australian TESOL*, 5, 52-61.

Literacy.

1432. Hooper, N. (1983). Correcting ESL compositions. *TECFORS*, 6(1), 7-10. [ERIC ED 267 650].

Suggests reducing the burden of correcting by indicating what needs to be corrected and allowing peers to discuss and rewrite papers in a workshop format.

Error Treatment.

1433. Horn, V. (1974). Using the "Ananase Tales Technique" for compositions. *TESOL Quarterly*, 8, 37-42.

Describes procedure by which students rewrite paragraphs from folktales, making step-by-step changes that gradually increase in difficulty of form.

Control/Classroom Activities.

1434. Horn, V. (1969). Teaching logical relationships in written discourse. *TESOL Quarterly*, 3, 291-296.

Claims that understanding of logical relationship among sentences is necessary in reading expository prose. Identifies some basic logical relationship markers and suggests using them as a teaching aid in comprehension of written compositions.

Coherence/Reading-Writing Relations.

1435. Hornberger, N. H. (1990). Creating successful learning contexts for biliteracy. *Penn Working Papers in Educational Linguistics*, 6(1), 1-21.

An ethnographic study compares how two elementary teachers created successful learning environments for two communities of Puerto Rican and Cambodian students.

Literacy/Hispanic/Cambodian/Elementary.

1436. Hornberger, N. H. (1989). Continua of biliteracy. *Review of Educational Research*, 59, 271-296.

Presents a model of bilteracy involving social contexts, individual development, and use of media that form micro-macro continua (e.g., oral-literate,L1-L2 transfer, simultaneous-successive, convergent-divergent scripts, etc.) covering the functions and status of literacy in various situations in North America and elsewhere where people routinely switch between two languages.

Literacy/Reading-Writing Relations.

1437. Horning, A. S. (1987). *Teaching writing as a second language.* Carbondale, IL: Southern Illinois University Press.

Proposes that the written form of English is essentially a second language for inexperienced native writers and that students learn written English essentially as other adults develop second language skills.
NS-NNS Comparisons.

1438. Horowitz, D. M. (1991). ESL writing assessments: Contradictions and resolutions. In L. Hamp-Lyons (Ed.), *Assessing second language writing in academic contexts* (pp. 71-85). Norwood, NJ: Ablex.
Advances the position that writing ability varies from task to task and discipline to discipline to such an extent that a single written performance, especially large-scale, is insufficient to predict success.
Assessment/Task.

1439. Horowitz, D. M. (1990). Fiction and nonfiction in the ESL/EFL classroom: Does the difference make a difference? *English for Specific Purposes*, 9, 161-168.
Raises questions about the appropriateness teaching of literature in ESL courses and how such a practice fits into the debate over discourse communities and literacy.
Literacy/Discourse Communities/Literature

1440. Horowitz, D. M. (1989a). Function and form in essay examination prompts. *RELC Journal*, 20(2), 23-35.
Analyzes two hundred eighty-four essay examination prompts for discoursal characteristics of the genre expected in the answer. Finds four types: comparison, cause-effect, process, and argument which are applied to classroom activities.
Examination Essays/Prompts.

1441. Horowitz, D. M. (1989b). The undergraduate research paper: Where research and writing meet. *System*, 17, 347-357.
Describes the process of undergraduate research and writing.
Academic Writing/Research Writing.

1442. Horowitz, D. M. (1988). To see our texts as others see it: Toward a social sense of coherence. *JALT Journal*, 10(2), 91-100.
Argues that the L2 writer needs intensive analysis of specific genres in order to learn the interpretative standards of a community for the purpose of interpreting written text.
Coherence/Audience/Reading-Writing Relations.

1443. Horowitz, D. M. (1986a). The author responds to Liebman-Kleine . . .[In The Forum]. *TESOL Quarterly*, 20, 788-790.
Responds to Liebman-Kleine's defense of process teaching that the cognitive preoccupation of process research neglects the social nature of writing, especially the demands of specific audiences.
Audience.

1444. Horowitz, D. M. (1986b). The author responds to Hamp-Lyons . . .[In The Forum]. *TESOL Quarterly*, 20, 796-797.
While accepting most of Hamp-Lyons' arguments, author claims that she has misrepresented him as rejecting the process approach itself instead of the uncritical acceptance of the approach which was his intention.

Process Instruction.

1445. Horowitz, D. M. (1986c). Essay examination prompts and the teaching of academic writing. *English for Specific Purposes*, *5*, 107-120.

Examines the organizational frames from a survey of two hundred eighty-four university essay examination prompts from fifteen academic departments. Suggests classroom uses for typology.

Prompts/Academic Writing.

1446. Horowitz, D. M. (1986d). Process, not product: Less than meets the eye. *TESOL Quarterly*, *20*, 141-144.

Criticizes the process approach to teaching writing, maintaining that it does not equip students for all university writing situations.

Process Instruction.

1447. Horowitz, D. M. (1986e). What professors actually require: Academic tasks for the ESL classroom. *TESOL Quarterly*, *20*, 445-462.

Surveys and categorizes academic writing tasks at several universities. Discusses controlled nature of tasks and suggests ways of implementing these in EAP classroom.

Academic Writing/Task/University.

1448. Horowitz, D. M. (1985, October). *Once is not enough: Writing from multiple sources*. Paper presented at the 5th Annual Meeting of the Midwest Teachers of English to Speakers of Other Languages, Milwaukee, WI [ERIC ED 267 655].

Offers a technique for teaching ESL students to use multiple sources as input to writing. A series of questions, related to multiple reading material, generates answers to successive paragraphs or sections for a final paper.

Assignments/Reading-Writing Relations.

1449. Horowitz, D. M., & McKee, M. B. (1984). Methods for teaching academic writing. *TECFORS*, *7*(2), 5-11.

Advocate use of analytic and critical thinking activities as generalized pre-writing strategies for argumentative writing.

Academic Writing.

1450. Hottel-Burkhart, N. (1984, March). *The disambiguating tasks of four essay topics*. Paper presented at the 18th Annual TESOL Convention, Houston, TX.

Shows that the demands of subject matter affect the structure of essays. In particular, anaphor and topic foregrounding vary with disambiguating tasks presented as essay topics to advanced non-native writers.

Advanced/Task/Topic.

1451. Hottel-Burkhart, N. (1982, May). *Research in L2 composition: The importance of L1 data*. Paper presented at the 16th Annual TESOL Convention, Honolulu, HI.

Presents results of a qualitative and quantitative analyses of an equal number of French and English essays by adult French Canadians. Results show essay length, number of cohesive ties, and overall L2 proficiency correlate with writing ability in French.

French/L1 Influence.

1452. Houghton, D. (1980a). Contrastive rhetoric. *English Language Research Journal*, *1*,

79-91.
>Introduces the field of contrastive rhetoric, discussing methods of making reliable contrastive analysis.
>Contrastive Rhetoric.

1453. Houghton, D. (1980b). The writing problems of Iranian students. In G. M. Greenall, & J. E. Price (Eds.), *Study modes and academic development of overseas students* (pp. 79-90). London: The British Council.
>Reviews sociolinguistic and contrastive linguistic aspects that could be responsible for peculiarly Iranian mistakes in student writing.
>Literacy/Contrastive Rhetoric/Iran.

1454. Houghton, D., & Hoey, M. (1983). Linguistics and written discourse: Contrastive rhetoric. *Annual Review of Applied Linguistics*, *3*, 2-22.
>Surveys central themes of contrastive rhetoric and their application to the teaching and learning of a target language.
>Contrastive Rhetoric.

1455. Houston, R. D. (1991, March). *Creating voices: The realities of college composition*. Paper presented at the 25th Annual TESOL Convention, New York, NY.
>Discusses how to help students develop voice which is both personal and academic in real college writing assignments.
>Voice/University.

1456. Howard, T., & Dedo, D. R. (1989, November). *Cultural criticism and ESL composition*. Paper presented at the 79th Annual NCTE Convention, Baltimore, MD. [ERIC ED 317 062].
>Argues that ESL composition teachers should act not as guardians of "correct" English but as cultural or ideological critics.
>Culture.

1457. Howe, P. M. (1990). The problem of the problem question in English for Academic Legal Purposes. *English for Specific Purposes*, *9*, 215-236.
>Analyzes schemas in twenty scripts by law students and professors responding to a legal problem.
>ESP.

1458. Howe, P. M. (1988). Teaching examination techniques at Buckingham. In P. C. Robinson (Ed.), *Academic writing: Process and product* (pp. 61-62). London: Modern English Publications/British Council.
>Illustrates the resulting deterioration of language in essay exams when students are subjected to high levels of anxiety.
>Examination Essays/Anxiety.

1459. Hoye, M. (1989). The effects of summary writing on the reading comprehension of American and ESL University freshman. *Dissertation Abstracts International*, *49*(11), 3291A.
>Evaluates the effectiveness of a summarization task on the comprehension or learning strategy for content area material by university freshmen. Positive correlations were found between ability to write a summary and reading comprehension scores as well as quantitative differences between good and poor

summary writers.
Summary Writing/NS-NNS Comparisons/Reading-Writing Relations.

1460. Hu, Z. L., Brown, D. F., & Brown, L. B. (1982). Some linguistic differences in the written English of Chinese and Australian students. *Language Learning and Communication*, *1*(1), 39-49.
Finds no significant differences in the overall distribution of cohesive devices in the English writing of Chinese and native English Australian students, except preference for conjunction by Chinese and for lexical cohesion by Australian students.
Cohesion/Chinese.

1461. Huang, H. J. (1991). The role of L1-L2 translation in the L2 writing curriculum. *Rassegna Italiana di Linguistica Applicata*, *23*(3), 105-127.
Describes the relationship between translation and writing and translation and curriculum. Claims that a translation-based writing program played a positive role in an advanced course for Chinese ESL students.
Translation/Reading-Writing Relations.

1462. Hubbard, P. (1984). Alternative outlining techniques for ESL composition. *CATESOL Occasional Papers*, *10*, 59-68. [ERIC ED 253 065].
Suggests two outlining ideas: box outlining and the card outline, to help ESL students with rhetorical and logical patterns of academic written English.
Invention/Academic Writing.

1463. Huckin, T. N. (1992, March). *Teaching research writing to nonnative speakers: A Dutch experience*. Colloquium presented at the 26th Annual TESOL Convention, Vancouver, BC.
Describes experiences with Dutch students in a two week 40 hour course on technical writing in Holland.
Technical Writing/Dutch.

1464. Huckin, T. N. (1991). *Technical writing and professional communication for nonnative speakers of English*. (Second Ed.). St. Louis, MO: McGraw.
An advanced textbook for science and technology college students preparing to write in their academic disciplines.
University/Technical Writing/ESP/Textbook.

1465. Huckin, T. N. (1988, March). *The many-splendoured life of abstracts*. Paper presented at the 39th Annual CCCC Meeting, St. Louis, MO.
Summary Writing

1466. Huckin, T. N., & Olsen, L. (1984). The need for professionally orented ESL instruction in the United States. *TESOL Quarterly*, *18*, 273-294.
Argues for the need for specialized instruction in writing and speaking if ESL students are to go from academic to professional success.
ESP/Teacher Preparation.

1467. Huddlestone, R. D. (1971). *The sentence in written English*. Cambridge: Cambridge University Press.
Reference work to syntactic structures in written scientific English.
ESP/Syntactic Structures.

1468. Hudelson, S. (1989a). A tale of two children: Individual differences in ESL children's writing. In D. M. Johnson, & D. H. Roen (Eds.), *Richness in writing: Empowering ESL students* (pp. 84-99). NY: Longman.

Describes the development of writing in two ESL children. Conclusions show that environment is crucial to writing. ESL children do display individual differences in personality traits, cognitve and social styles. Utilizing their native language helps them acquire English as a second language.

Children/Bilingual.

1469. Hudelson, S. (1989b). *Write on: Children writing in ESL*. Englewood Cliffs, NJ: CAL/Prentice-Hall.

Discusses how to incorporate writing in a whole language approach to the writing development of young ESL learners who, it is argued, learn to write in ways similar to their English peers. Also finds writing in one's native language may benefit writing in L2.

Children/Whole Language/NS-NNS Comparisons.

1470. Hudelson, S. (1988a). Children's writing in ESL. In *ERIC Digest* Washington, DC: TESOL.

In the belief that writing is similar for both first and second language learners, prescribes providing opportunities during class for ESL children to use writing to carry out tasks that are meaningful to them, such as keeping a diary or journal. Assessment should be based on daily classroom activities and may include keeping writing folders with all of each student's work.

Children.

1471. Hudelson, S. (1988b). Writing in a second language. *Annual Review of Applied Linguistics*, 9, 210-222.

In a review of research, discusses the application of a process oriented model in the second language classroom. Among the areas of concentration of current research are writing processes, second language classroom instruction, and second language writing.

Review.

1472. Hudelson, S. (1986). ESL children's writing: What we've learned, what we're learning. In P. Rigg, & D. S. Enright (Eds.), *Children and ESL: Integrating perspectives* (pp. 23-54). Washington, DC: TESOL.

Uses writing by four young ESL learners in order to exemplify past and present developments in understanding second language writing by children.

Children.

1473. Hudelson, S. (1984). Kan yu ret an rayt en Ingles: Children become literate in English as a second language. *TESOL Quarterly*, 18, 221-238.

Advocates that classroom practice needs to keep pace with recent research on second-language reading and writing development in children, providing teachers and curriculum planners with multiple possibilities for innovations. Findings suggest that: (1) even children who speak virtually no English read English print in the environment; (2) ESL learners are able to read English with only limited control over the oral system of the language; (3) the experiential and cultural background of the

ESL teacher has a strong effect on reading comprehension; and (4) child ESL learners, early in their development of English, can write English and can do so for various purposes.

Curriculum/Children/Literacy.

1474. Hudelson, S. (1983, March). *Janice: Becoming a writer of English*. Washington, DC: ERIC/FLL. [ERIC ED 249 760].

Case study of a native Spanish-speaking second-grader learning English in a Florida public school. Focuses on the classroom environment in which she was learning English, her writing development, her perceptions of writing in English and how they changed over time, and her struggles in the face of expectations of her writing by her teacher and others.

Hispanic/Elementary.

1475. Huebner, T., & Pearson, C. C. (1986, March). *Oral and written performance: Indications of baseline linguistic competence?* Paper presented at the 20th Annual TESOL Convention, Anaheim, CA.

Examines the nature of linguistic variation across genres and modes in the interlanguage of university ESL students.

Speaking-Writing Relations/Variation.

1476. Huffman, D. T., & Goldberg, J. R. (1987). Using word processing to teach EFL composition. *System, 15*, 169-176.

Reviews the use of selected word processing programs for EFL composition.

Word Processing.

1477. Hugg, S. (1980, May). *A method of individualizing instruction in English for Science and Technology*. Paper presented at the Annual NAFSA Meeting, St. Louis, MO.

ESP.

1478. Hughes, A., & Lascaratou, C. (1982). Competing criteria for error gravity. *ELT Journal, 36*, 175-182.

Compares the criteria employed by three groups of judges assessing the gravity of sentence errors made by Greek-speaking student writers. Greek teachers of English tend to appeal to violations of basic rules when encountering errors whereas NESs use intelligibility almost exclusively as their criteria. NES teachers use both criteria with a preference for intelligibility.

Error Gravity/NS-NNS Comparisons/Greek.

1479. Hughes, E. (1986, March). *Using holistic grading with ESL students*. Paper presented at the 37th Annual CCCC Meeting, New Orleans, LA.

Assessment/Scoring/Holistic.

1480. Hughey, J. B. (1990). Testing ESL composition. In D. Douglas (Ed.), *English language testing in U.S. colleges and universities* Washington, DC: National Association of Foreign Student Affairs.

Discusses the standards and expectations in developing ESL writing tests, the kind of tests that exist and what can be deduced from their results.

Evaluation/Assessment.

1481. Hughey, J. B. (1987, April). *Topic development in the writing class*. Paper presented at the 21st Annual TESOL Convention, Miami Beach, FL.

Examines strategies for developing writing topics.
Topic.

1482. Hughey, J. B., & Hartfiel, V. F. (1988, March). *Creating complete writing assignments*. Paper presented at the 22nd Annual TESOL Convention, Chicago, IL.
Workshop on creating realistic and meaningful writing assignments using reading-writing connection assignments.
Assignments/Reading-Writing Relations.

1483. Hughey, J. B., & Wormuth, D. R. (1985, April). *One step beyond: The oral presentation of writing*. Paper presented at the 19th Annual TESOL Convention, New York, NY.
Discusses how to teach students to translate writing into effective speech.
Speaking-Writing Relations.

1484. Hughey, J. B., & Wormuth, D. R. (1982, May). *Heuristics: Focus on writing as process*. Paper presented at the 16th Annual TESOL Convention, Honolulu, HI.
Maintains that rhetoric is needed in ESL writing beyond pattern practice and editing.
Process Instruction.

1485. Hughey, J. B., Wormuth, D. R., Hartfiel, V. F., & Jacobs, H. L. (1983). *Teaching ESL composition: Principles and techniques*. Rowley, MA: Newbury House.
Advocates the theory of writing as creative process and presents exercises that use this theory to develop certain principles of writing, especially purpose, audience awareness, and evaluation. Aims at facilitating students to write independently.
Evaluation/Assessment.

1486. Huizenga, J., Snellings, C. M., & Francis, G. B. (1990). *Basic composition for ESL: An expository workbook*. (Third Ed.). Boston: Heinle & Heinle.
A text that seeks to improve basic writing skills of students by treating six academic purposes through controlled creativity.
Beginners/Textbook.

1487. Huizenga, J., & Thomas-Ruzic, M. (1990). *Writing workout: A program for new students of English*. Boston: Heinle & Heinle.
Offers intensive step-by-step writing instructions with student writing samples. The activities in each unit build on one another and offer discussion, vocabulary, sentence- and paragraph-level tasks for prewriting, writing, and follow-up. The text is organized around five themes that address adult students' life experiences and interests -- home, health, family shopping, and travel.
Beginners/Textbook.

1488. Humes, A., & Cronnell, B. (1980, March). *English writing requirements for bilingual students in grades K-6*. Paper presented at the 14th Annual TESOL Convention, San Francisco, CA.
Provides a description of skills required of bilingual students in the monolingual English classroom.
Hispanic/Elementary/Bilingual.

1489. Hunt, K. W. (1970a). Do sentences in the second language grow like those in the first? *TESOL Quarterly, 4*, 195-202.

Raises the question of the universality and comparative rate of development of main clause embedding in the syntax of ESL students.
Sentence Combining.

1490. Hunt, K. W. (1970b, March). *Do sentences in the second language grow like those in the first?* Paper presented at the 4th Annual TESOL Convention, San Francisco, CA.
Suggests using sentence embedding drills in second language instruction.
Syntactic Development.

1491. Huntington, L. B. (1993, April). *Developing an ear for writing: Compositions and cassette recorders*. Paper presented at the 27th Annual TESOL Convention, Atlanta, GA.
Demonstrates how to use the cassette recorder with early student drafts to correct grammar errors.
Listening-Writing Relations.

1492. Huntley, H. S. (1992). *Feedback strategies in intermediate and advanced second language composition: A discussion of the effects of error correction, peer review, and student-teacher conferences on student writing and performance*. Washington, DC: ERIC/FLL. [ERIC ED 355 809].
Reviews feedback strategies currently in use with intermediate and advanced ESL learners, including error correction and alternatives in conferencing and peer review.
Feedback/Peer Response/Conferencing.

1493. Huntsinger, J. L. (1992, March). *Teaching composition to native Americans: Ideas for the classroom*. Paper presented at the 43rd Annual CCCC Meeting, Cincinnati, OH.
Amer-Indian.

1494. Hurley, D. S. (1993, April). *Evaluating an expertise-based college writing course*. Paper presented at the 27th Annual TESOL Convention, Atlanta, GA.
Describes a college course on academic writing in which students write all genre-based assignments on a single topic about which they become experts.
University/Curriculum.

1495. Huss, R. L. (1993, April). *Reexamining instructional assumptions: Beginning writing and young ESL students*. Paper presented at the 27th Annual TESOL Convention, Atlanta, GA.
An ethnographic study discusses discrepancies between a teacher's instructional assumptions and the literacy reality Punjabi-speaking Pakistani children in a British primary school
Punjabi/Children/Literacy.

1496. Huss, R. L. (1991). Among diverse worlds: An ethnographic study of young children becoming literate in English as a second language in a British multi-ethnic primary school. *Dissertation Abstracts International, 53*, 397A.
The writing of 5 and 6 year-old second language learners who integrate literacy knowledge from school, home, and religious school, may acquire literate competence without learning to speak well.

Children/Speaking-Writing Relations.

1497. Hutchinson Weidauer, M. (1990). *Modern impressions: Writing in our times.* Boston: Heinle & Heinle.

A progressive series of modules on cross-cultural issues for the low advanced student.

Textbook/Advanced.

1498. Hutchinson-Eichler, M., & Earle-Carlin, S. (1992, March). *Does teaching grammar for composition work?* Paper presented at the 26th Annual TESOL Convention, Vancouver, BC.

Presents results of a study comparing university students' ability to control and correct errors and achieve syntactic variety before and after a ten-week grammar course.

Grammar/University.

1499. Hvitfeldt, C. (1992). Oral orientations in ESL academic writing. *College ESL, 2*(1), 29-39.

Reports finding "residual orality" in the EFL writing of Malay college students. Recommends the use of student oral ability to transform their reading and writing into an academic style.

Speaking-Writing Relations/Contrastive Rhetoric/Malay.

1500. Hvitfeldt, C. (1986, November). *Guided peer critique in ESL writing at the college level.* Paper presented at the Annual Meeting of the Japan Association of Language Teachers of International Conference on Language Teaching and Learning, Seirei Gakuen, Hamamatsu, Japan. [ERIC ED 282 438].

Describes a college-level composition course based on peer critique in Malaysia. Suggests that limiting peer critique to the organization and content areas is more effective than the critique of mechanics and grammaticality.

Peer Response/Malay.

1501. Hwang, H. J. (1991). The development of English writing proficiency among Korean students from ninth-grade to college juniors. *Dissertation Abstracts International, 52*(11), 3814A.

Evaluates essays written by Korean students from ninth grade through junior year in college and analyses them for syntactic development as well as syntactic and semantic errors. Finds a clear writing developmental pattern: scores increase as grades and practice increase. As proficiency increased, error ratios decreased while error-free T-units and mean T-unit length increased. Lexical errors are the most frequent semantic type, whereas article omission and incorrect verb usage are the most frequent grammatical types across all grades.

Korean/Development/T-Unit.

1502. Hyland, K. (1990a). A genre description of the argumentative essay. *RELC Journal, 21*(1), 66-78.

Proposes a descriptive rhetorical framework for a genre approach to the argumentative essay for the purpose of instructing EFL/ESL students who lack such knowledge.

Argumentation/Genre.

1503. Hyland, K. (1990b). Providing productive feedback. *ELT Journal, 44,* 279-285.

    Suggests "minimal marking" strategy and taped commentary as alternatives to encourage students to act on feedback.

    Feedback.

1504. Hyland, K. (1983). ESL computer writers: What can we do to help? *System, 21,* 21-30.

    Argues that the positive effects of using word processing to teach ESL writing depends on the support offered in the learning environment. Offers four principles for such support.

    Word Processing.

I

1505. Idris, A. A. (1982). An analysis of the thematic structure and system of logical relations in English and Malay expository texts. *Dissertation Abstracts International, 43*(8), 2651A.

    Compares the thematic structures and system of logical or semantic relations (rheme) in expository texts in English and Malay. Findings show: (1) expository texts in both languages are usually deductively developed; (2) conjectures are predominant markers of theme in both languages followed by parallelism of structure in English and adverbials in Malay; (3) rheme generally relates higher level thematic units, superordinate-subordinate relations between themes more marked in Malay than English.

    FSP/Malay.

1506. Ike, N. J. (1990). From brainstorming to creative essay: Teaching composition writing to large classes. *English Teaching Forum, 28*(2), 41-43.

    Outlines an approach that addresses the problem of teaching writing to large classes.

    Large Classes.

1507. Ike, N. J. (1989). Fostering creativity in essay writing through group work. *English Teaching Forum, 27*(1), 45-47.

    Advocates a six step procedure for groups to follow to overcome the tendency to avoid pre-writing.

    Invention.

1508. Ilson, R. (1962). The dicto-comp: A specialized technique for controlling speech and writing in language learning. *Language Learning, 12,* 299-301.

    A passage presented verbally to a class is given back by students, one sentence at a time, in their own words or in the original. This differs from summary in that as many details as possible are included.

    Classroom Activities/Speaking-Writing Relations.

1509. Indrasuta, C. (1988). Narrative styles in the writing of Thai and American students. In A. C. Purves (Ed.), *Writing across languages and cultures: Issues in contrastive rhetoric* (pp. 206-226). Newbury Park, CA: Sage.

    Examines narrative style in writing: (1) in English by American students; (2)

in Thai by Thai students; (3) in English by Thai students. Finds that Thai students are influenced by culture rather than linguistic factors and transfer conventional rhetorical styles of L1 into L2.
Contrastive Rhetoric/Narration/Thai.

1510. Indrasuta, C. (1987). A comparison of the written compositions of American and Thai students. *Dissertation Abstracts International, 48*(7), 1681A.
Examines the similarities and differences in narrative written discourse of American English and Thai students and studies if written language in English by Thai students will be similar to the target language or to the first language. Findings indicate that similarities between the groups are due to the common characteristic of the language systems and common characteristics of pattern of written discourse. Differences in writing in English as a first language or a second language are due to cultural rather than linguistic factors.
Narration/Thai/Culture.

1511. Ingberg, M. (1987). Finnish-Swedish paragraph patterns in EFL student compositions. In I. Lindblat, & M. Ljund (Eds.), *Proceedings from the Third Nordic Conference for English Studies, Vol. 2* (pp. 417-426). Stockholm: Almqvist & Wiksell.
Analysis of 15 argumentative EFL essays by first-year university students in Sweden shows, contrary to a linear expository model, the presence of explicit thesis statements twice as frequently in the main body and conclusion as in the introduction of essays.
Coherence/Paragraph/Swedish/Finnish.

1512. Inghilleri, M. (1989). Learning to mean as a symbolic and social process: The story of ESL writers. *Discourse Processes, 12*(3), 391-411.
Describes composing process of two ESL writers whose teachers espoused the process approach. This study highlights the conflicts that emerge for students and teachers in their attempt to negotiate meaning.
Interaction/Process Research.

1513. Ingram, B., & King, C. (1989, March). *Changing beginning writer's engraved-in-stone outlook toward composition.* Paper presented at the 23rd Annual TESOL Convention, San Antonio, TX.
Discusses how creative structured activities help to overcome "once is enough" syndrome among inexperienced writers.
Beginners/Psychology.

1514. Ingram, B., & King, C. (1988). *From writing to composing: An introductory composition course for students of English.* NY: Cambridge University Press.
Text utilizes a process approach to composition through a variety of activities and topics. Pictures, compositions, maps, dialogues, diagrams, surveys, and long-range projects are some of the features used to stimulate students to become fluent and confident writers of English. Uses pair and group work exercises to introduce concepts and to help students generate ideas for composition.
University/Beginners/Textbook.

1515. Ingram, B., & King, C. (1987, April). *Peer-sharing for beginning-level compositions.* Paper presented at the 21st Annual TESOL Convention, Miami Beach, FL.

Offers suggestions to help beginners share work-in-progress which provide incentives to create and polish compositions.

Beginners/Collaboration.

1516. Ingram, B., & King, C. (1985, April). *Teaching composition to beginners: Incorporating a process-centered component.* Paper presented at the 19th Annual TESOL Convention, New York, NY.

Describes process-centered writing practices at the beginning-level that are interwoven with skill building activities that lend lexical and syntactic support to the writing process.

Process Instruction/Beginners.

1517. Inman, M. E. (1988, March). *Questioning writing: A flow chart approach to composition.* Paper presented at the 22nd Annual TESOL Convention, Chicago, IL.

A process of continual questioning while writing samples from varied sources can help develop intuitions about different purposes in writing.

Invention.

1518. Inness, D. K. (1987). An error analysis of the use of limiting, specifying, distinguishing, quantifying, and zero determiners in the writing of university students of English as a second language. *Dissertation Abstracts International, 48*(5), 1136A.

Examines the frequency of correct and incorrect grammatical usage of determiners in a sample of 117 in-class compositions by college ESL students from twenty-seven countries. The most frequently used category was specifying (classified according to their phoric status) and the most frequent error was in the use of quantifying determiners.

Error Analysis.

1519. Intaraprawat, P. (1988). Metadiscourse in native English speakers' and ESL students' persuasive essays. *Dissertation Abstracts International, 49*(7), 1720A.

Analyzes the patterns of metadiscourse features in persuasive essays written by college students. Findings indicate that metadiscourse features can be used as an indication of writing proficiency and are necessary in constructing coherent texts and creating writer-reader relationship.

University/Persuasion/Metacognition.

1520. Irvine, P., & Basham, C. S. (1982, May). *Peer interaction and writing in ESL.* Paper presented at the 16th Annual TESOL Convention, Honolulu, HI.

Shows how helping another to clarify meaning is a skill to be learned for either bilingual Navajo or traditional international students.

Peer Response/Amer-Indian.

1521. Irvine, P., & Elsasser, N. (1989). The ecology of literacy: Negotiations of writing standards in a Caribbean setting. In B. A. Rafoth, & D. L. Rubin (Eds.), *The social construction of written communication* (pp. 304-320). Norwood, NJ: Ablex.

Examines the "writing crisis" at the College of the Virgin Islands. Claims that the "falling standards" are a result of a clash between the dominant academic standards of the U.S. and the local and regional system. States the need for the development of a model of education that is built on an indigenous notion of literacy.

Literacy/Standards.

1522. Isidro Y Santos, A. (1937). *The development of written English expression of Filipino children: Part of a dissertation for the Ph.D.* Chicago: University of Chicago Press.

More than 1500 compositions written by Filipino children in grades 3-7 show development across grades in terms of vocabulary growth, development of linguistic structures, and a decrease in errors at the sentence level. The rate of growth is more rapid in the last two grades as is improvement in quality and content.

Filipino/Children.

1523. Italia, P. G. (1991). The curriculum loop: The role of the Writing Task Force in curriculum development at CUNY. *Teaching English in the Two-Year College, 18*(3), 186-190.

Discusses how the CUNY ESL writing curriculum was shaped by a Writing Task Force.

Curriculum.

J

1524. Jacobs, G. (1989). Miscorrection in peer feedback in writing class. *RELC Journal, 20*(1), 68-76.

Reports on a study investigating miscorrection in group writing activities. The subjects were eighteen third-year English majors in Thailand enrolled in a course devoted seventy per cent to writing and thirty per cent to reading. The findings of the study, in which learners gave feedback to their peers' writing, are consistent with studies of miscorrection in spoken activities.

Feedback/Responding/Thai.

1525. Jacobs, G. (1987). First experiences with peer feedback on compositions: Student and teacher reaction. *System, 15*, 325-333.

Reports experience with peer feedback in a process approach to EFL composition in Thailand. Groups tended to use their native language to discuss writing.

Feedback.

1526. Jacobs, G. (1985). Quickwriting: A technique for invention in writing. *ELT Journal, 40*, 282-290.

Recommends quickwriting or "free writing" as an invention technique useful in the EFL composition class to increase quantity of student writing. Discusses the advantages of quickwriting, such as concentrating on content rather than form and generating ideas. Quickwriting helps ESL writers think in the target language, write under pressure of time, and compose longer essays. Describes techniques of integrating quickwriting into writing class and presents the basic procedures and modeling steps. Limitations of quickwriting are also discussed.

Invention/Instruction.

1527. Jacobs, G., & Zhang, S. (1989, April). *Peer feedback in second language writing instruction: Boon or bane?* Paper presented at the Annual AERA Meeting, San Francisco, CA.

Feedback/Peer Response.

1528. Jacobs, H. L., & Zinkgraf, S. A. (1980, March). *Reliability and validity of the ESL Composition Ability Profile (ECAP)*. Paper presented at the 14th Annual TESOL Convention, San Francisco, CA.

    Reports high rater reliability in a sample of more than 750 essays.

    Assessment/Raters.

1529. Jacobs, H. L., Zinkgraf, S. A., Wormuth, D. R., Hartfiel, V. F., & Hughey, J. B. (1981). *Testing ESL composition: A practical approach.* Rowley, MA: Newbury House.

    A comprehensive discussion of composition testing and procedures for developing a composition testing program with step-by-step procedures for the evaluation of ESL student compositions based on a 100-point analytic scale, the ESL Composition Profile.

    Evaluation/Assessment.

1530. Jacobs, R. A. (1988, March). *Questioning writing: A flow chart approach to composition.* Paper presented at the 22nd Annual TESOL Convention, Chicago, IL.

    Statistical measures of syntactic complexity are inadequate because they ignore the role and organization of context in academic exposition and literary prose.

    Objective Measures/Syntactic Development.

1531. Jacobs, S. E. (1990). Building hierarchy: Learning the language of the science domain, ages 10-13. In U. M. Connor, & A. M. Johns (Eds.), *Coherence in writing: Research and pedagogical perspectives* (pp. 151-168). Alexandria, VA: TESOL.

    Claims that for children, learning the expository style of science, which is hierarchical in structure, is almost akin to learning a foreign language. Examines the writing of children in grade six and concludes that a child's personalized, embedded first language is important in learning the disembedded, academic language.

    Children/Register/ESP.

1532. Jacobs, S. E. (1982). *Composing and coherence: The writing of eleven premedical students.* Washington, DC: Center for Applied Linguistics. [ERIC ED 223 101].

    A comparative study of the science writing (a biology course) of eleven university students, five of whom spoke English as a second language. Found that their writing follows an information order reflecting how they memorized information. Both student populations had more difficulty with larger composing concerns than with the mechanics of language, especially connecting ideas with specific information relationships.

    Coherence/ESP/NS-NNS Comparisons.

1533. Jacobs, S. E. (1982, May). *On learning to write academic essays: Case studies.* Paper presented at the 16th Annual TESOL Convention, Honolulu, HI.

    Discusses weekly writing of a native and a nonnative for a biology course.

    Content/Cohesion.

1534. Jacobs, S. E. (1981). Rhetorical information as prediction. *TESOL Quarterly, 15,* 237-249.

    Claims that measures like the T-unit only provide information about surface and grammatical features but not rhetorical connectedness. Examines writing samples of ESL and native speaking students and argues that text grammar should show

connectives, not just as conjunctions but as predictions.
NS-NNS Comparisons/Coherence/Cohesion.

1535. Jacobs, S. E., & Brady, S. (1988, March). *Teacherless writing groups: Speaking and writing, ages 9-12*. Paper presented at the 22nd Annual TESOL Convention, Chicago, IL.

Writing groups teach children the social roles of responding and helping.
Group Work/Children.

1536. Jacoby, J. (1985). Training writing center personnel to work with international students: The least you should know. *Writing Lab Newsletter, 10*, 1-6.

Discusses problems tutoring international university students.
Tutoring.

1537. Jafarpur, A. (1991). Cohesiveness as a basis for evaluating compositions. *System, 19*, 459-465.

Reports a study using the T-unit to assess "functional fluency." Indices of cohesion correlate with writing quality in essays by 38 advanced EFL students in Iran.
Cohesion/Iran/Evaluation

1538. James, C. (1976). Judgments of error gravities. *English Language Teaching Journal, 31*, 116-124.

Examines native and non-native teachers' perceptions of errors by studying their markings of written work in English as a foreign language. Finds that native teachers are more tolerant towards errors than non-native teachers.
Error Gravity.

1539. James, J. P. (1993). *Write it down*. Burlingame, CA: Alta.

A textbook on the complete writing process for low-level students.
Textbook/Beginners.

1540. James, K. (1984). The writing of theses by speakers of English as a foreign language: The results of a case study. In R. Williams, J. M. Swales, & J. Kirkman (Eds.), *Common ground: Shared interests in ESP and communication studies* (pp. 99-113). Oxford: Pergamon.

A case study of a Brazilian student writing a thesis on the sociology of medicine illustrates problems in two broad areas: communication breakdowns and communication blurs.
Brazil/Research Writing.

1541. James, K. (1988). E.A.P.--- E.S.P.--- Self-sustaining growth. In P. C. Robinson (Ed.), *Academic writing: Process and product* (pp. 75-84). London: Modern English Publications/British Council.

Describes a course to address the problem of how to develop special subject writing ability when students represent a variety of disciplines. The five complementary elements of the methodology presented are: use of model paragraphs, classification of language items, systermatic collection of persnal reading examples by students, and essay tests.
Courses/Academic Writing.

1542. James, M. O. (1992, March). *L2 writing: Is fluency a predictor?* Paper presented at the 26th Annual TESOL Convention, Vancouver, BC.

Reports the results of four weeks of observation and self-reporting about the role of fluency in L2 writing proficiency.

Fluency/Classroom Research.

1543. James, M. O. (1989, March). *Creative approaches to "publishing" student writing.* Paper presented at the 23rd Annual TESOL Convention, San Antonio, TX.

Showcase displays, slide presentations, and video productions as well as the class newsletter are discussed.

Student Publications.

1544. Jamieson, J., & Silva, T. (1984, March). *The controlled research paper: A positive, practical alternative.* Paper presented at the 18th Annual TESOL Convention, Houston, TX.

Claims that controlling the topic and source material allows more energy to be devoted to the writing process.

Research Writing/Control.

1545. Jang, M. (1980, May). *Standardized tests and writing performance.* Paper presented at the Annual NAFSA Meeting, St. Louis, MO.

Assessment.

1546. Janopoulos, M. (1993). Comprehension, communicative competence, and construct validity: Holistic scoring from an ESL perspective. In M. M. Williamson, & B. A. Huot (Eds.), *Validating holistic scoring for writing assessment: Theoretical and empirical foundations* (pp. 303-325). Cresskill, NJ: Hampton Press.

Argues that comprehension plays a significant role in the construct validity of holistically scored ESL texts. Two experiments show that holistically trained ESL raters comprehend or recall more (and different degrees of) content from higher quality than lower quality ESL tasks.

Assessment/Holistic.

1547. Janopoulos, M. (1992a). University faculty tolerance of NS and NNS writing errors: A comparison. *Journal of Second Language Writing, 1*(2), 109-121.

Describes a study in which university faculty rated 24 sentences containing errors commonly committed by NNS writers on a 6-point scale of tolerance. Results were mixed, but faculty were generally more tolerant of NNS errors than they were of errors perceived as made by NSs.

Error Gravity/NS-NNS Comparisons.

1548. Janopoulos, M. (1992b, March). *Writing across the curriculum and the NNS student.* Paper presented at the 26th Annual TESOL Convention, Vancouver, BC.

Explores issues concerning NNS performance in writing across the curriculum programs, especially examination performance, error perception by faculty, and meeting standards.

WAC.

1549. Janopoulos, M. (1991a, March). *Faculty perceptions of writing quality: Same errors, different standards?* Paper presented at the 25th Annual TESOL Convention, New York, NY.

Finds in a survey of faculty at a midwestern university greater tolerance of the

errors of ESL writers than comparable errors by NES writers.
Error Gravity/NS-NNS Comparisons.

1550. Janopoulos, M. (1991b). *Using written recall protocols to measure aspects of holistic assessment of second language writing proficiency: The effect of task awareness* . Washington, DC: ERIC/CLL. [ERIC ED 335 869].

Finds that recall studies of the holistic reading process should use naive rather than focused subjects to avoid interference from the recall task.
Assessment/Holistic.

1551. Janopoulos, M. (1989). Reader comprehension and holistic assessment of second language writing proficiency. *Written Communication*, 6(2), 218-237.

Holistic reading is widely used to assess the proficiency of non-native speaking writers. However, ESL professionals have questioned how native speaking raters will comprehend NNS texts. Results show that readers of the better written text recalled better.
Assessment.

1552. Janopoulos, M. (1986). The relationship of pleasure reading and second language writing proficiency. *TESOL Quarterly*, 20, 763-768.

Examines if correlation exists between L1 and/or L2 pleasure reading and L2 writing proficiency in adult subjects. Findings indicate: (1) no correlation between total pleasure reading (L1 and L2) and L2 writing proficiency and (2) heavy pleasure readers in L2 were more proficient writers in L2.
Reading-Writing Relations.

1553. Jaramillo, B. L. (1974). *The mechanics of writing: A language laboratory manual for foreign students*. Ann Arbor: University of Michigan Press.

Thirty lessons on punctuation and other mechanical conventions in writing that can be used in a language laboratory to supplement a writing class for beginning ESL learners.
Beginners/Textbook.

1554. Jarrett, J. M., Giles-Lee, M., & Mbalia, D. D. (1990). *Pathways: A text for developing writers*. NY: Macmillan.

Text and workbook combination incorporates grammar into the writing instruction and includes a writing inventory for students to evaluate their own work. Pre- and post-tests permit students to gauge their progress.
Grammar/Textbook.

1555. Jayaswal, S. (1988, March). *Peer review beyond the classroom: The evolving student handbook*. Paper presented at the 22nd Annual TESOL Convention, Chicago, IL.

Sugggests that freshman composition students learn about audience by writing their own student handbook.
Audience/Peer Response.

1556. Jenkins, M. (1986). *Writing: A content approach to ESL composition*. Englewood Cliffs, NJ: Prentice Hall.

A content-oriented text for intermediate to advanced ESL students, focusing on rhetoric as well as specific content areas.
Advanced/Textbook.

1557. Jenkins, S. M. (1985, April). *A contrastive study of business letter writing styles: English, French, Japanese*. Paper presented at the 19th Annual TESOL Convention, New York, NY.
   See Jenkins & Hinds, 1987.
   Contrastive Rhetoric/Japanese/French.

1558. Jenkins, S. M., & Assaf, M. (1986, March). *The L2 writer and the process approach to writing*. Paper presented at the 20th Annual TESOL Convention, Anaheim, CA.
   Reports research on knowledge factors in the discovery process of L1 and L2 writers.
   Background Knowledge/NS-NNS Comparisons.

1559. Jenkins, S. M., & Hinds, J. (1987). Business letter writing: English, French, and Japanese. *TESOL Quarterly, 21*, 327-350.
   Examines the form and content of business letters in English, French, and Japanese and states that even though the surface structures of the three are very similar, American business letters are reader-oriented, French are writer-oriented, and Japanese business letters take a middle ground between the two.
   Contrastive Rhetoric/Business Writing/Japanese/French.

1560. Jenkins, S. M., Jordan, M. K., & Campbell, D. (1992, March). *Teaching technical writing: Whose responsibility is it?* Paper presented at the 26th Annual TESOL Convention, Vancouver, BC.
   Discusses respective responsibilities of writing and content area faculty and current models for programs on writing in technical disciplines.
   Technical Writing/WAC.

1561. Jenkins, S. M., Jordan, M. K., & Weiland, P. O. (1993). The role of writing in graduate Engineering education: A survey of faculty beliefs and practices. *English for Specific Purposes, 12*, 51-67.
   Finds that students never do a great deal of writing in Engineering courses.
   ESP/Engineering.

1562. Jensen, C. (1984, March). *A survey of ESL pre-freshman composition courses*. Paper presented at the 18th Annual TESOL Convention, Houston, TX.
   Presents results of a nation-wide survey of skills, methods, and materials used in preparing ESL students for freshman English.
   Research/Freshman Composition.

1563. Jeske, D. P. (1981). Talking on paper? An antidote. *CATESOL Occasional Papers, 7*, 84-93. [ERIC ED 210 922].
   Presents a structured approach using model essays to teach basic elements of expository prose for ESL students who "talk on paper" in an informal, ungrammatical, and disorganized fashion.
   Speaking-Writing Relations.

1564. Jewinski, J. (1988). Grammar by any other name: Structuralism in the classroom. In G. H. Irons (Ed.), *Second language acquisition: Selected readings in theory and practice* (pp. 163-170). Ontario, Canada: The Canadian Modern Language Review.
   Offers self-correction techniques for students after they develop their ideas coherently.

Grammar.

1565. Jex, W. W. (1988). Microcomputers and English language instruction: A few years later. *CALICO Journal*, 5(3), 84-89.

Reports experiences in the intensive program at NYU, using microcomputers and word processing.

Computers/Word Processing.

1566. Jex, W. W., & Engel, D. (1986, May). *Processing language: Word processing in an ESL writing class*. Paper presented at the Annual NAFSA Meeting, San Antonio, TX.

1567. Jie, G., & Lederman, M. J. (1988). Instruction and assessment of writing in China: The National Unified Entrance Examination for Institutions of Higher Education. *Journal of Basic Writing*, 7(1), 47-60.

A dialogic essay between two program directors about writing assessment in China and the U.S.

Assessment/Chinese.

1568. Jilbert, K. A. (1991, November). *Vygotsky and the bilingual child: A new look at old ideas*. Paper presented at the 81st Annual NCTE Convention, Seattle, WA.

Psychology.

1569. Jisa, H., & Scarcella, R. C. (1982, May). *Getting it together: An analysis of written discourse markers*. Paper presented at the 16th Annual TESOL Convention, Honolulu, HI.

Examines problems of adult ESL writers using discourse markers such as linear organizers.

Cohesion.

1570. John, B. (1988, March). *Academic writing: When persistence meets resistance*. Paper presented at the 22nd Annual TESOL Convention, Chicago, IL.

Describes how one instructor overcame resistance to a required technical writing course.

Affect/Technical Writing.

1571. Johns, A. M. (1994). Using classroom and authentic genres: Student initiation into academic writing. In D. D. Belcher, & G. Braine (Eds.), *Academic writing in a second language: Essays on research and pedagogy*. Norwood, NJ: Ablex.

Discusses issues in the teaching and learning of classroom genres (e.g., the essay examination) and of authentic genres of academic disciplines (e.g., the research paper). Describes an academic task portfolio that integrates the two genres in order to prepare students for diverse audiences and discourse expectations.

Genre/Academic Writing.

1572. Johns, A. M. (1993a). Reading and writing tasks in English for Academic Purposes classes: Products, processes and resources. In J. G. Carson, & I. Leki (Eds.), *Reading in the composition classroom: second language perspectives* Boston: Heinle & Heinle.

Relates task to three aspects of students' work: the products students write (target tasks), the operations (or processes) necessary to produce products, and the resources available to students while generating their texts. Discusses various approaches to each of these task elements and relates findings to English for Academic Purposes adjunct class.

Reading-Writing Relations/Task.

1573. Johns, A. M. (1993b). The reading-writing relationship: A review of literature. In P. Hashemipour, D. Barrutia, R. Maldonado, & M. van Naerssen (Eds.), *Studies in honor of Tracy D. Terrell*. St. Louis, MO: McGraw-Hill.

A review of recent L1 and L2 literature relating reading and writing in terms of parallel processes, schema activation, audience analysis and prediction. Also discussed is the influence of reading upon writing -- and of writing upon reading. Implications for teaching, in light of Natural Approach pedagogy, are suggested.

Reading-Writing Relations.

1574. Johns, A. M. (1993c). Too much on our plates: A response to Terry Santos' "Ideology in compositions: L1 and ESL". *Journal of Second Language Writing*, 2, 83-89.

Stresses the need for ESL teachers and theorists to shape an ideology distinct from L1 composition teaching while agreeing with Santos's evaluation of the preference for pragmatism instead of ideology.

Ideology.

1575. Johns, A. M. (1993d). Toward developing a cultural repertoire: The case study of a Lao college freshman. In D. E. Murray (Ed.), *Diversity as resource: Redefining cultural literacy* (pp. 183-201). Washington, DC: TESOL.

A case study of a female Laotian student who maintains cultural integrity while succeeding in the American academic milieu. Reports several key text-handling and learning strategies in relation to new literacy tasks.

Academic Writing/Culture/Laotian.

1576. Johns, A. M. (1993e). Written argumentation for real audiences: Suggestions for teacher research and classroom practice. *TESOL Quarterly*, 27, 75-90.

Suggests ways to teach and research the production of authentic argumentation for real audiences, stimulated by interviews with successful bilingual engineering writers.

Argumentation/Engineering.

1577. Johns, A. M. (1993f, April). *Academic reading and writing tasks: products, processes, and resources*. Paper presented at the 27th Annual TESOL Convention, Atlanta, GA.

Discusses tasks and resources in designing academic reading and writing materials.

Reading-Writing Relations/Materials.

1578. Johns, A. M. (1992a). Academic English: What can we do? *Journal of Intensive English Studies*, 6, 61-69.

Outlines current approaches to EAP and delineates what can and cannot be done effectively.

Academic Writing.

1579. Johns, A. M. (1992b). Toward developing a cultural repertoire: The case study of a Lao college freshman. In D. E. Murray (Ed.), *Diversity as resource: Redefining cultural literacy* (pp. 183-201). Arlington, VA: TESOL.

A case study of a female Laotian student who maintains cultural integrity while succeeding in the American academic milieu. Reports several key text-handling and learning strategies in relation to new literacy tasks.

EAP/Culture/Laotian.

1580. Johns, A. M. (1992c). *Using classroom and authentic genres: Student initiation into academic writing*. Unpublished manuscript, San Diego State University, San Diego, CA.

Discusses the issues in teaching and learning classroom genres (e.g., the essay examination) and authentic genres of disciplines (e.g., the research paper). Describes an academic task portfolio that integrates the two genres in order to prepare students for diverse audiences and discourse expectations.

Genre.

1581. Johns, A. M. (1992d, March). *Developing techniques for ESL adjunct classes*. Paper presented at the 26th Annual TESOL Convention, Vancouver, BC.

Adjunct.

1582. Johns, A. M. (1991a). English for specific purposes (ESP): Its history and contributions. In M. Celce-Murcia (Ed.), *Teaching English as a second or foreign language* (pp. 67-77). NY: Newbury/HarperCollins.

Discusses the ESP movement -- language teaching designed for specific learners and language learning purposes. ESP bears on writing insofar as it makes use of extensive analyses of lexical, syntactic, and rhetorical forms and functions.

ESP.

1583. Johns, A. M. (1991b). Faculty assessment of ESL student literacy skills: Implications for writing assessment. In L. Hamp-Lyons (Ed.), *Assessing second language writing in academic contexts* (pp. 167-179). Norwood, NJ: Ablex.

Offers criteria and suggestions for academic writing tests drawn from a report on a series of interviews with two faculty from the same discipline about the nature of academic literacy.

Assessment/Literacy.

1584. Johns, A. M. (1991c). Interpreting an English competency examination: The frustrations of an ESL science student. *Written Communication*, 8(3), 379-401.

Reports a case study of a Vietnamese student who writes successfully in general education and biology classes, but who continues to fail the English department's writing competency examination. Identifies student problems and the weaknesses of the test.

Evaluation/Vietnamese/ESP.

1585. Johns, A. M. (1991d, March). *Task representation in writing: teaching and testing issues*. Paper presented at the 25th Annual TESOL Convention, New York, NY.

Reports on case studies of three Asian students whose repeated failures on English department tests can be traced to difficulties comprehending prompts as well as representating tasks and audiences.

Task/Examination Essays.

1586. Johns, A. M. (1990a). Coherence as a cultural phenomenon: Employing ethnographic principles in the academic milieu. In U. M. Connor, & A. M. Johns (Eds.), *Coherence in writing: Research and pedagogical perspectives* (pp. 209-226). Alexandria, VA: TESOL.

Describes the use of "the journalog" in a writing adjunct class attached to a course on Western Civilization for linguistically diverse university students. Uses this technique to help students become ethnographers by examining: (1) the roles that they and their teacher played; (2) the major topics of the course and relations to each other; (3) what they considered as conventions of academic writing; and (4) the ways of using reading for writing. Ultimately helps students juxtapose their own approaches with expectations of the academic discourse community and therefore is a successful learning experience.

Curriculum/ Discourse Communities.

1587. Johns, A. M. (1990). L1 composition theories: Implications for developing theories of L2 composition. In B. Kroll (Ed.), *Second language writing: Research insights for the classroom* (pp. 24-36). Cambridge: Cambridge University Press.

Argues that complete L2 theories of composition need to account for writer, reality, audience, and language. In these terms, the essay reviews process, interactive, and social constructivist concerns.

Theory/Review.

1588. Johns, A. M. (1988a). The discourse communities' dilemma: Identifying transferable skills for the academic milieu. *English for Specific Purposes*, 7(1), 55-60.

Raises the problem that generalized English skills taught in EAP courses may not transfer to specific academic disciplines into which students subsequently enter.

Discourse Communities.

1589. Johns, A. M. (1988b). Two commentaries on Ruth Spack's "Initiating ESL Students into the Academic Discourse Community: How Far Should We Go?": A reader reads . . . [In The Forum]. *TESOL Quarterly*, 22, 705-707.

Opposes Spack's view of limiting ESL writers to general rather than specific academic writing tasks and audiences.

Academic Writing/WAC.

1590. Johns, A. M. (1988c, March). *Using schema-theoretical principles to teach the summary*. Paper presented at the 22nd Annual TESOL Convention, Chicago, IL.

Discusses a technique in which students slot context ideas in preparing a summary of problem/solution passage.

Summary Writing/Background Knowledge.

1591. Johns, A. M. (1987a). On assigning summaries: Some suggestions and cautions. *TECFORS*, 10(2), 1-5.

Discusses ways of teaching summarizing and the relevance of audience in choosing a type.

Summary Writing/Audience.

1592. Johns, A. M. (1987b, March). *Teaching a problem-solution text to ESL and basic writing students*. Paper presented at the 38th Annual CCCC Meeting, Atlanta, GA.

Text Analysis/NS-NNS Comparisons.

1593. Johns, A. M. (1986a). Coherence and academic writing: Some definitions and suggestions for teaching. *TESOL Quarterly*, 20, 247-266.

Two definitions of coherence: text-based and reader-based, are found in the current literature on coherence in ESL students' compositions. Suggests that both approaches should be taken into consideration by ESL writing teachers. Proposes prompt deconstruction as the initial step in the first draft and "top down" evaluation of the thesis in relationship to the prompt as a helpful revision strategy.

Coherence/Academic Writing/Revision.

1594. Johns, A. M. (1986b). The ESL student and the revision process: Some insights from schema theory. *Journal of Basic Writing*, 5(2), 70-80.

Suggests the use of schema-theoretical approach in improving the writing of ESL students in a basic writing class. Presents revisions by Chinese-speaking student using this approach.

Revision/Schema/Chinese.

1595. Johns, A. M. (1986c, March). *Writing task demands and evaluation in academic classrooms*. Paper presented at the 20th Annual TESOL Convention, Anaheim, CA.

Discusses faculty responses to questionnaire about important factors in evaluating academic writing.

Task/Standards.

1596. Johns, A. M. (1985a). Academic writing standards: A questionnaire. *TECFORS*, 8(1), 11-15. [ERIC ED 267 650].

Publishes a questionnaire surveying both tasks and grading criteria in academic writing courses.

Academic Writing/Task/Grading.

1597. Johns, A. M. (1985b). Summary protocols of "underprepared" and "adept" university students: Replications and distortions of the original. *Language Learning*, 35, 495-512.

Compares summarizing skills of underprepared students with mainstream adult students. Findings indicate that underprepared students: (1) omit a number of main ideas from their summaries; (2) include more sentence-level reproductions than combinations of idea units; (3) do not differ significantly from other groups in balance and distribution of idea units.

Summary Writing/University.

1598. Johns, A. M. (1985c, April). *Examining coherence problems in ESL writing*. Paper presented at the 19th Annual TESOL Convention, New York, NY.

Uses theoretical studies on coherence to examine coherence problems of university level ESL students.

Coherence/University.

1599. Johns, A. M. (1984). Textual cohesion and the Chinese speaker of English. *Language Learning and Communication*, 3, 69-74.

Corroborates Hu, Brown, and Brown's (1982) finding that Chinese university EFL students overuse additive conjuncts.

Cohesion/Chinese.

1600. Johns, A. M. (1983). "Relevance" and the ESL writing, reading class. *TECFORS*, 6(4), 1-2. [ERIC ED 267 649].

Claims that writing activities in ESL classes will be more successful if students can see their relevance to other academic subjects. Describes an effective adjunct class program where this principle has been applied.
WAC/Curriculum.

1601. Johns, A. M. (1981, March). *Using native speaker English-for-Business materials in ESL*. Paper presented at the 15th Annual TESOL Convention, Detroit, MI.
Discusses curricular materials that can be adopted for writing class use -- especially case, letter, memo, and report writing.
Materials/ESP/Business Writing.

1602. Johns, A. M. (1980a). Cohesion in written business discourse: Some contrasts. *The ESP Journal*, *1*, 35-44.
Examines distinctive cohesive items in business letters, reports, and textbooks. Concludes that each category has cohesive ties (lexical cohesion being most common), but generalizations cannot be made about classifications.
Cohesion/Business Writing.

1603. Johns, A. M. (1980b). Preventing global discourse errors: Problems and approaches to ESOL writing. *CATESOL Occasional Papers*, *6*, 65-70. [ERIC ED 200 060].
Examines errors committed by college-level ESL students in the area of cohesion and suggests using models to teach connectives.
Errors/Cohesion/University.

1604. Johns, A. M. (1980c, March). *Necessary academic English: A survey*. Paper presented at the 14th Annual TESOL Convention, San Francisco, CA.
Faculty responses to questionnaires at one university suggest what is needed to succeed academically.
Academic Writing/Standards.

1605. Johns, A. M. (1979a). A comparison of cohesive elements in American business and non-native speaker written discourse. *Dissertation Abstracts International*, *40*(4), 1927A.
Analyzes the cohesive elements in the written discourse in English of five non-native speaking groups and compares results with the cohesive elements in two modes of American business writing. Findings indicate mode of discourse important in selecting cohesive elements.
Cohesion/Text Analysis/Business Writing.

1606. Johns, A. M. (1979b, March). *Cohesive errors in the discourse of non-native speakers*. Paper presented at the 13th Annual TESOL Convention, Boston. [ERIC ED 200 060].
Uses Halliday & Hasan (1976) to classify errors in cohesion in 365 pieces of writing. Finds that lexical cohesion is the most frequently used cohesive device while errors in conjunction are the most frequent error type.
Cohesion/Error Analysis.

1607. Johns, A. M., & Mayes, P. (1990). An analysis of summary protocols of university ESL students. *Applied Linguistics*, *11*, 253-271.
Finds no significant differences in a textual analysis of the idea units from written protocols by ESL college students at two proficiency levels. Suggests

paraphrasing, sentence-combining, and creating theses and generalizations as appropriate pedagogy for improving ability to summarize.
Summary Writing/Academic Writing.

1608. Johnson, C. V. (1985). The composing processes of six ESL students. *Dissertation Abstracts International*, *46*(5), 1216A.

Interviews and composing aloud protocols of six advanced ESL college students (3 Spanish-speakers and 3 Japanese-speakers) show a wide variety of individual composing styles and problems. Most students used their native language in planning and metacommentary to some extent. As a group, L1 used more when writing about their home countries than about the U.S. Results suggest diversity among ESL students and complexity of the relation between language and writing.
L1 Influence/Hispanic/Japanese.

1609. Johnson, D. M. (1988a). ESL children as teachers: A social view of second language use. *Language Arts*, *65*(2), 154-163.

Suggests using ESL students to peer tutor native speaking children. Studies show that this method promotes L2 vocabulary development and greater interaction between ESL and native speaking children.
Vocabulary/Interaction.

1610. Johnson, D. M. (1988b, March). *Social context and language use in peer reviews*. Paper presented at the 22nd Annual TESOL Convention, Chicago, IL.

Analyzes peer review texts in a linguistically mixed university content course. Shows how students attempt to use socially appropriate language.
Peer Response.

1611. Johnson, D. M. (1992a). Interpersonal involvement in discourse: Gender variation in L2 writers' complimenting strategies. *Journal of Second Language Writing*, *1*(3), 195-215.

A set of 35 peer-review papers written by advanced L2 women writers showed less use of four female-female complimenting strategies than in papers by L1 women writers.
Style/Gender/NS-NNS Comparisons.

1612. Johnson, D. M. (1992b, March). *Perceiving writing quality through gender lenses*. Paper presented at the 26th Annual TESOL Convention, Vancouver, BC.

Reports the results of a study of the role of gender in assessing the writing of 49 ESL graduate students. Finds patterns of gender bias.
Assessment/Variation/Gender.

1613. Johnson, D. M. (1989). Enriching task contexts for second language writing: Power through interpersonal roles. In D. M. Johnson, & D. H. Roen (Eds.), *Richness in writing: Empowering ESL students* (pp. 39-54). NY: Longman.

Claims research to have shown that traditional teacher-centered instruction of writing for ESL students is not as effective as a social-interactional view. States that teachers can vary roles by giving students control over topics, expanding on social purposes of students' writing, and using students as teachers, all of which empower students.
Task/Social.

1614. Johnson, D. M., & Roen, D. H. (Eds.). (1989). *Richness in writing: Empowering ESL students* NY: Longman.

    An anthology of eighteen essays deals with ways of empowering ESL students through richness in writing, especially in K-12 classrooms. Part I describes creating enriching contexts for composing. Part II deals with rhetorical issues of L2 writing and shows how writing can be enhanced through principles of authenticity, audience, topic and purpose. Part III suggests using ESL students' rich cultural experience in writing.

    Elementary/Secondary School.

1615. Johnson, J. A. (1993). *Writing strategies for ESL students*. Boston: Heinle & Heinle.

    Textbook combines a review of grammar and mechanics with instruction in how to write paragraph and themes for academic contexts.

    University/Grammar/Textbook.

1616. Johnson, J. A. (1979, March). *The ESL student's struggle with written English*. Paper presented at Meeting of the College English Association. n.p. [ERIC ED 193 968].

    Proposes composition courses in ESL that address the specific problems of non-native speakers and discusses several approaches to teaching it.

    Courses.

1617. Johnson, K. E. (1992). Cognitive strategies and second language writers: A re-evaluation of sentence combining. *Studies in Second Language Acquisition, 1*(1), 61-75.

    Analysis of think-aloud protocols of nine advanced second language writers who completed controlled and open sentence-combining tasks suggests that sentence combining stimulalated higher and lower level cognitive strategies.

    Sentence Combining/Cognition.

1618. Johnson, K. (1983). Communicative writing practice and Aristotelian rhetoric. In A. Freedman, I. Pringle, & J. Yalden (Ed.), *Learning to write: First language, second language* (pp. 247-257). NY: Longman.

    Claims that teaching of communicative writing should aim at expressing intents within contexts. Highlights implications for teachers and syllabus designers.

    Communicative Writing.

1619. Johnson, K. (1982a). Communicative writing practice and Aristotelian rhetoric. In K. Johnson (Ed.), *Communicative syllabus design and methodology* (pp. 201-213). Oxford: Pergamon Press.

    Outlines an approach to writing that takes account of non-stereotyped nature of communication by including inductive, contextualized activities related to analysis of textual passages.

    Rhetoric/Communicative Writing.

1620. Johnson, K. (1982b). Five principles in a "communicative" exercise type. In K. Johnson, *Communicative syllabus design and methodology* (pp. 163-175). Oxford: Pergamon Press.

    Five principles for communicative material design: information transfer, information gap, jigsaw, task dependency, and correction for content -- are defined and illustrated.

Materials.

1621. Johnson, K. (1982c). Teaching appropriateness and coherence in academic writing. In K. Johnson, *Communicative syllabus design and methodology* (pp. 176-182). Oxford: Pergamon Press.

Presents a teaching sequence for the classifying function to illustrate how functional appropriateness and coherence can be taught.

Coherence/Communicative Writing.

1622. Johnson, K. (1981). Writing. In K. Johnson, & K. Morrow (Eds.), *Communication in the classroom: Applications and methods for a communicative approach* (pp. 93-107). Essex, England: Longman.

Suggests commmunicative activity sequences for preparing students to write free compositions and other ideas to stimulate paragraph level writing.

Communicative Writing.

1623. Johnson, M. (1981). Writing to learn and learning to write. *TECFORS*, *4*(3), 6-7. [ERIC ED 267 647].

Discusses how writing leads to involvement and learning.

Process Instruction.

1624. Johnson, M. A. (1988). Word processing in the English as a second language classroom. In J. L. Hoot, & S. B. Silvern (Eds.), *Writing with computers in the early grades* (pp. 107-121). NY: Teachers College Press.

Discusses the contribution of the computer as a communication facilitator for the early elementary ESL classroom. Focuses on using the computer within an LEA approach.

Children/Computers.

1625. Johnson, M. A. (1986). Effects of using the computer as a tool for writing on the vocabulary, reading, and writing of first and second-grade Spanish-speaking students. *Dissertation Abstracts International*, *47*(6), 2099-3000A.

Finds that children write longer stories, edit, explore, and revise more with the use of computers.

Computers/Elementary/Hispanic.

1626. Johnson, P. (1992). Cohesion and coherence in compositions in Malay and English. *RELC Journal*, *23*(2), 1-17.

Finds differences in coherence but not cohesion among good and weak Malay ESL essays and differences in both among comparable NES essays.

Coherence/Cohesion/Malay.

1627. Johnson, P. (1991, March). *Interaction of reading/writing strategies for comprehension and communication*. Paper presented at the 25th Annual TESOL Convention, New York, NY.

Conferences with ESL readers/writers suggests that reading academic texts facilitates writing expository prose in the categories of information, transaction, and process.

Reading-Writing Relations/Conferencing.

1628. Johnson, P. (1986). Acquisition of schema for comprehension and communication: A study for the reading-writing relationship in ESL. *RELC Journal*, *17*(1), 1-13.

Tests the hypothesis that acquisition of a western expository genre is easier if the same information is presented in narrative form (i.e., underlying schema). Inexperienced ESL writers recalled more in narrative than expository mode whereas experienced ESL writers performed the same in either mode. Concludes that inexperienced students employed "schema assimilation" (i.e., where expository material is adapted to fit narrative schema) in contrast to experienced students who used "schema accomodation" (i.e., where narrative genre is adapted and changed to fit a new expository genre).
Schema/Reading-Writing Relations.

1629. Johnson, P. (1985). Time for the basic basics: One-to-one conferencing with E.S.L. students. *TECFORS*, *8*(3), 7-12. [ERIC ED 267 650].
Provides advice about how to go about conferencing with ESL students.
Conferencing.

1630. Johnson, P. (1983, March). *A contrastive analysis of academic writing and technical writing and its methodological implications*. Paper presented at the 17th Annual TESOL Convention, Toronto, Ontario.
Outlines register differences to aid the teaching of technical writing to ESL students.
Technical Writing/Register.

1631. Johnson, P. (1982). Sentence combining: A summary and bibliography. *ERIC/CLL News Bulletin*, *5*(2), 3-4.
Argues that sentence-combining practice must begin at the student's level of linguistic competence because the learner cannot rely on an innate sense of grammaticality and that despite the benefits for syntactic fluency, should not replace a total writing course which needs to address the entire writing process.
Sentence Combining/Bibliography.

1632. Johnson, P., & Mileham, J. (1985, April). *Testing skills in expository writing through reading comprehension*. Paper presented at the 19th Annual TESOL Convention, New York, NY.
Gives a multiple choice exam that tests writing through reading.
Assessment/Objective Measures.

1633. Johnson, T., & Sheetz-Brunetti, Y. (1984). *English pyramids: Using hierarchical diagrams for communication activities*. Washington, DC: ERIC/FLL. [ERIC ED 249 816].
Claims that using a pyramid diagram as a visual representation of the way English speakers and writers organize ideas for comparison with discourse organization in other cultures can solve a common problem of ESL students, namely, inability to organize ideas hierarchically. Illustrates with a class activity that uses the pyramid for teaching concept hierarchies is a sentence-level exercise using the Chinese zodiac to organize ideas about personality traits and practice the pattern expected in English prose.
Contrastive Rhetoric/Organization.

1634. Johnston, S. A. (1985). An approach to the teaching of academic writing. *ELT Journal*, *39*, 248-252.

Recommends use of alternative research sources such as interviews when teaching the research paper in China where library resources may be scarce or inaccessible.
Academic Writing/Chinese.

1635. Johnston, S. S., & Zukowski-Faust, J. (1985). *Keys to composition: A guide to writing for students of English as a second language.* (Second Ed.). NY: Harcourt Brace Jovanovich.
Textbook intended to prepare students for a positive academic writing experience by teaching them to recognize and use tools for writing and the forms used by successful writers.
Intermediate/Textbook.

1636. Johnston, S. S., & Zukowski-Faust, J. (1980, March). *Composition testing: How to be objective.* Paper presented at the 14th Annual TESOL Convention, San Francisco, CA.
Offers multiple choice test for placement and diagnostic purposes.
Assessment/Objective Measures.

1637. Jollife, D. A. (1992). Writers and their subjects: Ethnologic and Chinese composition. In S. P. Witte, N. Nakadate, & R. D. Cherry (Eds.), *A rhetoric of doing: Essays on written discourse in honor of James L. Kinneavy* (pp. 261-275). Carbondale, IL: Southern Illinois University Press.
As part of a contrastive ethnological analysis with the American composition classroom, author shows that Chinese composition students when choosing and developing writing topics are shaped by their political, cultural, institutional, curricular and instructional contexts to call on authority, tradition and conform to the collective cause.
Chinese/Topic/Rhetoric.

1638. Jolly, D. (1984). *Writing tasks.* NY: Cambridge University Press.
Contains theory and exercises for teaching writing in the classroom, based on the notion that writing is primarily social in purpose. Offers models and practice at text-type level and, thereby, claims "to develop students' ability to write whole texts using the appropriate form, style, and language."
Materials/Intermediate.

1639. Jones, C. S. (1988, March). *Analytic components of holistic ratings of ESL compositions.* Paper presented at the 39th Annual CCCC Meeting, St. Louis, MO.
Evaluation.

1640. Jones, C. S. (1985a, April). *Discourse synthesis in first and second language composition.* Paper presented at the 19th Annual TESOL Convention, New York, NY.
Discourse Analysis/NS-NNS Comparisons.

1641. Jones, C. S. (1985b). Problems with monitor use in second language composing. In M. Rose (Ed.), *When a writer can't write: Studies in writer's block and other composing process problems* (pp. 96-118). NY: Guilford.
Discusses nonlinguistic sources of difficulties in second language composing in the light of Krashen's Monitor theory. Explores the composing processes of

monitor overusers and underusers. Reports a descriptive case study of two ESL learners.
Monitoring.

1642. Jones, C. S. (1983, March). *Some composing strategies of second language writers*. Paper presented at the 17th Annual TESOL Convention, Toronto, Ontario.
Strategies.

1643. Jones, C. S. (1982a). Attention to rhetorical information while composing in a second language. In C. C. Campbell, V. Flashner, T. Hudson, & J. Lubin (Eds.), *Proceedings of the Los Angeles Second Language Research Forum: Vol. II.* (pp. 130-143). Los Angeles, CA: UCLA.

Compares the writing process of two ESL writers (skilled and unskilled) who had similar linguistic proficiencies. Their composing processes differed at the cognitive (separability of ideas and expressions), rhetorical (text-bound vs. text-free), and syntactic (subordination/coordination patterns) levels.
Process Research.

1644. Jones, C. S. (1982b, May). *Composing in a second language: A process study*. Paper presented at the 16th Annual TESOL Convention, Honolulu, HI.

Reports a study of seven ESL students, using videotape and think aloud techniques. Finds similarities between L1 and L2 in planning and content organization of essays.
Process Research.

1645. Jones, C. S. (1980a). *Collecting data on the writing process of L2 writers*. Paper presented at the Annual Meeting of Ontario TESL Association, Ottawa, Ontario.
Process Research.

1646. Jones, C. S. (1980b). *The composing processes of an advanced ESL writer*. Paper presented at the Annual Meeting of the Ottawa TESL Association, Ottawa, Ontario.
Advanced/Process Research.

1647. Jones, C. S., & Tetroe, J. (1987). Composing in a second language. In A. Matsuhashi (Ed.), *Writing in real time: Modeling production process* (pp. 35-57). Norwood, NJ: Ablex.

Discusses the findings of a study of six Spanish-speaking students' composing strategies which show that the writing process in L1 is transferred to L2 writing tasks. Focuses on planning strategies of both L1 and L2 writers and argues that L2 composing is not different from L1 composing.
Hispanic/Strategies/L1 Influence/Planning.

1648. Jones, C. S., & Tetroe, J. (1983, March). *Observing ESL writing*. Paper presented at the 17th Annual TESOL Convention, Toronto, Ontario.
Process Research.

1649. Jones, D. (1988). *Knowing opportunities: Some possible benefits and limitations of dialogue journals in adult second language learning*. Unpublished master's thesis, School for Inteernational Living, Brattleboro, VT.
Dialogue Journals.

1650. Jones, J. (1991, November). *Benefits and issues involved in using portfolios with ESL students*. Paper presented at the 81st Annual NCTE Convention, Seattle, WA.

Assessment/Portfolios.

1651. Jones, P. E. (1981). *A descriptive analysis of the written English of EL Paso bilinguals*. Unpublished master's thesis, University of Texas, El Paso, TX.
Hispanic/Bilingual.

1652. Jones, P. M. (1988). *Knowing opportunities: Some possible benefits and limitations of dialogue journals in adult second language instruction*. Unpublished master's thesis, School for International Training, Brattleboro, VT.
Offers an evaluation of dialogue journals from the point of view of teaching experience and a review of current research.
Dialogue Journals.

1653. Jordan, M. K. (1981). Some associated nominals in technical writing. *Journal of Technical Writing and Communication*, (251-262),
Examines concept of "associated nominal" in the coherence of a text and highlights its role in student's writing development.
Syntactic Structures/Technical Writing/Cohesion.

1654. Jordan, R. R. (1988). The introductory paragraph in economics essays and examinations. In P. C. Robinson (Ed.), *Academic writing: Process and product* (pp. 63-66). London: Modern English Publications/British Council.
Discusses a native-speaking subject tutor's description of an "ideal introduction" in the light of data from essays and exams by 137 overseas students preparing to study economics in a British university. Contrary to expectations, students did not signal either the organization or the content of their essays (although they did so in their exam answers).
Academic Writing/Introductions

1655. Josephson, M. I. (1989). "Marking" EFL compositons: A new method. *English Teaching Forum*, 27(3), 28-32.
Describes a system -- the compform markchart -- that accomplishes an error analysis, error categorization, and error count in an efficient manner.
Evaluation/Error Analysis.

K

1656. Kachru, Y. (1982). Linguistics and written discourse in particular languages: Contrastive studies: English and Hindi. *Annual Review of Applied Linguistics*, 3, 50-69.
Examines the various approaches to discourse analysis in general and to English and South Asian languages in particular. Describes grammatical structure of Hindi and the influence of sociocultural factors in constructing and interpreting discourse with implications for theoretical, empirical, and pedagogical research.
Contrastive Rhetoric/Hindi.

1657. Kachru, Y. (1988). Writers in Hindi and English. In A. C. Purves (Ed.), *Writing across languages and cultures: Issues in contrastive rhetoric* (pp. 109-137). Newbury Park, CA: Sage.
Illustrates difference in conventions of register in selected pieces of written

expository texts in Hindi. Claims that differences are not categorical and that rhetorical pattern of Hindi is not always spiral but also linear.
Contrastive Rhetoric/Hindi.

1658. Kaczmarek, C. M. (1980). Scoring and rating "essay tasks". In J. W. Oller, & K. Perkins (Eds.), *Research in language testing* (pp. 151-159). Rowley, MA: Newbury.
Shows that subjective methods of assessing writing work as well as objective scoring techniques and are strongly correlated with other measures of ESL proficiency. Teacher judgments seemed reliable.
Evaluation.

1659. Kadar-Fulop, J. (1988). Culture, writing, and curriculum. In A. C. Purves, *Writing across languages and cultures: Issues in contrastive rhetoric* (pp. 25-50). Newbury Park, CA: Sage.
Presents a conceptual analysis of the relationship between culture, writing, and curriculum. Claims that mother tongue and foreign language instruction can cultivate both loyalty toward language of instruction and a sense of the multi-lingual character of the cultural tradition.
Culture/Curriculum.

1660. Kadesch, M. C., Kolba, E. D., & Crowell, S. C. (1989, March). *Helping students get from textbook to test or paper*. Paper presented at the 23rd Annual TESOL Convention, San Antonio, TX.
Incorporating what students have read into their writing requires a redefinition and expansion of the role of prewriting.
Invention/Reading-Writing Relations.

1661. Kadesh, M. C., Kolba, E. D., & Crowell, S. C. (1991). *Insights into academic writing: Strategies for advanced students*. Reading, MA: Addison Wesley/Longman.
Uses authentic college readings for critical thinking at the advanced level. Units feature pre-writing, drafting, rhetorical features, and checklists for editing. Text starts with self-expression and end with the research paper.
University/Reader.

1662. Kalaja, P., & Leppanen, S. (1992, March). *Process writing and computer conferencing in EFL*. Paper presented at the 26th Annual TESOL Convention, Vancouver, BC.
Presents results of an experiment studying the effects of computer conferences in a freshman process writing course on the quality of writing and on student attitudes.
Computers/Conferencing.

1663. Kamanya, E. (1988). The nonnative English writer. *Writing Lab Newsletter, 12*, 7-8.
Advocates encouraging ESL writers to "think in English" instead of translating from their first language.
L1 Influence.

1664. Kambal, M. O. (1980). An analysis of Khartoum University students' composition errors with implications for remedial English in the context of Arabicization. *Dissertation Abstracts International, 41*(4), 1570A.
Analyzes syntactic errors in written English compositions of Sudanese

students. Discusses noun phrase and verb phrase errors.
Errors/University/Arabic/Sudanese.

1665. Kameen, P. T. (1983). Syntactic skill and ESL writing quality. In A. Freeman, I. Pringle, & J. Yalden (Eds.), *Learning to write: First language/second language* (pp. 162-170). NY: Longman.

Finds that T-unit length and clause length are reliable discriminators between "good" and "poor" writing in 50 randomly chosen ESL compositions. Also notes that use of passive voice associated with highly valued essays.
Objective Measures/Assessment.

1666. Kameen, P. T. (1981, March). *How to use the T-unit yardstick in your classroom.* Paper presented at the 15th Annual TESOL Convention, Detroit, MI.

Regards the T-unit as a tool for analyzing student writing.
Objective Measures/Assessment/T-Unit.

1667. Kameen, P. T. (1979, March). *Syntactic skill and ESL writing.* Paper presented at the 13th Annual TESOL Convention, Boston.

Quantitative indices, such as T-unit length, clause length, and passive voice seem to discriminate between "good" and "poor" ESL compositions.
Objective Measures/T-Unit/Assessment.

1668. Kameen, P. T. (1978). A mechanical, meaningful, and communicative framework for ESL sentence combining exercises. *TESOL Quarterly, 12*, 395-401.

States the theoretical foundation for sentence-combining in intermediate and advanced ESL writing classes. Describes a three-stage sequencing of exercises within Paulston's framework of mechanical, meaningful, and communicative exercises.
Sentence Combining/Intermediate/T-Unit.

1669. Kamel, B. N. (1983). Arguing in English as a second language: A study of the speech act performance of Arabic speakers. *Dissertation Abstracts International, 45*(1), 104A.

Examines the effects of sociocultural factors on the acquisition of speech acts (argumentation) by Arabic speaking learners of English. Findings show interference of mother tongue and culture at the level of illocutionary force and discourse rules and at the level of idiomatic usage.
Arabic/Argumentation/Speaking-Writing Relations.

1670. Kamel, G. W. (1989). Argumentative writing by Arab learners of English as a foreign and second language: An empirical investigation of contrastive rhetoric. *Dissertation Abstracts International, 50*(3), 677A.

A quasi-experimental study examines the argumentative writing in Arabic and English by EFL and ESL Arab learners. Results show that participants produced significantly more T-units, more audience adaptation units and more claims, warrants and data (Toulmin, 1959) in their native language than in the target language. Also, ESL Arab students seem to outperform EFL Arab students in writing in English. Concludes that rhetorical ability is attributable to exposure, writing experience, and linguistic proficiency in target language rather than to L1 rhetorical influence.
Arabic/Argumentation/Contrastive Rhetoric.

1671. Kamisli, S. (1993). Word processing and the writing process: A case study of five

Turkish English as a second language (ESL) students. *Dissertation Abstracts International, 53*(12), 4238A.

Describes how five Turkish ESL students adapted to (a) using computers to write and (b) a process-oriented approach to learning to write. The study concludes that the students became more at ease with writing with computers than with pen and paper. Also, peer collaboration occurred in a less structured learning/teaching writing environment.

Word Processing/Turkish.

1672. Kang, S. M. (1993). A practical approach to teaching expository writing to ESP students. *English Teaching Forum, 31*(2), 32-33.

Advises limiting ESP writing initially to expository writing taught in a read-analyze-write approach in order to overcome the problem of substituting translation for creation.

ESP/Exposition.

1673. Kangas, J. A., & Reichelderfer, N. (1987). *Persistence by successful and nonsuccessful remedial and nonremedial English-as-a-Second-Language students: A longitudinal study.* (Research Report No. 65). Washington, DC: ERIC/FLL. [ERIC ED 289 539].

Finds that success in college reading and writing courses was one of the most significant factors in the persistence of native and non-native as well as remedial and non-remedial students (N=1264) in college.

Reading-Writing Relations/NS-NNS Comparisons.

1674. Kantor, R. N. (1989, March). *Writing without transition words: Forcing students to explore options.* Paper presented at the 23rd Annual TESOL Convention, San Antonio, TX.

Discusses techniques to encourage shift from over-reliance on transition words to lexical and grammatical options.

Style/Usage.

1675. Kantor, R. N. (1987, March). *Topic development for the Test of Written English.* Paper presented at the 38th Annual CCCC Meeting, Atlanta, GA.

Assessment/TWE/Topic.

1676. Kantor, R. N. (1985, April). *Topic management: Problems of sentence boundaries, transition, and reference.* Paper presented at the 19th Annual TESOL Convention, New York, NY.

Finds use of transitions, referential expressions, and placement of sentence boundaries as the key to native-like control in writing.

Topic/Style/Usage.

1677. Kantor, R. N., & Belcher, D. D. (1988, March). *Synergistic grammar instruction: Combining classroom and conference-based instruction.* Paper presented at the 22nd Annual TESOL Convention, Chicago, IL.

Suggests activities that combine tutorial and classroom grammar instruction to optimize the acquisition of advanced structures for ESL composition students.

Grammar.

1678. Kaplan, J. D., & Palhinha, E. M. G. (1982). Non-native speakers of English and their composition abilities: A review and analysis. In W. E. Frawley (Ed.), *Linguistics and literacy* (pp. 425-458). NY: Plenum.

In a survey of non-native college students, the majority report that their strongest writing skill is grammar and their weakest is style. Advocates the teaching of style.

Style.

1679. Kaplan, R. B. (1992). Contrastive rhetoric. In W. Bright (Ed.), *International encyclopedia of linguistics, volume 1* (pp. 302-303). NY: Oxford University Press.

Defines CR as "the notion that the organization of written text is substantially different in different languages" and describes some premises and problems with the research tradition.

Contrastive Rhetoric.

1680. Kaplan, R. B. (1991). Concluding essay: On applied linguistics and discourse analysis. *Annual Review of Applied Linguistics*, *11*, 199-204.

Summarizes contribution of this special volume on discourse analysis to applied linguistics, defined as "the uses and users of texts -- the social contexts in which users interact and the problems associated with such interaction at the personal, social, and political levels".

Discourse Analysis.

1681. Kaplan, R. B. (1990). Writing in a multilingual/multicultural context: What's contrastive about contrastive rhetoric? *The Writing Instructor*, *10*, 7-18.

Advocates cultural sensitivity through contrastive rhetoric to the native patterns brought by second writers language to the new context.

Contrastive Rhetoric.

1682. Kaplan, R. B. (1988). Contrastive rhetoric and second language learning: Notes toward a theory of contrastive rhetoric. In A. C. Purves (Ed.), *Writing across languages and cultures: Issues in contrastive rhetoric* (pp. 275-304). Newbury Park, CA: Sage.

Traces the history of contrastive rhetoric and text analysis, enumerates the evidence that contrastive rhetoric examines, and suggests pedagogical implications.

Contrastive Rhetoric.

1683. Kaplan, R. B. (1987a). Cultural thought patterns revisited. In U. M. Connor, & R. B. Kaplan (Eds.), *Writing across languages: Analysis of L2 text* (pp. 9-22). Reading, MA: Addison-Wesley.

Briefly reviews Kaplan (1966) and reiterates that rhetorical patterns are culture-specific. States the need for a sound theoretical model to study written texts.

Contrastive Rhetoric.

1684. Kaplan, R. B. (1987b, April). *Fact and counter-fact: An exploration in Chinese writing*. Paper presented at the 21st Annual TESOL Convention, Miami Beach, FL.

Contrastive Rhetoric/Chinese.

1685. Kaplan, R. B. (1986a). Culture and the written language. In J. M. Valdes (Ed.), *Culture bound: Bridging the cultural gap in language teaching* (pp. 8-19). Cambridge: Cambridge University Press.

Explores the impact of the invention of writing and technological

developments on the relation between human beings and information and on the structure and content of language. Indicates a close tie between culture and written language and that spoken and written language influence each other.
Culture/Contrastive Rhetoric.

1686. Kaplan, R. B. (1986b). On the structure of text and its pedagogical implications. *Lenguas Modernas*, *13*, 67-78.
Discusses what makes writing a complex process in order to determine what needs to be included in a course in composition.
Text Analysis/Contrastive Rhetoric

1687. Kaplan, R. B. (1984). Reading and writing: Assumptions and presuppositions. *The American Language Journal*, *2*(2), 39-48.
Discusses reasons why the renaissance in the teaching of reading and writing to ESL students is warranted.
Contrastive Rhetoric.

1688. Kaplan, R. B. (1983a). Contrastive rhetorics: Some implications for the writing process. In A. Freedman, I. Pringle, & J. Yalden (Eds.), *Learning to write: First language, second language* (pp. 139-161). NY: Longman.
Reprints Kaplan (1982).
Contrastive Rhetoric.

1689. Kaplan, R. B. (1983b). An introduction to the study of written texts: The discourse "compact". *Annual Review of Applied Linguistics*, *3*, 138-151.
Examines the history of writing and the presuppositions that history seems to impose on the pedagogical process. Concludes that individuals from differing linguistic systems come to the writing process with different ideas about both the process and the product.
Contrastive Rhetoric.

1690. Kaplan, R. B. (1983c). Reading and writing, technology and planning: To do what and with what and to whom? In J. E. Alatis, H. Stern, & P. Strevens (Eds.), *GURT '83: Applied linguistics and the preparation of second language teachers -- Toward a rationale* (pp. 242-254). Washington, DC: Georgetown University Press.
Elaborates concepts about writing that teachers need to know.
Teacher Preparation.

1691. Kaplan, R. B. (1982a). Contrastive rhetoric: Some implications for the writing process. *English Teaching and Learning*, *6*, 24-38.
Posits that speakers of different languages use characteristic devices to present information, to establish the relationships among ideas, to show the centrality of one idea as opposed to another, to select the most effective means of presentation, and to develop topic and realize focus.
Contrastive Rhetoric.

1692. Kaplan, R. B. (1982b, May). *A proficiency examination of writing skills used for placement in freshman-level ESL courses*. Paper presented at the 40th Annual NAFSA Meeting, Seattle, WA.
Assessment/Placement.

1693. Kaplan, R. B. (1981). Error in advanced-level discourse. *TECFORS*, *4*(3), 2-3.

Argues that error gravity at the advanced discourse level cannot be identified with a single linguistic constituent, function, or factor.
Contrastive Rhetoric/Error Gravity.

1694. Kaplan, R. B. (1978a). Contrastive rhetorics: Further speculations. Paper presented at the Joint Conference of the American Association of Applied Linguistics and the Linguistic Sociey of America, Boston, MA. [ERIC ED 172 582].
Discusses L1 interference in textual focus or how the writer orients readers to what is prominent information in a text. Significant differences in NES and NNES performance on a discourse completion task suggests differing assumptions about shared knowledge between writer and reader underlying the concept of focus.
Contrastive Rhetoric/NS-NNS Comparisons.

1695. Kaplan, R. B. (1978b). On the notion of topic in written discourse. *Australian Review of Applied Linguistics*, *1*(2), 1-10. [ERIC ED 171 146].
Suggests that a coherent text consists of discourse blocs which are made up of discourse units that are joined using bloc signals. Claims that this has important implications for language teaching, particularly the teaching of scientific and technological discourse.
Contrastive Rhetoric/Topic.

1696. Kaplan, R. B. (1977). Contrastive rhetoric: Some hypotheses. *ITL: Journal of Applied Linguistics*, 39, 62-72.
Presents fundamental definitions of textual discourse and its elements with sample text rewritten to illustrate these principles.
Contrastive Rhetoric.

1697. Kaplan, R. B. (1976). A further note on contrastive rhetoric. *Communication Quarterly*, *24*(2), 12-19.
Offers a preliminary taxonomy of syntactic devices used to provide "linearity" in English discourse blocs in contrast to differing rhetorical patterns reported in the writing of other cultures.
Contrastive Rhetoric/Syntactic Structures.

1698. Kaplan, R. B. (1971). Composition at the advanced ESL Level: A teacher's guide to connected paragraph construction for advanced-level foreign students. *English Record*, *21*(4), 53-64.
Gives practical procedures for students to generate topics and organize ideas in the advanced composition class.
Paragraph/Advanced.

1699. Kaplan, R. B. (1970a). *The anatomy of rhetoric: Prolegomena to a functional theory of rhetoric*. Philadelphia: Center for Curriculum Development.
Republishes material from Kaplan's earlier articles (1966, 1967, 1968, 1969, 1970, 1971) within a revised relativistic framework of contrastive rhetoric.
Contrastive Rhetoric.

1700. Kaplan, R. B. (1970b). Notes toward an applied rhetoric. In R. C. Lugton (Ed.), *Preparing the EFL teacher: A projection for the 1970's* (pp. 45-74). Philadelphia: Center for Curriculum Development.
Discusses how rhetoricians such as Pitkin (1968) and Christensen (1967)

provide a dynamic way to analyze discourse which is illustrated by analyses of passages from Bronowski, Macauley, and an essay by a Thai learner of English.
Contrastive Rhetoric/Text Analysis/Thai.

1701. Kaplan, R. B. (1968). Contrastive rhetoric: Teaching composition to the Chinese student. *Journal of English as a Second Language*, *3*(1), 1-13.
Claims that the traditional Chinese "eight-legged" essay which was once required in civil-service examinations impacts on the writing of Mandarin-speaking writers of English.
Contrastive Rhetoric/Chinese.

1702. Kaplan, R. B. (1967a). Contrastive rhetoric and the teaching of composition. *TESOL Quarterly*, *1*, 10-16.
Discusses parallelism, a characteristic of Koranic style, that is found to influence the writing and revision of advanced Arab learners of English.
Arabic/Contrastive Rhetoric/Style.

1703. Kaplan, R. B. (1967b, April). *Contrastive rhetoric and the teaching of composition: On seeing the world through language-colored glasses*. Paper presented at the 1st TESOL Convention, Miami Beach, FL.
See previous item.
Contrastive Rhetoric.

1704. Kaplan, R. B. (1966a). A contrastive-rhetoric approach to reading and writing. In R. B. Kaplan (Ed.), *Selected conference papers of the Association of Teachers of English as a Second Language* (pp. 85-93). NY: NAFSA/University of Southern California Press.
Discusses philosophical background for his view that rhetoric and logic are cultural phenomena. Illustrates contrast between a typical "linear" English paragraph development and parallelism in Semitic languages and the ESL writing of an Arabic-speaking student.
Contrastive Rhetoric/Reading-Writing Relations/Arabic.

1705. Kaplan, R. B. (1966b). Cultural thought patterns in inter-cultural education. *Language Learning*, *16*, 1-20.
First statement of the contrastive rhetoric notion. Examines paragraph development of various groups of ESL students and postulates a distinct rhetorical and cultural thought pattern for each cultural group. Suggests practical ways of teaching rhetorical structure of English to ESL students.
Contrastive Rhetoric/Paragraph.

1706. Kaplan, R. B., d'Anglejan, A., Cowan, J. R., Kachru, B., & Tucker G. Richard (Eds.). (1983). *Annual Review of Applied Linguistics* Rowley, MA: Newbury House.
Issue devoted exclusively to cross-linguistic analysis of written discourse, mainly essays on particular language contrasts, with bibliographies. See Houghton & Hoey (1983), Leap (1983), Kachru (1983), Hinds (1983), Chang (1983), Tsao (1983), Pandharipande (1983), and Kaplan (1983) for specific studies.
Contrastive Rhetoric/Review/Bibliography.

1707. Kaplan, R. B., & Grabe, W. (1991). The fiction in science writing. In H. Schroder (Ed.), *Subject-oriented texts: Language for special purposes and text theory* (pp. 199-

217). Berlin: deGruyter.

Argues that text structural differences exist both between and within languages and reviews research examining the rhetorical nature of science writing.

Contrastive Rhetoric/Text Analysis.

1708. Kaplan, R. B., & Shaw, P. A. (1984). *Academic English: Exploring and creating discourse*. Rowley, MA: Newbury House.

Textbook with varied readings and exercise suitable for college bound international student who needs to improve reading and writing of academic texts through attention to elements and patterns of discourse.

Textbook/Advanced.

1709. Kasser, C. (1993, April). *Teaching rhetoric and grammar in content-based writing courses*. Paper presented at the 27th Annual TESOL Convention, Atlanta, GA.

Describe methods of incorporating patterns students need into courses on focued on specific content or themes.

Rhetoric/Grammar/Courses.

1710. Katchen, J. E. (1982). A structural comparison of American English and Farsi expository writing. *Papers in Linguistics: International Journal of Human Communication (Edmonton, Canada)*, 15(3), 165-180.

Compares the structural characteristics of American English and Farsi expository writing. Finds that (1) Farsi introductions and conclusions were not as explicitly or clearly stated as were those in American essays, and (2) that Farsi paragraphs, unlike the American English equivalents, lacked topic sentences in initial positions and statements of supporting evidence to follow up.

Contrastive Rhetoric/Farsi.

1711. Katz, A. (1988). Issues in writing proficiency assessment: The academic context. In P. Lowe, & C. W. Stansfield (Eds.), *Second language proficiency assessment: Current issues* (pp. 178-201). Englewood Cliffs, NJ: Prentice Hall Regents.

Discusses the changing role of academic writing in the foreign language learning context and describes TWE, holistic scoring and portfolio assessment.

Assessment/Holistic/Portfolios.

1712. Katz, A. M. (1988). Responding to student writers: The writing conferences of second language learners. *Dissertation Abstracts International*, 49(6), 1394A.

Examines the contextual and interactional factors in conferencing nonnative English speaking writers. The writing conference was found to be a neutral vehicle that served the agenda of the teachers in the context of their individual, overall framework of teaching.

Hispanic/Conferencing/Responding.

1713. Katz, A. M. (1986, March). *Teaching style in writing classrooms: Four distinct institutional contexts*. Paper presented at the 20th Annual TESOL Convention, Anaheim, CA.

Reports research that shows how teaching style affects way techniques and procedures are applied.

Style.

1714. Katz, A. M. (1985, March). *Student attitudes toward writing: First language/second*

language. Paper presented at the 36th Annual CCCC Meeting, Minneapolis, MN.
Psychology/NS-NNS Comparisons.

1715. Kaufman, L. M. (1988). Tense alternation by native and non-native English speakers in narrative discourse. *Dissertation Abstracts International, 49*(1), 84A.

Study describes tense variation in the description of past events by native and non-native speakers. Non-natives produce significantly more non-past tense verbs forms with past time meaning.
Hispanic/Narration/NS-NNS Comparisons.

1716. Kayfetz, J. L., & Blass, L. J. (1981). Can naive judges recognize improvement in ESL compositions? *TESL Reporter, 14*(4), 77-82.

Naive judges (i.e., non-English teachers) assessed the progress of ESL students' writing ability at four distinct proficiency levels. Results indicate that those at the very beginning and at the low-advanced levels improved the most. However, fewer than half the students at the intermediate and the high-advanced levels were judged better at the end of seven weeks of instruction.
Assessment/IEP.

1717. Kayfetz, J. L., Blass, L. J., & Cato, J. (1980, March). *Can naive judges recognize improvement in ESL compositions?* Paper presented at the 14th Annual TESOL Convention, San Francisco, CA.

Argues that focus should be placed on global writing skills since people outside English are primarily content-oriented.
Assessment/Raters.

1718. Kearney, B. A. (1989, March). *Academic discourse community: Initiation and participation through research writing.* Paper presented at the 23rd Annual TESOL Convention, San Antonio, TX.

Shows that research writing course is appropriate for preparing ESL students to participate in academic culture.
Discourse Communities/Research Writing.

1719. Keh, C. L. (1991). Teaching grammar as a process in the process of writing. *English Teaching Forum, 29*(1), 17-21.

Reviews the teaching of grammar and tells where it might be taught in the process.
Grammar.

1720. Keh, C. L. (1990a). Design for a process-approach writing course. *English Teaching Forum, 28*(1), 10-12.

Outlines a course for adults who want to use a process approach.
Process Instruction/Chinese.

1721. Keh, C. L. (1990b). Feedback on the writing process: A model and methods for implementation. *ELT Journal, 44*, 294-304.

Discusses peer feedback, conferencing, and written comments in a model of feedback within the process approach.
Feedback.

1722. Keh, C. L. (1989). How I use the dicto-comp. *English Teaching Forum, 27*(1), 39-40.

Describes how she uses dicto-comp -- a form of controlled writing -- in high school classses in Hong Kong.
Control/Secondary School.

1723. Keller, M. A., & Mirano-Neto, N. (1987, April). *Responding to students' writing: A pilot study* . Urbana, IL: ERIC/RCS.

A study investigates whether twenty pre-intermediate students are affected by a change of approaches to writing. Reports the process approach was more effective than traditional error correction.
Responding.

1724. Kelly, C. A. (1986). *Introductory guide to ESL writing.* Unpublished master's thesis, California State University, Sacramento, CA.
Teacher Preparation.

1725. Kelly, P. (1986). How do ESL students compose? *Australian Review of Applied Linguistics*, *9*(2), 94-119.

A study of the composing processes of 9 adult professional L2 writers shows that more proficient writers composed in larger chunks and revised more than less proficient writers.
Process Research.

1726. Kempf, M. K. (1975). A study of English proficiency level and the composition errors of incoming foreign students at the University of Cincinnati during 1969-1974. *Dissertation Abstracts International*, *36*(6), 3636A.

Analyzes the correlation between the native language background, English proficiency levels, and errors in written English by ESL students. Results show significant differences among native languages with respect to nine error categories. Analyzes error types of Chinese students and indicates role of redundancy in the etiology of errors.
Error Analysis/Chinese.

1727. Kenkel, J. (1991, March). *The pragmatics of argumentation and contrastive rhetoric.* Paper presented at the 25th Annual TESOL Convention, New York, NY.

Analyzes English language newspaper editorials from India, Singapore, and the US, using European pragmatic analysis.
Argumentation/Text Analysis/Contrastive Rhetoric.

1728. Kennedy, B. L. (1993a). Non-native speakers as students in first-year composition classes with native speakers: How can writing tutors help? *Writing Center Journal*, *13*, 27-38.

Describes tutorial activities that may be used to solve five problems ESL students have in composition class.
Tutoring.

1729. Kennedy, B. L. (1993b, April). *The role of topic in writing.* Paper presented at the 27th Annual TESOL Convention, Atlanta, GA.

Discusses the difference in quality between personal and academic topics in ESL writing.
Topic.

1730. Kennedy, B. L. (1992, March). *Writing and synthesis: A multi-cultural approach.*

Paper presented at the 26th Annual TESOL Convention, Vancouver, BC.

Describes the development of a process writing text for university NS and NNS students, which is not culturally-biased.

Materials/Culture.

1731. Kennedy, G. D. (1987). Expressing temporal frequency in academic English. *TESOL Quarterly, 21*, 69-86.

Presents a method for finding out how the communicative notion of temporal frequency (i.e., how many times or how often) is expressed in written academic English. Examination of three hundred linguistic devices reveals that temporal subordination is the most frequently used set of structures. Advocates frequency of register use as the criteria for determining the incorporation of temporal markers in ESL materials.

Register/Syntactic Structures.

1732. Kenyon, D. (1987, April). *Putting the writing process into classroom practice.* Paper presented at the 21st Annual TESOL Convention, Miami Beach, FL.

Workshop for teachers unfamiliar with the writing process.

Process Instruction.

1733. Kenyon-Nord, A. (1990). A brand new view: Language development and creative writing for elementary ESL students. *Writing Notebook: Creative Word Processing in the Classroom, 8*(1), 18-19.

Gives a computer lesson to help elementary ESL students new to school feel more comfortable in their environment.

Computers/Elementary.

1734. Kerr, J. Y. K. (1956). *Common errors in written English: An analysis based on essays by Greek students.* London: Longmans & Green.

Identifies the most common errors in a database of 1,000 English essays written by Greek students.

Error Analysis/Greek.

1735. Kerrigan, W. J., & Metcalf, A. A. (1987). *Writing to the point: Six basic steps.* (Fourth Ed.). NY: Harcourt Brace Jovanovich.

Intermediate/Textbook.

1736. Kessler, C., & Quinn, M. E. (1983, March). *Acquisition of second-language literacy by a Gujarati speaker: A longitudinal case-study.* Paper presented at the 17th Annual TESOL Convention, Toronto, Ontario.

Describes the acquisition of literacy-related processes by a 16 year-old ESL high school student in southwestern U.S.

Literacy/Secondary School.

1737. Keyes, J. R. (1984). Peer editing and writing success. *TESOL Newsletter (Supplement No, 1: Writing and composition), 18*(1), 11-12.

Claims that the writing activity for high school ESL students in which peers act as editors follows learning principles of Kenneth Bruffee, Thom Hawkins, and Carl Rogers.

Middle School/Peer Response/Editing.

1738. Keyes, J. L. (1983). A syntactical approach for teaching writing to English as a second language Hispanic college students. *Dissertation Abstracts International, 43*(12), 3836A.

    Analyzes results of a study that used a specifically designed manual to teach the syntactical features of written English to ESL students.

    Hispanic/Materials/Syntactic Structures.

1739. Khalil, A. M. (1989). A study of cohesion and coherence in Arab EFL college student writing. *System, 17*, 359-371.

    Analyzes cohesion (Halliday & Hasan, 1976) and coherence (Grice, 1975) in twenty English single paragraph compositions written by Arab EFL freshmen students. Finds that students overuse reiteration of the same lexical item as a cohesive device but underuse other lexical and grammatical cohesive devices. On the other hand, the lack of coherence is linked to insufficient information about the assigned topic.

    Arabic/Cohesion/Coherence.

1740. Khalil, A. M. (1985). Communicative error evaluation: Evaluation and interpretation of written errors of Arab EFL learners. *TESOL Quarterly, 19*, 335-351.

    Semantically rather than syntactically deviant utterances are judged less intelligible and interpretable by native speakers.

    Errors/Assessment.

1741. Khalil, A. M. (1984). Communicative error evaluation: A study of American native speakers' evaluations and interpretations of deviant utterances written by Arab EFL learners. *Dissertation Abstracts International, 45*(11), 3339A.

    Discusses the pedgogical implications of native speaker judgments of written errors by Arab EFL learners.

    Error Gravity.

1742. Kharma, N. N. (1986). Composition problems: Diagnosis and remedy. *English Teaching Forum, 24*(3), 21-24.

    Suggests that stylistic difficulties as well as rhetorical problems encountered by second language writers can be remedied by using reading materials, written exercises on style, punctuation, and information ordering as well as model passages as guides.

    Contrastive Rhetoric.

1743. Khattak, M. I. (1993). Teaching students to write a research-project proposal. *English Teaching Forum, 31*(1), 40-41.

    Shares a worksheet (Carosso, 1986) for analyzing audience and ideas for selecting a topic before writing a research-project proposal.

    Audience/Technical Writing.

1744. Khattak, M. I. (1991). English teachers can teach technical writing. *English Teaching Forum, 29*(2), 34-35.

    Argues that it is possible to teach students in several areas without becoming expert in technical subjects.

    Technical Writing.

1745. Khered, M. O. H. (1983). Measuring the syntactic maturity in the written English of Arab students at four proficiency levels and establishing an EFL index of development. *Dissertation Abstracts International*, *44*(4), 1010A.

    Examines writing samples of Arab college students for syntactic maturity towards establishing an EFL index of development. Findings show: (1) similarities and differences in the developmental stages between EFL students and American school children; and (2) similarities between EFL learners and adult second language learners of French and German. Establishes criteria for EFL index as percentage of error-free T-units, number of words in error-free T-units, and grammatical errors.

    Arabic/Syntactic Development/Proficiency.

1746. Kifle, Y. (1990). Stylistics, pedagogy, and Ethiopian writing in English: An activity-based approach to teaching literature in EFL. *Dissertation Abstracts International*, *52*(1), 99A.

    Proposes to use Ethiopian writings in English as sample texts for stylistic analysis in university EFL courses as a way of integrating literature and language teaching and bridging the cross-lingual and cross-cultural barriers in the Ethiopian situation.

    Ethiopia/Literature/Style.

1747. Kikuchi, K. (1978). *Teaching English composition to Japanese students*. Unpublished master's thesis, Hunter College, CUNY, New York, NY.

    Contrastive Rhetoric/Japanese.

1748. Kim, I. H. (1983). An analysis of errors in English compositions written by selected Korean and Thai students: Its implications for teaching writing in EFL classrooms. *Dissertation Abstracts International*, *44*(6), 1714A.

    Studies errors in written compositions of Korean and Thai students by categorizing their degree of unintelligibility according to native speakers' intuitions. Findings show that native speakers: (1) are more sensitive to word than form errors; (2) evaluated errors according to syntax and context; (3) considered noun errors more serious than verb errors; (4) were tolerant of minor errors.

    Error Gravity/Thai/Korean.

1749. Kim, W. S. (1991). The role of metacognitive skills in young ESL students' writing revisions. *Dissertation Abstracts International*, *52*(5), 1668.

    Both self-regulation and self-awareness training were effective in enhancing 5th- and 6th-grade ESL writers' metacognitive and writing skills. Positive changes (although not statistically significant) occurred in their revision skills.

    Metacognition/Revision/Computers.

1750. Kimball, J. (1985, April). *Listening to write: New ways to create prose*. Paper presented at the 19th Annual TESOL Convention, New York, NY.

    Shows how to integrate music and poetry with the composition process.

    Listening-Writing Relations.

1751. Kimball, M. C. (1980, March). *Suggestions for the advanced ESL composition course*. Paper presented at the 14th Annual TESOL Convention, San Francisco, CA.

    Demonstrates how to teach students to make the transition from controlled practice to free writing.

    Control/Advanced.

1752. King, C., & Cowart, R. (1993, April). *Essential elements of a multi-disciplinary academic writing course.* Paper presented at the 27th Annual TESOL Convention, Atlanta, GA.

  Describes a credit-bearing multi-disciplinary course featuring four streams of academic writing for graduate students.

  Courses/Graduate Students.

1753. Kinsella, P. L. (1985). *The techniques of writing.* (Fourth Ed.). NY: Harcourt Brace Jovanovich.

  Beginners/Textbook.

1754. Kirkhoff, K., Mallett, B. A., & Sankovich, A. A. (1983, March). *Teaching strategies for Chinese students in ESL composition: Adapting from native language rhetorical patterns to American ones.* Paper presented at the 17th Annual TESOL Convention, Toronto, Ontario.

  Interviews plus contrastive analysis of texts and products suggest persistent native patterns in expository writing of advanced Chinese ESL students.

  Chinese/Advanced/Contrastive Rhetoric.

1755. Kirkland, E. R. (1980, November). *Language experience and the limited and non-English-speaking child.* Paper presented at meeting of the California Reading Association, Sacramento, CA. [ERIC ED 197 286].

  Gives procedures and reasons for teaching limited and non-English-speaking children to read and write English by using the language experience approach. Important factors in LEA include 1) pupil-teacher dictation, 2) individual key vocabularies, 3) alphabet learning, 4) writing independently, and 5) using good literature as a motivator.

  Children/LEA.

1756. Kirkland, M. R. (1993, April). *Considerations in teaching incorporation of prior research in writing.* Paper presented at the 27th Annual TESOL Convention, Atlanta, GA.

  Offers a framework for teaching source-text-reader relationships, especially how to incorporate prior research into successful writing.

  Academic Writing.

1757. Kirkland, M. R., & Reid, F. C. (1982, May). *Sentence combining -- Phase II.* Paper presented at the 16th Annual TESOL Convention, Honolulu, HI.

  Advises using sentence combining at the intermediate level for teaching effective expression of relationships and flexibility of expression.

  Sentence Combining/Intermediate.

1758. Kirkland, M. R., & Saunders, M. A. (1989, March). *Maximizing student performance in summary writing: Managing cognitive load.* Paper presented at the 23rd Annual TESOL Convention, San Antonio, TX.

  Presents an approach to maximizing student performance in writing summaries which involve significant cognitive constraints.

  Summary Writing.

1759. Kirkland, M. R., & Saunders, M. A. (1991). Maximizing student performance in summary writing: Managing the cognitive load. *TESOL Quarterly, 25,* 105-122.

  Provides overview of constraints that make summary writing a fundamental

cognitive academic activity.
Academic Writing/Summary Writing.

1760. Kirn, E. (1991). *A competency-based reading-writing book.* St. Louis, MO: McGraw-Hill.
Contains everyday reading material -- ads, signs, letters, schedules -- supplemented by survival writing tasks.
Adult Education/Beginners/Textbook.

1761. Kitagawa, M. M. (1989). Letting ourselves be taught. In D. M. Johnson, & D. H. Roen (Eds.), *Richness in writing: Empowering ESL students* (pp. 70-83). NY: Longman.
Claims that ESL learners write and learn best when they are in control of the learning task and when teachers let themselves be taught. States that such an approach empowers students by giving them authority and voice.
Control.

1762. Kitchin, D. A. (1991). Case study of ESL community college students using computer-based writing tools in a composition course. *Dissertation Abstracts International, 52*(4), 1240A.
Describes experiences and consequences for ESL community college students of using pre-writing, word processing, and grammar-analysis software. Qualitative data shows that the eight participants were positive and enthusiastic about their experience which is confirmed by gains found in the length and quality of the essays they wrote over a semester. Argues for incorporation of word processing in ESL classes.
Computers/Word Processing.

1763. Klassen, B. R. (1977). Sentence-combining exercises as an aid to expediting syntactic fluency in learning English as a second language. *Dissertation Abstracts International, 37*(10), 6258A.
Examines the effects of sentence-combining exercises on development of syntactic maturity in ESL students. Study confirms that sentence-combining can expedite language development of ESL students.
Sentence Combining.

1764. Klassen, C., & Burnaby, B. (1993). "Those who know": Views on literacy among adult immigrants in Canada. *TESOL Quarterly, 27,* 377-397.
Examines the language and literacy needs of immigrants to Canada, presenting a qualitative study of a group of Latin American adults which suggests that literacy needs exist in Spanish and English.
Literacy/Hispanic.

1765. Kleber, R. E. (1986, March). *Creative writing in ESL, low intermediate to advanced.* Paper presented at the 20th Annual TESOL Convention, Anaheim, CA.
Proposes a "contrastive new rhetoric" that goes beyond arrangement to analyze cultural contrasts of process.
Intermediate/Culture.

1766. Klein, G. K. (1979, March). *ESL and NL composition: Equivalent is not equal.* Paper presented at the 13th Annual TESOL Convention, Boston.

Presents a case study of a student enrolled concurrently in an ESL and a native speaker course.
NS-NNS Comparisons.

1767. Kleinmann, H. H., & Selekman, H. R. (1981). The use and sequencing of dicto-comp exercises. *English Language Teaching Journal*, *35*(2), 191-194.

The dicto-comp exercise consists of a passage which is read several times to students who follow an outline of the reading. After the final reading, students are asked to reproduce the passage in writing, adhering as closely as possible to the original version. A handout gives brief directions, an outline which arranges cues in the order in which they are used in the composition, and a graphic representation of the paragraphing of the finished product.
Classroom Activities/Control.

1768. Kleinmann, H. H., & Selekman, H. R. (1979, March). *The use and sequencing of dicto-comp exercises*. Paper presented at the 13th Annual TESOL Convention, Boston.

Describes how to stimulate writing by using a structured version of the dicto-comp exercise first introduced by Ilson (1962) and Riley (1970).
Listening-Writing Relations.

1769. Klobusicky-Mailander, E. (1990). Putting the computer to work in your writing class. *ELT Journal*, *28*, 2-7.

Discusses how to organize effective work for the novice in a computer lab.
Computers.

1770. Knapp, D. (1972). A focused efficient method to relate composition correction to teaching aims. In H. B. Allen, & R. Campbell (Eds.), *Teaching English as a second language* (pp. 213-221). NY: McGraw-Hill.

Provides a checklist for evaluating writing that assumes students learn from their successes.
Evaluation.

1771. Knapp, J. (1982, May). *Alternatives to rhetoric in the ESL composition class*. Paper presented at the 16th Annual TESOL Convention, Honolulu, HI.

Argues in favor of a process approach rather than teaching the rhetorical modes.
Process Instruction.

1772. Knepler, H., & Knepler, M. (1993). *Crossing cultures: Readings for composition*. (Fourth ed.). NY: Maxwell Macmillan.

Collection of sixty cross-cultural readings, progressing from highly subjective selections to essays in the standard modes of discourse from which students draw to write about themselves and then to generalize about experiences.
University/Textbook.

1773. Knepler, M. (1984). Impromptu writing to increase fluency. *TESOL Newsletter (Supplement No. 1: Writing and Composition)*, *18*(1), 15-16.

Describes how impromptu writing and student discussions on each other's papers can benefit ESL writing, making it more communicative, more individual, and more interesting.

Classroom Activities/Fluency.

1774. Kobayashi, H. (1984). Rhetorical patterns in English and Japanese. *TESOL Quarterly, 18,* 737-738.

Study reports that rhetorical patterns as well as type and placement of a general statement in expository and narrative essays by Japanese students (N=226) show relative cultural preferences. Japanese students writing in Japanese wrote specific statements before general ones, whereas their American peers chose the reverse pattern. Japanese advanced ESL students in the U.S fell between these two groups but Japanese non-English majors in Japan reflected the specific before general pattern. Concludes that Japanese ESL learners tend to use first language patterns
Contrastive Rhetoric/Japanese.

1775. Kobayashi, H., & Rinnert, C. (1992). Effects of first language on second language writing: Translation vs. direct composition. *Language Learning, 42,* 183-215.

Finds greater syntactic complexity in translations by 48 Japanese university students than in their English compositions. Lower but not higher proficiency students benefited from translation whereas higher-level students made more meaning relevant errors in translations than in their direct writing.
L1 Influence/Translation.

1776. Kobayashi, H., & Rinnert, C. (1990). *Effects of first language on second language writing: Translation versus direct writing.* Paper presented at the 24th Annual TESOL Convention, San Francisco, CA.

Investigates the effect of first language on the quality and quantity of translations and direct compositions by Japanese university students.
Japanese/L1 Influence/Task.

1777. Kobayashi, H. (1985). Rhetorical patterns in English and Japanese. *Dissertation Abstracts International, 45*(8), 2425A.

Examines compositions of American college students, Japanese ESL students, Japanese EFL students, and Japanese students writing in Japanese. Results show each group used different rhetorical patterns, and Japanese ESL students wrote closer to American students writing in English and Japanese EFL students to Japanese students writing in Japanese.
Contrastive Rhetoric/Japanese.

1778. Kobayashi, T. (1992). Native and nonnative reactions to ESL compositions. *TESOL Quarterly, 26,* 81-110.

Investigates how NESs and Japanese native speakers evaluate and edit ESL compositions written by Japanee college students. Finds that NESs were stricter about grammaticality but gave more positive evaluations than did Japanese evaluators.
Error Gravity/NS-NNS Comparisons.

1779. Kobayashi, T. (1990). *Native and non-native reactions to ESL compositions.* Unpublished master's thesis, University of Hawaii, Honolulu, HI.

See previous item.
Error Gravity/NS-NNS Comparisons.

1780. Koch, B. J. (1984). Comments on Karyn Thompson-Panos and Maria Thomas-Ruzic's "The least you should know about Arabic: Implications for the ESL writing instructor"-- a reader reacts. *TESOL Quarterly, 18,* 542-545.

Claims that Thompson-Panos and Thomas-Ruzic's evaluation does not go far enough to explain discourse strategies. Criticizes the ethnocentricity of Shouby (1951) and reviews her own research on repetition in Arabic prose which is persuasive by creating presence, that is, affective proximity.

Contrastive Rhetoric.

1781. Kocher, S., Chenoweth, A., & Era, K. (1991, March). *Cultural expectations in persuasive writing.* Paper presented at the 25th Annual TESOL Convention, New York, NY.

A study of the grading behavior of native English and Japanese teachers rating persuasive essays in Japanese and their English translations suggests differential expectations by examiners.

Assessment/Contrastive Rhetoric/Persuasion/Japanese.

1782. Koda, K. (1991, April). *Achieving discourse proficiency in second language composition.* Paper presented at the Annual Meeting of the AERA, Chicago, IL.

Proficiency.

1783. Koda, K. (1987, April). *Effects of L1 literacy skills on the development of L2 literacy.* Paper presented at the Annual AERA Meeting, Washington, DC.

Literacy.

1784. Kohn, J. (1988, March). *Comparing resident and non-resident ESL writers.* Paper presented at the 22nd Annual TESOL Convention, Chicago, IL.

Reports research on variable performance in composition due to use of oral style, comprehension of cultural inference, and response to teacher expectations.

Speaking-Writing Relations/Culture/LOR.

1785. Kolls, M. R. (1992, March). *Portfolio assessment: A feasibility study.* Paper presented at the 26th Annual TESOL Convention, Vancouver, BC.

Reports the results of a pilot study concerning the use of portfolios in language arts class in California.

Assessment/Portfolios/Secondary School.

1786. Konecni, E. (1978). Contrastive analysis of the rhetoric of scientific and technical English and Macedonian. In M. T. Trimble, L. Trimble, & K. Drobnic (Eds.), *English for specific purposes: Science and technology* (pp. 167-176). Corvalllis, OR: Oregon State University.

Compares paragraph structures in two technical rhetorics.

Technical Writing/Paragraph/Macedonian.

1787. Konneker, B. H., & Perkins, K. (1983, March). *Advanced ESL composition: No place for sentence-combining.* Paper presented at the 17th Annual TESOL Convention, Toronto, Ontario.

Concludes that sentence-combining is not productive at the L2 advanced level of proficiency on the basis of a study in which experimental students were trained in sentence-combining and controls in traditional rhetorical instruction.

Advanced/Sentence Combining.

1788. Konneker, B. H., & Perkins, K. (1981, March). *Testing the effectiveness of sentence-combining for ESL composition.* Paper presented at the 15th Annual TESOL

Convention, Detroit, MI.

> Reports an experiment in which student writing, after treatment with sentence-combining exercises by Memering and O'Hare, was measured for qualitative (i.e., holistic) and quantitative (i.e., Test of Ability to Subordinate) gains.
> Sentence Combining.

1789. Kosel, L., Martin, V. V., Ostler, S. E., & Petraglia, J. (1993, April). *The many faces of contrastive rhetoric.* Colloquium presented at the 27th Annual TESOL Convention, Atlanta, GA.

> Colloquium discusses (a) grading criteria, (b) reading-writing relations, (c) rhetorical forms, and (d) process and cognition across cultures.
> Contrastive Rhetoric.

1790. Koshi, A. K. (1992). *Discoveries: Reading, thinking, writing.* Boston: Heinle & Heinle.

> Presents reading, writing, critical thinking, and grammar as an integrated whole and employs both process and product approaches to writing.
> Textbook.

1791. Koshi, A. K. (1986, March). *Cloze as a measure of writing proficiency.* Paper presented at the 21st Annual TESOL Convention, Miami Beach, FL.

> Reports a study showing the superiority of a cloze over a discourse type grammar test as a measure of writing proficiency.
> Assessment/Proficiency.

1792. Kotecha, P. (1991). Problem solving and report writing for second language engineering students. *Journal of Technical Writing and Communication, 21,* 165-173.

> Describes a report writing unit for South African engineering students.
> Technical Writing.

1793. Kowal, K. H. (1987). Embracing the Tao: Peter Elbow re-contextualized -- A review essay. *TECFORS, 10,* 6-13.

> Reviews use of Elbow's Embracing contraries for Asian students.
> Review/Asian.

1794. Kowitz, J., Aebersold, J. A., Schwarte, B., & Smith, E. L. (1981, March). *Extemporaneous writing and the development of critical writing.* Paper presented at the 15th Annual TESOL Convention, Detroit, MI.

> Describes how to make timed writing more than an assessment instrument by using analytic procedures to heighten awareness.
> Assessment/Time.

1795. Kraft, C., & Lee, S. (1992, March). *The computer lab: A writer's tool.* Paper presented at the 26th Annual TESOL Convention, Vancouver, BC.

> Discusses the benefits and effective usage of a computer lab for writing instruction.
> Computers/Laboratory.

1796. Krahnke, K., Al-Jamhoor, A., & Khranke, K. (1992, March). *A cross-cultural analysis of written discourse.* Paper presented at the 26th Annual TESOL Convention, Vancouver, BC.

Reports a discourse analysis of the formal writing of forty Saudi and Japanese essays written in L1 and L2. Cross-linguistic comparisons indicate similarity between L1 and L2, signficant individual variation, and moderate similarity within cultural groups.
L1-L2 Comparison/Arabic/Japanese.

1797. Krapels, A. R. (1990a, March). *Contrastive rhetorics and ESL writing*. Paper presented at the 41st Annual CCCC Meeting, Chicago, IL.
Contrastive Rhetoric.

1798. Krapels, A. R. (1990b). The interaction of first and second language composing: Processes and rhetorics. *Dissertation Abstracts International, 51*(12), 4045A.
Attempts to discover and describe the relationships between L1 and L2 composing of five advanced level ESL writers who speak either Spanish, Chinese, or Arabic. The analysis of a variety of products and an assortment of data by the three participants suggest that (1) L2 composing process reflects L1 composing; (2) composing in L1 is more fluent than in L2; and (3) L2 composing is influenced by the first language rhetoric for introducing, elaborating, and concluding essays.
Hispanic/Chinese/Arabic.

1799. Krapels, A. R. (1990c). Second language writing process research. In B. Kroll (Ed.), *Second language writing: Research insights for the classroom* (pp. 37-56). Cambridge: Cambridge University Press.
Presents an overview of research on the process of composing in a second language, including a number of unpublished dissertations.
Review.

1800. Krapels, A. R. (1987, November). *Facilitating success in the ESL writing classroom*. Paper presented at the 77th Annual NCTE Convention, Los Angeles, CA.
Language Development.

1801. Krapels, A. R. (1985, March). *Contrastive rhetorics in the ESL writing class: Pragmatics and process*. Paper presented at the 36th Annual CCCC Meeting, Minneapolis, MN.
Contrastive Rhetoric.

1802. Krapels, A. R., & El-Komi, M. (1986, March). *Researcher and researchee: Two perspectives on composition research*. Paper presented at the 21st Annual TESOL Convention, Miami Beach, FL.
Discusses an ethnographic research project investigating composing processes and contrastive rhetoric from the points of view of the teacher/researcher and student/subject.
Ethnographic Research/Contrastive Rhetoric.

1803. Krashen, S. D. (1991). Reading, writing, form and content. *Georgetown University Round Table on Languages and Linguistics, 1990* (pp. 364-376). Washington, DC: Georgetown University Press.
Argues that cognitive rather than linguistic development occurs <u>through</u> writing, implying instruction in second language writing should focus on "enterprises," in Frank Smith's sense (1988) of students solving real problems.
Cognition/Reading-Writing Relations.

1804. Krashen, S. D. (1984). *Writing: Research, theory, and applications*. Oxford: Pergamon Press.

    Reviews what is known about learning to write with special attention to the role of reading and how second language acquisition and composing are involved.

    Reading-Writing Relations.

1805. Kreeft, J. E. (1984). Dialogue journal writing and the acquisition of grammatical morphology in English as a second language. *Dissertation Abstracts International*, *46*(10), 3019A.

    Examines dialogue journal writing of beginning ESL students to determine the acquisition of grammatical morphology. Findings show acquisition of morphology influenced by: (1) universal cognitive processes; (2) features of second language input; (3) first language background; and (4) strategies employed by individual learners.

    Dialogue Journals/Syntactic Development/Children.

1806. Kreeft, J. E., Shuy, R., Staton, J., Reed, L., & Morroy, R. (1984). *Dialogue writing: Analysis of teacher-student interactive writing in the learning of English as a second language*. Washington, DC: ERIC/CAL. [ERIC ED 252 097].

    Reports on an NIE-funded study of the linguistic development of sixth-grade ESL students writing dialogue journals in class.

    Dialogue Journals/Elementary/Language Development.

1807. Kresovich, B. M. (1990). Timed writing practice for Japanese university students in an EFL setting. *Bulletin of College of Education, University of the Ryukyus*, *37*(1), 121-128. [ERIC ED 330 212].

    Argues that exercises requiring more rapid writing by novice writers can overcome the constraints of debilitating early training of Japanese students. Discusses a six-step procedure for such exercises.

    Japanese/Time.

1808. Kresovich, B. M. (1989). Sentence combining activities for Japanese university students. *Southern Review*, *4*, 140-149. [ERIC ED 322 743].

    Describes seven activities to help college-level Japanese ESL students develop intuitions about English grammar and practice the rhetoric of written English. Activities are contextualized and progressively less controlled.

    Japanese/Sentence Combining.

1809. Kresovich, B. M. (1988). The journal assignment in composition class at a Japanese University. *Bulletin of College of Education, University of the Ryukyus*, *33*(1), 1-15. [ERIC ED 311 731].

    Discusses journal writing in an English composition class at a Japanese university.

    Assignments/Journal Writing.

1810. Krishnaswamy, R. (1990, March). *Cross-cultural influences on strategies of cohesion*. Paper presented at the 24th Annual TESOL Convention, San Francisco, CA.

    Unlike the linear structure of English writing that employs metonymic modes of cohesion, prose in Indian languages structures spirally, using metaphoric modes of cohesion. In 19th century Hindi narrative, the new metonymic prose model of

English gets superimposed upon an anterior mode of a metaphoric nature producing a split narrative.
Hindi/Contrastive Rhetoric/Narration.

1811. Kroll, B. (1993a, April). *Broadening composition programs: Bringing ESL agendas to non-ESL faculty*. Paper presented at the 27th Annual TESOL Convention, Atlanta, GA.

Discusses how to facilitate faculty development of L1 teachers who experience problems with increasing numbers of non-native immigrant students in their classes.
University/Teacher Preparation.

1812. Kroll, B. (1993b, April). *ESL students in non-ESL classes: Intimidated or integrated*. Paper presented at 44th Annual Convention of CCCC, San Diego, CA.
NS-NNS Comparisons.

1813. Kroll, B. (1993c). Teaching writing IS teaching reading: Training the new teacher of ESL composition. In J. G. Carson, & I. Leki (Eds.), *Reading in the composition classroom: Second language perspectives* (pp. 61-81). Boston: Heinle & Heinle.

Claims that knowledge of reading theory enables teacher trainees and experienced teachers to focus on the relevant and necessary connections between the production and interpretation of texts.
Reading-Writing Relations/Teacher Preparation.

1814. Kroll, B. (1992, March). *Research agenda for ESL writing: A decade of TESOL convention in review*. Paper presented at a colloquium at the 26th Annual TESOL Convention, Vancouver, BC.

Discusses the growth and distribution of types of TESOL conference presentations on writing and composition during the last decade. Notes a dramatic increase in the total number of presentations with more data-based papers and teacher materials or pedagogy largely responsible for the increase.
Review.

1815. Kroll, B. (1991a). Teaching writing in the ESL context. In M. Celce-Murcia (Ed.), *Teaching English as a second or foreign language* (pp. 245-263). Second Ed. NY: Newbury/HarperCollins.

Discusses concerns of ESL teachers, such as course placement, curricular principles, syllabus design, interrelation of writing and reading, creating assignments, and responding to student writing.
Teacher Preparation.

1816. Kroll, B. (1991b). Understanding TOEFL's Test of Written English. *RELC, 22*(1), 20-33.

Discusses the evolution of TWE, the development of topics, and scoring procedures.
Assessment/TWE/Scoring.

1817. Kroll, B. (1990a). Introduction. In B. Kroll (Ed.), *Second language writing: Research insights for the classroom* (pp.1-10). Cambridge: Cambridge University Press.

Notes the manner in which the discipline of composition has developed in the last 25 years and cautions that we should not presume that the act of writing in one's first language is the same as writing in a second language.

Reviews.

1818. Kroll, B. (Ed.). (1990b). *Second language writing: Research insights for the classroom.* Cambridge: Cambridge University Press.

Offers thirteen original articles, written by recognized scholars in the field, which cover major, current issues in teaching writing to non-native speakers. The articles are research-based (either qualitative or qualitiative in type) and involve practical implications for classroom teachers. Included are: a history of the evolution of approaches to the teaching of second language writing (Silva), current paradigm typologies of teaching (Johns), a survey of research (Krapels), key issues in teacher response (Leki) and assessment (Hamp-Lyons), and a description of trhe reading-writing relation (Eisterhold). It also contains specific studies on topical structure analysis (Connor, and Farmer), assignments (Kroll), the composing process of second language writers (Friedlander), teacher response to student writing (Fathman, & Whalley), student processing of feedback (Cohen, & Cavalcanti) and the use of information from sources (Campbell).

Research/Theory/Instruction

1819. Kroll, B. (1990c). The rhetoric/syntax split: Designing a curriculum for ESL students.

Proposes we separate for the purposes of placement rhetoric and syntax in scoring essays.

Assessment/Rhetoric

1820. Kroll, B. (1990d). What does time buy? ESL students performance on home versus class compositions. In B. Kroll (Ed.), *Second language writing: Research insights for the classroom* (pp.140-154). Cambridge: Cambridge University Press.

Study finds that providing an extended amount of time at home to produce an essay does not in and of itself lead to a better performance.

Assignments/Time

1821. Kroll, B. (1989, March). *Direct assessment of first and second language writing skills.* Paper presented at the 40th Annual CCCC Meeting, Seattle, WA.

Explains methodology used to rate essay samples written in both L1 and in ESL by native speakers of Japanese and Chinese and to identify critical feature of quality prose.

Assessment/Japanese/Chinese.

1822. Kroll, B. (1988a, March). *Graduate preparation for future ESL writing teachers.* Paper presented at the 22nd Annual TESOL Convention, Chicago, IL.

Reviews some graduate course offerings on teaching ESL writing.

Teacher Preparation.

1823. Kroll, B. (1988b, March). *Issues in teacher training for ESL writing instruction.* Paper presented at the 39th Annual CCCC Meeting, St. Louis, MO.

Identifies the nature of material covered in graduate courses for ESL writing teacher trainees.

Teacher Preparation.

1824. Kroll, B. (1987a, March). *Graduate students in ESL writing classes: Assignments to meet the challenge.* Paper presented at the 38th Annual CCCC Meeting, Atlanta, GA.

Gives assignments suited to graduate EFL students with focus on their content-area kowledge and writing needs.
Graduate Students/Assignments.

1825. Kroll, B. (1987b, April). *What writing teachers want to know: Making training count.* Paper presented at the 21st Annual TESOL Convention, Miami Beach, FL.
Reports the results of a survey of current and prospective ESL teachers about teacher training needed for success in the classroom.
Teacher Preparation.

1826. Kroll, B. (1985a, March). *The plus rhetoric minus syntax syndrome in ESL students.* Paper presented at the 36th Annual CCCC Meeting, Minneapolis, MN.
Suggests classroom strategies for dealing with ESL students who exhibit persistent grammatical problems despite ability to control essay organization.
Rhetoric/Errors.

1827. Kroll, B. (1985b). *What does time buy? Syntactic accuracy and discourse fluency in ESL composition.* Washington, DC: ERIC/FLL. [ERIC ED 257 075].
A comparison of 50 in-class and 50 out-of-class ESL compositions reveals no significant difference in correctness or relation of correctness to discourse fluency.
Assignments/Time.

1828. Kroll, B. (1983, March). *Training writing teachers: A bibliographic review.* Paper presented at the 17th Annual TESOL Convention, Toronto, BC.
Introduces and assesses for ESL writing teachers 10 composition teaching manuals designed for teachers of native speakers.
Teacher Preparation/Materials.

1829. Kroll, B. (1982a, March). ESL consciousness raising for teachers of native speakers. Paper presented at the 33th Annual CCCC Meeting, San Francisco, CA.
Suggests aspects of second language learning that English composition teachers should be aware of when teaching non-native students.
Teacher Preparation.

1830. Kroll, B. (1982b). Levels of error in ESL compositions. *Dissertation Abstracts International*, *43*(10), 3307A.
Compares the compositions written by twenty-five freshman students from different language backgrounds in a limited amount of time (a class period) to those written outside of class or with 10-14 days preparation time. Finds no relationship between the quality of the essays as measured by holistic evaluation and quanititative measures of errors. Apparently, the time factor alone does not influence either the syntactic or discourse properties of ESL compositions.
Errors/Time/Assignments.

1831. Kroll, B. (1979a, March). *An analysis of advanced ESL compositions in freshman English.* Paper presented at the 13th Annual TESOL Convention, Boston.
Discusses in-class and at-home essays in a university course.
Assignments/University.

1832. Kroll, B. (1979a). Learning and acquisition: Two paths to writing. *English Education*, *11*(2), 83-90.
Discusses the relationship of Krashen's theory (1978) to individual variation

in writing performance.
Theory.

1833. Kroll, B. (1979c). A survey of the writing needs of foreign and American college freshmen. *English Language Teaching Journal, 33*(3), 219-226.

To help curriculum planners develop writing programs, a three-part questionnaire was designed to determine the past, present, and future writing needs that students should be exposed to. The survey involved 35 university students enrolled in freshman English sections specifically restricted to international students and 20 students in a regular freshman English course for native speakers.
Needs/University.

1834. Kroll, B. (1978). Sorting out writing problems. In C. Blatchford, & J. Schachter (Eds.), *On TESOL '78: EFL policies, programs, practices* (pp. 176-182). Washington, DC: TESOL.

Calls for more dialogue between contemporary rhetoricians and applied linguists in order to improve teacher awareness of both fields.
Teacher Preparation.

1835. Kroll, B. M. (1989, March). *Cross-cultural influences on strategies of cohesion.* Paper presented at the 40th Annual CCCC Meeting, Seattle, WA.
Assessment/NS-NNS Comparisons.

1836. Kroll, B. M., & Schafer, J. C. (1984). Error analysis and the teaching of composition. In S. L. McKay (Ed.), *Composing in a second language* (pp. 135-144). Rowley, MA: Newbury House.
Reprints Kroll & Schafer (1978).
Error Analysis/Language Development.

1837. Kroll, B. M., & Schafer, J. C. (1978). Error analysis and the teaching of composition. *College Composition and Communication, 29,* 242-248.

Claims that the shift towards the process approach in ESL composition helps view errors as developmental and the product of intelligent cognitive strategies.
Error Analysis/Language Development.

1838. Kroll, B. M., & Schafer, J. C. (1977, March). *The development of error analysis and its implications for the teaching of composition.* Paper presented at the 28th Annual CCCC Meeting, Kansas City, MO. [ERIC ED 145 482].

Suggests that error analysis in composition courses is helpful since students learn from their mistakes which is, therefore, an important part of the process of writing.
Error Analysis/Feedback.

1839. Kuhlman, N. A. (1982, May). *Basic competency writing tests: What do we learn?* Paper presented at the 16th Annual TESOL Convention, Honolulu, HI.

Suggests that diagnositic categorization rather than holistic assessment has greater advantages for evaluating Spanish-English bilinguals.
Hispanic/Assessment.

1840. Kuhlman, N. A. (1980, March). *The bilingual student: Writing competencies.* Paper presented at the 14th Annual TESOL Convention, San Francisco, CA.

Discusses characteristics of Hispanic limited-English speaking students in 8th

and 10th grades and freshman college levels.
Hispanic.

1841. Kumpf, L. E. (1987). Structuring narratives in a second language: Descriptions of rhetoric and grammar. *Dissertation Abstracts International, 47*(10), 3749A.

Examines the relationship of narrative structure and grammatical form in the writing of three Japanese and three Spanish speakers. Hierarchical characteristics of their discourses are found very individual in choice of signals, functions, and strategies for fulfilling the discourse purposes. Also, time references and aspect are grammatically systematic.

Narration/Organization/Japanese/Hispanic.

1842. Kunz, L. A. (1991). *26 steps: Controlled composition for intermediate and advanced ESL students*. Old Tappan, NJ: Prentice Hall Regents.

Forty-eight short passages offered for copying and rewriting in a controlled composition text.

Beginners/Intermediate/Textbook.

1843. Kunz, L. A., & Munch, H. (1985). *26 steps: Controlled composition for intermediate and advanced language development*. (Second, revised ed.). Hayward, CA: Alemany Press.

Forty-eight short passages offered for copying and rewriting in a controlled composition text.

Beginners/Intermediate/Textbook.

1844. Kupper-Herr, G. (1983). *Pre-writing activities in an ESL writing program*. Unpublished master's thesis, University of Hawaii, Manoa, HI.

Invention.

1845. Kutz, E. (1986). Between students' language and academic discourse: Interlanguage as middle ground. *College English, 48*, 385-396.

Extends the concept of "interlanguage" as a means of assessing students' existing competency in L1 and L2 to the acquisition of academic discourse.

Interlanguage/Academic Writing.

1846. Kutz, E., Groden, S., & Zamel, V. (1993). *The discovery of competence: Teaching and learning with diverse student writers*. Portsmouth, NH: Heinemann Boynton/Cook.

Chronicles the way authors changed their thinking about how to teach writing and how they redesigned their writing classroom as an environment for collaborative inquiry by students and teachers. The thesis is the discovery by teachers through inquiry which recognizes and helps develop student competence as users of language. This book offers new approaches to evaluation, program design, and the multicultural curriculum for all, including ESL, teachers of writing.

Teacher Preparation/Collaboration.

1847. Kuure, L. (1987). Cohesion and strategies in student composition. In I. Lindblat, & M. Ljund (Eds.), *Proceedings from the Third Nordic Conference for English Studies, Vol. 2* (pp. 427-436). Stockholm: Almqvist & Wiksell.

The emphasis on spoken rather than written language in EFL secondary school teaching in Finland may be responsible for the intermediary form of student writing, characterized by positive politeness (involvement) and strong assumption of shared knowledge with a reader.

Cohesion/Finnish/Speaking-Writing Relations.

1848. Kwah, P. F. (1988). *The relationship between reading and writing in English as a second language.* Unpublished master's thesis, University of Texas, Arlington, TX.

Study focuses on whether ESL students' L2 writing ability correlates with their L2 reading ability and with the amount of pleasure reading done in their L1 and L2. Results indicate a strong positive relationship between L2 writing ability and L2 reading ability. The relationship between L2 writing ability and the amount of pleasure reading in L2 was non-significant. Less competent writers tend to read more in their native language. This study provided some evidence to support the assumption that there is a relationship between reading and writing in a second language.

Reading-Writing Relations.

1849. Kwan-Terry, A., Cook, C., & Ragan, P. H. (1988). *Interactive writing: An advancewd course in writing skills.* NY: Prentice Hall International.

Designed for students at the National University of Singapore who can command the grammar of English, but who need to study how different parts of a paragraph interact and how different paragraphs interact according to the writer's purpose to form a coherent and organized text.

Advanced/Textbook.

1850. Kwok, H., & Chan, M. M. (1975). Creative writing in English: Problems faced by undergraduates in the English department, University of Hong Kong. *Topics in Culture Learning*, *3*, 13. [ERIC ED 116 470].

Describes difficulties of Chinese-speaking undergraduate students in a creative writing course in English.

Creative Writing/Chinese.

L

1851. Lachman, A. W. (1990, March). *Unsilencing international voices.* Paper presented at the 41st Annual CCCC Meeting, Chicago, IL.

Voice.

1852. Lachman, A. W. (1988, March). *"Why Euthanasia is Killing Me": Provoking student writing.* Paper presented at the 22nd Annual TESOL Convention, Chicago, IL.

Demonstrates how ethical issues lend themselves to highly motivated writing.

Motivation/Topic.

1853. Lackstrom, J., Selinker, L., & Trimble, L. (1973). Technical rhetorical principles and grammatical choice. *TESOL Quarterly*, *7*, 127-136.

Defines rhetoric in English for Science and Technology (EST) and shows the impact of rhetorical principles on article use and tense choice.

ESP/Rhetoric.

1854. Lacy, R. (1984, March). *In class and out-of-class writing tasks: Their role in the evaluation of non-native speakers.* Paper presented at the 18th Annual TESOL

Convention, Houston, TX.

    Reports an experiment with college level international students in which holistically evaluated out-of-class essays were better than similarly assessed in-class essays on a midterm. Despite this difference, students performed nearly the same on an in-class final exam.

    Time/Assignments.

1855. Lado, A. L. (1992). Literacy levels of adult Spanish speakers: A key factor in beginning ESL literacy. *Dissertation Abstracts International*, *52*(9), 3205A.

    Interviews with Spanish-speaking adults indicate low levels of L1 literacy among those studying ESL at the beginning level several years after having arrived in the U.S.

    Literacy/Beginners/Spanish.

1856. Lado, R. (1955). *Annotated bibliography for teachers of English as a foreign language*. Washington, DC: US Government.

    A bibliography of 721 items covering many aspects of ESL/EFL teaching between 1946 and 1954 lists no items on ESL writing.

    Bibliography.

1857. Lai, E. F. K. (1993). The effect of a summer reading course on reading and writing skills. *System*, *21*, 87-100.

    An intensive 4-week reading program for 226 Hong Kong secondary students seemed to improve their writing as well as their reading.

    Reading-Writing Relations/Secondary School/Chinese.

1858. Lai, E. F. K. (1986). Self-access remedial work in writing and the computer. *English Teaching Forum*, *24*(3), 29-30.

    Shares experiences devising remedial error-correction exercises for weak writers in Hong Kong high schools.

    Computers/Secondary School/Error Treatment.

1859. Lai, P. C. (1986). The revision processes of first-year students at the National University of Singapore. *RELC Journal*, *17*(1), 71-84.

    Analyzes preliminary and subsequent drafts of L2 texts by Chinese university students, using the Faigley & Witte's taxonomy. Finds a substantial number of revisions per person. However, nearly 80% of these changes were formal or meaning preserving. Later drafts, however, tended toward more text-based changes and at a higher syntactic level.

    Chinese/Revision/University.

1860. Lai, P. C., & Ngooi, C. A. (1991). How journal writing improved our English classes. *English Teaching Forum*, *29*(3), 43-45.

    Testifies to the effectiveness of journal writing.

    Journal Writing.

1861. Laing, D., & van den Hoven, A. (1986). *A comparative study of the syntactic maturity and surface control of grade 8 Francophones writing in English*. Paper presented at the 4th International Conference on the Teaching of English, Ottawa, Ontario. [ERIC ED 285 409].

    Francophone eighth-graders compare favorably (more words per T-unit and clauses per T-unit) with equivalent Anglophone groups in syntactic maturity and limited aspects of writing proficiency.

Syntactic Development/French.

1862. Lam, C. Y. P. (1992). Revision processes of college ESL students: How teacher comments, discourse types, and writing tools shape revision. *Dissertation Abstracts International, 52*(12), 4248A.

Seeks to find out how ESL writers revise and what affects their revisions. Two intact classes of ESL college writing (including five case studies) were asked to write and revise in three types of discourse: expressive, transactional, and expressive. Moreover, two of the cases wrote and revised on computers in contrast to two who used pen and paper. Most ESL students realized that revision entails both content and mechanical changes. Teacher comments and computers seem to affect revision but discourse type did not.

Revision/Feedback/Computers.

1863. Lamp, S. A. (1984, March). *Teaching ESL students to edit: The forgotten skill.* Paper presented at the 18th Annual TESOL Convention, Houston, TX.

Suggestions offered for training students to edit all possible errors.

Editing.

1864. Lamp, S. A. (1980, March). *Planning diagnostic writing tests.* Paper presented at the 14th Annual TESOL Convention, San Francisco, CA.

Focuses on three methods of creating effective writing tests.

Assessment.

1865. Lanauze, M., & Snow, C. (1989). The relation between first- and second-language writing skills: Evidence from Puerto Rican elementary school children in bilingual programs. *Linguistics and Education, 1,* 323-339.

Assesses picture description writing in two languages by 38 fourth and fifth graders in a Spanish-English bilingual program. Finds evidence for the transfer of academic and literacy skills from L1 to L2 before their L2 oral-aural skills have fully developed.

Hispanic/Elementary.

1866. Land, R. E. (1992, March). *In the writing classroom: A survey of writing axioms.* Colloquium presented at the 26th Annual TESOL Convention, Vancouver, BC.

Finds a lack of consensus among ESL teachers, teaching assistants, and English professors about their definitions of writing.

Approaches.

1867. Land, R. E. (1987, March). *Research challenges of linguistically heterogeneous writing classes.* Paper presented at the 38th Annual CCCC Meeting, Atlanta, GA.

Research.

1868. Land, R. E., & Whitley, C. A. (1989). Evaluating second language essays in regular composition classes: Toward a pluralistic US rhetoric. In D. M. Johnson, & D. H. Roen (Eds.), *Richness in writing: Empowering ESL students* (pp. 284-293). NY: Longman.

Claims that in evaluating ESL compositions, teachers should not only go beyond sentence-level mechanics but also beyond the notion of the "one correct"

rhetorical pattern. States the need for teachers to change the way they read, respond, and evaluate by accomodating to more kinds of rhetorical patterns.
Evaluation/Teacher Preparation.

1869. Land, R. E., & Whitley, C. A. (1986, April). *Influences of second-language factors on the performance of freshman writers*. Paper presented at the Annual Meeting of the AERA, San Francisco, CA.
NES readers are most negatively influenced by ESL students' patterns of organization learned in their native language rhetorical communities.
Readers/Assessment/L1 Influence.

1870. Lane, J., & Lange, E. (1992). *Writing clearly: An editing guide*. Boston: Heinle & Heinle.
Guided instruction and practice in strategies for reducing errors.
Textbook.

1871. Lange, E. (1993, April). *Creating computer-based grammar exercises for a composition class*. Paper presented at the 27th Annual TESOL Convention, Atlanta, GA.
Demonstrates how to create computer-based grammar exercises for the classroon by using word processing.
Grammar/Computers.

1872. Lange, E. (1988, March). *Training non-ESL teachers to evaluate the ESL basic writer's papers*. Paper presented at the 39th Annual CCCC Meeting, St. Louis, MO.
Teacher Preparation.

1873. Lapkin, S. (1983). The English writing skills of French immersion pupils in grade five. *Canadian Modern Language Review*, *39*, 24-33.
Found similarities in English writing abilities of immersion and non-immersion students.
Children/French/Research.

1874. Lapp, R. E. (1987a). Using quickwriting to facilitate the writing process of intermediate and advanced ESL students: Part I. *TECFORS*, *10*(1), 1-5.
The first part of a two part series explains how to train and manage ESL writers in a technique for prewriting.
Invention/Intermediate/Advanced.

1875. Lapp, R. E. (1987b). Using quickwriting to facilitate the writing process of intermediate and advanced ESL students: Part II. *TECFORS*, *10*(2), 9-13.
Second of a two-part series discusses how to use this technique to aid drafting, revising and evaluating writing.
Process Instruction/Evaluation.

1876. Lapp, R. E. (1984). *The process approach to writing: Towards a curriculum for international students*. Unpublished master's thesis, University of Hawaii, Honolulu, HI.
Presents a rationale and outline for the curriculum of a writing course for international students who require pre-freshman remedial writing. The strategies and behaviors characteristic of skilled and unskilled native and non-native writers are presented in a series of eleven tables corresponding to different phases of the writing

process.
Curriculum/Process Instruction/University.

1877. Lapp, R. E. (1983, March). *Teaching the composing process.* Paper presented at the 17th Annual TESOL Convention, Toronto, Ontario.
Describes a classroom program for learning to write by writing.
Courses/Process Instruction.

1878. Lapp, R. E., & Diffley, F. (1988, March). *Responding to student writing: Teacher feedback for extensive revision.* Workshop presented at the 22nd Annual TESOL Convention, Chicago, IL.
Suggests ways to give oral and written feedback on student writing.
Responding.

1879. Lapp, R. E., Perrin, C., Cervantes, R., Heuring, D. L., & Gordon, D. (1984, March). *Responding to student writing: Teacher feedback for extensive revision.* Demonstration at the 18th Annual TESOL Convention, Houston, TX.
Suggests procedures and techniques, especially modeling how to give appropriate feedback, to ensure worthwhile activities.
Responding.

1880. Lapp, R. E., Pervin, C., Roulon, K., & Taylor, S. (1987, April). *The writing cycle? Heuristics for teaching the writing process.* Paper presented at the 21st Annual TESOL Convention, Miami Beach, FL.
Writing cycle heuristics, strategies specific to different moments are illustrated in this workshop.
Process Instruction.

1881. Larkin, G., & Shook, R. (1978, October). *Interlanguage, the monitor, and sentence combining.* Paper presented at the Los Angeles Second Language Research Forum, Los Angeles, CA. [ERIC ED 169 779].
Examines the effects of sentence combining exercises on relative clause formation in writing in English by Cantonese-speaking students. Results show that sentence combining exercises did not result in longer relative clauses.
Sentence Combining/Chinese/Language Development.

1882. Larsen-Freeman, D. (1979, March). *Length and accuracy analysis of ESL learners' writing.* Paper presented at the 13th Annual TESOL Convention, Boston. [ERIC ED 175 290].
Reports results of three studies seeking an efficient means of measuring development.
Objective Measures/Language Development.

1883. Larsen-Freeman, D. (1978). An ESL index of development. *TESOL Quarterly, 12,* 439-448.
Reports that the average number of words per error-free T-unit in written compositions by ESL students is a suitable additional measure (Larsen-Freeman & Strom, 1977) of a learner's second language proficiency.
Evaluation/Objective Measures.

1884. Larsen-Freeman, D. (1978, April). *An ESL index of development.* Paper presented at the 12th Annual TESOL Convention, Mexico City, Mexico.

Reports results of a pilot study of 48 ESL compositions by university students. Average number of words per T-unit correlates significantly with ESL proficiency.
T-Unit/Syntactic Development.

1885. Larsen-Freeman, D., & Strom, V. (1977). The construction of a second language acquisition index of development. *Language Learning*, *27*, 123-134.

Examines compositions written by forty-eight ESL students in order to determine an index of second language proficiency. Results indicate that the most suitable measures of written language at the sentence level were the average length of T-units and the total number of error-free T-units per composition.
Evaluation/Objective Measures.

1886. Larson, D. N., & Smalley, W. A. (1972). Learning to read and write. In *Becoming bilingual: A guide to language learning* (pp. 312-338). South Pasadena, CA: William Carey Library.

Focuses primarily on the differences posed for learners by a native language orthographic system that contrasts with English.
Orthography.

1887. Latief, M. A. (1991). Assessment of English writing skills for students of English as a foreign language at the Institute of Teacher Training and Education (Ikip-Malang) Indonesia. *Dissertation Abstracts International*, *51*(12), 40008.

Evaluates the effectiveness of one department's writing curriculum on the quality of EFL student writing. Neither the rhetoric and coherence nor the syntactic complexity of descriptive papers, as measured by primary trait scoring, improved significantly. But seniors wrote longer and better (again, measured by primary trait scoring) argumentative papers.
Indonesian/Curriculum/Evaluation.

1888. Latona, M. (1985, March). *A communicative use of journal writing in ESL and basic writing classes*. Paper presented at the 36th Annual CCCC Meeting, Minneapolis, MN.

Journal Writing.

1889. Latulippe, L. D. (1992). *Writing as a personal product*. Englewood Cliffs, NJ: Regents/Prentice Hall.

Textbook for international students planing to enter a university within a semester. Treats writing as both a process and a product. Includes chapters and exercises on choosing topics, deciding on an audience, preparing a writing plan, persuading an audience, and preparing a research paper.
Advanced/Textbook.

1890. Laube, L. (1992, March). *Underlife in ESL writing class: Insights for teachers*. Paper presented at the 43rd Annual CCCC Meeting, Cincinnati, OH.

Documents patterns of resistance with anecdotes from apprentice teachers and student journals.
Teacher Preparation/Resistance.

1891. Laurencio, D. E. (1984). The effect of using writing models on the writing performance of secondary English as a second language students. *Dissertation Abstracts International*, *44*(9), 2698A.

Examines whether use of writing models has significant effect on writing performance of ESL students. Results show writing models do effect writing performance.

Models.

1892. Laurencio, D. E., & Walker Defelix, J. (1984, March). *The effect of models on the writing performance of secondary English as a second language students.* Paper presented at the 18th Annual TESOL Convention, Houston, TX.

After being taught a combination of writing models, an experimental group wrote significantly better papers than a control group regardless of instruction received.

Models/Secondary School.

1893. Lautamatti, L. (1990). Coherence in spoken and written discourse. In U. M. Connor, & A. M. Johns (Eds.), *Coherence in writing: Research and pedagogical perspectives* (pp. 29-40). Alexandria, VA: TESOL.

Describes two facets of discourse coherence: propositional coherence and interactional coherence. Claims that formal writing/speech is usually characterized by propositional coherence and informal speech/writing by interactional coherence. Studies their relation to the discourse topic and finds that both are often present in different degrees in both formal and informal speech and writing.

Coherence/Speaking-Writing Relations/TSA.

1894. Lautamatti, L. (1987). Observations on the development of the topic of simplified discourse. In U. M. Connor, & R. B. Kaplan (Eds.), *Writing across languages: Analysis of L2 text* (pp. 87-114). Reading, MA: Addison-Wesley.

Examines aspects of topical development in written discourse on basis of text and its simplified version. Implications for foreign language reading comprehension stated.

Coherence/TSA.

1895. Lawgali, K. (1993, April). *Using portfolios in the advanced writing class.* Paper presented at the 27th Annual TESOL Convention, Atlanta, GA.

Presents a sample portfolio to illustrate the process of selection and learning.

Portfolios/Advanced.

1896. Lawrence, M. S. (1976). *Reading, thinking, writing: A text for students of English as a second language.* Ann Arbor, MI: University of Michigan Press.

Textbook integrates reading and writing and concentrates on grammar and vocabulary of logical relationships. Exercises in making extrapolations, manipulating and imposing order on data, and synthesizing information.

Intermediate/Textbook.

1897. Lawrence, M. S. (1973). Enquiry method and problem solving in EFL classroom. *TESL Reporter*, 5(1), 1-2, 12. [ERIC ED 077 287].

Maintains that the enquiry method of teaching composition is particularly effective with advanced students because its cognitive orientation draws on the intelligence of the students.

Classroom Activities.

1898. Lawrence, M. S. (1972). *Writing as a thinking process.* Ann Arbor, MI: University of Michigan Press.

Textbook for intermediate and advanced ESL students based on a semantic and cognitive approach to writing. Provides exercises focusing on <u>what</u> is being written about and <u>how</u> to organize one's writing.

Advanced/Textbook.

1899. Lawrence, M. S. (1971, March). *Writing as an active thinking process*. Paper presented at the 5th Annual TESOL Convention, New Orleans, LA.

Transfer of knowledge can be acheived by viewing writing as a conscious thinking process not as an end product. This method is accomplished through question formulation and problem solving/data manipulation.

Cognition.

1900. Lay, N. D. (1992, March). *Writing beyond ESL*. Paper presented at the 43rd Annual CCCC Meeting, Cincinnati, OH.

Describes two collaborative programs at CUNY.

Programs.

1901. Lay, N. D. (1983). *Making the most of English: An intermediate reading-writing text for ESL students*. San Diego, CA: Harcourt Brace Jovanovich.

Offers a text integrating reading and writing at the intermediate level.

Intermediate/Textbook/Reading-Writing Relations.

1902. Lay, N. D. (1982). Composing processes of adult ESL learners: A case study. *TESOL Quarterly*, *16*, 406.

Examines the composing processes of four Chinese-speaking ESL learners by an analysis of their written products and their talk-aloud protocols. Describes the similarities and differences between the composing processes in a first and second language and the influence of the first language in the composing in second language.

Process Instruction/Chinese.

1903. Lay, N. D. (1983). Native language in the composing process. In B. Kwalick, M. Silver, & V. Slaughter (Eds.), *Selected papers from the 1982 conference "New York writes: Kindergarten through college"* (pp. 17-21). NY: CUNY Instructional Resource Center.

Reports several findings from a study of the products, interviews, and think-aloud processes of five Chinese students who first wrote an essay in Chinese and then several in English. Among these are the use of the native language in pre-writing and the role of topics in inducing language switches.

L1 Influence/Chinese.

1904. Lay, N. D. (1978). *Chinese thought and Chinese language: Effects on students' writings*. Washington, DC: ERIC/FLL. [ERIC ED 166 275].

Posits conceptual and grammatical variation in writing Chinese and English. Suggests topics, methods, and structures for teaching Chinese students' to improve their writing.

Culture/Chinese.

1905. Lay, N. D. (1975). Chinese language interference in written English. *Journal of Basic Writing*, *1*(1), 50-61.

Presents key written errors made by Chinese learners and an English-

Mandarin contrast table to help teachers identify persistent errors.
Chinese/Grammar.

1906. Lay, N. D. (1974, March). *Preliminary research on a contrastive guide to teach English to Chinese immigrant students*. Paper presented at the 8th Annual TESOL Convention, Denver, CO.

Compiles a list of specific structural interference problems encountered by university students.
Chinese/L1 Influence.

1907. Lazarton, A. (1992). Linking ideas with and in spoken and written discourse. *IRAL, 30*(3), 191-206.

Analyzes a corpus of 7000 instances of <u>and</u> in 12 samples of spoken and written language to determine what kinds of elements are connected, what types of connections are made, and what semantic relations are expressed.
Cohesion/Speaking-Writing Relations.

1908. Leach, P. (1987). Passive resistance. *Journal of Applied Linguistics, 3*, 51-65.

An analysis of essays by thirty-five Hong Kong intermediate students indicates that particularly difficult English verbal groups, such as passives, are avoided by non-native writers. Discusses possible interlingual factors contributing to this "passive resistance".
Strategies/Chinese.

1909. Leader, L. (1992, March). *Student newspaper computer applications: Not just desktop publishing*. Demonstration presented at the 26th Annual TESOL Convention, Vancouver, BC.

Demonstrates how students can use Macintosh software for news gathering, drafting, editing, page design, and graphics.
Student Publications/Computers.

1910. Leap, W. (1982). Linguistics and written discourse in particular languages: Contrastive studies: English and American Indian Languages. *Annual Review of Applied Linguistics, 3*, 24-37.

Discusses factors related to written Indian language discourse and Indian English language literacy, especially the issue of error in speech and writing.
Amer-Indian/Errors/Speaking-Writing Relations.

1911. Leavelle, C. A. (1984). *A functional analysis of connectives in English composition: Implications for the teaching of English as a second language*. Unpublished master's thesis, North Texas State University, Denton, TX.

Claims that connectives in English are not merely dependent on syntax but are a part of the continuum of semantic dependency. Suggests measures to teach connectives to ESL students that will take into account semantic and pragmatic factors.
Cohesion.

1912. Leavitt, H. D., & Sohn, D. A. (1990). *Look, think & write*. Littlewood, IL: NTC Publishing Group.

Beginning writers in this texbook are encouraged to record their observations about 130 thought-provoking photographs with accuracy and imagination, and to plan,

organize, and write expository essays.
Beginners/Textbook.

1913. Lebauer, R. S. (1990a). *A collaborative computer-assisted reading and writing project: Dynamic stories* . Urbana, IL: ERIC/RCS. [ERIC ED 321 546].

Describes the rationale, preparation, and implementation of a project in which students collaborate to create stories. This collaboration realistically requires brainstorming, peer feedback, and revising. Ultimately, student-created stories become part of a permanent "library" of programs.
Computers/Reading-Writing Relations/Collaboration.

1914. Lebauer, R. S. (1990b, March). *Dynamic stories: Collaborative computer assisted reading and writing*. Paper presented at the 24th Annual TESOL Convention, San Francisco, CA.

See previous item.
Computers/Reading-Writing Relations/Collaboration.

1915. Lebauer, R. S., & Scarcella, R. C. (1991, March). *Strengthening the reading/writing connection*. Paper presented at the 25th Annual TESOL Convention, New York, NY.

Shows how to strengthen the literacy relationship by creating activities that provide reading as comprehensible input, require reader reactions to texts, and develop writer-oriented readers.
Reading-Writing Relations.

1916. Lebauer, R. S., Scarcella, R. C., & Stern, S. (1990). *Reactions: Multi-cultural reading-based writing modules*. Englewood Cliffs, NJ: Prentice Hall Regents.

A process approach to writing is integrated with other skills in an intermediate to advanced textbook featuring multicultural readings.
Textbook/Intermediate.

1917. Lederman, M. J. (1988). Why test? *Journal of Basic Writing*, 7(1), 38-46.

Finds similarities between reasons for testing in contemporary America and in traditional and modern China.
Assessment/Chinese.

1918. Lee, C. E. (1990). Korean high school seniors' oral and literate comprehension and production skills in English. *Dissertation Abstracts International*, 51(9), 3004-3005A.

Tests the hypothesis that Korean subjects, forty high school seniors, perform better in literate comprehension and production than in aural comprehension and production. Conclusions on production measures (picture descriptions) are that (1) subjects wrote more than they spoke in both English and Korean; (2) produced slightly more written words in English and slightly more spoken words in Korean; and (3) made more errors in speaking than in writing.
Korean/Speaking-Writing Relations.

1919. Lee, G. W. (1990). *Analysis of errors in the compositions written by nonnative English speakers*. Unpublished master's thesis, East Texas State University, Commerce, TX.
Error Analysis.

1920. Lee, M. (1984). Brainstorming as an aid to writing. *TESL Canada Journal, 1*(2), 78-79.
> Discusses how to increase student writing proficiency with brainstorming.
> Invention.

1921. Lee, M. (1976). Some common grammatical errors made in written English by Chinese students. *CATESOL Occasional Papers, 3*, 115-119.
> Reviews grammatical errors found in the writing of Chinese students.
> Chinese/Error Analysis.

1922. Lee, N. S., & Sender, B. (1981, March). *Linking adult education and community college writing skills in ESL.* Paper presented at the 15th Annual TESOL Convention, Detroit, MI.
> Discusses general writing objectives and curricular models to facilitate the transition from one program to another.
> Programs.

1923. Lee, W. (1973). *Intrusions from Chinese in compositions by Hong Kong students.* Unpublished master's thesis, UCLA, Los Angeles, CA.
> Discusses the influence of Chinese stylistics, such as preference for formal symmetry and regular rhythm, in the writing of Chinese students in Hong Kong.
> Chinese/Style/Contrastive Rhetoric.

1924. Lee, Y. C. (1993). Revision breakdowns in academic writing of Chinese graduate-level ESL students. *Dissertation Abstracts International, 54*(3), 844-855A.
> An analysis of multiple revisions of one self-chosen academic writing assignment by five Chinese graduate students reveals that subjects had very limited English language ability, limited ability to detect errors, and difficulty using a wide variety of strategies for revising.
> Chinese/Graduate Students/Editing.

1925. Lefkowitz, N. (1986). *From process to product: Writing from experience for beginning and intermediate ESL students.* Englewood Cliffs, NJ: Prentice Hall Regents.
> Text provides students with communicative practice in the skills needed for the entire writing process from planning to revision. It combines both process and product approaches as well as self-discovery techniques.
> Beginners/Intermediate/Textbook.

1926. Lehman, R. (1991, April). *Comparing the meaning of national ratings in an International Assessment of Writing Achievement.* Paper presented at the Annual Meeting of the AERA, Chicago, IL.
> Assessment.

1927. Leimkuhler, M. (1992, March). *Cohesion in adult Korean and native English speaker's writing.* Poster presented at the 26th Annual TESOL Convention, Vancouver, BC.
> Shows comparison of the cohesive ties (reference, conjunction, reiteration) in expository essays of college-level Korean and native English speakers. Koreans used many more pronouns and conjunctive terms but significantly fewer repetitions and synonyms.

Korean/Cohesion/Exposition/University.

1928. Leimkuhler, M. (1990). *Anaphoric cohesion in the writing of adult Korean ESL subjects and native speakers of English*. Unpublished master's thesis, University of Illinois, Urbana-Champaign, IL.

Finds differences in use of cohesive devices attributable to L1, topic choice, and essay content.

Text Analysis/Cohesion/Korean.

1929. Leki, I. (1993). Reciprocal themes in ESL reading and writing. In J. G. Carson, & I. Leki (Eds.), *Reading in the composition classroom: Second language perspectives* (pp. 9-32). Boston: Heinle & Heinle.

Introduces current issues in reading and writing, arguing that the field is on the verge of a major shift in perspective.

Reading-Writing Relations.

1930. Leki, I. (1992a, March). *Current issues in ESL writing: The reading/writing connection*. Paper presented at the 43rd Annual CCCC Meeting, Cincinnati, OH.

Issues discussed include the transfer of literacy skills, the role of culturally-determined attitudes in acquiring such skills, the kinds of reading and writing activities in use, and how to use reading for writing and learning.

Reading-Writing Relations.

1931. Leki, I. (1992b, March). *Research agendas for ESL writing: Changing perspectives on L2 reading and writing*. Paper presented at a Colloquium at the 26th Annual TESOL Convention, Vancouver, BC.

Outlines seven research areas for developing social perspectives on reading-writing relationships.

Reading-Writing Relations/Research.

1932. Leki, I. (1992c). *Understanding ESL writers: A guide for teachers*. Portsmouth, NH: Boynton/Cook.

Presents the findings of research about the special characteristics, qualities, and situations of ESL students for writing teachers without a significant amount of contact with the teaching of writing to ESL students. Covers acquisition models, ESL/ NES differences, ESL characteristics, classroom expectations and behaviors, composing strategies, contrastive rhetoric, errors, and responding.

Teacher Preparation.

1933. Leki, I. (1991a). Building authorial expertise through sequenced writing assignments. *TESOL Journal, 1*(2), 19-23.

Describes a five-assignment sequence that helps students become authorities on a topic.

Assignments/Topic.

1934. Leki, I. (1991b). A new approach to advanced ESL placement testing. *Journal of the Council of Writing Program Administrators, 14*, 53-68.

Proposes an innovative alternative to traditional ESL placement testing.

Placement.

1935. Leki, I. (1991c). The preference of ESL students for error correction in college-level writing classes. *Foreign Language Annals, 24*, 203-218.

Theory notwithstanding, the majority of ESL students surveyed in freshman composition want all their errors corrected, suggesting that they equate good writing with error-free writing.

Error Treatment.

1936. Leki, I. (1991d). Teaching second language writing: Where we seem to be. *English Teaching Forum*, *29*(2), 8-11.

Discusses some of the changes that have come about in the teaching of writing in a second language.

Instruction.

1937. Leki, I. (1991e). Twenty-five years of contrastive rhetoric: Text analysis and writing pedagogies. *TESOL Quarterly*, *25*, 123-143.

Reviews development and problems of contrastive rhetoric as well as benefits for the classroom.

Contrastive Rhetoric/Review.

1938. Leki, I. (1990a). Coaching from the margins: Issues in written response. In B. Kroll (Ed.), *Second language writing: Research insights for the classroom* (pp. 57-68). Cambridge: Cambridge University Press.

Summarizes issues involved in studying written response to compositions.

Responding.

1939. Leki, I. (1990b). The technical editor and the non-native speaker of English. *Technical Communication*, *37*(2), 148-152.

Advises technical editors who work with the materials of non-native writers about current views toward second language acquisition, especially studies of contrastive rhetoric that suggest culturally dictated styles of presenting written materials.

Editing.

1940. Leki, I. (1989a). *Academic writing: Techniques and tasks*. NY: St. Martin's Press.

Designed for students learning to write in academic contexts, this textbook encourages drafting and redrafting, invention, journal writing, feedback and the application of these writing processes to analyzing, evaluating, and arguing.

University/Textbook.

1941. Leki, I. (1989b, March). *Matching perceptions: Student and teacher evaluation of writing*. Paper presented at the 23rd Annual TESOL Convention, San Antonio, TX.

Studies the degree to which student perceptions of good writing are shared by ESL writing teachers.

Standards.

1942. Leki, I. (1985a). Linking writing journals to writing in the ESL classroom.Part II. *TECFORS*, *8*(5), 1-6.

Continues TECFORS,8 (3).

Journal Writing.

1943. Leki, I. (1985b). Linking writing journals to writing in the ESL classroom.Part I. *TECFORS*, *8*(3), 13-15. [ERIC ED 267 650].

Reviews strengths and weaknesses of three kinds of writing journals.

Journal Writing.

1944. Leki, I., Belcher, D. D., Newstetter, W. C., Prior, P. A., & Connor, U. M. (1993, April). *Attractions, dangers, and issues in qualitative writing research.* Paper presented at the 27th Annual TESOL Convention, Atlanta, GA.

Discusses some key issues in conducting qualitative research: problems of identity, ideology, and contrastive textual analysis.

Research.

1945. Leki, I., Gertzman, A., Rowe Henry, A., Cumming, A. H., & Nunan, D. (1993, April). *Complexities of ESL writing: Reports of qualitative research.* Paper presented at the 27th Annual TESOL Convention, Atlanta, GA.

Qualitative research studies by recreating the writing world of ESL students enable teachers and researchers to experience the complexity of student engagement with educational institutions.

Research.

1946. Leone, E. (1989, March). *Scorer training and consensus-building for college placement compositions.* Paper presented at the 23rd Annual TESOL Convention, San Antonio, TX.

Describes a workshop for persons outside ESL who need to be trained to score ESL compositions for placement purposes.

Assessment/University/Placement.

1947. Leonhardt, N. L. (1985). The effects of assigned versus open topics on the writing scores of university-level nonnative English speakers. *Dissertation Abstracts International, 46*(10), 2951A.

Examines the effects of topic choice on ESL essay writing. Findings show: (1) no relationship between topics and subscores of the writing test; and (2) high correlations between TOEFL subscores and totals as well as ESL composition profile subscores and total scores.

Evaluation/Topic.

1948. Lesikin, J. (1989, March). *The social consequences of evaluating ESL writing.* Paper presented at the 23rd Annual TESOL Meeting, San Antonio, TX. [ERIC ED 308 700].

Discusses the social implications of evaluating the writing of ESL students in the context of the Hegemony Theory, a radical and critical view of schooling, which identifies schools as an agency of socialization. Maintains that ESL writing teachers must sensitize themselves to these social implications by looking into three areas: (1) who establishes the evaluation criteria, (2) what the evaluation criteria are, and (3) how the evaluation criteria sre used, including when evaluation is carried out and by whom.

Socio-Political Theory.

1949. Less, P. (1992, March). *Responding to Japanese writers: Eating artichokes with noble minds.* Poster presented at the 26th Annual TESOL Convention, Vancouver, BC.

Displays writing samples showing expressions of Japanese thought and culture.

Japanese/Responding.

1950. LeTourneau, M. S. (1985). Typical ESL errors and tutoring strategies. *Writing Lab*

Newsletter, (5-8),

Presents certain inflectional and grammatical errors as common to ESL students and advises how to deal with them.

Errors/Tutoring.

1951. Leung, L. (1984). The relationship between first-and second-language writing. *Language Learning and Communication*, 3(2), 187-202.

Questionnaires administered to forty Chinese secondary school students and their teachers at four grade levels reveal a close relationship between L1 and L2 writing. Some L2 writing problems can be traced to L1 problems.

Chinese/Secondary School/LI Influence.

1952. Levenston, E. A. (1978). Error analysis of free composition: The theory and practice. *Indian Journal of Applied Linguistics*, 4(1), 1-11.

Using an algorithm developed by S. Pitt Corder as a basis for providing data for describing idiosyncratic dialects, this study claims to offer a new approach to error analysis. Procedure is to construct a set of well-formed sentences having the same meaning as the original from a base essay written by a learner. This is followed by composing a <u>reformulation</u>, essentially an editing process. This method of going from text to reconstruction is suggested for use in the language classroom.

Error Analysis/Feedback/Reformulation.

1953. Leverson, S. (1979). Teaching reading and writing to limited and non-English speakers in secondary schools. *English Journal*, 68, 38-42.

Discusses the language experience approach to reading and writing and describes how such an approach would benefit limited and non-English speaking high school students.

Reading-Writing Relations/Secondary School.

1954. Levine, I. W. (1976). *Developing a sequential program for the teaching of writing and composition for foreign-born Spanish speaking high school bilingual students*. Unpublished master's thesis, Hunter College, CUNY, New York, NY.

Hispanic/Programs/Secondary School.

1955. Levinson, J. (1987, April). *Identifying linguistic needs of upper-level ESL students*. Paper presented at the 21st Annual TESOL Convention, Miami Beach, FL.

Distinguishes treatable structural deficiencies in the writing of upper-level students from those that are not responsive to direct instruction.

Advanced/Syntactic Structures.

1956. Levy, M. (1990). Concordances and their integration into a word-processing environment for language learners. *System*, 18, 177-188.

Describes how language learners might use concordances, such as MicroConcord, along with on-line dictionaries, thesauruses, style checker and word processing to help ESL students develop their written language learning.

Computers/Programs/Word Processing.

1957. Lewitt, P. J. (1990). How to cook a tasty essay: The secret of real rewriting. *English Teaching Forum*, 28(1), 2-4.

Provides a metaphor to guide rethinking about the teaching of writing to a more learner-centered mode.

Japanese.
1958. Lewis, P. (1990). Language experience approach for ESL students. *Adult Learning, 1*(5), 27.

ESL learners need to be in control of the words they use to create texts that become their reading materials.
LEA/Adult Education.

1959. Li, N. Y. K. (1990, July). *Writing with pen or computer? A study on ESL secondary school learners*. Paper presented at the 5th Annual World Conference on Computers in Education, Sydney, Australia. [ERIC ED 322 720].

Hong Kong eighth-graders wrote better and longer essays (about 200 each) with computers than their peers who wrote by hand (N=40). Only a few of the essays, however, accounted for the significant differences found. Neither group, however, felt that writing in English was either easy or enjoyable.
Computers/Secondary School/Chinese.

1960. Li, X. M. (1993). A celebration of tradition or of self? An ethnographic study of teachers' comments on student writing in America and in China. *Dissertation Abstracts International, 53*(11), 3829A.

Surveys writing teachers (N=60) in China and the U.S. about the quality of self-selected writing samples of four writing teachers (2 from each country) who were also interviewed in depth. Finds and interprets some commonly held criteria for "good writing" but also shows that there are substantial "national" differences between teachers in both countries. Results imply that cultural bias may inadvertently affect teachers as readers and judges of EFL writing.
Chinese/Reader/NS-NNS Comparisons.

1961. Li, X. (1990). Various ways of correcting written work. *English Teaching Forum, 28*(1), 34-36.

Gives several techniques for correcting compositions.
Feedback/Chinese.

1962. Liao, T. S. H. (1984). A study of article errors in the written English of Chinese college students in Taiwan. *Dissertation Abstracts International, 45*(7), 2017A.

Examines and classifies errors in usage of articles in written English by Chinese-speaking students. Attributes errors to underteaching/underlearning rather than interference of mother tongue.
Error Analysis/Chinese.

1963. Libben, G. (1982). *Some fundamentals of ESL composition analysis*. Unpublished master's thesis, Concordia University, Montreal, Canada.

1964. Lidman, W. J. (1981). *Developing written communication skills in the Jackson Township Bilingual Program*. Unpublished master's thesis, Keane State College, Keane, NJ. [ERIC ED 215 576].

Studies how teaching methods, language development, and self-image are related to the under-achievement of bilingual elementary school students.
Elementary.

1965. Lieber, P. E. (1984, March). *Tense shifts in college students' narrative writing*. Paper presented at the 18th Annual TESOL Convention, Houston, TX.

An analysis of narrative protocols written by native and ESL college students shows need to control tense shifting caused by action shifts and commentary story line interaction.
Narration/Syntactic Structures.

1966. Lieber, P. E. (1981, October). *Superordinate terms in expository writing*. Paper presented at the Annual Conference of New York State English to Speakers of Other Languages and Bilingual Educators Association, Rochester, NY. [ERIC ED 214 389].

Stresses the importance of teaching ESL students the appropriate use of superordinates and hyponyms that will help them in their academic writing. Suggests using literature on reading comprehension for techniques for presenting, practicing and differentiating superordinates.
Coherence/Instruction.

1967. Liebman, J. D. (1992a). Toward a new contrastive rhetoric: Differences betweeen Arabic and Japanese rhetorical instruction. *Journal of Second Language Writing*, *1*(2), 141-165.

Reports results of a survey of Japanese and Arabic ESL students about how writing is taught in their cultures: in Japan emphasis is on the expressive function, whereas in Arab countries, transactional writing receives more attention.
Contrastive Rhetoric.

1968. Liebman, J. D. (1992b, March). *ESL and NES writing communities' conceptions of academic writing*. Paper presented at the 43rd Annual CCCC Meeting, Cincinnati, OH.

Argues that dichotomies between both process and product as well as EAP and WAC obscure what each area does well and ignores the gaps in our knowledge.
NS-NNS Comparisons.

1969. Liebman, J. D. (1991, March). *A history of ESL writing theory and pedagogy*. Paper presented at the 42nd Annual CCCC Meeting, Boston, MA.
Instruction/Theory.

1970. Liebman, J. D. (1988a). Contrastive rhetoric: Students as ethnographers. *Journal of Basic Writing*, *7*(2), 6-27.

Discusses the application of contrastive rhetoric to the teaching of writing by both ESL and NES students. The organization of the papers did not reveal any cultural differences between the students but differences were found in the students' approaches to the material.
Contrastive Rhetoric/NS-NNS Comparisons.

1971. Liebman, J. D. (1988b, March). *Using the Myers-Briggs Type Indicator in ESL writing classes*. Paper presented at the 22nd Annual TESOL Convention, Chicago, IL.

Finds a personality preference test to be useful to both students and teachers.
Learning Styles.

1972. Liebman, S., Van Slyke, A., & Desbonnet, K. (1985, April). *Guiding their way: Composition development for ESL students*. Paper presented at the 19th Annual TESOL Convention, New York, NY.

Presents a sequence of writing exercises that lead students from prewriting through organizing the in-class theme.
Control/Exercises.

1973. Liebman-Kleine, J. D. (1987a, March). *The student/researcher: An ethnographic study of contrastive rhetoric*. Paper presented at the 38th Annual CCCC Meeting, Atlanta, GA.

1974. Liebman-Kleine, J. D. (1987b). Teaching and researching invention: Using ethnography in ESL writing classes. *ELT Journal, 41*, 104-111.

A small-scale study of the invention preferences of advanced ESL students reveals a range of techniques used from hierarchical treeing to open-ended, exploratory techniques.
Invention/Ethnographic Research.   See Liebman-Kleine, 1988.

1975. Liebman-Kleine, J. D. (1987c, March). *Towards a contrastive new rhetoric: A rhetoric of process*. Paper presented at the CCCC Convention, Atlanta, GA. [ERIC ED 281 194].

Examines the cultural differences and similarities in discourse production of a native and a non-native freshman composition class.
Contrastive Rhetoric/NS-NNS Comparisons.

1976. Liebman-Kleine, J. D. (1986a). In defense of teaching process in ESL composition . . .[In The Forum]. *TESOL Quarterly, 20*, 783-788.

Responds to Horowitz (1986) which purportedly espouses an academic vs. process approach to writing. Author emphasizes differences among process approaches and claims that process approach isubsumes academic writing.
Process Instruction.

1977. Liebman-Kleine, J. D. (1986b, March). *Toward a contrastive new rhetoric -- A rhetoric of process*. Paper presented at the 20th Annual TESOL Convention, Anaheim, CA. [ERIC ED 271 963].

Reports a survey of 77 nonnative writers with highly variable prior rhetorical training. Results suggest that the influence of culture on the rhetoric of NNS writing may be due to previous training in writing.
Contrastive Rhetoric/Process Research.

1978. Light, R. L., & Fan, L. Y. (1989). *Contemporary world issues: An interactive approach to reading and writing*. Boston: Heinle & Heinle.

Text emphasizes communication and interaction by utilizing a variety of readings, supplemented with charts, graphs, tables, and maps, from contemporary publications. Exercises provide practice in skimming, scanning, predicting, note-taking, analyzing, and summarizing. Pre-writing activities offer practice in exploring, analyzing, and presenting ideas about the readings. All activities allow students to compare their own experiences and opinions about the topics.
University/Advanced/Textbook.

1979. Ligon, F., & Tannebaum, E. (1990). *Picture stories*. NY: Addison Wesley/Longman.

This text provides language and literacy activities for low beginner young adults with little or no literacy skills. Students write stories related to those presented

in text which are related to experiences of immigrant families.
Beginners/Textbook.

1980. Lim, H. P. (1983a). The development of syntax in the writing of university ESL students. *TESOL Quarterly*, *17*, 313-314.

Studies syntactic complexity in ESL writing of one hundred twenty students. Examines the relationship of free-writing and rewriting. More proficient students were more expressive in both free-writing and rewriting.
Assessment/Objective Measures.

1981. Lim, H. P. (1983b). Using T-unit measures to assess writing proficiency of university ESL students. *RELC Journal*, *14*(2), 35-43.

T-unit measures were used to assess both free writing and rewriting abilities of sixty ESL students, representing three levels of proficiency. Results indicate that measures used in evaluating writing will have to be error-free if they are to discriminate accurately between compositions written by ESL students.
Assessment/ Objective Measures.

1982. Lim, H. P. (1982). The development of syntax in the writing of university ESL students. *Dissertation Abstracts International*, *43*(4), 1133A.

Examines the free-writing and re-writing of ESL students at three proficiency levels to arrive at an index of syntactic development in English as a second language. Findings show mean error-free T-units per sentence as the best index, followed by mean words per error-free T-unit and then by mean words per T-unit.
Language Development/Free Writing/Revision.

1983. Lin, C. C. (1990). The structures of English and Chinese narratives written by college students in Taiwan. *Dissertation Abstracts International*, *50*(7), 2036A.

Finds quantitative differences in the number of episodes written in English rather than in Chinese by native Chinese-speaking college students.
L1-L2 Comparison/Chinese/Narration.

1984. Lindeberg, A. C. (1987). A functional role analysis of expository and argumentative student essys in EFL. In I. Lindblat, & M. Ljund (Eds.), *Proceedings from the Third Nordic Conference for English Studies, Vol. 1* (pp. 175-190). Stockholm: Almqvist & Wiksell.

Finds differing patterns of sequences of discourse functions in good and poor expository and argumentative essays by business/economics EFL students in Sweden.
Academic Writing/Coherence/Text Analysis.

1985. Lindeberg, A. C. (1986a). Cohesion and coherence in short expository essays. In H. Ringbom, & M. Rissanen (Eds.), *Proceedings from the Second Nordic Conference for English Studies* (pp. 199-207). Abo, Finland: Abo Akademi Foundation Research Institute.

1986. Lindeberg, A. C. (1986b). Functional role analysis applied to narrative and non-narrative student essays in EFL. In *NORDWRITE reports I: Trondheim papers in applied linguistics* (pp. 26-45). Trondheim, Norway: University of Trondheim.
Coherence/Text Analysis.

1987. Lindeberg, A. C. (1985a). Abstraction levels in student essays. *Text: An Interdisciplinary Journal for the Study of Discourse*, *5*(4), 327-346.

Presents a model for analyzing the depth of development in student writing, which helps differentiate between good and poor essays. The method emphasizes functional relations between segments of text.
Coherence/Text Analysis.

1988. Lindeberg, A. C. (1985b). Cohesion, coherence patterns, and EFL essay evaluation. In N. E. Enkvist (Ed.), *Coherence and composition: A symposium* (pp. 67-92). Abo, Finland: Research Institute of the Abo Akademi Foundation.
Illustrates a method (following Lieber, 1980) for measuring coherence by type of cohesive tie in the linear development of themic and rhemic information that is useful for describing good as well as not so coherent essays.
Coherence/Text Analysis.

1989. Lindemann, E. (1988). *Longman bibliography of composition and rhetoric, 1986.* NY: Longman.
Annual classified listing of scholarship on written English and its teaching for American compositionists, including 97 items related to ESL published before 1986.
Bibliography.

1990. Lindemann, E. (1987). *Longman bibliography of composition and rhetoric, 1984-1985.* NY: Longman.
Annual classified listing of scholarship on written English and its teaching for American compositionists, including 134 items related to ESL published in 1984-85.
Bibliography.

1991. Lindemann, E., & Fleming, S. M. (1992). *CCCC bibliography of composition and rhetoric, 1990.* Carbondale, IL: NCTE/Southern Illinois Press.
Annual classified listing of scholarship on written English and its teaching for American compositionists, including 85 items related to ESL published in 1990.
Bibliography.

1992. Lindemann, E., & Fleming, S. M. (1991). *CCCC bibliography of composition and rhetoric, 1989.* Carbondale, IL: CCCC/Southern Illinois Press.
Annual classified listing of scholarship on written English and its teaching for American compositionists, including 61 items related to ESL published before 1989.
Bibliography.

1993. Lindemann, E., & Harding, M. B. (1991). *CCCC bibliography of composition and rhetoric, 1988.* Carbondale, IL: CCCC/Southern Illinois Press.
Annual classified listing of scholarship on written English and its teaching for American compositionists, including 56 items related to ESL published in 1988.
Bibliography.

1994. Lindemann, E., Monroe, S., & O'Quinn, T. (1990). *CCCC bibliography of composition and rhetoric, 1987.* Carbondale, IL: CCCC/Southern Illinois Press.
Annual classified listing of scholarship on written English and its teaching for American compositionists, including 75 items related to ESL published in 1987.
Bibliography.

1995. Lindfors, J. W. (1988a). From helping hand to reciprocity to mutuality: Dialogue journal writing with Zulu students. *Journal of Learning, 1*(1), 63-85.
Dialogue Journals/Zulu.

1996. Lindfors, J. W. (1988b). From 'talking together" to "being together in talk". *Language Arts*, *65*(2), 135-141.

    Discusses how dialogue journals were used with Zulu students in South Africa.

    Dialogue Journals/Zulu.

1997. Lindfors, J. W. (1988c). Zulu students' questioning in dialogue journals. *Questioning Exchange*, *2*(3), 289-304.

    Finds abundance, variety and sincerity in the English dialogue journal questioning by Zulu sixth graders in South Africa.

    Dialogue Journals/Zulu.

1998. Lindsay, D. B. (1984a). *Cohesion in the compositions of ESL and English students*. Unpublished master's thesis, UCLA, Los Angeles, CA.

    In a study of a single timed composition by NES and NNS college students, finds that ESL students use more cohesive ties than NESs. Also, poorly rated NNSs make more errors in the use of cohesion. Error-free cohesive ties may measure quality of writing.

    Cohesion/NS-NNS Comparisons.

1999. Lindsay, D. B. (1984b, March). *A qualitative analysis of the cohesion in ESL and English compositions*. Paper presented at the 18th Annual TESOL Convention, Houston, TX.

    Results show developmental stages in acquisition and interesting differences between native and non-native writers.

    Cohesion/NS-NNS Comparisons.

2000. Lindstrom, M. (1981). *Native speaker reaction to stylistic errors in writing: An error evaluation*. Unpublished master's thesis, Colorado State University, Fort Collins, CO.

    Error Gravity/Style.

2001. Linnarud, M. (1986). *Lexis in composition: A performance analysis of Swedish learners' written English*. Lund, Sweden: Liber Forlag Malmo.

    Compares the difference in lexis in writing by seventeen-year-old Swedish learners and NES by counting lexical individuality, sophistocation, variation, and density in texts. Factors are evaluated by teachers. Results indicate that NES write longer essays with greater lexical values than Swedish learners in the same time. While Swedish and NES teachers are equallly sensitive to errors, native university teachers have a higher corrrelation with lexical individuality than do Swedish teachers or 'naive' native speakers.

    Lexis/Swedish/NS-NNS Comparisons.

2002. Linnarud, M. (1983). On lexis: The Swedish learner and the native speaker compared. *Jyvaskyla Cross-Language Studies*, *10*, 249-261.

    Examines possibility that lexis accounts for perceived difference between EFL compositions and native compositions written by same age students. Measures of lexis applied to each composition were: lexical originality, use of conventional syntagms, idioms, and collocations, lexical sophistication, lexical variation, and lexical density. Within the Swedish learner group a significant relation was found between lexical

originality, lexical sophistication, and use of collocations. Also notes that outside of the number of errors, second language writers were much less original than native speakers. This was due both to lack of vocabulary originality and lack of topic originality. The second-language writers often used circumlocution to express something for which a fixed expression exists.
Lexis/Text Analysis/Swedish.

2003. Linnarud, M. (1978). Cohesion and communication in the target language. *Interlanguage Studies Bulletin (Utrecht)*, *3*(1), 23-33.

Examines the effect on the native speaker of the presence or absence of overt error in written free communication and offers a contrastive analysis of meaning cohesion in a sample of data from Swedish learners. Finds frequency, density and variation in cohesion use linked to quality of essays.
Cohesion/Swedish.

2004. Linnarud, M. (1977). Some aspects of style in the source and the target language. *Papers and Studies in Contrastive Linguistics*, *7*, 85-94.
Style.

2005. Linnarud, M. (1975). *Lexis in free production: An analysis of the lexical texture of Swedish students' written work*. (Swedish-English Contrastive Studies Report No. 6). Lund, Sweden: Lund University.
See Linnarud, 1986.
Cohesion.

2006. Linse, C. (1988, March). *Don't phone: Write!* Paper presented at the 22nd Annual TESOL Convention, Chicago, IL.
Demonstrates letter writing activities for elementary ESOL students.
Letter Writing/Elementary.

2007. Lintermann-Rygh, I. (1985). Connector density -- An indicator of essay quality? *Text*, *5*(4), 347-357.

Describes a preliminary descriptive study of Norwegian students' writing performance in L1 and EFL based on the Trondheim corpus of applied linguistics. Connector density is not a useful variable for performance analysis of compositions written in Norwegian (L1).
Cohesion/Norwegian.

2007. Liontas, J. I. (1989). Using authentic materials to develop functional proficiency in writing. In B. T. Frye, & F. W. J. Medley, Jr. (Eds.), *Perspectives and horizons. Dimension: Language 89* NC: Report of Southern Conference on Language Teaching.

Illustrates how to adapt realia from the target culture to the learner's immediate environment in order to teach the processes and principles of writing holistically.
Materials.

2008. Liou, H. C. (1992a). An automatic text analysis project for EFL writing revision. *System*, *20*, 481-492.

Describes an English grammar text analysis program for Chinese students in Taiwan.
Computers/Grammar/Chinese.

2009. Liou, H. C., Wang, S. H., & Yuli, H. Y. (1992b). Can grammatical CALL help EFL writing instruction? *CALICO Journal, 10*(1), 23-44.

    An experiment compares the use of CALL courseware, designed for error analysis, drill, and remediation, with paper-and-pencil homework assignments. Finds that grammatical CALL was not detrimental when combined with classroom writing instruction.

    Computers/Grammar/Chinese.

2010. Liou, H. C. (1992c). Investigation of using text-critiquing programs in a process-oriented writing class. *CALICO Journal, 10*(4), 17-38.

    A quasi-experimental study (N=39) leads to the claim that text-analysis programs, such as Grammatik, may be beneficial to learners when revising if careful design and attention is provided.

    Computers/Process Instruction/Chinese.

2011. Liou, H. C. (1991, March). *Computer-assisted writing revision: A progress report.* Paper presented at the 25th Annual TESOL Convention, New York, NY.

    Discusses the development of a grammar program to help students with their revisions.

    Computers/Grammar/Chinese.

2012. Lipp, E. (1990). *From paragraph to term paper: A reading and composition text for advanced students.* Boston: Heinle & Heinle.

    Text helps students refine their reading and writing skills by offering a review of effective strategies. The readings cover a wide range of topics from computer dating to environmental programs.

    University/Advanced/Textbook.

2013. Lipp, E. (1983, October). *Bridging the culture gap: The first phase of training writing lab tutors to work with ESL students.* Paper presented at the Midwest Writing Centers Conference, Iowa City, IA. [ERIC ED 241 958].

    Offers an in-service program focusing on six areas of concern to help writing lab staffs work more effectively with ESL students.

    Writing Center/Tutoring.

2014. Lites, E. (1993, April). *Designing the business writing curriculum.* Paper presented at the 27th Annual TESOL Convention, Atlanta, GA.

    Describes the skills and assignments in curricula of university and workplace programs.

    Business Writing.

2015. Lites, E., & Lehman, J. P. (1991). *Visions: An academic writing text.* Englewood Cliffs, NJ: Prentice Hall Regents.

    Uses a process-oriented approach to prepare pre-university ESL students in academic and technical fields for academic writing. Progresses from sentence and paragraph construction to creating short compositions with many exercises and related activities.

    Intermediate/Textbook.

2016. Little, G. D. (1989, March). *The practical application of contrasting texts.* Paper presented at the 23rd Annual TESOL Convention, San Antonio, TX.

Outlines a course for advanced ESL speakers that uses contrasting rhetorical patterns.
Contrastive Rhetoric/Advanced.

2017. Littlejohn, A. (1988). *Company to company: A new approach to business correspondence in English*. NY: Cambridge University Press.
Instructs ESL learners on writing business correspondence by using a discussion-based approach.
Intermediate/Business Writing/Textbook.

2018. Littlejohn, A., & Hicks, D. (1987). Task-centered writing activities. In C. N. Candlin, & D. Murphy (Eds.), *Language learning tasks* (pp. 69-92). Englewood Cliffs, NJ: Prentice-Hall International.
Presents criteria for and samples of task-based writing activities -- especially simulations which are task-specific, decision-oriented and implemented in real time.
Task.

2019. Lloyd, D. J. (1950). A "linguistic" approach to English composition. *Language Learning*, *3*, 109-116.
Advocates using English as a subject matter in ESL composition rather than focusing on correct usage as purportedly occurs in freshman composition for native speakers.
NS-NNS Comparisons.

2020. Lo, W. A. Y., & Mohan, B. A. (1980, March). *"Cultural thought patterns," writing, and Chinese students*. Paper presented at the 14th Annual TESOL Convention, San Francisco, CA.
Argues against Kaplan's (1966b) thesis which attributes distinctive thought patterns to individual cultures. Deficiencies in the writing of Hong Kong students in Vancouver are attributed, rather, to lack of education in paragraph organization.
Chinese/Contrastive Rhetoric.

2021. Lockhart, C., & Ng, P. (1993a, April). *The appropriacy of peer feedback for ESL writers*. Paper presented at the 27th Annual TESOL Convention, Atlanta, GA.
Finds that students are capable of proving feedback that is worthwhile for the development of effective composing strategies.
Peer Response.

2022. Lockhart, C., & Ng, P. (1993b). How useful is peer response? *Perspectives*, *5*(1), 17-29.
Investigates student perspectives on peer response among first-year Hong Kong college students involved in semi-autonomous groups. Finds peer response useful to students' audience awareness and feedback on ideas.
Peer Response/Hong Kong.

2023. Long, D. R., & Harlow, L. L. (1988). The newspaper and the five skills. *New challenges and opportunities. Dimensions: Languages 87*. Columbus, OH: Report of the Southern Conference on Language Teaching. [ERIC ED 336 939].
Gives the advantages of using newspapers as input to second language writing and cross-cultural analysis.
Newspaper/Materials.

2024. Long, M. N. (1971). A varied approach to a writing course in English. *RELC Journal*, *2*(2), 43-61.
> Suggests ways to use an audiotape as a prompt to writing practice.
> Responding.

2025. Longmire, K. L. (1986, March). *The influence of imaginative literature on ESL writing*. Paper presented at the 20th Annual TESOL Convention, Anaheim, CA.
> Suggests that using imaginative literature to generate writing leads to improvement.
> Literature.

2027. Lope, D. (1991). From reading to writing strategies. *English Teaching Forum*, *29*(4), 42-44.
> Gives a three-stage classroom procedure for linking reading and writing, illustrated with material from biotechnology.
> Reading-Writing Relations.

2028. Lott, B. (1963). Guided composition. *English Language Teaching*, *18*(1), 102-104.
> Gives a lesson to aid transition from controlled to free composition. Students write successive sentences on the board and receive feedback one sentence at a time. Afterwards, students write out the composition from memory.
> Classroom Activities/Control.

2029. Love, A. (1990, April). *Teaching communication skills to science students at tertiary level in Zimbabwe: Teaching "scientific discourse" or "textualization"?* Paper presented at the World Congress of Applied Linguistics (International Association of Applied Linguistics), Thessalonika, Greece. [ERIC ED 324 919].
> Claims that problems in meeting the requirements of scientific discourse outweigh errors of linguistic competence for university science students in Zimbabwe.
> ESP/Zimbabwe.

2030. Love, B. (1983). *A study in contrastive rhetoric: Implications for teaching composition to ESL students*. Unpublished master's thesis, University of Wyoming, Laramie, WY.
> Contrastive Rhetoric.

2031. Loveday, L. (1983). Rhetoric patterns in conflict: The sociocultural relativity of discourse-organizing processes. *Journal of Pragmatics*, *7*(2), 169-190.
> Discusses cultural diversity in the sequencing of superstructural (Van Dijk, 1977) discourse patterns.
> Pragmatics/Rhetoric/Culture.

2032. Low, M. (1991, March). *Analyzing news coverage as a task-based writing assignment*. Paper presented at the 25th Annual TESOL Convention, New York, NY.
> Demonstrates an assignment which analyzes several publications' coverage of the same event.
> Assignments/Advanced/Task.

2033. Lu, M. Z. (1987). From silence to words: Writing as struggle. *College English*, *49*, 437-448.
> Reports the psychological and political struggles one woman experienced as a student growing up bilingual and biliterate in China before the end of the Cultural Revolution.

Sociocultural Factors/Literacy/Chinese.
2034. Lucas, T. F. (1992). Diversity among individuals: Eight students making sense of classroom journal writing. In D. E. Murray (Ed.), *Diversity as resource* (pp. 202-232). Alexandria, VA: TESOL.

Describes the diverse ways in which eight students from six different countries responded to journal writing in two university classes.
Journal Writing.

2035. Lucas, T. F. (1991). Individual variation in students' engagement with a genre. *The CATESOL Journal, 4,* 7-39.

Studies the differences among ESL adult students and their adaptability to in-class journal writing assignments requiring description.
Journal Writing/Variation.

2036. Lucas, T. F. (1990). Personal journal writing as a classroom genre. In J. K. Peyton (Ed.), *Students and teachers writing together: Perspectives on journal writing* (pp. 101-123). Alexandria, VA: TESOL.

Reports a case study of nine adult ESL students who learned the conventions of the dialogue journals "genre" and felt positively affected by the experience.
Dialogue Journals/Affect.

2037. Lucas, T. F. (1988a, March). *Beyond language "and" culture: Individual variation in students' engagement with a written genre.* Paper presented at the 22nd Annual TESOL Convention, Chicago, IL. [ERIC ED 304 005].

Findings of a study of the role of individual differences in the journal writing of adult ESL students indicate that differences, such as past writing experience and personality, had a greater influence than cultural background on students' approaches to a journal writing task.
Culture/Journal Writing.

2038. Lucas, T. F. (1988b). Personal journal writing in an ESL writing class: Teaching, learning, and adapting to the genre conventions. *Dissertation Abstracts International, 49*(3), 420A.

Study examines the role of personal journal writing in the ESL composition classroom. Analysis of procedures and qualitative research were used to determine the extent of students' adaptation to the conventions of writing as presented to them. These conventions include elements of form, function, audience, and content, and were taught both implicitly and explicitly. Concludes that classroom personal journal writing facilitates acquisition of such genre conventions.
Journal Writing/Genre.

2039. Lund, S. (1982, May). *The advanced composition workshop: Modifying Garrison for ESL.* Paper presented at the 16th Annual TESOL Convention, Honolulu, HI.

Garrison's conference method (1974) can be modified to accomodate the limited fluency and absence of native intuitions of ESL writers.
Conferencing.

2040. Luo, Y. Y. (1989). From craft to art -- How to teach composition. *English Teaching Forum, 27*(4), 26-28.

Offers comments on various aspects of teaching writing and Chinese learners.

Chinese.

2041. Lux, P. A. (1991). Discourse styles of Anglo and Latin American college student writers. *Dissertation Abstracts International*, 52(6), 2128A.

Compares essays by Spanish-speaking students written in Spanish and English and Anglo-American students written in English and Spanish in order to test the contrastive rhetoric hypothesis (Kaplan, 1966). Products were analyzed for rhetorical structure, for sentence-level sytntactic forms, and by means of a factored multivariate analysis. Results show significant differences in the written discourse styles of the four groups which are best explained by cultural and developmental influences.

Hispanic/Contrastive Rhetoric.

2042. Lux, P. A. (1990, March). *Discourse characteristics of Anglo/Latin university-student compositions*. Paper presented at the 24th Annual TESOL Convention, San Francisco, CA.

Presents the results of a study comparing the writing style of 120 first-year students from universities in Quito, Ecuador and Tempe, Arizona. Both global and local discourse features in the students' compositions are analyzed and implications for cross-cultural communication are discussed.

Hispanic/Culture.

2043. Lynch, T.(1988). Teaching examination answer writing: Process, product or placebo? In P. C. Robinson (Ed.), *Academic writing: Process and product* (pp. 53-60). London: Modern English Publications/British Council.

Discusses the writing component -- focusing on examination answer writing -- of a short-term, intensive course required of overseas students at a univerity in the United Kingdom. Materials, classroom procedures as well as reactions from students and tutors are summarized.

Courses/Examination Essays.

M

2044. MacDonald, A., & MacDonald, G. (1993, April). *Helping ESL students pass English placement exams*. Paper presented at 44th Annual Convention of CCCC, San Diego, CA.

Placement.

2045. MacDonald, G., & MacDonald, A. (1992, March). *Composition for career exploration*. Paper presented at the 26th Annual TESOL Convention, Vancouver, BC.

Points out that academic topics related to career majors tend to motivate advanced students.

Topic/Motivation/Advanced.

2046. MacDonald, M. G., & Hall, C. (1991, March). *How are ESL writing teachers trained?* Paper presented at the 25th Annual TESOL Convention, New York, NY.
See next item.

Research/Teacher Preparation.

2047. MacDonald, M. G., & Hall, C. (1990, March). *Training the next generation of ESL writing teachers*. Paper presented at the 24th Annual TESOL Convention, San

Francisco, CA.

Examines responses to a survey of 151 TESL-related teacher training programs to determine the influence of current research and practices in rhetoric/composition on training procedures. The study considers the role of first language research, TESL topics central to the writing process, and procedures in the ESL classroom.

Teacher Preparation.

2048. Mace-Matluck, B. J., Dominquez, D., Holtzman, W. J., & Hoover, W. (1983). *Language and literacy in bilingual instruction.* (National Institute of Education Final Report No. 400-80-0043). Austin, TX: Southwest Regional Educational Development Laboratory.

Hispanic/Literacy.

2049. MacGowan-Gilhooly, A. (1992). *Achieving clarity in English: A whole-language book.* Dubuque, IA: Kendall Hunt.

The second book of a series intended for basic and ESL college writers who have achieved fluency in writing. Provides whole-language activities for reading, writing and research, and instructional and reference material.

University/Textbook.

2050. MacGowan-Gilhooly, A. (1991a). *Achieving fluency in English: A whole-language book.* Dubuque, IA: Kendall Hunt.

The first in a series for basic and ESL college writers who need to learn to read and write fluently. Takes a whole language approach and encourages students to read 1000 pages of fiction, keep a reading journal and a writing journal and write a 10,000 word "book" of their own.

University/Textbook.

2051. MacGowan-Gilhooly, A. (1991b). Fluency before correctness: A whole language experiment in college ESL. *College ESL, 1*(1), 37-47.

Describes a three course sequence on ESL reading and writing, based on a whole language approach to college ESL.

Whole Language/University/Reading-Writing Relations.

2052. MacGowan-Gilhooly, A. (1991c). Fluency first: Reversing the traditional ESL sequence. *Journal of Basic Writing, 10*(1), 73-87.

Describes a whole language approach to writing and reading at the college level, which enables students to become fluent in reading and writing before achieving formal accuracy.

Fluency/Literacy.

2053. Macha, D. H. (1977, May). *Teaching freshman English to native and non-native students: Some similarities and some differences.* Paper presented at the National Convention of NAFSA, New Orleans, LA. [ERIC ED 149 603].

Claims that linguistic differences between native and non-native students have made many English instructors adopt different instructional methods for the two groups. Suggests, however, that there are similarities and presents techniques that are workable in a mixed group.

Freshman Composition/NS-NNS Comparisons.

2054. Macha, D. H., & Angelis, P. J. (1976, August). *An annotated bibliography of materials for teaching advanced written skills in English as a second language*. Washington, DC: ERIC/FLL. [ERIC ED 132 823].

Contains lists of textbooks for teaching of written skills to ESL university students. First section contains texts designed exclusively for second language learners and second section contains texts for native speakers that have been found useful for non-native speakers.

Bibliography/Advanced.

2055. Mackay, R. (1993). Approximating completeness. *Language and Communication*, *13*(1), 67-79.

A review of an anthology, Asian voices in English edited by Chan & Harris, explores the difficulty of full expression of cultural identity through writing in a second language.

Literature/Asian.

2056. Mackie, A., & Bullock, C. (1990). Discourse matrix: A practical tool for ESL writing teachers. *TESL Canada Journal*, *8*(1), 67-76.

Shows how a technique developed by Nold & Davis (1980) and Coe (1988) allows for contrastive rhetorical analysis in the classroom.

Contrastive Rhetoric.

2057. MacNealy, M. S. (1988, March). *Starting from scratch: Establishing an ESL writing program at a small university*. Paper presented at the 39th Annual CCCC Meeting, St. Louis, MO.

Programs.

2058. MacNealy, M. S. (1987, March). *ESL speaking and writing abilities: Can one predict the other?* Paper presented at the 38th Annual CCCC Meeting, Atlanta, GA.

Proficiency/Speaking-Writing Relations.

2059. Maftoon-Semnani, P. (1979). A contrastive study of the rhetorical organization of American English and Persian expository paragraphs written by published writers in each language. *Dissertation Abstracts International*, *40*(3), 1318A.

Examines the content of expository paragraphs written in English and in Persian to determine the differences in rhetorical organization. Quantitative and qualitative analyses reveal significant differences in rhetorical patterns of the two languages.

Contrastive Rhetoric/Persian/Exposition.

2060. Maguire, M. H. (1991, November). *Seeing ourselves as readers and responders of the reading and writing of bilingual children*. Paper presented at the 81st Annual NCTE Convention, Seattle, WA.

Bilingual/Responding.

2061. Maguire, M. H. (1987). Is writing a story in a second language that much more complex than in a first language? Children's perceptions. *Carleton Papers in Applied Language Studies*, *4*, 17-65.

Describes a study of the perceptions of writing stories in English and French during one school year by six bilingual 10-11 year-old children. Two cases illustrate the complexity of the writing in two languages. One demonstrates similar patterns

across two language systems and social texts; another exhibits patterns which vary interlinguistically and between the two social texts.
Children/French.

2062. Maher, J. C. (1981). Guided poetry composition. *English Language Teaching Journal, 35*(3), 168-171.

Describes several poetic devices in using poetry composition in ESL classes to practice writing skills.
Creative Writing/Control.

2063. Mahmoud, A. A. (1983). A functional analysis of written compositions of Egyptian students of English and the implications of the notional-functional syllabus for the teaching of writing. *Dissertation Abstracts International, 44*(5), 1439A.

Compares cohesion and coherence strategies in written English by Egyptian college students and by native speakers of English. Results show: (1) Egyptian compositions use fewer synonyms and lexical collocations; (2) Egyptian compositions use a lower level of connectedness; and (3) Egyptian compositions rarely use formal closure and have inappropriate conjunctives. Proposes strategies for teaching cohesion and coherence.
Arabic/Cohesion/NS-NNS Comparisons.

2064. Maier, P. (1992). Politeness strategies in business letters by native and non-native English speakers. *English for Specific Purposes, 11*, 189-205.

Finds striking differences in the politeness strategies used by NES and NNSs in business letters, including less formal but more direct strategies used by NNSs.
Business Writing/NS-NNS Comparisons.

2065. Makinen, K. (1993, April). *Topical depth and writing quality in student EFL compositions*. Paper presented at the 27th Annual TESOL Convention, Atlanta, GA.
See next item.
Topic/TSA.

2066. Makinen, K. (1992). Topical depth and writing quality in student EFL composition. *Scandanavian Journal of Educational Research, 36*(3), 237-247.

Reports research on the relation of topical depth and writing quality in the EFL writing of 24 secondary students. Good quality essays are associated with essay topics that are evenly developed across levels in a topical structure analysis.
Topic/TSA.

2067. Makino, S. (1978). Paragraph -- Is it a legitimate unit? -- A case study from English and Japanese. In R. Brown, & H. Steinmann (Eds.), *Rhetoric 1979* (pp. 238-296). Minneapolis, MN: University of Minnesota Center for Advanced Studies in Language, Style, and Literary Theory. [ERIC ED 155 950].

Argues for legitimacy of paragraphs as a linguistic unit on the grounds that pronominalization makes crucial use of paragraph, that surface constituent structure of paragraph is evident from recipe and medical discourses, and that there is a deep paragraph structure because ambiguous discourse relies on paragraphing for interpretation.
Contrastive Rhetoric/Paragraph/Japanese.

2068. Malcolm, D. (1982). *A comparison of English compositions by native and non-native*

speakers. Unpublished master's thesis, Concordia University, Montreal, Canada.
NS-NNS Comparisons.

2069. Malkoç, A. M. (1971). *TESOL bibliography: Abstracts of ERIC publications and research reports*. Washington, DC: TESOL.

Gives six items on ESL writing and composition.
Bibliography.

2070. Mallett, B. A. (1983, March). *Contextual influences on shifts in verb tenses*. Paper presented at the 17th Annual TESOL Convention, Toronto, Ontario.

Outlines method for teaching tense shifts at the discourse level, frequently troublesome for advanced ESL composition students.
Advanced/Syntactic Structures.

2071. Mallett, B. A., & Holshuh, L. W. (1983, March). *Reading task complexity for advanced-level ESL writers*. Paper presented at the 17th Annual TESOL Convention, Toronto, Ontario.

Ordering composition assignments by degree of complexity reduces the task overload for advanced ESL writers dealing simultaneously with control of grammar, lexical production, rhetorical effectiveness in expository writing.
Assignments/Task.

2072. Mangelsdorf, K. (1992). Peer reviews in the ESL composition classroom: What do the students think. *ELT Journal, 46*, 274-284.

Advanced ESL writing students (n=40) report that peer reviews can be helpful during the drafting process as long as the task is carefully structured.
Peer Response.

2073. Mangelsdorf, K. (1989). Parallels between speaking and writing in second language acquisition. In D. M. Johnson, & D. H. Roen (Eds.), *Richness in writing: Empowering ESL students* (pp. 134-145). NY: Longman.

Claims that, traditionally, speaking and writing have been separated in L2 curriculum. Posits that despite differences between speaking and writing, the many parallels offer opportunities for classroom discussions that serve as a means of empowering students in their writing.
Speaking-Writing Relations.

2074. Mangelsdorf, K., Roen, D. H., & Taylor, V. (1990). ESL students' use of audience. G. Kirsch, & D. H. Roen (Eds.), *A sense of audience in written communication* (pp. 231-247). Newbury Park, CA: Sage.

Examines ESL students' perceptions of audience and the way these perceptions are reflected in the revision of their writing. Concludes that ability to interact effectively with audience enables students to simultaneously enter discourse communities and find their own voices.
Rhetoric/Audience.

2075. Mangelsdorf, K., & Schlumberger, A. L. (1992). ESL student response stances in a peer-review task. *Journal of Second Language Writing, 1*(3), 235-254.

Examines the stances taken by 60 EFL freshman composition students toward peer writers of texts. Finds three stances: Interpretative, collaborative, and prescriptive (most popular).

Peer Response.
2076. Mangelsdorf, K., & Schlumberger, A. L. (1989, March). *Contrastive rhetoric in the ESL writing classroom*. Paper presented at the 23rd Annual TESOL Convention, San Antonio, TX.
Claims that lessons in contrastive rhetoric improved the writing of a class of advanced ESL students in comparison to a class who did not receive those lessons.
Contrastive Rhetoric/Advanced.
2077. Mangelsdorf, K., & Taylor, V. (1987, March). *Using heuristics to respond to advanced ESL composition students*. Paper presented at the CCCC Meeting, Atlanta, GA. [ERIC ED283 377].
Revision heuristics found successful only with better writers in a small sample.
Revision/Advanced.
2078. Mann, R. P. (1986). A statistical survey of transitional device usage among writers of English as a second language and native writers of English. *Dissertation Abstracts International, 47*(5), 1636A.
Examines the transitional devices in written English used by Arabic-speaking, Chinese-speaking, Spanish-speaking and native-speakers of English of three proficiency levels. Results show: (1) significant differences in variation in distribution of transitional devices by different language backgrounds; (2) difference in position of devices by different language backgrounds; and (3) no significant differences between proficiency levels.
NS-NNS Comparisons/Hispanic/Chinese/Arabic/Cohesion.
2079. Manuel, C. C., & Fernández, R. C. (1986). An imaginative approach to teaching writing. *English Teaching Forum, 24*(3), 40-42.
Offers several inventive exercises of an imaginative kind to motivate students to write.
Motivation.
2080. Marino, M. (1986). Writing techniques. *English Teaching Forum, 24*(3), 28.
Makes nine suggestions for teaching writing without books to college students in Thailand.
Thai.
2081. Markley, R. W. (1981). *Handwriting workbook: Handwriting and letter recognition practice for learners of the English alphabet*. Englewood Cliffs, NJ: Prentice Hall.
For learner whose native language does not use a Roman alphabet, this workbook offers exercises to practice cursive writing and letter recognition.
Handwriting/Textbook.
2082. Markstein, L. (1991, November). *Portfolio assessment: Background and introduction*. Paper presented at the 81st Annual NCTE Convention, Seattle, WA.
Assessment/Portfolios.
2083. Markstein, L. (1987). *Write now!: Business writing*. Englewood Cliffs, NJ: Prentice Hall.
Textbook for entry-level business writing.
Beginners/Business Writing/Textbook.
2084. Markstein, L., Withrow, J., Brookes, G., & Price, S. (1992, March). *A portfolio*

assessment experiment for college ESL students. Paper presented at the 26th Annual TESOL Convention, Vancouver, BC.

Describes the use of an experimental portfolio assessment in an ESL program where the curriculum is integrated.

Assessment/Portfolios/University.

2085. Marler, M. G. (1983). The impact of parallelism: A rationale for teaching parallel structure at all ESL levels. *TESL Reporter*, *16*(1), 7-13.

Makes a case for the importance of teaching parallelism and applies it to ESL writing.

Rhetoric/Classroom Activities.

2086. Marquez, E. J. (1979). The simultaneous teaching of grammar and paragraph structure. *RELC Journal*, *10*(2), 36-43.

Discusses classroom activities for writing descriptive and narrative paragraphs along with grammar exercises.

Paragraph/Grammar.

2087. Marshall, H. W. (1982, May). *GLUE: A useful concept for eliminating fragments and run-ons*. Paper presented at the 16th Annual TESOL Convention, Honolulu, HI.

Presents a series of exercises in which students monitor their own clause connectors.

Cohesion/Error Treatment.

2088. Marshall, H. W. (1981, October). *GLUE: A useful concept for eliminating fragments and run-ons*. Paper presented at the Annual Conference of the New York State English to Speakers of Other Languages and Bilingual Educators Association, Rochester, NY. [ERIC ED 210 926].

Discusses a series of exercises meant to help advanced ESL students avoid sentence fragments and run-on lines by self-monitoring their writing using a reference list of GLUE words (i.e., term used for all connectors) and by identifying their relation to subject-verb units.

Error Treatment/Cohesion.

2089. Marshall, M. J. (1986, March). *Writing without tears: Advanced composition for academic success*. Paper presented at the 20th Annual TESOL Convention, Anaheim, CA. [ERIC ED 271 962].

Describes a conferencing approach that increases quantity, confidence, and responsibility.

Conferencing/Advanced/Academic Writing.

2090. Marshall, S. (1991). A genre-based approach to the teaching of report-writing. *English for Specific Purposes*, *10*, 2-13.

Discusses the use of a genre approach to report writing and feedback evaluation in an engineering course.

Report Writing/Papua New Guinea.

2091. Martin, A. R. (1990). Teaching writing as a tool for learning with adult ESL students: A case study. *Dissertation Abstracts International*, *51*(10), 3304A.

Evaluation of the amount, fluency, and quality of writing in various contexts by three adult students with varying degrees of initial literacy suggests improvement

in their written language literacy over eight months.
Adult Education/Content.

2092. Martin, A. V. (1986, March). *Relationships in writing: An interdisciplinary perspective*. Paper presented at the 20th Annual TESOL Convention, Anaheim, CA.

Interdiscipinary research on information relationships supports the teaching of relationships such as definition and summary.
Summary Writing.

2093. Martin, A. V. (1983, March). *ESL students' perceptions of L1-L2 differences in organizing ideas*. Paper presented at the 17th Annual TESOL Convention, Toronto, Ontario.

Presents a study of how advanced ESL students in six L1 groups perceived the similarities/differences in formal organization in their L1 and in English.
Advanced/Organization/Perceptions.

2094. Martin, A. V. (1980). Proficiency of university-level advanced ESL students and native speakers of English processing hierarchical information in context. *Dissertation Abstracts International*, *40*(10), 5425-5426A.

Designs an instrument, an extended cloze passage (full-sentence deletion with multiple choice alternatives), to measure hierarchical and spatial/chronological ability in text processing. Native and non-native speaking university freshman and advanced ESL students were found to significantly differ from each other. Factors other than English language proficiency are suggested, including willingness to adopt certain organizational patterns found in U.S. university settings. Suggests that formal written English be regarded from cultural perspectives to aid ESL students.
NS-NNS Comparisons/Text Analysis.

2095. Martin, C., Seltzer, S., Kimmelman, J., & Krantz, H. (1985). *Exploring American English: Writing skills for classroom and career*. Boston: Heinle & Heinle.

Text offers the ESL student a variety of rhetorical modes for practice. It also contains realistic role-playing exercises for conversation practice, and a unit on "Writing in the World Outside".
Advanced/Textbook.

2096. Martin, J. R. (1989). *Factual writing: Exploring and challenging social reality*. Oxford: Oxford University Press.

Offers a systemic linguistic approach to children's writing development and instruction that applies to language education generally. Discusses the nature and functions of factual writing within the cultural experience of Australia education
Teacher Preparation/Children.

2097. Martin, J. E. (1991). *Contrastive rhetoric: Implications of a revised approach to text*. Washington, DC: ERIC/FLL. [ERIC ED 329 118].

Suggests the study of pragmatic differences in contrastive rhetoric is more fruitful than the study of formal arrangement.
Contrastive Rhetoric/Pragmatics.

2098. Martin, M. (1992, March). *Pondering before pouncing: Responding to advanced academic writing*. Paper presented at the 26th Annual TESOL Convention, Vancouver, BC.

Discusses the complexity and diagnostic difficulty of many advanced written errors, such as time, aspect, voice, theta-roles, logic, and lexis and suggests ways to deal with them appropriately.
Responding/Advanced/Errors.

2099. Martin-Betancourt, M. E. (1986). The composing processes of Puerto Rican college students of English as a second language. *Dissertation Abstracts International, 47*(7), 2577A.
Describes the composing processes of Puerto Rican ESL college students. Verbal protocols indicate that the ESL composing processes resemble L1 composing processes. Planning, transcribing, and reviewing are non-linear and recursive, although individual differences in the way these processes are carried out have been noticed.
Hispanic/Process Research/University.

2100. Maruta, S. (1990). *An assessment of composition writing proficiency of form four students at a selected secondary school in Zimbabwe*. Unpublished master's thesis, Iowa State University, Ames, IA.
Zimbabwe/Secondary School.

2101. Marwin, N. (1984, March). *The use of logical connectors in the writing of Chinese and American graduate students*. Paper presented at the 18th Annual TESOL Convention, Houston, TX.
Explores the Chinese EFL learners' use of four semantic categories of logical connectors at the syntactic and discourse levels in various modes.
NS-NNS Comparisons/Chinese/Cohesion.

2102. Marwin, N., & Hochstein, D. (1993, April). *Meeting the advanced writing needs of international graduate students*. Paper presented at the 27th Annual TESOL Convention, Atlanta, GA.
Describes the results of a study of graduate student writing needs beyond the EAP level and a course designed to meet those needs.
Graduate Students/Courses.

2103. Maschler, T. (1990). *Turning the kaleidoscope in the E.S.L. classroom*. Unpublished master's thesis, School for International Living, Brattleboro, VT. [ERIC ED 332 534].
Gives ideas about reading and writing poetry in the ESL classroom.
Creative Writing/Literature.

2104. Masny, D., & Foxall, J. (1993). Writing apprehension in L2. *TESOL Matters, 3*(1), 9. [ERIC ED 352 844].
Investigates writing preferences, writing apprehension and academic achievement among 28 junior college ESL writers. Both low achievers and low apprehensive students were more concerned about form than content. Highly apprehensive writers preferred not to take more writing.
Affect.

2105. Masny, D., & Foxall, J. (1992, March). *Writing apprehension in L2*. Paper presented at the 26th Annual TESOL Convention, Vancouver, BC.
Reports results of study of high and low apprehension intermediate level ESL

writers.
Anxiety/Intermediate.

2106. Mason, B. (1993, April). *The effect of extensive reading on writing*. Paper presented at the 27th Annual TESOL Convention, Atlanta, GA.

Reports a study on the effect of extensive reading (measured by cloze and written summaries) on writing quality.
Reading-Writing Relations.

2107. Mason, C. (1987, April). *Group processes at the word processor*. Paper presented at the 21st Annual TESOL Convention, Miami Beach, FL.

Advocates group composing of papers.
Computers/Word Processing/Collaboration.

2108. Massa, J. L. (1990). The development of academic literacy in a dialogical ESL classroom: Three case studies. *Dissertation Abstracts International*, *51*(12), 4046A.

A year-long case study traces the development of academic literacy in three ESL students. Provides an in-depth description of the learner's response to a dialogic classroom, including the establishment of "other identity," forms of resistance, and awareness of "academic ethoi".
Discourse Communities/Ethnographic Research.

2109. Master, P. (1991). Active verbs with inanimate subjects in scientific prose. *English for Specific Purposes*, *10*, 15-33.

Suggests ways to teach Asian students in EST how to use inanimate subjects with active verbs and the semantic bounds of Engish anthropomorphism.
ESP/Asian.

2110. Master, P. (1981). Teaching English for Science and Technology (EST) through technical writing. *CATESOL Occasional Papers*, *7*, 42-60. [ERIC ED210 920].

Describes how to create a syllabus for a technical writing course for non-technically trained ESL teachers.
Technical Writing/ESP.

2111. Matalene, C. (1987). The author responds to Crew . . . [In The Forum]. *College English*, *49*, 830-831.

Clarifies the point of her essay -- the cultural impact of Chinese rhetoric.
Rhetoric/Chinese.

2112. Matalene, C. (1986). Carolyn Matalene responds to Thomas . . . [In The Forum]. *College English*, *49*, 846-848.

Discusses additional experiences teaching students in China.
Rhetoric/Chinese.

2113. Matalene, C. (1985). Contrastive rhetoric: An American writing teacher in China. *College English*, *47*, 789-808.

Contrasts traditional Chinese and modern western rhetorics and argues for the recognition of the limits of western rhetoric in teaching Chinese students as well as an appreciation of other rhetorical systems.
Culture/Rhetoric/Chinese.

2114. Mather, S. (1991, March). *New strategy for improving students' writing skills explored*. Paper presented at the 25th Annual TESOL Convention, New York, NY.

Discusses the effectiveness of a strategy for helping deaf students better manage the cognitive demands of the writing process.

Cognition/Hearing-Impaired.

2115. Matta, W. B. (1992). University writing and the nonnative speaker of English: A preliminary case study of selected United States high school graduates. *Dissertation Abstracts International, 53*(4), 1084A.

Studies the holistic quality, errors, and t-units on two tasks written by four foreign-born and four native-born university freshman who graduated from U.S. high schools. Unsurprisingly, NNESs as a group had lower holistic scores and made relatively greater numbers of vocabulary usage errors than native controls. Neither error assessment nor t-unit measures, however, distinguished between the groups except for a minority subgroup for whom vocabulary skills correpsonds with holistic quality.

NS-NNS Comparisons/Vocabulary.

2116. Mattar, H. E. (1989). A cross-sectional error analysis study of the common writing errors made by adult Arabic-speaking EFL learners in Bahrain. *Dissertation Abstracts International, 50*(10), 3171A.

Cites evidence of avoidance of the passive voice and relative clause in the written English of Bahraini students. Also finds that the gravity and frequency of errors as judged by native and non-native EFL teachers are unrelated. Teachers do not appear to use frequency as the prime criteria for judging the gravity of errors.

Error Analysis/Arabic.

2117. Matthews, D., & McNamara, M. J. (1984, March). *Synthesizing the process, rhetorical and grammar-based approaches to ESL composition teaching.* Paper presented at the 18th Annual TESOL Convention, Houston, TX.

Argues for a synthesis of process and form-oriented instruction to ESL composition.

Approaches/Instruction.

2118. Matthews, D., & Rodby, J. (1984, March). *ESL students and essay exams: Pedagogy based on a needs analysis.* Paper presented at the 18th Annual TESOL Convention, Houston, TX.

Dicusses strategies to help ESL students meet the demand for essay exam writing in specific models and under time constraints.

Examination Essays/Time.

2119. Matthews, S. (1980, March). *Application and cognitive approach of combined methods for basic cursive handwriting instruction.* Paper presented at the 14th Annual TESOL Convention, San Francisco, CA.

Offers suggestions about physical, psychological, and technical aspect of teaching handwriting to ESL students.

Handwriting.

2120. Matthies, B. (1988). The non-native speaker of English learns to write -- somehow. In G. H. Irons (Ed.), *Second language acquisition: Selected readings in theory and practice* (pp. 171-181). Ontario, Canada: The Canadian Modern Language Review.

Presents an eclectic combination of techniques from controlled to functional,

depending on the level of the learners' ability.
Approaches.

2121. Matusmura, E., & Schwarte, B. (1984, March). *The ability of ESL students to self-monitor their writing*. Paper presented at the 18th Annual TESOL Convention, Houston, TX.

Investigates the ability of 31 ESL students to monitor and correct grammatical errors in articles and main verbs.
Editing/Error Treatment.

2122. Mauranen, A. (1993). Contrastive ESP rhetoric: Metatext in Finnish-English economic texts. *English for Specific Purposes*, *12*, 3-22.

Describes a contrastive textlinguistic study of texts written by Anglo-American and Finnish academics. The former use more metatext (i.e., text about text) than do Finnish writers, which shows a more explicit presence of writer in the text.
ESP/Finnish/Contrastive Rhetoric.

2123. Maxwell-Paegle, M. A., & Parker, B. (1992, March). *Guided composition techniques for advanced ESL writing classes*. Paper presented at the 26th Annual TESOL Convention, Vancouver, BC.

Shows how to use guided composition techniques at the advanced level.
Control.

2124. May, B. A. (1984). Effective instruction for teaching basic writing skills with computer-assisted language learning in an English as a second language program. *Dissertation Abstracts International*, *45*(12), 3616A.

Develops and pilot tests a three-stage teacher training model for the instruction of basic writing skills for ESL students supported by computer-assisted language learning. Results validate the model.
Computers/Teacher Preparation.

2125. McAlister, E. (1981, March). *Using film as composition -- The ESL classroom*. Paper presented at the 15th Annual TESOL Convention, Detroit, MI.

Demonstrates an experiment for getting students to write clear descriptions of objects and geographical locations.
Film.

2126. McAlpine, L. (1989). Teacher-as-reader: Oral feedback on ESL student writing. *TESL Canada Journal*, *7*(1), 62-67.

Describes an oral feedback procedure (a think aloud protocol) to show students how a reader makes sense of a text.
Feedback.

2127. McCagg, P. (1990). Toward understanding coherence: A response proposition taxonomy. In U. M. Connor, & A. M. Johns (Eds.), *Coherence in writing: Research and pedagogical perspectives* (pp. 111-127). Alexandria, VA: TESOL.

Presents a response proposition taxonomy as an extension of the propositional analysis technique to account for readers' prior knowledge and reasoning strategies that play a major role in their making inferences. Demonstrates use of taxonomy and states pedagogical implications, especially for second language readers.
Reading-Writing Relations/Coherence.

2128. McCall, D. M. (1992). Story completion as a writing exercise. *English Teaching Forum, 30*(4), 42-43.

Shows how a story completion task was used with Hungarian students.
Assignments/Hungarian.

2129. McClure, E., Branstine, Z., & Platt, E. (1990). Tense and aspect in the written English narrative of monolingual American and bilingual Mexican fourth, sixth, ninth, and twelfth graders. In L. Bouton, & Y. Kachru (Eds.), *Pragmatics and language learning. Vol. 1* (pp. 209-220). Urbana-Champaign: University of Illinois Press.

NS-NNS Comparisons/Children/Hispanic.

2130. McCretton, E., & Rider, N. (1993). Error gravity and error hierarchies. *IRAL, 31*(3), 172-188.

NNS teachers were more severe and consistent than NES teachers when judging errors in 25 sentences containing seven types of errors. Both groups, however, ranked errors similarly.
Error Gravity/NS-NNS Comparisons.

2131. McCurdy, P. (1992, March). *What do students do with composition feedback?* Paper presented at the 26th Annual TESOL Convention, Vancouver, BC.

Reports the results of a survey of the nature of feedback received by students and how they process it. Findings suggest the need for training in learning strategies in order to more effectively use the feedback.
Feedback/Revision.

2132. McDaniel, B. A. (1985, March). *Ratings vs. equity in the evaluation of writing.* Paper presented at the 36th Annual CCCC Meeting, Minneapolis, MN. [ERIC ED 260 459].

Discusses findings of a study conducted to determine the differences between the responses of evaluators of large-scale tests toward essays written by ESL students and those written by non-ESL students. The discrepancy in the way evaluators respond to native and non-native students' essays indicates that a better definition of "good" and "bad" writing is required.
NS-NNS Comparisons/Assessment/Raters.

2133. McDaniel, B. A. (1980). Contrastive rhetoric: Diagnosing problems in coherence. *The English Quarterly, 13*(3), 65-75.

Reports a study of writing styles of professional journals from various disciplines which show varying degrees of coherence.
Contrastive Rhetoric/Coherence.

2134. McDevitt, D. (1989). How to cope with spaghetti writing. *ELT Journal, 43*, 19-23.

Suggests how to recognize and revise errors of subordination and coordination.
Error Treatment.

2135. McDonough, S. (1985). Academic writing practice. *ELT Journal, 39*(4), 241-247.

Discusses application of academic writing exercises for EFL students in postgraduate courses. The emphasis of the course is on speed and confidence. Students are involved in preparing their own questions which are then rewritten by the teacher in the examination format.

Academic Writing.

2136. McDonough-Kolb, M., Grossman, A. N., & Martone, D. (1990, March). *Problems and possibilities: Connecting culture, writing and conversation.* Paper presented at the 24th Annual TESOL Convention, San Francisco, CA.

Workshop enacts, explores, and analyzes various classroom and conference strategies in which conversation is a vehicle for the development of multicultural students' writing.

Speaking-Writing Relations/Conferencing.

2137. McDough, V., McNerney, M., & Mendelsohn, D. J. (1984, March). *Grading adult students' essays: It's less of a nightmare than you think.* Paper presented at the 18th Annual TESOL Convention, Houston, TX.

Demonstrates use of a quick, reliable, and valid instrument for assessing placement and achievement essays.

Evaluation/Adult Education.

2138. McGarrell, H. M., Baltra, A., Friedlander, A. C., Phinney, M., & Liou, H. C. (1993, April). *Writing with computers: From process to product.* Colloquium presented at the 27th Annual TESOL Convention, Atlanta, GA.

Panelists discuss various topics in current research on writing with computers in ESL classes.

Computers.

2139. McGirt, J. D. (1984). *The effect of morphological and syntactic errors on the holistic scores of native and non-native compositions.* Unpublished master's thesis, UCLA, Los Angeles, CA.

Error Analysis/Evaluation/NS-NNS Comparisons.

2140. McGrail, L. (1989, March). *Project FOCUS: Writing through pictures.* Paper presented at the 23rd Annual TESOL Convention, San Antonio, TX.

Describes a participatory photography/writing project.

Project Work.

2141. McGreal, R. (1986). Word processors and the teaching of writing. *English Teaching Forum, 24*(3), 39-40.

Suggests that the use of word processing for beginners helps convey a sense of form and structure and a sense of detachment from their errors.

Computers/Word Processing.

2142. McGroarty, M., & Scott, S. (1993). Reading, writing, and roles in U.S. adult literacy textbooks. *TESOL Quarterly, 27,* 563-573.

Discusses briefly how a sample of widely used adult literacy textbooks teach and use writing.

Materials/Adult Education/Literacy.

2143. McIver, B. (1987). Teaching writing: The autobiographical approach. *English Teaching Forum, 25*(3), 49.

Urges alternating between practices of reading and writing autobiographies.

Reading-Writing Relations.

2144. McKay, H., & Abigail, T. (1993). *Write after: Group projects as pre-writing activities.* Burlingame, CA: Alta.

Offers preparation for paragraph writing for low-intermediate adults and young adults with little formal experience with writing.

Textbook/Group Projects/Invention.

2145. McKay, J. R. (1988, March). *Using the same essay placement test for native and non-native speakers of English*. Paper presented at the 39th Annual CCCC Meeting, St. Louis, MO.

Assessment/NS-NNS Comparisons.

2146. McKay, S. L. (1993a). Examining L2 composition ideology: A look at literacy education. *Journal of Second Language Writing, 2,* 65-81.

Discusses three assumptions about literacy in L2 composition ideology: social practice, plurality, and power.

Ideology/Literacy.

2147. McKay, S. L. (1993b). Sociocultural factors in teaching composition to Pacific Rim writers. In M. N. Brock, & L. W. Walters (Eds.), *Teaching composition around the Pacific Rim: Politics and pedagogy* (pp. 1-14). Clevedon, ENG: Multilingual Matters.

Claims that knowledge of certain social conventions, namely the morphosyntactic, rhetorical, semantic and topicl, is essential for Pacific Rim students to be considered effective writers in a western cultural context.

Asian/Socio-Cultural Factors.

2148. McKay, S. L. (1989). Topic development and written discourse accent. In D. M. Johnson, & D. H. Roen (Eds.), *Richness in writing: Empowering ESL students* (pp. 253-262). NY: Longman.

Examines essays written on the same topic by Chinese students in China and by foreign students in U.S.A. Findings show topic development influenced by cultural experiences, social and educational policies.

Topic/Chinese.

2149. McKay, S. L. (1986, March). *Topic development and written discourse accent*. Paper presented at the 20th Annual TESOL Convention, Anaheim, CA. [ERIC ED 272 031].

Finds common themes in essays written by Chinese students in PRC in response to the same writing topic.

Chinese/Contrastive Rhetoric/Topic.

2150. McKay, S. L. (Ed.). (1984). *Composing in a second language*. Rowley, MA: Newbury House.

Reprints ESL articles by Hendrickson (1980), Kaplan (1966), Kroll & Schafer (1978), Raimes (1983), Robinett (1972), Taylor (1981), Watson-Reekie (1982), Weissberg & Buker(1978), and Zamel (1983) as well as several by L1 writing scholars.

Approaches.

2151. McKay, S. L. (1983, March). *Some limitations in teaching composition*. Paper presented at the 17th Annual Convention of TESOL, Toronto, Ontario. [ERIC ED 275 151].

States that writing is such a complex process that teachers are limited in ways

to help students with knowledge about topic and about audience, with selection of suitable methods for writing, and with self-evaluation. Suggests ways teachers can help students help themselves.
Topic/Audience.

2152. McKay, S. L. (1982). A focus on pre-writing strategies. In M. Hines, & W. Rutherford (Eds.), *On TESOL '81* (pp. 89-95). Washington, DC: TESOL.
Examines pre-writing strategies for transactional writing, including considerations of audience.
Invention.

2153. McKay, S. L. (1981a). ESL/remedial English: Are they different? *English Language Teaching Journal, 35*(3), 310-315.
Suggests reasons why writing problems of ESL students are not dealt with adequately in remedial courses for native speakers.
Curriculum/University.

2154. McKay, S. L. (1981b). Pre-writing activities. *TECFORS, 4*(3), 1-2. [ERIC ED 267 647].
Offers three reasons for using pre-writing activities.
Invention.

2155. McKay, S. L. (1981c). Using films as a pre-writing activity. *TESOL Newsletter, 15*(4), 27-28.
Discusses the advantages of using films to stimulate writing and gives a heuristic for the film Le Haricut to illustrate how various themes may be explored.
Film/Invention.

2156. McKay, S. L. (1979a). Communicative writing. *TESOL Quarterly, 13*, 73-80.
Presents a method for teaching writing that fosters communicative aspects as well as grammatical correctness, suggesting situations (The Traffic Officer, The Consumer Protection Agency Investigator, The Civil Engineer, and The Art Teacher) to stimulate the writer while generating practice of some grammatical structures.
Approaches.

2157. McKay, S. L. (1979b). A notional approach to writing. *CATESOL Occasional Papers, 5*, 11. [ERIC ED 187 146].
Presents sample notional writing materials geared towards writing academic papers for advanced ESL students. Importance of peer correction highlighted.
Materials.

2158. McKay, S. L., & Weinstein-Shr, G. (1993). English literacies in the U.S.: National policies, personal consequences. *TESOL Quarterly, 27*, 399-430.
Discusses the pressure to become literate in English in the U.S. and the tendency for the acquisition of L2 literacy to be associated with native language loss.
Literacy.

2159. McKee, M. B. (1984). Academic writing vs. composition. *MEXTESOL Journal, 8*(3), 7-14. [ERIC ED 249 807].
Argues that ESL teachers should prepare students for academic writing since it differs from what is usually done in composition classes.
Academic Writing/Hispanic.

2160. McKee, M. B. (1982, February). Sentence-combining -- not if or when, but how. In J. R. Boyd, & J. F. Haskell (Eds.), *Selected papers from the Tenth Illinois TESOL/BE Annual Convention*. Illinois TESOL/BE. [ERIC ED 224 350]

   Compares two methods of teaching English as a second language: open sentence combining practice that uses group discussions and a more traditional method. Results indicate the group that followed open sentence combining showed greater syntactic maturity and fewer errors than the other group. Also examines relationship between syntactic maturity and improvement in reading comprehension.
   Sentence Combining.

2161. McKenzie, J. (1986, March). *Teaching composition through literature*. Paper presented at the 20th Annual TESOL Convention, Anaheim, CA.

   Basing writing tasks on literature provide ESL students with models for language structure.
   Literature/Task.

2162. McKinley, S. (1975). *Connectives in composition for ESL students*. Unpublished master's thesis, University of Florida, Gainesville, FL.
   Cohesion.

2163. McLaughlin, D. (1985). *Literacy in Navajoland: Functions and effects of power*. Paper presented at the Annua Ethnography in Education Research Forum, Philadelphia, PA. [ERIC ED 257 324].

   Gives a detailed description of language use (Navajo and English) in a rural New Mexico community. Usually the community used English for writing and Navajo for speech despite the existence of a vernacular script.
   Amer-Indian/Speaking-Writing Relations.

2164. McLaughlin, D., & Leap, W. (1991, April). *What Navajo students know about written English and sources for their knowledge*. Paper presented at the Annual AERA Meeting, Chicago, IL.
   Amer-Indian.

2165. McLaughlin, J., & Turner, K. (Eds.). (1988). *Leaves: Written by students of English as a second language* . Bloomington, IN: ERIC/RCS. [ERIC ED 300 521].

   Shares a collection of stories written by adult ESL learners in England.
   Creative Writing/Student Publications.

2166. McLeod, A. (1986). Critical literacy: Taking control of our own lives. *Language Arts, 63*(1), 37-50.

   Describes a literacy program for ESL high school students based on discussion of social issues. A pilot group of students (age 11-16) showed significant improvement in writing and literacy skills.
   Secondary School/Literacy.

2167. McMurray, D. (1976). *Teaching advanced composition to foreign students*. Unpublished master's thesis, California State University, Fresno, CA.
   Advanced.

2168. McMurtrey, M. (1983, March). *Situational appropriateness for the ESL writer*. Paper presented at the 17th Annual TESOL Convention, Toronto, Ontario.

   A research study of ten ESL graduate students given a situation and asked to

write letters to form different audiences shows differences in each writer's awareness of their audience.
University/Audience.

2169. McMurtrey, M. (1982, May). *Procedures for developing audience awareness in the composing process*. Paper presented at the 16th Annual TESOL Convention, Honolulu, HI.

Intensive group interviews and biographical narratives help students gain audience awareness.
Audience.

2170. McNamara, M. J. (1991, March). *Teaching essay exam writing strategies within a process approach*. Paper presented at the 25th Annual TESOL Convention, New York, NY.

Discusses test preparation study skills, invention, organizing, writing, and editing techniques.
Examination Essays.

2171. McNamara, M. J. (1990). *Work in progress*. Boston: Heinle & Heinle.

Offers a step-by-step approach to writing process with concern for topic, purpose, audience and main idea.
Textbook/Advanced.

2172. McNamara, T. F. (1990). Item response theory and the validation of an ESP test for health professionals. *Language Testing, 7*, 52-76.

Grammar found to be the best predictor of performance on the writing subtest of the Australian Occupational English Test. Researcher suggests that raters may have tacitly agreed in order to weigh control of linguistic features heavily despite the absence of confirmation in the criteria used.
Assessment.

2173. Meath-Lang, B. (1990). The dialogue journal: Reconceiving curriculum and teaching. In J. K. Peyton (Ed.), *Students and teachers writing together: Perspectives on journal writing* (pp. 3-17). Alexandria, VA: TESOL.

Experiences with both deaf and second language learners suggest that dialogue journals "can be the foundation and enactment of a truly reconceived, student-centered language program".
Dialogue Journals/Responding.

2174. Meath-Lang, B., & Albertini, J. (1985, April). *Writing from experience: Dialogue journals as a teaching tool*. Paper presented at the 19th Annual TESOL Convention, New York, NY.

Workshop on the theory and practice of dialogue journals in ESL and TED classrooms.
Dialogue Journals.

2175. Meiden, W. (1951). The resume composition. *Modern Language Journal, 35*, 104-112.

Distinguishes two types of free composition: original composition and resume composition, and recommends ways to teach the latter.
Free Writing.

2176. Mejia, J. A. (1989, March). *A Chicano context: A Mexican-American writing pedagogy*. Paper presented at the 40th Annual CCCC Meeting, Seattle, WA.
Hispanic/Instruction.
2177. Mellor, E. R., & Ramirez, M. G. (1993, April). *Creative written expression within the whole language classroom*. Paper presented at the 27th Annual TESOL Convention, Atlanta, GA.

Shows techniques for developing language and promoting written expression at various stages of the writing process through the whole language approach.
Whole Language.
2178. Mellor, E. R., & Ramirez, M. G. (1989, March). *Creative writing in a bilingual classroom, or any classroom*. Paper presented at the 23rd Annual TESOL Convention, San Antonio, TX.

Suggests that creative writing fulfills many learning purposes.
Creative Writing.
2179. Mellor, K. L. (1979). *Teaching English composition to international students*. Unpublished master's thesis, Wichita State University, Wichita, KS.
2180. Mellor, K. L., & Broadhead, G. L. (1982). *Generative rhetoric in ESL composition classes*. Washington, DC: ERIC/FLL. [ERIC ED 241 959].

Finds improvements in ESL student sentence-combining as a result of treatment with Christensen's generative rhetoric.
Generative Rhetoric.
2181. Meloni, C. (1983). *What do university ESL students write about in dialogue journals?* Washington, DC: ERIC/CLL. [ERIC ED 240 885].

Gives a topical analysis of seven ESL dialogue journals. Finds no clear pattern of topics in the categories academic, personal, cultural, interpersonal, and general interest.
Dialogue Journals/Topic.
2182. Menasche, L. (1984a). Discourse mode, enabling metaphors, and styles of closure in the composing process: Two case studies based on interruption interviews. *Dissertation Abstracts International, 46*(5), 1217A.

Examines the effects of mode on composing process and the ways writers represent composing to themselves. Two expressive and two explanatory papers whose composing was interrupted at 5 and 20-minute intervals were compared. Each writer's personal approach to writing appears to account for major variations in their writing. Also suggests that each writer has a personal set of "enabling metaphors."
Style/Process Research.
2183. Menasche, L. (1984b). The two dreams of Ahmed Fu-Chin Sanchez. *TESOL Newsletter (Supplement No. 1: Writing and Composition), 18*(1), 12.

An imaginary creation of responses by the "archetypal foreign student" to a research paper assignment.
Research Writing/Assignments.
2184. Menasche, L. (1984c). *Writing a research paper*. Ann Arbor, MI: University of Michigan Press.

A guide to familiarize the intensive English student with the conventions of

the English language research paper. It breaks the research and writing processes into a series of manageable activities with corresponding exercises.
Research Writing/Textbook.

2185. Menasche, L. (1983, March). *ESL writers and the research paper: Teaching materials that meet the need*. Paper presented at the 17th Annual TESOL Convention, Toronto, Ontario.
Discusses principles for preparing structured activities for teaching ESL writers research writing.
Research Writing.

2186. Menasche, L., & Vernick, J. A. (1987, April). *Writing in ESL: Ideas for classroom activities*. Paper presented at the 21st Annual TESOL Convention, Miami Beach, FL.

Discusses a video presentation of activities to stimulate and support student writing.
Classroom Activities.

2187. Mendelsohn, D. J. (1983). The case for considering syntactic maturity in ESL and EFL. *International Review of Applied Linguistics in Language Teaching, 21*, 299-311.

Maintains that measuring syntactic error alone is inadequate and that syntactic maturity should also be considered. Discusses ways of measuring syntactic maturity in spoken English of non-native speakers and examines the relationship of syntactic error to syntactic maturity.
Evaluation/Objective Measures.

2188. Mendelsohn, D. J., Beyers, J., McNerney, M., Tyacke, M., & Carrier, M. (1992). *Real Writing*. San Diego, CA: Dominie Press.
Integrates in a single book true-to-life oral and written language functions, such as expressing an opinion.
Textbook/Intermediate.

2189. Mendelsohn, D. J., & Cumming, A. H. (1987a, April). *Professors' ratings of language use and organization in compositions*. Paper presented at the 21st Annual TESOL Convention, Miami Beach, FL.
Engineering, literature, and ESL professors rank ordered two sets of specifically modified compositions at eight-month intervals.
Assessment/Rating.

2190. Mendelsohn, D. J., & Cumming, A. H. (1987b). Professors' ratings of language use and rhetorical organization in ESL compositions. *TESL Canada Journal, 5*(1), 9-26.
Reports a small-scale study of the criteria three groups of faculty at a Canadian university use to assess ESL writing. While faculty in ESL, English, and Engineering show consistent high levels of agreement in ranking the same ESL papers, certain differences in criteria used seem to exist between faculty in different fields and even among faculty in a single discipline.
Assessment/Rating.

2191. Mendelsohn, D. J., & Tyacke, M. (1982, May). *Successful procedures for rapid assessment of writing and speaking*. Paper presented at the 16th Annual TESOL

Convention, Honolulu, HI.

Results of a pilot study show that the English Composition Ability Profile (Jacobs, et al., 1980) is the best instrument among six procedures tested.

Assessment.

2192. Mendiola, S. E. (1984). Written English of Mexican-American students: A study of grammar, structure, and organization. *Dissertation Abtracts International, 45*(6), 1760A.

A comparison of the linguistic characteristic of English compositions by bilingual Spanish college freshmen indicates that English dominant bilinguals outperformed Spanish dominant bilinguals. Objective measures (e.g., no. of words, sentences, T-units, etc.) account for 40% of the variance in holistic scores. Variations in standard English attributed to demographic and sociolinguistic factors.

Objective Measures/Hispanic/T-Unit.

2193. Menke, G. E. (1982b, May). *Using sentence combining in technical English.* Paper presented at the 16th Annual TESOL Convention, Honolulu, HI.

Develops exercises at both the sentence and discourse levels for technical English.

Sentence Combining/Technical Writing.

2194. Menke, G. E. (1981, March). *Using sentence-combining in ESL advanced composition.* Paper presented at the 15th Annual TESOL Convention, Detroit, MI.

Expresses view contrary to Zamel (1980) in claiming that sentence combining is useful in explaining and clarifying rhetorical processes.

Sentence Combining/Advanced.

2195. Menke, S. A. (1982a, May). *The noun phrase: A cohesive force in written discourse.* Paper presented at the 16th Annual TESOL Convention, Honolulu, HI.

Identifies the noun phrase as a cohesive force that makes for naitve-like writing.

Style/Syntactic Structures.

2196. Mercado, C. I. (1991). Native and second language literacy: The promise of a new decade. In A. A. Ambert (Ed.), *Bilingual education and English as a second language: A research handbook, 1988-1990* NY: Garland.

Reviews the findings from research on the nature and development of biliteracy as well as instructional practices between 1988 and 1990.

Review/Literacy/NS-NNS Comparisons.

2197. Mercado, C. I., & Torres, M. (1993, April). *Approaches in literacy/biliteracy for limited English proficient.* Paper presented at the 27th Annual TESOL Convention, Atlanta GA.

Discusses an innovative approach to literacy/biliteracy of sixth graders.

Literacy/Children.

2198. Merchler, G., Hayes, Curtis W., & Villareal, I. A. (1982, May). *Reaching writing rewards: Composition for speakers of other languages.* Paper presented at the 16th Annual TESOL Convention, Honolulu, HI.

Presents a mini-course for elementary and junior high school ESL teachers.

Elementary/Middle School.

2199. Merrill, C. (1976, March). *Chicano compositions: Interference, interlanguage, integration.* Paper presented at the 29th Annual CCCC Meeting, Philadelphia, PA. [ERIC ED 131 501].
   Examines the characteristics of the Chicano dialect in the writing of Chicano freshman by using contrastive and error analysis. Findings show the need to distinguish between actual features of Chicano dialect and idiosyncratic errors.
   Hispanic/Error Analysis/L1 Influence.

2200. Mettler, S. (1983). Exercise language options: Speech into writing--and back. *TESOL Newsletter, 17*(5), 1, 3-4.
   Argues that current theory can justify teaching students about their stigmatized errors, called image-breakers, and how active monitoring of these fossils can expand and modify their interlanguage.
   Speaking-Writing Relations.

2201. Mettler, S. (1982, May). *Exercising language options: Speech into writing and back.* Paper presented at the 16th Annual TESOL Convention, Honolulu, HI.
   Claims that control of standard English can result from systematically contrasting speech and writing.
   Speaking-Writing Relations/Standards.

2202. Meyers, A. (1988). *Writing with confidence.* (Third Ed.) Glenview, IL: Scott, Foresman/Little Brown.
   Offers instruction at sentence, paragraph, and essay levels.
   University/Textbook.

2203. Michel, A. J. (1989). A case study of the composing processes of advanced Spanish, Chinese, and Arabic ESL writers. *Dissertation Abstracts International, 49*(11), 3252.
   Five participant from each language group were videotaped writing in four modes (narration, description, exposition, and argumentation). A variety of results based on questionnaires, interviews, and other analyses of the data are presented. ESL writers were unconcerend about purpose, overlapped their writing processes, and used L1 processes. They were largely concerned with surface problems, edited or proofread as revision, lacked audience awareness, and drafted infrequently
   Advanced/Process Research.

2204. Miller, D. C. (1980, March). *An aid to the seemingly helpless speller.* Paper presented at the 14th Annual TESOL Convention, San Francisco, CA.
   Advises using a spelling chart to correct ESL errors due to graphophonemic interference from the native language.
   Spelling/Error Treatment.

2205. Miller, J. R. (1987). Teaching term-paper skills to university students. *English Teaching Forum, 25*(2), 13-17.
   Suggests ways of more efficiently teaching term paper skills such as limiting the scope of the research, providing lists of topics to choose from, teaching students how to take notes from primary and secondary sources, outlining, and writing rough to final drafts.
   University/Research Writing.

2206. Miller, L. D. (1983, March). *Writing anxiety: Friend or foe in the EFL classroom?*

Paper presented at the 17th Annual TESOL Convention, Toronto, Ontario.

Reports finding of a study of EFL freshman composition writers. Anxiety plays has different effects on the quality of composition and on academic achievement, which is partially explained by affective and educational assumptions of students and their teachers.

Affect.

2207. Miller, L. D., & Zaki, A. (1982, May). *Research paper syllabus: Discovery of discourse and cognitive correspondences.* Workshop presented at the 16th Annual TESOL Convention, Honolulu, HI.

Workshop deals with designing research writing course for advanced ESL students.

Research Writing.

2208. Miller, M. (1984, March). *Dialogue journals: Communicative competence through written interaction.* Paper presented at the 18th Annual TESOL Convention, Houston, TX.

Discusses the affective and practical advantages of written conversation between students and teachers.

Dialogue Journals.

2209. Miller, M., & Thompson, C. (1984, March). *Catching them up: Strengthening reading and writing abilities for Arabic-speaking students with skewed skills.* Paper presented at the 18th Annual TESOL Convention, Houston, TX.

Discusses curriculum needed to balance differences between developed orality yet undeveloped literacy among Arab intermediate ESL learners.

Reading-Writing Relations/Arabic.

2210. Miller, R. E. (1990). Solving the Chinese puzzle: Reconstructing English as a second language writing programs in response to Asian students' needs. *Master's Abstracts International, 28*(4), 487.

A survey of Asian students at a small liberal arts college suggests the need for a new writing program that addresses the characteristics of American academic writing.

Asian/Needs.

2211. Milman, J. (1993). Something to write about: Linking ESL and content courses in a Pacific Rim university. In M. N. Brock, & L. W. Walters (Eds.), *Teaching composition around the Pacific Rim: Politics and pedagogy* (pp. 117-129). Clevedon, ENG: Multilingual Matters.

Examines the effectiveness of using a content-bsed approach for the teaching of reading and writing to Asian/Pacific students. Results suggest that linking English instruction with content class instruction is successful.

Content.

2212. Min, C. K. (1990). The effects of assignments in ESL/EFL compositions. *Dissertation Abstracts International, 50*(8), 2473A.

A study of Korean ESL learners indicates preferences for writing on subjective topics; reports superior performance when students were provided with little information on assignments.

Assignments/Korean.

2213. Mitchell, C. J. (1990). Ideology and practice: The acquisition of academic literacy in a university ESL (English as a second language) writing class. *Dissertation Abstracts International, 51*(2), 495A.

Investigates ethnographically the acquisition of academic literacy within a university ESL writing class. The study analyzes the linguistic interaction between the teacher and four students and critically reviews the relationship between the teaching practices and the student success or lack of success. Concludes that student success or lack of success relates to prior experience with the academic context, prior writing ability as well as student oral interaction in the context of the writing conferences used in this study.

Academic Writing/Conferencing.

2214. Mittan, R. (1989a). The peer review process: Harnessing students' communicative power. In D. M. Johnson, & D. H. Roen (Eds.), *Richness in writing: Empowering ESL students* (pp. 207-219). NY: Longman.

Claims that peer reviews make use of students' communicative powers and shows ways to implement them in their writing. Describes theoretical basis of peer reviews and suggests ways of using the process.

Feedback/Peer Response.

2215. Mittan, R. (1989b, March). *A peer review process for ESL composition: Some whys and some ways*. Paper presented at the 40th Annual CCCC Meeting, Seattle, WA.

See previous item.

Peer Response.

2216. Mixon, M., & Breyer, J. (1993, April). *Turning them onto writing by using feature films*. Paper presented at the 27th Annual TESOL Convention, Atlanta GA.

Describes procedures for using contemporary films to motivate advanced writers to produce better papers.

Motivation.

2217. Mlynarczyk, R. K. (1991). Is there a difference between personal and academic writing? *TESOL Journal, 1*(1), 17-20.

Argues that initiating writing with personal topics ultimately strengthens the quality of college-level academic prose.

Academic Writing/Assignments.

2218. Mlynarczyk, R. K. (1990, March). *Personal and academic writing: A false dichotomy?* Paper presented at the 24th Annual TESOL Convention, San Francisco, CA.

Suggests that the commonly held distinction between "personal" and "academic" writing implies a clear-cut opposition that does not hold up when examined in the light of actual practice and suggests ways to prepare ESL students to respond appropriately in many different writing contexts.

Academic Writing.

2219. Mlynarczyk, R. K., & Haber, S. B. (1990). *In our own words: A guide with readings for student writers*. NY: St. Martin's Press.

Uses writing by students as a bridge between personal and academic writing.

Offers opportunities for students to express their attitudes toward and experiences with writing. A variety of writing strategies are introduced and material for self-evaluation and peer response are included.
Advanced/Textbook.

2220. Moe, H. (1983). EST rhetoric: A pedagogical model for Norway's senior secondary schools. *Dissertation Abstracts International, 43*(8), 2652A.
Presents a pedagogical model for instruction in EST for Norwegian senior secondary school science programs, adopted from research in EST and adapted to the target population.
ESP/Secondary School/Norwegian.

2221. Moesser, A. (1974, March). *Where does the written accent go?* Paper presented at the 8th Annual TESOL Convention, Denver, CO.
Discusses the lack of preparation in bilingual education for the teaching of writing.
Bilingual.

2222. Mohamed, M. A. (1986). Ellipsis: A contrastive study of Swahili and English discourse. *Dissertation Abstracts International, 47*(6), 2145A.
Examines translations in Swahili and English for use of ellipsis, reference, and substitution. Results show significant differences and similarities in these domains.
Swahili/Cohesion.

2223. Mohan, B. A. (1986a). The author responds to Gregg . . . [In The Forum]. *TESOL Quarterly, 20*, 358-361.
Criticizes Gregg (1986) for lack of evidence and discusses circularity of some cross-cultural research.
Contrastive Rhetoric/Research.

2224. Mohan, B. A. (1986b). The author responds to Ricento . . . [In The Forum]. *TESOL Quarterly, 20*, 569-573.
Responds to Ricento's criticism (1986) that he has discarded Kaplan's description of the Chinese paragraph without offering another model. Claims his purpose was to call for more rigorous studies of Chinese expository prose not to offer his own model.
Contrastive Rhetoric/Chinese.

2225. Mohan, B. A., & Lo, W. A. Y. (1985). Academic writing and Chinese students: Transfer and developmental factors. *TESOL Quarterly, 19*, 515-534.
Argues against the claim that organizational patterns in Chinese writing differ significantly from those in English. A comparison of writing practices of Chinese students in Hong Kong and British Columbia schools shows that emphasis is placed on sentence-level rather than discourse-level concerns. Teachers need to realize that language transfer should not be treated as an obstacle in writing of Chinese students.
Contrastive Rhetoric/Organization/Chinese.

2226. Mohr, E. V. (1972, February). *Writing = ESL + problems*. Paper presented at the 6th Annual TESOL Convention, Washington, DC.
Reviews why the teaching of writing is more difficult than the teaching of spoken language to ESL students.

Speaking-Writing Relations.

2227. Molinsky, S. J., & Bliss, B. (1990). *Access: Fundamentals of literacy and communication*. Englewood Cliffs, NJ: Prentice Hall.

Text is designed for adults and secondary school students with limited or no literacy skills. It helps students gain access to beginning level coursework.

Secondary School/Beginners/Adult Education/Textbook.

2228. Moll, L. C. (1989). Teaching second language students: A Vygotskian perspective. In D. M. Johnson, & D. H. Roen (Eds.), *Richness in writing: Empowering ESL students* (pp. 55-69). NY: Longman.

Discusses the relevance of Vygotsky's theory of the zone of proximal development for teaching writing to ESL students. Describes three ESL classrooms where this principle is seen operating below the surface and stresses its value in providing a social organization of instruction and in facilitating students to make meaning of experience.

Theory/Classroom Activities.

2229. Monson, P. M. R. (1992). Correlations between acculturation variables and English achievement levels for Mexican-American elementary students. *Dissertation Abstracts International, 52*(7), 2445A.

Surveys one hundred Mexican-American elementary students in grades 3-6 to find out what sociocultural variables contribute to the success of those who achieve a high level of English literacy. Girls who had Anglo friends had significantly better English literacy skills.

Hispanic/Elementary/Literacy/Acculturaton.

2230. Montalvan, R., & Anderson, D. (1992, March). *The LSP summer seminar on teaching writing*. Paper presented at the 26th Annual TESOL Convention, Vancouver, BC.

Describes a 60-hour professional development seminar for Phillipine teachers on how to teach LEP students to write, emphasizing activities and motivation.

Teacher Preparation/Phillipines.

2231. Montano-Harmon, M. R. (1991). Discourse features of written Mexican Spanish: Current research in contrastive rhetoric and its implications. *Hispania, 74*(2), 417-425.

Compares compositions written in Spanish by secondary school students in Mexico with those written by Anglo-American students in the U.S.

Hispanic/Contrastive Rhetoric.

2232. Montano-Harmon, M. R. (1988). Discourse features in the compositions of Mexican, English-as-a-second-language, Mexican-American Chicano, and Anglo high school students: Considerations for formulations of educational policies. *Dissertation Abstracts International, 50*(5), 1235A.

Attempts to identify differences in discourse features in expository compositions by four groups of high school students. Discourse features in composition by English-dominant Mexican-American/Chicano students were significantly different from others. Their texts show prevalence of oral discourse features and, consequently, non-standard English rather than interference from Spanish. Since their failure to distinguish between oral and written codes distinguishes

these students from Spanish-dominant learners, more suitable educational policies and programs should be developed.
Hispanic/Secondary School.

2233. Moody, K. W. (1965). Controlled composition frames. *English Language Teaching*, *19*(4), 146-155.
Suggests five stages for student writing with each step progressively less controlled.
Control/Beginners.

2234. Moore, L. (1986). Teaching students how to evaluate writing. *TESOL Newsletter*, *20*(5), 23-24.
Presents guidelines for peer evaluation which begin with group evaluations of anonymous works and move to evaluation of students' writing.
Evaluation/Feedback/Peer Response.

2235. Moore, L., Schneider, M. L., & Werner, P. (1990). Summary writing strategies of ESL writers. *TESOL Newsletter*, *24*(2), 33-35.
Presents a study which examines the effects of instruction on summary writing and the strategies used by students in summary writing. Finds students wrote significantly longer summaries after one semester of instruction and main strategies they used were: copy, paraphrase, invention, and reference to author/text.
Summary Writing.

2236. Moore, R. (1986, March). *Writing without composing: A visual perspective*. Paper presented at the 20th Annual TESOL Convention, Anaheim, CA.
Endorses and suggests activities for writing that promotes visual knowledge of the L2.
Style.

2237. Moragné e Silva, M. L. (1992a, March). *Comparing first and second language composing processes*. Paper presented at the 43rd Annual CCCC Meeting, Cincinnati, OH.
Reviews a wide range of research from Zamel forward on the role of L1 in the L2 composing process.
L1 Influence/Process Research.

2238. Moragné e Silva, M. L. (1992b, March). *First and second language composing processes across tasks*. Paper presented at the 26th Annual TESOL Convention, Vancouver, BC.
Reports an 18-month case study of an adult writer composing in two languages and responding to a variety of tasks.
Process Research/Task/Portugese.

2239. Moragné e Silva, M. L. (1991). Cognitive, affective, social, and cultural aspects of composing in a first and second language: A case study of one adult writer. *Dissertation Abstracts International*, *52*(12), 4249A.
A 14-month longitudinal case study of a Portugese adult composing a variety of academic and non-academic tasks in Portugese (L1) and English (L2). Finds cross-linguistic similarities in problem representation, goal creation, and high-level planning and evidence of complex interaction between L1 and L2, depending on the language

base of content and structural knowledge used in writing. Task familiarity had the largest effect on the composing process.

Portugese/Process Research/L1-L2 Comparison.

2240. Moragné e Silva, M. L. (1989). A study of composing in a first and second language. *Texas Papers in Foreign Language Education, 1*(2), 132-151.

The complexity of second language composing is explored in a six-month case study of a Portugese-speaking ESL writer. Protocols and interviews show striking similarities in the processes used in the two languages. Differences occurred in the efficiency of attaining high level goals in L2 because of an occasional inability to translate, controlled low-level skills, and difficulty structuring L1 knowledge.

L1-L2 Comparison/Portugese.

2241. Moragné e Silva, M. L. (1988). Is the process of composing in a second language similar to composing in the first? *Texas Papers in Foreign Language Education, 1*(1), 16-25.

A review of the L1 and L2 literature leads to the conclusion that the current data cannot answer the question of similarity with any certainty. Suggests, however, that the composing process of NESs is not always generalizable and that there is a high degree of transfer of composing skills from L1.

L1-L2 Comparison.

2242. Moragné e Silva, M. L. (1987, March). *Effects of the writing experience on first and second language composing: A case study*. Paper presented at the 38th Annual CCCC Meeting, Atlanta, GA.

L1-L2 Comparison/Process Research/Portugese.

2243. Moragné e Silva, M. L. (1986, March). *First and second language composing process: A case study*. Paper presented at the 20th Annual TESOL Convention, Anaheim, CA.

Case study of a writer, using think-aloud procedures and post-composing interviews, shows marked similarities in skilled writer's successful attainment of goals in L1 and L2.

L1-L2 Comparison/Process Research/Portugese.

2244. Morcos, D. A. (1985). *A linguistic study of coordination and subordination in the writing of Arabic-speaking ESL students*. Unpublished master's thesis, University of New Orleans, New Orleans, LA.

Arabic/Syntactic Structures.

2245. Morgan, E. J. (1992, March). *Indicators of writing quality in Malaysian and American compositions*. Poster presented at the 26th Annual TESOL Convention, Vancouver, BC.

Describes a study comparing use of given-new contract and its relation to writing quality in compositions by Malaysian ESL and American freshman writers.

Malay/NS-NNS Comparisons/FSP.

2246. Morgan, E. J. (1990). The given-new contract in the compositions of Malaysian ESL writers as an indicator of writing quality. *Dissertation Abstracts International, 51*(4), 1142A.

Focuses on the particular difficulties that Malaysian ESL students have in

sequencing information in a particular order. Compositions in a persuasive mode were collected from freshman college EFL students in Kuala Lumpur. Repetition of propositional arguments and antecedents was compared to holistically scored writing quality. The best indicator of writing quality was the amount of new information for both Malays and Americans. Several cultural differences are also indicated.
FSP/Malay/NS-NNS Comparisons/Contrastive Rhetoric.

2247. Morow, P. R. (1989). Conjunct use in business news stories and academic journal articles: A comparative study. *English for Specific Purposes*, *8*, 239-254.
Offers a comparison of the use of conjunct connectives in business news stories and economics journal articles for ESP business courses.
ESP/Business Writing/Cohesion.

2248. Morrell, S., Fox, D. N., & Whittemore, R. (1992, March). *Writing with a purpose: Intercultural research through letter exchanges*. Paper presented at the 25th Annual TESOL Convention, New York, NY.
Describes a letter exchange between an anthropology class and an ESL classs seeking information for a research paper.
Letter Writing.

2249. Morrisroe, S. (1987, April). *Improving writing skills with a student-produced newsletter*. Paper presented at the 21st Annual TESOL Convention, Miami Beach, FL.
Finds students writing improvement when it results in a product.
Student Publications.

2250. Morroy, R. (1985). Teacher strategies: Linguistic devices for sustaining interaction in dialogue journal writing. *Dissertation Abstracts International*, *47*(10), 3750A.
Describes linguistic strategies used by teachers for most effective interactions in dialogue journals. Discusses implications for theory of discourse strategies.
Dialogue Journals/Responding.

2251. Moser, J., & Raphan, D. (1993). Russian students' writing: An adaptation of skills. *College ESL*, *3*(1), 43-52.
A self-report survey finds that Russian immigrant college students are focused and motivated learners. Interviews suggest that educational background is linked with ease with structure, organization, and analysis in L2 writing and a lack of a personal point of reference. Offers suggestions for helping students personalize their writing.
Russian.

2252. Moten, B., Soden, B., & Zuck, J. G. (1980, March). *Personal/educational/cultural presuppositions and written academic discourse*. Paper presented at the 14th Annual TESOL Convention, San Francisco, CA.
Presents the view that students need to unlearn inappropriate strategies for learning discourse.
Discourse Analysis.

2253. Mountainbird, P. (1989). Community college ESL students reflecting on thoughts and feelings about writing and themselves as writers: An exploratory study of metacognition. *Dissertation Abstracts International*, *49*(12), 3595A.
Provides information about attitudes, identity, and self-direction of adult

community college ESL writers.
University/Affect.

2254. Mowat, R. (1990). Should literacy students be asked to copy? *TESL Talk, 20*(1), 275-277.
Offers suggestions for helping students improve their handwriting.
Handwriting.

2255. Mukkatash, L. (1981). Wh-questions in English: A problem for Arab students. *IRAL, 19*(4), 317-332.
Discovers that Arab-speaking students did not invert the subject and verb or auxiliary when producing WH-questions in English and also frequently ommited do in auxiliary-less WH-questions.
Arabic/Error Analysis.

2256. Mullen, K. A. (1980). Evaluating writing proficiency. In J. W. Oller, & K. Perkins (Eds.), *Research in language testing* (pp. 160-170). Rowley, MA: Newbury.
Finds that only some pairs of experienced ESL teachers were reliable when rating essays on five scales of writing proficiency. Also, vocabulary usage found to play heaviest role in determining overall quality of compositions written.
Evaluation/Proficiency.

2257. Mullen, K. A. (1977). Using rater judgments in the evaluation of writing proficiency for non-native speakers of English. In H. D. Brown, C. Yorio, & R. Crymes (Eds.), *On TESOL '77: Teaching and learning ESL--Trends in research and practice* (pp. 309-318). Washington, DC: TESOL.
Readers can, but do not always, agree on the rating of compositions.
Assessment/Rating.

2258. Munsell, P., & Clough, M. (1982, May). *Practical techniques for guiding advanced ESL writers*. Paper presented at the Annual NAFSA Meeting, Seattle, WA.
Advanced/Control.

2259. Munsell, P., & Clough, M. (1984). *A practical guide for advanced writers in English as a second language*. Boston: Heinle & Heinle.
Textbook offers three parts: section on basic organizational forms of writing, a second section on developmental rhetorical and gramamtical skills, and a third section on academic skills.
Advanced/Textbook.

2260. Murray, D. (1988, March). *Strategies for collaborative writing*. Paper presented at the 22nd Annual TESOL Convention, Chicago, IL.
Presents strategies for providing opportunities to learn to write collaboratively.
Collaboration.

2261. Mustapha, S. Z. (1991). Reading and writing in a specific environment: The Malaysian experience. *Dissertation Abstracts International, 52*(9), 3233A.
Investigates how ten Malaysian college students (Malay, Chinese, Indian) read in order to learn by analyzing think-aloud protocols, retellings, and free writing data.
Reading-Writing Relations/Malaysia.

2262. Myers, C. (1989, March). *From culture shock to academic writing competence*. Paper presented at the 23rd Annual TESOL Convention, San Antonio, TX.

Demonstrates a series of materials to help students paraphrase, quote, and incorporate reading knowledge.

Research Writing.

2263. Myers, G. (1988). The social construction of science and the teaching of English: An example of research. In P. C. Robinson (Ed.), *Academic writing: Process and product* (pp. 143-150). London: Modern English Publications/British Council.

ESP/Ethnographic Research/Scientific Writing.

2264. Myers, S. A. (1993). In search of the genuine article: A cross-linguistic investigation of the development of the English article system in written compositions of adult ESL students. *Dissertation Abstracts International*, *53*(7), 2352A.

A study of the use of definite and indefinite article in 900 compositions written by 475 adult ESL students from nine different language backgrounds but at different proficiency levels shows a strikingly similar development for students whose L1 contains articles and also a clear similarity among students whose L1 do not have articles.

Usage/Development.

N

2265. Narain, M. (1991, March). *Non-native speakers: Some problems of language usage.* Paper presented at the 42nd Annual CCCC Meeting, Boston. [ERIC ED 334 588].

Reports that Asian ESL students experience problems with self-identity, usage questions, and choice of grammatical voice.

Grammar/Asian.

2266. Nashaat, K. (1992, March). *Guided group composition using the overhead projector.* Paper presented at the 25th Annual TESOL Convention, New York, NY.

Shows how and when to guide a group of students inexperienced with the writing process.

Instruction.

2267. Nathan Dryden, I. J. (1988). The composing processes of five Malaysian ESL/EFL college writers: A multi-method approach. *Dissertation Abstracts International*, *48*(10), 2563 A.

A multi-method approach using case studies, process tracing, naturalistic and quasi-product approaches was adopted to access the thinking processes during composing of five Malaysian ESL/EFL students. The findings show that reviewing and "talking and writing" were the main elements of the writing process. All students viewed writing as a recursive process involving continuous planning, translating, and revising. Grammar was not the primary concern.

Process Research/Malay/University.

2268. Nathenson-Mejia, S. (1992). Writing in a second language: Negotiating meaning through invented spelling. *Language Arts*, *66*(5), 516-526.

Studies the invented spellings of Spanish-speaking Mexican first-graders who wrote captions to pictures in a bilingual program. Concludes that children used their knowledge of Spanish orthography while negotiating spellings in English.

Spanish/Children/Spelling.

2269. Nation, P., & Benz, C. (1993, April). *Designing student conferences for writing and speech classes*. Paper presented at the 27th Annual TESOL Convention, Atlanta, GA.

>Demonstrates conferencing and other classroom techniques and tools applicable to both skills.
Speaking-Writing Relations/Conferencing.

2270. National Clearinghouse on Literacy Education (1991). *Dialogue journal bibliography: Published books, articles, reports and dissertations about dialogue journal research and use*. Washington, DC: ERIC/CLE. [ERIC ED 333 722].

>Provides more than 90 references to various documents on dialogue journals.
Dialogue Journals/Bibliography.

2271. Nattinger, J., & DeCarrico, J. S. (1992). *Lexical phrases and language teaching*. Oxford: Oxford University Press.

>Presents a language teaching program that draws from research on the use of unanalyzed language fragments, in particular the unit lexical phrase, in predictable social contexts. A chapter on teaching reading and writing suggests how this theory applies to three genres of written discourse: the formal essay, the informal letter, and the business letter.
Reading-Writing Relations/Genre.

2272. Neff, J. A. (1993, April). *Discourse development in Spanish EFL writing*. Paper presented at the 27th Annual TESOL Convention, Atlanta, GA.

>Compares grammatical and rhetorical factors in expository compositions written by NESs and three levels of EFL learners in Spain.
Spanish/Exposition.

2273. Neill, D. R. (1982). *Guidelines for developing an advanced level ESL writing syllabus*. Unpublished master's thesis, University of Hawaii, Honolulu, HI.
Advanced/Courses.

2274. Nelson, E. S. (1983). A spelling flow-chart. *TESOL Newsletter, 17*(1), 23.

>Displays a flow chart that guides students through a series of yes-no decisions in spelling -ing, -ed, -s forms.
Spelling.

2275. Nelson, G. L. (1993). Reading and writing: Integrating cognitive and social dimensions. In J. G. Carson, & I. Leki (Eds.), *Reading in the composition classroom: Second language perspectives* (pp. 315-330). Boston: Heinle & Heinle.

>A summary and integration of the papers in this volume argues that reading and writing are cultural, social, and contextual.
Reading-Writing Relations/Review.

2276. Nelson, G. L. (1992a, March). *ESL peer review groups: A case study*. Paper presented at the 43rd Annual CCCC Meeting, Cincinnati, OH.

>Discusses study observing six interactions of four students reviewing each others' writing of a paragraph. Finds that the social dimension of their interaction was the strongest but not necessarily most beneficial factor.
Peer Response.

2277. Nelson, G. L. (1992b, March). *ESL writing groups: A case study*. Paper presented at the 26th Annual TESOL Convention, Vancouver, BC.

Presents an analysis of a four-person writing group using Fanselow's FOCUS system (1987) for describing classroom observations.

Classroom Research/Writing Groups.

2278. Nelson, G. L., & Keenan, J. B. (1979, March). *Technical writing: PSI method*. Paper presented at the 13th Annual TESOL Convention, Boston.

Describes application of the Personalized System of Instruction (PSI) to the teaching of technical writing to international students.

Technical Writing.

2279. Nelson, G. L., & Murphy, J. M. (1993a). Peer response groups: Do L2 writers use peer comments in revising their drafts? *TESOL Quarterly*, 27, 135-142.

A study of a four-person intermediate level peer-response group suggests that when writers interact with their peers in a cooperative manner, they are likely to use peer revisions in their revising.

Peer Response/Revision.

2280. Nelson, G. L., & Murphy, J. M. (1993b, April). *Writing groups and the less proficient ESL student*. Paper presented at 44th Annual Convention of CCCC, San Diego, CA.

See next item.

Writing Groups.

2281. Nelson, G. L., & Murphy, J. M. (1993c). Writing groups and the less proficient ESL student. *TESOL Journal*, 2(2), 23-26.

Reports on a study of a low-intermediate writing group (N=4) in a ten-week writing course. The students identified at least one major area needing improvement in 91% of the writing sampled when compared with trained raters. This ability to identify macrolevel problems (i.e., organization, development, and topic sentences) although not microlevel problems (repetition, parallel structure, etc.) suggests what low proficient writing groups can do effectively.

Writing Groups.

2282. Nelson, G. L., & Murphy, J. M. (1992). An L2 writing group: Tasks and social dimensions. *Journal of Second Language Writing*, 1(3), 171-194.

In a case study of one L2 writing group for six weeks, finds that students stayed on task by discussing each other's texts but that group dynamics were less than ideal.

Peer Response.

2283. Nelson, M. P. (1991). *At the point of need: Teaching basic and ESL writers*. Portsmouth, NH: Boynton/Cook.

Emphasizes similarities between writing process and problems of native and nonnative writers. Recommends the same process-based workshop approach for both populations, based on research over a five year period in the context of a university writing center.

NS-NNS Comparisons/Teacher Preparation.

2284. Nelson, M. W. (1985a). Teaching "writing" to ESL students: A process-based approach. *WATESOL Working Papers*, 2(Fall-Winter 1984-85), 12-25. [ERIC ED 267

586].
Describes a college-level composition course based on freewriting and writing strategies. The course consists of three segments: drafting, revising, and fine tuning. Each segment plays an important role in preparing ESL writers for the next stage of composing. Grammar and mechanics as well as structure and rules are de-emphasized.

Curriculum/Approaches.

2285. Nelson, M. W. (1985b, March). *Using small-group writing tutorials with ESL and basic students*. Paper presented at the 36th Annual CCCC Meeting, Minneapolis, MN.

Group Work/Tutoring.

2286. Nelson, M. W. (1983). From "composition" to "writing "-- revising an EFL tradition. *WATESOL Working Papers*, *1*, 53-67. [ERIC ED 244 509].

Distinguishes "composition" -- a product-oriented approach whose focus is on form -- from "writing" -- a process-oriented approach whose focus is on content. Describes a successful instructional approach for native and non-native speakers of English where "writing" is emphasized.

Process Instruction.

2287. Neu, J., & Scarcella, R. C. (1991). Word processing in the ESL writing classroom: A survey of student attitudes. Patricia Dunkel (Ed.), *Computer-assisted language learning and testing: Research issues and practice* (pp. 169-187). NY: Newbury/Harper Collins.

Attempts to determine empirically whether positive results exist for NNES students using computers in ESL writing class and whether students like it. The Asian refugee immigrants (N=54) studied were enrolled in university ESL writing classes and most used word processing almost three-fourths of the time. Results show that, indeed, they believe their writing benefited from the use of computers. Also, most students had a positive attitude toward learning and using word processing.

Computers/Word Processing.

2288. Neumann, A. (1978). *Analysis of interference and development factors in college freshman compositions*. Unpublished master's thesis, Pan American University, Brownsville, TX.

Examines effect of first-language interference on the English composition skills of college students. Student written errors were examined in the light of interference factors as represented by native language status and development factors as represented by the number of years of study in high school English. The findings point out the greater impact of developmental factors although previous views in the literature favored interference.

Hispanic/Error Analysis/L1 Influence.

2289. Nevarez, H. O., Berk, V. B., & Hayes, C. W. (1979). The role of handwriting in TESOL. *TESOL Newsletter*, *13*(1), 25-26.

Suggests reasons and activities for teaching cursive skills to Arabic-speaking students.

Handwriting/Arabic.

2290. Nevo, D. (1986). Comments on Stansfield: A history of the Test of Written English -- The developmental year. *Language Testing, 3*(2), 235-236.

Points out that ETS may have sacrificed validity for reliability of TWE by using general writing topics.

Assessment/TWE.

2291. Newsham, G. S. (1978). Compositions, not essays or rhetoric. *TESL Talk, 9*, 41-45.

Argues that rhetoric, essay, and composition are not the same because each has a different history, purpose, and text structure. The composition is the easiest and most practical form to teach in a writing class for students of English as a second language.

Rhetoric.

2192. Newsham, G. S. (1977). *The paragraph in French and English*. Unpublished doctoral dissertation, Universite de Montreal, Faculte des Sciences et de 'Education.

Studies sentences in 24 paragraphs from French and English college textbooks for freshman according to Halliday's theme/rheme distinction. Finds a variety of mixed patterns rather than a single overall text pattern. Two patterns were common to French; a combination of two patterns characteristic of English paragraphs.

Contrastive Rhetoric/French.

2293. Newton, J. (1990). Electronic tutoring and ESL students' writing: The experience at York University's computer-assisted writing centre. In M. L. Craven, R. Sinyor, & D. Paramskas (Eds.), *CALL: Papers and reports* (pp. 87-89). La Jolla, CA: Athelstan.

Evaluates the effectiveness of electronic tutoring with ESL students.

Writing Center/Computers.

2294. Ney, J. W. (1977, April). *Miscue analysis: The writing of three Hispanic-American students in a class of twenty fourth-graders*. Paper presented at the 11th Annual TESOL Convention, Miami Beach, FL.

Finds little qualitative difference between Hispanic and non-Hispanic student miscues (Goodman, 1973).

Hispanic/Error Analysis/Elementary.

2295. Ney, J. W., & Fillerup, M. (1980). *The effects of sentence combining on the writing of ESL students at the university level*. Washington DC: ERIC/FLL. [ERIC ED 193 961].

Reports a quasi-experimental study of the effects of sentence-combining training on the syntactic development of ESL freshmen. ESL college students who received sentence-combining practice in addition to controlled exercises showed significantly greater syntactic development, but did not improve overall writing proficiency.

University/Sentence Combining.

2296. Ng, B. (1966). An analysis of the compositions of bilingual children in the fifth grade. *Dissertation Abstracts International, 27*(11), 3632A.

Compositions written by 356 fifth-grade Chinese bilingual students show that their structural patterns in English are related to the degree of their bilingualism

Chinese/Children/Bilingual.

2297. Nickell, S. S. (1986). Writing conferences on the computer. *CALICO Journal*, *3*(3), 29-30, 36.

Computer conferences help teachers spot the precise level of student difficulties.

Computers/Conferencing.

2298. Nishimura, Y. K. (1986). Prose-organizing studies of Japanese college students: A contrastive analysis. *Descriptive and Applied Linguistics*, *19*, 207-218.

Analyzes the differences in prose-organization strategies of native speakers of Japanese and English. The study supports the claim that American writers use the "linear" strategy. The major difference observed lies in attitudes toward the ending of the text: American writers end the text with a definite conclusion whereas Japanese writers avoid making a point at the end of their writing.

Contrastive Rhetoric/Organization/Japanese.

2299. Nishio, Y. (1991). *Longman ESL literacy*. NY: Addison Wesley/Longman.

Focuses on developing competency in reading and writing in English for preliterate and semi-literate students.. Oral/aural skills give a foundation to function effectively at home, school, and work.

Beginners/Textbook.

2300. Nkamana, D. G. (1975). *A proposed program in English composition for first year Bantu junior high school students*. Unpublished master's thesis, UCLA, Los Angeles, CA.

Programs/Bantu/Middle School.

2301. Noguchi, R. R. (1988, November). *Unconscious linguistc knowledge: Using what students already know to correct some persistent sentence-level errors*. Paper presented at the 78th Annual NCTE Convention, St. Louis, MO.

2302. Norman, U. (1990). Testing writing skills in the literature class. *English Teaching Forum*, *28*(1), 45-46.

Discusses materials for intermediate writing.

Literature/Intermediate/Turkish.

2303. Norment, N. (1987, March). *Organizational structures and grammatical variations of Haitian, Greek, and Vietnamese students*. Paper presented at the 38th Annual CCCC Meeting, Atlanta, GA.

Vietnamese/Haitian/Greek/Contrastive Rhetoric.

2304. Norment, N.(1986). Organizational structure of Chinese subjects writing in Chinese and in ESL. *Journal of the Chinese Language Teachers Association*, *21*(3), 49-72.

Uses the Milic Logical Categories test to measure the organizational structures of thirty narrative and expository essays in English by native Chinese speakers. Finds a high degree of resemblance of structures across modes and subjects, concluding that the pattern of organization of writing is determined by the language background of writers.

Rhetoric/Chinese/Organization.

2305. Norment, N.(1984). Contrastive analyses of organizational structures and cohesive elements in native and ESL Chinese, English, and Spanish writing. *Dissertation Abstracts International*, *45*(1), 172A.

Investigates the differences and similarities in the organization of events by freshman in expository and narrative compositions written in their native language (English, Chinese, and Spanish), and by Chinese-speaking and Spanish-speaking students in English. Findings show distinct organizational structures for each language, a transfer of thess structures into the second language, and mode of discourse as a factor in students' writing proficiency.
Hispanic/Chinese/Contrastive Rhetoric/Narration.

2306. Norment, N. (1982). *Contrastive analyses of organizational structures and cohesive elements in English, Spanish (ESL) and Chinese (ESL) students' writing in narrative and expository modes*. Urbana, IL: ERIC/RCS. [ERIC ED 269 764].
Examines the kind of cohesive devices employed in English texts written by native Chinese, Spanish, and English-speaking adult college students. Finds patterns for each language group representative of organizational schemes suggested by Kaplan (1966). Also finds greater use of cohesive devices in narrative than expository modes across language groups.
Contrastive Rhetoric/Cohesion/Chinese/Spanish.

2307. Norton, R. F. (1982). *A comparison of thinking and writing patterns in Korea and the U.S.* (AFS Occasional Paper in International Learning No.12). NY: American Field Service International/Intercultural Programs. [ERIC ED 290 648].
Reports the results of research showing preference for induction as a writing style by Korean essayists in contrast to deductive preference by American writers.
Contrastive Rhetoric/Korean.

2308. Norton, R. F. (1979). A contrastive analysis of Korean and American writing styles: As expressed in expository essays. *Dissertation Abstracts International*, *39*(11), 6600A.
Examines five Korean and five American essays for features of organizational patterns. Results show English has a deductive-linear pattern while Korean has an inductive, linear pattern.
Organization/Exposition/Korean.

2309. Notess, M. H. (1984, March). *Using inductive assignments to teach technical and academic discourse forms*. Demonstration at the 18th Annual TESOL Convention, Houston, TX.
Shows how to teach conventions of an unfamiliar written form inductively.
Technical Writing/Conventions.

2310. Nurss, J. R. (1989, March). *Assessment of written language acqusition in young LEP students*. Paper presented at the 23rd Annual TESOL Convention, San Antonio, TX.
Presents a whole language theory of assessment of kindergarten and primary children.
Elementary/Whole Language.

O

2311. Obah, T. Y. (1993). Learning from others in the ESL writing class. *English Quarterly*, *25*(1), 8-13.
Shows how combining pair work, peer feedback, and features of the group

approach enables students to improve their writing.
Collaboration.

2312. Obeidat, H. A. (1986). An investigation of syntactic and semantic errors in the written composition of Arab EFL learners. *Dissertation Abstracts International, 47*(9), 3415A.

Examines syntactic and semantic errors in the writing of Arabic-speaking EFL students. Findings reveal some errors: (1) can be attributed to mother tongue interference, (2) are often caused by sociocultural factors, (3) allude to universal grammar of learners, and (4) are part of the developmental process of all ESL/EFL learners irrespective of language background.

Error Analysis/Arabic.

2313. O'Brien, M. (1993, April). *Content reading and writing for EST*. Paper presented at the 27th Annual TESOL Convention, Atlanta, GA.

Describes a course using authentic texts and writing assignments to reinforce content.

ESP/Reading-Writing Relations.

2314. O'Brien, M. (1983, March). *The classroom teacher and the case study: The perils and possibilities of conducting your own research*. Paper presented at the 17th Annual TESOL Convention, Toronto, Ontario. [ERIC ED 234 611].

Discusses potential sources of invalidity in teacher-research studies of their own classrooms, illustrated by a study done in an ESL writing class.

Research.

2315. O'Brien, M., & McDonough, J. (1989, March). *Integrating speaking and writing in the beginning ESL classroom*. Paper presented at the 23rd Annual TESOL Convention, San Antonio, TX.

A semi-controlled interview with preceding exercises helps beginning ESL/EFL students with the grammar and vocabulary they need to express themselves in writing.

Speaking-Writing Relations/Beginners/Control.

2316. O'Brien, T. (1987). Writing for continuous assessment or examinations -- A comparison of style. In P. C. Robinson (Ed.), *Academic writing: Process and product* (pp. 67-74). London: Modern English Publications/British Council.

Describes research-in-progress on formal and informal features of the linguistic performance of psychology students who wrote essay examinations under timed conditions compared to untimed essays on similar topics.

Academic Writing/Time/Style.

2317. O'Conner, F. (1989). *Express yourself in written English*. Littlewoood, IL: NTC Publishing Group.

Text directs students to develop both conceptual and technical skills in writing in a worktext format. It features exposure to model paragraphs and compositions which are analyzed and manipulated. It also provides exercises for students to outline paragraphs and compositions as well as writing exercises.

Intermediate/Textbook.

Part 2: Background materials, methodology, 1953-1963. Washington, DC: CAL.
Lists 24 items in a section on "Composition, Spelling, and Writing".
Bibliography/Methods.

2323. Ohannessian, S. (1964). *Reference list of materials for English as a second language. Part 1: Texts, readers, dictionaries.* Washington, DC: CAL.
Describes numerous textbooks for use in teaching writing and other skills.
Bibliography/Textbook.

2324. Ohannessian, S., Pedtke, D. A., Erwin, B., & Malkoç, A. M. (1969). *Reference list of materials for English as a second language. Supplement: 1964-1968.* Washington, DC: CAL.
Lists 26 textbooks on composition, handwriting, and spelling for ESL students.
Bibliography/Textbook.

2325. Oi, K. M. (1984). Cross-cultural differences in rhetorical patterning: A study of Japanese and English. *Dissertation Abstracts International, 45*(8), 2511A.
Compares writing in English by Japanese students, writing in English by American college students, and writing in Japanese by Japanese students for cohesive devices, organizational principles, and cultural rhetorical tendencies. Findings show each group employs a distinct rhetorical tradition in writing in their native language and that Japanese students writing in English transfer rhetorical pattern of Japanese into English.
Organization/Cohesion/Japanese/University.

2326. Okamura, F. (1976). *Contrastive rhetoric of English and Japanese.* Unpublished master's thesis, UCLA, Los Angeles, CA.
Contrastive Rhetoric/Japanese.

2327. Oller, J. W., & Ziahosseiny, S. M. (1970). The contrastive analysis hypothesis and spelling errors. *Language Learning, 20,* 183-189.
Examines validity of strong, moderate, and weak versions of the contrastive analysis hypothesis by comparing spelling errors of ESL students whose native language used a Roman alphabet with those whose native language used a non-Roman alphabet. Results indicate a more moderate Contrastive Analysis Hypothesis predicts spelling errors based on "interference" of similar patterns due to false generalizations.
Research/Spelling.

2328. Olshtain, E. (1991). Functional tasks for mastering the mechanics of writing and going just beyond. In M. Celce-Murcia (Ed.), *Teaching English as a second or foreign language* (Second Edition) (pp. 235-245). NY: Newbury/HarperCollins.
Discusses how to gradually teach beginners the mechanics of writing -- letter and word recognition, spelling, punctuation and capitalization -- within a communicative framework.
Beginners/Mechanics/Children.

2329. Olson, D. R. (1983, March). *Literacy as a second language.* Paper presented at the 17th Annual TESOL Convention, Toronto, Ontario.
Argues that literacy in a first language is a second language, requiring the learning of a range of devices for referring to language, that is, metalanguage.
NS-NNS Comparisons/Literacy.

2330. Oluwadiya, A. (1992). Some pre-writing techniques for student writers. *English Language Forum, 30*(4), 12-15, 32.

    Discusses pre-writing ideas and how they apply to the Nigerian secondary school classroom.

    Invention/Nigerian/Secondary School.

2331. O'Malley, J. M., & Kupper, L. (1989, April). *A production system for writing in a foreign language.* Paper presented at the Annual AERA Meeting, San Francisco, CA.

    Psychology.

2332. O'Malley, J. M., & Pierce, L. V. (1992, March). *Portfolio development: Experiences from the field.* Paper presented at the 26th Annual TESOL Convention, Vancouver, BC.

    Assesses teacher responses to the use of portfolios at the elementary, intermediate, and secondary levels.

    Assessment/Portfolios.

2333. Onaka, N. (1984). Developing paragraph organization skills at the college level. *English English Teaching Forum, 22,* 14-22.

    Discusses the role of paragraph organization in teaching English to Japanese university students. Describes several pedagogical problems resulting from rhetorical differences between English and Japanese and presents techniques of paragraph development in English.

    Contrastive Rhetoric/Paragraph/Japanese.

2334. Ong Kiam Ann, A. (1977). Dictation as a technique for teaching composition. *RELC Journal, 8*(2), 85-90.

    Suggests dictation techniques of listen-and-write, listen-and-modify, listen-and-answer, and listen-and-complete.

    Listening-Writing Relations.

2335. Orge, C. (1978). *A new approach to writing for the ESL student.* Unpublished master's thesis, Hunter College, CUNY, New York, NY.

    Approaches.

2336. Ortblad, D. (1980). Teaching writing by an "anticipation method." D. L. Bouchard, & L. J. Spaventa (Comps.), *A TEFL anthology: Selected articles from the English Teaching Forum, 1973-78* (pp. 191-193). Washington, DC: International Communication Agency.

    Proposes an "anticipation method," which in contrast to controlled writing, encourages guessing of meaning and structure from contextual clues provided in EST passages.

    Methods/ESP.

2337. Osburne, A. G., & Dowd, J. L. (1987). Teaching Chinese students to write essay examinations and papers. *TECFORS, 10,* 1-5.

    Describes techniques to remedy negative features of Chinese students' writing on examinations.

    Examination Essays/Chinese.

2338. Osburne, A. G., & Harss-Covaleski, S. L. (1992). Translation in the ESOL composition class. *College ESL, 2*(2), 33-44.

Does spontaneous writing of an entire text in L2 rather than translation from L1 produce superior results? An experiment compared spontaneous composition in English with translation into English by nine high intermediate-advanced ESL adults writing two timed cause-effect topics. Concludes that there are no substantial qualitative or quantitative differences between the written products.

Translation/L1-L2 Comparison.

2339. Oshima, A., & Hogue, A. (1991). *Writing academic English.* (Second Ed.). Reading, MA: Addison-Wesley.

Offers an integrated approach to grammar, rhetoric, as well as sentence and paragraph structure. Chapters give step-by step-procedures for each of the traditional modes, offer model essays, convention rules, dictocomps, and grammar.

Intermediate.

2340. Oshima, A., & Hogue, A. (1990). *Introduction to academic writing.* White Plains, NY: Addison Wesley/Longman.

Integrates grammar and rhetoric as well as sentence and paragraph writing for the intermediate level with pre-writing activities as well as emphasis on mechanics.

Textbook/Intermediate.

2341. Oster, J. (1990, March). *Rigidity . . . Resistance . . . Emergence: A Chinese engineer becomes a writer.* Paper presented at the 24th Annual TESOL Convention, San Francisco, CA.

A case study spanning several years, illustrated with excerpted papers and interviews, documents a student's development from William Perry's (1968) Stage One Dualism to increased openness, relativism, analysis, expressiveness, and eventually a journalism manuscript.

Chinese/Development.

2342. Oster, J. (1987). *From reading to writing: A rhetoric and reader.* (Second Ed.). Boston: Heinle & Heinle.

Text is designed for ESL students in freshman composition courses in order that they may achieve the proficiency levels necessary for success in college. The text is organized into rhetorical modes with a variety of professional and student models. It includes critical thinking exercises, a research paper chapter, and a basic sentence review to help students overcome troublespots.

University/Textbook.

2343. Oster, J. (1984, March). *The rhetoric of the visual: Using non-verbal stimuli to teach rhetorical and analytic skills.* Demonstration at the 18th Annual TESOL Convention, Houston, TX.

Uses cartoons, ads, and surrealist painting to teach aspects of rhetoric.

Media.

2344. Oster, J. (1985a). The ESL composition course and the idea of a university. *College English, 47,* 66-76.

Describes an ESL composition course that attempts to engage foreign students in two-way communication about the idea of a university through reading, writing, and discussion. Shows how such an approach can help eliminate foreign students'

misconceptions about life in the United States and Americans' misconceptions about their culture and attitudes.
Curriculum/University.

2345. Oster, J. (1985b, April). *A graduation follow-up of ten former freshmen.* Paper presented at the 19th Annual TESOL Convention, New York, NY.
Examines the effect of writing intensive courses on writing ability after four years.
Research/IEP.

2346. Oster, J., Brodkey, D. G., Brosnahan, I., Goldstein, L. M., McKay, J. R., Perkins, L., Reid, J. M., & Smith, J. M. (1987, April). *The freshman composition administrator's session.* Colloquium presented at the 21st Annual TESOL Convention, Miami Beach, FL.
Focuses on relations to departments and teachers in programs.
Administration.

2347. Osterloh, K. H. (1980). Intercultural differences and communicative approaches to foreign language teaching in the Third World. *Studies in Second Language Acquisition, 3,* 64-70.
Claims that learners from different cultures, especially the Third World, bring to the English text different concepts about the text, about the author and about personal and collective opinions. Emphasizes need for revising materials used in the Third World and relating them to learner's environment and culture.
Contrastive Rhetoric.

2348. Ostler, S. E. (1990, March). *The contrastive rhetorics of Arabic, English, Japanese, and Spanish.* Paper presented at the 24th Annual TESOL Convention, San Francisco, CA.
A discourse bloc analysis of 160 essays displays the rhetorical patterns found in prose written in English by Arabic, Japanese, and Spanish speakers writing in English, and native English speakers. The results demonstrate that there are culturally-coded rhetorical differences in the organization of prose across these languages.
Contrastive Rhetoric/Arabic/Japanese/Spanish.

2349. Ostler, S. E. (1988). A study of contrastive rhetoric of Arabic, English, Japanese, and Spanish. *Dissertation Abstracts International, 49*(2), 245A-246A.
Uses four populations to test the Contrastive Rhetoric Hypothesis. A discourse block analysis of essays (N=160) by NESs and Arabic, Japanese, and Spanish learners shows distinctive rhetorical patterns, especially with regard to the comparative degree of development of the organizational parts, i.e., introduction, body, and conclusion. Each of the four languages also has a characteristic syntactic preference pattern: most notably, passives and nominalizations in NES essays, parallel constructions and relatives in Arabic learners' essays, and length and sentential elaboration in Spanish learners' essays.
Contrastive Rhetoric/NS-NNS Comparisons.

2350. Ostler, S. E. (1987). English in parallels: A comparison of English and Arabic prose. In U. M. Connor, & R. B. Kaplan (Eds.), *Writing across languages: Analysis of L2 text* (pp. 169-185). Reading, MA: Addison-Wesley.

Studies expository essays written in English by Saudi Arabian students. Findings indicate that rhetorical style of classical Arabic is present in English essays written by Arabic students. Suggests using distinctions to help students improve their essays.

Rhetoric/Exposition/Arabic.

2351. Ostler, S. E. (1986a). Writing problems of international students in the composition classroom. *The Writing Instructor, 5,* 178-189.

Outlines and addresses some potential cultural problems of international students in American composition classes.

Culture.

2352. Ostler, S. E. (1986b, March). *Teaching library and research strategies in palatable chunks.* Paper presented at the 20th Annual TESOL Convention, Anaheim, CA.

Discusses a syllabus for a research writing course.

Research Writing/Courses.

2353. Ostler, S. E. (1985, April). *The relationship of L1 literacy to L2 reading and writing.* Paper presented at the 19th Annual TESOL Convention, New York, NY.

Attempts to determine correlation between value of literate modality in native language and L2 literacy after a year of intensive English.

Literacy/Reading-Writing Relations.

2354. Ostler, S. E., & Kaplan, R. B. (1982, May). *Contrastive rhetoric revisited.* Paper presented at the 16th Annual TESOL Convention, Honolulu, HI.

Reexamines Kaplan's notion in the light of recent research and criticism.

Contrastive Rhetoric.

2355. Ostler, S. E. (1981). *English in parallels: A study of Arabic style.* Unpublished manuscript, University of Southern California, Los Angeles, CA.

Finds that Arabic student writing in English has more T-units and discourse blocs, reflecting emphasis on finite clauses characteristic of written Arabic, than a sample of English published text.

Contrastive Rhetoric/Arabic/Style.

2356. Ostler, S. E. (1980). A survey of academic needs for advanced ESL. *TESOL Quarterly, 14,* 489-502.

Based on a survey of IEP graduates at a large university, recommends adjustments to the advanced level of intensive programs to be more field-specific in reading and writing.

Academic Writing/IEP.

2357. Ouaouicha, D. (1987). Contrastive rhetoric and the structure of learner-produced argumentative texts in Arabic and English. *Dissertation Abstracts International, 47*(9), 3339A.

Investigates the structure of argumentative texts written by Americans and Moroccans in both Arabic and English. One hundred essays were analyzed using a system developed from Toulmin (1959). The same structures were found in both languages as were substantiation structures with implicit and explicit warrants. American subjects, however, showed audience awareness and emotional appeal

significantly more often than did the Moroccans. These features were attributed to training rather than the influence of the native language.
NS-NNS Comparisons/Argumentation/Contrastive Rhetoric/Arabic.

2358. Ounvichit, T. (1988). *Contrastive expository writing: Thai and English*. Unpublished master's thesis, Mahidol University, Bangkok, Thailand.
Contrastive Rhetoric/Exposition/Thai.

2359. Ovaiza, S. (1976). The teaching of spelling. *English Language Teaching Journal, 30*, 219-224.
Outlines a procedure for teaching spelling to students of English as a second language.
Spelling.

2360. Owens, R. J. (1970). Teaching English composition. *RELC Journal, 1*(1), 119-126.
Suggests that poor standards of written English can be attributed to unrealistic expectations and confusion between teaching the English essay as an art form and composition to ESL students.
Standards.

P

2361. Pack, A. C., & Hendrichsen, L. E. (1992). *Sentence combination: Writing, combining, and editing standard English sentences*. (Second Ed.). Boston: Heinle & Heinle.
A sentence writing exercise book for intermediate proficiency learners.
Intermediate/Textbook.

2362. Pack, A. C., & Hendrichsen, L. E. (1979, March). *Teaching ESL/SESD students to write-combine standard English sentences*. Paper presented at the 13th Annual TESOL Convention, Boston.
Uses Allen's sector analysis to teach writing.
Grammar.

2363. Pack, A. C. (1977, April). *A research project on the use of sector analysis in remedial English writing classes*. Paper presented at the 11th Annual TESOL Convention, Miami Beach, FLA.
Reports success of Robert Allen's sector analysis with a variety of university students.
Grammar.

2364. Padron, Y. N., & Bermudez, A. B. (1987, April). *Examining Hispanic students' perceptions of writing instruction*. Paper presented at the Annual AERA Meeting, Washington, DC.
Hispanic/Perceptions.

2365. Pagurek, J. (1984). *Writing workshop: Paragraph and sentence practice*. Boston: Heinle & Heinle.
A practical manual that teaches writing techniques such as generalizing, talking about differences, enumerating, defining, and expressing cause and result.
Intermediate/Textbook.

2366. Paine, M. J. (1976). Variation in the use of written exercises. *English Language Teaching Journal, 30*, 326-332.

    Discusses problems encountered by elementary grade ESL students doing uncontextualized written exercises in numbered lists from a course book. Suggests possible remedies.

    Elementary.

2367. Paiva, J. L., & O'Donnell, T. D. (1991). *Independent writing.* (Second Ed.). Boston: Heinle & Heinle.

    Textbook presents an ordered, cumulative approach to writing. Each lesson begins with a writing discussion, is followed by a cyclical progression of activities that simulate the composing process, and adds a structural review and other exercises.

    Textbook/Intermediate.

2368. Paiva, J. L., & O'Donnell, T. D. (1980). *Independent writing. (Second Ed.).* Boston: Heinle & Heinle.

    Textbook presents an ordered, cumulative approach to writing. Each lesson begins with a writing discussion, is followed by a cyclical progression of activities that simulate the composing process, and adds a structural review and other exercises.

    Textbook/Intermediate.

2369. Palmer, J. D. (1988). Discourse, register, and the teaching of writing: An orientation. In G. H. Irons (Ed.), *Second language acquisition: Selected readings in theory and practice* (pp. 182-191). Ontario, Canada: The Canadian Modern Language Review.

    Discusses how the organization of written discourse differs markedly from that of spoken discourse and how the dimensions of register need to be presented to ESL students.

    Register/Speaking-Writing Relations/Conventions.

2370. Palmer, J. D. (1980). How a paragraph hangs together. *English Teaching Forum, 18*(2), 16-19.

    Suggests ways to teach cohesion.

    Cohesion/Paragraph.

2371. Paltridge, B. (1992). EAP placement testing: An integrated approach. *English for Specific Purposes, 11*, 243-268.

    Describes the development of a placement test which includes a subjectively scored writing component with a specific prompt that calls for a problem-solution text.

    Placement/Evaluation.

2372. Pandharipande, R. (1982). Linguistics and written discourse in particular languages: Contrastive studies: English and Marathi. *Annual Review of Applied Linguistics, 3*, 118-136.

    Analyzes the discourse features of English and Marathi pointing out the similarity and difference in the two languages and predicts possible difficulties of Marathi learners of English as a second language. Notes that sociocultural, syntactic, and organizational factors determine form and function of discourse.

Contrastive Rhetoric/Marathi.

2373. Parasher, S. V. (1977). Focus on learners' English: A case study of Hindi-speaking first year students' performance. *CIEFL Bulletin (Central Institute of English and Foreign Languages)*, *13*, 41-57. [ERIC ED 185 867].

Identifies some of the written errors made by Hindi-speaking EFL students. The source of errors is traced to overgeneralization, negative transfer from first language, pressure of one English construction on another, and overdrilling of certain items. Suggests using errors as source for remediation.

Error Analysis/Hindi.

2374. Park, Y. M. (1988). Academic and ethnic background as factors affecting writing performance. In A. C. Purves (Ed.), *Writing across languages and cultures: Issues in contrastive rhetoric* (pp. 261-274). Newbury Park, CA: Sage.

Examines the writing of both native and non-native speakers of English in different academic disciplines for the influence of academic and ethnic background and the effects of topic variation on writing performance.

Variation/Topic/NS-NNS Comparisons.

2375. Parkhurst, C. (1990). The composition process of science writers. *English for Specific Purposes*, *9*, 169-179.

Discusses the writing processes of native and non-native science writers in a process-oriented composition class.

ESP/NS-NNS Comparisons.

2376. Parkhurst, C. (1988, March). *Science writing: Content, form, and process differences and teaching implications*. Paper presented at the 22nd Annual TESOL Convention, Chicago, IL.

Discusses writing for science and technology, the academic major of nearly 40% of ESL students.

ESP.

2377. Parkhurst, C. (1985). Using C.A.L.L. to teach composition. In P. Larson, E. L. Judd, & D. S. Messerschmitt (Eds.), *On TESOL: A brave new world for TESOL* (pp. 255-260). Washington, DC: TESOL.

Gives examples of non-drill programs for proofreading.

Curriculum/Computers/Editing.

2378. Parkhurst, C., Price, K., & Fryman, J. (1985, April). *A computerized writing lab: Reactions, problems, solutions*. Paper presented at the 19th Annual TESOL Convention, New York, NY.

Computers/Writing Center.

2379. Parks, S., Thibadeau, S., & Brassard, M. L. (1984, March). *Process instruction and the writing competency of elementary Arab ESL learners: A case study*. Paper presented at the 18th Annual TESOL Convention, Houston, TX.

Reports improvements in writing ability of 16 Arabic-speaking adult students at the elementary level in an intensive program after eight-week treatment focusing on consciousness of the composing process.

Arabic/Beginners/Process Instruction.

2380. Partridge, K. L. (1981). *A comparison of the effectiveness of peer vs. teacher evaluation for helping students of ESL to improve the quality of their written compositions*. Unpublished master's thesis, University of Hawaii, Honolulu, HI.

Finds that teacher evaluation is more effective than peer evaluation for helping college-level ESL students improve the quality of their essay drafts.

Feedback/University.

2381. Paschal, G. (1990). German and English academic genres: A contrastive study of astronomical sublanguage and discourse. *Dissertation Abstracts International, 51*(9), 3060A.

Examines a corpus of three scientific academic genres (scholarly articles, textbook chapters, encyclopedia entries) in German and English. Finds that the texts possess parallel as well as divergent sets of lexical and syntactic features, having discourse functions correlated to the roles of writer, reader, and purpose of texts. Proposes an analytic model of genres, embedded in forums, and demonstrates how the lexical, syntactic, and discourse style is conventionalized within respective forums.

Genre/German/Text Analysis.

2382. Patkowski, M. S. (1989). What are we rating when we rate holistically? In J. D. Macero, B. J. Agor, & N. Tumposley (Eds.), *Realizing the dream: Selected conference proceedings of the annual meeting of the New York State TESOL* (pp. 63-71). NY: NY TESOL. [ERIC ED 314 955].

Finds that holistic ratings agree with a measure of "conformity to correct prose," a technique based on error counting, in that they give the same ranks to five essays from five ability levels. The by-product of the technique is a grammatically correct version of essays that can be used as feedback.

Assessment/Holistic/Rating

2383. Patkowski, M. S. (1981, March). *"Acquisition" exercises for ESL writing*. Paper presented at the 15th Annual TESOL Convention, Detroit, MI.

Suggests that dictation, paragraphing, and precis-writing are acquisition-oriented in Krashen's sense due to their holistic nature.

Classroom Activities.

2384. Patrie, J. (1989). The use of the tape recorder in an ESL composition programme. *TESL Canada Journal, 6*(2), 87-90.

Reports giving more and better feedback when using a tape recorder.

Feedback.

2385. Patthey-Chavez, G. G. (1988, April). *Writing opinions in high school: A comparison of Anglo and Latino students' texts*. Paper presented at the 11th Annual Meeting of the American Association of Applied Linguistics, New Orleans, LA.

Finds that NESs us more markers of discourse to introduce examples than Latino writers.

Spanish/Secondary School.

2386. Paul, M. (1985). Workplace simulations: A strategy for audience-centered writing. *TECFORS, 8*(5), 1-5. [ERIC ED 267 650].

Discusses a course which uses the theme of work and simulations of writing tasks from the workplace for a college class of immigrants and refugees.

Task.

2387. Paul, P. (1987). Perspectives on using American Sign Language to teach English as a second language. *Teaching English to Deaf and Second Language Students*, *5*(3), 10-16.
> Argues for using ASL to teach English literacy skills.
> ASL/Literacy.

2388. Pauliukonis, N. R., & Brown, M. S. (1993, April). *Using ASL as a basis for written essay development*. Paper presented at the 27th Annual TESOL Convention, Atlanta, GA.
> Describes how the customary restricted writing of hearing-impaired students is overcome by creating a bilingual(deaf-hearing) exchange as a preparation to write formal college essays.
> Hearing-Impaired.

2389. Paulston, C. B. (1972). Teaching writing in the ESOL classroom: Techniques of controlled composition. *TESOL Quarterly*, *6*, 33-59.
> Describes theoretical issues and classroom procedures for teaching writing in an EFL context.
> Control/Classroom Activities.

2390. Paulston, C. B. (1970). Teaching footnotes and bibliographic entries to foreign students: A tagmemic approach. *English Language Teaching*, *24*(3), 279-283.
> Gives a technique for teaching appropriate documentation of sources in a research paper.
> Research Writing.

2391. Paulston, C. B. (1967). The use of model passages in a program of guided composition. In B. W. Robinett (Ed.), *On Teaching English to Speakers of Other Languages: Papers read at the TESOL conference, New York City, March 17-19, 1966. Series III.* (pp. 149-153). Washington, DC: TESOL.
> Describes a program of guided composition and the preparation of suitable materials.
> Control.

2392. Paulston, C. B., Henderson, R. T., Furey, P. R., & Call, M. E. (1983). *Writing: Communicative activities in English*. Englewood Cliffs, NJ: Prentice-Hall.
> Offers a controlled composition textbook organized around grammatical structures and topics centered on the lives of community-college students.
> Intermediate/Advanced/Textbook.

2393. Pavelich, J. L. (1978). Organizing special classes for foreign students in the technical writing course. *Technical Writing Teacher*, *5*(2), 55-58.
> Describes a remedial writing program for foreign students lacking technical writing skills.
> Curriculum/Technical Writing.

2394. Payne, R., & McTeague, F. (1976). Developing literacy skills in adolescents and adults. *TESL Talk*, *7*, 60-82.
> Provides meaningful problem-solving exercises for teaching English as a second language to adult learners.

Classroom Activities.

2395. Paznik-Bondarin, J., & Baxter, M. (1987). *Write and write again: A worktext with readings*. NY: Macmillan.

A process-oriented text that helps ESL writers integrate reading, writing, critical thinking, grammar, and vocabulary skills. Contains model essays and guidelines for every stage of the writing process. Writing exercises and assignments are at the end of each chapter.

Advanced/Textbook.

2396. Pearson, C. C. (1981). Introducing advanced concepts of reading and writing in the beginning ESL class. *TECFORS*, *4*(3), 5-7. [ERIC ED 267 647].

Uses balloon diagram to illustrate the way "advanced" skills and concepts can be introduced earlier in ESL writing development.

Beginners/Reading-Writing Relations.

2397. Pearson, C. C., & Hubbard, P. (1992). The writing assignments and writing problems of doctoral students: Faculty perceptions, pedagogical issues, and needed research. *English for Specific Purposes*, *11*, 33-49.

A survey of first-year NES and NNS doctoral students in humanities, social sciences, and natural sciences finds they have problems with writing at the global level and need discipline-specific instruction.

Graduate Students/NS-NNS Comparisons.

2398. Pearson, C. C., & Hubbard, P. (1988, March). *Faculty expectations on required writing tasks in doctoral coursework*. Paper presented at the 22nd Annual TESOL Convention, Chicago, IL.

Implications for ESL pedagogy are drawn from a survey across doctoral disciplines.

Academic Writing/Graduate Students/Task.

2399. Pearson, S. (1983). The challenge of Mai Chung: Teaching technical writing to the foreign-born professional in industry. *TESOL Quarterly*, *17*, 383-399.

Identified technical writing needs of EFL students and stated their implications for course design and materials development. She also argued that recent research in reading technical English can be applied to the teaching of technical writing.

Curriculum/Technical Writing.

2400. Pech, W. C., & Buckingham, T. (1980). Writing from experience: A composition program for intermediate students. In D. L. Bouchard, & L. J. Spaventa (Comps.), *A TEFL anthology: Selected articles from the English Teaching Forum, 1973-78* (pp. 194-198). Washington, DC: International Communication Agency.

Gives a model application of the language experience approach to writing.

Approaches/Intermediate.

2401. Peitzman, F. (1988, March). *Pushing for advanced literacy: Helping transitional ESL writers gain authority*. Paper presented at the 39th Annual CCCC Meeting, St. Louis, MO.

Literacy.

2402. Peitzman, F. (1986, March). *Reformulation: What benefits for the advanced ESL writer?* Paper presented at the 37th Annual CCCC Meeting, New Orleans, LA.

Discusses Cohen's (1982;1983) idea of revision interaction between non-native writers and native revisers.
Revision.

2403. Penfield, J. (1981, November). *Literacy development in bilingual contexts Mexican-Americans*. Paper presented at the Annual Meeting of the American Association for Applied Linguistics, New York, NY. [ERIC ED 212 439].
Examines writing samples of Mexican-American university students learning English as a second language, for linguistic aspects of Chicano English likely to cause difficulty in the acquisition of standard written English. Results show that difficulty in writing due to dialect background, lack of familiarity with English writing system, and the interference of Spanish.
Hispanic/Literacy/L1 Influence.

2404. Pennington, M. C. (1993a). A critical examination of word processing effects in relation to L2 writers. *Journal of Second Language Writing*, 2, 227-255.
A comprehensive review of the L1 and L2 scholarship assesses the effects of word processing on ESL writer. Identifies seven variables of method and context which contribute to conflicting results. Concludes that under certain conditions, word processing benefits the nonnative writer.
Word Processing/Review.

2405. Pennington, M. C. (1993b). Exploring the potential of word-processing for nonnative writers. *Computers and the Humanities*, 27(3), 149-163.
Claims that word processing and the associated instructional environment can benefit nonnative writers.
Word Processing.

2406. Pennington, M. C. (1992a). Beyond off-the-shelf computer remedies for student writers: Alternatives to canned feedback. *System*, 20, 423-437.
Argues against the use of grammar checkers and style analyzers by nonproficient writers and in favor of a wide range of emergent alternatives to computer-assisted feedback.
Computers/Feedback.

2407. Pennington, M. C. (1992b, March). *Reflecting on teaching and learning: Developing ESL writing teachers*. Paper presented at the 26th Annual TESOL Convention, Vancouver, BC.
Describes the evolution of a reflective/developmental focus for a graduate course aimed at training ESL writing teachers.
Teacher Preparation.

2408. Pennington, M. C. (1991a). Positive and negative potentials of word processing for ESL writers. *System*, 19, 267-275.
Argues that the users and circumstances of use, rather than properties of the medium itself, determine degree of success, since any potential benefit of the medium can also be a potential drawback.
Computers/Word Processing.

2409. Pennington, M. C. (1991b). A qualitative artifact analysis of the attributes of word processing for student writers. *Computer Assisted Language Learning*, 4(2), 93-105.

Outlines both the positive and negative usability claims made for computer use in teaching writing as a process by applying artifact analysis to the following wordprocessing tools: keyboard, visual display, printer, storage capacity, and text modification functions. Concludes that the capabilities of word processing combined with the attributes of the computer offer an array of potentials for the native and non-native student alike.

Word Processing/Process Instruction.

2410. Pennington, M. C. (1990a). An evaluation of word processing for ESL students. *University of Hawaii Working Papers in ESL, 9*(1), 77-113.

Finds that word-processing enhances the creative revision process of ESL students.

Computers/Word Processing.

2411. Pennington, M. C. (1990b, March). *Computer-oriented composition*. Paper presented at the 41st Annual CCCC Meeting, Chicago, IL.

Computers/Word Processing.

2412. Pennington, M. C., & Brock, M. N. (1991). Process and product approaches to computer-assisted composition. In M. C. Pennington, & V. Stevens (Eds.), *Computers in applied linguistics: An international perspective* (pp. 79-109). Clevedon, Eng: Multilingual Matters.

Reports research comparing two approaches to the individualised, tutorial use of computers as supplements to university-level ESL writing courses in Hawaii. Four subjects, divided between users of an experimental text analysis program (IBM's Critique) and recipients of conferencing and word processing wrote three compositions with each paper completed in a series of three sequential drafts over a three-week period. Results indicate that students who used text analysis drafted less, revised for meaning less, and edited no more thoroughly than the comparison group. Conferencing with word processing even for a short time may help promote several benefits.

Computers/Word Processing.

2413. Pennington, M. C., & So, S. (1993). Comparing writing process and product across two languages: A study of 6 Singaporean University student writers. *Journal of Second Language Writing, 2*, 41-63.

No clear relationship between the products and the processes of writing in two languages (Chinese or Japanese and English) was discovered among six female writers in Singapore. But similarities across languages in the individual processes used and a significant relationship between proficiency and text quality are noted.

Singapore/Process Research.

2414. Pennington, M. C., & Zhang, D. (1993). A survey of writing attitudes and activities of Chinese graduate students at a U.S. university. In M. N. Brock, & L. W. Walters (Eds.), *Teaching composition around the Pacific Rim: Politics and pedagogy* (pp. 75-89). Clevedon, ENG: Multilingual Matters.

Results of a survey of Chinese graduate students in the U.S. about writing in English and themselves as writers indicate that attitudes are generally positive.

Chinese/Graduate Students.

2415. Peppin, S. M., & Krumm, M. L. (1978, April). *Using iconographics to develop an individualized writing component*. Paper presented at the 12th Annual TESOL Convention, Mexico City, Mexico.

Shows a series of writing activities that help students evaluate and organize data from iconographic material and then process it using appropriate rhetorical devices in their compositions.

Assignments.

2416. Peregoy, S. F., & Boyle, O. F. (1993). *Reading, writing & learning in ESL: A resource book for K-8 teachers*. NY: Longman.

Aims to provide a theoretically sound practical resource for K-8 teachers. Separate chapters concern classroom strategies for teaching writing as a process and the use of writing and reading across the curriculum to promote discovery, comprehension, and retention of information

Children/WAC/Process Instruction.

2417. Peretz, A. S. (1986). Summary writing for EFL students of science and technology. *English Teaching Forum*, 24(3), 31-32.

Presents procedures for teaching summarizing to prepare students for the real world in science and technology.

Summary Writing.

2418. Perez, C. G. (1979, March). *Syntactic complexity in the writing of bilinguals -- school children and adults*. Paper presented at the 13th Annual TESOL Convention, Boston.

Analyzes rewriting of controlled passages by Spanish-speaking monolinguals and bilinguals in Puerto Rico.

Hispanic/Bilingual/T-Unit.

2419. Perkins, K. (1986, November). *A proposed research program for ESL composition evaluation*. Paper presented at the 76th NCTE Convention, San Antonio, TX. [ERIC ED 290 155].

Proposes a comprehensive research program for studying the evaluation of ESL composition.

Evaluation/Research.

2420. Perkins, K. (1984). A regression analysis of direct and indirect measures of English as a second language written compositions. *Occasional Papers -- University of Essex, Department of Linguistics*, 29, 113-123.

Uses the Test of Ability of Subordinate (TAS) as the indirect measure and holistic scores of free writing samples as the direct measure in order to establish the relationship between these two measures of ESL writing proficiency. Results show that both measures account for substantial variance in a direct measure variable.

Evaluation/Scoring.

2421. Perkins, K. (1983). On the use of composition scoring techniques, objective measures, and objective tests to evaluate ESL writing ability. *TESOL Quarterly*, 17, 651-671.

Discusses the advantages and disadvantages of three scoring methods: holistic, analytic, and primary-trait. Concludes that no method is perfect in evaluating ESL writing ability: holistic scoring is not reliable due to the differences in judgment among raters, analytic method neglects the text as a whole, while primary-trait

method takes up too much time and is difficult to use
Evaluation/Scoring.

2422. Perkins, K. (1982a, May). *An analysis of the robustness of composition scoring schemes*. Revised version of a paper presented at the 16th Annual TESOL Convention, Honolulu, HI. [ERIC ED 217 723].

Studies the efficiency of holistic scoring, analytical scoring, and an objective diagnostic (Davidson's Test of Ability to Subordinate) in assessing compositions by using these measures to analyze compositions written by advanced ESL students. Results show that the analytical variable accounted for 89% of variance.
Assessment/Objective Measures.

2423. Perkins, K. (1982b). *The application of a stylistic metric to English as a second language compositions*. Washington, DC: ERIC/FLL. [ERIC ED 225 383].

Presents evidence for the concurrent validity in ESL composition of a stylistic measure defining complexity, first proposed by Joseph Williams (1979).
Assessment/Style.

2424. Perkins, K. (1982c). The Test of Ability to Subordinate: Predictive and concurrent validity for attained ESL composition. In T. Culhane, C. K. Braley, & D. K. Stevenson (Eds.), *Proceedings of the Fourth International Language Testing Symposium of the Interuniversitare Sprachtestgruppe held at the University of Essex, 14-17 September 1981* (pp. 104-112). Colchester: University of Essex, Department of Language and Linguistics. [ERIC ED 217 734].

Finds no significant correlation between syntactic development as measured by Davidson's Test of Ability to Subordinate (TAS) and overall writing ability (using different scoring methods). TAS had predictive but not concurrent validity. Holistic scores and analytical scores correlated significantly with most other variables.
Objective Measures/TAS

2425. Perkins, K. (1980a, April). *Input vs. intake in an advanced ESL composition class*. Paper presented at the 14th Annual Meeting of TESOL, San Francisco, CA. [ERIC ED 193 930].

Examines the correlation between input from a course syllabus for advanced ESL students containing exercises in paragraph organization, logical organzation, use of subordinating conjunctions, of main clauses, of coordinating conjunctions, and intake as manifested in linguistic products. Results show significant improvement in all areas of input except subordinating conjunctions.
Advanced/Courses.

2426. Perkins, K. (1980b). Using objective methods of attained writing proficiency to discriminate among holistic evaluations. *TESOL Quarterly, 14*, 61-69.

Describes a study which used ten objective measures to evaluate writing proficiency of advanced ESL students. Results indicate that only those objective measures which take the absence of errors into account discriminated among holistic evaluations of experienced ESL teachers.
Evaluation/Scoring/Advanced.

2427. Perkins, K., & Brutten, S. R. (1990). Writing: A holistic or atomistic entity? *Journal of Basic Writing, 9*(1), 75-84.

Decides in favor of holistic over atomistic approaches because an empirical study failed to disclose the separation of skills as traditionally believed.
Approaches/Research.

2428. Perkins, K., & Brutten, S. R. (1988, March). *An information -- processing approach to measure organization in ESL writing*. Paper presented at the 22nd Annual TESOL Convention, Chicago, IL.

Reports an approach that distinguishes good from poor writers in organizing information.
Assessment.

2429. Perkins, K., Brutten, S. R., Larson, R. L., Miller, L. D., & Ross, S. B. (1985, April). *Teaching and testing ESL writing skills*. Colloquium at the 19th Annual TESOL Convention, New York, NY.

Discusses use of objective tests and holistic evaluation in intensive as well as college composition courses.
Evaluation/Pedagogy.

2430. Perkins, K., & Homburg, T. J. (1980). Three different statistical analyses of objective measures of attained ESL writing proficiency to discriminate among holistic evaluations. In R. Silverstein (Ed.), *Proceedings of the Third International Conference on Frontiers in Language Proficiency and Dominance Testing* (pp. 326-337). Carbondale, IL: Southern Illinois University.

Finds that two performance variables among a number of objective measures examined, namely total errors and errors per T-unit, discriminated significantly between three different holistic evaluations.
Evaluation/Objective Measures.

2431. Perkins, K., & Konneker, B. H. (1982). *Content and methodology for ESL composition teachers*. Washington, DC: ERIC/FLL. [ERIC ED 219 926].

Provides an overview of theory and practice in English as a second language. Includes sample syllabi on freshman composition and technical writing for ESL students, composition correction guides, sample evaluation form and a sample grade sheet.
Pedagogy.

2432. Perkins, K., & Leahy, R. (1978). Using objective measures of composition to compare native and non-native compositions. *Occasional Papers on Linguistics*, 6, 306-317.

Native compositions contain significantly more error-free T-units and non-native compositions contain significantly more errors per T-unit. However, objective measures fail to discriminate holistic evaluations.
Assessment/Objective Measures.

2433. Perkins, K., & Parish, C. (1984, April). *Direct versus indirect measures of writing proficiency: Research in ESL composition*. Paper presented at the Annual Meeting of the Illinois Teachers of English to Speakers of Other Languages, Chicago, IL. [ERIC ED 243 306].

Analyzes writing proficiency of ESL students using two indirect measures -- Test of the Ability to Subordinate (TAS), Revision and Editing Test (RET) -- and a

direct measure -- holistic evaluation. Results showed (1) TAS has higher reliability and validity than RET; (2) holistic scoring profile guide and RET provide similar criterion-related information.
Assessment/Objective Measures.

2434. Perkins, L., & Scarcella, R. C. (1986). Coming out of the cabbage badge: Relying on what you've got -- linguistic fallback. *TECFORS, 9*(4), 1-9.

Discovers through text analysis (n=120) and observation that permanent resident college students in the U.S. tend to fall back on the their knowledge of spoken rather than written English whereas international students transfer their rhetorical skills in writing from their L1 cultural norms. Argues that this provides evidence for Newmark's (1966) ignorance and Krashen's (1982) input hypotheses.
Speaking-Writing Relations/LOR/Culture.

2435. Perry, W., & Thornburg, L. (1992, March). *Western writing in Eastern Europe: A context for conflict*. Paper presented at the 26th Annual TESOL Convention, Vancouver, BC.

Reports experiencing but resolving conflict between teacher's expectations about rhetorical organization in student writing and student resistance to adopting western modes in a university level academic writing course.
Hungarian/University/Resistance.

2436. Pery-Woodley, M. P. (1991). Writing in L1 and L2: Analysing and evaluating learners' texts. *Language Teaching, 24*, 69-83.

Presents a critical survey of research focusing on analysis of learners' texts.
Review/Text Analysis/NS-NNS Comparisons.

2437. Pery-Woodley, M. P. (1990). Contrasting discourses: Contrastive analysis and a discourse approach to writing. *Language Teaching, 23*(3), 143-151.

Describes developments in contrastive linguistics since it has broadened to include discourse linguistics.
Discourse Analysis/Text Analysis.

2438. Pery-Woodley, M. P. (1989). Textual designs: Signaling coherence in first and second language academic writing (Vols. I and II). *Dissertation Abstracts International, 51*(8), 2668A.

Develops a framework for the analysis of the signalling of textual structure. Utilizes it to evaluate what may hinder coherence in learner texts. Specific syntactic features and characteristics make up four clusters of features: topic identification, salience and "chunkability," relations between chunks, and text-type appropriateness. Finds that French and English native texts use different devices to signal textual structure and use the same devices differently.
Text Analysis/Coherence/French.

2439. Pery-Woodley, M. P. (1987). Non-nativeness in second language texts: The syntax factor. T. Bloor, & J. Norrish (Eds.), *Written language: Papers from the Annual Meeting of the British Association for Applied Linguistics* (pp. 130-142). London: Center for Information on Language Teaching and Research.

Compares a set of native English texts, native French texts and non-native (French) English papers for how sentence syntax realizes or affects textual functions.

Concludes that there is considerable difference in text-building devices used by native writers of French and English including different ways of foregrounding/ backgrounding information, creating linkage for topic continuity, and distributing "marked structures," such as passives and clefts.
Text Analysis/Syntactic Structures/French.

2440. Peters, B. (1986). Ghosts, demons and chicken bones: Dramatic writing in the ESL classroom. *TESL Talk, 16*(1), 26-33.
Describes an experimental writing project implemented in an Italian language school. Writing skills were taught as an integral part of learning a second language. The use of dramatic improvisations, discussion, script-performance, monologues, and dialogue writing allowed for integrating oral and written practice. Six categories of perception -- focus, classification, contrast, sequencing, physical context and change -- were used to practice writing strategies.
Curriculum.

2441. Peterson, H. M. (1976). *Development of curriculum for teaching English composition to college students of English as a second language.* Unpublished master's thesis, Hunter College, CUNY, New York, NY.
Curriculum/Programs/University.

2442. Peterson, M. P. (1993, April). *A perfect match: Writing tasks in a reading class.* Paper presented at the 27th Annual TESOL Convention, Atlanta, GA.
Discusses writing assignments developed for advanced ESL reading class.
Reading-Writing Relations/Assignments.

2443. Peterson, P. W. (1989, March). *Becoming bilingual in an academic setting: Memory for text.* Paper presented at the 23rd Annual TESOL Convention, San Antonio, TX.
Finds differences in native and nonnative memory for text based on written summaries of a geography lecture.
NS-NNS Comparisons.

2444. Peterson, R. D. (1976). *The influence of visualization exercises on the ability of speakers of English as a second language to write with emotional impact.* Unpublished master's thesis, UCLA, Los Angeles, CA.
Classroom Activities.

2445. Pettinari, C. (1984, March). *Contrastive rhetoric in context: Discourse analysis in a cross-cultural setting.* Paper presented at the 18th Annual TESOL Convention, Houston, TX.
Describes how differences in the relationship between writers and audience in organizational contexts appear to influence the choice of information in surgical reports in English, Spanish, and Spanish-English interlanguage.
Hispanic/ESP.

2446. Peyton, J. K. (1993a). *Dialogue journals: Interactive writing to develop language and literacy.* Washington, DC: ERIC/LL. [ERIC ED354 789].
An ERIC Digest describes briefly and comprehensively the use of dialogue journals or written conversations in which teachers and students communicate with each other and the wide range of ages and educational settings to which it has been applied.

Dialogue Journals.
2447. Peyton, J. K. (1993b, April). *Dialogue journal writing: Instructional materials for teacher training*. Paper presented at the 27th Annual TESOL Convention, Atlanta, GA.
    Demonstrates how to use a new workshop packet, text, and handbook.
    Dialogue Journals.
2448. Peyton, J. K. (1990a). Dialogue journal writing and the acquisition of English grammatical morphology. In J. K. Peyton (Ed.), *Students and teachers writing together: Perspectives on journal writing* (pp. 67-97). Alexandria, VA: TESOL.
    A ten month study finds that five sixth grade beginning ESL students read and write meaningful messages long before they master its forms and structures. Daily dialogue journal writing is a rich resource for teachers to follow their students' progress.
    Dialogue Journals/Development.
2449. Peyton, J. K. (1990b). Introduction. In J. K. Peyton (Ed.), *Students and teachers writing together: Perspectives on journal writing* (pp. ix-xv). Alexandria, VA: TESOL.
    Dialogue journals offer a means for teachers to "ensure that students' experiences with writing involve them in meaningful communication and foster their language development".
    Dialogue Journals/Responding.
2450. Peyton, J. K. (Ed.). (1990c). *Students and teachers writing together: Perspectives on journal writing* Alexandria, VA: TESOL.
    Five essays by different teachers show how dialogue journals can relate significantly to curriculum, classrooms, and collaboration.
    Dialogue Journals.
2451. Peyton, J. K. (1988). *The effect of teacher strategies on students' interactive writing: The case for dialogue journals*. Los Angeles, CA: UCLA Center for Language Education and Research. [ERIC ED 298 763].
    Indicates that student-initiated topics are the best way to develop dialogue journals for elementary students.
    Dialogue Journals/Topic/Elementary.
2452. Peyton, J. K. (1988, March). *Beyond writing assignments: The influence of communicative context on ESL students' writing*. Paper presented at the 22nd Annual TESOL Convention, Chicago, IL.
    Compares the quantity and maturity of writing in three assigned and three unassigned entries in dialogue journals. The assigned tasks varied in topic control, audience, and purpose. Findings suggest that ESL students may explore and demonstrate a more complete range of their writing abilities in unassigned writing about personally chosen topics than in assigned writing about teacher-selected topics.
    Topic/Task/Dialogue Journals/Elementary.
2453. Peyton, J. K. (1987). *Dialogue journal writing with limited English proficient students*. Los Angeles, CA: CLEAR. [ERIC ED 287 308].
    Provides a short guide in question-answer format to using dialogue journal

writing for the development of LEP students.
Dialogue Journals.

2454. Peyton, J. K. (1986). Literacy through written interaction. *Passage*, 2(1), 24-29. [ERIC ED 273 097].
Describes ways of using dialogue journals with ESL writers. The interactional and communicative character of dialogue journals develop literacy skills in a natural way and provide students with informal, student-centered, meaningful written conversation.
Dialogue Journals/Literacy.

2455. Peyton, J. K. (1985, July). *Questions in ESL classrooms: New perspectives from written interaction*. Revised version of a paper presented at the 7th Annual Summer Meeting of TESOL, Washington, DC. [ERIC ED 287 308].
Reports questioning patterns in the dialogue journal interactions of two groups of sixth graders which differs from typical classroom discourse in that both participants introduce topics and ask questions. Variation is related to proficiency level.
Dialogue Journals/Interaction.

2456. Peyton, J. K., & Mackinson-Smyth, J. (1989). Writing and talking about writing: Computer networking with elementary students. In D. M. Johnson, & D. H. Roen (Eds.), *Richness in writing: Empowering ESL students* (pp. 100-119). NY: Longman.
Describes the use of the computer network for interactive writing by hearing-impaired ESL students. Shows the efficacy of this method through examples where students not only write but talk about their writing and thus peer-tutor. Claims this method has implications for all ESL students.
Computers/Networking/Hearing-Impaired.

2457. Peyton, J. K., & Reed, L. (1990). *Dialogue journal writing with nonnative English speakers: A handbook for teachers*. Alexandria, VA: TESOL.
Defines what dialogue journals are and illustrates strategies and uses with different students.
Dialogue Journals/Teacher Preparation.

2458. Peyton, J. K., & Richardson, G. (1988, March). *Beyond writing assignments: An expanded view of students' abilities*. Paper presented at the 22nd Annual TESOL Convention, Chicago, IL.
Finds that unassigned writing is as mature as assigned writing in sixth grade ESL dialogue journals.
Dialogue Journals/Topic/Elementary.

2459. Peyton, J. K., & Seyoum, M. (1989). The effect of teacher strategies on ESL students' writing: The case of dialogue journals. *Research in the Teaching of English*, 23, 310-334.
Finds that the teacher achieves collaborative interaction in the dialogue journals of sixth grade ESL students by responding to topics initiated by students and by making statements expressing opinions.
Dialogue Journals/Collaboration.

2460. Peyton, J. K., & Staton, J. (Eds.). (1991). *Writing our lives: Reflections on dialogue journal writing with adults learning English* Old Tappan, NJ: Regents Prentice Hall. [ERIC ED 333 763].

Guide to dialogue journal use primarily for teachers and tutors in adult literacy settings. Fourteen chapters, authored by different individuals, in five parts, introduce and describe the uses of dialogue journals, explain working with beginning writers and the training of teachers and tutors, and give the benefits for students and teachers.

Dialogue Journals/Adult Education/Literacy.

2461. Peyton, J. K., Staton, J., Richardson, G., & Wolfram, W. (1990). The influence of writing task on ESL students' written production. *Research in the Teaching of English*, 24, 142-171.

Finds that ESL elementary students demonstrate a more complex range of writing abilities in unassigned writing about self-chosen topics.

Task/Topic.

2462. Pfingstad, N. (1984). Showing writing: Modeling the process. *TESOL Newsletter (Supplement No. 1: Writing and Composition)*, 18(1), 1-3.

Describes the use of modeling in helping students through the process of writing English as a second language and highlights the benefits of this method.

Classroom Activities.

2463. Phap, D. T. (1980). *A contrastive approach for teaching English as a second language to Indochinese students*. San Antonio, TX: Intercultural Development Research Association. [ERIC ED 205 018].

Manual presents dissimilar features of English and Indochinese which are likely to pose problems for Indochinese learners of English. Presents cultural background of Indochinese students and explores ways of teaching English morphology, phonology, syntax, reading, vocabulary, and composition.

Contrastive Analysis/Indochinese.

2464. Pharis, K. E. (1988, March). *A graduate faculty view of foreign graduate student writing*. Paper presented at the 22nd Annual TESOL Convention, Chicago, IL.

Compares graduate faculty evaluation of organization, content, and grammar of EFL writers with that of independent evaluators.

Evaluation.

2465. Pharis, K. E. (1987). A study of faculty perceptions of foreign graduate student writing. *Dissertation Abstracts International*, 48(7), 1682A.

Investigates the reliability and criteria used by faculty in judging the quality of eight student essays.

Assessment/Raters.

2466. Phinney, M. (1993). *Process your thoughts: Writing with computers*. Boston: Heinle & Heinle.

Text and software with topical organization, authentic readings, exercises and a balance of process and product approaches to writing with a computer.

Textbook/Computers.

2467. Phinney, M. (1992, March). *ESL writers and computers: Helping the helpers*. Paper presented at the 25th Annual TESOL Convention, New York, NY.

Shows how to adapt writing software for ESL students.
Computers.

2468. Phinney, M. (1991a). Computer-assisted writing and writing apprehension in ESL students. In P. Dunkel (Ed.), *Computer-assisted language learning and testing: Research issues and practice* (pp. 189-204). NY: Newbury/HarperCollins.

Reports the results of a two-phase study of ESL students' perceptions of writing apprehension in English and how this is affected by writing with a computer. Results indicate that using a computer to write did reduce writing apprehension, helped students with timeliness, improved attitudes, and enhanced perception of ability to cope with complex material. Computers, however, may encourage a tendency for ESL students to prematurely edit.
Anxiety/Computers.

2469. Phinney, M. (1991b). Studying the computer writing process. *TESOL Matters, 1*(6), 15.

Describes how to record keystrokes (using macros on a word processor) made by students as they write on a computer in order to review with them their own writing strategies.
Computers/Word Processing.

2470. Phinney, M. (1991c). Word processing and writing apprehension in first and second language writers. *Computers and Composition, 9*(1), 65-82.

Neither L1 nor L2 writers reduced their apprehension simply by using a computer in a first-year composition class. L2 writers but not L1 writers reduced their blocking behaviorsthat used computers.
Word Processing/Affect/NS-NNS Comparisons.

2471. Phinney, M. (1989, July). *Computer-assisted writing and writing apprehension in ESL students*. Paper presented at the Pennsylvania State University Conference on Rhetoric and Composition, University Park, PA.
Computers/Programs.

2472. Phinney, M. (1989). Computers, composition, and second language teaching. In M. C. Pennington (Ed.), *Teaching languages with computers: The state of the art* (pp. 81-96). La Jolla, CA: Athelstan.

Relates that modest benefits rather than inflated expectations accrue to second language writers who use word processing. Explores using the computer as a writing aid in ways other than word processing.
Computers/Word Processing.

2473. Phinney, M., & Khouri, S. (1993). Computers, revision and ESL writers: The role of experience. *Journal of Second Language Writing, 2*, 257-277.

Four case studies find that experience with a computer rather than writing proficiency more strongly determines the computer writing strategies of advanced ESL writers. More computer experience, for example, is tied with more time revising and more semantic changes to text.
Computers/Word Processing/Revision.

2474. Phinney, M., & Khouri, S. (1991). *ESL writers and computers: Proficiency, experience, and revision*. Paper presented at the 7th Annual Conference on

Computers and Writing, Biloxi, MS.

Reports the results of a study of the way ESL students write on a computer and how their processes changed with computer experience.

Computers/Word Processing/Revision.

2475. Phinney, M., & Mathies, C. (1990). ESL student responses to writing with computers. *TESOL Newsletter*, *24*(2), 30-31.

Examines ESL students' use of and attitude towards using the computer in writing. Finds that although most ESL students use computer for editing, they felt computers took some of the tedium out of writing and therefore relieved some of their anxiety in writing.

Computers/Word Processing/Feedback.

2476. Phinney, M., & Mathies, C. (1987, April). *Writing and revising with computers in ESL composition*. Paper presented at the 21st Annual TESOL Convention, Miami Beach, FL.

Finds that longer and more complex papers as well as more time spent writing and revising result from two semesters of incorporating word processing in ESL composition classes.

Computers/Word Processing/Revision.

2477. Phooi, C. L. (1986). The revision processes of first-year students at the National University of Singapore. *RELC Journal*, *17*(1), 71-84.

Describes revision changes in meaning, operation, syntax, and stage (Faigley & Witte, 1981) in three essays by eighty-two Chinese-speaking students. Students concentrated on surface meaning, lower syntactic levels, and cognitively easier operations.

Revision/Chinese.

2478. Pica, T. (1986). An interactional approach to the teaching of writing. *English Teaching Forum*, *24*(3), 6-11.

Discusses three traditional approaches to the teaching of writing: models approach, process approach, and an integrated approach. Suggests that an interactional approach supplements rather that replaces the above. Emphasis is now placed on both gaining control and providing opportunities for self-expression.

Approaches.

2479. Pica, T. (1984). Second language acquisition theory in the teaching of writing. *TESOL Newsletter*, *18*(2), 5-6.

Describes two activities which demonstrate ways in which students can engage in meaningful communication through writing as a way of giving feedback to each other.

Peer Response/Feedback.

2480. Pickard, V. (1993, April). *Empowering novice writers: Can concordancers contribute?* Paper presented at the 27th Annual TESOL Convention, Atlanta, GA.

Describes a course in which students designed their own learning materials, employed concordancers to identify writing problems, and analyzed expert samples of writing.

Courses/Beginners/Computers.

2481. Picus, M. (1985, March). *Foreign students in native speaker classes -- What do we do with them?* Paper presented at the 36th Annual CCCC Meeting, Minneapolis, MN.

    Culture.

2482. Picus, M. (1983a). When Asians write: What to expect in grammar. *TECFORS*, *6*(5), 1-3. [ERIC ED 267 650].

    Says that Chinese and Vietnamese students have problems with perception of English word classes and word forms.

    Chinese/Vietnamese/Errors.

2483. Picus, M. (1983b). *The writing strategies of Vietnamese students*. Unpublished master's thesis, University of Houston, Houston, TX.

    Examines the ESL writing of eight Vietnamese-speaking students, using error analysis, revision analysis, and a recursive model of writing. Finds that most subjects do not find or correct errors in essays once they have been committed to paper. Attributes this to shutting down of the monitor to give a sense of completion.

    Vietnamese/Error Analysis/Revision.

2484. Picus, M. (1982). The writing strategies of ESL students. *TECFORS*, *5*(5), 7-8. [ERIC ED 267 648].

    Finds a diversity of writing strategies in the revisions of eight Vietnamese university students, although they shared the common practice of ceasing to monitor after physically completing a draft.

    Vietnamese/Strategies.

2485. Pimsarn, P. (1986). The reading and writing relationship: A correlational study of English as a second language learners at the collegiate level. *Dissertation Abstracts International*, *47*(8), 2974A.

    Studies the correlation between reading and writing abilities of ESL college students finding a statistically significant relationship between reading and writing ability levels. The data consisted of standardized reading tests, comparison/contrast writing sample, and a questionnaire adminstered to 40 ESL students in a freshman English course.

    Reading-Writing Relations.

2486. Pincas, A. (1970). Writing in paragraphs. *English Language Teaching*, *24*, 182-185.

    Advises new teachers to use paragraph patterns from the beginning of language learning.

    Beginners/Paragraph.

2487. Pincas, A. (1964). Teaching different styles of written English. *English Language Teaching*, *18*(2), 74-81.

    Proposes extension of "multiple substitution technique" to teach different written registers.

    Style.

2488. Pincas, A., & Allen, K. (1982). *Writing in English: Books 1, 2, 3*. London: Macmillan.

    A series of three texts with progressively more challenging exercises to help learners of English at the beginning, intermediate, and advanced levels gain the

necessary skills for effective written communication. The series progresses from simple sentence combining to essay writing to using different writing styles.
Secondary School/Textbook.

2489. Piper, A. (1991, March). *What's the matter with my essay?* Paper presented at the 25th Annual TESOL Convention, New York, NY.

Raises questions about the effectiveness of group work for learning to write.
Group Work.

2490. Piper, A. (1989a). Writing instruction and the development of ESL writing skills: Is there a relationship? *System, 17*(2), 211-222.

Reiterates how instruction affects how learners write, how teachers' attitudes and social interaction in the classroom affect the quality of writing, and how development and feedback constrain the process.
Instruction.

2491. Piper, A. (1987). Helping learners to write: A role for the word processor. *ELT Journal, 41,* 119-125.

Discusses the advantages of word processing in an intermediate multilingual EFL class. Word-processing helps EFL writers pay more attention to the structure of the text and to grammar. Positive contributions of word processors to the composing skills of EFL students are discussed in terms of class management and language learning motivation.
Computers/Word Processing/Intermediate.

2492. Piper, A. (1986). Computers and the literacy of the foreign language learner: A report on EFL learners using the word-processor to develop writing skills. *VEA Papers in Linguistics, 25*(6), 145-161.

Discusses the use of word-processor in a small multilingual group of EFL learners. The initial lessons in using computers involve both the acquisition of word-processor metalanguage and practice with specific linguistic structures such as the present perfect tense. Using computers has motivating effects on EFL learners
Computers/Word Processing.

2493. Piper, T. (1989b). *Written language growth in a multi-ethnic classroom.* Paper presented at the Second Language Research Forum, Los Angeles, CA. [ERIC ED 308 528].

Compares texts written by bilingual, ESL, and monolingual second graders (eight each), according to a psycholinguistic coding scheme. The use of descriptive language was most popular, except among bilinguals who speculated and generalized more.
Children/NS-NNS Comparisons.

2494. Pitcher, B., & Ra, J. B. (1967, February). *The relation between scores on the TOEFL and ratings of actual theme writing* . (ETS Statistical Report 67-9). Princeton, NJ: ETS.

To determine the degree to which TOEFL scores, especiallly the writing ability scores, correlate with ratings of writing ability, 310 international students wrote four themes that were correlated with all parts of the TOEFL. Writing ability, English structure, and vocabulary seem to be excellent predictors of theme writing.

Assessment/TWE.

2495. Poggi, C. (1992, March). *The novel in the ESL composition class*. Paper presented at the 25th Annual TESOL Convention, New York, NY.

Presents teacher's experience teaching a novel in a community college ESL course.

Literature.

2496. Poh, S. C. (1988, March). *Equal opportunity and ESL for limited English proficiency domestic students*. Paper presented at the 22nd Annual TESOL Convention, Chicago, IL. [ERIC ED 325 036].

Suggests special needs of Asian immigrants in college ESL programs.

Asian/University.

2497. Polak, J. (1992, March). *How to get students to write without knowing it*. Poster presented at the 26th Annual TESOL Convention, Vancouver, BC.

Shares two spontaneous, ungraded projects which resulted in writing for audience and publication since students had autonomy to be creative.

Project Work/Student Publications.

2498. Pollitt, A., & Hutchinson, C. (1987). Calibrated graded assessments: Rasch partial credit analysis of performance writing. *Language Testing*, *4*, 72-92.

Assessment/Scoring.

2499. Polycarpou, S., & Shoemaker, C. (1992, March). *The process approach: It's for beginning writers, too!* Paper presented at the 26th Annual TESOL Convention, Vancouver, BC.

Argues that empowerment occurs for beginning writers who benefit from exercises that enhance the writing process.

Process Instruction/Beginners.

2500. Ponder, R., & Powell, W. W. (1989). *Sourcebooks as content-bearing instruction in intensive ESL programs*. Washington, DC: ERIC/FLL. [ERIC ED 307805].

Proposes the use of sourcebooks in the advanced EL composition class in a dual instructional program: one centered on content and the other on skills development. A sourcebook project units langue proficiency with background knowledge and can serve as a primary source of a research paper.

IEP/Advanced.

2501. Port, R. J. (1967). Controlled, guided, and free writing. *TESL Reporter*, *1*(4), 3. [ERIC ED 184 351].

Claims that free-writing serves no purpose for ESL student and leads to reinforced errors. Suggests using controlled and guided writing and to begin with exercises involving simple substitutions.

Free Writing/Control.

2502. Porter, D. M. (1989, March). *Comparison of narrative structures in written student narratives*. Paper presented at the 23rd Annual TESOL Convention, San Antonio, TX.

Compares the rhetorical functions of narrative structures written by Hispanic and Indonesian students.

Narration/Hispanic/Indonesian.

2503. Porter, D. W. (1985). Sentence combining with students of English as a second language. *Dissertation Abstracts International, 45*(7), 2018A.

Compares sentence-combining of ESL students with that of native speakers. Results show significant differences and, therefore, suggests changes in texts and exercises for ESL students. Tests the effects of such revised texts on sentence-combining of ESL students. Results show increase in structures taught but also increase in errors. Concludes that these exercises must be supplemented by grammar instruction.

Sentence Combining/NS-NNS Comparisons.

2504. Porter, D. (1990). Precis writing in the ESL classroom. *Journal of Reading, 33*(5), 381.

Suggests that precis writing contributes to critical thinking and ability to learn from text.

Summary Writing.

2505. Posner, B. (1981, October). *Teaching writing to ESL students*. Paper presented at the Annual Conference of New York Educators Association, Rochester, NY. [ERIC ED 216 529].

Presents suggested exercises for teaching writing to beginning, intermediate, advanced, and transitional level ESL students.

Exercises.

2506. Potter, L. D. (1981). American Indian children and writing: An introduction to some issues. In B. Cronnell (Ed.), *The writing needs of linguistically different students* (pp. 129-160). Los Alamitos, CA: Southwest Regional Laboratory for Educational Research and Development.

Endorses development of first language reading and writing skills in Pueblo Indian communities, based on Wolfram et al. (1979).

Literacy/Amer-Indian.

2507. Poulsen, E. (1993, April). *Analyzing collaborative writing processes from split-screen video recordings*. Paper presented at the 27th Annual TESOL Convention, Atlanta GA.

Investigates the text production of nine different pairs writing on computers, using a split-screen technique. Focus is on how pairs use different processes in collaborating.

Collaboration/Computers.

2508. Poulsen, E. (1991). Writing processes with word processing in teaching English as a foreign language. *Computers & Education, 16*, 77-81.

Presents preliminary results from 3-year qualitative study of Danish intermediate level students using word processing in the process writing classroom. Students did little planning and changed from one process level to another.

Word Processing/Process Research/Danish.

2509. Povey, J. F. (1969a, March). *Creative writing in BIA schools*. Paper presented at the 3rd Annual TESOL Convention, Chicago, IL.

Creative writing shows native American students that the second language can be a vehicle for their own concerns.

Amer-Indian/Creative Writing.

2510. Povey, J. F. (1969b). Creative writing in BIA schools. *TESOL Quarterly, 3,* 305-308.

Believes that a creative writing program as described encourages both validity of native culture and adaptation to the Anglo world.
Amer-Indian/Creative Writing.

2511. Povey, J. F. (1969c). Cultural self-expression through English in American Indian schools. *Florida FL Reporter, 7*(1), 131-132, 164.

Discusses the Allen project which encourages Navajo students to write about themselves and their culture in English as a way of empowering themselves linguistically.
Amer-Indian.

2512. Powell, J., & Vilagra, O. (1991, March). *ESL academic writing: A visual process.* Paper presented at the 25th Annual TESOL Convention, New York, NY.

Presents instructional techniques for teaching composition to ESL students in an academic setting.
Academic Writing/Instruction.

2513. Powell, J., & Vilagra, O. (1990, March). *TESOL: Picture writing (from basic literacy to academic writing).* Paper presented at the 24th Annual TESOL Convention, San Francisco, CA.

Describes a project which involves the use of a story-board and a vocabulary list to help ESL adult learners. States the learning objectives, teaching procedures, and the results of previous classroom applications.
Adult Education.

2514. Powell, W. W. (1980). ESL and composition: A report. *TESOL Newsletter, 14*(3), 15-16.

Summarizes papers on writing presented at a regional NAFSA conference devoted to professionalism in international education.
Review.

2515. Powers, J. K. (1993a, April). *Helping the graduate thesis writer through faculty and writing center collaboration.* Paper presented at the 44th Annual Meeting of the Conference on College Composition and Communication, San Diego, CA. [ERIC ED 358 466].

Develops a trialogue model of collaboration between faculty advisors, writing center staff, and ESL graduate students who need assistance with theses and research writing.
Graduate Students/Writing Center/Collaboration.

2516. Powers, J. K. (1993b). Rethinking writing center conferencing strategies for the ESL writer. *Writing Center Journal, 13*(2), 39-47.

Suggests adapting collaborative conferencing strategies, including a need for intervention, as a solution to problems ESL writers pose for NES tutors in writing centers.
Conferencing/Writing Center.

2517. Powers, J. K. (1993c, April). *The role of the writing center in ESP/EAP.* Paper presented at the 27th Annual TESOL Convention, Atlanta, GA.

Summarizes data survey on the role of university writing centers in preparing ESL writers for academic writing.

Writing Center.

2518. Praninskas, J. (1965). Controlled writing. In V. F. Allen (Ed.), *On Teaching English to Speakers of Other Languages: Papers read at the TESOL Conference, Tucson, AZ, May 8-9, 1964. Series I.* (pp. 146-148). Champaign, IL: NCTE.

Describes controlled writing as one way to teach students "not particularly interested in learning to write, and those who are convinced that they can't".

Control.

2519. Prater, D. L. (1988, April). *Using writing activities to enhance comprehension and retention of content area reading in ESL students.* Paper presented to the Annual AERA Meeting, New Orleans, LA.

Reading-Writing Relations.

2520. Preston, W. (1982). Poetry ideas in teaching literature and writing to foreign students. *TESOL Quarterly, 16,* 489-502.

Presents an adaptation of two poetry ideas for teaching poetry writing to intermediate-level Thai secondary English teachers.

Creative Writing/Thai/Secondary School/Intermediate.

2521. Pretzer, W. L., & Karle, D. (1989, March). *Foreign teaching assistants as college composition teachers: Issues.* Paper presented at the 23rd Annual TESOL Convention, San Antonio, TX.

Reports results of nationwide survey of English departments.

Freshman Composition.

2522. Price, V. (1986, March). *ESL placement testing: Who and what do which tests test?* Paper presented at the 37th Annual CCCC Meeting, New Orleans, LA.

Assessment.

2523. Prince, E. (1993). *Write more! An intermediate writing text.* Boston: Heinle & Heinle.

Combines grammar principles, rhetorical modes, and writing mechanics with cross-cultural readings.

Textbook/Intermediate.

2524. Prince, E. (1991). *Write soon! A beginning text for ESL writers.* Boston: Heinle & Heinle.

A beginning text for adult as well as young adult ESL writers. Teaches the student how to print and write the English alphabet and offers practice in basic sentence structure. Prepares the student for the college and/or business environment by gradually increasing the level of difficulty of the writing tasks. Focuses on grammatical accuracy; the grammar rules are highlighted and set apart for easy reference. Also includes paragraphs and essays on various topics to serve as models.

Beginners/Secondary School/Adult Education/Textbook.

2525. Prior, P. A. (1993). Contextualizing writing and response in graduate seminars: A sociohistoric perspective on academic literacies. *Dissertation Abstracts International, 53*(7), 2281A.

An ethnographic study of four graduate seminars (Sociology, Geography, American Studies, and Agricultural Economics) seeks to understand how academic writing aand response is cued, produced, and responded to in context and over time. Presents a comparison of how the topical content of talk and text in the four seminars reflected participants' multiple contexts and histories. In depth case analyses are also given of (a) how oral response influenced revision of a dissertation prospectus, and (b) a student's conference paper across multiple episodes of written response and revision.
Graduate Students/Ethnographic Research/Academic Writing.

2526. Prior, P. A. (1992, March). *Redefining task: Academic writing in six graduate courses*. Paper presented at the 26th Annual TESOL Convention, Vancouver, BC.

Reports an ethnographic study of NES and ESL students writing in five disciplines. Results suggest that understanding an academic writing task requires examination of how task is cued, produced, and responded to in context and over time. The relationship between classroom context, student writing, and professor response are complexly intertwined.
Task/NS-NNS Comparisons.

2527. Prochnow, S. B. (1989, March). *Developing rhetorical descriptors of ESL writing assessment*. Paper presented at the 23rd Annual TESOL Convention, San Antonio, TX.

Develops rhetorical descriptors to complement a linguistically-centered essay rating scale.
Assessment/Scoring.

2528. Prochnow, S. B., & Hamp-Lyons, L. (1990, March). *Assessing writing: Holistic plus, more for your money*. Paper presented at the 24th Annual TESOL Convention, San Francisco, CA.

Presents a new coding system for the MELAB composition test, which reports raters' judgments that certain features of a particular composition are strikingly different from its overall level of writing quality. The paper discusses coding frequency, reader reliability, and the results of a user survey.
Assessment/Scoring.

2529. Proctor, S., & Arndt, V. (1992, March). *Team writing: It's a natural for peer feedback*. Paper presented at the 26th Annual TESOL Convention, Vancouver, BC.

Reports that peer feedback is considered more helpful and valued when two or more students work together to produce one paper.
Collaboration/Peer Response.

2530. Prodromou, L. P. (1989). All coherence gone: Literature and EFL. In *A Forum anthology, Volume IV: Selected articles from the English Teaching Forum, 1984-1988* (pp. 229-235). Washington, DC: USIA, Bureau of Educational and Cultural Affairs.

Gives two lesson plans related to teaching literature as a variety of English and how to talk and write about it.
Cohesion/Literature.

2531. Pruna, R. G. (1959). English composition practice in Cuba. *Language Learning, 9*, 67-70.

Describes a college writing course in Cuba in which literacy was promoted by frequent practice writing the paraphrase, precis, and paragraph as well as sentences.

Hispanic/Courses/University.

2532. Pryzant, P., & Picus, M. (1984, March). *From deference to detachment: American rhetorical styles for Asian students*. Paper presented at the 18th Annual TESOL Convention, Houston, TX.

Notes extreme patterns of deference and involvement in rhetorical styles of Indo-Chinese students in advanced composition courses.

Asian/Style.

2533. Purves, A. C. (1992). Reflections on research and assessment in written composition. *Research in the Teaching of English, 26*(1), 108-122.

Discusses the IEA study of native composition in fourteen countries. Reports project failed to achieve comparability because (1) writing on a few tasks cannot represent writing ability, (2) one shot drafting session is insufficient, and (3) rater judgments are subjective. As a consequence, claims most assessments only measure PDQ (Perceived Drafting Quality).

Assessment/IEA.

2534. Purves, A. C. (1991, April). *Levels and patterns of performance in written compositions in 14 systems of education*. Paper presented at the Annual Meeting of the AERA, Chicago, IL.

Assessment.

2535. Purves, A. C. (1988a). Introduction. In A. C. Purves (Ed.), *Writing across languages and cultures: Issues in contrastive rhetoric* (pp. 9-21). Newbury Park, CA: Sage.

Provides a brief introduction to a volume of cross-cultural studies and examines the theoretical and methodological issues involved in contrastive rhetoric research.

Contrastive Rhetoric/Culture.

2536. Purves, A. C. (Ed.). (1988b). *Writing across languages and cultures: Issues in contrastive rhetoric* Newbury Park, CA: Sage.

A collection of eleven essays that treat the impact of culture on writing in a foreign language. Volume includes theoretical considerations, differences in national writing styles, rhetorical transfer, and contrastive rhetoric.

Contrastive Rhetoric/Culture.

2537. Purves, A. C. (1986). Rhetorical communities, the international student, and basic writing. *Journal of Basic Writing, 5*(1), 38-51.

Reports the results of a case study of an Arabic-speaking international student who gradually learned to write academic essays. States that different cultures have many rhetorical and interpretative communities.

Arabic/University/Academic Writing.

2538. Purves, A. C. (1984). In search of an internationally-valid scheme for scoring compositions. *College Composition and Communication, 35*, 426-438.

Develops a scoring scheme of eight features on a particular topic to evaluate writing in international settings. Claims, however, that such a scheme is limited and

must take into account cross-cultural differences of writer and reader.
Evaluation/IEA.

Q

2539. Qoqandi, A. M. Y. (1984). Measuring the level of syntactical growth of Saudi twelfth graders in EFL writing using T-unit analysis. *Dissertation Abstracts International, 46*(4), 916A.

Finds that mode of writing (expository vs. letter writing) rather than type of program (science vs. humanities) has a significant impact on Arab EFL students' written syntactic development.
T-Unit/Arabic/Secondary School.

R

2540. Rabideau, D. (1993). *Integrating reading and writing into adult ESL instruction.* Washington, DC: ERIC/NCLE. [ERIC ED 358 749].

An ERIC Digest describes some major practices in teaching reading and writing to adult ESL students. These include whole language techniques in reading and writing instruction that provides practice, permits experimentation, and allows learners to set goals.
Reading-Writing Relations/Adult Education.

2541. Rabura, T. G. (1991). *Dialogue journal writing with elementary school students learning English as their second language.* Unpublished master's thesis, Central Washington University, Ellensburg, WA.
Dialogue Journals/Elementary.

2542. Radecki, P. M., & Swales, J. M. (1988). ESL student reaction to written comments on their written work. *System, 16,* 355-365.

Finds the attitudes of ESL students at a major university toward feedback is mixed. Responses to a survey were categorized 46% as receptors, 41% semi-resisters, and 13% resisters. Follow-up interviews suggested that the more students progress from being English language learners to apprentices in their disciplines, the more restricted is the role assigned to the language teacher.
Feedback.

2543. Radell, R. (1983, March). *Integrating conversation and composition: Techniques for emphasizing the composing process.* Paper presented at the 17th Annual TESOL Convention, Toronto, Ontario.
Meaningful dialogue accomplishes pre-writing objectives.
Invention/Speaking-Writing Relations.

2544. Radford, W. L. (1969). The blackboard composition. *English Language Teaching, 24*(1), 49-54.

On a chosen topic, a class offers one sentence at a time to the teacher who records the emerging composition or story on the blackboard.
Paragraph/Secondary School.

2545. Ragan, P. H. (1989). Applying functional grammar to teaching the writing of ESL.

WORD: Journal of the International Linguistic Association, 40(1-2), 117-124.

Discusses classroom methodology that employs the systemic linguistic perspective of Halliday to teach writing more effectively to university nonnative speakers of English. Concludes that ESL students can more profitably analyze text that they have produced during task-oriented, conceptualized language-related activities. Also claims that classroom interaction is facilitated by a systemic perspective.

Text Analysis/University.

2546. Rahman, M. A. (1990). Some effects of computers on ESL writing. *Dissertation Abstracts International, 51*(8), 2719A.

Examines whether international ESL students in an intensive program improve their writing skills when they use word processing on four writing assignments. A repeated measures design determined that there was no significant difference in the errors or revisions made between essays produced on computers and those produced by typewriter or pen. Concludes that computers neither improve nor adversely affect the writing of ESL students.

Computers/Word Processing.

2547. Railey, K., Devine, J., & Boshoff, P. P. (1992, March). *Implications of cognitive models in L1 and L2 writing*. Paper presented at the 43th Annual CCCC Meeting, Cincinnati, OH. [ERIC ED 346 455].

Investigates student knowledge of cognition in first and second language writing. Results indicate that all writers have metacognitive models, clustering around (a) grammar and correctness, (b) communications/audience sensitivity, and (c) personal voice/expressiveness as well as either a single focus or a complex focus template for composing.

Metacognition.

2548. Raimes, A. (1993). The author responds to Canagarajah . . .[In The Forum]. *TESOL Quarterly, 27*, 306-310.

Defends the pluralism of her approach to ESL writing, that is, advocating balanced interest in form, content, writer, and reader, as both accurately reflecting the field and serving the interests of adult students who formulate their own values and political views.

Instruction.

2549. Raimes, A. (1992a). The author responds to Connor . . .[In The Forum]. *TESOL Quarterly, 26*, 179-180.

Suggests that ETS is now but has not always been open to criticism of its tests.

TWE.

2550. Raimes, A. (1992b). The author responds to Traugott, Dunkel, and Carrell . . .[In The Forum]. *TESOL Quarterly, 26*, 186-190.

Offers further commentary on who, what, and how research is conducted on the TWE, advocating more independent research that examines the effectiveness of TWE and more open discussion of research results.

Assessment/TWE.

2551. Raimes, A. (1992c). *Exploring through writing: A process approach to ESL composition*. (Second Ed.). NY: St. Martin's Press.

    A college composition text for intermediate to advanced learners has three parts: processes, grammar troublespots, and materials (i.e. pictures and readings on five subject areas).

    University/Textbook.

2552. Raimes, A. (1992d). *Grammar troublespots: An editing guide for ESL students*. (Second Ed.). NY: St. Martin's Press.

    Provides a brief guide to grammatical areas which are most troublesome to ESL students. Twenty-one troublespots are presented with self-diagnostic flow charts, explanations, and exercises to help students learn to edit.

    University/Editing/Textbook.

2553. Raimes, A. (1992e). Instructional balance: From theories to practices in teaching writing. In J. E. Alatis (Ed.), *Georgetown University Round Table on Languages and Linguistics 1991* (pp. 223-238). Washington, DC: Georgetown University Press.

    Characterizes the current state of affairs in L2 composition as more controversy than commonality between balanced and unbalanced stances. Describes approaches through form, writer, content, and audience and their corruptions.

    Instruction/Approaches.

2554. Raimes, A. (1992f, March). *In the writing classroom: Evaluation*. Paper presented at the 26th Annual TESOL Convention, Vancouver, BC.

    Discusses the lack of objective criteria or consensus about good writing. Explores how the use of portfolios and of holistic assessment tend to flatten out subjective elements.

    Evaluation/Portfolios.

2555. Raimes, A. (1991a). Errors: Windows into the mind. *College ESL*, *1*(2), 55-64.

    Suggests strategies that encourage students to recognize and repair their errors.

    Errors/Feedback.

2556. Raimes, A. (1991b). Out of the woods: Emerging traditions in the teaching of writing. *TESOL Quarterly*, *25*, 407-430.

    Finds that the search for a new approach during the last twenty-five years has led to successive focuses on the writer and the writing processes, on academic content, and on the reader's expectations. Five difficult issues and emerging traditions are noted.

    Instruction.

2557. Raimes, A. (1990a). *How English works: A grammar handbook with readings*. NY: St. Martin's Press.

    Offers grammatical instruction based on published readings which are glossed and from which examples and exercises are drawn. Readings include selections from non-fictional essays dealing with various content. Focused writing tasks elicit structure and authentic student writing is available for editing practice.

    Grammar/Textbook.

2558. Raimes, A. (1990b). The TOEFL test of written English: Causes for concern. *TESOL*

Quarterly, 24, 427-442.

Expresses several concerns about ETS's Test of Written English, including the lack of topic choice, the comparability of topic types, the lack of distinction between graduate and undergraduate students, the scoring system, the question of what the test measures, the question of the necessity of two tests and the backwash effect of the TWE.

Assessment/TWE.

2559. Raimes, A. (1988a). On filters, hinges, and windows. In L. Z. Smith (Ed.), *Audits of meaning: A festschrift in honor of Ann E. Berthoff* (pp. 169-181). Portsmouth, NH: Boynton/Cook.

Addresses native writing teachers who need to know about ESL writers. Discusses how ESL students learn, how their cultural and rhetorical knowledge contributes to their writing, and how their errors reveal their strategies for learning and composing.

NS-NNS Comparisons.

2560. Raimes, A. (1988b, March). *Responding to students' written errors: Looking at cases*. Paper presented at the 22nd Annual TESOL Convention, Chicago, IL.

Surveys current research on teacher response and examines examples of student explanations of their errors.

Responding

2561. Raimes, A. (1988c). The texts for teaching writing. In B. K. Das (Ed.), *Materials for language learning and teaching* (pp. 41-58). Singapore: SEAMEO RELC.

Criticizes most ESL writing textbooks as insensitive to current theory in either content or instructional approach. Suggests that the real focus of writing instruction should be on primary, that is authentic, student and teacher, texts.

Textbook/Materials.

2562. Raimes, A. (1988d, March). *Windows into the mind: Working with ESL students' errors*. Paper presented at the 39th Annual CCCC Meeting, St. Louis, MO.

See Raimes, 1991a.

Errors/Feedback.

2563. Raimes, A. (1987a). Language proficiency, writing ability, and composing strategies: A study of ESL college student writers. *Language Learning, 37*, 439-468.

Think-aloud protocols show similarities between composing strategies of L2 and basic L1 writers. However, L2 writers are more willing to correct their writing and engage in interaction with the emerging texts yet these composing strategies show little correspondence with either writing ability or language proficiency.

NS-NNS Comparisons/Strategies.

2564. Raimes, A. (1987b). Why write? From purpose to pedagogy. *English Teaching Forum, 25*(4), 36-41.

Reviews why teachers ask students to write and states they ask them to write for reinforcement, training, imitation, communication, fluency, and learning.

Instruction.

2565. Raimes, A. (1987c, April). *Why write? Perspectives on purpose and pedagogy*. Paper presented at the 21st Annual TESOL Convention, Miami Beach, FL.

Examines six pedagogical purposes for writing, finding writing to learn to be comprehensive enough to include all purposes and types of writing.
Instruction.

2566. Raimes, A. (1986a). Teaching ESL writing: Fitting what we do to what we know. *Writing Instructor*, *5*, 153-166.
Advises teachers to make their own syntheses between process and product, after examining the contradictory advice of current research on the one hand and ESL writing textbooks on the other.
Materials.

2567. Raimes, A. (1986b, March). *Teaching ESL composition: What we know and what we do*. Paper presented at the 37th Annual CCCC Meeting, New Orleans, LA.
See previous item.
Review/Textbook.

2568. Raimes, A. (1985a, March). *An investigation of the composing processes of ESL remedial and non-remedial students*. Paper presented at the 36th Annual CCCC Meeting, Mineapolis, MN.
See next item.
Process Research.

2569. Raimes, A. (1985b, April). *An investigation of how ESL students write*. Paper presented at the 19th Annual TESOL Convention, New York, NY. [ED 271 965].
Examines the writing processes in English of non-native speakers with different linguistic backgrounds. Concludes that some common patterns emerge when using think-aloud protocols, proficiency tests, and interviews.
Process Research.

2570. Raimes, A. (1985c). What unskilled ESL writers do as they write: A classroom study of composing. *TESOL Quarterly*, *19*, 229-258.
Studies the composing processes of eight unskilled ESL writers in a university setting. This study gathers data by using a questionnaire, a standardized proficiency test, holistic scores on essays, and spoken protocols. The findings suggest that even though there are similarities among writers there are too many differences to generalize about the group.
Process Research/University.

2571. Raimes, A. (Ed.). (1984c). *TESOL Newsletter (Supplement No. 1): Writing and Composition*, *18*(1), 1-16.
Special issue provides nine pedagogical articles on ESL writing/composition, plus brief tips for ESL writing teachers.
Instruction.

2572. Raimes, A. (1984d, March). *Two studies of the composing process in a second language and the implications for teaching*. Paper presented at the 35th Annual CCCC Meeting, New York, NY.
Process Research.

2573. Raimes, A. (1983a). Anguish as a second language? Remedies for composition teachers. In A. Freedman, I. Pringle, & J. Yalden (Eds.), *Learning to write: First language, second language* (pp. 258-272). NY: Longman.

Claims that for many ESL students writing causes anguish since it is regarded by many teachers only as a mechanical task of writing correctly. Suggests as a remedy assignments that involve thinking and concentrate on making meaning.
Anxiety.

2574. Raimes, A. (1983b). *Techniques in teaching writing.* Oxford: Oxford University Press.
Focuses on techniques, such as using pictures, reading material, all language skills, practical writing tasks, copnmtrolled writing, organization, and ways of responding to student writing.
Classroom Activities/Responding/Teacher Preparation

2575. Raimes, A. (1983c). Tradition and revolution in ESL teaching. *TESOL Quarterly, 17,* 535-552.
Suggests that ESL teaching is in the middle of a paradigm shift. Discusses view of those challenging traditional areas and highlights possibilities for future research.
Theory.

2576. Raimes, A. (1981a, March). *Critical issues in retraining faculty to teach composition.* Paper presented at the 32nd Annual CCCC Meeting, Dallas, TX.
Teacher Preparation.

2577. Raimes, A. (1981b, March). *Topics for composition: Purpose, audience, and process.* Paper presented at the 15th Annual TESOL Convention, Detroit, MI.
Workshop considers how, why, and for whom topics are written.
Topic.

2578. Raimes, A. (1980, March). *Breaking the barrier of the sentence.* Paper presented at the 31st Annual CCCC Meeting, Washington, DC.

2579. Raimes, A. (1979a, March). *A grammar for composition: The grammar of coherence.* Paper presented at the 13th Annual TESOL Convention, Boston.
Discusses lexical and syntactic devices useful in written discourse and suggests classroom activities to help implement discourse elements.
Style.

2580. Raimes, A. (1979b, April). *A faculty's response to teaching writing in the subject areas.* Paper presented at the 30th Annual CCCC Meeting, Minneapolis, MN.
Content.

2581. Raimes, A. (1978a). *Focus on composition.* NY: Oxford University Press.
Textbook for intermediate learners combines syntactic and rhetorical foci in each lesson with content from art, culture, journalism, and literature.
Intermediate/Textbook.

2582. Raimes, A. (1978b). *Problems and teaching strategies in ESL composition (If Johnny has problems, what about Juan, Jean and Ywe-Han?)* Language in Education, Theory and Practice No. 14Englewood Cliffs, NJ: Prentice-Hall. [ERIC ED 175 243].
Discusses similarities and differences between teaching composition to native English speakers and ESL students. Discusses the problems language learners encounter when they write.

NS-NNS Comparisons.
2583. Raimes, A. (1976a). Composition: Controlled by the teacher, free for the student. In J. F. Fanselow, & M. Hines (Ed.), *On TESOL '76* (pp. 183-194). Washington, DC: TESOL.

Claims that the division between and sequencing of controlled and free composition in intermediate-advanced ESL writing classes is not productive. Suggests allowing students to write freely in a controlled situation.
Control/Fluency.

2584. Raimes, A. (1976b, March). *Not control vs. freedom but control with freedom: A model for ESL composition instruction.* Paper presented at the 10th Annual TESOL Convention, New York, NY.

Workshop suggests a three-level approach to teaching compositon: (1) free composition tasks stimulated by art, literature, science, and culture, (2) back-up practice with focused attention to syntactic structures, (3) follow-up free compositions.
Methods/Control.

2585. Raimes, A. (1975, December). *The ESL student in freshman composition.* Paper presented at the Annual Modern Languages Association Meeting, San Francisco, CA.

University.

2586. Raimes, A., Persky, C., & Sayre, J. (1982, March). *Getting them to do it: The politics, procedures, and problems of faculty involvement in writing across the curriculum.* Paper presented at the 33rd Annual CCCC Meeting, San Francisco, CA.
WAC/Politics.

2587. Raimes, A., Zamel, V., Brookes, G., Gaskill, W. H., Jacobs, S. E., Reid, J. M., Widdowson, H. G., Taylor, B. P., & White, R. V. (1985, March). *Key questions about writing.* Colloquium at the 19th Annual TESOL Convention, New York, NY.

Participants discuss ways to reconcile process-oriented teaching and academic demands, applying process at various levels, and responding to student writing.
Process Instruction/Academic Writing.

2588. Raimes, A., Zamel, V., Brookes, G., Land, R. E., Taylor, B. P., & White, R. V. (1992, March). *In the writing classroom: An interactive colloquium.* Colloquium presented at the 26th Annual TESOL Convention, Vancouver, BC.

Annual colloquium discusses the nature of academic writing, effects of institutional constraints, faculty relations, and the teaching of writing to beginners.
Instruction/Research.

2589. Raimes, A., Zamel, V., Brookes, G., Land, R. E., Spack, R., Taylor, B. P., & White, R. V. (1993, April). *Key questions about writing: An interactive colloquium.* Paper presented at the 27th Annual TESOL Convention, Atlanta, GA.

Distinguished panelists respond to key questions about composition.
Process Instruction.

2590. Rainey, K. (1990). Teaching technical writing to non-native speakers. *Technical Writing Teacher, 17*(2), 131-135.

Describes four techniques found to be effective in teaching technical writing

to nonnative speakers.
Technical Writing.

2591. Rainsbury, R. (1978). Teaching composition at the beginning level: A promising approach. In R. L. Light, & A. H. Osman (Eds.), *Collected papers in teaching English as a second language and bilingual education* (pp. 69-75). New York: Teachers College, Columbia University.

Describes a set of lessons that introduce a beginning ESL class to writing in English. The students who were young adults received 12 hours of instruction in grammar per week. The use of grammar-oriented materials is defended by explaining that grammar patterns must be mastered by non-native speakers of English.
Beginners/Materials/Grammar.

2592. Rainsbury, R. (1977). *Written English: An introduction for beginning students of English as a second language.* Englewood Cliffs, NJ: Prentice-Hall.

Intensive practice for beginners with the mechanics of written English -- spelling and punctuation -- and sentence-combining and clause-making.
Beginners/Textbook.

2593. Ramaglia, J. (1988, April). *Writing (ESL) in accounting.* Paper presented at the Eastern Michigan University Conference on Languages for Business and the Professions, Ann Arbor, MI. [ERIC ED 304 905].

Describes a technique for assisting students in accounting while improving writing ability.
Business Writing.

2594. Ramani, E. (1990, March). *Draft to draft: Teaching the scientific research paper.* Paper presented at the 24th Annual TESOL Convention, San Francisco, CA.

Describes a research writing course based on successive drafts of an important paper by a leading Indian scientist. Students use these drafts to recover and refine their own tacit knowledge of public scientific discourse and produce through peer interview and reformulation procedures, their own drafts of research papers.
Research Writing/Scientific Writing.

2595. Ramsey, R. D. (1983, March). *Teaching native and non-native speakers together in professional communication courses.* Paper presented at the 17th Annual TESOL Convention, Toronto, Ontario.

Discusses strategies and techniques for teaching mixed populations in business communication and technical writing courses.
Technical Writing/Business Writing.

2596. Rankin, D. S. (1984). Comments on Patricia Carrell's "Cohesion is not coherence" -- a reader reacts . . . [In The Forum]. *TESOL Quarterly, 18,* 158-161.

Defends Halliday and Hasan's theory of cohesion (1976) by demonstrating the deficiency of ESL materials lacking cohesiveness. Suggests that textual emphasis helps ESL students.
Cohesion.

2597. Raphael, C. B. (1983). *Rhetorical reader for ESL writers.* Boston: Heinle & Heinle.

A cross-disciplinary collection of unabridged essays arranged by rhetorical mode with activities designed to extend vocabulary and develop reading

comprehension.
University/Textbook.

2598. Rapp, L. C. (1988, March). *Proofreading skills and writing proficiency: Error detection, editing accuracy, and linguistic competence.* Paper presented at the 22nd TESOL Conference, Chicago, IL. [ERIC ED 307 802].

More proficient ESL writers are better at detecting errors than treating them accurately.
Error Treatment/Editing.

2599. Ray, B. M., & Jiang, W. (1993, April). *Should students use bilingual dictionaries in process writing?* Paper presented at the 27th Annual TESOL Convention, Atlanta, GA.

Examines writing problems among East Asian students (Chinese, Japanese, Korean) traceable to student dependency on bilingual dictionaries.
Asian/Dictionaries.

2600. Ray, R. E. (1989). World view and academic discourse: An analysis of ESL writing. In P. Downing, S. Lima, & M. Noonan (Eds.), *Milwaukee Studies on Language. Selected papers from the 17th annual University of Wisconsin Milwaukee linguistics symposium: Literacy and linguistics* Vol. 3, (pp. 27-33).

Radially dissimilar "structures of expectation" (Tannen, 1979) explain why forty Arab ESL students failed a writing proficiency exam given by the English Department at a midwestern university. An analysis of their essays reveals that Arab writers neither directly address the topic nor give an appropriate academic response to the topic, two key aspects noted by exam readers as part of the world view valued in the humanities.
Arabic/Academic Writing/Discourse Communities.

2601. Ray, R. E. (1987). Academic literacy and nonnative writers. *Dissertation Abstracts International*, 48(11), 2852A.

On the basis of a textual analysis of writing exams and a four-year case study of Arab ESL students, proposes a cultural explanation of difficulties that non-native writers have meeting academic literacy standards, such as inability to pass proficiency exams and meeting English Department expectations.
Standards/Culture/Arabic.

2602. Rayburn, K. R. (1989, March). *Contrastive rhetoric: Using Kaplan in the classroom.* Paper presented at the 23rd Annual TESOL Convention, San Antonio, TX.

Gives a demonstration for diagnosing contrastive rhetoric (CR) and involving students in CR in the classroom.
Contrastive Rhetoric.

2603. Raymond, R. (1993). Monitoring and grammatical morpheme accuracy in the English composition of Japanese university students. *Dissertation Abstracts International*, 53(9), 3193A.

An investigation of the cognitive strategy of monitoring grammatical form finds that less-error-prone (LEP) students monitor grammatical form in a different way than more-error prone (MEP) students writing EFL compositions. Furthermore, training in focus-on-grammatical form improved the performance of all MEPs but not for all LEPs.

Japanese/Monitoring/Error Treatment.

2604. Read, J. (1991). The validity of writing test tasks. In S. Anivan (Eds.), *Current developments in language testing*

Argues that the influence of prior knowledge should be considered in constructing writing tests. Suggests three types of ESL test writing situations depend on the degree of prior knowledge permitted: independent task (i.e., topic given without preparation or support), guided task (i.e., content support provided), and experience task (providing content and skills before writing).

Task/Background Knowledge.

2605. Read, J. (1990). Providing relevant content in an EAP writing test. *English for Specific Purposes*, 9, 109-121.

Considers how best to elicit samples of writing for assessment in an EAP proficiency test: using guided and experience tasks were superior to independent ones.

Academic Writing/Assessment/Task.

2606. Read, J. (1989, March). *Providing background knowledge in an EAP writing test*. Paper presented at the 23rd Annual TESOL Convention, San Antonio, TX.

Describes development of an EAP writing test that controls for background knowledge by providing relevant knowledge about each topic before the task is undertaken.

Assessment/Topic.

2607. Reeder, N. J., & Flanagan, K. (1992, March). *Summing it up: Teaching preacademic summary and paraphrase*. Paper presented at the 26th Annual TESOL Convention, Vancouver, BC.

Presents a model of how to teach summary and paraphrase writing to university-bound students.

Summary Writing.

2608. Regent, O. (1985). A comparative approach to the learning of specialized written discourse. In P. Riley (Ed.), *Discourse and learning* (pp. 105-120). NY: Longman.

Shows how scientific English discourse is not constructed in the same way as scientific French discourse.

ESP/Contrastive Rhetoric/French.

2609. Reid, F. C., & Kirkland, M. R. (1983, March). *Reading for writing: The utilization of some material*. Paper presented at the 17th Annual TESOL Convention, Toronto, Ontario.

Suggests a series of tasks for the high intermediate and advanced ESL levels that gradually lead students from re-expression of an author's material to incorporation of such materials in their own writing.

Task/Reading-Writing Relations.

2610. Reid, J. M. (1993a). Historical perspectives on writing and reading in the composition classroom. In J. G. Carson, & I. Leki (Eds.), *Reading in the composition classroom: Second language perspectives* (pp. 33-60). Boston: Heinle & Heinle.

Traces the historical use of reading in the ESL writing classroom. Discusses

typical practices and their theoretical assumptions and changes in reading and writing paradigms with their pedagogical implications.
   Reading-Writing Relations.
2611. Reid, J. M. (1993b). *Teaching ESL composition.* Englewood Cliffs, NJ: Prentice-Hall.

   A comprehensive guide for students training to become ESL writing teachers. It provides historical and theoretical information as a foundation for the discussion of a full range of curricular and pedagogic issues in basic, intermediate, and advanced ESL writing courses.
   Teacher Preparation.
2612. Reid, J. M. (1993c, April). *Multiple audiences for ESL writers.* Paper presented at 44th Annual CCCC Meeting, San Diego, CA.
   Audience.
2613. Reid, J. M. (1993d, April). *Reading in an ESL classroom.* Paper presented at the 27th Annual TESOL Convention, Atlanta, GA.
   Workshop describes how reading is currently used in composition classrooms, underlying assumptions, classroom practices as well as examples of exercises and activities.
   Reading-Writing Relations.
2614. Reid, J. M. (1992a). A computer text-analysis of four cohesive devices in English discourse by native and nonnative writers. *Journal of Second Language Writing,* 1(2), 79-107.
   Using the Writer's Workbench, finds frequent cooccurrence of four cohesive devices in 768 essays (two tasks) written in English by native speakers of Arabic, Chinese, Spanish, and English.
   Cohesion/NS-NNS Comparisons.
2615. Reid, J. M. (1992b). The reading-writing connection in the ESL composition classroom. *Journal of Intensive English Studies,* 6, 27-51.
   Discusses models of reading in the writing classroom and reports an exploratory action research study of an advanced ESL composition class.
   Reading-Writing Relations.
2616. Reid, J. M. (1992c, March). *Collaborative learning and the ESL writing tutorial.* Paper presented at the 26th Annual TESOL Convention, Vancouver, BC.
   Collaboration.
2617. Reid, J. M. (1992d, April). *The ESL writer: Developing a sense of audience.* Paper presented at the 43rd Annual CCCC Meeting, New York, NY.
   Describes the lack of knowledge most ESL students have about the academic audience for whom they must write and suggests ways of informing them about that audience.
   Academic Writing/Audience.
2618. Reid, J. M. (1990a). *Multiple audiences for ESL writers: The peer editor program.* Paper presented at the Wyoming Conference on English, Laramie, WY.
   Presents how to start and implement a peer editing program matching native speakers with ESL students. Suggests the importance and value of multiple audiences

in writing.
Collaboration/Peer Response.

2619. Reid, J. M. (1990b). Responding to different topic types: A quantitative analysis from a contrastive rhetoric perspective. In B. Kroll (Ed.), *Second language writing: Research insights for the classroom* (pp. 191-210). Cambridge: Cambridge University Press.

Author uses discourse analysis to identify the quantitative differences in the syntax and lexicon of 768 responses to four writing assessment tasks. Students with Arabic, Chinese, English, and Spanish language backgrounds differed.
Topic/Contrastive Rhetoric.

2620. Reid, J. M. (1990c, March). *Composition in the computer classroom: A descriptive study*. Paper presented at the 24th Annual TESOL Convention, San Francisco, CA.

Describes experiences of teachers and students during the first year of a computer classroom; suggestions for designing such a classroom as well as planning for the differences in the pedagogical situation.
Computers/Instruction.

2621. Reid, J. M. (1990d, May). *An update on the Test of Written English*. Paper presented at the National NAFSA Conference, Portland, OR.

Presents the latest research on the Test of Written English and responds to controversy surrounding the test.
TWE/Evaluation.

2622. Reid, J. M. (1989a). English as a second language composition in higher education: The expectations of the academic audience. In D. M. Johnson, & D. H. Roen (Eds.), *Richness in writing: Empowering ESL students* (pp. 220-234). NY: Longman.

Claims that many advanced ESL students are not aware of academic conventions in writing. Suggests that teachers make students aware of expectations and use contrastive rhetoric to help students see differences between writing in their native languages and in English. Presents exercises to help demystify the experience and guide students towards writing for an academic audience.
Contrastive Rhetoric/Audience/Academic Writing.

2623. Reid, J. M. (1989b). Quantitative differences in English prose by Arabic, Chinese, Spanish and English writers. *Dissertation Abstracts International, 50*(3), 672A.

Examines 768 essays by four language background groups in order to see if their products reflect distinct discourse patterns valued in those cultures. A computer-text analysis program (Writer's Workbench) analyzed fourteen variables in the essays on four prompts. Finds many significant differences for different language backgrounds.
Hispanic/Arabic/Chinese/Contrastive Rhetoric.

2624. Reid, J. M. (1989c, March). *Demystifying teaching: Writing rituals and post-mortems*. Paper presented at the 40th Annual CCCC Meeting, Seattle, WA.

Discusses ways to make writing clear and worthwhile for students. Includes metacognitive exercises to help students discover what they are learning.
Instruction/Metacognition.

2625. Reid, J. M. (1989d, March). *The ESL teacher as cultural informant*. Paper presented at the 40th Annual CCCC Meeting, Seattle, WA.

States that the ESL teacher must be cognizant of and able to teach the demands of academic writing. Suggests that teachers research academic writing tasks, audience expectations, and task demands in order to inform their students of the needs of the U.S. academic audience.

Academic Writing/Task.

2626. Reid, J. M. (1989e, March). *The ESL writing teacher as change agent.* Paper presented at the 23rd Annual TESOL Convention, San Antonio, TX.

Discusses the role of the writing teacher as change faciliator and the need for student-teacher collaboration.

Collaboration.

2627. Reid, J. M. (1988). *The process of composition.* (Second Ed.). Englewood Cliffs, NJ: Prentice-Hall.

Textbook for advanced intensive language program students and/or remedial or community college sheltered ESL composition classes. Focuses on English for Academic Purposes in that it provides academic writing tasks and formats.

Textbook/University.

2628. Reid, J. M. (1987a). *Basic writing.* (Second Ed.). Englewood Cliffs, NJ: Prentice Hall.

Designed for students who are false beginners, whose knowledge of English is limited, or whose writing is more underdeveloped than other language skills. Text organized thematically around student experiences. Contains numerous opportunities to write through a variety of exercises.

Beginners/Textbook.

2629. Reid, J. M. (1987b). ESL composition: The expectations of the academic audience. *TESOL Newsletter, 21*(2), 34.

Discusses two considerations in writing, purpose and audience, stating that teachers are not trying to change the way students think, but only to change the way they present their ideas.

Contrastive Rhetoric.

2630. Reid, J. M. (1987c). The Writer's Workbench and ESL composition. *Computers and Composition, 4,* 53-63.

Describes how to adapt a computer program for ESL students and considers limitations as strength.

Curriculum/Computers.

2631. Reid, J. M. (1987d, March). *The new TOEFL writing examination.* Paper presented at the 38th Annual CCCC Meeting, Atlanta, GA.

Describes the research and development of the TOEFL Test of Written English, including preparation, pre-testing, scoring guide development, and the administration of the TWE.

TWE/Evaluation.

2632. Reid, J. M. (1987e, April). *Does ESL writing differ quantitatively?* Paper presented at the 21st Annual TESOL Convention, Miami Beach, FL.

Analyzes a large sample of essays with the Writer's Workbench for

quantifiable differences that correlate with language background, holistic evaluation, and topic types.
   Syntactic Structures/Style.

2633. Reid, J. M. (1987f, April). *Text-analysis program: Which ones work?* Paper presented at the 21st Annual TESOL Convention, Miami, FL.
   Description of 76 variables "counted" or responded to by the Writer's Workbench. Discussion of the responses and variables most and least helpful for ESL writing students.
   Computers/Text Analysis.

2634. Reid, J. M. (1986). Using the Writer's Workbench in ESL composition teaching and testing. In C. W. Stansfield (Ed.), *Technology and language testing* (pp. 167-188). Washington, DC: TESOL.
   Reports that college ESL writers who used Writer's Workbench significantly improved editing and writing skills compared to those who did not have access to it the text-analysis software. But a number of other variables not studied may have contributed to this outcome.
   Computers/Programs.

2635. Reid, J. M. (1985a). The author responds to Spack. . . [In The Forum]. *TESOL Quarterly*, *19*, 398-400.
   Defends teaching outlining as part of the invention process for pre-university ESL students.
   Invention.

2636. Reid, J. M. (1985b, April). *Computer text-analysis in ESL composition: A research report*. Paper presented at the 19th Annual TESOL Convention, New York, NY.
   Reports an investigation into the possibilities of using word processors and text analysis software (Writer's Workbench) with ESL students to determine (1) if international students can learn to use computer equipment; (2) if students feel time invested is worthwhile; and (3) if ESL students' problems with writing American academic prose can be remedied with this type of assistance.
   Computers/Text Analysis.

2637. Reid, J. M. (1985c). *Using the Writer's Workbench in ESL composition and teaching*. Paper presented at the 7th Annual Language Testing Research Colloquium, Princeton, NJ.
   Presentation of statistical analysis of a small corpus of ESL essays to demonstrate the strengths and weaknesses of the Writer's Workbench as a text-analyzer of ESL writing.
   Text Analysis/Computers.

2638. Reid, J. M. (1984a). Comments on Vivian Zamel's "The composing process of advanced ESL students: Six case studies" -- A reader reacts . . . [In The Forum]. *TESOL Quarterly*, *18*, 149-153.
   Claims that Zamel's study (1983) is limited since it is based on very advanced ESL students. Stresses the need for intensive English programs for students to achieve minimal proficiency in academic prose before advancing to the level Zamel describes.

Curriculum/Advanced.

2639. Reid, J. M. (1984b). ESL composition: The linear product of American thought. *College Composition and Communication, 35*, 449-452.

    Discusses problems in written communication due to cultural differences. Gives examples of different approaches to writing in Japan, Iran, USA, Middle East, and South America. Proposes ESL writing curriculum which prepares ESL students to write according to American reader's expectations.

    Curriculum/Culture.

2640. Reid, J. M. (1984c). The radical outliner and the radical brainstormer: A perspective on composing processes. *TESOL Quarterly, 18*, 529-534.

    States that there is no single composing process -- some students resort to pre-planning and making outlines and others resort to brainstorming.

    Invention.

2641. Reid, J. M. (1984d, May). *CAI in ESL composition: The Writer's Workbench system.* Paper presented at the Annual NAFSA Meeting, Snowmass, CO.

    Describes a computerized text analysis software and how it can apply to compositions.

    Computers.

2642. Reid, J. M. (1984e, May). *The ESL writer and the audience.* Paper presented at the Annual NAFSA Conference, Denver, CO.

    Workshop for public school teachers about ESL students, their problems, surprises, and solutions.

    Teacher Preparation/Audience.

2643. Reid, J. M. (1983, May). *ESL composition: Process and product.* Paper presented at the Annual NAFSA Meeting, Cincinnati, OH.

    An introduction to the controversy surrounding the process-product continuum. Recommends a balanced approach to the use of process and product in the ESL writing classroom.

    Process Instruction.

2644. Reid, J. M. (1982). Intermediate ESL composition: The use of specific detail and the point paragraph outline. *American Language Journal, 1*, 25-40. [ERIC ED 240 826].

    Presents a curriculum for intermediate composition for ESL students using levels of specificity as an organizing principle and provides sample exercises.

    Curriculum/Intermediate.

2645. Reid, J. M. (1981, March). *How to grade compositions "intuitively," reliably, and validly.* Paper presented at the 15th Annual TESOL Convention, Detroit, MI.

    Demonstrates a process of evaluation and ranking based on criteria of grammatical accuracy, organization, and content.

    Assessment.

2646. Reid, J. M., Kroll, B., Pennington, M. C., Jacobs, H. L., & Constantinides, J. C. (1982, May). *Issues and approaches in ESL composition.* Colloquium presented at the 16th Annual TESOL Convention, Honolulu, HI.

    Colloquium presents several viewpoints on major theoretical and practical issues of instruction.

Instruction.

2647. Reid, J. M., & Lindstrom, M. (1985). *The process of paragraph writing.* (Second Ed.). Englewood Cliffs, NJ: Prentice Hall Regents.

A handbook on the essentials of paragraph construction which includes authentic student writing examples for novice writers. Each chapter addresses basic thinking and ordering techniques for successful academic writing.

Intermediate/Textbook.

2648. Reid, J. M., & Lindstrom, M. (1984, March). *CAI in ESL composition: Using the Writer's Workbench with international students.* Paper presented at the 18th Annual TESOL Convention, Houston, TX.

Reports results from use of text-editing and text-analyzing software by small group of intermediate and advanced intensive English students.

Computers/Intermediate.

2649. Reid, J. M., Lindstrom, M., McCaffrey, M., & Larson, D. (1983). Computer-assisted text analysis for ESL students. *CALICO Journal, 1*(3), 40-42.

Found that ESL students in an intensive program could benefit from using word processors and text-editing software, despite the fact that the quality of their writing rated holistically did not improve significantly over a semester.

Curriculum/Computers.

2650. Reid, J. M., & O'Brien, M. (1984). The application of holistic grading in an ESL writing program. *The American Language Journal, 2*(1), 53-64.

Presents a holistic rubric and scoring sheet used in an intensive program to evaluate ESL writing.

Assessment/Holistic/IEP.

2651. Reid, J. M., & O'Brien, M. (1981, March). *The application of holistic grading in an ESL writing program.* Paper presented at the 15th Annual TESOL Convention, Detroit, MI. [ERIC ED 221 044].

Results confirm validity of holistic evaluation in assessing ESL writing.

Assessment/Holistic.

2652. Reid, J. M., & Powers, J. K. (1993). Extending the benefits of small-group collaboration to the ESL writer. *TESOL Journal, 2*(4), 25-32.

Describes university-level writing tutorials that offer experience with multiple audiences and building community as a way to solve writing problems.

Collaboration.

2653. Reid, J. M., & Strunk, V. L. (1984, March). *Audience expectation exercises for ESL writing classes.* Paper presented at the 18th Annual TESOL Convention, Houston, TX.

Offers several exercises to help ESL writers improve their decisions about reader expectations.

Audience/Exercises.

2654. Reitzel, A., & Behrens, C. (1993, April). *Dear pen pal: Letters for authentic communication and analysis.* Paper presented at the 27th Annual TESOL Convention, Atlanta, GA.

Describes a pen pal program between IEP students and TESL teacher

preparation students.
Letter Writing.

2655. Rentz, M. D. (1992). *The reader's journal: Authentic reading for writers*. Englewood Cliffs, NJ: Regents/Prentice Hall.

Includes a collection of reading selections chosen by students and varying in subject, length, and difficulty.
IEP/Textbook.

2656. Retten, S. (1992, March). *Evaluating student essays: Peer evaluation and self-assessment*. Paper presented at the 26th Annual TESOL Convention, Vancouver, BC.

Discusses how peer evaluation and self-assessment reduce the amount of paperwork confronting writing teachers.
Evaluation.

2657. Reynolds, E., & Mixdorf, M. (1990). *Confidence in writing: A basic text*. (Second Ed.). San Diego, CA: Harcourt, Brace Jovanovich.

Textbook presents a five-step procedure in each chapter to help novice writers learn to write with confidence. The procedure is to brainstorm, write a topic sentence, outline, draft, and revise. Chapters become successively more complex and academically oriented. The final chapters include supplementary readings for practice in summary writing and a handbook giving information about grammar and mechanics.
Beginners/Textbook.

2658. Reynolds, P. R. (1993). Evaluating ESL and college composition texts for teaching the argumentative rhetorical form. *Journal of Reading, 36*(6), 474-480.

Discusses criteria for evaluating ESL college textbooks that teach argumentation in the light of the possibility of contrastive rhetoric.
Argumentation/Materials.

2659. Reynoso, W. D. (1987, November). *Blacks, Hispanics, and Asians in the English classroom: A linguistic approach to a problem*. Paper presented at the 77th Annual NCTE Convention, Los Angeles, CA.
Hispanic/Asian.

2660. Rhynes, E. J. (1985). *Discovering the writer's voice: E.S.L. students and the writing process*. Unpublished master's thesis, University of Victoria, Victoria, BC.
Voice/Process Instruction.

2661. Rice Martha K., & Burns, J. U. (1986). *Thinking-writing: An introduction to the writing process for students of ESL*. Englewood Cliffs, NJ: Prentice Hall.

Gives logical steps for creating a paragraph. Uses the rhetorical forms of description, classification, function, process, comparison and contrast, example, and reason. Stresses the importance of thinking before writing in order to achieve unity and cohesion.
Intermediate/Textbook.

2662. Ricento, T. (1987a). Aspects of coherence in English and Japanese expository prose. *Dissertation Abstracts International, 48*(7), 1754A.

Compares coherence markers in English and Japanese expository texts and examines the degree to which native speakers access formal schemata in reordering scrambled paragraphs of these texts. Analysis of texts reveal cross-linguistic similarities and differences in coherence markers. Results of paragraph reordering exercises show (1) certain rhetorical patterns familiar to both Japanese and English native speakers while some only familiar to Japanese native speakers; and (2) bilingual native Japanese speakers accessed formal schemata appropriate for English expository prose when reading English translations of Japanese texts.

Coherence/Japanese/Exposition/Schema.

2663. Ricento, T. (1987b, April). *Coherence in English and Japanese expository prose.* Paper presented at the 21st Annual TESOL Convention, Miami Beach, FL.

Analyzes reader evaluations of twenty newspaper editorials within a model of coherence.

Japanese/Coherence/Contrastive Rhetoric.

2664. Ricento, T. (1986). Comments on Bernard Mohan and Winnie Au-Yeung Lo's "Academic writing and Chinese students: Transfer and developmental factors" . . . [In The Forum]. *TESOL Quarterly, 20,* 595-568.

In response to Mohan and Lo (1985), claims that while they have pointed out loopholes in earlier studies in contrastive rhetoric, they themselves make assertions without supporting evidence.

Contrastive Rhetoric

2665. Ricento, T., Kaplan, R. B., Eggington, W. G., Dantas, M., Grabe, W., & Montano-Harmon, M. R. (1989, March). *Contrastive rhetoric: Current research and pedagogical implications.* Paper presented at the 23rd Annual TESOL Convention, San Antonio, TX.

Colloquium presents findings of contrastive studies of discourse from more than six languages.

Contrastive Rhetoric.

2666. Richard-Amato, P. (1989, March). *Using reaction dialogues to develop writing skills in ESL.* Paper presented at the 23rd Annual TESOL Convention, San Antonio, TX.

Recommends reaction dialogues to encourage students, especially reluctant writers, to stretch to higher levels of meaning and expression through writing.

Invention/Speaking-Writing Relations.

2667. Richards, J. C. (1979). Rhetorical and communicative styles in the new varieties of English. *Language Learning, 29,* 1-26.

Points out that the indigenization of English includes new written communicative styles coined by creative writers of English as a second language who grapple with the problems raised by new varieties of English.

Professional Writing.

2668. Richards, R. T. (1988). Thesis/dissertation writing for EFL students: An ESP course design. *English for Specific Purposes, 7*(3), 171-180.

Describes an intensive English for Specific Purposes (ESP) thesis-writing course which focuses on total discourse learning needs and uses an interactive model of needs analysis.

Curriculum/ESP.

2669. Richards-Apatiga, A. R. (1988, March). *ESL basic writers: Are writing centers responding?* Paper presented at the 22nd Annual TESOL Convention, Chicago, IL.
    Discusses what happens to ESL students when they visit one university's writing center.
    Writing Center.

2670. Richmond, J. W. (1981, March). *Righting wrongs in writing.* Paper presented at the 15th Annual TESOL Convention, Detroit, MI.
    Surveys techniques for handling errors in student writing.
    Error Treatment.

2671. Richmond, K. C. (1985a). Prose models and the ESL writing lesson. *CATESOL Occasional Papers, 11*, 31-40. [ERIC ED 263 765].
    Claims that the use of prose models in the ESL writing class can eliminate some problems inherent in the process-based class. Prose models provide a rich source of rhetorical patterns and improve students' repertoire of phrases and vocabulary. Exposure to many prose models introduces variety and eliminates mechanistic and formulaic application of models in writing.
    Imitation/Prose Models.

2672. Richmond, K. C. (1985b, May). *Prose models and the ESL writing lesson.* Paper presented at the 16th Annual Meeting of CATESOL, San Diego, CA. [ERIC ED 263 765].
    Claims, contrary to most proponents of the process approach, that prose models can be used to help ESL writers if a large enough number of exemplars is employed.
    Prose Models/Imitation.

2673. Richmond, K. C. (1984, March). *Teacher-induced errors.* Paper presented at the annual meeting of CATESOL, San Jose, CA. [ERIC ED 244 516].
    Claims that many ESL students have inaccurate assumptions about writing since they have little prior experience in writing; teachers overlook this and mislead students by overemphasizing one aspect of writing which leads to teacher-induced errors. Suggests ways to avoid these errors.
    Errors/Responding.

2674. Ridpath, S. (1992). The use of computers in the tutoring process: Overcoming communication obstacles between tutor and the ESL student. *Writing Lab Newsletter, 17*(3), 7-8.
    Describes how the technique called "cooperating audience" (working alongside the composing student at a computer) applies to the tutoring of an ESL student.
    Tutoring/Computers/Revision.

2675. Rigg, P., & Hudelson, S. (1984, March). *Language experience for reading and writing.* Paper presented at the 18th Annual TESOL Convention, Houston, TX.
    Advocates language experience approach to eliciting reading and writing for non-literate ESL learners.
    LEA/Literacy/Children.

2676. Riley, K. I. (1989, March). *The case against ESL tracking in freshman composition.* Paper presented at the 23rd Annual TESOL Convention, San Antonio, TX.

Argues that tracking ESL students in freshman composition while apparently a boon actually raises disturbing questions.

Freshman Composition/Politics.

2677. Riley, K. I. (1985, April). *Five strategies for beginning composition.* Paper presented at the 19th Annual TESOL Convention, New York, NY.

Presents five strategies for teaching "authoring" instead of secretarial skills at the beginning level.

Beginners.

2678. Ringbom, H. (1977, February). *Spelling errors and foreign language learning strategies.* Paper presented at the Conference of Contrastive Linguistics and Error Analysis, Stockholm, Sweden. [ERIC ED 148 103].

Examines the English spelling errors made by native-speaking Finns and Swedish-speaking Finns and relates these to the pronunciation of the intended words. Suggests that difference in spelling errors of both groups may be due to the near-phonemic spelling system of Finnish.

Error Analysis/Spelling/Finnish/Swedish.

2679. Rinvolucri, M. (1983). Writing to your students. *ELT Journal, 37,* 16-21.

States benefits and limitations of a letter-correspondence method used by a teacher to learn more about students in order to plan syllabus for subsequent term.

Syllabus Design.

2680. Rittershofer, J. S. (1987). The nominal reference system in the interlanguage of Japanese students' writing in English: A discourse analysis. *Dissertation Abstracts International, 48*(1), 119A.

Examines compositions written by high-intermediate to low-advanced Japanese students writing in English for characteristics of the nominal system in their interlanguage. Study shows a developmental movement from native language to target language.

Japanese/Discourse Analysis.

2681. Riverol, A. (1983). *The action reporter.* Hayward, CA: Alemany Press.

Adapts an approach to language acquisition activities derived from news-reporting, such as interviewing. It features a step-by-step guide for developing communication skills as well as activities to enhance those skills. Students learn to draw upon their own resources to speak, write, and communicate.

Secondary School/Intermediate.

2682. Rivers, W. J. (1987). Story writing: A comparison of native and L2 discourse. In J. P. Lantolf, & A. Labarca (Eds.), *Research in second language learning: Focus on the classroom* (pp. 195-211). Norwood, NJ: Ablex.

An analysis of written protocols by American university students learning elementary German. They performed a narration task in both languages showing greater emphasis on self-regulatory activities than on communication which corroborates in another language the findings of Frawley & Lantolf (1985) for beginning ESL writers.

Research/Narration/Beginners.

2683. Rivers, W. M., & Temperley, M. S. (1978). *A practical guide to the teaching of*

English as a second or foreign language. NY: Oxford University Press.

Two chapters give numerous exercises that illustrate the "skill-getting /skill-using" approach to teaching written communication.

Instruction.

2684. Rizzo, B., & Villafane, S. (1975). Spanish influence on written English. *Journal of Basic Writing, 1*(1), 62-71.

Finds that the same kinds, if not number, of errors in the written English of native Spanish-speaking students occur in the writings of native New Yorkers. For Hispanic students, the effort to analogize produces errors when the structure of the two languages diverge.

Hispanic/Errors.

2685. Roach, W. L. (1989a, March). *Choosing and using -- poetry and prose in the ESL composition class.* Paper presented at the 40th Annual Convention CCCC Meeting, Seattle, WA.

Literature.

2686. Roach, W. L. (1989b). Incorporating American literature into the English as a second language college composition classroom. *Dissertation Abstracts International, 49*(10), 2955A.

As a result of incorporating literature, reading but not writing ability improved in a specially designed one-semester ESL college composition course.

Curriculum/Literature.

2687. Robb, T. N., Ross, S. B., & Shortreed, I. (1986). Salience of feedback on error and its effect on EFL writing quality. *TESOL Quarterly, 20,* 83-95.

Direct methods of error-treatment do not improve compositions, according to a study of four groups of EFL writers each of whom was provided with a different type of error-feedback (full-correction, abbreviated code system, uncoded feedback, and inaugural feedback). However, there was a gradual increase in the mean score. The authors conclude that more salient error-feedback treatments do not have significant effects on revisions.

Error Treatment/Feedback.

2688. Robbins, M. (1977). *Error explorations: A procedure for examining written interlanguage performance.* Unpublished master's thesis, UCLA, Los Angeles, CA.

Error Analysis.

2689. Robinett, B. W. (1972). On the horns of a dilemma: Correcting compositions. In J. E. Alatis (Ed.), *Studies in honor of Albert H. Markwardt* (pp. 143-151). Washington, DC: TESOL.

Describes a composition grading checklist intended to create a more positive approach for teachers and learners.

Grading/Feedback.

2690. Robinson, J. H. (1993, April). *Contrastive rhetoric and the East Asian student.* Paper presented at the 27th Annual TESOL Convention, Atlanta, GA.

Analyzes the rhetorical structures of L1 and L2 papers by Chinese and Japanese students.

Contrastive Rhetoric/East Asian.

2691. Robinson, J. H., Anderson, J., Basena, D. M., Blumhardt, D., Frindethie, M. K., & Missaghie, S. (1990, October). Contrastive rhetoric and tutoring ESL writers. In D. Healy (Comp.), *Centers for collaboration: Diversity for the new decade. Selected proceedings of the 32nd annual conference of the Midwest Writing Association, St. Cloud, MN* (pp. 77-90). Minneapolis: Midwest Writing Association. [ERIC ED 333 426].

    Reviews Kaplan's (1966) four patterns and draws implications for tutoring ESL writers so they transform their writing from the pattern of one culture to that of the other.

    Contrastive Rhetoric/Tutoring/Academic Writing.

2692. Robinson, J. O. (Comp.). (1969). *An annotated bibliography of modern language teaching. Books and articles, 1946-1967* London: Oxford University Press.

    Ten pedagogical references are listed in a section on the teaching of composition.

    Bibliography.

2693. Robinson, P. C. (Ed.). (1988). *Academic writing: process and product* London: Modern English Publications/British Council.

    Collection of seventeen papers selected from the 1985 SELMOUS (Special English Language Materials for Overseas English Students) Conference on Academic Writing held at Reading University. The papers, generally, concern themselves with the process of writing especially at the university level.

    Academic Writing/ESP.

2694. Robinson, P. (1987). Projection into dialogue as a composition strategy. *ELT Journal, 41*, 30-36.

    Discusses decision-making processes involved in drafting and revising business letters.

    Business Writing/Process Instruction.

2695. Robinson, T. H. (1986, March). *Evaluating foreign students' written English: A research report*. Paper presented at the 20th Annual TESOL Convention, Anaheim, CA.

    Reports research on the effect of academic background on ratings of corrected ESL compositions.

    Assessment/Rating.

2696. Robinson, T. H. (1985). Evaluating foreign students' compositions: The effects of rater background and of handwriting, spelling, and grammar. *Dissertation Abstracts International, 45*(3), 2951A.

    The raters' background as well as the handwriting and spelling of Arabic-speaking, Chinese-speaking, and Spanish-speaking students in some situations affected the evaluation of compositions and produced fluctuations in score correlations.

    Hispanic/Arabic/Chinese/L1 Influence.

2697. Robinson, T. H. (1982). Holistic scoring of essays. *TECFORS, 5*(2), 7-9.

    Reviews one university's procedures for holistically scoring ESL essays.

    Assessment/University.

2698. Robinson, T. H., & Madrey, L. (1986b). *Active writing*. Boston: Heinle & Heinle.

Intended to help prepare students for writing at the college freshman level. Writing is taught as a process and students are encouraged to identify their purpose and audience, be creative, and revise their drafts. The topics covered are the same as those American students would read except that American cultural assumptions are avoided.

Advanced/University/Textbook.

2699. Robinson, T. H., & Skinner, A. A. (1984, March). *The process log: A tool for students and teachers to bring composing alive in the EFL writing classroom.* Paper presented at the 18th Annual TESOL Convention, Houston, TX.

Discusses variety of ways to use process logs in the EFL writing class in order to help expand repertoire of composing strategies.

Logs.

2700. Robinson-Fellag, L., & Watson, L. T. (1989, March). *Tools for L2 writing.* Paper presented at the 23rd Annual TESOL Convention, San Antonio, TX.

Demonstrates how to sequence writing activities to stimulate content, organization, and vocabulary while still considering process.

Classroom Activities.

2701. Rodby, J. (1992). *Appropriating literacy: Writing and reading as a second language.* Portsmouth, NH: Heinemann-Boynton/Cook.

This book aims to address the topic of reading and writing education for ESL students at all levels. It draws broadly on interdisciplinary fields in order to provide a social constructivist reading of ESL literacy as a social practice. It maintains that teaching practices should be shaped by a social perspective, offering a dialectical framework based on Bakhtin and Vygotsky which is applied to Bulosan's autobiography America is in the Heart. The metaphor of communitas is used to encourage teachers to read their NNES students' texts differently.

Literacy/Social.

2702. Rodby, J. (1990). The ESL writer and the kaleidoscopic self. *Writing Instructor, 10,* 42-50.

Suggests that writing in English engages the ESL student in a dialectic of identity and difference. Recommends that differences should be promoted rather than ignored.

Culture.

2703. Rodby, J. (1989). A polyphony of voices: The dialectics of social interaction and ESL literacy practices. *Dissertation Abstracts International, 50*(5), 1239A.

Criticizes ESL literacy practices as being too cognitive and individual and insufficiently social. Argues, on the basis of Vygotsky and Bakhtin, for a social/dialectical view of ESL. Supports this view with the writing of African, Chicanom, and other writers and illustrates position with a detailed analysis of the autobiography of the Philippine poet Carlos Bulosan.

Social/Literacy.

2704. Rodby, J. (1988a, March). *The ESL writer and the kaleidoscopic self.* Paper presented at the 39th Annual CCCC Meeting, St. Louis, MO.

See Rodby, 1990.

Literacy/Social.
2705. Rodby, J. (1988b, November). *Writing an image/composing a word: Videotape projects for ESL students*. Paper presented at the 78th Annual NCTE Convention, St. Louis, MO.
Project Work.
2706. Rodby, J. (1987). *Writing by choice: Intermediate composition for students of ESL*. Englewood Cliffs, NJ: Prentice Hall.
Text provides theory-based instruction for nonnative students through introduction to step-by-step strategies and structures of written English.
Intermediate/Textbook.
2707. Rodby, J. (1986, March). *Community and communitas: Social interaction in ESL writing development*. Paper presented at the 37th Annual CCCC Meeting, New Orleans, LA.
See Rodby, 1992.
Literacy/Social.
2708. Rodby, J. (1984). Chapters rerouted and exercises undone. *Writing Instructor, 3*, 89-94.
Offers suggestions, based on textbook materials, for helping English as a second language students to learn to write coherent English.
Classroom Activities.
2709. Roderman, W. H. (1990). *Writing 1: Getting started*. Hayward, CA: Alemany Press.
Beginning writers are lead step-by-step through the stages of prewriting, composing, revising, editing, and publishing. It includes activities from brainstorming to critiquing that can be done individually, in pairs, or in groups. Students are encouraged to collaborate.
Beginners/Textbook.
2710. Rodman, L. (1978). ESL in freshman English. *English Quarterly, 11*, 138-146.
The English as a second language program conducted within the freshman English curriculum at the University of British Columbia focuses on grammar and composition. Also identifies three problems that high schools can help the university to resolve.
Curriculum.
2711. Rodoni, E. (1993, April). *Personal and group journals: A research agenda for teacher/students*. Paper presented at the 27th Annual TESOL Convention, Atlanta, GA.
Workshop offers a forum for the exchange of ideas about this popular instructional method as a basis for setting a possible research agenda.
Journal Writing.
2712. Rodriguez, E. (1991). Articulation: The community college task in teaching ESL writing. *The CATESOL Journal, 4*, 97-101.
Suggests improvements in ESL programs intending to be equivalent to regular freshman writing courses.
Curriculum.
2713. Rodriguez-Diaz, D. B. (1989, November). *Microcomputers in ESL instruction*. Paper

presented at the 79th Annual NCTE Convention, Baltimore, MD.
Computers.

2714. Rodriques, R. J. (1975a). A comparison of the written and oral English syntax of Mexican-American bilingual and Anglo-American monolingual fourth and ninth grade students. *Dissertation Abstracts International, 35*(9), 6123-4A.

Finds few significant differences between language, level, or mode for the syntactic features measured.

Speaking-Writing Relations/Spanish/Children.

2715. Rodriques, R. J. (1975b). A comparison of the written and oral syntax of Mexican-American bilingual and Anglo-American monolingual fourth and ninth grade students. In R. Crymes, & W. E. Norris (Eds.), *On TESOL '74: Selected papers from the 8th Annual TESOL convention* (pp. 103-107). Washington, DC: TESOL.

Discusses results of measuring sentence complexity and syntactic-morphological variations between groups.

Hispanic/NS-NNS Comparisons.

2716. Rodriques, R. J. (1974, March). *A comparison of the written and oral syntax of Mexican-American bilingual and Anglo-American monolingual fourth and ninth grade students*. Paper presented at the 8th Annual TESOL Convention, Denver, CO.

Discusses results of measuring sentence complexity and syntactic-morphological variations between and within groups.

Hispanic/NS-NNS Comparisons/Speaking-Writing Relations.

2717. Rodriquez, A. (1988). Research in reading and writing in bilingual education and English as a second language. In A. A. Ambert (Ed.), *Bilingual education and English as a second language: A research handbook, 1986-1987* (pp. 61-117). NY: Garland.

Reviews separately reading and writing research for limited English proficiency students.

Review/Bilingual/Literacy.

2718. Roen, D. H. (1991). ESL writing teachers at work. *Journal of Intensive English Studies, 5,* 19-35.

Gives 20 suggestions for using prewriting to explore fiction and 8 guidelines for responding to student writing.

Invention/Responding.

2719. Roen, D. H. (1989). Developing effective assignments for second language writers. In D. M. Johnson, & D. H. Roen (Eds.), *Richness in writing: Empowering ESL students* (pp. 193-206). NY: Longman.

Suggests that effective writing assignments for ESL students are ones that have real purposes with real and interested audiences, help students in viewing and developing processes that experienced writers use, and provide feedback first on content and then form, thus helping students tackle rhetorical concerns.

Assignments/Audience/Process Instruction.

2720. Roen, D. H., & Mangelsdorf, K. (1988, March). *Composing processes for ESL students: More than meets the eye*. Paper presented at the 39th Annual CCCC Meeting, St. Louis, MO.

2721. Rojas, P. M. (1968). Writing to learn. *TESOL Quarterly*, 2, 127-129.
>Describes six types of drill for controlling writing at the beginner level.
>Beginners/Control.

2722. Rollin, M. F. (1985). *Three factors in the written production of limited English writers in freshman composition courses at U. T. El Paso*. Unpublished master's thesis, University of Texas, El Paso, TX.
>Presents a profile of 30 limited English writers who are between ESOL and English composition classes. Concludes that multiple reasons exist for underachievement of limited English writers, especially the sociocultural context, and that reading is a major consideration in improving the writing performance of these students.
>Hispanic/University/Reading-Writing Relations.

2723. Rooholamine, S. D. (1986). A cultural manual in English as a foreign language for advanced students from Iran. *Dissertation Abstracts International*, 47(9), 3343A.
>Addressed to prospective Persian teachers of EFL at advanced levels in Iranian colleges, this study advocates the teaching of American culture as necessary to prepare non-natives for the differences they encounter in the US. Proposes writing exercises to facilitate cultural awareness, using a contrastive rthetoric approach.
>Curriculum/Culture/Persian.

2724. Rooks, G. M. (1989). *Paragraph power: Communicating ideas through paragraphs*. Englewood Cliffs, NJ: Prentice Hall.
>Explores paragraph structure and development with particular focus on topic sentences, subject development, and the summary sentence. Discusses various rhetorical modes, as well as grammar and outline procedures. Offers many exercises.
>Intermediate/Textbook.

2725. Rooks, G. M. (1988). *Share your paragraph: The process approach to writing*. Englewood Cliffs, NJ: Prentice Hall Regent.
>Helps students develop strategies for pre-writing and obtaining feedback, for writing and revising, and for thinking critically. Students learn from the process of peer editing and use their own writing to learn as well.
>Advanced/Textbook.

2726. Root, C. B. (1993, April). *Finding wild mind: Tales from people who wrote*. Paper presented at the 27th Annual TESOL Convention, Atlanta, GA.
>Suggests with reference to Zen that the power of expressive writing leads to self-revelation.
>Expressive Writing.

2727. Root, C. B. (1992, March). *Thanks for the memories: Creating a class book*. Poster presented at the 26th Annual TESOL Convention, Vancouver, BC.
>Displays finished arts-based class memory book.
>Creative Writing/Student Publications.

2728. Root, C. B. (1979). The use of personal journals in the teaching of ESOL. *TESL Reporter*, 12(2), 3-5.
>Presents four arguments for adopting daily, out-of class writing assignments as an adjunct to the writing classs.

Assignments/Journals.
2729. Rorschach, E. G. (1989, March). *A new ESL curriculum: Fluency first*. Paper presented at the 40th Annual CCCC Meeting, Seattle, WA.
Whole Language/Fluency.
2730. Rorschach, E. G. (1986). The effects of readers' awareness: A case study of three ESL student writers. *Dissertation Abstracts International, 47*(12), 14311A.
Examines the writing of three advanced ESL college students in a basic writing course to see the influence of audience awareness on revisions. Students were interviewed for choices they had made and outside readers responded to writers. Findings show students influenced more by teacher's idea of grammatical correctness and that instruction hindered their fluency.
Audience/Revision/University.
2731. Rorschach, E. G. (1985, March). *The effects of reader awareness on ESL writers*. Paper presented at the 36th Annual CCCC Meeting, Minneapolis, MN. [ED 260 447].
Examines the writing of three ESL writers in a basic writing class in order to check the validity of the assumption that ESL writers experience difficulties composing the five-paragraph essay due to cross-cultural interference. The case study of one of the students indicates that the writer has a clear idea of the five-paragraph essay but cannnot discuss ideas in depth according to the readers' expectations
Culture.
2732. Rorschach, E. G., & MacGowan-Gilhooly, A. (1993, April). *The fluency first project: Looking at students' writing*. Paper presented at the 27th Annual TESOL Convention, Atlanta, GA.
Workshop to discuss evaluative criteria for a program focused on fluency before correctness.
Fluency/Evaluation.
2733. Rorschach, E. G., Rakijas, M., & Benesch, S. (1984). Cohen's reformulating comps prompts questions (Letter to the Editor). *TESOL Newsletter, 18*(3), 17.
Questions whether the value of the technique of having a native reformulate a nonnative composition if there are changes in the meaning of the original student essay.
Reformulation.
2734. Rorschach, E. G., Tillyer, A., Moreno, A., & Verdi, G. (1992, March). *Research on ESL composition instruction: The fluency-first approach*. Paper presented at the 26th Annual TESOL Convention, Vancouver, BC.
Reports longitudinal data and case study results of a fluency-first college composition program. Since 1983 more students pass the course, fewer repeat it, and fewer prior courses are required each year.
Programs/Fluency.
2735. Rosario, G. D. (1978). *A typewriting course for students taking English as a second language*. Unpublished master's thesis, California State University, Long Beach, CA.

Courses.

2736. Rosow, L. V. (1992). Group journals, a short pitch for a panacea. *TESOL Matters*, 2(2), 15.

   Discusses using a whole-language based group journal process (Frye, Hollingsworth, Horan & Stewart, 1989) in the ESL classroom.

   Journals/Whole Language.

2737. Ross, C. N. G. (1979). Contrast conjoining in English, Japanese, and Mandarin Chinese. *Dissertation Abstracts International*, *39*(10), 6105A.

   Examines the use of "contrast conjoining" in English, Japanese, and Mandarin Chinese and explains differences in terms of syntactic, semantic, and pragmatic aspects in the three languages.

   Cohesion/Chinese/Japanese.

2738. Ross, D. A. (1982). Topic schemas: A cognitive approach to writing assignments. *TECFORS*, *5*(5), 4-7. [ERIC ED 267 648].

   Distinguishes between controlling topic assigment and selecting it and offers topic schemas--skeletal topic assignments--for students to complete.

   Topic/Assignments.

2739. Ross, J. (1968). Controlled writing: A transformational approach. *TESOL Quarterly*, *2*, 253-261.

   Gives a transformational grammatical approach to controlling writing by using productive technique of sentence building and a recognition technique of identifying faulty sentence constructions.

   Control.

2740. Ross, J. (1967). Controlled composition. In D. G. Wigglesworth (Ed.), *Selected conference papers of the Association of Teachers of English as a Second Language* (pp. 47-49). Los Altos, CA: NAFSA/Language Research Associates' Press.

   Suggests ways to prepare material so as to control the syntactic patterns in paragraph writing.

   Control/Paragraph.

2741. Ross, S. B., & Robb, T. N. (1987, April). *The reading approach to composition: Testing the input hypothesis*. Paper presented at the 21st Annual TESOL Convention, Miami Beach, FL.

   Compares writing quality of Japanese EFL students who were taught international extensive reading instead of sentence-combining and journal writing.

   Japanese/Reading-Writing Relations.

2742. Ross, S. B., Robb, T. N., & Shortreed, I. (1988). First language composition pedagogy in second language classroom: A reassessment. *RELC Journal*, *19*(1), 29-48.

   Reports the effectiveness of journal writing but not sentence combining or reformulation.

   Journals/Reformulation/Sentence Combining.

2743. Rosser, C. F. (1989). The response of college teachers to undergraduate foreign-student writing. *Dissertation Abstracts International*, *50*(4), 890A.

   NES college teachers have a positive attitude and are generally tolerant toward ESL writers, focusing primarily on content for their evaluation.

WAC/Responding.

2744. Rothschild, D., & Klingenberg, F. (1990). Self and peer evaluation of writing in the intensive ESL classroom. *TESL Canada Journal*, *8*(1), 52-65.

One study shows some increase in learners' awareness of criteria for good writing when evaluation is brought into the classroom.

Assessment/Peer Response.

2745. Rottweiler, G. P. (1984). Systematic cohesion in published general academic English: Analysis and register description. *Dissertation Abstracts International*, *45*(8), 2512-2513A.

Studies systemic cohesion in a sample of published academic texts (Halliday and Hasan, 1976). Finds five major results including the omnipresence of cohesion in all sentences, the greater frequency of lexical cohesion, differences in distribution across text locations, and systematic relations with Gray's (1977) concept of core assertion.

Cohesion/Register.

2746. Rowland, J. C., & Van Gelder, L. O. (1968). *An annotated bibliography on the college teaching of English: 1963-1965*. Champaign, IL: NCTE.

Only one of 241 citations relates to EFL writing.

Bibliography.

2747. Rowland, J. C., Van Gelder, L. O., & McKiernan, J. (1966). *An annotated bibliography on the college teaching of English: 1957-1963*. Champaign, IL: NCTE.

Bibliography.

2748. Roy, A. M. (1989). Developing second language literacy: A Vygotskyan perspective. *Journal of Teaching Writing*, *8*, 91-98.

Presents Vygotskyian terms for second language composing.

Literacy/Psychology.

2749. Roy, A. M. (1988). ESL concern for writing program administrators: Problems and policies. *WPA: Journal of the Council of Writing Program Administration*, *11*(3), 17-28.

Distinguishes three types of programs for traditional international students, recent immigrants, and bilingual students. Suggests that a writing program serving these populations should have courses that utilize social contexts for writing, teachers knowledgeable about both writing and language, and assessment sensitive to language and literacy development.

Curriculum/Administration.

2750. Roy, A. M. (1986, March). *Literacy and empowerment in ESL composition*. Paper presented at the 37th Annual CCCC Meeting, New Orleans, LA.

Literacy.

2751. Roy, A. M. (1983, March). *Prewriting techniques*. Paper presented at the 17th Annual TESOL Convention, Toronto, Ontario.

Says that pre-writing activities reduce blocking and help ESL students test ideas, move into a topic, generate details, and plan organizing strategies.

Invention/Anxiety.

2752. Rua-Larsen, M. (1988). *An integrated reading/writing curriculum for secondary and*

postsecondary ESL students. Unpublished master's thesis, SUNY, Oswego, NY.
Curriculum/Secondary School/Reading-Writing Relations.

2753. Rubenstein, J. S., & Gubbay, J. M. (1990). *Essentials of reading and writing English: Books 1, 2, 3*. Littlewood, IL: NTC Publishing Group.

Consists of three workbooks for teaching adults to master reading and writing through presentation of original stories which are to be read aloud and written.
Adult Education/Textbook.

2754. Rubin, D. L., Goodrum, R., & Hall, B. (1990). Orality, oral-based culture, and the academic writing of ESL learners. *Issues in Applied Linguistics*, *1*(1), 56-76.

Argues that ESL learners from oral-based cultures can learn to reintegrate their native discourse strategies after becoming aware of the differences between oral and written codes in English.
Speaking-Writing Relations/Culture.

2755. Ruetten, M. K. (1993, April). *Evaluating ESL students' performance on competency exams*. Paper presented at 44th Annual Convention of CCCC, San Diego, CA.
Evaluation.

2756. Ruetten, M. K. (1991). Reading problematical ESL placement essays. *College ESL*, *1*(2), 37-47.

Studies 17 problematical ESL placement essays, especially unbalanced essays, in order to determine how they depart from readers' expectations and what might be done about it.
Holistic/Evaluation.

2757. Ruetten, M. K. (1989, March). *Holistic evaluation of problem essays in ESL*. Paper presented at the 40th Annual CCCC Meeting, Seattle, WA.
Evaluation.

2758. Ruetten, M. K. (1987, November). *ESL students' perceptions of teacher comments*. Paper presented at the 77th Annual NCTE Convention, Los Angeles, CA.
Feedback/Perceptions.

2759. Rupp, J. H., & Rayburn, K. R. (1989, March). *Cultural influences and the writing process*. Paper presented at the 23rd Annual TESOL Convention, San Antonio, TX.

Demonstrates that topic generation, brainstorming, revision and peer editing are a challenge for the culturally diverse classroom.
Culture.

2760. Russell, A. (1992, March). *Motivating reading and writing students with electronic mail*. Paper presented at the 26th Annual TESOL Convention, Vancouver, BC.

Describes how using E-Mail motivates students to communicate and collaborate on reading and writing.
Computers/Reading-Writing Relations.

2761. Russikoff, K., & Pilgreen, J. (1993, April). *Seeking input: Reading and writing revision strategies as tools*. Paper presented at the 27th Annual TESOL Convention, Atlanta, GA.

Discusses research on a hierarchy of literacy revision strategies with pedagogical applications.
Reading-Writing Relations/Revision.

2762. Russo, G. M. (1988). Writing: An interactive experience. In W. M. Rivers (Ed.), *Interactive language teaching* (pp. 83-92). New York: Cambridge University Press.

Discusses how writing is an interactive activity in which students are involved with one another, with instructors, and other members of the community. Describes four types of interactive writing: Class, group, individual, and community writing which students can use to express themselves.

Interaction.

2763. Rybowski, T. (1986). Paraphrasing as an aid to writing. *English Teaching Forum*, *24*(3), 38-39.

Advises the teaching of parphrasing to beginning students.

Summary Writing.

S

2764. Sa'adeddin, M. (1989). Text development and Arabic-English negative interference. *Applied Linguistics*, *10*, 36-51.

Problems of negative transfer for Arab-speaking EFLwriters attributed to differences in text development in Arabic and English in that Arabic texts utilizes the aural mode to a greater extend whereas English texts emphasize the visual mode.

Text Analysis/Arabic.

2765. Sage, H., Markstein, L., Blanton, L. L., Leki, I., & Broukal, M. (1993, April). *Reading in the writing classroom.* Colloquium presented at the 27th Annual TESOL Convention, Atlanta, GA.

Panel explores issues related to research and instruction in reading and writing from different points of view.

Reading-Writing Relations.

2766. Saksena, A. (1984). Linguistic models, pedagogical grammars, and ESL composition. *International Review of Applied Linguistics*, *22*, 137-143.

Presents negative consequences of using pedagogical grammars of English dominated by theoretical models. Suggests integrating composition principles into pedagogical grammar drills.

Grammar.

2767. Salebi, M. Y. (1986). The effects of a teaching method based on contrastive analysis to reduce written errors in English made by Arab students. *Dissertation Abstracts International*, *47*(4), 1226A.

Investigates the effectiveness of a teaching method based on contrastive analysis to reduce written errors in English of Arab students. Findings show method does benefit students.

Errors/Instruction.

2768. Salimbene, S. (1986, March). *Writing as interaction: An approach to reader-directed prose.* Paper presented at the 20th Annual TESOL Convention, Anaheim, CA.

Workshop explores writing as social interaction by experiencing both writer and reader perspectives.

Audience.

2769. Sally, O. (1976). The teaching of spelling. *English Language Teaching Journal, 30*, 219-224.
>Claims that spelling errors are a serious source of errors for Sri Lankan students. Describes a systematic exercise to help students master English spelling.
>Errors/Spelling/Sri Lanka.

2770. Saltzman, S. A. (1993, April). *Writing literary research papers: Five steps for ESL students*. Paper presented at the 27th Annual TESOL Convention, Atlanta, GA.
>Shows a five-step procedure for writing literary research papers on independent research topics.
>Research Writing/Literature.

2771. Saltzman, S. A. (1988, March). *Student-inspired revision*. Paper presented at the 22nd Annual TESOL Convention, Chicago, IL.
>Discusses self-motivation in revision.
>Revision.

2772. Sammander, A. R. (1987). A comparison of spoken with written texts with respect to error and non-error cohesive ties and syntactic structures of adult Arabic-speaking learners of English as a foreign language. *Dissertation Abstracts International, 48*(5), 1138A.
>Spoken and written texts by Arabic-speaking high and low-scoring EFL students did not show significant differences in cohesion and syntactic structures. Low-scorers produced more errors because they took more risks.
>Arabic/Cohesion/Speaking-Writing Relations/Errors.

2773. Samonte, A. L. (1970). Techniques in teaching writing. *RELC Journal, 1*(1), 127-138.
>Offers some practical solutions to teaching freshman composition in the Phillipines.
>Phillipines.

2774. Sampson, D. E., & Gregory, J. F. (1991). A technological primrose path? ESL students and computer-assisted writing programs. *College ESL, 1*(2), 29-36.
>Illustrates problems that can arise when style check software is used by basic ESL writers.
>Word Processing.

2775. Sampson, G. P. (1981). A functional approach to teaching writing. *English Teaching Forum, 19*(2), 10-13.
>Discusses classroom tasks that have a product, audience, function, and linguistic focus.
>Task.

2776. Sampson, G. P. (1980). Teaching the written language using a functional approach. *TESL Talk, 11*, 38-44.
>Suggests using individualized reading and writing tasks in a functional approach to teaching English as a second language.
>Approaches.

2777. Samuda, N. (1978). *Teaching college composition to students of English as a second or foreign language*. Unpublished master's thesis, University of Texas, Austin, TX.

Pedagogy/University.

2778. Samuel, M. (1988). Towards a genuine approach to composition writing. *English Teaching Forum*, 26(2), 28-33.

Describes an approach to teaching writing that includes vivid description, sensory experience, and anything that involves real life experience.

Approaches.

2779. Samway, K. D. (1989, March). *Teachers and students as literary pen pals: An odyssey*. Paper presented at the 23rd Annual TESOL Convention, San Antonio, TX.

Discusses a three-way correspondence between an ESOL teacher, her students, and a researcher-teacher.

Elementary.

2780. Samway, K. D. (1987a). The formal evaluation of children's writing: An incomplete story. *Language Arts*, 64, 289-298.

Researcher finds strengths in the writing of a Puerto Rican elementary student in an ESOL class that are not revealed by formal evaluation of his writing.

Children/Assessment.

2781. Samway, K. D. (1987b). The writing process of non-native English speaking children in the elementary grades. *Dissertation Abstracts International*, 49(3), 451A.

Describes the writing processes, revision techniques, and evaluation criteria of elementary aged non-native English speakers (grades 2-6) who engage in meaningful, message-oriented writing experiences in ESOL classrooms. Reports group-differentiated findings due to age and experience, variation in childrens' writing styles, and substantial teacher influence on children's writing.

Elementary/Process Research.

2782. Samway, K. D. (1986, March). *How can I get them to write?* Paper presented at the 20th Annual TESOL Convention, Anaheim, CA.

Workshop discusses techniques for students who are reluctant to write.

Children/Affect.

2783. Samway, K. D., Alvarrez, L. P., Mackinson-Smyth, J., Peyton, J. K., & Taylor, D. (1988, March). *Writing as reflection at the elementary level*. Paper presented at the 22nd Annual TESOL Convention, Chicago, IL.

Colloquium discusses growth of children's powers of written reflection.

Children.

2784. Samway, K. D., & Taylor, D. (1993). Inviting children to make connections between reading and writing. *TESOL Journal*, 2(3), 7-11.

Offers a variety of activities reflecting the value of collaborative language and literacy environments for children.

Children/Reading-Writing Relations.

2785. Samway, K. D. (1993). "This is hard, isn't it?" Children evaluating writing. *TESOL Quarterly*, 27, 233-258.

Describes the criteria used by nonnative English-speaking children (grades 2-6) when evaluating writing, based on the results of 14 in-depth interviews.

Children/Evaluation.

2786. Sanaou, R. (1984). The use of reformulation in teaching writing to ESL students.

Carleton Papers in Applied Language Studies, 1, 139-146.
Discusses technique popularized by Cohen, 1983a.
Reformulation.

2787. Sanborn, J. (1987). Obstacles and opportunities: Sentence combining in advanced ESL. *Journal of Basic Writing, 6*(2), 60-71.
Emphasizes the usefulness of sentence-combining for the advanced ESL student.
Sentence Combining/Advanced.

2788. Sanchez, L. L. (1992, March). *English writing in the workplace in a bilingual setting.* Paper presented at the 26th Annual TESOL Convention, Vancouver, BC.
Reports findings from a study of English writing in business and industrial settings in Puerto Rico.
Hispanic/Bilingual/Business Writing.

2789. Sanchez-Escobar, A. (1984). A contrastive study of the rhetorical patterns of English and Spanish writing. *Dissertation Abstracts International, 45*(5), 1321A.
Analyzes, compares and contrasts the organization of English and Spanish paragraphs and essays. Findings show similarities and differences in both languages. The major stylistic feature of English was linear and Spanish digressive.
Hispanic/Organization/Style.

2790. Sanchez-Escobar, A. (1981). *An analysis of current composition theories and their application to teaching Spanish-speaking students.* Unpublished master's thesis, George Peabody College for Teachers, Nashville, TN.
Hispanic/Instruction.

2791. Sanchez-Villamil, O. I. (1991). The effects of two metacognitive strategies on intermediate ESL college students' writing. *Dissertation Abstracts International, 52*(5), 1670A.
Investigates the effect of two metacognitive strategy treatments on the writing of intermediate ESL students being instructed by means of different teaching methods: process writing and reading-writing interface. Both the text structure awareness treatment and the strategic self-monitoring treatment did not yield statistically significant differences. Neither did the study show any significant differences between the effect of either teaching method on writing quality.
Meta-cognition/Instruction.

2792. Sanctis, D. D. (1985, September). The problem with "formal" research papers. *WATESOL Working Papers, 2*, 68-78. [ERIC ED 267 591].
Discusses some of the difficulties experienced by advanced ESL writers in the process of composing formal research papers. Most problems have to do with introductions and conclusions. Suggestions for teaching include more emphasis on reseach techniques, group revisions, note-taking, elimination of all required reading assignments, limiting the number of sources required, and increasing the amount of time for thinking.
Advanced/Research Writing/University.

2793. Sandberg, K. C. (1967). Drills for writing laboratories. In D. G. Wigglesworth (Ed.), *Selected conference papers of the Association of Teachers of English as a Second*

Language (pp. 53-57). Los Altos, CA: NAFSA/Language Research Associates' Press.

Describes a writing laboratory designed on principles of the aural-oral language laboratory. Gives several model drills for this context.

Drills/Laboratory.

2794. Sandberg, K. C. (1972, February). *Priorities in teaching writing: Strategies for bridging the gap.* Paper presented at the 6th Annual TESOL Convention, Washington, DC.

Suggests need for a new approach to bridge gap between audiolingual skills and advanced writing ability.

Methods.

2795. Sansone, R. (1993, April). *Letter writing develops skills and self-confidence.* Paper presented at the 27th Annual TESOL Convention, Atlanta, GA.

Discusses how academic writing needs are addressed by letter writing in high-interest whole language program.

Letter Writing.

2796. Santana-Seda, O. S. (1975). A contrastive study in rhetoric: An analysis of the organization of English and Spanish paragraphs written by native speakers of each language. *Dissertation Abstracts International, 35*(10), 6681A.

Analyzes and contrasts organization of English and Spanish paragraphs written by university students. Results indicate: (1) predominance of co-ordinate sequence in Spanish and subordinate sequences in English; (2) more non-sequential sentences in Spanish than in English; (3) majority of non-sequential sentences in Spanish were within paragraphs while in English started a new paragraph; yet (4) difference in occurrence of non-sequential sentences is not statistically significant.

Hispanic/Contrastive Rhetoric/University.

2797. Santiago, R. (1971). A contrastive analysis of some rhetorical aspects of the writing in Spanish and English of Spanish-speaking college students in Puerto Rico. *Dissertation Abstracts International, 31*(12), 6368A.

Examines the logical relations in sentences and paragraphs in the writing in Spanish and English by Spanish-speaking students in Puerto Rico. Findings show no significant differences between the writing in the two languages.

Hispanic/Contrastive Rhetoric/L1-L2 Comparison.

2798. Santos, T. A. (1993). Response to Ann M. Johns. *Journal of Second Language Writing, 2,* 88-90.

Responds to Johns' reading of her view of ideology in composition.

Ideology.

2799. Santos, T. A. (1992a). Ideology in composition: L1 and ESL. *Journal of Second Language Writing, 1*(1), 1-15.

Gives four reasons why L2 composition research, unlike L1 composition, is not political.

Politics.

2800. Santos, T. A. (1992b, March). *Research agendas for ESL writers: Will ESL writing move in a sociopolitical direction?* Paper presented at Colloquium at the 26th Annual

TESOL Convention, Vancouver, BC.
Claims that ESL writing is aligned with the more practical discipline of applied linguistics rather than with that of Literature, which explains why questions of ideology and politics -- currently fashionable in L1 composition -- are not yet influential in L2 composition.
Politics.

2801. Santos, T. A. (1992c, March). *What do we teach when we teach ESL writing?* Paper presented at the 26th Annual TESOL Convention, Vancouver, BC.
Describes and evaluates the teaching of writing as a medium and/or as a subject.
Approaches.

2802. Santos, T. A. (1988). Professor's reaction to the academic writing of nonnative-speaking students. *TESOL Quarterly*, 22, 69-90.
Reports reactions of one hundred seventy-eight professors from the Physical Sciences, Social Sciences, and Humanities to compositions written by two ESL students. The main responses were that: (1) more experienced professors and American professors are more tolerant of errors than younger professors and non-native professors, and (2) lexical errors considered more serious than content errors. Suggests need for emphasis on vocabulary improvement and lexical selection.
Error Gravity/Lexis/Evaluation.

2803. Santos, T. A. (1986, March). *Professors' reactions to the writing of nonnative students*. Paper presented at the 20th Annual TESOL Convention, Anaheim, CA.
Reports negative reactions to two compositions by a spectrum of professors.
Assessment/Error Gravity.

2804. Santos, T. A. (1985). Professors' reactions to the academic writing of non-native-speaking students. *Dissertation Abstracts International*, 46(8), 2283A.
Examines attitudes of professors toward academic writing of non-native-speaking students. Results show: (1) language seems to have been more important than content; (2) rank order for errors was comprehensibility, irritation and acceptability; (3) lexical errors considered most serious; (4) non-science professors more tolerant of errors than science professors; and (5) age and native language of professors are significant variables in their rating.
Error Gravity/Responding.

2805. Sarantos, R. L. (1974). Advanced composition. *Modern English Journal*, 5, 51-56.
An excerpt from a course for advanced students designed to teach proficiency in English composition by providing activities specifically geared to the elimination of native language interference.
Curriculum/LI Influence/Advanced.

2806. Sarantos, R. L. (1971). *Advanced composition: English as a second language*. Miami, FL: Dade County Public Schools. [ERIC ED 063 825].
Describes a course in which students prepare outlines of what they read and listen, write paragraphs, compositions, and term papers in order to eliminate first language interference.
L1 Influence/Advanced.

2807. Sarig, G. (1993). Composing a study-summary: A reading-writing encounter. In J. G. Carson, & I. Leki (Eds.), *Reading in the composition classroom: Second language perspectives* (pp. 161-182). Boston: Heinle & Heinle.

    Investigates the processes involved in reading and writing summaries of L1 and L2 texts; finds intricate, cyclical proceses and transfer of skills.

    Reading-Writing Relations/Summary Writing.

2808. Sarig, G. (1988). *Composing a study-summary: A reading-writing encounter*. Paper presented at the 22nd Annual TESOL Convention, Chicago, IL.

    Discusses the outcomes of a particular reading-writing connection.

    Summary Writing.

2809. Sarkar, S. (1978). The use of pictures in teaching English as a second language. *ELT Journal*, *32*(3), 175-180.

    Describes the effectiveness of using visual aids to teach English as a foreign language.

    Classroom Activities/Media.

2810. Sarwar, Z. (1991, March). *Teaching writing in large classes*. Paper presented at the 25th Annual TESOL Convention, New York, NY.

    Describes objectives, outlines, materials, and student samples from a fifty-hour reading/writing course for over 100 volunteer students.

    Large Classes.

2811. Sarwar, Z. (1992, March). *Teaching writing in large classes*. Paper presented at the 26th Annual TESOL Convention, Vancouver, BC.

    See next item.

    Large Classes.

2812. Sasser, L., & Cromwell, C. (1987, November). *Testimony: Writing cooperatively*. Paper presented at the Annual Meeting of CATESOL, Los Angeles, CA. [ERIC ED 317 046].

    A lesson plan and materials based on the story "Testimony" provides an opportunity for cooperative reading and writing.

    Collaboration/Reading-Writing Relations.

2813. Sato, C. J. (1990, March). *Discourse-based grammar in the writing conference*. Paper presented at the 24th Annual TESOL Convention, San Francisco, CA.

    An approach to university process writing courses is presented which adopts a 'focus on form' and 'grammatical consciousness-raising' by using discourse-based grammar. The paper reports on a project in which writing conferences were designed to make salient to learners discourse constraints or morphosyntax.

    Conferencing/Grammar.

2814. Sato, T. (1990). Revising strategies in Japanese students' writing in English as a foreign language. *Dissertation Abstracts International*, *51*(6), 2005A.

    Examines the quality ratings of the final revision of picture-prompted stories written by 90 Japanese college EFL students. Results show that the total number of successful revisions rather than the total number of revisions significantly differentiated the good from the poor-rated final drafts.

    Japanese/Revision.

2815. Saunders, M. A. (1992). The fail-safe micro research paper. *WATESOL Working Papers*, 27-36.
    A revised version of Saunders, 1986.
    Research Writing.

2816. Saunders, M. A. (1991). The effectiveness of direct instruction on the abilities of selected nonnative English speakers to produce written paraphrases of English texts. *Dissertation Abstracts International*, 52(5), 1670-1671A.
    Attempts to find out whether "semantic mapping," i. e., the use of graphic representation, or traditional textbook instruction improved intermediate-level proficiency students' ability to paraphrase. Results with a small number of subjects suggest that the graphic presentation significantly improves performance.
    Paraphrase Writing/Methods.

2817. Saunders, M. A. (1986). The fail-safe micro research paper. *WATESOL Working Papers*, 3, 1-9 . [ERIC ED 274 201].
    Reports successful experience abbreviating the research paper assignment in a step-by-step procedure for intermediate ESL students.
    Research Writing/IEP/Intermediate.

2818. Saward, C. (1981, March). *Developing a student-written newspaper for advanced composition class*. Paper presented at the 15th Annual TESOL Convention, Detroit, MI.
    Discusses strategies for designing and implementing a newspaper project.
    Project Work.

2819. Sayers, D. (1989). Bilingual sister classes in computer writing networks. In D. M. Johnson, & D. H. Roen (Eds.), *Richness in writing: Empowering ESL students* (pp. 120-133). NY: Longman.
    Describes a collaborative project between two bilingual sister classes, using a computer writing network for creating the required functional writing environment. Claims that the computer assisted both groups in adopting their approaches to writing in order to get the most out of the learning experience.
    Computers/Networking/Bilingual.

2820. Sayers, D. (1986). Sending messages: Across the classroom and around the world. *TESOL Newsletter, Supplement on computer-assisted learning*, 20(1), 7-8.
    Describes how to use two writing tools -- Dialogue Maker and the Computer Chronicle Newswire on the Apple II -- in order to facilitate interactive writing for young learners.
    Computers.

2821. Scane, J., Guy, A. M., & Wenstrom, L. (1991). *Think, write, share: Process writing for adult education*. Toronto: OISIE Press.
    Offers help introducing process instruction in adult ESL and ABE classes by guiding teachers through the tasks of process writing and advising about establishing co-operation.
    Teacher Education.

2822. Scarcella, R. C. (1993). *Power through written words*. Boston: Heinle & Heinle.
    A high-intermediate textbook in the Tapestry series, offering multicultural

reading modules to explore facets of personal and societal power.
Textbook/Intermediate.

2823. Scarcella, R. C., Lebauer, R. S., Albright, Ron, & Kumpf, L. E. (1988, March). *Limitations of personal computers in ESL writing instruction.* Paper presented at the 22nd Annual TESOL Convention, Chicago, IL.

Describes limitations and how to overcome them.
Computers.

2824. Scarcella, R. C., & Lee, C. (1989). Different paths to writing proficiency in a second language? A preliminary investigation of ESL writers of short-term and long-term residence in the United States. In Miriam R. Eisenstein (Ed.), *The dynamic interlanguage: Empirical studies in second language acquisition* (pp. 137-154). NY: Plenum.

Compares the expository writing of Korean-born university students with varying lengths of residence in the US in order to determine if LOR affects either the route or the speed of English written language acquisition. Finds, in general, that long-term learners wrote better organized essays, containing fewer lexical errors than their short-term peers (implying different stages of development) while they may be nonetheless be at similar morpho-syntactic stages.
Proficiency/LOR/Korean.

2825. Scarcella, R. C., & Lee, C. (1988, March). *Helping Korean students overcome their ESL writing problems.* Paper presented at the 22nd Annual TESOL Convention, Chicago, IL.

See previous item.
Korean.

2826. Scarcella, R. C. (1984a). Cohesion in the writing development of native and non-native English speakers. *Dissertation Abstracts International, 45*(5), 1386A.

Compares the use of cohesive devices in expository essays of thirty native and eighty non-native English speakers. Results suggest that cohesive devices are not what determine coherence but native speakers and advanced ESL students achieved coherence through different structural and pragmatic means.
Cohesion/Exposition.

2827. Scarcella, R. C. (1984b). How writers orient their readers in expository essays: A comparative study of native and non-native English writers. *TESOL Quarterly, 18,* 671-688.

Describes a study of how writers orient their readers in expository essays. The essays of thirty native speakers and eighty non-native were analyzed in an attempt to judge the orienting skills of both groups. The results indicate that non-native speakers are more limited in their ability to orient readers.
Coherence/Audience.

2828. Scarcella, R. C. (1984c, March). *Transfer and the organization of written text: A study in contrastive rhetoric.* Paper presented at the 18th Annual TESOL Convention, Houston, TX.

Reports striking organizational differences in the impromptu expository essays written during a one-hour period by 20 monolingual English speakers and 20

Taiwanese learners of English.
Transfer/Contrastive Rhetoric/Chinese.

2829. Scarcella, R. C., Neu, J., & Allbright, R. (1987, April). *Word processing in the academic writing curriculum*. Paper presented at the 21st Annual TESOL Convention, Miami Beach, FL.
Describes how using computers helps students invent, edit, and revise.
Computers/Word Processing/Academic Writing.

2830. Schaetzel, K. (1988, March). *Preparing ESL students for university writing proficiency exams*. Paper presented at the 22nd Annual TESOL Convention, Chicago, IL.
Presents teaching strategies for helping ESL students prepare for writing trests.
Assessment/IEP.

2831. Schaetzel, K. (1987, March). *Helping ESL students become research and library literate*. Paper presented at the 38th Annual CCCC Meeting, Atlanta, GA.
Research Writing.

2832. Schafer, J. C. (1978). Text-building in English and Vietnamese: A comparative rhetorical analysis, Volumes 1 and 2. *Dissertation Abstracts International, 39*(6), 3555A.
Examines and applies Becker's model of text analysis to an English and a Vietnamese text. Model claims that understanding of text is based on co-text, pre-text, intention, and context. Presents model as useful instructional approach in teaching reading, writing, and English as a second language.
Text Analysis/Vietnamese.

2833. Schafer, J. S. (1983). Linguistic descriptions of speaking and writing and their impact on composition pedagogy. *Journal of Advanced Composition, 4*, 85-106.
Surveys investigations that contrast speaking with writing and concludes that helping students imitate speech in their writing is a proper goal for advanced composition classes.
Speaking-Writing Relations.

2834. Scharer, G. D. E. (1980). Letter writing in an advanced service-English course. In D. L. Bouchard, & L. J. Spaventa (Comps.), *A TEFL anthology: Selected articles from the English Teaching Forum, 1973-78* (pp. 205-210). Washington, DC: International Communication Agency.
Proposes teaching comparative styles of letter writing in a course intended where English is a language of administration and business.
ESP/Letter writing.

2835. Schecter, S., & Harklau, L. (1992, March). *Writing in a non-native language: Past, present, and future*. Paper presented at the 26th Annual TESOL Convention, Vancouver, BC.
Synthesizes findings from research on writing in a non-native language.
Review.

2836. Schecter, S., & Harklau, L. (1991). *Writing in a non-native language: An annotated bibliography* . (Technical Report 51). Berkeley, CA: National Center for Study of Writing and Literacy. [ERIC ED 343 429].

A classified bibliography provides detailed annotations for 170 data-based studies written before 1991 in five areas: text features, proficiency development, the writing process, the relation of NNS writing to other language skills, and instructional factors.

Bibliography.

2837. Schenck, M. J. (1988). *Read, write, revise: A guide to academic writing*. NY: St. Martin's Press.

Combines readings about American culture and instruction in writing to give freshman ESL students a guide to the writing process. Each chapter includes vocabulary, idioms, journal writing, pre-writing, collaborative work, drafting, peer reviewing, and revising.

University/Textbook.

2838. Scheraga, M. (1990). *Practical English writing skills: A complete guide to writing in English*. Littlewood, IL: NTC Publishing Group.

Textbook addresses writing skills that are necessary to function successfully in everyday life. Tasks include leaving messages, writing thank-you notes, preparing resumes, and writing letters.

Beginners/Adult Education/Textbook.

2839. Scheraga, M., & Maculaitis, J. D. (1985, April). *Righting writing -- from fear to fiction*. Paper presented at the 19th Annual TESOL Convention, New York, NY.

Demonstrates progression of lessons for high school ESL from dictation to student publications.

Secondary School/Instruction.

2840. Schick, R. M., & De Masi, M. (1991, April). *Predicting writing performance across countries*. Paper presented at the Annual Meeting of the AERA, Chicago, IL.

Assessment.

2841. Schiller, J. L. (1990). Writing in L1, writing in L2: Case studies of the composing processes of five adult Arabic-speaking ESL writers. *Dissertation Abstracts International, 50*(9), 2883A.

Five ESL college writers composed aloud and were extensively interviewing about their past educational experiences and their perception of writing. Four of these writers show no significant differences between their L1 and L2 patterns of composing.

L1-L2 Comparison/Arabic.

2842. Schlumberger, A. L. (1989, March). *The role of contrastive rhetoric in ESL writing classrooms*. Paper presented at the 40th Annual Convention CCCC Meeting, Seattle, WA.

Contrastive Rhetoric.

2843. Schlumberger, A. L. (1988, March). *Rhetorical analysis: A composition assignment promoting awareness of language and culture*. Paper presented at the 39th Annual CCCC Meeting, St. Louis, MO.

Assignments/Culture.

2844. Schlumberger, A. L., & Clymer, D. (1987, March). *What to do in composition classes when you have ESL students and no ESL expertise*. Paper presented at the

38th Annual CCCC Meeting, Atlanta, GA. [ERIC ED 283 382].

Presents suggestions for nonspecialist teachers dealing with ESL students. Claims that process methodology is very relevant for ESL composition classes.

Process Instruction/Teacher Preparation.

2845. Schlumberger, A. L., & Clymer, D. (1989a). Tailoring composition classes to ESL students' needs. *Teaching English in the Two-Year College, 16*(2), 121-128.

Makes suggestions for composition teachers who have ESL students but lack formal training in teaching English as a second language: placement by holistically scored essays, thematic organization of courses, and attention to all language skills with fewer required papers.

Curriculum/University.

2846. Schlumberger, A. L., & Clymer, D. (1989b). Teacher training through teacher collaboration. In D. M. Johnson, & D. H. Roen (Eds.), *Richness in writing: Empowering ESL students* (pp. 146-159). NY: Longman.

Describes benefits of a training program for graduate assistant teachers which uses a collaborative context for helping them evaluate papers, develop materials, form questions for the final exam and design the curriculum.

Teacher Preparation.

2847. Schlumberger, A. L., & Mangelsdorf, K. (1989, March). *Reading the context*. Paper presented at the 23rd Annual TESOL Convention, San Antonio, TX. [ERIC ED 304 945].

Examines impact of awareness of contrastive rhetoric on writing quality in a second language. Concludes no significant difference due to awarenesss, although context enhanced by knowledge of linguistic and rhetorical forms is a valid objective in ESL writing instruction.

Contrastive Rhetoric.

2848. Schneider, M. L. (1989, March). *Collaboration inside and outside of college writing class*. Paper presented at the 23rd Annual TESOL Convention, San Antonio, TX.

Reports a year-long ethnographic study of collaboration among college ESL writers. Gives a framework, examples, and activities to illustrate the research.

Ethnographic Research.

2849. Schneider, M. L. (1985, April). *How do passing essays pass?* Paper presented at the 19th Annual TESOL Convention, New York, NY.

Explores the difference between good writing and the appearance of good writing, through an analysis of a group of passing essays.

Evaluation.

2850. Schneider, M. L. (1984, March). *Judging writing quality: Does cohesion make a difference?* Paper presented at the 18th Annual TESOL Convention, Houston, TX.

Reports on a study of the extent to which cohesive devices contribute to holistic judgments of writing quality.

Evaluation/Cohesion.

2851. Schneider, M. L., & Connor, U. M. (1990). Analyzing topical structure in ESL essays: Not all topics are equal. *Studies in Second Language Acquisition, 12*, 411-427.

Replicates Connor & Schneider (1988); finds that two topical structure variables -- proportion of sequential and parallel topics in essays -- differentiate the highest from the lower-rated ESL essays.
Coherence/TSA.

2852. Schneider, M. L., & Riggles, J. (1989, March). *Topical structure analysis as a revision strategy.* Paper presented at the 23rd Annual TESOL Convention, San Antonio, TX.
Reports study of the effectiveness of teaching topical structure analysis as a text-based revision strategy on the quality of advanced ESL compositions.
Revision/TSA.

2853. Scholtz, C. M. (1982, May). *An advanced reading and writing course for science students.* Paper presented at the 16th Annual TESOL Convention, Honolulu, HI.
Describes an integrated course for advanced Chinese students in the PRC.
Courses/Reading-Writing Relations/Chinese.

2854. Schreiber, M. (1985). An authentic writing experience. *TESOL Newsletter, 19*(2), 14.
Advices giving advanced students tasks resembling those required in their academic courses. Suggests an example from a course for students of literature.
Task/Literature.

2855. Schroder, H. (1991). Linguistic and text-theoretical research on languages for special purposes. In H. Schroder (Ed.), *Subject-oriented texts: Language for special purposes and text theory* (pp. 1-47). Berlin: deGruyter.
Reviews developments in text-centered LSP (Languages for Special Purposes) research, especially prominent in Europe. Provides a comprehensive classified, unannotated bibliography of the field.
Review/Bibliography/ESP.

2856. Schroen, C., Carroll, S., & Garkov, J. G. (1992, March). *Audio peer review in ESL composition.* Paper presented at the 26th Annual TESOL Convention, Vancouver, BC.
Describes a two-phase process using audiotape peer response and reports results of an experiment to evaluate its success.
Peer Response/Advanced.

2857. Schumann, F. M. (1975). Collective storywriting: Teaching creative writing to ESL children. M. K. Burt, & H. C. Dulay (Eds.), *On TESOL '75: New directions in second language learning, teaching, and bilingual education* (pp. 300-304). Washington, DC: TESOL.
Relates how children developed a booklength story as a classroom activitiy with the teacher's guidance.
Creative Writing/Children.

2858. Schwabe, G. T. (1989, March). *Transfer of native language patterns in ESL student writing.* Paper presented at the 23rd Annual TESOL Convention, San Antonio, TX.
Discusses potential effects upon writing of culturally different reader/writer responsibilities as well as structural contrasts.
Transfer/Culture.

2859. Schwarte, B., & Matsumura-Lothrop, E. (1987). The self-monitoring of articles and verbs in ESL written production. *MinneTESOL Journal, 6*, 29-51. [ERIC ED 336 979].

Studies the ability of 31 advanced ESL students to monitor their use of article and verb errors in composition immediately and after delay. Results show that 25% of verb errors and 15% of article errors were corrected without assistance with half the corrections occuring immediately following production.

Editing/Error Treatment.

2860. Scott, C. T. (1965). Some remarks on the teaching of composition. In R. P. Fox (Ed.), *The 1964 conference papers of the Association of Teachers of English as a Second Language of the National Association of Foreign Student Affairs* (pp. 43-48). NY: NAFSA/University of Southern California Press.

Raises questions of objectives and techniques for teaching composition which go beyond traditional ESL instruction.

Instruction.

2861. Scott, M. S., & Tucker, G. R. (1974). Error analysis and English-language strategies of Arab students. *Language Learning, 24*, 69-97.

Examines and classifies errors of Arabic speaking students in a low intermediate intensive English course at the American University of Beirut in order to describe learners' transitional grammar. Finds more verb errors in speaking and more article errors in writing than vica-versa. Total errors seem to decline over time.

Error Analysis/Arabic.

2862. Scull, S. (1987). *Critical reading and writing for advanced ESL students.* Englewood Cliffs, NJ: Prentice Hall.

Introduces the various rhetorical modes and methods of writing used in college and business. Offers a range of readings, analysis of sample student essays, as well as illustrations of common errors in grammar and punctuation.

University/Textbook.

2863. Secord, M. A. (1978). *A categorization of transitional expressions in English.* Unpublished master's thesis, UCLA, Los Angeles, CA.

Cohesion.

2864. Seda, I., & Abramson, S. (1990). English writing development of young, linguistically different learners. *Early Childhood Research Quarterly, 5*(3), 379-391.

An examination of the emergence of English writing among thirty-one children, including Hmong and Laotian kindergartners. Suggests that native and nonnative children experience similar stages of development and that a transactional relationshp exists bertween their oral and written language.

Children/Development/Speaking-Writing Relations.

2865. Segal, M. K., & Pavlik, C. (1993). *Interactions II: A writing process book.* (Second Ed.). St. Louis, vMO: McGraw-Hill.

Second writing text in a four-level, integrated notional-functional textbook series that guides students through the writing process from paragraphs to compositions treating life-skills and practical topics.

Textbook.

2866. Segal, M. K., & Pavlik, C. (1985). *Interactions I: A writing process book.* (Second

Ed.). St. Louis, MO: McGraw-Hill.

First of two writing levels in a notional-functional basal textbook series encourages students to write from experience, to explore ideas, and to edit emphasizing life-skills through academic topics.

Intermediate/Textbook.

2867. Seidhofer, B. (1990, March). *Summary judgments: Perspectives on reading and writing*. Paper presented at the annual IATEFL meeting, Dublin, Ireland. [ERIC ED 321 571].:

Reports on two kinds of summary writing.

Summary Writing/Reading-Writing Relations.

2868. Seitz, J. E. (1990, March). *Making a difference: What ESL students teach us about teaching*. Paper presented at the 41st Annual CCCC Meeting, Chicago, IL.

2869. Sekara, A. T. (1988). A student-centered report-writing program. *English Teaching Forum*, 26(2), 8-11.

Describes an individualized writing program for advanced ESP report writing, that emphasizes acquiring library skills, building self-esteem through writing, and shifting the active role from the teacher to the student.

Programs/Research Writing.

2870. Selinker, L. (1973, May). *Formal written communication and ESL*. Paper presented at the 7th Annual TESOL Convention, San Juan, Puerto Rico.

Describes rhetorical principles governing multisentential units in discourse.

Rhetoric/Register.

2871. Selinker, L., Kumaravadivelu, B., & Miller, D. (1985). Second-language composition teaching and research: Towards a "safe rule" perspective. *Papers in Applied Linguisitics -- Michigan*, 1(1), 53-83.

Discusses findings of three previous studies and examines process approach to teaching paragraph writing to native and non-native students. Proposes using explicit "safe rules" statements in teaching composition. Analysis of data collected from a course in academic compositions shows that discussion of specific "safe rules" is helpful in overcoming problems in writing. The need for determining learners' interlanguage outcomes empirically is stressed

ESP/Paragraph.

2872. Selinker, L., & Lakshmanan, U. (1990, March). *Consciousness-raising strategies in the rhetoric of writing development*. Paper presented at the 24th Annual TESOL Convention, San Francisco, CA.

Extends consciousness-raising (C-R) strategies from oral syntactic development to rhetorical and written dimensions. Data, gathered in academic contexts, suggest that understanding of rhetorical structures does not guarantee appropriate productive use. The presenters see evidence of apparent fossilized rhetorical interlanguage structures becoming open to destabilization (=acquisition) through C-R when there is merging of known academic content with specific pedagogical input.

Interlanguage/Speaking-Writing Relations.

2873. Selinker, L., Todd-Trimble, M., & Trimble, L. (1978). Rhetorical function-shifts in

EST discourse. *TESOL Quarterly, 12*, 311-320.

Discusses two methods of English of Science and Technology (EST) paragraph development: rhetorical process and rhetorical function-shift development. Sets up hypotheses to account for explicit and implicit information in some EST function-shift paragraphs.

ESP/Rhetoric.

2874. Selinker, L., Todd-Trimble, M., & Trimble, L. (1976). Presuppositional information in ESL discourse. *TESOL Quarterly, 10*, 281-290.

Claims that the reason many non-native speakers find it difficult to comprehend total discourse of English of Science and Technology, even when they know the vocabulary, is because they lack presuppositional or implicit information.

ESP/Background Knowledge.

2875. Selinker, L., & Trimble, L. (1980). Scientific and technical writing: The choice of tense. In D. L. Bouchard, & L. J. Spaventa (Comps.), *A TEFL anthology: Selected articles from English Teaching Forum, 1973-78* (pp. 269-273). Washington, DC: International Communication Agency.

Discusses the rhetorical functions embodied in the choice of tenses in EST materials.

ESP/Rhetoric.

2876. Selinker, L., & Trimble, L. (1974). Formal written communication and ESL. *Journal of Technical Writing and Communication, 4*(2), 81-91.

Discusses research showing the relation between rhetorical function and gramamtical tense choice and how to teach it.

ESP.

2877. Selinker, L., Trimble, L., & Bley-Vroman, R. (1974). Presupposition and technical rhetoric. *English Language Teaching Journal, 29*, 59-65.

Studies the rhetorical function of presuppositions in scientific and technical discourse and their grammatical realizations. Claims that the cover errors of non-native speakers using English of science and technology arise because of lack of understanding of the correlation of the two.

Technical Writing/Background Knowledge.

2878. Semke, H. D. (1984). Effects of the red pen. *Foreign Language Annals, 17*, 195-202.

Studies the effects of four methods of correcting writing assignments. Finds that the progress of students is enhanced by writing practice alone and not by sentence-level corrections. This study recommends that a considerable amount of free writing can help students become better writers.

Feedback/Errors.

2879. Semke, H. D. (1982). *Free-writing -- help or hindrance?* Paper presented at the Annual Meeting of the American Council on the Teaching of Foreign Languages, New York, NY. [ERIC ED 228 850].

Free Writing

2880. Seng, M. W. (1985). Teach writing right on the overhead projector. *TESL Reporter, 18*(1), 3.

Discusses how to use the overhead projector.
Classroom Activities.

2881. Severino, C. (1993a). The "doodles" in context: Qualifying claims about contrastive rhetoric. *The Writing Center Journal, 14*(1), 44-62.
Discusses problems with Kaplan's (1966) original "doodle" study, sugggesting how in EFL contexts student pedagogical histories play against school writing through which rhetorics are transmitted.
Contrastive Rhetoric/Writing Center.

2882. Severino, C. (1993b). ESL and native-English speaking writers and pedagogies. *The Writing Center Journal, 13*(2), 63-70.
Reviews some recent works discussing the differences between native and non-native writers in order to suggest relevance to the writing center.
NS-NNS Comparisons/Writing Center.

2883. Severino, C. (1993c). The sociopolitical implications of response to second language and second dialect writing. *Journal of Second Language Writing, 2*, 181-201.
Defines a continuum of three stances for responding to L2/ESL writing: separatist, accomodationist, and assimilationist and shows how these stances are applicable to the writing of three university students: an international student from Japan, and immigrant from Korea, and an African-American student.
Politics/Responding.

2884. Seward, B. H. (1982). *Writing American English*. Old Tappan, NJ: Prentice Hall Regents.
A workbook for handwriting.
Handwriting/Textbook.

2885. Seward, B. H. (1972). Teaching an advanced composition lesson. *TEFL, 6*(4), 1-2.
Describes a course that uses student-selected topics, multiple drafts, use of field trips and visual aids to enable students to write better.
Process Instruction.

2886. Shabrami, C. J. T. (1988). The role of first language background and major in the development of the expository writing of Japanese and Hispanic graduate students. *Dissertation Abstracts International, 49*(8), 2135A.
Studies the influence of first-language and academic field on the development of English expository writing ability. Results indicate: (1) fluency is more function of topic than a developmental trend; and (2) writing of all groups improves over time, due to the quantity of writing tasks in their disciplines.
Hispanic/Japanese/Exposition.

2887. Shaffer, M. J. (1976). *A composition book: Three chapters and outline (for ESL)*. Unpublished master's thesis, University of Arizona, Flagstaff, AR.
Pedagogy/Materials.

2888. Shakir, A. (1991). Coherence in EFL student-written texts: Two perspectives. *Foreign Language Annals, 24*, 399-411.
Twenty-four EFL secondary school teachers in Jordan who assessed two English expository essays by Arabic-speaking college writers found predominantly sentence level weakness when an independent analysis using current discourse

Coherence/Arabic/Responding.

2890. Shank, C. C. (1986). *Approaching the needs of adult illiterate ESL students*. Unpublished master's thesis, Georgetown University, Washington, DC. [ERIC ED 316 061].

Reviews seven areas in the literature on the learning proceses of adults not literate in their first language.

Literacy/Adult Education.

2891. Sharma, V A. (1982). Syntactic errors as indices of developing language proficiency in Arabic speakers writing English at the intermediate and advanced levels of English as a second language. *Dissertation Abstracts International*, 42(9), 3986A.

Explores use of syntactic errors in the category of finite verb phrase, the relative clause and T-unit or sentence for defining intermediate and advanced levels of second language proficiency. Results show that nature of writing task and syntactic complexity seem to provide best methods for identifying language proficiency.

Proficiency/Objective Measures/Arabic.

2892. Sharma, V. A. (1979a, March). *Errors and syntactic complexity at two levels of ESL*. Paper presented at the 13th Annual TESOL Convention, Boston.

An investigation of verb errors and relative clause errors by Arabic-speaking learners suggests that writing as a mode affects meaurement of syntactic complexity.

Arabic/Error Analysis/Syntactic Development.

2893. Sharma, V. A. (1979b). *Syntactic maturity: Assessing writing proficiency in a second language*. Paper presented at the International Conference on Frontiers in Language Proficiency and Dominance Testing, Carbondale, IL. [ERIC ED 185 105].

Describes a study in which Hunt and O'Donnell's Aluminium Passage was administered to sixty ESL students. Students rewrote to improve the paragraph of 32 short single-clause sentences. Analysis of resulting paragraphs found that error-free T-units and words per error-free T-unit were the most valid measures of syntactic proficiency.

Objective Measures/Syntactic Development.

2894. Sharpsteen, L., & Etter, A. (1992, March). *Teaching composition skills in context: The Tropical Rainforest*. Paper presented at the 26th Annual TESOL Convention, Vancouver, BC.

Demonstrates a thematic unit based on the Knowledge Framework, which develops thinking skills with composition.

Content.

2895. Sharwood Smith, M. (1980). New directions in teaching written English. In D. L. Bouchard, & L. J. Spaventa (Comps.), *A TEFL anthology: Selected articles from the English Teaching Forum, 1973-78* (pp. 211-216). Washington, DC: International Communication Agency.

Advocates teaching written English as communication, working with texts and exercises based on the principle of dynamic polarity.

Communicative Writing.

2896. Sharwood Smith, M. (1974). Experimental formats for exercises in written English. *TESOL Quarterly*, 8, 43-52.

Presents five exercise types intended to promote written communication and

the manipulation of text.
Communicative Writing.

2897. Sharwood Smith, M. (1973). Teaching written English for communication. *RELC Journal*, *4*(2), 48-56.

Argues that problem-solving character of written English requires learner to communicate intentions. Describes some principles, e.g. dynamic polarity, for constructing communicative writing exercises.
Communicative Writing.

2898. Shaw, P. M. (1991). Science research students' composing processes. *English for Specific Purposes*, *10*, 186-206.

Structured interviews with 22 ESL dissertation writers about their composing processes suggests that purpose and audience are especially problematic.
ESP/Graduate Students.

2899. Shaw, P. A. (1982, May). *The place of fluency in the writing skill*. Paper presented at the 16th Annual TESOL Convention, Honolulu, HI.

A replication of Briere's study (1966) supports the notion that fluency can be developed without deterioration in accuracy.
Fluency/Accuracy.

2900. Shaw, P. M., & Donaldson, A. S. (1990, March). *But how can I not copy?* Paper presented at the 24th Annual TESOL Convention, San Francisco, CA.

Describes an approach to training learners to use sample Ph.D. dissertations in their own composing. Emphasizes the role of the EFL specialist in teaching writing for other disciplines within the wider process-product framework.
Research Writing/WAC.

2901. Sheal, P. R., & Wood, S. (1981). Proof-reading as a means of reducing student errors. *English Language Teaching Journal*, *35*(4), 405-407.

Advocates attention to proof-reading, although the results of a pilot project on the effectiveness of proofreading exercises to reduce common student errors were not as dramatic as anticipated.
Errors/Editing.

2902. Sheehan, T. (1986). *Comp one: An introduction composition workbook for students of ESL*. Englewood Cliffs, NJ: Prentice Hall Regents.

Provides a series of progressive lessons in three skill areas: sentence mechanics and grammar, rhetorical patterns, and spelling. Examples and illustrations help students to understand and practice each skill.
Beginners/Textbook.

2903. Shen, F. (1989). The classroom and the wider culture: Identity as a key to learning English composition. *College Composition and Communication*, *40*, 459-466.

Relates personal clashes between background in Marxist Chinese education and the requirements of English composition as well as efforts to reconcile them.
Culture/Chinese.

2904. Shen, Y., & Crymes, R. (1965). *Teaching English as a second language: A classified bibliography*. Honolulu, HI: East-West Center Press.

A section on writing and composition lists 29 items, mostly textbooks.

Bibliography/Textbook.

2905. Sheorey, R. (1992, March). *Goof gravity index of American and Mexican ESL teachers*. Paper presented at the 26th Annual TESOL Convention, Vancouver, BC.

Reports the results of a study comparing error perception of American and Mexican ESL teachers. Evaluates eight error categories in light of "goof gravity indices" for both groups.

Hispanic/Error Gravity/Evaluation.

2906. Sheorey, R. (1985, April). *Goof gravity in ESL: Native vs. non-native perceptions*. Paper presented at the 19th Annual TESOL Convention, New York, NY.

Compares error perception of ESL teachers in U.S. and India evaluating eight categories of grammatical errors in ESL compositions.

NS-NNS Comparisons/India/Error Gravity.

2907. Sheorey, R. (1978). An investigation of the problems in second language discourse structure and its pedagogical implications in the teaching of English as a second language at the advanced level. *Dissertation Abstracts International, 39*(4), 2107A.

Examines the discourse structures of advanced ESL students writing in English and relates them to the discourse structures in their native languages. Presents a pedagogical model based on approaches of Christensen, Pike, Becker, and Rodgers and suggests guidelines for use of this model.

Discourse Analysis.

2908. Sheorey, R., & Rothenheber, P. (1993, April). *Hyping writing skills with HyperCard*. Paper presented at the 27th Annual TESOL Convention, Atlanta, GA.

Shows how to use a Macintosh computer program to develop the writing skills of LEP students.

Computers.

2909. Sheorey, R., & Ward, M. (1984, March). *Using non-ESL teachers' perceptions of error gravity in correcting ESL compositions*. Paper presented at the 18th Annual TESOL Convention, Houston, TX.

Reports results of judgments by a large sample of college professionals in various technological fields about eight common ESL errors.

Error Gravity.

2910. Sheraga, M., & Maculaitis, J. D. (1985, April). *Righting writing -- from fear to fiction*. Paper presented at the 19th Annual TESOL Convention, New York, NY.

Demonstrates how a teacher can bring students from dictation to editing and publishing a collection of their own work.

Student Publications.

2911. Sherman, J. (1992). Your own thoughts in your own words. *ELT Journal, 46*, 190-198.

Discusses different cultural attitudes toward the function of the written word and the writer's purpose as experienced by an English teacher in the Italian educational system.

Italian/Academic Writing.

2912. Sherrard, C. (1989). Teaching students to summarize: Applying textlinguistics. *System, 17*, 1-12.

Uses the macrostructure model of Van Dijk and Kintsch (1978) to analyze and improve the teaching of summarizing skills to students of translation and interpretation.
Summary Writing.

2913. Shezi, G. T. (1991). *An investigation into the kinds and amounts of writing tasks assigned in some Black South African secondary and high schools*. Unpublished master's thesis, Iowa State University, Ames, IA.
South Africa/Secondary School/Task.

2914. Shih, M. (1992, March). *Grammar editing strategies for ESL writers*. Paper presented at the 25th Annual TESOL Convention, New York, NY.
Poster session presents strategies for students to improve their self-correction of common ESL errors.
Editing/Grammar.

2915. Shih, M. (1986a, March). *Content-based approaches to teaching academic writing*. Paper presented at the 20th Annual TESOL Convention, Anaheim, CA.
Defines five approaches to teaching academic writing based on writing tasks assigned in American university courses.
Academic Writing/University.

2916. Shih, M. (1986b). Content-based approaches to teaching academic writing. *TESOL Quarterly, 20*, 617-648.
Describes five content-based approaches to teaching academic writing. Invention strategies are discussed for use in the classroom instead of the normal practice from patterns and guidelines are given for designing content-based writing courses.
Courses/Academic Writing.

2917. Shih, M. (1984, March). *An integrated skills approach for advanced ESL composition*. Demonstration at the 18th Annual TESOL Convention, Houston, TX.
Gives guidelines for developing a program that integrates skills to help advanced ESL writers to summarize synthesize, and evaluate issues in writing assignments.
Advanced.

2918. Shih, M. (1983, March). *Responding to writing: How can feedback prompt ESL students to develop revision and editing skills?* Workshop at the 17th Annual TESOL Convention, Toronto, Ontario.
Presents common techniques for structuring feedback.
Feedback/Revision.

2919. Shih, M., & Johns, A. M. (1989, March). *EAP course design and the issue of transferable skills*. Paper presented at the 23rd Annual TESOL Convention, San Antonio, TX.
Examines course design of a predictive and a reactive model for EAP.
Courses/Academic Writing.

2920. Shindler, J. (1987, April). *Facing in-class writing: A process for advanced ESL writers*. Paper presented at the 21st Annual TESOL Convention, Miami Beach, FL.
Uses an in-class exam essay to show how to encourage self-questioning in a

six step process for advanced ESL writers.
Advanced/Assignments.

2921. Shindler, J. (1983, March). *Letting go: Designing the intermediate-advanced ESL composition class for college bound students*. Paper presented at the 17th Annual TESOL Convention, Toronto, Ontario.

Suggests encouraging real world involvement in campus activities, such as preparing a monthly foreign students column for the newspaper.
Intermediate/Advanced.

2922. Shinoda, Y. (1983). Some practical advice on teaching English technical writing to foreign students. *Technical Writing Teacher, 10*, 140-147.

Examines some of the educational bases underlying the difficulties English as a second language poses for Japanese and other foreign students and how these affect instructional approaches for technical writing teachers. Discusses three factors to keep in mind when teaching foreign students: technical and semi-technical terms, grammar, and rhetoric.
Technical Writing/Japanese.

2923. Shishin, A. (1985). Rhetorical patterns in letters to the editor. *Journal of the Aichi Institute of Technology, 20*, 17-28. [ERIC ED 288 350].

Dismisses the view that cultures are limited to one rhetorical pattern and claims that both linear and non-linear patterns are common in both Japanese and English discourse. Recommends explicit teaching of both patterns based on the assumption that the awareness of rhetorical conventions enables non-native writers to learn new conventions faster.
Rhetoric/Japanese.

2924. Shoemaker, C. (1993a). *Write ideas: A beginning writing text*. Boston: Heinle & Heinle.

A topically-organized process approach with personal stories as starting points.
Textbook/Beginners.

2925. Shoemaker, C. (1993b). *Write in the middle*. Orlando, FL: Harcourt Brace & World.

Guides intermediate level students through the writing process using invention techniques, journal writing, summarizing, thesis writing, and revision.
Textbook/Intermediate.

2926. Shoemaker, C. (1985). *Write in the corner*. NY: Harcourt Brace Jovanovich.

Textbook is based on the view that all writing is personal as well as a process.
Secondary School/Textbook.

2927. Shook, R. (1978). Sentence combining: A theory and two reviews. *TESL Reporter, 11*(3), 4. [ERIC ED 159 894].

Describes the theory underlying sentence-combining and reviews two practice books.
Sentence Combining.

2928. Sides, M. N. (1988, March). *Collaborative learning: Teaching writing in the refugee classroom*. Paper presented at the 39th Annual CCCC Meeting, St. Louis, MO.
Collaboration/Refugees.

2929. Silber, P. (1979). Teaching written English as a second language. *College*

Composition and Communication, 30, 296-300.
   Advises students to imitate the pattern practice and rigid structures in order to realize how writing conveys a message to the reader and to recognize that there is a fundamental distinction between spoken and written language.
   Approaches.

2930. Silva, T. (1993a, April). *ESL students in freshman composition: Placement issues.* Paper presented at the 27th Annual TESOL Convention, Atlanta, GA.
   Describes three models for providing freshman composition to NNSs.
   Placement/Freshman Composition.

2931. Silva, T. (1993b, April). *Resources for prospective teachers of ESL writers.* Paper presented at 44th Annual Convention of CCCC, San Diego, CA.
   Teacher Preparation.

2932. Silva, T. (1993c). Toward an understanding of the distinct nature of L2 writing: The ESL research and its implications. *TESOL Quarterly, 27*, 657-677.
   An examination of 72 research reports indicates salient differences in both the composing processes and text features of L1 and L2 writing.
   L1-L2 Comparison/Review.

2933. Silva, T. (1992a). L1 vs. L2 writing: ESL graduate students' perceptions. *TESL Canada Journal, 10*(1), 27-47.
   A classroom based study explores how ESL graduate students perceive the differences between writing in English and their native language and how such perceptions should be reflected in teacher practices.
   L1-L2 Comparison/Perceptions.

2934. Silva, T. (1992b, March). *Current issues in ESL writing: Differences in written texts of ESL and NES writers.* Paper presented at the 43rd Annual CCCC Meeting, Cincinnati, OH.
   Summarizes thirty-seven reports of empirical research suggesting that while ESL and NES are very similar, ESL texts are distinct in quality, fluency, accuracy, structure, and style.
   NS-NNS Comparisons/Review.

2935. Silva, T. (1992c, March). *Research agendas for ESL writing: Differences in ESL and NES writing.* Paper presented at a Colloquium at the 26th Annual TESOL Convention, Vancouver, BC.
   Reviews and analyzes 37 reports comparing NES and NNS writing patterns.
   NS-NNS Comparisons.

2936. Silva, T. (1991, March). *Comparing composing processes: ESL and NES freshman writers.* Paper presented at the 25th Annual TESOL Convention, New York, NY.
   Perceptions of personal, product, and process variables differ between ESL and NES and between Spanish and Chinese ESL writers.
   NS-NNS Comparisons/Spanish/Chinese.

2937. Silva, T. (1990a). A comparative study of the composing of selected ESL and native English-speaking freshman writers. *Dissertation Abstracts International, 51*(10), 3397A.
   Seeks to identify variables which distinguish the composing of ESL and NES

freshman writers. Data include interviews as well as introspective and retrospective protocols, and compositions by six first-semester freshmen from English, Spanish, and Chinese first language groups. Reports significant differences between these populations in terms of experience, process, and product variables.
NS-NNS Comparisons/University.

2938. Silva, T. (1990b). Second language composition instruction: Developments, issues, and directions in ESL. In B. Kroll (Ed.), *Second language writing: Research insights for the classroom* (pp. 11-23). Cambridge: Cambridge University Press.
Provides a chronological review of the major studies that have influenced the teaching of composition to ESL students. Advocates principled evaluation of approaches and the development of comprehensive models.
Review/Instruction.

2939. Silva, T. (1990c, March). *Comparing the composing of ESL and native English speaking freshman writers*. Paper presented at the 41st Annual CCCC Meeting, Chicago, IL.
Reports finding salient differences in several case studies of the written products as well as writing processes of native and non-native college students.
NS-NNS Comparisons/Research.

2940. Silva, T. (1989a, March). *A critical review of ESL composing process research*. Paper presented at the 23rd Annual TESOL Convention, San Antonio, TX. [ED 305 820].
Interprets finding and critiques the methods in 22 research reports on composing by college ESL students.
Review.

2941. Silva, T. (1989b, March). *A review of the research on the evaluation of ESL writing*. Paper presented at 40th Annual CCCC Meeting, Seattle, WA. [ERIC ED 309 643].
Discusses the basic issues in the field of ESL writing assessment, including the use of various instruments, indirect measures, correlational results and other language testing matters.
Evaluation/Review.

2942. Silva, T. (1988a). Comments on Vivian Zamel's "Recent research on writing pedagogy": A reader responds . . . [In The Forum]. *TESOL Quarterly*, 22, 517-520.
Questions Zamel's assumption (1987) that LI and L2 writing are essentially the same phenomenon and her advocacy of qualitative research.
Review.

2943. Silva, T. (1988b, March). *Research on the composing process of ESL writers: A review and critique*. Paper presented at the 39th Annual CCCC Meeting, St. Louis, MO.
Critical review of many empirical studies of ESL composition which have appeared in the last decade discerning trends, patterns, and methodological concerns.
Review.

2944. Silva, T. (1987, March). *ESL composition: An historical perspective*. Paper presented at the 38th Annual CCCC Meeting, Atlanta, GA. [ERIC ED 282 242].
Summarizes research in ESL composition from 1945; proposes model for instruction based on the basic variables of second language writing.

Review/Instruction.
2945. Silva, T. (1986, March). *Making connections: Independent research, the writing classroom, and the ESL student*. Paper presented at the 37th Annual CCCC Meeting, New Orleans, LA.

Reports on research writing at the advanced IEP level, especially how research materials on a topic chosen by students can be developed into acceptable expository prose.
Research Writing/IEP/Advanced.
2946. Silva, T., & Reichelt, M. (1993a). Selected bibliography of recent scholarship in second language writing. *Journal of Second Language Writing*, 2, 173-177.

Tri-annual review in JSLW classifies and summarizes 18 research-oriented reports on writers, texts, and instruction from 1991-92. Some studies on second languages other than English are included.
Bibliography.
2947. Silva, T., & Reichelt, M. (1993b). Selected bibliography of recent scholarship in second language writing. *Journal of Second Language Writing*, 2, 279-285.

Presents summaries of 23 recent research-oriented studies on writers, processes, texts, audience and assessment, reading and writing, and instruction in second language writing published in 1992-93. Includes some non-ESL/EFL references.
Bibliography.
2948. Silva, T., & Reichelt, M. (1992). Selected bibliography of recent scholarship in second language writing. *Journal of Second Language Writing*, 2, 91-95.

This first installment of a tri-annual classified survey in JSLW selects and annotates 19 recent research reports, articles, and dissertationspublished in 1991-92 on various topics concerning second language writing.
Bibliography.
2949. Silver, C. (1991). Word processing with a syntheziser and ESL students. *Computers in Education*, 8(6), 18-19.

Describes a project which uses a word processor with voice synthesizer to facilitate language patterns.
Word Processing.
2950. Silver, N. W. (1990). The effect of word processing on self-esteem and quality of writing among beginning English as a second language (ESL) students. *Dissertation Abstracts International*, 51(12), 4047A.

Investigates the effect of using word processing on the self-esteem and quality of writing of beginning ESL students in a secondary school. Four classes (N=66), divided between students who received word processing in a computer center and those who had only the recursive developmental learning sequence treatment, were studied in a quasi-experiment that used a pre-test/post-test design. Word processing improved the quality of writing but did not provide a significant positive effect upon student self-esteem.
Computers/Instruction/Secondary School.
2951. Simmen, E. (1978, April). *From event to essay: The intercultural experience through*

composition. Paper presented at the 12th Annual TESOL Convention, Mexico City, Mexico.

Suggests that writing can be used to reduce "culture shock" experienced by international students. Two assignments are offered: a BEFORE-DURING-AFTER composition which puts the writer into an incident reflecting contrasting cultures and a HERE-and-THERE composition (e.g. relaxing in parks) that investigates dissimilarities in apparently common experiences.

Culture/Topic.

2952. Simmonds, P. (1985). A survey of English language examinations. *ELT Journal, 39*, 33-42.

Compares twenty-three American and British ESL examinations, including methods of teaching writing.

Evaluation/Review.

2953. Simon, S. T. (1976). *Teaching writing to advanced ESL students*. Unpublished master's thesis, Hunter College, CUNY, New York, NY.

Advanced.

2954. Simpson, E. (1982). Tutoring the non-native student in the regular school program. In C. Carter (Ed.), *Non-native and nonstandard dialect students* (pp. 49-50). Urbana, IL: NCTE.

Uses a tutoring program to cope with placement of two Cambodian students in a high school remedial writing class.

Secondary School/Tutoring/Cambodian.

2955. Sims, B. R., & Guice, S. (1992). Differences between business letters from native and non-native speakers of English. *The Journal of Business Communication, 29*(1), 23-39.

Compares 214 letters of inquiry about admission to graduate study in English by NS and NESs in a test of the assumption that cultural factors affect communication.by NESs deviated less from US business norms. NNSs letters were significantly more polite, contained more unnecessary personal and professional information, and a significantly greater number of inappropriate requests.

Business Writing/NS-NNS Comparisons.

2956. Sims, D. M. (1979). Teaching written English to adult ESL students: Some critical annotations of current teacher materials. *TESL Reporter, 12*(2), 6.

Materials.

2957. Sindermann, G., & Horsella, M. (1989). Strategy markers in writing. *Applied Linguistics, 10*(4), 438-446.

Translation/Hispanic.

2958. Singh, F. B. (1988, March). *The teaching of writing and the foreign-born writing teacher: Some implications for ESL programs*. Paper presented at the 39th Annual CCCC Meeting, St. Louis, MO.

2959. Singleton, C. (1983). *Sentence combining for the intermediate level ESL students* . Washington, DC: ERIC/FLL. [ERIC ED 267 622].

Presents a method of teaching composition to intermediate ESL students based on sentence combining. The course consists of four segments: using, varying, and rearranging connectors; ordering thoughts; choosing and varying styles; and eliminating faulty constructions. Sentence combining is the central focus, and vocabulary, grammar, and punctuation are deemphasized.

Sentence Combining/Intermediate/Courses.

2960. Siripham, S. (1989). An investigation of syntax, semantics and rhetoric in the English writing of 15 Thai graduate students. *Dissertation Abstracts International*, 50(4), 941A.

Analyzes the syntactic and semantic errrors as well as style in essays by fifteen Thai students on "My First Week's Experience in the U.S." Finds that Thai students were unaware of rhetorical style in English but made errors in syntax and semantics. The most frequent were verb errors in syntax and awkward expression in semantics.

Thai/Error Analysis/Style.

2961. Sistrunk, S. A. (1987). *Coordination and subordination in Arabic-speaking students' English writing*. Unpublished master's thesis, University of Kansas, Lawrence, KS.

Arabic/Syntactic Structures.

2962. Siu, K. P. (1986). *The effects of mode on syntactic and rhetorical complexity for EFL students at three grade levels*. Unpublished master's thesis, Chinese University of Hong Kong, Hong Kong. [ERIC ED 274 163].

Study explores narrative and argumentative writing by Hong Kong secondary and university students. Subjects were forty university English majors, forty Form four, and forty Form six secondary students. Students in these grade levels experienced difficulty in using the argumentative mode at the syntactic and rhetorical levels. The investigation concludes that students of English as a foreign language have not been taught the necessary rhetorical skills to write argumentative compositions and suggests that the needed academic skill be consciously taught in the classroom.

Chinese/Argumentation/Narration.

2963. Sivall, J. (1987). Inter-school correspondence: A rationale and an invitation. *TECFORS*, 10, 14-15.

Describes a newsletter exchange among three Canadian ESL programs.

Audience/Student Publications.

2964. Skelton, J., & Pindi, M. (1987). Acquiring a new context: Zairean students struggle with the academic mode. *English for Specific Purposes*, 6, 121-131.

Distinguishes types of transfer in the written interlanguage of Zairean economics students who have a high tolerance for transfer and errors.

Zairean/Error Analysis.

2965. Skibniewski, L. (1988). The writing processes of advanced foreign language learners in their native and foreign languages: Evidence from thinking aloud and behavior protocols. *Studia Anglica Posnaniensia*, 21, 177-186.

Studies the nature of writing processes through the expository prose of skilled, unskilled, and average student Polish EFL writers using their native and foreign language. Finds differences in the writing processes of skilled and unskilled writers in both languages.

Process Research/L1-L2 Comparison/Polish.

2966. Skibniewski, L., & Skibniewski, M. (1986). Experimental study: The writing process of intermediate/advanced foreign language learners in their foreign and native languages. *Studia Anglica Posnaniensia, 19*(3), 143-163.

Investigates stages of the writing process of freshman students (N=21) writing descriptive essays in English and Polish. Finds the same stages as well as rates of composing by subjects in NL and FL; but skilled and unskilled writers differed.
L1-L2 Comparison/Polish.

2967. Skidmore, C. (1993). *Process writing portfolio program.* Burlingame, CA: Alta.

A folder for written work using a portfolio system with reference guides and checklists.
Textbook/Portfolios.

2968. Slager, W. R. (1972). Classroom techniques for controlling composition. In K. Croft (Ed.), *Readings on English as a second language* (pp. 232-243). Cambridge, MA: Winthrop.

Suggests several controlled exercises for paragraph writing.
Control/Classroom Activities.

2969. Slager, W. R. (1966). Controlling composition: Some practical classroom techniques. In R. B. Kaplan (Ed.), *Selected conference papers of the Association of Teachers of English as a Second Language* (pp. 77-85). NY: NAFSA/University of Southern California Press.

Presents ten ways to teach controlled composition beyond the sentence level.
Control.

2970. Smadi, O. M. (1986). A focused efficient method for teaching composition. *English Teaching Forum, 24*(3), 35-36.

Advocates a procedure in which the teacher focuses on previously determined objectives and the gradually progresses from oral practice to written compositon.
Arabic.

2971. Smalley, R. L., & Reutten, M. K. (1993). *Refining composition skills: Rhetoric and grammar for ESL students.* (Third Ed.). Boston: Heinle & Heinle.

Combines practice in rhetorical strategies and techniques with a review of grammar. Appendices provide a handbook for writing, grammar, and mechanics.
University/Grammar/Textbook.

2972. Smith, A. (1992, March). *Evaluating ESL composition: Does a holistic approach really work?* Paper presented at the 26th Annual TESOL Convention, Vancouver, BC.

Reports research showing the value of holistic scoring for global assessment and its weakness for evaluating local problems.
Evaluation/Holistic.

2973. Smith, A. (1993, April). *Teaching successful revision strategies in the ESL writing classroom.* Paper presented at the 27th Annual TESOL Convention, Atlanta, GA.

Reports a videotaped protocol analysis of revision by novice and expert NES and ESL writers. Stage, level, stype, and purpose of revision are considered.
Revision//NS-NNS Comparisons.

2974. Smith, M. S. (1976). Writing versus speech. *English Language Teaching Journal, 31*, 17-19.

    Claims that traditionally the importance of speaking in a foreign language is stressed over writing, yet writing improves speech. States that vocabulary and structures are more important then pronunciation and are common to both writing and speech.

    Speaking-Writing Relations.

2975. Smith, M. (1992, March). *Contexts for writing on the border: The community and the constraints of Hispanic freshman writers.* Paper presented at the 43rd Annual CCCC Meeting, Cincinnati, OH.

    Hispanic/University.

2976. Smith, R. M. (1981). Individualizing composition in a heterogeneous class. *TECFORS, 4*(4), 4-6. [ERIC ED 267 647].

    Reports sucessfully adapting the Personlized System of Instruction (PSI) to the teaching of technicl writing for ESL students.

    ESP.

2977. Smith, W., Conrad, S. M., Frodesen, J. M., Goldstein, L. M., Holten, C. A., Katz, A. M., & Negrey, B. (1993, April). *Colloquium on conversational interaction in the writing conference.* Colloquium presented at the 27th Annual TESOL Convention, Atlanta, GA.

    Colloquium consists of four presentations on the discourse/conversational analysis of ESL writing conferences. Oral and written negotiation, NS-NNS negotiation, individual conferencing styles, and the pedagogical purposes of conference talk are treated.

    Conferencing.

2978. Smith, W., & Frodesen, J. M. (1991, March). *Student writers' use of peer feedback in essay revision.* Paper presented at the 25th Annual TESOL Convention, New York, NY.

    Reports a study of the attention and use made of peer feedback by developmental ESL writing students (N=48).

    Peer Response/Revision.

2979. Smithies, M. S. (1981). Formal style in an oral culture: Problems at the university level. *English Language Teaching Journal, 35*, 369-372.

    Discusses the problem of shifting from oral to written forms in Third World ESL countries is illustrated by students at the University of Technology in Papua New Guinea. Gives examples of informal usage of written English that contains too much slang contrasted with overly formal English.

    Speaking-Writing Relations/ Papua New Guinea.

2980. Smithies, M. S. (1972). The teaching of writing. *Bulletin of the English Language, 2*(1), 9-30.

    Criticizes free writing for encouraging the production of errors. Remedy is to provide controlled exercises, drills on sentences and mechanics which are applied to letter writing.

    Control/Error Treatment.

2981. Smithies, M. S., & Holzknecht, S. (1981). Errors in Papua New Guinea written English at the tertiary level. *RELC Journal, 12*(2), 10-34.

    Multilingual students show a wide range of errors in English.

    Error Analysis.

2982. Smoke, T. (1992). *A writer's workbook: An interactive writing text for ESL students.* (Second Ed.). NY: St. Martin's Press.

    Each of fifteen chapters presents a main reading intended to interest students followed by discussion activities and opportunities to debate, write, or do further reading. Exercises in each chapter deal with invention, strategies, form, development, revising, and editing. Several alternate ways of using the textbook are suggested.

    Advanced/Textbook.

2983. Smoke, T. (1991). Becoming an academic insider: One student's experience of attaining academic success in college. *Dissertation Abstracts International, 52*(6), 2055A.

    Presents a four-year case study of a female developmental ESL student who moves from academic outsider to insider. Her success is attributed to her development, first, of a community of allies who provided assistance with writing, advice about academic problems, and support and, second, to her integration of her prior knowledge with her new learning.

    University/Chinese/Academic Writing.

2984. Smoke, T. (1988, March). *Using photographs to teach academic writing.* Paper presented at the 22nd Annual TESOL Convention, Chicago, IL.

    Historical photographs, family and native country as well as "Polaroid-type" pictures are effective in creative context for teaching rhetorical patterns.

    Materials.

2985. Smoke, T. (1987a, March). *What happens after the developmental writing ESL courses.* Paper presented at the 38th Annual CCCC Meeting, Atlanta, GA.

    See next item.

    Curriculum.

2986. Smoke, T. (1987b). What happens beyond the developmental writing/ESL course? In G. Brookes, & J. Gantzer (Eds.), *Improving the odds: Helping ESL students succeed. Selected papers from the 1987 CUNY ESL Council Conference, New York, NY* (pp. 24-27). NY: CUNY Resource Center. [ERIC ED 328 068].

    A follow-up study finds that early intervention is necessary if ESL students are to succeed in college.

    Curriculum.

2987. Smolten, L., & Munson, S. (1993, April). *Teacher training in the use of portfolios.* Paper presented at the 27th Annual TESOL Convention, Atlanta, GA.

    Focuses on training prospective ESL teachers in holistic assessment and the use of portfolios.

    Evaluation/Teacher Preparation.

2988. Snell, D., & Pitillo, A. (1993, April). *Student composition feedback: Do ESL and EFL instructors differ?* Paper presented at the 27th Annual TESOL Convention, Atlanta, GA.

Compares comments on the writing of ESL and EFL university students by four teaches in each environment.
Feedback/Japanese.

2989. Snow, M. A., & Brinton, D. M. (1988). The adjunct model of language instruction: An ideal EAP framework. In S. Benesch (Ed.), *Ending remediation: Linking ESL and content in higher education* (pp. 33-52). Washington, DC: TESOL.
Describes the rationale for and the implementation of an adjunct model of language instruction in which English/ESL courses are linked with content courses. Suggests applications of this model to other ESL/EFL settings.
Programs/Adjunct.

2990. Snow, M. A., & Brinton, D. M. (1984, March). *Linking ESL courses with university content courses: The adjunct model*. Paper presented at the California Association of Teachers of English, San Jose, CA. [ERIC ED 244 515].
Advocates integrating ESL writing with other university courses across the curriculum.
Academic Writing/Content.

2991. Snyder, B., & Auerbach, B. (1986). *Bridges: From sentence to paragraph*. San Diego, CA: Harcourt Brace Jovanovich.
A thematically and grammatically focused textbook emphasizing writing beyond the sentence.
Beginners/Secondary School/Textbook.

2992. So, W. Y. (1986). Integrating first language and second language approaches to writing. *Dissertation Abstracts International, 47*(4), 1308A.
A survey of the research on English composition and ESL writing serves as the basis for proposing an integrated approach to ESL writing instruction.
Instruction.

2993. So, W. Y. (1980, March). *Toward a more effective method in ESL writing*. Paper presented at the 14th Annual TESOL Convention, San Francisco, CA.
Reports success with a program that combines Krashen's monitor model and Curran's Counseling Learning to improve individual writing performance.
Methods.

2994. Soh, B., & Soon, Y. (1991). English by E-Mail: Creating a global classroom via the medium of computer technology. *ELT Journal, 45*, 287-292.
Describes a project that attempts to improve written communicatiojn and cross-cultural awareness, by using E-mail telecommunications between Singapore and Quebec.
Computers.

2995. Sohn, D. A., & Enger, E. (1990). *Writing by doing*. (Second Ed.). Littlewood, IL: NTC Publishing Group.
Text directly involves students in the writing process in a step-by-step approach from the basics to more sophistocated tasks.
Intermediate/Textbook.

2996. Sokmen, A. A. (1988). Taking advantage of conference-centered writing. *TESOL Newsletter, 22*(1), 1, 5.

Discusses the Garrison (1974) format for creating a conference-centered course.
Conferencing/Syllabus Design.

2997. Sokolik, M., & Tillyer, A. (1992). Beyond portfolios: Looking at student projects as teaching and evaluation devices. *College ESL, 2*(2), 47-51.

Outlines the advantages for students and teachers of writing projects, i.e., lengthy, unified pieces of writing on a single theme or topic whether research-oriented, essayist or creatively.
Project Work/Assessment.

2998. Soter, A. O. (1988). The second language learner and cultural transfer in narration. In A. C. Purves (Ed.), *Writing across languages and cultures: Issues in contrastive rhetoric* (pp. 177-205). Newbury Park, CA: Sage.

Examines the narratives written in English by Vietnamese, Arabic-speaking Lebanese, and native-speaking Australian students. Results indicate ESL writers bring their own cultural experiences and knowledge of language to their writing and reading and encode meanings in ways different from the target language.
Vietnamese/Arabic.

2999. Soter, A. O. (1985). Writing: A third language for second language learners: A cross-cultural discourse analysis of the writing of school children in Australia. *Dissertation Abstracts International, 46*(11), 3274A.

Examines discourse and style in the narrative writing of native and non-native speakers at two grade levels. Results show a weak tendency for students from different language backgrounds to use different patterns of story development.
NS-NNS Comparisons/Style/Elementary/Narration.

3000. Southard, B., Caldwell, V., & Southard, S. G. (1984, March). *The use of cloze procedure as a predictor of writing ability.* Paper presented at the 18th Annual TESOL Convention, Houston, TX.

Findings strongly suggest cloze is a significant predictor of ESL writing ability from placement in college level composition courses.
Assessment.

3001. Southard, S. G. (1982). *Technical writing and beginning ESL students: A workshop approach.* Paper presented at the International Technical Communication Conference, Boston. [ERIC ED 226 352].

Describes a technical writing workshop for ESL students. Suggests ways of overcoming difficulties caused by students limited English proficiency.
Technical Writing.

3002. Spaan, M. (1993). The effect of prompt in essay examinations. In D. Douglas, & C. Chappelle (Eds.), *A new decade of language testing research* (pp. 98-122). Alexandria, VA: TESOL.

Finds that the choice between prompts did not have a significant effect on holistically-scored essays by eighty-eight ESL students writing two essays as part of the MELAB.
Prompts/Assessment.

3003. Spaan, M. (1989, March). *Essay tests: What's in a prompt?* Paper presented at the

23rd Annual TESOL Convention, San Antonio, TX.
Investigates the effect of topic types on writer, essay, and graders.
Assessment/Prompts.

3004. Spack, R. (1993a). *The international story: An anthology with guidelines for reading and writing about fiction.* NY: St. Martin's Press.
Offers 22 complete short stories written by authors from 17 countries, background and discussion activities, and advice for writing interpretive and critical essays.
Textbook/Literature.

3005. Spack, R. (1993b). Student meets text, text meets student: Finding a way into academic discourse. In J. G. Carson, & I. Leki (Eds.), *Reading in the composition classroom: Second language perspectives* (pp. 183-196). Boston: Heinle & Heinle.
Argues that academic writing is not detached and impersonal but is rather an engaging and personal process of seeking knowledge and understanding.
Academic Writing/Reading-Writing Relations.

3006. Spack, R. (1991, March). *The subject matter of a writing class.* Paper presented at the Colloquium on Writing at the 25th Annual TESOL Convention, New York, NY.
Content.

3007. Spack, R. (1990a). *Guidelines: A cross-cultural reading-writing text.* NY: St. Martin's Press.
Integrates a variety of readings, including several that cover cross-cultural topics, with a progression of increasingly challenging writing assignments based on the readings.
University/Textbook.

3008. Spack, R. (1990b, March). *Writing in academic settings: Addressing three populations.* Paper presented at the Colloquium on Writing at the 24th Annual TESOL Convention, San Francisco, CA.
Academic Writing/University.

3009. Spack, R. (1988a). The author responds to Braine . . . [In The Forum]. *TESOL Quarterly, 22,* 703-705.
Rejects Braine's call for teaching the writing of other disciplines.
Advanced/University.

3010. Spack, R. (1988b). The author responds to Johns . . . [In The Forum]. *TESOL Quarterly, 22,* 707-708.
Reiterates that teaching writing in disciplines should be done only by those well-versed in the subject matter.
Advanced/Curriculum/Academic Writing.

3011. Spack, R. (1988c). Initiating ESL students into the academic discourse community: How far should we go? *TESOL Quarterly, 22,* 29-51.
Provides a detailed review of research in L1 writing programs and defines "academic writing" and writing across curriculum. Claims that ESL teachers should not teach writing in the disciplines but should rather concentrate on general principles of inquiry and rhetoric and writing from other texts. Emphasis on strategies for academic writing and on form.

Academic Writing/Discourse Communities.
3012. Spack, R. (1988d, March). *Writing workshop for teachers*. Workshop presented at the 22nd Annual TESOL Convention, Chicago, IL.
Workshop.
3013. Spack, R. (1987, March). *Academic discourse communities*. Paper presented at the Colloquium on Writing at the 21st Annual TESOL Convention, Miami Beach, FL.
Discourse Communities.
3014. Spack, R. (1986, March). *Errors and explanations*. Paper presented at the Colloquium on Writing at the 20th Annual TESOL Convention, Anaheim, CA.
Errors.
3015. Spack, R. (1985). Literature, reading, writing, and ESL: Bridging the gaps. *TESOL Quarterly, 19*, 703-726.
Discusses the academic, intellectual, cultural, and linguistic benefits of using literature in an ESL program. It also examines the current research on reading and composing in relation to literature and describes a literature and compositon course for ESL students.
Curriculum/Literature.
3016. Spack, R. (1984a). Comments on Joy Reid's "The radical outliner and the radical brainstormer: A perspective on composing processes" . . . [In The Forum]. *TESOL Quarterly, 19*, 396-398.
Argues that Reid's "radical outlining" is linear rather than generative.
Invention.
3017. Spack, R. (1984b). Invention strategies and the ESL college composition student. *TESOL Quarterly, 18*, 649-670.
In light of a review of invention research, author discusses a variety of discovery techniques and provides a rationale for teaching invention in a writing class. Uses a student's notes to justify how invention strategies can help students generate better ideas.
Invention.
3018. Spack, R. (1983a, March). *The use of student-teacher working journals in ESL composition*. Paper presented at the 17th Annual TESOL Convention, Toronto, Ontario.
See next item.
Journal Writing.
3019. Spack, R., & Sadow, C. (1983b). Student-teacher working journals in ESL freshman composition. *TESOL Quarterly, 17*, 575-593.
Recommends journal writing in ESL composition class as an effective method of introducing expressive writing in an expository writing course. The student-teacher working journals are based not on personal topics but on subjects discussed in class, and therefore, constitute a non-threatening approach to writing which leads to generating and sharing of ideas, contemplation of and commitment to writing.
Journal Writing.
3020. Spack, R., & Sadow, C. (1988, March). *Writing workshop for teachers*. Paper presented at the 22nd Annual TESOL Convention, Chicago, IL.

Presents a workshop aimed to stimulate writing in response to reading.
Reading-Writing Relations.

3021. Spack, R., & Sadow, C. (1984, March). *Creating techniques in ESL freshman composition*. Paper presented at the 18th Annual TESOL Convention, Houston, TX.

Shows how inventing techniques can be a stimulating way to begin composition courses so that students discover ideas for their papers and decide what they want to communicate.
Invention.

3022. Speers, K., & Tarini, C. (1992, March). *Feedback for advanced students*. Paper presented at the 26th Annual TESOL Convention, Vancouver, BC.

Presents findings comparing the effect of feedback of two types (directive comments and correction symbols) on second draft revisions of college ESL compositions.
Revision/Feedback/Advanced.

3023. Spencer, D. H. (1981, December). *The reality of written examinations and realism in preparing for them*. Paper presented at the Conference of the International Association of Teachers of English as a Foreign Language, London, England. [ERIC ED 214 393].

Claims that written examinations are the best indicators of student's language ability. Suggests ways that teachers can help students prepare for these examinations.
Assessment/Examination Essays.

3024. Spencer, D. H. (1965). Two types of guided composition exercise. *English Language Teaching*, 19(4), 156-158.

Advises that written pattern practice encompass whole sentence revision and word substitution at the paragraph level to contextualize exercises.
Control.

3025. Spiegel-Podnecky, J. (1989). *Literacy points*. Burlingame, CA: Alta.

Introduces basic English literacy skills in reading and writing with sequenced learning steps. Plenty of exercises in listening, speaking, reading, and writing focusing on sound/symbol relationships, comprehension, vocabulary development, writing of words, sentences, and paragraphs.
Adult Education/Textbook.

3026. Srivastava, R. N. (1989). Literacy. *Annual Review of Applied Linguistics*, 10, 81-102.

Mentions several key studies on applied linguistics and writing in the context of a review of the diverse perspectives that have developed over the last decade on the nature and function of literacy around the world.
Literacy/Review.

3027. St. John, M. J. (1987). Writing process of Spanish scientists publishing in English. *English for Specific Purposes*, 6, 113-120.

Finds that rereading is the only recursive element and that revision is limited to local concerns for precise equivalents in English for Spanish expressions in the composing processes of a group of Spanish researchers.
Hispanic/ESP/Process Research.

3028. Stack, J. (1988, March). *Holistic evaluation of student writing*. Paper presented at the 22nd Annual TESOL Convention, Chicago, IL.
>Workshop explores evaluation and assumptions underlying holistic evaluation.
>Assessment/Holistic.

3029. Staczek, J. (1992, March). *Speech patterns in academic writing*. Paper presented at the 26th Annual TESOL Convention, Vancouver, BC.
>Examines linguistic devices in the academic writing of L1 and advanced L2 learners. Shows that writers use a mixture of registers to take advantage of speech through lexical and syntactic choices.
>Speaking-Writing Relations/NS-NNS Comparisons.

3030. Stahlheber, E., & Selinker, L. (1991). Rhetorical consciousness raising and applied discourse analysis: Evaluating an EAP writing center/clinic/lab/workshop via the case study method. *Papers in Applied Linguistics -- Michigan*, 6(1), 60-67.
>A case study of the effect of explicit, individualized instruction in rhetorical/grammatical awareness on the writing in English of a Chinese doctoral student in physical chemistry. Improvements were found in his dissertation writing.
>Chinese/ESP.

3031. Stairs, A. (1990). Questions behind the question of vernacular education: A study in literacy, native language, and English. *English Quarterly*, 22(3-4), 103-124.
>Attempts to assess the relative proficiency of vernacular-educated third- and fourth-grade Canadian children on the basis of analytic measures of writing in Inuktitut (L1) and English (L2). Correlational results suggest that the introduction of English L2 writing is associated with more impoverished Inuktitut writing.
>Amer-Indian/Children.

3032. Stalker, J. W., & Stalker, J. C. (1989). The acquisition of rhetorical strategies in introductory paragraphs in written academic English: A comparsion of NNSs and NSs. In S. M. Gass, C. Madden, D. Preston, & L. Selinker (Eds.), *Variations in second language acquisition, Volume 1: Discourse and pragmatics* (pp. 144-152). Clevedon, UK: Multilingual Matters.
>Find neither sentence nor discourse level features when comparing a literary response essay by five native and five non-native speakers of English.
>Paragraph/Discourse Analysis.

3033. Stalker, J. W., & Stalker, J. C. (1988). Comparison of pragmatic accomodation of nonnative and native speakers in written English. *World Englishes*, 7(2), 119-128.
>Analyzes writing by novice freshman native and nonnative speakers of English. No differences are reported at the sentence level but at the discourse level nonnative students are reported to produce more coherent and clearer essays. Development of discourse level strategies should be the primary concern of the instructor.
>Discourse Analysis.

3034. Stall, J. (1988, March). *ESL entry level students can write, too!* Paper presented at the 22nd Annual TESOL Convention, Chicago, IL.
>Adult entry level ESL students can begin learning English through writing.
>Beginners.

3035. Stanley, J. (1992). Coaching student writes to be effective peer evaluators. *Journal of Second Language Writing*, *1*(3), 217-233.
> The quality of peer interactions can be significantly improved by preparing students more thoroughly for group work.
> Peer Response.

3036. Stanley, N. (1980, March). *Writing workshops in the ESL composition classroom*. Paper presented at the 14th Annual TESOL Convention, San Francisco, CA.
> Explains how to change writing class into a writing workshop.
> Workshop.

3037. Stansfield, C. W. (1986). A history of the Test of Written English: The developmental years. *Language Testing*, *3*(2), 224-234.
> Discusses the development of the TOEFL essay test.
> Assessment/TWE.

3038. Stansfield, C. W., & Ross, J. (1988a). A long-term agenda for the Test of Written English. *Language Testing*, *5*, 160-186.
> Outlines basic issues in determining the validity and reliability of the TWE.
> TWE/Research.

3039. Stansfield, C. W., & Ross, J. (1988b, March). *A long term research agenda for the Test of Written English*. Princeton, NJ: Educational Testing Service.
> Outlines basic issues in the determination of the validity and reliability of the TWE in order to guide the conceptualization and design of future research.
> Assessment.

3040. Stansfield, C. W., Scott, M. L., & Kenyon, D. (1991, March). *Development and validation of a Spanish-English translation exam*. Paper presented at the 25th Annual TESOL Convention, New York, NY.
> Reports on the Spanish-English Verbatim Translation Exam developed by CAL for the federal government to select employees for translation competency.
> Assessment/Hispanic/Translation.

3041. Stansfield, C. W., & Webster, R. (1986). The new TOEFL writing test. *TESOL Newsletter*, *20*(5), 17-18.
> Outlines the types of writing questions, method of scoring, and the outcomes of the TOEFL Test of Written English.
> Assessment/TWE.

3042. Stanton, M. (1986). A painless exercise in revision. *TESL Reporter*, *19*(4), 80.
> Describes how revising a group essay can make an exercise in revision less threatening and therefore more rewarding.
> Revision.

3043. Stanulewicz, D. (1992). Letters: Guess who has written to you. *English Teaching Forum*, *30*(4), 44-46.
> Gives several ideas for interesting letter-writing activities in the classroom.
> Letter Writing/Classroom Activities.

3044. Staton, J., & Peyton, J. K. (1986). *History of dialogue journals and dissertation abstracts*. Washington, DC: ERIC/FL. [ERIC ED 294411].
> Discusses the origin of the idea of dialogue journals in 1964 in a course taught

by Leslee Reed as well as a five dissertations that have studied related aspects and applications of dialogue journals.
Dialogue Journals/Review.

3045. Staton, J., Shuy, R., & Kreeft, J. E. (1983). *Analysis of dialogue journal writing as a communicative event, vols. I and II*. Washington, DC: CAL. [ERIC ED 214 196; 214 197].

Reports an analysis of student-teacher dialogue journals, which are seen as a link between natural competence in oral discourse and a developing competence in written language.
Dialogue Journals/Research.

3046. Staub, D., & Tickle, A. (1993, April). *Action research on peer editing: What do students think?* Paper presented at the 27th Annual TESOL Convention, Atlanta, GA.

Reports results of a study of student preferences in peer editing.
Peer Response/Editing.

3047. Steed, J. F. (1980). Getting the connection. In D. L. Bouchard, & L. J. Spaventa (Comps.), *A TEFL anthology: Selected articles from the* English Teaching Forum, *1973-78* (pp. 217-219). Washington, DC: International Communication Agency.

Discusses the teaching of logical connectors.
Cohesion.

3048. Steer, J. (1989, March). *Teaching the research paper: Some interactive techniques*. Paper presented at the 23rd Annual TESOL Convention, San Antonio, TX.

Recommends integrating dialogue journals, oral paraphrasing activities, and paired interviews into research writing for ESL students.
Research Writing.

3049. Steer, J. (1988, March). *Dialogue journal writing for academic purposes*. Paper presented at the 22nd Annual TESOL Convention, Chicago, IL. [ERIC ED 295 479].

Developing a sense of purpose and audience leads to academic writing.
Dialogue Journals/Academic Writing.

3050. Steffensen, M. S. (1989, March). *Relating reading and writing: Metadiscourse in dialogue journals*. Paper presented at the 23rd Annual TESOL Convention, San Antonio, TX.

Discusses differences in the use of dialogue journals for responding to reading and for writing on self-selected topics.
Dialogue Journals/Reading-Writing Relations.

3051. Steffensen, M. S. (1986, March). *Teaching composition and culture with the dialogue journal*. Paper presented at the 20th Annual TESOL Convention, Anaheim, CA.

Points out that dialogue journals increase fluency as well as mechanical skills.
Culture/Dialogue Journals.

3052. Steinhaus, K., & Peirce, B. N. (1991, March). *Avoiding unpleasant surprises when developing essay test questions*. Paper presented at the 25th Annual TESOL Convention, New York, NY.

Reviews promising test questions that yielded unscoreable responses on the

TWE.
Assessment/Prompts/TWE.

3053. Steinhaus, K., Reid, J. M., Kroll, B., & Kantor, R. N. (1989, March). *Essay topic development: The TOEFL-TWE collaborative approach*. Workshop presented at the 23rd Annual TESOL Convention, San Antonio, TX.

Examines how topics have been and can be developed for the Test of Written English (TWE).
Assessment/Topic.

3054. Stenstrom, A. B. (1975a). Grammatical errors in teacher trainees' written work. *Swedish-English Contrastive Studies*, 7, 16. [ERIC ED 145 703].

Analyzes and categorizes written errors made by teacher trainees in Sweden.
Error Analysis/Teacher Preparation/Swedish.

3055. Stenstrom, A. B. (1975b). *Grammatical errors in teacher trainees' written work*. Washington, DC: ERIC/FLL. [ERIC ED 145 703].

Classifies sentence-level grammatical errors attributable to various sources. Most of the errors, however, did not affect comprehensibility according to NESs.
Swedish/Errors.

3056. Stephens, M. K. (1989). A comparison of models used to describe article use in the writing of ESL students. *Dissertation Abstracts International*, 50(5), 1239A.

Applies several analytical models to a corpus of articles used in the entrance examination essays of thirty-three Taiwanese computer science graduate students. Study concludes that models by Jack Richards and Thomas Shu-hui Liao provide the most valid and accurate descriptions of English article use.
Usage/Chinese.

3057. Stephens, R., & Knepler, M. (1981, March). *Teaching composing to ESL students: What, when, why, and how*. Paper presented at the 15th Annual TESOL Convention, Detroit, MI.

Presents theory and materials for teaching composing in all levels of an ESL program.
Materials/Theory.

3058. Stephenson, B. C. (1989). Responsive writing. *English Teaching Forum*, 27(4), 45-46.

Finds that an antedote to dullness with fluency is to encourage observation while writing in class.
Zimbabwe/Description.

3059. Stevens, V. (1984). Implications of research and theory concerning the influence of control on the effectiveness of CALL. *CALICO Journal*, 2(1), 28-33, 48.

Describes a computer-asssisted research project into writing errors of ESL college students. The analysis of errors identified the most common errors and patterns of errors in the writing of particular language groups. The errors in verb agreement, parts of speech, article use, tenses, and prepositions are discussed.
Computers/Error Analysis.

3060. Stevens, V., Pennington, M. C., Murison-Bowie, S., Jordan, G., & Johns, T. (1993, April). *Text analysis and data driven learning in the classroom*. Colloquium presented at the 27th Annual TESOL Convention, Atlanta, GA.

Surveys how to use computers to analyze texts so as to serve learning from input in a bottom-up manner, and critiques the use with nonnative students of grammar checkers and concordancers

Computers.

3061. Stevenson, D. W. (1983). Audience analysis across cultures. *Journal of Technical Writing and Communuication*, 319-330.

Addresses the relevance and importance of understanding cultural implications of teaching technical writing to non-native speakers.

Technical Writing.

3062. Stice, R. (1984, March). *Cultural differences in composition correction: A Chinese (PRC)-American comparison.* Paper presented at the 18th Annual TESOL Convention, Houston, TX.

A study of ten American and ten Chinese teachers examining compositions shows tendency to look for different types of errors, perhaps due to differing conceptions of language and language instruction.

NS-NNS Comparisons/Chinese.

3063. Stokes, E. (1984). An ESL writing workshop. *TESOL Newsletter (Supplement No, 1: Writing and composition)*, *18*(1), 4-5.

Describes the theory and implementation of a writing workshop for ESL students. Stresses the importance of peer conferences and discussion of writing experiences among students in the workshop.

Workshop/University.

3064. Stone, B., & Failer, S. (1989, March). *Process writing with computers: Making it work.* Paper presented at the 23rd Annual TESOL Convention, San Antonio, TX.

Discusses learning center procedures for nonacademic ESL program.

Computers/Writing Center.

3065. Storla, S. R. (1993, April). *Writing for critical thinking: Problem solving and information transfer.* Paper presented at the 27th Annual TESOL Convention, Atlanta, GA.

Demonstrates two writing-based critical thinking activities for the classroom.

Strategies/Classroom Activities.

3066. Storla, S. R. (1987). The role of reading materials in university composition: Causes for native users of English and for ESL students. *Dissertation Abstracts International*, *48*(5), 1138A.

Explores the way reading and writing interact in the literacy-based curriculum.

Reading-Writing Relations/Curriculum.

3067. Storla, S. R. (1986, March). *Special considerations in the selection and use of reading materials for ESL composition classes.* Paper presented at the 37th Annual CCCC New Orleans, LA.

Reading-Writing Relations.

3068. Storla, S. R. (1984, March). *The revision component of the writing process in the ESL composition class.* Paper presented at the 18th Annual TESOL Convention, Houston, TX.

Reports a study of revision changes made by advanced ESL students in their compositions.

Revision/Advanced.

3069. Stout, B. (1987, March). *Ideas about writing that EFL students bring to our classes.* Paper presented at the 38th Annual CCCC Meeting, Atlanta, GA.

3070. Stratton, F. (1978). Designing a communicative writing syllabus for university level, advanced learners of English as a second or foreign language. *TESL Talk, 9,* 46-54.

Focuses on the input of a communicative writing syllabus that can be organized in terms of "rhetorical coherence," defined as the function and the act a piece of writing fulfills, and "text-forming resources" or the resources in English for making a piece of writing a text.

Syllabus Design/University/Advanced.

3071. Stratton, L., Reid, J. M., & Lindstrom, M. (1984, March). *Tutorials: Solution to some ESL writing problems.* Paper presented at the 17th Annual TESOL Convention, Toronto, Ontario.

Suggests that scheduled student tutorial conferences offer all the advantages of native speaker conferences.

Conferencing.

3072. Strei, G. J. (1987). Selecting and preparing meaningful and communicative exercises for the ESL writing class. In C. Cargill (Ed.), *A TESOL professional anthology: Grammar and composition* (pp. 91-98). Littlewood, IL: National Textbook Co.

Compares mechanical drills with meaningful and communicative exercises, arguing that while the former may help the beginner, ultimately, only by contextualizing language through meaningful communicative activity can the learner prepare for real-life tasks.

Communicative Writing/Beginners.

3073. Strei, G. J. (1973, May). *A contrastive study of the written discourse of English and Spanish.* Paper presented at the 7th Annual TESOL Conference, San Juan, Puerto Rico.

Finds that the majority of subjects transferred their mother tongue composition form English to Spanish and vica-versa.

Hispanic/Contrastive Rhetoric.

3074. Strei, G. J. (1972). *A contrastive study of the structure of rhetoric in English and Spanish composition.* Unpublished master's thesis, McGill University, Montreal, Quebec.

See previous item.

Hispanic/Contrastive Rhetoric.

3075. Strother, J. B. (1993, April). *Effect on text topic on L2 writer's syntactic choices.* Paper presented at the 27th Annual TESOL Convention, Atlanta, GA.

Argues that the topic or semantic context is the primary factor determining a writer's syntactic choices irrespective of language background or content expertise.

Topic/Syntactic Structures.

3076. Strother, J. B. (1992, March). *Effect of test topic on L2 writer's syntactic choices.* Paper presented at the 26th Annual TESOL Convention, Vancouver, BC.

Presents evidence from two studies indicating that the topic or semantic context is the primary factor determining a writer's syntactic choices regardless of the writer's language background or subject matter expertise.
Topic/Syntactic Structures.

3077. Strother, J. B., & Ulijin, J. M. (1989). L1 and L2 syntactic structuring in ESP writing: Reading aspects and an error analysis. In C. Laurén, & M. Nordman (Eds.), *Special language: From humans thinking to thinking machines* (pp. 347-361). Clevedon, UK: Multilingual Matters.

Analyzes the syntactic choices of ESP writers depending on their language background and their knowledge of the subject as well as Dutch-English errors and reading comprehension in EST. Syntactic differences between common language syntactic structures and those characteristic of science and technology, especially in computer science texts, have little significance for reading time and comprehension.
ESP/Syntactic Structures/Dutch.

3078. Sugimoto, E. (1978). Contrastive analysis of English and Japanese technical rhetoric. In M. T. Trimble, L. Trimble, & K. Drobnic (Eds.), *English for specific purposes: Science and technology* (pp. 177-197). Corvallis, OR: Oregon State University.

Studies the paragraph in comparative specialized texts in Japanese and English on the basis of the Selinker/Trimble model.
Technical Writing/Japanese.

3079. Suid, M., & Lincoln, W. (1993). *Recipes for writing*. Burlingame, CA: Alta.

A sourcebook for teachers who want to supplement their writing curriculum with 48 motivating activities.
Textbook/Elementary.

3080. Suksaeresup, N. (1980). A survey of current practices and recommendations for improved instruction in English composition teaching in Thai teacher training colleges. *Dissertation Abstracts International, 41*(4), 1548A.

Studies teaching practices in English composition by Thai teachers based on a questionnaire sent to teacher training colleges. Makes suggestions in areas of curriculum planning, departmental administration, teacher responsibility, teaching effectiveness, and teacher training.
Thai/Teacher Preparation.

3081. Sullivan, K. E. (1993). *Paragraph practice: Writing the paragraph and the short composition*. (Sixth Ed.). Reading, MA: Addison-Wesley.

A textbook for guided writing practice with opportunities to use pre-writing techniques. Moves from topic sentences to full paragraphs to short essays. It also offers suggestions to get student writers started.
Intermediate/Textbook.

3082. Sulzmann, H. (1978). Writing as self-discovery: Teaching writing skills to non-native speakers. *TEAL Occasional Papers, 2*, 13. [ERIC ED 157 388].

Demonstrates use of first-person point of view to teach writing to adult ESL students. Suggests helping students to correct their own errors and to improve structures.
Classroom Activities.

3083. Sun, M. C. (1990). Code switching and writing in a second language: A study of Chinese students writing in English. *Dissertation Abstracts International, 50*(8), 2475A.

Discusses the positive role of thinking in the first language as an aid to drafting and the holistic exploration of ideas.

Chinese/L1 Influence.

3084. Sunday, B. R. (1986). The non-native speaker in Freshman English: A second language teacher's viewpoint. *Journal of Clinical Reading: Research and Programs, 2*(1), 15-17.

Suggests that college English programs can improve the cultural bias of reading and writing assignments.

University/Culture/Materials.

3085. Sunday, B. R. (1982, October). *Cohesive characteristics of sample texts produced by secondary bilingual students.* Paper presented at the conference of the Ohio TESOL Association for Bilingual/Multicultural Education, Dayton, OH. [ERIC ED 222 084].

Analyzes the cohesive strategies used by secondary students, using the Halliday and Hasan (1976) method of categorizing semantic units. Results provide information on both errors and mastery of cohesive devices.

Cohesion/Secondary School.

3086. Sunderman, P. W. (1987). Teaching writing skills to ESL students in applied scientific and technical fields. In C. Cargill (Ed.), *A TESOL professional anthology: Grammar and composition* (pp. 99-120). Littlewood, IL: National Textbook Co.

Provides advice on curriculum and lesson planning for ESL teachers without science background, based on the research literature in ESP. The focus is on teaching writing courses to ESL students while they are taking academic courses in applied scientific and technological subjects.

ESP/University.

3087. Sunderman, P. W. (1985). *Connections: Writing across disciplines.* NY: Holt, Rinehart and Winston.

Focuses on writing skills pertinent to academic study, giving emphasis to interests and major fields of study of ESL students, that is, those having a scientific, technical, business, and agricultural base.

University/Textbook.

3088. Susini, S. (1980, March). *Beyond the ESL writing class.* Paper presented at the 14th Annual TESOL Convention, San Francisco, CA.

Discusses how to cope with problems of mixed "remedial" classes.

NS-NNS Comparisons.

3089. Swain, M. (1993). The output hypothesis: Just speaking and writing aren't enough. *The Canadian Modern Language Review, 50,* 158-164.

Hypothesizes that language acquisition may occur by producing either spoken or written language in that learners are forced to recognize what they do not know or know only partially. Their response may be to ignore it; search their knowledge to close the gap; or identify it and pay attention to relevant input. Suggests that a particular genre of collaborative activities: discussion of the target language itself, may be especially useful.

Output Hypothesis/Speaking-Writing Relations.

3090. Swain, M., & Lapkin, S. (1989, April). *First language literacy and its relation to third language learning*. Paper presented at the Annual AERA Meeting, San Francisco, CA.

Literacy/L1 Influence.

3091. Swales, J. M. (1992a). Discourse community and the evaluation of written text. J. E. Alatis (Ed.), *Language, community, and social meaning* (pp. 316-323). Washington, DC: Georgetown University Press.

Discusses the problematic nature of evaluating ESL texts, especially the fact that they are locally evaluated.

Discourse Communities/Evaluation.

3092. Swales, J. M. (1992b, March). *Teaching research writing to nonnative speakers: Roles of instructor*. Colloquium presented at the 26th Annual TESOL Convention, Vancouver, BC.

Discusses the roles that a teacher may play from general to specific in teaching research writing.

Research Writing.

3093. Swales, J. M. (1990a). *Genre analysis: English in academic and research settings*. Cambridge, MA: Cambridge University Press.

Approaches post-secondary training in academic English from an ESP and discourse analysis perspective. Gives both theory and practice that focuses on discourse community, textual genre, and task in academic writing.

Academic Writing/Audience/Task/Genre.

3094. Swales, J. M. (1990b). Nonnative speaker graduate engineering students and their introductions: Global coherence and local management. In U. M. Connor, & A. M. Johns (Eds.), *Coherence in writing: Research and pedagogical perspectives* (pp. 187-207). Alexandria, VA: TESOL.

Presents a performance analysis of introductions in the academic writing produced by nonnative graduate engineering students. Claims that making students aware of expectations of readers in terms of elements in a research introduction will help them create global coherence and therefore overall comprehensibility.

Text Analysis/Coherence/ESP.

3095. Swales, J. M. (1988, March). *English as an international language of research*. Paper presented at the 39th Annual CCCC Meeting, St. Louis, MO.

Genre/Research Writing.

3096. Swales, J. M. (1987). Utilizing the literatures in teaching the research paper. *TESOL Quarterly, 21*, 41-68.

Presents an approach to the teaching of research English based on four bodies of literature: the sociology of science, citation analysis, technical writing, and English for academic purposes. Reviews present knowledge on the research paper, schema, and "process" vs. "product" controversy.

Research Writing.

3097. Swales, J. M. (1984). Research into the structure of introductions to journal articles and its application into the teaching of academic writing. In R. Williams, J. M. Swales, & J. Kirkman (Eds.), *Common ground: Shared interests in ESP and communications studies* (pp. 77-86). Oxford: Pergamon.

   Investigates the predictable structure of the article introduction and shows how this analysis applies to the teaching of academic writing to L1 and L2 students.
   ESP/Academic Writing

3098. Swales, J. M. (1982). Examining examination papers. *English Language Research Journal (Birmingham)*, 3, 9-25.

   A pilot study analyses the prompts from six examination papers in chemistry, finding seven categories of question-types. Each question averages three parts with each part consisting of a single or double instruction. The "describe"/"explain" type was most frequent.
   Academic Writing/Examination Essays.

3099. Swales, J. M., & Horowitz, D. M. (1988, March). *Genre-based approaches to ESL and ESP materials.* Paper presented at the 22nd Annual TESOL Convention, Chicago, IL.

   Advocates attention to genre in developing EAP task-based materials.
   Genre/EAP/Materials.

3100. Sweedler-Brown, C. O. (1993a). The effects of ESL errors on holistic scores assigned by English composition faculty. *College ESL*, 3(1), 53-69.

   Discovers a statistically significant difference in ratings of unmodified and corrected holistically scored essays by English composition teachers.
   Error Gravity/Holistic/Raters.

3101. Sweedler-Brown, C. O. (1993b). ESL essay evaluation: The influence of sentence-level and rhetorical features. *Journal of Second Language Writing*, 2, 3-17.

   Are experienced writing teachers untrained in ESL more strongly influenced by grammatical and syntactic proficiency or by rhetorical aspects of writing? This study finds that sentence-level errors were the most influential factor when grading both NES developmental and ESL essays holistically.
   Evaluation.

3102. Sweedler-Brown, C. O. (1992, March). *Discourse vs sentence-level influences in ESL essay evaluation.* Paper presented at the 26th Annual TESOL Convention, Vancouver, BC.

   After sentence level errors are corrected in the essays of high intermediate ESL writers, study finds that those receiving low analytic scores on grammar-mechanics correlate strongly with holistic grades, while high organization and development analytic scores showed no correlation.
   Assessment.

3103. Sweedler-Brown, C. O. (1991). *Sentence-level error: How significant is ESL essay evaluation?* Paper presented at the 25th Annual TESOL Convention, New York, NY.

   Finds (1) a strong correlation between holistic scores and low analytic scores

analytic scores in essays by high-intermediate ESL writers.
Assessment/Errors/Intermediate.

3105. Sweedler-Brown, C. O. (1989, March). *Developing relationships between reading and writing for ESL students*. Paper presented at the 40th Annual CCCC Meeting, Seattle, WA.
Reading-Writing Relations.

3106. Sween, M. (1980). *An approach for teaching the illiterate ESL student how to read and write*. Unpublished master's thesis, School for International Training, Brattleboro, VT.
Literacy.

T

3107. Tabor, K. (1984). Gaining successful writing in the foreign language classroom. *Foreign Language Annals*, *17*, 123-124.

Suggests that activities such as prewriting and brainstorming, peer evaluation and conferencing in which students repond to their own writing are helpful in teaching EFL students to write in the target language.
Process Instruction.

3108. Taborek, E., & Adamowski, E. (1984). To seal up one's mouth three times: Understanding the education and linguistic differences that confront Chinese students in ESL writing classes. *TESL Talk*, *15*(3), 88-95.

Discusses the differences between Canadian and Hong Kong educational systems and their implications for Canadian teachers of writing who have Chinese students in their classes. Gives a limited contrastive analysis of Chinese and English related to writing problems faced by Chinese ESL students. To help Chinese students organize their essays according to English readers' expectations, such techniques as group work, brainstorming, sentence combining, and parts of speech identification are used.
Contrastive Rhetoric/Chinese.

3109. Tadros, A. A. (1984). Prediction as an aspect of the structuring of didactic text and its implications for the teaching of reading and writing. In J. M. Swales, & H. Mustafa (Eds.), *ESP in the Arab world* (pp. 52-67). University of Aston: The Language Studies Unit.

Gives an analysis of textual signals that predict occurrences of linguistic events (Hoey, 1979) in an English economics textbook.
Arabic/Text Analysis/ESP.

3110. Tadros, A. A. (1980). A look beyond the sentence. In D. L. Bouchard, & L. J. Spaventa (Comps.), *A TEFL anthology: Selected articles from* English Teaching Forum, *1973-78* (pp. 220-226). Washington, DC: International Communication Agency.

Describes some techniques for analyzing expository paragraphs in economics and social studies.
ESP/Paragraph.

3111. Tagong, K. (1992). Revising strategies of Thai students: Text-level changes in essays written in Thai and in English. *Dissertation Abstracts International*, *52*(8), 2849A.

Examines 24 drafts of expressive and argumentative essays written in two

languages, using Faigley & Witte's (1981) system. Finds that Thai students made few changes in both languages. Most changes were meaning-preserving; few meaning-changing. L1 reported to influence pre-writing and idea generation.
Thai/Revision/L1 Influence.

3112. Tagong, K. (1991). Revising strategies of Thai students: Text-level changes in essays written in Thai and in English. *Dissertation Abstracts International*, *52*(8), 2849A.
Examines 24 drafts of expressive and argumentative essays written in two languages, using Faigley & Witte's (1981) system. Finds that Thai students made few changes in both languages. Most changes were meaning-preserving; few meaning-changing. L1 reported to influence pre-writing and idea generation.
Thai/Revision/L1 Influence.

3113. Takala, S. (1988). Origins of the international study of writing. In T. P. Gorman, A. C. Purves, & R. E. Degenhart (Eds.), *The IEA study of written composition I: The international writing tasks and scoring scales* (pp. 3-14). NY: Pergamon Press.
Describes the purposes of the IEA study of native composition in 14 countries as: (1) to contribute to the conceptualization of the domain of writing; (2) to develop an internationally appropriate set of writing tasks and a system for assessing compositions; (3) to describe recent developments and the current state of instruction in written composition; and (4) to identify factors that explain differences and patterns in the performance of written composition.
Evaluation.

3114. Takala, S. (1986, May). *Testing writing ability: A review*. Paper presented at a language testing symposium in honor of John B. Carroll and Robert Lado, Quiryat Anavim, Israel.
Argues that writing should not be considered secondary to speaking and that the testing of EFL writing should follow native language writing research.
Review/Evaluation.

3115. Takala, S., & Vahapassi, A. (1985). *International study of written composition*. Bloomington, IN: ERIC/RCS. [ERIC ED 257 096].
Addresses problems relating to the construction of native writing tasks, the allocation of writing tasks, and the scoring of student scripts in the IEA project in which fourteen countries collaborated. The most appropriate scoring system combined a holistic, overall-impression with an analytical marking. It was concluded that in spite of a great effort the scoring metric was too elastic to allow robust cross-national comparisons of scores on any one task or group of tasks.
Assessment/IEA/Scoring.

3116. Takano, S. (1993). The transfer of L1 rhetoric in L2 texts and its implications for second language teaching. *Journal of Intensive English Studies*, *7*, 43-83.
Discusses the conflict caused by cross-cultural (Japanese and English) rhetorical discrepancies, specifically of transfer of topic-comment discourse and Japanese paragraphing. A study of two English paragraphs written by 10 Japanese native speakers (graded by American and Japanese judges using culture-specific evaluative guidelines) suggests transfer of Japanese rhetorical strategies does indeed occur.
Transfer/Contrastive Rhetoric/Japanese.

3117. Takashima, H. (1987). To what extent are non-native speakers qualified to correct free composition? A case study. *British Journal of Language Teaching*, 25(1), 43-48.

Finds that Japanese judges are unable to detect rhetorical deviance in a study of corrections of a Japanese student's essay.

NS-NNS Comparisons/Error Gravity/Japanese.

3118. Taki El Din, S. R. (1987). The effectiveness of sentence combining practice on Arab students' overall writing quality and syntactic maturity. *Dissertation Abstracts International*, 47(8), 3022A.

Reports results of a preliminary study designed to determine the effectiveness of sentence combining in an EFL composition course on the syntactic maturity and overall quality of EFL students in the United Arab Emirates. Concludes tentatively that sentence combining has positive effects on the quality of writing due to problems in the design of the study.

Sentence Combining/Arabic.

3119. Talburt, S. (1992, March). *Reinventing lives: Soviet women speak in dialogue journals*. Paper presented at the 26th Annual TESOL Convention, Vancouver, BC.

Explores the journal stories of Soviet emigre women which suggest the need for greater connection with their American communities.

Dialogue Journals/Russian.

3120. Tamez, J. D., & Weiland, P. O. (1991, March). *Collaborative conferences: ESL teachers and graduate students interact*. Paper presented at the 25th Annual TESOL Convention, New York, NY.

Shows how the proper use of questioning techniques enables the teacher to promote independent writing.

Conferencing/Interaction.

3121. Tanchotikul, S. (1992). How to teach a narrative. *English Teaching Forum*, 28(4), 39-40.

Suggests a way to make writing more meaningful.

Narration/Secondary School/Thai.

3122. Tapla, E. (1992, March). *Hypothetical topics: Effects on syntactic complexity, accuracy, and fluency*. Paper presented at the 26th Annual TESOL Convention, Vancouver, BC.

Reports results of a study of learner essays which were hypothetical, timed, and field-specific. Results indicate hypothetical topic essays were less syntactically complex, less accurate, and of a sub-par quality.

Assessment/Prompts.

3123. Tarone, E., Downing, B., Cohen, A. D., Gillette, S., Murie, R., & Dailey, B. (1993). The writing of southeast Asian-American students in secondary school and university. *Journal of Second Language Writing*, 2, 149-172.

Southeast Asian-American immigrant children in 8th-, 10th-, and 12th-grade mainstream secondary school classes scored the same on essays as nonnative university students, although not as good as native-speaking university students. Age of arrival is reported as the most important factor to correlate with the immigrant group's success in the four writing traits measured.

Asian/Secondary School.

3124. Tarone, E., Dwyer, S., Gillette, S., & Icke, V. (1981). The use of the passive in two astrophysics journal papers. *ESP Journal*, 1(2), 123-140.

Finds that writers of journal articles in astrophysics use the passive voice for several definite, systematic functions in their discourse.
ESP.

3125. Tarpley, F. (1991, March). *Cross-cultural styles in college composition*. Paper presented at the 25th Annual TESOL Convention, New York, NY.
Interviews with twenty ESL graduate students indicate that writing in ESL requires different styles and organizational plans as well as language codes due to differing audience expectations.
Culture/Style.

3126. Tawake, S., & Smith, L. E. (1993). Write like an author: Pacific and Asian literatures as a resource for teaching composition. In M. N. Brock, & L. W. Walters (Eds.), *Teaching composition around the Pacific Rim: Politics and pedagogy* (pp. 35-47). Clevedon, ENG: Multilingual Matters.
Recommends the use of culturally relevant creative readings for the teaching of composition. Presents sample exercises.
Asian/Literature.

3127. Taylin, V. (1988, March). *ESL composers' use of audience awareness*. Paper presented at the 39th Annual CCCC Meeting, St. Louis, MO.
Audience.

3128. Taylor, B. P. (1981). Content and written form: A two-way street. *TESOL Quarterly, 15*, 5-13.
Argues that writing, even for ESL students who have not acquired full linguistic proficiency, does not follows a strict sequence of steps: plan- outline- write. Advises emphasis on content rather than form. Also points out that students write better on personal topics than on teacher-assigned topics or when following a controlled exercise.
Approaches/Control/Beginners.

3129. Taylor, B. P. (1980, March). *Content and written form: A two-way street*. Paper presented at the 14th Annual TESOL Convention, San Francisco, CA.
Emphasizes the role of revision in essay writing as a dynamic creative process of give and take between content and form.
Revision.

3130. Taylor, B. P. (1978). Teaching composition skills and low-level ESL students: Cause-effect and comparison-contrast. In B. W. Robinett (Ed.), *1976-77 papers in ESL: Selected conference papers of the National Association for Foreign Student Affairs, ATESL section* (pp. 31-34). Washington, DC: NAFSA.
Presents suggestions for teaching students to write paragraphs containing sentences reflecting two types of specific relationships.
Paragraph/Academic Writing.

3131. Taylor, B. P. (1976a, March). *Composition and the elementary ESL student*. Paper presented at the 10th Annual TESOL Convention, New York, NY.
Proposes to teach free composition to beginning ESL students and offers exercises in treating paragraphs.
Beginners/Free Writing.

3132. Taylor, B. P. (1976b). Teaching composition to low-level ESL students. *TESOL*

Quarterly, 10, 309-319.

Suggests students write early in their language training and not wait until they gain advanced linguistic proficiency. Suggests writing activities such as fill-in-blanks, sentence completion, answering questions, dialogue completion, and paragraph development through question answering for beginning ESL writers.

Classroom Activities/Beginners.

3133. Taylor, B. P., Raimes, A., Smith, F., Widdowson, H. G., & Zamel, V. (1983, March). *Writing in English as a second language: A colloquium.* Colloquium presented at the 17th Annual TESOL Convention, Toronto, Ontario.

Seven leading researchers review current developments in research on second language composing in this annual colloquium.

Review.

3134. Taylor, B. P., Zamel, V., Brookes, G., Raimes, A., & Spack, R. (1986, March). *Practical considerations in teaching writing as a process.* Colloquium presented at the 20th Annual TESOL Convention, Anaheim, CA.

Considers process syllabus, response procedures, and writing development in this annual colloquium.

Process Instruction.

3135. Taylor, B. P., Zamel, V., Auerbach, E. R., Brookes, G., Hudelson, S., Mohan, B. A., & Spack, R. (1987, April). *Current trends and issues in the teaching of writing.* Colloquium presented at the 21st Annual TESOL Convention, Miami Beach, FL.

Annual colloquium addresses issues of process instruction, content-based teaching, literacy, and reading-writing relationships.

Review.

3136. Taylor, C. (1992, March). *Recent developments in the Test of Written English.* Paper presented at the 26th Annual TESOL Convention, Vancouver, BC.

Discusses recent developments based on research in the TWE program.

Assessment/TWE.

3137. Taylor, C., & Henning, G. H. (1990, March). *Current research on the TOEFL Test of Written English.* Paper presented at the 24th Annual TESOL Convention, San Francisco, CA.

Provides an overview of the Test of Written English research agenda and four current TWE research projects. Two studies examine the relationship between the TWE scores and writing ability; two others examine the psychometric characteristics of the TWE.

Assessment/TWE.

3138. Taylor, C. M., & Hart, M. J. (1978, April). *Advanced composition models: Practical structural development through imitative writing.* Paper presented at the 12th Annual TESOL Convention, Mexico City, Mexico.

Suggests a synthesis of skills is essential for preparing advanced level students for university work.

Advanced/University.

3139. Taylor, E. A. (1976). *Writing assignments at the American University in Cairo.* Unpublished master's thesis, UCLA, Los Angeles, CA.

Assignments.

3140. Taylor, G. (1986). Errors and explanations. *Applied Linguistics*, 7, 144-166.

Attempts to systematize what constitutes a good error analysis, based on the idea that errors need to be explained as part of the process of writing rather than merely identified and syntactically described.

Errors.

3141. Taylor, G., & Chen, T. (1991). Linguistic, cultural, and subcultural issues in contrastive discourse analysis: Anglo-American and Chinese scientific texts. *Applied Linguistics*, 12, 319-336.

Based on an analysis of introductions to scientific articles by three groups of physical scientists (Anglo-American and Chinese writing in English as well as Chinese writing in Chinese), this study finds that there is no Chinese way of writing science that is attributable to features of the Chinese language system itself. Yet significant discourse variations occur among all groups examined.

Contrastive Rhetoric/Chinese.

3142. Taylor, V., & Mangelsdorf, K. (1988, March). *ESL writing processes: Adapting to the academic writing community*. Paper presented at the 22nd Annual TESOL Convention, Chicago, IL.

Describes a student guide to ESL composition developed to help undergraduates meet the rhetorical expectations of the American academic community.

Discourse Communities.

3143. Tedick, D. J. (1993, April). *A multidimensional exploration of raters' judgments of ESL writing*. Paper presented at the 27th Annual TESOL Convention, Atlanta, GA.

Finds that raters do not always conform to scoring guidelines when judging ESL writing but rather approach scoring with individual styles.

Raters/Evaluation.

3144. Tedick, D. J. (1990). ESL writing assessment: Subject matter knowledge and its impact on performance. *English for Specific Purposes*, 9, 123-143.

Finds that a field-specific topic is better than a general topic in discriminating the writing proficiency of one hundred-five ESL students in a university English placement essay test.

Academic Writing/Assessment/Topic.

3145. Tedick, D. J. (1989a). The effects of topic familiarity on the writing performance of nonnative writers of English at the graduate-level. *Dissertation Abstracts International*, 49(9), 2569A.

The subject matter of topics used in large-scale writing assessment may influence writing performance. Argues that general topics do not allow writers to use their prior knowledge and, therefore, do not elicit responses that accurately reflect their ability. Essays by 105 ESL subjects at three ESL course levels differed significantly, both quantitatively and qualitatively, on a topic in the subjects' field of study rather than on a general topic.

Topic/Background Knowledge.

3146. Tedick, D. J. (1989b, April). *Second language writing assessment: Bridging the gap between theory and practice*. Paper presented at the Annual AERA Meeting, San

Francisco, CA.
Assessment.

3147. Tedick, D. J., & Dubetz, N. (1991, April). *Differences between ESL students' writing on two topics: A look at linguistic features*. Paper presented at the Annual Meeting of the AERA, Chicago, IL.
Topic/Syntactic Structures.

3148. Tedick, D. J., & Mathison, M. A. (1991, April). *Comparing topics: The rhetoric of ESL college placement essays*. Paper presented at the 25th Annual TESOL Convention, New York, NY.
Provides a rhetorical analysis of ESL graduate students' writing performance on a general and a field-specific topic.
Assessment/Prompts.

3149. Tedick, D. J., & Mathison, M. A. (1990, April). *Subject-matter knowledge and its impact on ESL students' writing: A descriptive analysis*. Paper presented at the Annual AERA Meeting, Boston.
Content.

3150. Teel, T. L. (1971). *A sociolinguistic study of Spanish linguistic interference and non-standard grammatical phenomena in the written English of selected Mexican-American bilinguals*. Unpublished master's thesis, University of Texas, El Paso.
Written errors by Spanish-English bilinguals from lower SES backgrounds exhibit non-standard dialect features, such as omission of -ed past tense marker on verbs.
Spanish/Errors.

3151. Tegey, M. (1984, September). A structured approach to teaching composition. *WATESOL Working Papers*, 2, 1-11. [ERIC ED 267 585].
Warns against the exclusive use of process-based approach to the teaching of ESL composition, since college-bound ESL writers are often confused by the loosely structured and creative process approach. Recommends a more systematic method based on a structured approach to advanced compostion teaching which uses eight writing stages, each including both thinking and writing.
Control/University.

3152. Teich, N. (1987). Transfer of writing skills: Implications of the theory of lateral and vertical transfer. *Written Communication*, 4(2), 193-208.
Discusses applications of the theory of lateral and vertical transfer
(Gagne 1965) to writing. Claims that the theory is compatible with the distinction between declarative and procedural cognitive processes and the pedagogy that combines both student-centered and direct, content-oriented instruction. Recommends practical procedures combining both mechanics and journal skills (the lateral transfer) and higher-order knowledge (the vertical transfer) for improving classroom instruction.
Transfer.

3153. Teich, N. (1985, March). *Transfer of writing skills: How the concept of transfer can help teachers of ESL and basic writing*. Paper presented at the 36th Annual CCCC Meeting, Minneapolis, MN. [ERIC ED 257 057].
Argues for student-centered assignments that recognize both the audience and the student's prior knowledge.

Transfer/Content.

3154. Templin Richards, R. (1988, March). *Thesis/dissertation writing for ESL students: ESP course design*. Paper presented at the 22nd Annual TESOL Convention, Chicago, IL.

Describes a four-week ESP course for EFL graduate students.

ESP/Research Writing/Courses.

3155. Teng, C. (1991). Grammar, imitation, and process: How teaching methods affect what Chinese students learn about written English. *Dissertation Abstracts International, 52*(2), 452-453A.

Study investigates causes of problems that Chinese students have writing cohesive, well-developed English prose. Discovers through protocol analysis, observations, and analysis of written products that students combine drafting and writing into a single step, spend no time on pre-writing, and focused on correctness of individual sentences as they write. Traditional writing education in China which stresses grammar and paragraph level models is associated with these writing problems of Chinese students.

Chinese/Process Research.

3156. Teng, W. H. (1990). Typical errors of Taiwanese students of English as a foreign language (EFL) as perceived by native English speakers and Taiwanese EFL teachers. *Dissertation Abstracts International, 52*(2), 452A.

In order to determine what the effect is of typical errors made by Taiwanese students, a test was administered to sixty native English speakers and seventy-two Taiwanese ESL teachers. Results indicate that native speakers are more lenient in rating errors than are Chinese teachers. Both groups regarded errors in fundamental structures as serious and believe that errors of spelling and article use are less serious. Yet NES judges were most concerned about "intelligibility" whereas Taiwanese judges were lenient of such interference errors.

Error Gravity/Chinese.

3157. Terdal, M. S. (1985). Learning to read and write in English: Case studies of two Southeast Asian students in a northwest urban school. *Dissertation Abstracts International, 46*(11), 3276A.

Examines perceptions about reading and writing of two high school students from Southeast Asian backgrounds. Findings show some connection between reading and writing theory and, therefore, its implications for the ESL classroom. Also presents dichotomy that sometimes exists between a teacher's perceptions and a student's expectations.

Secondary School/Reading-Writing Relations.

3158. Terdal, M. S., Fox, D. N., Wang, C., & Zhou, M. (1988, March). *Chinese students in American universities: Conflicting reading and writing strategies*. Paper presented at the 22nd Annual TESOL Convention, Chicago, IL.

Describes training in reading and writing of Chinese EFL students.

Reading-Writing Relations/Chinese.

3159. Terdy, D., & Bercovitz, L. (1989). *Home English literacy for parents: An ESL family curriculum*. Washington, DC: Office of Bilingual Education and Minority Language Affairs. [ERIC ED 313 926].

A literacy curriculum encourages parent involvement.

Literacy/Children/Curriculum.
3160. Terry, R. M. (1992). Teaching and evaluating writing as a communicative skill. *Foreign Language Annals*, *1*, 43-54.

Advocates using writing to develop communication as well as the traditional purpose as a support skill and discusses how to do it.
Communicative Writing.

3161. Tesdell, L. (1984). ESL spelling errors. *TESOL Quarterly*, *18*, 333-334.

Investigates spelling errors in fifty-six compositions written by students from different language backgrounds. The results suggest no evidence that spelling pedagogy should vary from language group to language group.
Error Treatment/Spelling.

3162. Tetroe, J., & Jones, C. S. (1984, April). *Transfer of planning skills in second language writing*. Paper presented at the Annual Meeting of the AERA, New Orleans, LA.
Transfer/Planning.

3163. Tetroe, J., & Jones, C. S. (1983, March). *Planning and revising in adult ESL students*. Paper presented at the 34th Annual CCCC Meeting, Detroit, MI.
Process Research/Planning/Revision.

3164. Thabet, A. A. (1984). Cohesion in EFL programs: A computational linguistics approach. *Dissertation Abstracts International*, *44*(10), 3053A.

Analysis with TXTPRO, a text processing program, shows lack of cohesion in Egyptian EFL textbooks and programs which contributes to weakness in writing.
Cohesion/Arabic/Computers.

3165. Thaipakdee, S. (1992). Relationships among writing quality, attitudes toward writing, and attitudes toward computers in a computer-mediated technical writing class for English as a Foreign Language students. *Dissertation Abstracts International*, *53*(4), 1135.

Surveys anxiety, attitudes toward writing, attitudes toward computer use, and revision practices among 23 ESL students in a technical writing class. Claims that students with more positive attitudes toward writing and computer usefulness tended to produce better writing. Students who said they revised more frequently also had better attitudes toward writing than those who did not. On the other hand, neither time nor computer anxiety, confidence, or preference is reported to affect performance.
Computers/Affect/Technical Writing.

3166. Thaiss, C. J., & Kurylo, C. (1981). Working with the ESL student: learning patience, making progress. *The Writing Center Journal*, *1*(2), 41-46.
Writing Center.

3167. Tharu, S. (1974). The person and the process in the product: A focus on the teaching of writing. *CIEFL Bulletin (Central Institute of English and Foreign Languages)*, *10*, 36-46. [ERIC ED 185 840].

This article maintains that a student can learn to write well only if he believes in himself and in the value of his own responses. Hence, the student is encouraged to express himself by writing about his own experiences. Samples and analyses of student writing demonstrate this point.
Motivation.

3168. Thomas, G. K. (1986). A comment on "Contrastive rhetoric: An American writing teacher in China." *College English*, *48*, 844-845.

  Relates two experiences teaching Chinese students which support Matalene (1985) claim that Chinese learners rely mainly on memory and imitation.

  Contrastive Rhetoric/Chinese.

3169. Thomas, H. (1984). Developing the stylistic and lexical awareness of advanced students. *ELT Journal*, 187-191.

  Describes three revision and text-analysis exercises, illustrated by materials translated into English from Hungarian.

  Advanced/Style/Hungarian.

3170. Thomas, J. (1992, August). *The affective experience of ESL writers*. Unpublished doctoral dissertation, Indiana University of Pennsylvania, Indiana, PA.

  This study is a naturalistic description of the affective experiences of ESL learners in two intensive classes composing. Finds that emotions play an important but diverse role in the composing process of ESL writers, both the result of a causal cognition and an instigator of action. The study also suggests an interrelationship among emotions experienced and self-efficacy and self-esteem.

  Affect/IEP/Ethnographic Research.

3171. Thomas, J. (1993). Countering the "I can't write English" syndrome. *TESOL Journal*, *2*(3), 12-15.

  Suggests how to help students who believe they are incapable of writing.

  Affect.

3172. Thomas-Ruzic, M., & Norloff, C. (1993, April). *Reformulation of compositions: An interactive project in teacher education*. Paper presented at the 27th Annual TESOL Convention, Atlanta, GA.

  Shows how to apply the technique of reformulation to teacher education.

  Reformulation/Teacher Preparation.

3173. Thomas-Ruzic, M., & Thompson-Panos, K. (1980). Contrastive features of Arabic and English and their practical applications. *Colorado Working Papers in Linguistics and Language Teaching*, *2*, 120-128.

  Contrastive Rhetoric/Arabic.

3174. Thomas-Ruzic, M., & Thompson-Panos, K. (1984). The author responds to Koch. *TESOL Quarterly*, *18*, 545-547.

  Responds to Koch's reply (1984) and commends her work on Arabic rhetoric. Claims that in evaluating two pieces of writing one tends to take one point of view and so had described Arabic as it appears to Americans. Argues that this does not mean a lack of cultural sensitivity.

  Contrastive Rhetoric/Arabic.

3175. Thompson, M. (1986, March). *Literacy in a Creole context: Teaching freshman English in Jamaica*. Paper presented at the 37th Annual CCCC Meeting, New Orleans, LA. [ERIC ED 276 054].

  Recommends conceptualizing in native language, switching codes, and praticing reading and writing extensively.

  Creole/Freshman Composition.

3176. Thompson, R. M. (1990). Writing-proficiency tests and remediation: Some cultural differences. *TESOL Quarterly*, *24*, 99-102.

Reports data about how international students coped with holistically graded writing exams required for graduation at a public comminity college. The study finds that students from Latin America do less well than either students from Southeast Asia or the Middle East both on mandated essay exams and in academic preparation, suggesting the need for instruction in full-length essay writing.

Hispanic/Evaluation.

3177. Thompson, R. M. (1984, March). *Holistic methods for building fluency in academic English*. Demonstration at the 18th Annual TESOL Convention, Houston, TX.

Finds native and non-native writers can be united in composition courses after only one course devoted to boosting, confidence, fluency, and proficiency for ESL students if a holistic rather than analytic approach is adopted.

NS-NNS Comparisons.

3178. Thompson-Panos, K., & Thomas-Ruzic, M. (1983). The least you should know about Arabic: Implications for the ESL writing instructor. *TESOL Quarterly*, *17*, 609-623.

Analyzes contrastive features of written Arabic and English such as the contrasting alphabets, vowel systems, spelling conventions, syntactic coordination and subordination, and rhetorical organization. Discusses writing deficiencies of Arab ESL students. Suggests that familiarity with students' errors can help to improve the writing of Arab students at the university level.

Contrastive Rhetoric/Arabic/University.

3179. Thompson-Panos, K., & Thomas-Ruzic, M. (1981, March). *Hidden communication and the Arab and his language*. Paper presented in a panel (interaction in Saudi Arabia) at the Annual SIETAR Conference, Vancouver, BC.

Contrastive Rhetoric/Arabic.

3180. Thonus, T. (1993). Tutors as teachers: Assisting ESL/EFL students in the Writing Center. *Writing Center Journal*, *13*(2), 13-26.

Tutoring/Writing Center.

3181. Thornburg, L., & Perry, W. (1992, March). *Western writing in Eastern Europe: A context for conflict*. Paper presented at the 26th Annual TESOL Convention, Vancouver, BC.

Presents an approach to teaching university-level academic writing in Hungary with a focus on resolving differences in teacher and student expectations about rhetorical modes.

Hungarian/Academic Writing.

3182. Tillyer, A., & Sokolik, M. (1993). Beyond portfolios: A practical look at student projects as teaching and evaluation devices (part 2). *College ESL*, *3*(1), 80-87.

Describes how to use projects with lower proficiency learners and how projects may be used for evaluation and teaching with higher-level classes.

Project Work.

3183. Tipton, S. (1987). *The effectiveness of topical structure analysis as a revision strategy for ESL writers*. Unpublished master's thesis, Ohio University, Athens, OH.

Shows the effectiveness in using topical structure analysis as a teaching method to help students check and revise their own writing for coherence.

Revision/TSA.
3184. Tom, A., & McKay, H. (1989). *Writing warmups*. Hayward, CA: Alemany Press.

A resource book containing prewriting activities which help students understand the writing process. The activities are designed to let the students become aware of the available options they have as writers and to give them practice in making decisions. The text is divided into two parts: "Focusing Activities" dealing with audience, purpose, focus, and point of view; and "Organizing Activities" dealing with classification, sequence, cause and effect, and comparison and contrast.

Secondary School/Textbook.

3185. Tomlinson, B. (1983). An approach to the teaching of continuous writing in ESL classes. *ELT Journal, 37*, 7-15.

Describes a seven-stage method for teaching writing: free writing, analysis, presentation, controlled writing, guided writing, free writing, and modeling.

Methods.

3186. Tommola, J., & Lehtio, P. (1987). An information-rich environment for the production of expository texts in English. In I. Lindblat, & M. Ljund (Eds.), *Proceedings from the Third Nordic Conference for English Studies, Vol. 2* (pp. 437-451). Stockholm: Alinqvist & Wiksell.

Describes the design of a computer technology system that provides an information-rich environment for producing expository texts. Produces facilitations of FL writing development, of psycholinguistic skills, and enrichment of learning.

Computers/Text Analysis.

3187. Tormakangas, K. (1991, April). *Predictions of performance in written compositions at three age levels -- A comparison using structural equations*. Paper presented at the Annual Meeting of the AERA, Chicago, IL.

Assessment.

3188. Touchie, H. Y. (1983). Transfer and related strategies in the acquisition of English relative clauses by adult Arab learners. *Dissertation Abstracts International, 44*(4), 1075A.

Examines the written production of English relative clauses by 102 Arab ESL learners. Findings show a number of factors working together in the shaping of the interlanguage -- native language, target language, transfer and other perceptual and production strategies and language universals.

Arabic/Syntactic Structures.

3189. Tracy, G. E. (1990). The effect of sentence-combining practice on syntactic maturity and writing quality in ESL students in freshman composition. *Dissertation Abstracts International, 50*(9), 2777A.

Claims that extensive practice with sentence-combining is required if students are to achieve maximum improvement in syntacitc development and writing quality.

Sentence Combining.

3190. Traugott, E. C., Dunkel, P., & Carrell, P. L. (1992). An acknowledgment of concern and a concern for lack of acknowledgment . . . [In The Forum]. *TESOL Quarterly, 26*, 180-185.

Addresses perceived inadequacies in Raimes's criticism of the research agenda for

TWE from the point of view of the TOEFL Research Committee.
Assessment/TWE.

3191. Traurig, V. (1978). *A study in second language composition: An emphasis on quantity*. Unpublished master's thesis, University of Pittsburgh, Pittsburgh, PA.
Fluency.

3192. Traxler, C. B. (1990, April). *Direct writing assessment of nontraditional students: Construct validity of the TOEFL TWE*. Paper presented at the Annual Meeting of the AERA, Boston.
Assessment.

3193. Treuba, H. T. (1989). Organizing classroom instruction in specific sociocultural contexts: Teaching Mexican youth to write. In S. R. Goldman, & H. T. Treuba (Eds.), *Becoming literate in English as a second language* (pp. 235-252). Norwood, NJ: Ablex.
Reports encouraging results from an action research project that sought to improve writing instructions for minority, largely Hispanic junior high school students in the San Diego area. Teachers, trained in ethnography, developed and implemented new writing modules for their classrooms.
Hispanic/Middle School/Ethnographic Research.

3194. Treuba, H. T., Moll, L. C., Diaz, S., & Diaz, R. (1984). *Improving the functional writing of bilingual secondary school students*. Urbana, IL: NCTE. [ERIC ED 240 862].
Describes a junior high school writing curriculum for Hispanic bilinguals.
Hispanic/Middle School/Bilingual.

3195. Tribble, C. (1991, March). *Appropriate models: Electronic texts and the teaching of writing*. Paper presented at the 25th Annual TESOL Convention, New York, NY.
Demonstrates practical ways to use machine-readable texts in the ELT classroom.
Computers.

3196. Tricomi, E. (1986). Krashen's second-language acquisition theory and the teaching of edited American English. *Journal of Basic Writing*, 5(2), 59-69.
Suggests that writing teachers could use research on second language acquisition as a guide to the teaching of the mechanics of writing and help students gain control over edited American English.
Editing.

3197. Trimble, L. (1985). *English for science and technology: A discourse approach*. Cambridge: Cambridge University Press.
Treats all aspects of scientific and technological texts from lexis to rhetoric, explains how to teach numerous features discussed, and offers many assignments and exercises to practice the skills discussed.
Technical Writing/ESP/Rhetoric.

3198. Tripp, E. L. (1982). Forty, foreign -- and freshman. In C. Carter (Ed.), *Non-native and nonstandard dialect students* (pp. 46-48). Urbana, ILL: NCTE.
Relates how to match an ESL student with a native speaking peer as a tutor.
University/Tutoring.

3199. Tsao, F. F. (1982a). Linguistics and written discourse in particular languages: Contrastive studies: English and Chinese. *Annual Review of Applied Linguistics*, 3, 99-117.
Reviews contrastive studies of English and Mandarin Chinese beyond the level

of the sentence. These include analyses of cohesion, functional sentence perspective, and preferred stylistic structures.
Contrastive Rhetoric/Chinese.

3200. Tsao, F. F. (1982b). *Topic chains in Chinese.* Unpublished manuscript, Chinese University of Hong Kong, Hong Kong.
[See next item].
Contrastive Rhetoric/Chinese/Topic.

3201. Tucker, A. (1991). *Decoding ESL: International students in the American college classroom.* NY: McGraw Hill.
Discusses experiences teaching writing and literature to international students. Chapters explore the cross-cultural reading of Persian-speaking students, a Greek writer's idiolect, the motivation of a Chinese woman from Taiwan, the acquisition of article usage by a Russian student, Japanese and American rhetorical preferences, and native and nonative encounters with literature written in English. The hermeneutics of reading ESL texts shows how American teachers can question their own cultural preconceptions.
University/Literature/Textbook.

3202. Tucker, A. (1986, March). *Japanese expository patterns, or ten ways to avoid an argument.* Paper presented at the 37th Annual CCCC Meeting, New Orleans, LA.
Japanese/Exposition.

3203. Tucker, R. W. (1983, March). *Conversation to composition: A transitioning technique.* Paper presented at the 17th Annual TESOL Convention, Toronto, Ontario.
Offers techniques: questioning strategies, focused interviews, and structured notes, which utilize conversational ability in the improvement of writing.
Speaking-Writing Relations.

3204. Tyler, A., & Raffel, S. (1983, March). *Advanced ESL writing: An alternative approach.* Workshop presented at the 17th Annual TESOL Convention, Toronto, Ontario.
Advocates an approach that centers assignments within a rhetorical context, emphasizes transition from personal to academic writing, and offers a proof-reading method for college ESL composition.
Advanced/University.

U

3205. Ulijin, J. M., & Strother, J. B. (1987). Interlanguage and EST writing: some syntactic evidence. *English for Specific Purposes*, 6(2), 99-112.
A comparison of technical writing by Dutch and American students shows a preference for scientific register above common language.
Technical Writing/Dutch/Register.

3206. Ultsch, S., Orkin, N. S., & Tragant, E. (1989, March). *Students' preferences for various written error corrections: An exploration.* Paper presented at the 23rd Annual TESOL Convention, San Antonio, TX.
Discusses student responses to questionnaires concerning their preferences.
Error Treatment/Preferences.

3207. Urzua, C. (1987). "You stopped too soon": Second language children composing and revising. *TESOL Quarterly, 21*, 279-304.

    A year-long observational study of four Southeast Asian children writing in English shows attention to aspects of abstract, context-reduced language in their writing and revising.

    Children/Revision/Southeast Asian.

3208. Urzua, C. (1985, April). *"You stopped too soon": Composing in L2 children*. Paper presented at the 19th Annual TESOL Convention, New York, NY.

    Reports a longitudinal study of four southeast Asian children as they wrote and revised various pieces of writing.

    Children/Asian.

3209. Urzua, C., Serna, I. A., & Hudelson, S. (1992, March). *Personal reasons for writing in a second language*

    Poster presented at the 26th Annual TESOL Convention, Vancouver, BC.

    Data from a longitudinal study in K-3 suggests that children acquiring literacy in L1 who are free to choose the language and purpose of engaging in literacy events acquire literacy in L2 as a by product.

    Children/Literacy.

3210. Usovicz, E. (1986, March). *Advanced writing skills: Toward the acquisition of style*. Paper presented at the 20th Annual TESOL Convention, Anaheim, CA.

    Workshop demonstrates importance of choice in written expression.

    Advanced/Style.

3211. Uzawa, K., & Cumming, A. H. (1989). Writing strategies in Japanese as a foreign language: Lowering or keeping up the standards. *The Canadian Modern Language Review, 46*, 178-194.

    A case study portrays the composing strategies of four Canadian adults who were learning Japanese. They wrote an expository task in their mother tongue before transposing their intended text into a distinctly foreign language. Protocol analysis shows contrary tendencies. Subjects used compensatory strategies to "keep up the standard" they attain in their mother tongue but also engage strategies to "lower the standard" because of restricted knowledge in the foreign language.

    L1 Influence/Japanese.

V

3212. Vahapassi, A. (1988). The problem of selection of writing tasks in cross-cultural study. In A. C. Purves (Ed.), *Writing across languages and cultures: Issues in contrastive rhetoric* (pp. 51-78). Newbury Park, CA: Sage.

    Examines native writing tasks in school exit examinations of several countries and compares them to a general model of written discourse. Findings used to develop writing tasks for the IEA Writing Study.

    Evaluation/IEA.

3213. Valdes, G. (1992). Bilingual minorities and language issues in writing: Toward professional responses to a new challenge. *Written Communication, 9*, 85-136.

Distinguishes writing needs of fluent/functional bilinguals from those of ESL students and mainstream native writers. Calls for bilingual research by bilingual writers.
Bilingual/Research.

3214. Valdes, G. (1991). *Bilingual minorities and language issues in writing: Toward professional responses to a new challenge* (Technical Report No. 54). Berkeley, CA: Center for the Study of Writing. [ERIC ED 341 067].
See next item.
Bilingual/Research.

3215. Valdez Pierce, L., & O'Malley, J. M. (1991, March). *Using a portfolio approach to monitor academic language development*. Paper presented at the 25th Annual TESOL Convention, New York, NY.
A workshop presents portfolio development and analysis for integrated assessment of limited English proficient students.
Assessment/Portfolios/Children.

3216. Van Haalen, T. G. (1990). *Efficacy of word processing as a writing tool for bilingual elementary school students: A pilot study*. Washington, DC: ERIC/FLL. [ERIC ED 318 233].
Finds no clear-cut relations between bilingualism, field-sensitivity/insensitivity, and computer writing strategies among English monolingual and Spanish bilingual fourth-graders.
Elementary/Word Processing/Spanish.

3217. Van Haalen, T. G. (1990). Writing and revising: Bilingual students' use of word processing. *Dissertation Abstracts International, 52*(2), 418-419A.
Study compares 22 balanced bilingual Mexican-American fifth-grade students and their monolingual peers. Two handwritten compositions and two word processed compositions were analyzed for revision types (Bridwell 1980) and strategies (Bermudez and Padron, 1987) employed. Subjects made significantly more revisions, except for surface errors, with pencil and paper than with the computer. Bilingual females revised more and used more expert strategies than bilingual males; monolingual females reported using fewest expert strategies.
Computers/Hispanic/Revision/Word Processing.

3218. van Pletzen, B. F. (1992, March). *Incorporating the English idiom into the ESL writing instruction*. Paper presented at the 26th Annual TESOL Convention, Vancouver, BC.
Emulation of idiomatic English in writing creates a significant improvement, it is claimed, in voice and readability of ESL writing.
Speaking-Writing Relations/Voice/Style.

3219. Van Schaik, J. D. (1978, April). *A comparison of advanced ESL and freshman composition textbooks*. Paper presented at the 12th Annual TESOL Convention, Mexico City, Mexico. [ERIC ED 171 513].
Reports a national survey and content analysis of a sample of textbooks used throughout the U. S. in freshman composition and ESL courses. Results indicate that the content of ESL texts differs in both the amount and type of composition instruction offered. Also discovers an apparent discrepancy between expressed ESL composition goals and actual practices.

Materials/Textbook.
3220. Van Wart, M., & Johnson, J. (1986, May). *Word processing as a component of advanced ESL curriculum*. Paper presented at the Annual NAFSA Meeting, San Antonio, TX.
Computers/Word Processing.
3221. Vance, K. (1987, April). *Integrate writing courses with technology courses for international students*. Paper presented at the 21st Annual TESOL Convention, Miami Beach, FL.
Discusses successful program for Arabic-speaking students.
Arabic/ESP.
3222. Vander Lei, E. A. (1987, April). *Defining the ESL composing process: 33 retrospective analyses*. Paper presented at the 21st Annual TESOL Convention, Miami Beach, FL.
Finds two similarities and three unique characteristics between ESL and native speaker composing processes.
NS-NNS Comparisons.
3223. Vanetti, L., & Jurich, D. (1990). A context for collaboration: Teachers and students writing together. In J. K. Peyton (Ed.), *Students and teachers writing together: Perspectives on journal writing* Alexandria, VA: TESOL.
Describes how the design and implementation of a personal journal writing class created a new role, namely collaboration, for the teachers.
Dialogue Journals/Responding/Collaboration.
3224. Vanetti, L., & Jurich, D. (1985, April). *The missing link: Connecting journals to academic writing*. Paper presented at the 19th Annual TESOL Convention, New York, NY.
Presents lessons that link journal writing with academic writing as a means for students to discover the writing process.
Cohesion/Journal Writing.
3225. Vann, R. J. (1981). Bridging the gap between oral and written communication in EFL. In B. Kroll, & R. J. Vann (Eds.), *Exploring speaking-writing relationships: Connections and contrasts* (pp. 154-167). Urbana, IL: NCTE.
Presents a model that relates speech and writing in the development of a learner of English as a foreign language. Elaborates on implications for teachers and researchers.
Speaking-Writing Relations.
3226. Vann, R. J. (1979a). Oral and written syntactic relationships in second language learning. In C. A. Yorio, K. Perkins, & J. Schachter (Eds.), *On TESOL '79: The learner in focus* (pp. 322-329). Washington, DC: TESOL.
A study of 28 ESL students correlates their L2 proficiency with the syntactic features of written stories and oral retellings about a short, silent film. Multiple regression analysis shows that the error-free t-unit in writing has the strongest correlation with TOEFL scores.
Speaking-Writing Relations.
3227. Vann, R. J. (1979b, March). *Oral and written syntactic relationships in second language learning*. Paper presented at the 13th Annual TESOL Convention, Boston.
Studies data from Arabic-speaking learners who differentiate oral and written styles in a manner similar to native speakers.

Arabic/NS-NNS Comparisons/Speaking-Writing Relations.

3228. Vann, R. J. (1979c). A study of the relationship of the oral and written English of adult Arab speakers. *Dissertation Abstracts International, 39*(9), 5484A.

Examines (1) the relationship between the oral and written language of adult Arabic EFL learners; and (2) the reliability of widely used indices of syntactic maturity. Results show (a) there is a correlation between oral and written proficiency; (b) mean length of error-free T-units was best index for writing and the ratio of error-free T-units combined with oral mean length of T-units accounts for the largest amount of variance in oral language; and (c) certain correspondences between second language learning and first language acquistion.

Speaking-Writing Relations/Arabic/Syntactic Development.

3229. Vann, R. J., Lorenz, F. O., & Meyer, D. M. (1991). Error gravity: Faculty response to errors in the written discourse of nonnative users of English. In L. Hamp-Lyons (Ed.), *Assessing second language writing in academic contexts* (pp. 181-195). Norwood, NJ: Ablex.

Confirms evidence of error hierarchy in faculty responses found in Vann, Meyer, and Lorenz (1984). Faculty are unified in seeing errors as more or less serious but vary predictably, primarily according to academic discipline, in response to certain kinds of errors.

Error Gravity.

3230. Vann, R. J., Meyer, D. M., & Lorenz, F. O. (1984). Error gravity: A study of faculty opinion of ESL errors. *TESOL Quarterly, 18*, 427-440.

Describes the reaction and response of a cross-section of university faculty members to twelve common written errors by non-native speakers of English. This study was designed to determine which sentence-level errors are judged to be more serious and discover what factors influence this judgment. The findings suggest evidence of a hierarchy of errors predicted by factors of the age and academic discipline of faculty judge.

Error Gravity.

3231. Varonic, E. M. (1985, March). *Patterns in non-native writing*. Paper presented at the 36th Annual CCCC Meeting, Minneapolis, MN.

Organization.

3232. Vaughan, C. (1991). Holistic assessment: What goes on in the raters' minds? In L. Hamp-Lyons (Ed.), *Assessing second language writing in academic contexts* (pp. 111-125). Norwood, NJ: Ablex.

Analyzes think-aloud protocols of nine raters when assessing six ESL essays. While some essays are clearly judged according to guidelines, others -- especially borderline cases -- elicit personal criteria in judgments. Study implies that raters do not adhere to a single, unified method.

Assessment/Responding.

3233. Verdorn, B. J. (1982). *Don't throw it away: Junk mail in the adult ESL class*. Unpublished master's thesis, Hunter College, CUNY, New York, NY. [ERIC ED 218 949].

Junk mail is useful as class material for, among other reasons, learning various

types of letter-writing styles.
Materials/Adult Education.

3234. Vergara, E. C. (1982, May). *Undergraduate scientific writing in an ESL setting*. Paper presented at the 16th Annual TESOL Convention, Honolulu, HI.
Describes a practical approach for Phillipine agriculture students.
ESP/Phillipines.

3235. Vetter, D. (1991). Discourses across literacies: Personal letter writing in a Tuvaluan context. *Language and Education*, 5(2), 125-145.
Discusses the transfer across literacies of discourse conventions specific to personal letter writing in Tuvalu (a South Pacific nation) among vernacular and Tavaluan Engish biliterates.
South Pacific/Contrastive Rhetoric/Letter Writing.

3236. Vilamil, O., & Carrasquillo, A. (1988). *Assessing writing in the ESL classroom*. Washington, DC: ERIC/FLL. [ERIC ED 301 032].
Discusses language learning and composition for the ESL writing teacher in Puerto Rico.
Hispanic/University.

3237. Vincent, S. (1990). Motivating the advanced learner in developing writing skills: A project. *ELT Journal*, 44(4), 272-278.
A classroom project for advanced writers at the fifth-year university level in Poland illustrates how interest and motivation to write for the real world can develop the ability to write.
Motivation/Project Work/Polish.

W

3238. Wagner, H. (1982). Kids can be ESL teachers. In C. Carter (Ed.), *Non-native and nonstandard dialect students* (pp. 62-65). Urbana, IL: NCTE.
Seventh-graders provided teacher with useful suggestions for helping two ESL students mainstreamed in their classroom.
Elementary.

3239. Wald, B. (1989). The development of writing skills among Hispanic high school students. In S. R. Goldman, & H. T. Treuba (Eds.), *Becoming literate in English as a second language* (pp. 155-185). Norwood, NJ: Ablex.
Investigates the similarities and differences between the skills of early and late learners of both spoken and written English among advanced high school graduates in the Hispanic bilingual community of Greater East Los Angeles. Provides further support for "read-first" and "write-first" (i.e. before speaking) theories of literacy instructions.
Hispanic/Secondary School/Literacy.

3240. Walker, C. (1982). Milk o leche? In C. Carter (Ed.), *Non-native and nonstandard dialect students* (pp. 17-27). Urbana, IL: NCTE.
Suggestions for individualizing writing work in a remedial college course for a Spanish-speaking ESL student.
Hispanic/University/Classroom Activities.

3241. Walker, M., & Raupp, M. (1985). *Write! Write! Guided composition for English language students*. (Second Ed.). Reading, MA: Addison-Wesley.

   Twenty lessons dealing with everyday life, which stimulate reading and writing in increasingly complex ways. Each lesson builds on previous ones and has three levels of difficulty.

   Beginners/Textbook.

3242. Walker, P. (1976). An approach to creative writing. *TESL Talk*, 7, 87-90.

   Describes an experiment which uses the "theme approach" to language teaching.

   Creative Writing.

3243. Wall, A. P. (1983, March). *The pre-writing stage in advanced ESL composition*. Paper presented at the 17th Annual TESOL Convention, Toronto, Ontario.

   Indicates that the pre-writing stage of advanced ESL composition is the appropriate point to introduce journals, wet ink writing, visual and auditory invention prompts among other invention strategies

   Invention/Advanced.

3244. Wall, D. (1984, March). *Writing for academic purposes --- Helping overseas students interpret university writing demands*. Paper presented at the 18th Annual TESOL Convention, Houston, TX.

   Recommends a course prior to enrollment that can clear up student misconceptions about academic writing requirements and practice judging and producing by subject teacher criteria.

   Academic Writing/University.

3245. Wall, D. (1982, May). *A pre-sessional academic writing course for graduate students in economics*. Paper presented at the 16th Annual TESOL Convention, Honolulu, HI.

   Presents an investigation of criteria used by subject specialists in assessing L2 writers majoring in that discipline.

   Assessment/ESP.

3246. Wall, D., Nickson, A., Jordan, R. R., Allwright, J., & Houghton, D. (1988). Developing student writing -- a subject tutor and writing tutor compare points of view. In P. C. Robinson (Ed.), *Academic writing: Process and product* (pp. 117-129). London: Modern English Publications/British Council.

   For a panel discussion, presents the responses of one subject matter and three writing tutors to a student's term paper on urban unemployment. Panel members discussed their reactions to the student paper as well as the tutor reactions. The student essay is appended to Robinson (1988).

   Feedback/Academic Writing/Tutoring.

3247. Wallace, D. (1987). *Dialogue journals: A tool for ESL teaching*. Urbana, IL: ERIC/RCS. [ERIC ED 280 316].

   Describes effective use of dialogue journals in the ESL classroom for the purpose of enhancing fluency and developing a sense of realistic communication.

   Dialogue Journals/Fluency.

3248. Wallace, R. B. (1985). English for specific purposes in ESL undergraduate composition classes: Rationale. *Dissertation Abstracts International*, 46(5), 1218A.

   Suggests an ESP approach to teaching writing to ESL students, based on a review and criticism of ESL composition courses and on feedback from faculty regarding their expectations of writing by ESL students.

University/ESP.

3249. Wallace, R. B. (1988a, March). *Native and non-native sentence combining: A study in differences*. Paper presented at the 39th Annual CCCC Meeting, St. Louis, MO.

Sentence Combining/NS-NNS Comparisons.

3250. Wallace, R. B. (1988b, April). *Teaching English for professionals: English for Specific Purposes in ESL undergraduate composition courses*. Paper presented at the Eastern Michigan University Conference on Languages for Business and the Professions, Ann Arbor, MI.

Describes an adaptation of the British model for teaching ESP.

ESP/Technical writing.

3251. Wallace, R. B. (1987). Teaching audience to advanced ESL technical writers. *Exercise Exchange*, *33*(1), 19-21.

Students follow a six-step procedure for making paper airplanes which serve as instructions for the semester to follow.

Classroom Activities/Audience.

3252. Wallace, R. B. (1986). Listening and writing skills in the ESL composition class. *Exercise Exchange*, *32*(1), 33-34.

Gives a six-step exercise in writing instructions to make a paper airplane.

Listening-Writing Relations.

3253. Walsh, C. (1987). Language, meaning and voice: Puerto Rican students' struggle for a speaking consciousness. *Language Arts*, *64*, 198-206.

Examines student strategies employed to deal with tensions between school and community discourses.

Hispanic/Discourse Communities.

3254. Walsleben, M. C. (1989). The effect of integrative/instrumental motivation on the expository writing of unskilled English as a second language writers. *Dissertation Abstracts International*, *49*(8), 2098A.

Investigates how different types of motivation affect ability to write in the expository academic mode of 82 unskilled ESL writers. Finds that writing is significantly correlated with an ESL writer's integrative motivation but not affected by only a 30-minute lesson on expository writing.

Affect/Exposition.

3255. Walters, K. (1988, November). *Composition and literacy theory and research: A brief overview of affective factors*. Paper presented at the 78th Annual NCTE Convention, St. Louis, MO.

Affect.

3256. Walters, K. (1985, April). *Topical structure in the English essays of Arabic speakers*. Paper presented at the 19th Annual TESOL Convention, New York, NY.

Reports research on the culturally-influenced topical structure (Witte, 1983) of English compositions by Arabic-speaking students.

Culture/Arabic/TSA.

3257. Walters, L. W. (1993a). A descriptive study of Asian American basic writers.

Dissertation Abstracts International, 53(6), 2132A.

A qualitative study of Asian Americans unable to pass a university writing competence test suggests that cultural heritage, family influence, and prior educational experience contributed to their unsuccessful literacy practices.

Asian/Ethnographic Research.

3258. Walters, L. W. (1993b). A diary study of Asian American basic writers or why do I get question mark looks? In M. N. Brock, & L. W. Walters (Eds.), *Teaching composition around the Pacific Rim: Politics and pedagogy* (pp. 61-74). Clevedon, ENG: Multilingual Matters.

Suggests using journals/diaries to better understand Asian American immigrants and their attitudes toward learning a second language and culture.

Asian American/Culture/Journal Writing.

3259. Walton, C., & Congrave, C. (1986, March). *Establishing and using an ESL microcomputer writing center*. Paper presented at the 20th Annual TESOL Convention, Anaheim, CA.

Finds that secondary LEP students can make the transition to mainstream classes through the use of computers for writing.

Secondary School/Computers/Word Processing.

3260. Walworth, M., & Staton, J. (1985, April). *Content-focused use of dialogue journals*. Paper presented at the 19th Annual TESOL Convention, New York, NY.

Content-focused dialogue journals are useful in guiding reading and for acquiring appropriate schemata.

Dialogue Journals/Content.

3261. Wang, C. (1992). Paragraph organization in English and Chinese academic prose: A comparative study. *Dissertation Abstracts International, 53*(3), 796A.

Analyzes a sample of paragraphs in academic journals written in two languages: English and Chinese, using interactional analysis (Tirkkonen-Condit, 1985) as a measure. Finds that Chinese and English academic writing are basically similar in method insofar as English paragraphs favor deductive organization whereas Chinese paragraphs are evenly divided between deductive, inductive, and mixed modes. However, individual stylistic variation was greater among Chinese writers.

Paragraph/Chinese.

3262. Wang, M. (1987). An unconventional approach to composition teaching. *TECFORS, 10*(1), 6-8.

Describes ease of extensive writing, fast writing, and intensive writing of which only the last is graded by the teacher.

Instruction.

3263. Wardell, D. (1990, June). *Writing: The development of coherent rhetorical forms in advanced learners of a second language*. Paper presented at the 20th Annual Meeting of the Communication Association of Japan, Tokyo, Japan. [ERIC ED 321 558].

Describes a program for advanced ESL students in Japan that attends to rhetorical patterns for developing students' writing skills on business-specific topics.

Japanese/Advanced/Business Writing.

3264. Watabe, M., Brown, C., & Ueta, Y. (1991). Transfer of discourse function: Passives in the writing of ESL and JSL learners. *IRAL, 29*(2), 115-134.

Presents strong evidence for the interplay and transfer of native language form and function of passive structures in ESL and Japanese as a second language.

L1 Influence/Syntactic Structures.

3265. Waters, K., & Williams, B. (1992, March). *Instructional aides: Language development through writing L1 and L2.* Paper presented at the 26th Annual TESOL Convention, Vancouver, BC.

Describes efforts to teach Yup'ik-speaking students in Alaska writing in their first language in order to develop their ability to write in English later.

Alaskan/Literacy.

3266. Watkins-Goffman, L. (1990, March). *The teaching of writing: A pedagogy of questions.* Paper presented at the 24th Annual TESOL Convention, San Francisco, CA.

Explores ways to help students learn to revise by forming questions about the content of student drafts. The approach encourages students to read drafts objectively, self-revise, and edit. Student drafts and audiotapes demonstrate the questioning techniques.

Questioning/Revision.

3267. Watkins-Goffman, L. (1987a). A case study of the second language writing process of a sixth-grade writing group. *Dissertation Abstracts International, 47*(8), 2932A.

A case study of eight sixth-grade ESL students investigates the writing processes and the interaction between the group and the researcher. The study corroborates current research which indicates that expressive writing started early to ensure sufficient exposure to vocabulary and to context of social interaction, as well as specific audience and purpose, has positive effects on the L2 writing process.

Process Research/Elementary.

3268. Watkins-Goffman, L. (1987b, April). *The composing process of eight sixth-grade ESL students.* Paper presented at the 21st Annual TESOL Convention, Miami Beach, FL.

Reports a case study of an ESL writing group, indicating acquisition process over a twelve-week period.

Process Research/Elementary.

3269. Watkins-Goffman, L. (1989). *The teaching of writing: A pedagogy of hidden questions.* Paper presented at the Annual Northeast Regional Conference of English in the Two-Year College, Albany, NY. [ERIC ED 328 914].

Suggests that ESL students can be trained in self-evaluation skills by using checklists to introduce revising as a process of reading to formulate questions about their texts.

Revision/Metacognition.

3270. Watkins-Goffman, L., & Berkowitz, D. (1990). *Thinking to write: A composing-process approach to writing.* Boston: Heinle & Heinle.

A composition text that offers the advanced ESL student topics to stimulate discussion and writing. It combines authentic reading material, grammar explanations, and discussing and composing techniques. Each chapter focuses on a particular rhetorical mode -- narration, description, argument, comparison/contrast, and research-paper writing. Students are encouraged to think about what they read and analyze what they

compose.
   Advanced/Textbook.
3271. Watkins-Goffman, L., & Cummings, V. (1993, April). *Teaching argument writing across cultures: Theory to practice*. Paper presented at the 27th Annual TESOL Convention, Atlanta, GA.
   Reviews instructional programs based on research findings across cultures on what helps students organize their thinking for writing argumentative essays.
   Argumentation.
3272. Watkins-Goffman, L., Velasquez, C., & Goffman, R. (1989). *Making your point: A process approach to argumentation*. Boston: Heinle & Heinle.
   Uses current topics in teaching learners how to defend positions through effective argumentation.
   Textbook/Advanced.
3273. Watkins-Goffman, L., Velasquez, C., & Goffman, R. (1988). *Making your point: A process approach to argumentation*. Boston: Heinle & Heinle.
   Uses current topics in teaching learners how to defend positions through effective argumentation.
   Textbook/Advanced.
3274. Watson, L. T. (1989, March). *Steps to peer responding for L2 writers*. Paper presented at the 23rd Annual TESOL Convention, San Antonio, TX.
   Students should be led through focused and systematic steps of examining their writing "top-down" rather than merely exchanging papers.
   Classroom Activities/Responding.
3275. Watson-Reekie, C. B. (1982). The use and abuse of models in the ESL writing class. *TESOL Quarterly, 16*, 5-14.
   Examines the traditional use of models in the ESL composition class and gives suggestions for using models not as an ideal product but as part of the process of writing.
   Models/Process Instruction.
3276. Watts, M. (1981). Writing poetry and learning English. *English Language Teaching Journal, 35*, 444-450.
   Describes a project that uses the writing of poetry to stimulate imagination. Finds that grammatical errors decrease while choice of lexical items remain difficult.
   Creative Writing.
3277. Weaver, L. R., & Padron, Y. N. (1993, April). *Examining teacher's perceptions and acceptance of writing strategy instruction for ESL students*. Paper presented at the Annual Meeting of the American Educational Research Association, Atlanta, GA.
   Teacher Beliefs//Strategies.
3278. Webb, S. J. (1988). Using figurative language in epistemic writing: The purposes and processes of first and second language writers. *Dissertation Abstracts International, 49*(11), 3353A.
   Studies figurative language production in the epistemic writing (i.e., writing to discover new knowledge) of seven university volunteers (three NNSs). Case studies based on protocol analysis and retrospective interviews describe the processes involved in producing and using figurative language along with the role in generating insight and the

purposes served. Results show that figurative language is a holistic process evoking a pattern that unifies experience, meaning, and unconscious elements. It also varies in degree of creativity from frozen to novel and is involved in generating insight in various ways.
L1-L2 Comparison/Literacy.

3279. Webb, S. S. (1992). Bibliography of writing texts. *WPA: Writing Program Administration*, 15(3), 78-98.
Provides annotations of 164 textbooks (copyrighted in 1992) for college writing, including ESL writing.
Bibliography/Textbook.

3280. Weeks, R. (1993, April). *The writing strategies inventory: An assessment and instructional instrument*. Paper presented at the 27th Annual TESOL Convention, Atlanta, GA.
Describes development and use of an instrument to assess the writing strategies of advanced ESL writers.
Objective Measures/Strategies.

3281. Weiner, L. R. (1978, April). *Teaching writing through the use of communicative objectives*. Paper presented at the 21st Annual TESOL Convention, Miami Beach, FL.
Views writing as suitable for communicative syllabus design.
Syllabus Design.

3282. Weinstein, G. (1984). Literacy and second language acquisition: Issues and perspectives. *TESOL Quarterly*, 18, 471-484.
Presents a theoretical examination of the relationship between literacy and second language acquisition. This paper also reviews a study conducted in a Thai refugee camp and suggests that a functional approach to literacy might be more valuable than a developmental approach.
Literacy/Theory/Southeast Asian.

3283. Weinstein-Shr, G. (1991). *Literacy and second language learners: A family agenda*. Washington, DC: ERIC/FLL.
Discusses a family-centered approach to improving the academic success through literacy of immigrant children
Literacy/Children.

3284. Weinstein-Shr, G. (1989). *From problem solving to celebration: Discovering and creatring meanings through literacy* . Washington, DC: ERIC/FLL. [ERIC ED 313 916].

Presents a case study of a teacher and three adult Hmong literacy students.
Literacy/Hmong.

3285. Weir, C. (1988). Academic writing -- Can we please all the people all the time? In P. C. Robinson (Ed.), *Academic writing: process and product* (pp. 17-34). London: Modern English Publications/British Council.
Surveys the problems experienced in academic writing by native and overseas students at British universities as well as the perception of their problems by tutoring staff. Tutor responses to twelve criteria are reported in detail. Relevance and adequacy of content is the most important criteria.

Academic Writing/NS-NNS Comparisons/Responding.

3286. Weir, C. (1983). *Identifying the language problem of overseas students in tertiary education in the United Kingdom.* Unpublished doctoral dissertation, University of London, London, ENG.

3287. Weissberg, R. C. (1992, March). *Analyzing develpmental speaking/writing interrelationships in adult ESL learners.* Paper presented at the 26th Annual TESOL Convention, Vancouver, BC.

A longitudinal study suggests that writing and speech develop differentially for the L1 literate ESL writer. Discusses procedures for identifying development and a differential model of adult L2 writing.

Speaking-Writing Relations.

3288. Weissburg, R. C. (1992, March). *Research speaking & writing in the applied life sciences: The graduate seminar presentation.* Paper presented at a Colloquium at the 26th Annual TESOL Convention, Vancouver, BC.

The oral discourse of students (both native and nonnative) in a science seminar is regarded as a distinct genre with some sections (e.g., Methodology and Results) more speech-like and other sections (Introduction and Discussion) more written-like.

Research Writing/Speaking-Writing Relations/Genre.

3289. Weissberg, R. C. (1990). On coherence: An interview with Ulla Connor and Ann Johns. *TESOL Newsletter, 24*(4), 8-9.

Editors discuss what their collection of papers, Coherence in Writing, offers and the audiences it is intended to serve.

Review.

3290. Weissberg, R. C. (1984). Given and new: Paragraph development models from scientific English. *TESOL Quarterly, 18,* 485-500.

Reports a study conducted to determine the ability of a set of descriptive models for paragraph development based on the given/new contract to describe paragraph structures in experimental research reports in English. Results show that the given/new principle of information distribution is a regular feature of the English paragraph. Applications of the models in ESL technical writing courses are discussed.

ESP/Models/Paragraph.

3291. Weissberg, R. C. (1989, March). *Measuring coherence: Is topical structure analysis the answer?* Paper presented at the 23rd Annual TESOL Convention, San Antonio, TX.

Reports results of a study applying Topical Structure Analysis to ESL compositions.

Coherence/TSA.

3292. Weissberg, R. C. (1982, May). *Information transfer in the teaching of academic writing.* Paper presented at the NAFSA, Long Beach, CA. [ERIC ED 292 100].

See Weissburg, 1984.

Academic Writing/Transfer/Content.

3293. Weissberg, R. C. (1978). Progressive decontrol through deletion: A guided writing technique for advanced learners in technical fields. *TESL Reporter, 11*(2), 1,4,14-15. [ERIC ED 150 856].

Presents a technique for progressively decontrolling the teaching of technical

writing in contrast to a grammatical method and a cognitive method.
Control/Advanced/ESP.

3294. Weissburg, R. C., & Buker, S. (1990). *Writing up research: Experimental research report writing for students of English.* Englewood Cliffs, NJ: Prentice Hall.

Designed for students of English for Specific Purposes or those involved in their own research, the text focuses on the forms and conventions of written reports and provides writing practice for each stage of the research report.
University/ESP/Textbook.

3295. Weissburg, R. C., & Buker, S. (1978, April). *Strategies for teaching the rhetoric of written EST.* Paper presented at the 12th Annual TESOL Convention, Mexico City, Mexico.

Describes teaching strategies employed in technical writing for Latin American students at a U.S. university.
Hispanic/Technical Writing.

3296. Weissburg, R. C., & Buker, S. (1978). Strategies for teaching the rhetoric of written English for science and technology. *TESOL Quarterly, 12*, 321-329.

Describes teaching strategies used in a technical writing class for Latin American students at New Mexico State University. States that focus is on correspondence between grammatical and rhetorical fuctions in English of Science and Technology.
Technical Writing/ESP.

3297. Wenden, A. L. (1992). Metacognitive strategies in L2 writing: A case for task knowledge. In J. E. Alatis (Ed.), *Georgetown University Round Table on Languages and Linguistics 1991* (pp. 302-322). Washington, DC: Georgetown University Press.

Reports an exploratory study of the use by eight ESL students of metacognitive strategies to regulate a writing task. The three most successful writers showed that it is necessary to know the task specifically in order to effectively plan, evaluate, and monitor L2 writing.
Metacognition/Task.

3298. Wenden, A. L. (1989, April). *The metacognitive strategies of ESL writers and their relationship to task knowledge.* Paper presented at the Annual AERA Meeting, San Francisco, CA.
Strategies.

3299. Wenzell, V., & Eleftherlou, A. (1993, April). *Why LEP adolescents can't write: A needs assessment.* Paper presented at the 27th Annual TESOL Convention, Atlanta, GA.

Investigates the causes of illiteracy in a study of 600 urban LEP junior high school students.
Literacy/Middle School.

3300. Werner, A. B. (1983, March). *Talk-write: A functional approach to teaching ESL composition.* Paper presented at the 17th Annual TESOL Convention, Toronto, Ontario.

Zoellner's talk-write approach to writing is compatible with the oral experience emphasis in TESOL practice.
Speaking-Writing Relations.

3301. West, G. K. (1980). That-nominal constructions in traditional rhetorical divisions of scientific research papers. *TESOL Quarterly, 14*, 483-488.

Examines relationship between "<u>that</u>-nominal" and the rhetorical structure of scientific papers. Results indicate significant differences between frequency of "<u>that</u>-nominal" and the rhetorical sections of English of Science and Technology. Pedagogical implications highlighted.
Technical Writing/ESP.

3302. Whalen, K. (1988). Pilot study on the nature of difficulties in written expression in a second language: Process or product? *Bulletin of the Canadian Association of Applied Linguistics, 10*(1), 51-57.

To determine the nature of writing problems in a second language, a comparison of first/second-language texts written by anglophone and francophone students was conducted. Students composing in a second language reported that the development of ideas and organization were constrained by linguistic difficulties.
LI Influence/French.

3303. Whalley, E., & Basham, C. S. (1986, March). *Teachers' responses to writing: What students prefer*. Paper presented at the 20th Annual TESOL Convention, Anaheim, CA.

Results of a questionnaire indicate preferences of Asian immigrants and Alaskan native students to different forms of composition correction.
Responding/Preferences/Asian/Alaskan.

3304. White, R. V. (1993). Laying it on the line. In M. N. Brock, & L. W. Walters (Eds.), *Teaching composition around the Pacific Rim: Politics and pedagogy* (pp. 130-149). Clevedon, ENG: Multilingual Matters.

Presents personal, pedagogic and academic insights gained from the experience of using journals, peer observation, student evaluations and student texts in teaching writing in Japan. See White, 1990.
EFL.

3305. White, R. V. (1992, March). *In the writing classroom: Effect of institutional contexts*. Paper presented at a Colloquium at the 26th Annual TESOL Convention, Vancouver, BC.

Discusses the nature of institutional constraints on the teaching of writing and how to deal with them.

3306. White, R. V. (1990). *Laying it on the line*. Washington, DC: ERIC: FLL. [ERIC ED 319 233].

Reports on using process-oriented writing curriculum with Japanese students.
Japanese/Process Instruction.

3307. White, R. V. (1988). Academic writing: Process and product. In P. C. Robinson (Ed.), *Academic writing: Process and product* (pp. 4-16). London: Modern English Publications/British Council.

Discovers in the American tradition of writing research principles and practices relevant to EAP -- especially the concern for unexpected outcomes characteristic of the process approach.
Process Research/Review.

3308. White, R. V. (1987). Approaches to writing. In M. H. Long, & J. C. Richards (Eds.), *Methodlogy in TESOL* (pp. 259-266). NY: Newbury.

Considers writing equal in importance to other language skills. Discusses

characteristics, levels, sequence, and appropriate types of exercises.
Approaches.

3309. White, R. V. (1980). *Teaching written English. Practical Language Teaching, No. 4.* Winchester, MA: Unwin & Allen.

A guide to ESL writing for teachers. It suggests ways to teach writing as a means of communication with correctness linked to stylistic appropriateness.
Teacher Preparation/Communicative Writing.

3310. White, S. (1980, March). *Error and contrastive analysis for Iranian ESL students.* Paper presented at the 14th Annual TESOL Convention, San Francisco, CA.

Examines twenty-five types of errors made in a sample of 75 essays by Iranian ESL students. Results suggest many errors due to contrast between languages.
Iran/Error Analysis.

3311. Whitehead, C. (1985). *A contrastive rhetoric of Arabic and English and its applications to the teaching of E. S. L. composition.* Unpublished master's thesis, University of Florida, Gainsville, FL.

Contrastive Rhetoric/Arabic.

3312. Whitley, C. A. (1987, March). *ESL students in regular writing classes: Listening to different voices.* Paper presented at the 38th Annual CCCC Meeting, Atlanta, GA.

3313. Widdowson, H. G. (1983). New starts and different kinds of failure. In A. Freedman, I. Pringle, & J. Yalden (Eds.), *Learning to write: First language, second language* (pp. 34-47). London: Longman.

Identifies some of the difficulties involved in writing, particularly in a foreign or a second language. Suggests using a methodology that views writing as an interactive process and to help learners use discourse process from their native language.
Communicative Writing.

3314. Widdowson, H. G. (1980). Conceptual and communicative functions in written discourse. *Applied Linguistics, 1,* 234-243.

Argues for the development in learners a capacity for using language for both thinking and acting so that they can exploit its meaning potential in discourse.
Communicative Writing.

3315. Widdowson, H. G. (1972). The teaching of English as communication. *ELT Journal, 27*(1), 15-19.

A classic statement of the view that the teaching of English should shift from its emphasis on formal to the communicative properties of language.
Communicative Writing.

3316. Wiener, L. R. (1979, March). *Teaching organization in writing: The argument and business letter.* Paper presented at the 13th Annual TESOL Convention, Boston.

Discusses American conventions for two forms which contrast with those in other cultures.
Contrastive Rhetoric/Argumentation/Business Writing.

3317. Wiener, L. R. (1978, April). *Teaching writing through the use of communicative objectives.* Paper presented at the 12th Annual TESOL Convention, Mexico City, Mexico.

Demonstrates a writing syllabus that focuses on communicative objectives.

Communicative Writing.

3318. Wigfield, J. (1991). *Gateway to English: Second steps.* (Second Ed.). Boston: Heinle & Heinle.

    This text further develops adult literacy skills based on dictation, survival skills, and topics of general interest to adults.

    Adult Education/Textbook.

3319. Wigfield, J. (1988). *First steps in reading and writing: A literacy workbook.* (2nd ed.). Boston: Heinle & Heinle.

    Designed to develop adult literacy as well as involve students in the learning process, the text uses pictures which are to be completed and matched with words. Students begin by copying letters in block style and moving on to lower case script.

    Adult Education/Textbook.

3320. Wiggin, B., & Bernstein, J. (1979). Technical writing in EFL: The journal article. *RELC Journal, 10*(2), 67-69.

    Describes a course to train agricultural researchers to write a journal article.

    ESP/Technical Writing.

3321. Wikborg, E. (1990). Types of coherence breaks in Swedish student writing: Misleading paragraph division. In U. M. Connor, & A. M. Johns (Ed.), *Coherence in writing: Research and pedagogical perspectives* (pp. 131-149). Alexandria, VA: TESOL.

    Examines Swedish students' writing for coherence breaks and identifies misleading paragraph divisions as the second most frequent cause of coherence breaks. Illustrates the importance of paragraphing in texts and classifies two types of misleading paragraphs: (1) change of topic within the paragraph and (2) unwarranted change of paragraph. Suggests ways teachers can help students overcome these problems.

    Paragraph/Coherence/Swedish.

3322. Wikborg, E. (1987). Uncertain inference ties in university student writing. In I. Lindblat, & M. Ljund (Eds.), *Proceedings from the Third Nordic Conference for English Studies, vol. 2* (pp. 453-467). Stockholm: Almquist & Wiksell.

    Impaired texts of inexperienced writers exhibit two types of uncertain inference ties: demonstrative and comparative inferences that cannot be identified and those insufficiently specified inferences of different degrees of recoverability. Recommend drafting and revising processes as remedy.

    Coherence/Swedish.

3323. Wikborg, E. (1985a). Types of coherence breaks in university student writing. In N. E. Enkvist (Ed.), *Coherence and composition: A symposium* (pp. 93-133). Abo, Finland: Research Institute of the Abo Akademi Foundation.

    Examines coherence breaks in one hundred forty-four essays by university students writing in Swedish. The five most frequent (in order) are -- uncertain inference ties, misleading paragraph divisions, misleading sentence connections, unspecified topic, and change or drift in topic -- are defined and exemplified.

    Coherence/Swedish.

3324. Wikborg, E. (1985b). Unspecified topic in university student essays. *Text: An Interdisciplinary Journal for the Study of Discourse, 5*(4), 359-370.

    Presents a definition of topic in terms of hierarchy, development, and function.

Illustrates usefulness of this division as a diagnostic instrument for unspecified topic in impaired texts by applying it to two student essays.
Coherence/Topic/Swedish.

3325. Wilcott, P. (1973). *Definiteness problems in the written English of Arabic speakers: A taxonomy with partial explanation*. Washington, DC: ERIC/FLL. [ERIC ED 121 052].
Finds frequent error types in article usage, especially omission of <u>the</u> in obligatory contexts and inclusion of <u>the</u> where no article is needed. These are attributed to the influence of Arabic L1.
Arabic/Errors.

3326. Wilcoxon, H. C. (1993, April). *Coherence and cohesion in writing by Chinese students*. Paper presented at the 27th Annual TESOL Convention, Atlanta, GA.
Studies errors with "conjunctive elements" and their sources made by Chinese students at two universities.
Chinese/Coherence/Cohesion.

3327. Wilcoxson, B. M. (1985). Some common concerns of reading and writing for ESL students. *Arizona English Bulletin, 27*, 125-128.
Urges the teaching of reading and writing as complementary skills.
Elementary/Reading-Writing Relations.

3328. Wiley, T. G. (1993). Discussion of Klassen & Burnaby and McKay & Weinstein-Shr: Beyond assimilationist literacy policies and practices. *TESOL Quarterly, 27*, 421-430.
Rejects the the assimilationist tendency to "see English literacy as the sole remedy for economic and social injustices".
Literacy.

3329. Willcott, P. (1974, March). *Advanced EFL and traditional goals of freshman composition: Some questions*. Paper presented at the 8th Annual TESOL Convention, Denver, CO.
Questions the efficacy of separating ESL freshmen from freshman composition in which, it is claimed, challenging rhetorical and cultural issues are raised.
Advanced.

3330. Willcott, P. (1973). *Definiteness problems in the written English of Arabic speakers: A taxonomy with partial explanation*. Washington, DC: ERIC/FLL. [ERIC ED 121 052].
Finds three major categories of error in the definite article usage in essay exams written by Arabic-speaking ESL students.
Error Analysis/Arabic.

3331. Williams, J. D. (1993, April). *Defining a developmental curriculum for a pluralistic society: The administrative challenges*. Paper presented at the 44th Annual Meeting of the Conference on College Composition and Communication, San Diego, CA. [ERIC ED 359 558].
Calls on directors of composition programs to alter the cognitive deficiency model and subskill orientation of mainstream basic writing courses in order to accomodate the influx of non-LEP ESL students who are now attending college and who need a challenging and progressive curriculum.
Curriculum.

3332. Williams, J. D., & Snipper, G. C. (1990). *Literacy and bilingualism.* New York:

Longman.

Presents an overview of theory and research associated with literacy and bilingualism and reviews techniques for implementation in the classroom.

Literacy/Bilingual.

3333. Williams, M. P. (1989). A comparison of the textual structures of Arabic and English written texts: A study in the comparative orality of Arabic. (Vols. I and II). *Dissertation Abstracts International, 50*(10), 3218A.

Uses both a systemic functional grammar approach and a Functional Sentence Perspective to analyze patterns of textual cohesion and text development in English and Arabic texts. The cohesion analysis shows that texts in Arabic have a tendency toward orality in that they make more prominent the addresser and addressee, avoid ellipsis, use a higher proportion of pronouns, display more repetition of clause structure, more repetition of lexical strings, and use more multifunctional connectors. On the other hand, English texts display greater cohesive synonymy items, more substitution. Moreover, English technical writing displays greater thematic complexity and different patterns of thematic connection between sentences.

Speaking-Writing Relations/Arabic/Cohesion.

3334. Williams, M. P. (1984). A problem of cohesion. In J. M. Swales, & H. Mustafa (Eds.), *English for Specific Purposes in the Arab world* (pp. 118-128). Birmingham, UK: University of Aston, Language Studies Unit.

Uses a systemic-functional approach to analyze patterns of cohesion and textual development in English and Arabic and finds differences in thematic repetition instead of the preference in English for discourse adjuncts and punctuation.

Cohesion/Arabic/Text Analysis.

3335. Williams, M. P. (1982). *A contrastive analysis of text cohesion and development in Arabic and English.* Unpublished master's thesis, University of Leeds, Leeds, ENG.

Confirms Kaplan's contrastive rhetoric hypothesis by reporting on experiences teaching and examining the writing of Arabic-speaking learners of English.

Cohesion/Arabic.

3336. Williams, R. M. E. (1978). *The effects of intensive practice in sentence-combining techniques on the syntactic fluency and overall writing quality of Japanese students learning English as a second language.* Unpublished master's thesis, Clemson University, Clemson, SC.

Studies the effects of sentence-combining exercises for fifteen minutes a session for ten sessions on the syntactic maturity of Japanese ESL students. Finds no significant growth in syntactic maturity and a decrease in quality of writing judged on five factors.

Syntactic Development/Sentence Combining/Japanese.

3337. Williamson, J. (1985). A guide to teaching writing skills to intermediate E.S.L. students. *TECFORS, 8*(5), 5-9. [ERIC ED 267 650].

Outlines an intermediate level course to help make the transition from sentence making to composing paragraphs.

Intermediate/Courses.

3338. Willoquet-Maricondi, P. (1992). Integrating ESOL skills through literature. *TESOL Journal, 1*(2), 11-14.

Short stories are used to promote the development of written and oral language skills among college ESL students.

Literature/University.

3339. Wilson, E. (1993, April). *External assessment of writing in community college ESL programs*. Paper presented at the 27th Annual TESOL Convention, Atlanta, GA.

Describes a method of assessing timed writing samples in a community college ESL program and discusses outcomes and feedback by students/faculty.

Evaluation.

3340. Wilson, E., & Nourse, J. (1993, April). *External assessment of writing in community college ESL programs*. Paper presented at the 27th Annual TESOL Convention, Atlanta GA.

Describes a method of external assessment of timed writing and placement in a communty college ESL program.

Assessment.

3341. Windsor, A. T. (1978). *The personal journal for ESL*. University of Hawaii, Honolulu, HI.

Journal Writing.

3342. Winer, L. (1992). "Spinach to chocolate": Changing awareness and attitudes in ESL writing teachers. *TESOL Quarterly*, 26, 57-80.

Uses data from student journals in a TESL writing practicum to trace the process by which practice of and reflection on specific activities change awareness of and attitudes toward writing and the teaching of writing. Argues for the need to integrate training and development in teacher education.

Teacher Preparation.

3343. Winer, L. (1983, March). *Error analysis in a Creole/English context*. Paper presented at the 17th Annual TESOL Convention, Toronto, Ontario.

Reports the first large-scale empirical study of errors in written composition by English Creole speakers.

Creole/Error Analysis.

3344. Winer, L. (1981, March). *Error analysis of written compositions of English Creole speakers*. Paper presented at the 15th Annual TESOL Convention, Detroit, MI.

Analyzes a large corpus of errors from secondary school students in the West Indies.

Creole/Error Analysis/Secondary School.

3345. Winer, L., & Steffensen, M. S. (1992). Cross-cultural peer dialogue journals in ESOL teacher education. *TESOL Journal*, 1(3), 23-27.

Dialogue journals can be useful in helping teachers in training acheive awareness of cross-cultural differences.

Dialogue Journals/Teacher Preparation.

3346. Winfield, F. E., & Barnes-Felfeli, P. (1982). The effects of familiar and unfamiliar cultural context on foreign language composition. *Modern Language Journal*, 66, 373-378.

Presents a study that examines the effects of familiar and unfamiliar cultural context on foreign language composition. Results show that familiar cultural context leads

to better writing.
Culture/Background Knowledge.

3347. Winfield, M. Y. (1989). *Fundamentally speaking: A focus on English as a second language* . Washington, DC: ERIC/FLL. [ERIC ED 319 241].
Techniques for teaching speaking and writing must be examined for cultural bias.
Speaking-Writing Relations/Culture.

3348. Wingfield, R. J. (1975). Five ways of dealing with errors in written composition. *English Language Teaching Journal*, 29, 311-313.
Claims that there are essentially five ways of dealing with errors and individual teachers must make their own choices of the most appropriate way of dealing with errors according to the needs of their classroom.
Error Treatment.

3349. Wink, J., & Towell, J. (1993). *Teacher research in a linguistically-diverse classroom.* Washington, DC: ERIC/RIE. [ERIC ED 359 779]).
Offers suggestions for conducting classroom research on writing issues relevant to ESL students.
Research.

3350. Winter, E. (1992, March). *Equalizing writing assessment for non-native speakers of English in the mainstream classroom.* Paper presented at the 43rd Annual CCCC Meeting, Cincinnati, OH.
Assessment.

3351. Wintergest, A. C. (1991, March). *Holistic scoring: An assessment measure for ESL writing proficiency.* Paper presented at the 25th Annual TESOL Convention, New York, NY.
A workshop shows how to adapt the TWE scoring guidelines to ESL programs.
Assessment/Holistic.

3352. Witbeck, M. C. (1976). Peer correction procedures for intermediate and advanced ESL composition lessons. *TESOL Quarterly*, 10, 321-326.
Describes four specific procedures for correcting student compositions and points out that peer correction will provide students with editing and revision skills, improve student-student and teacher-student oral communication, and help students understand errors as a necessary outcome of learning.
Error Treatment.

3353. Withrow, J. (1987). *Effective writing: Writing skills for intermediate students of American English.* NY: Cambridge University Press.
A writing practice book designed to help students develop their writing skills through problem solving activities. Tasks such as organizing ideas, selecting and ordering information, using reporting words, attitude words, and linking words and phrases, writing beginning and ending paragraphs, and punctuating sentences enables students to become aware of what a well-written text is. Each unit focuses on a different type of writing.
Intermediate/Textbook.

3354. Withrow, J., Brookes, G., & Cummings, M. C. (1987). Teachers talk about reading and writing connections. In G. Brookes, & J. Gantzer (Eds.), *Improving the odds: Helping*

ESL students succeed. Selected papers from the 1987 CUNY ESL Council Conference, New York, NY (pp. 9-13). NY: CUNY Resource Center. [ERIC ED 328 068].

    Gives responses from a larger sample of interviews of five teachers who discuss reading and writing.

    Reading-Writing Relations/University.

3355. Withrow, J., Brookes, G., & Cummings, M. C. (1990). *Changes: Readings for ESL writers*. NY: St. Martin's Press.

    An interactive reading/writing text for ESL students which focuses on the process approach. Designed to help students connect their thoughts and feelings with those expressed in the text and to then express themselves in writing.

    Reader/Textbook.

3356. Witt, B. (1991). Publishing student work to achieve multiple benefits. *TESOL Journal, 1*(1), 31,34.

    Offers suggestions about how to solicit, select and distribute publishable student work, based on experiences at the Chinle Schools -- a public school district in the center of the Navajo nation in Arizona.

    Student Publications/Collaboration/Amer-Indian.

3357. Wohl, M. (1985). *Techniques for writing: Composition*. (Second Ed.). Boston: Heinle & Heinle.

    Text emphasises styles and techniques of formal and informal writing, covering material through the term paper.

    University/Advanced/Textbook.

3358. Wolfram, W. (1979). *Variability in the English of two Indian communities and its effects on reading and writing*. Arlington, VA: CAL.

    Study of different age levels in two Pueblo Indian speech communities did not find consistent correlations between their non-standard English dialect and reading or writing errors.

    Amer-Indian/Errors.

3359. Wong, L. A., & Thomas, J. (1993). Nativization and the making of meaning. In M. N. Brock, & L. W. Walters (Eds.), *Teaching composition around the Pacific Rim: Politics and pedagogy* (pp. 15-27). Clevedon, ENG: Multilingual Matters.

    Claims that nativized lexical items in the writing of students in India and Singapore demonstrate creativity and attempts at conveying unique cultural experiences. To avoid stifling creativity by imposing western rhetorical patterns, authors suggest using the process approach to the teaching of writing to encourage students to use language creatively while striving for international norms.

    Asian/Lexis.

3360. Wong, R., Glendinning, E., & Mantell, H. (1987a). *Becoming a writer: Developing academic writing skills*. Reading, MA: Addison Wesley/Longman.

    Focuses on selecting, organizing, and expressing informtion accurately and effectively.

    Beginners/Textbook.

3361. Wong, R., Glendinning, E., & Mantell, H. (1987b). *Ready to write: A first composition textbook*. NY: Addison Wesley/Longman.

Textbook for beginners offers opportunities for sentence practice.
Beginners/Textbook.

3362. Wong, R., & Lucas, T. F. (1980, March). *Beyond advanced ESL composition: Writing the term paper*. Paper presented at the 14th Annual TESOL Convention, San Francisco, CA.

Describes a transitional writing course for students entering university.
Research Writing.

3363. Wong, R. Y. L. (1993). Strategies for the construction of meaning: Chinese students in Singapore writing in English and Chinese. *Dissertation Abstracts International, 53*(12), 4236A.

Chinese students from four secondary schools in Singapore report in response to questionnaires using similar strategies in L1 and L2 writing. They indicate greater difficulty with Chinese than English writing, reflecting greater ability in English. Think-aloud protocols (N=43) indicate both effective and ineffective writers use meaning-constructing strategies but differ in the quality of their use.
Singapore/Chinese/Strategies.

3364. Wong, S. l. C. (1988). What we do and don't know about Chinese learners of English: A critical review of selected research. *RELC Journal, 19*(1), 1-20.

Deals, in part, with the hypothesis that Chinese writers have a written discourse accent even when sentences are free of surface errors.
Chinese/Review/Contrastive Rhetoric.

3365. Wong, S. L. C. (1984, March). *Applying error analysis to materials development for advanced ESL writers*. Paper presented at the 18th Annual TESOL Convention, Houston, TX.

Suggests an approach, based on work with Asian immigrants and psycholinguistic principles, that supplements communicative writing tasks with the learner's cognitive role in rule formation.
Error Analysis/Advanced.

3366. Wong, S. D. (1992). Contrastive rhetoric: An exploration of proverbial references in Chinese student L1 and L2 writing. *Journal of Intensive English Studies, 6*, 71-90.

Supports Kaplan's hypothesis that language-specific culture variation occurs in the use of chengyu (i.e., "set phrases") by mature L2 learners who are fully literate in their L1.
Contrastive Rhetoric/Chinese.

3367. Wong, Y. K. (1993). Instruction in argumentative writing in Hong Kong secondary schools: A contrastive study of Chinese-English rhetoric. *Dissertation Abstracts International, 53*(10), 3515A.

Examines linguistic differences in "good" argumentative texts in English and Chinese. Argumentative texts in these languages differ in their use of rhetorical questions, references, and negatives. The layout of background information (brief in English; elaborate in Chinese) is a major difference between rhetorics.
Chinese/Argumentation/Contrastive Rhetoric.

3368. Wongkhan, S. (1991). The influence of ESL students' cultural schemata on the quality of their writing. *Dissertation Abstracts International, 52*(5), 1700A.

Compositions on native and foreign culture-specific stimuli by Thai and Japanese ESL students were examined for the quality and the quantity (word and proposition length) of their writing. Both groups performed significantly better writing (measured by the Composition Profile) about their native cultures, but the influence of cultural schemata on quantity of writing only existed for the most able Japanese students. Unexpectedly, Thai students wrote more propositions although of lower quality about the foreign culture stimuli.

Thai/Japanese/Culture/Schema.

3369. Wood, A. S. (1982). An examination of the rhetorical structures of authentic chemistry texts. *Applied Linguistics*, *3*, 121-143.

Describes the way preparatory and experimental articles in chemistry have typical linguistic rhetorical structures.

ESP/Rhetoric.

3370. Woods, D. (1989). Error correction and the improvement of language form. *TESL Canada Journal*, *6*(2), 60-73.

Discusses the complexities inherent in composition correction and some alternatives.

Responding.

3371. Woods, D. (1984). A process orientation in ESL writing. *Carleton Papers in Applied Language Studies*, *1*, 101-132. [ED 264 724].

Discusses the process-based approach to teaching the ESL composition course. Sees the process approach to writing as emphasizing non-linear, complex writing process based on brainstorming, drafting-feedback-revision cycle, reader awareness, monitoring, and problem-solving. The relationship between reading and writing is also emphasized.

Process Instruction.

3372. Woodward, M. R. (1981). A tutorial component in the ESL writing course. *English Language Teaching Journal*, *35*(2), 158-161.

Gives suggestions for applying a program of individual meetings to discussions with students.

Conferencing/Tutoring.

3373. Woodward, S. W. (1993). Easing into summary writing. *TESOL Journal*, *3*(2), 34.

Offers several suggestions for preparing students to be more effective at writing summaries without plagiarizing.

Summary Writing/Plagiarism.

3374. Wormuth, D. R., Jacobs, H. L., Hughey, J. B., & Hartfiel, V. F. (1979, March). *Evaluating and improving the wriitng proficiency of ESL students*. Paper presented at the 13th Annual TESOL Convention, Boston.

Workshop presents a holistic-analytic scheme for evaluating ESL compositions.

Assessment.

3375. Wrase, J. (1984). Connecting ideas in ESL writing. *TESOL Newsletter (Supplement No. 1: Writing and Composition)*, *18*(1), 6-8.

Describes practices for teaching the combining of sentences to advanced ESL students in a course for basic writers.

Sentence Combining/Advanced.

3376. Wright, J. T. (1971). Writing contextualized drills. *TEFL, 5*(2), 4-5.
> Argues that context-based drills, such as students building stories that demonstrate grammar problems, are better than substitution drill for practicing syntax for communication.
> Syntactic Development.

3377. Wu, T. Y. (1986). A practical ten-minute writing process. *English Teaching Forum, 24*(3), 28-29.
> Creates a writing activity for middle school students, based on Lozanov's Suggestopedia.
> Middle School.

3378. Wu, Y. (1993). First and second language writing relationship: Chinese and English. *Dissertation Abstracts International, 53*(12), 4303-4A.
> The attitudes held by Chinese ESL college student toward writing tasks in both Chinese and English were found to be significantly related to the scores received on writing samples. An analysis of those samples suggests several linguistic gaps in interlingual transfer, such as passive voice, and modifiers.
> L1-L2 Comparison/Chinese/Affect.

3379. Wyatt-Brown, A. M. (1993, April). *Psychoanalytic theory, whole language, and ESL writing*. Paper presented at the 27th Annual TESOL Convention, Atlanta, GA.
> Outlines ways to apply British object-relations theory to the writing classroom.
> Psychology.

3380. Wyatt-Brown, A. M. (1990). *Life after graduate school: Skill development for international scholarship* . Washington, DC: ERIC/FLL. [ERIC ED 319 241].
> Describes a course for ESL students seeking to publish and present papers in ELT.
> Research Writing/Technical Writing.

3381. Wyatt-Brown, A. M. (1988, March). *Mini-thesis writing course for international graduate students*. Paper presented at the 22nd Annual TESOL Convention, Chicago, IL.
> Describes a course on thesis writing.
> Graduate Students/Research Writing/ESP.

X

3382. Xu, G. Q. (1988). Inventing through discussing. *TESOL Newsletter, 22*(1), 19-21.
> Sugggests a technique in which each student makes a two-three minute presentation in a small group about a topic generated through other prewriting means. Group members can question, suggest, and comment in a collaborative effort at invention.
> Invention/Collaboration.

3383. Xu, G. Q. (1990). An ex post facto study of differences in the structure of standard expository paragraphs between written compositions by native and non-native speakers of English at the college level. *Dissertation Abstracts International, 51*(6), 1942A.
> Compares equal number of native and non-native writers in terms of their ability to recognize multi-level paragraphs and to write such paragraphs. Finds no significant

difference between compositions of college admitted students in terms of levels of generality (Christensen, 1965) or paragraph patterns (Coe, 1988) due to language background or educational level. But, the ability to recognize paragraph breaks correlates slightly with ability to develop multi-level paragraphs
Paragraph/Text Analysis/NS-NNS Comparisons.

3384. Xu, G. Q. (1989a). *ESL/EFL composition: A selected annotated bibliography* . Bloomington, IN: ERIC/RCS. [ERIC/RCS 309 645].
Gives an 80-item annotated bibliography, citing sources in a five-year period between 1983 and 1988.
Bibliography.

3385. Xu, G. Q. (1989b). *Helping ESL students improve un-English sentences in one-to-one conferencing* . Washington, DC: ERIC/FLL. [ERIC ED 304 003].
Suggests conferencing is effective in analyzing causes of writing errors.
Conferencing/Style/Error.

3386. Xu, G. Q. (1989c). *Instruction of EFL composition in China* . Washington, DC: ERIC/FLL. [ERIC ED 304 019].
Reports that at colleges and universities in China there is a predominant emphasis on form and a general devaluation of writing instruction.
Instruction/Curriculum/Chinese.

Y

3387. Yamashita, S. O. (1986). *A Japanese boy's acquisition of English grammatical morphemes in writing*. Unpublished master's thesis, University of Houston, Houston, TX.
The acquistition of grammatical morphemes is examined in the writing in English by a Japanese-speaking boy and compared with Krashen's (1977) 'Natural Order Hypothesis' and Hakuta's (1979) longitudinal case study of speech. Findings show some correlations with theories but also that morpheme use is often dependent on learner's L1.
Japanese/Speaking-Writing Relations.

3388. Yan, Z. (1990). Academic writing and Chinese ESP learners: Influence of previous English learning experience. In J. Wu, J. Gebhard, S. Wang, & M. Zhang (Eds.), *Proceedings of the Symposium on Intensive English Training in China* (pp. 266-275). Beijing, China: Beijing Education Press.
Finds that the vast majority of Chinese post-graduates ESP learners who had studied English since middle school had no formal training writing in English and instruction that was received restricted their beliefs about writing and its evaluation.
ESP/Chinese/Graduate Students.

3389. Yao, L. C. (1991). Writing in English for academic purposes: Case studies of four Taiwanese graduate students. *Dissertation Abstracts International, 52*(1), 101A.
A naturalistic study of four Taiwanese students entering a graduate program where they were writing in English to fulfill course requirements for the first time. Their reading for writing is dependent on their language proficiency as well as on the specific task at hand. Protocols revealed extensive dependence on planning in the first language,

translation, and inefficient processing. Plagiarism, a common practice, is attributed to socio-cultural backgound.
   Academic Writing/Chinese.

3390. Yap, A. (1978). '"The Singapore Writer and the English language" -- A comment. *RELC Journal*, 9(1), 87-88.
   Suggests use of Singapore English by Singapore writers is appropriate in resposne to suggestion by Crewe that standard English should be used.
   Standards/Singapore.

3391. Yau, M. S. S. (1991). The role of language factors in second language writing. W. M. Malave, & G. Duquette (Eds.), *Language, culture & cognition* (pp. 266-283). Clevedon, UK: Multilingual Matters.
   Does limited linguisitic proficiency of ESL writers in the second language have a direct effect on the content of L2 writing? A comparison of the cognitive and linguistic complexity of twenty ESL grade 9 (Hong Kong), twenty LI grade 9 (Canada), and twenty ESL grade 13 (Hong Kong) students, found that on cognitive measures the ESL grade 9 students were lowest and ESL grade 13 students the highest. On syntactic measures grade 9 ESLers were substantially lower and grade 13 ESLers not very different than L1 9th graders. A follow-up study attempted to control for school system difference and rhetorical transfer (from Chinese L1), finding essays written in Chinese were significantly higher in cognitive complexity. Results suggest that language ability does affect cognitive processing.
   Syntactic Structures/NS-NNS Comparisons/Chinese.

3392. Yau, M. S. S. (1989, March). *Quantitative comparison of L1 and L2 writing processes*. Paper presented at the 23rd Annual TESOL Convention, San Antonio, TX.
   Reports results of a study of the pause patterns and planning activities of L1 and L2 students, suggesting that lack of fluency in L2 constrains their writing processes.
   Planning/Fluency.

3393. Yau, M. S. S. (1988, March). *Improving ESL writing performance: An information processing perspective*. Paper presented at the 22nd Annual TESOL Convention, Chicago, IL.
   Offers two techniques, oral pre-writing and syntactic bridging, designed to overcome L2 writers limited proficiency.
   Task.

3394. Yau, M. S. S. (1983). *Syntactic development in the writing of ESL students*. Unpublished master's thesis, University of British Columbia, Vancouver, BC. [ERIC ED 234 618].
   Investigates the development of English language syntactic maturity among Chinese secondary school ESL students. Narrative and expository compositions written by sixty students at three grade levels were analyzed for increases in T-unit length, clause length, number of clauses per T-unit, and the use of nominals, adverbials, and coordinations within T-units. T-unit length was found to increase with grade level as well as from expository to narrative writing. Similarly, use of nominals and adverbials increased with grade level, with greater increases in the expository than in the narrative compositions. There was not a significant increase in use of coordinate structures between grade levels, indicating that this transformation is acquired early. The syntactic

development of the students showed a notable resemblance to that of native English speaking students, indicating the employment of common language learning strategies.

Chinese/Secondary School/Language Development.

3395. Yau, M. S. S., & Belanger, J. (1985). Syntactic development in the writing of EFL students. *English Quarterly*, *18*(2), 107-118.

Examines the syntactic complexity and grammatical transformations used by students of English as a foreign language. Suggests that they use and expand syntactic structures in a manner similar to native speakers.

Syntactic Development/NS-NNS Comparisons.

3396. Yau, M. S. S., & Belanger, J. (1984). The influence of mode on the syntactic complexity of EFL students at three grade levels. *TESL Canada Journal*, *2*(1), 65-76.

Corroborates earlier research on relationships between syntactic complexity and grade level and extends findings in relation of mode and syntax. Older students are more able to adjust their syntax to the demands of rhetorical task.

Syntactic Development/Children.

3397. Yli-Jokipii, H. (1991). Running against time and technology: Problems in empirical research into written business communication. K. Sajavaara, D. Marsh, & T. Keto (Eds.), *Communication and discourse across cultures and languages* (pp. 59-72). Jyvaskyla, Finland: Publications of the Association of Applied Linguistics of Finland.

Business Writing.

3398. Yobst, J., & Alvarez, M. (1992, March). *Prewriting activities for rhetorical pattern curricula*. Paper presented at the 26th Annual TESOL Convention, Vancouver, BC.

Demonstrate prewriting activities for academic ESL composition classes, including group and pair experiential work that creates need for writing in modes of compare/contrast, narration, cause/effect, classification, and opinion.

Invention/Rhetoric.

3399. Yobst, J., & Koch, R. S. (1993, April). *Grammar for composition: Course design and implementation*. Paper presented at the 27th Annual TESOL Convention, Atlanta, GA.

Describes the process of designing a grammar in composition course and a pilot study of the results.

Grammar.

3400. Yoder, L. (1984). Process or product? An exercise in both. *TECFORS*, *7*(2), 1-2. [ERIC ED 267 647].

Describes a course assignment, creating a book for another group of students, which leads pre-freshman ESL writers through inventing, organizing, and composing to the final document.

Process Instruction.

3401. Yontz, R. A. (1988). Frame anaphora: The definite article in discourse. *Dissertation Abstracts International*, *49*(5), 1133.

Devises a theory of frame anaphora (derived from Hawkins, 1978) to analyze definite article usage by native and nonnative writers. An in-depth analysis of Korean NNSs' writing shows they make both syntactic and pragmatic errors attributable to the complexity of the English article system.

Discourse Analysis/NS-NNS Comparisons/Korean.

3402. Yorio, C. (1989). The other side of the looking glass. *Journal of Basic Writing*, 8(1), 32-45.

Makes a case for principled compromise in dealing with the anxiety of ESL students and of attending to their perceptions of the coursework. Suggests accomodating to perceived need for more reading, more grammar, and more writring practice while engaging in learner training about teacher strategies in writing.

Anxiety/Programs.

3403. Yorkey, R. (1977). Practical EFL techniques for teaching Arabic-speaking students. In J. E. Alatis, & R. Crymes (Eds.), *The Human Factors in ESL* (pp. 57-85). Washington, DC: TESOL.

Compares Arabic and English from the phonological, morphological, grammatical and rhetorical perspectives and suggests ways for teaching writing to Arabic-speaking EFL students.

Contrastive Rhetoric/Arabic.

3404. Yoshida, N. J. (1983). Process-oriented instruction in composition. *ORTESOL Journal*, 4, 18-36. [ERIC ED 240 836].

Claims that there are many similarities in ways native speakers from remedial courses and ESL students approach writing. In light of this, suggests that process-oriented writing instruction for native speakers has relevance for ESL students.

Process Instruction/NS-NNS Comparisons.

3405. Yoshihara, K. (1981). *Grammar for writers of English as a second language*. Unpublished master's thesis, California State University, Hayward, CA.

Grammar.

3406. Young, A. B. (1982). The effects of English as a second language instruction on the T-units of language minority students. *Dissertation Abstracts International*, 43(2), 358A.

Examines the effects of ESL instruction on the syntactic maturity of ESL students. Results show positive correlation.

Instruction/Syntactic Development.

3407. Young, T. A. (1990). The dialogue journal: Empowering ESL students. *Writing Notebook: Creative Word Processing in the Classroom*, 8(1), 16-17.

Presents guidelines for implementing the use of dialogue journals for reading and writing.

Computers/Dialogue Journals.

3408. Yu, Z. Z. (1981). New methodology in journal writing: A trial method for teaching technical writing to non-native speaker-scientists at GSELC. *English for Specific Purposes*, 52, 6-11.

The Graduate School English Language Center in Beijing has used journal writing since 1980 to encourage scientists to practice writing.

ESP/Journal Writing.

Z

3409. Zacker, J. (1987, April). *Writing workshop: An ESL writing program that gets results*. Paper presented at the 21st Annual TESOL Convention, Miami Beach, FL.

Reports a useful technique for meaning oriented, student-centered learning. Workshop.

3410. Zacker, J. (1988, March). *Writing workshop: Ideas for highly motivating ESL writing tasks*. Paper presented at the 22nd Annual TESOL Convention, Chicago, IL.

Describes process-oriented, student-centered writing tasks for all levels of proficiency.

Process Instruction/Workshop.

3411. Zamel, V. (1993). Questioning academic discourse. *College ESL, 3*(1), 28-39.

Criticizes teaching academic language divorced from context, separating the personal from the academic, and the hierarchical model in which other disciplines dictate what is to be done in ESL composition. Suggests teaching toward points of commonality among discourses, allowing students to discover their commitments in an intellectual struggle with authentic work.

Academic Writing/Ideology.

3412. Zamel, V. (1992, March). *In the writing classroom: The nature of academic discourse*. Paper presented at the 26th Annual TESOL Convention, Vancouver, BC.

Discusses the need to resist reductionist and exclusionist classroom practices and to orient students to reclaim authority for their knowledge by reshaping content, connecting their own perspectives, and locating meaning in their own observations and discoveries.

Classroom Activities/Discourse Communities.

3413. Zamel, V. (1991). Acquiring language, literacy, and academic discourse: Entering ever new conversations. *College ESL, 1*(1), 10-18.

Theory as well as what students have to say suggest ways for ESL teachers to promote language and literacy development.

Literacy/Academic Writing.

3414. Zamel, V. (1990). Through students' eyes: The experiences of three ESL writers. *Journal of Basic Writing, 9*(2), 83-98.

A case study of three ESL student writers suggests the central role of student beliefs, expectations, and perspectives on writing instruction and the classroom contexts in which writing takes place.

Process Research.

3415. Zamel, V. (1989a). The teaching of writing: Toward a pedagogy of questions. In J. D. Macero, B. J. Agor, & N. Tumposley (Eds.), *Realizing the dream: Selected conference proceedings of the annual meeting of the New York State TESOL* (pp. 39-62). NY: NY TESOL. [ERIC ED 314 954].

A case study of two ESL students observed and interviewed over two semesters in the same pre-composition course taught by different teachers indicates contrasting models of instruction. Finds that posing a few answerless riddles appears to empower both students and teachers in the process of discovery.

Process Research.

3416. Zamel, V. (1989b, March). *Writing: Through students' eyes*. Paper presented at the 40th Annual Convention CCCC, Seattle, WA.

See Zamel, 1988c.

University/Process Research.

3417. Zamel, V. (1988a). The author responds to Silva . . . [In The Forum]. *TESOL Quarterly*, 22, 520-524.

Maintains that effective writing goes beyond L1/L2 differences and that ethnographic research is significant.

Process Instruction.

3418. Zamel, V. (1988b). Thinking beyond imagination: Participating in the process of knowing. In L. Z. Smith (Ed.), *Audits of meaning: A festschrift in honor of Ann E. Berthoff* (pp. 182-194). Portsmouth, NH: Boynton/Cook.

Outlines why what Berthoff calls a "pedagogy of exhortation" in ESL instruction and materials is ineffective and suggests an alternative paradigm, a "pedagogy of knowing," that values learners' individuality, engages students in writing about what they know and what they need to learn, and promotes the development of literateness.

Approaches/NS-NNS Comparisons.

3419. Zamel, V. (1988c, March). *Writing: Through students' eyes*. Paper presented at the 22nd Annual TESOL Convention, Chicago, IL.

A case study of experiences of an ESL student in different university level writing classrooms.

University/Process Research.

3420. Zamel, V. (1987). Recent research on writing pedagogy. *TESOL Quarterly*, 21, 697-715.

Presents an overview of the latest research on the composing processes from process-oriented research of individual students to surveys which indicate that the mechanistic surface-level approach to writing is still being used by many ESL teachers. Offers possible theories explaining the reliance on traditional, reductionist models.

Review.

3421. Zamel, V. (1986, March). *Corresponding with researcher-writers*. Paper presented at the 37th Annual CCCC Meeting, New Orleans, LA.

Collaboration/Research.

3422. Zamel, V. (1985a, March). *First language acquisition as a model for second language acquisition and the development of writing*. Paper presented at the 36th Annual CCCC Meeting, Minneapolis, MN.

NS-NNS Comparisons/Theory.

3423. Zamel, V. (1985b, March). *Integrating conceptual and language development in the teaching of ESL and basic writers*. Paper presented at the 36th Annual CCCC Meeting, Minneapolis, MN.

NS-NNS Comparisons/Cognition/Language Development.

3424. Zamel, V. (1985c). Responding to student writing. *TESOL Quarterly*, 19, 79-102.

Studies ESL teachers and how they respond to student written compositions. The findings indicate that teacher comments are similar and are usually very concerned with surface level error regardless of the draft and such reponses give the students a very limited view of writing.

Process Instruction/Responding.

3425. Zamel, V. (1984). The author responds to Reid. *TESOL Quarterly*, 18, 154-158.

Responds to Reid's argument and claims that what ESL students need is not only

practice with rhetorical patterns of English. States the need to apply Krashen's concept of "making meaning" to the ESL writing class.
Process Instruction.

3426. Zamel, V. (1983a). The author responds to Barnes . . . [In The Forum]. *TESOL Quarterly, 17,* 138-139.
Reiterates position that process-centered writing pedagogy is likely to lead to improved products, which is questioned in Barnes' response.
Process Instruction.

3427. Zamel, V. (1983b). The composing processes of advanced ESL students: Six case studies. *TESOL Quarterly, 17,* 165-188.
Investigates the composing processes of six advanced ESL writers at the post-freshman level. This study interviews and observes how advanced writers discover and create meaning. The findings indicate that methods that are prescriptive, formulaic, and overly concerned with error do not mirror how students actually write which is much more recursive and individual.
Process Research.

3428. Zamel, V. (1983c, March). *ESL writing: Implications from research in composition.* Paper presented at the 17th Annual TESOL Convention, Toronto, Ontario.
NS-NNS Comparisons.

3429. Zamel, V. (1983d). In search of the key: Research and practice in composition. In J. Handscombe, R. A. Orem, & B. P. Taylor (Eds.), *On TESOL '83: The question of control* (pp. 195-207). Washington, DC: TESOL.
Reviews process research in L1 and L2 as the "key" and suggests what teachers can do to implement these findings in their classrooms.
Process Instruction.

3430. Zamel, V. (1983e). *In search of the key: Research and practice in composition.* Paper presented at the 17th Annual TESOL Convention, Toronto, Ontario. [ERIC ED 275 152].
Shows how experienced writers see writing as a recursive process while inexperienced writers are more distracted by form and the final product. Suggests ways teachers can help students view writing as a creative process.
Process Instruction/NS-NNS Comparisons.

3431. Zamel, V. (1983f). Teaching those missing links in writing. *ELT Journal, 37,* 22-29.
Suggests more effective strategies for presenting cohesive devices than their usual presentation by functions. Claims that the functional approach ignores the semantic and syntactical restrictions of cohesive devices.
Cohesion.

3432. Zamel, V. (1982a, May). *Research on composing: Implications for ESL.* Paper presented at the 16th Annual TESOL Convention, Honolulu, HI.
Presents findings that suggest ESL composing is similar to NES composing.
NS-NNS Comparisons.

3433. Zamel, V. (1982b). Writing: The process of discovering meaning. *TESOL Quarterly, 16,* 195-209.
Classic article defining what the process approach means in ESL. The author

states that ESL students need ideas to explore and write about. Composition instruction should recognize the importance of generating, formulating, and refining one's ideas. Revision should become the main component of ESL writing instruction, and ESL teachers should intervene throughout the process.

Process Instruction/Revision.

3434. Zamel, V. (1981, March). *Writing sentences: Solving grammatical puzzles.* Paper presented at the 15th Annual TESOL Convention, Detroit, MI.

Maintains that techniques such as generative rhetoric and sentence expanding allow students to experience the writing of sentences as a puzzle-solving activity.

Grammar/Classroom Activities.

3435. Zamel, V. (1980). Re-evaluating sentence-combining practice. *TESOL Quarterly, 14,* 81-90.

Although sentence-combining practice improves the quality of writing, some important questions about its effectiveness may be raised. Cites numerous studies showing that the activity should not be used as a total course of instruction in the ESL classroom.

Sentence Combining.

3436. Zamel, V. (1976). Teaching composition in the ESL classroom: What we can learn from research in the teaching of English. *TESOL Quarterly, 10,* 67-76.

ESL teachers of writing should become aware of current research in the teaching of composition for L1 learners since it is applicable to L2 students. Writing involves a great deal more than knowing grammar. ESL teachers must determine the qualities that make a good writer and ESL students should write for self-expression and creativity.

Process Instruction/NS-NNS Comparisons.

3437. Zamel, V., Brookes, G., Cohen, A. D., Cumming, A. H., Johns, A. M., Land, R. E., Raimes, A., Spack, R., Taylor, B. P., & White, R. V. (1990, March). *Entering the 90's: Key questions about writing.* Colloquium presented at the 24th Annual TESOL Convention, San Francisco, CA.

An interactive colloquium discusses issues about writing that face teachers, researchers, and theorists in the coming decade.

Instruction/Theory/Research.

3438. Zamel, V., Raimes, A., Brookes, G., Johns, A. M., Land, R. E., Spack, R., & Taylor, B. P. (1991, April). *In the writing classroom: An interactive colloquium.* Colloquium presented at the 25th Annual TESOL Convention, New York, NY.

A panel of experienced writing teachers discuss aspects of classroom teaching, such as, what subject matter, what kinds of writing, how to approach errors, how to recognize growth, and so forth.

Process Instruction.

3439. Zeider, M., & Bensoussan, M. (1988). College students' attitudes towards written versus oral tests of English as a foreign language. *Language Testing, 5,* 100-114.

Students preferred written over oral tests because they were more pleasant, valuable, as well as less anxiety provoking and more reflective of comprehension. No meaningful relationship to performance was observed.

Evaluation/Preferences.

3440. Zellermayer, M. (1988). An analysis of oral and literate texts: Two types of reader-writer relationships in Hebrew and English. In B. A. Rafoth, & D. L. Rubin (Eds.), *The social construction of written communication* (pp. 287-303). Norwood, NJ: Ablex.

    Discusses ways that texts written in two different rhetorical communties (Hebrew and English) demonstrate considerations of thoughtfulness on the part of their respective audiences.

    Culture/Hebrew/Reader-Writer Relations.

3441. Zellermayer, M. (1986, March). *Second language writing: Shifting along the oral/literate continuum.* Paper presented at the 20th Annual TESOL Convention, Anaheim, CA.

    Discusses stylistic difference between English and Hebrew in terms of oral/literate aspects of writing.

    Hebrew/Style/Speaking-Writing Relations.

3442. Zhang, F. X., & Chen, S. J. (1989). Techniques to teach writing. *English Teaching Forum, 27*(2), 34-36.

    Describes how authors teach writing at a teacher's college in China.

    Chinese.

3443. Zhang, S. (1985). *The differential effects of source of corrective feedback on ESL writing proficiency.* Unpublished master's thesis, University of Hawaii, Honolulu, HI.

    Feedback.

3444. Zhang, S. (1987). Cognitive complexity and written production in English as a second language. *Language Learning, 37*(4), 469-481.

    Analysis of sixty-three written responses to questions at high and low cognitive levels shows that an increase in cognitive complexity increases syntactic complexity in the writing of intermediate ESL learners. Comparison of the written responses across the two levels also shows a reduction of the dispersion of error incidence.

    Cohesion/Chinese.

3445. Zhang, S., & Jacobs, G. (1989, March). *The effectiveness of peer feedback in ESL writing class.* Paper presented at the 23rd Annual TESOL Convention, San Antonio, TX.

    Two studies find that peer feedback contains little miscorrection but is as effective as teacher feedback in stimulating successful revision.

    Peer Response/Responding.

3446. Zhang, X. (1990, November). *Language transfer in the writing of Spanish-speaking ESL learners: Toward a new concept.* Annual Conference of the Three Rivers TESOL Association, Indiana, PA. [ERIC ED 329 129].

    Documents anamolies in the writing of Spanish students, which are attributed to transfer.

    Hispanic/Transfer.

3447. Zhang, X. (1993). English collocations and their effect on the writing of native and non-native college freshmen. *Dissertation Abstracts International, 53*(5), 1423A.

    Explores collocation as a source of fluency in writing by comparing the relation of collocation to writing quality. NES freshman writers performed better than NNS freshman writers on a measure of collocation and good writers within each group did significantly better than poor writers.

    Collocation/NS-NNS Comparisons.

3448. Zhao, H. (1992, March). *Textual, contextual, and extra-contextual knowledge in ESL composition*. Paper presented at the 43rd Annual CCCC Meeting, Cincinnati, OH.

Argues that a redefinition of grammatical knowledge helps students become better writers.

Background Knowledge/Grammar.

3449. Zhao, H. (1990, March). *The teaching of writing in China: An overview*. Paper presented at the 41st Annual CCCC Meeting, Chicago, IL.

Chinese.

3450. Zhu, H. (1993). Cohesion and coherence in Chinese ESL writing. *Dissertation Abstracts International*, 53(7), 2233A.

Compares essays by the same subjects (N=4) written in Chinese and English on two expository topics. Finds that Chinese essays depend more on lexical ties whereas English essays used more connectors. Chinese referential ties were often lexical repetition; English rely on pronouns and deictics. Also shows that Chinese essays are writer-centered, implicit and general, while English essays are reader-oriented and explicit.

Cohesion/Chinese/Coherence.

3451. Zhu, W. (1992, March). *The effects of peer revision ESL writing*. Paper presented at the 26th Annual TESOL Convention, Vancouver, BC.

Reports the results of a study on peer revision in ESL college writing.

Revision/Peer Response/University.

3452. Zidan, A. T. (1982). The effects of immediate presentation versus delayed presentation of the written form in the teaching of English as a foreign language to beginning students in Egypt. *Dissertation Abstracts International*, 43(9), 2913A.

Compares the differential effects of immediate and delayed presentation of the written form in the teaching of English as a foreign language as well as the effects of sex and I.Q. on achievement in the language skills. Results show (1) immediate presentation better than delayed presentation; (2) high I.Q. participants more successful than low I.Q. participants; (3) males better in writing and speaking but no significant difference between reading, listening, and overall; and (4) significant three-factor interaction of treatment, sex and I.Q. on written and oral production.

Instruction/Arabic.

3453. Ziv, N. D. (1982). Using peer groups in the composition classroom. In C. Carter (Ed.), *Non-native and nonstandard dialect students* (pp. 51-52). Urbana, IL: NCTE.

Describes peer response groups which provide native feedback to ESL students.

University/Peer Response.

3454. Zizi, K. (1988). Contrastive discourse analysis of argumentative and informative newspaper prose in Arabic, French, and English: Suggestions for teaching/learning English as a foreign language for journalistic purposes (EJP) in Morocco. *Dissertation Abstracts International*, 49(1), 86A.

Examines the discourse structure within and across Arabic, French, and English. Analyzes headlines for implicit knowledge, speech acts, and style in samples of argumentative and informative newspaper prose. Reports a number of comparative findings. For example, finds that informative prose is more repetitious in English than in Arabic but that Arabic argumentative prose is more repetitive than English argumentation.

Contrastive Rhetoric/ESP/Arabic/French.

3455. Zuck, J. G. (1969, March). *Communicative urgency: Reading and writing.* Paper presented at the 3rd Annual TESOL Convention, Chicago, IL.

Reading-Writing Relations.

3456. Zuck, J. G., & Oster, S. (1980, March). *Explorations in written discourse.* Paper presented at the 14th Annual TESOL Convention, San Francisco, CA.

Colloquium is devoted to specific but diverse aspects of writing.

Discourse Analysis.

3457. Zuckermann, G. (1987). The impact of writing activities on the teaching of reading to students of English as a foreign language. *Dissertation Abstracts International, 48*(2), 326A.

Hebrew-speaking students at the intermediate ESL level were trained in five different types of sentence writing exercises. Results indicate that sentence writing improved reading comprehension. The impact on grasping ideas within and between sentences suggests that reading and writing share the same processes.

Reading-Writing Relations/Hebrew.

3458. Zughoul, M. R., & Kambal, M. O. (1983). Objective evaluation of EFL composition. *International Review of Applied Linguistics in Language Teaching, 21*, 87-103.

Presents an evaluation method for dividing compositions into three components and describes a scoring mechanism for each component.

Evaluation/Objective Measures.

3459. Zughoul, M. R., & Kambal, M. O. (1978, April). *Objective evaluation of EFL compositions.* Paper presented at the 12th Annual TESOL Convention, Mexico City, Mexico.

Discusses attempt to develop an analytic scale that values structure, content, and organization equally.

Assessment/Scoring.

3460. Zutell, J., & Allen, V. G. (1988). The English spelling strategies of Spanish-speaking bilingual children. *TESOL Quarterly, 22*, 333-339.

Investigates spelling strategies of second-, third- and fourth-grade Spanish-speaking children in a transitional bilingual program. Finds that some word categories are more or less difficult to spell for some Spanish learners.

Hispanic/Children/Spelling.

3461. Zutell, J., & Allen, V. G. (1983, April). *English spelling strategies of Hispanic bilingual children.* Paper presented at the Annual AERA Meeting, Montreal, Quebec.

Spelling/Hispanic/Children.

INDEX OF NAMES

(Lists authors for main entries as well editors and
authors for anthologized essays)

Abadir, L. A., 1
Abdan, Abdulrahman A., 2
Abdulaziz, Helen T., 3
Abigail, Tom, 2144
Abi-Near, Jeannette, 4
Aboderin, Adewuyi Oyeyemo, 5
Abraham, R. G., 6
Abramson, Shareen, 2864
Abu-Humos, Omar Mustafa, 7
Abunowara, A. M., 8
Abu-Salim, Issam, 109
Achiba, M., 9
Ackert, Patricia, 10
Acton, William, 11
Acuna, Dagmar S., 12
Adamowski, Eleanor, 3106
Adams, Carole, 13
Adams, J., 15
Adams, Judith-Anne, 14
Adams, K., 15
Adamson, H. D., 16
Adjakey, Komi M., 17
Aebersold, Jo Ann, 1794
Afghari, Akbar, 18
Aghbar, Ali A., 19, 20, 21, 22, 23, 24, 25, 26
Agor, Barbara J., 379, 2382, 3413
Aguas, E. F., 27
Ahn, Byung-Kyoo, 28
Ahrens, C. O., 29
Aitches, Marian, 30
Alam, M. Badsha, 31
Alam, Mohammed, 25
Alamansa, Anita, 32
Alarmy, Virginia, 197
Alatis, James E., 1690, 2553, 2689, 3090, 3295, 3401
Al-Batal, Karen, 569

Albertini, John, 33, 2175
Albrechtsen, Dorte, 34
Albright, Ron, 2823
Alderson, J. Charles, 1302
Al-Falahi, H. A., 35
Alhaidari, Ahmed Omer, 36
Ali, Hisham A., 37
Al-Jabr, Abdulfattah Mohammad, 38
Al-Jamhoor, Abdulrahman, 1796
Al-Jubouri, Adnan J. R., 39
Allaei, Sara Kurtz, 40, 41, 42, 43
Allahyari, Kathryn Hall, 44
Allbright, Ronald, 2829
Allen, Harold B., 1770
Allen, Kate, 2488
Allen, Virginia French, 45, 46, 47, 48, 49, 765, 902, 2518
Allen, Virgina G., 50, 3458, 3459
Allen, Walter P., 51
Allison, Desmond, 52, 53
Allwright, Joan, 54, 3244
Allwright, Richard, 55
Almeida, Jose Carlos Paes de, 56
Alptekin, Cem, 57, 58
Alptekin, Margaret, 58
Alt, Ruth R., 59
Altaha, Fayez M., 931
Alvarez, Michelle, 3396
Alvarez, R. S., 60
Alvarrez, L. P., 2783
Aly, Mohamed Sayed, 61
Amato, Katya, 62
Ambert, Alba A., 2196
Amiri, P. M., 63, 64
Ammon, Paul, 65
Anakasiri, Sontaya, 66
Anderson, Damon, 67, 2230

Anderson, Janice, 2691
Anderson, Karen Hunter, 68, 69
Anderson, Mary Lynn, 70
Anderson, Pamela L., 71, 72, 73
Anderson, Peggy J., 74
Anderson, Roger, 75
Angelis, Paul J., 76, 77, 2054
Angerilli, Mark, 735
Angioletti, P. J., 78
Anivan, Scrinee, 1309
Antia, Balou, 79
Appel, Gabriela, 80
Applebee, Arthur, 430
Arani, Mahmoud Tabatabai, 81
Arapoff, Nancy, 86, 87, 88, 89
Arapoff-Cramer, Nancy, 82, 83, 84, 85
Arcinegas, Matilde, 90
Ard, Josh, 91
Arena, Louis A., 92, 93, 94, 889
Arkin, Marian, 95
Arnaudet, Martin L., 96, 97
Arndt, Valerie, 98, 99, 100, 2529
Aron, Helen, 101, 102
Arthur, Bradford, 103, 104
Asaad, Salah B., 105
Ascher, Allen, 106
Asenavage, Karen, 107
Assaf, Masium, 1558
Atari, Omar Fayez, 108, 109
Athey, Stephanie, 481
Atkinson, Dwight, 110, 1359
Auerbach, Barbara, 111, 2990
Auerbach, Elsa Roberts, 112, 559, 3133
Aungprethep, Chitra, 113
Austin, Julia Stutts, 114, 115, 116
Autonomous Metropolitan University, 117
Ayari, Salah, 118
Azabdaftari, Behrooz, 119, 120

Babayan, Diana, 121
Bacha, Nola S., 122, 1312

Bacheller, Franklin I., 123, 124, 125
Badawi, Mary, 126
Badger, Richard, 127
Bahtia, A. T., 128
Bailey, Kathleen M., 394, 397, 1291, 1380
Bailey, Luke, 129
Bailey, Nathalie H., 130, 1007, 1008, 1009
Bajek, Michele M., 131
Ball, Wendy E., 132
Ballajthy, Ernest, 133
Ballard, Brigid, 134, 135
Ballif, M., 302
Ballwey, Linda Williams, 136
Baltra, A., 2138
Bamberg, Betty, 1299
Bander, Robert G., 137, 138
Bang, Hwa-Ja Park, 139
Bannai, Hideko, 140, 141
Barclay, Gwen, 919
Bardovi-Harlig, Kathleen, 142, 143, 144, 145
Barker, David, 146
Barkho, Leon Y., 147
Bar-Lev, Zev, 148
Barnes, Greg A., 149
Barnes, Linda Laube, 150, 151
Barnes, Mary Ellen, 152
Barnes-Felfeli, P., 3344
Barnwell, D., 153
Barrett, Mary Ellen, 96, 97, 154, 155
Barrutia, D., 1573
Bartelo, Dennise M., 156, 157, 158
Bartelt, H. Guillermo, 159, 160, 161, 162, 163, 559
Barton, Ellen L., 164
Basena, David M., 2691
Basham, Charlotte S., 165, 166, 167, 168, 169, 170, 171, 172, 1520, 3301
Basil, A. Ali, 842

Baskoff, Florence S., 173, 174, 175, 176
Bassett, Lisa, 177, 178
Bataineh, Ruba Fahmi, 179
Batchelor, Karen, 180
Bates, Linda N., 181, 182, 183, 184, 185
Batterman, Henry, 1225
Bauder, Thomas, 186
Bauer, Evelyn, 891
Bauer, W. J., 187
Baumhover, Mary Jo, 188
Baxter, Milton, 2395
Bayley, Robert J., 189
Bean, Martha, 190
Bear, Jean Munro, 191, 192
Beazley, Malcolm R., 193
Bebout, L. J., 194
Becher-Costa, Silvia, 797
Beck, Robert D., 195
Beene, Lynn, 196
Begay, Valavia, 197
Behrens, Christel, 2654
Behrens, L., 198
Beker, Christopher, 199
Belanger, Joe, 3393, 3394
Belanger, Monique, 460
Belanoff, Pat, 629
Belcher, C., 200
Belcher, Diane D., 201, 202, 203, 204, 205, 206, 207, 208, 209, 210, 211, 212, 650, 1571, 1677, 1944
Belcher, Lynne Renee, 213, 214, 719
Bell, James H., 215, 216
Beller, Sheryl V., 217
Belnar, Judith, 218
Benander, Ruth, 219
Benesch, Sarah, 220, 221, 222, 223, 224, 225, 226, 227, 228, 229, 230, 380, 908, 1227, 1406, 2733, 2988
Benitez, Ricardo, 231
Benson, Beverly A., 232, 233, 438, 439, 440, 441
Bensoussan, Marsha, 3437
Benton, Kay Hutchison, 234
Benz, Cheryl, 235, 2269
Bercovitz, Laura, 3157
Berens, Gayle L., 236, 237
Berezovsky, Helen, 967
Berg, Catherine, 238, 239
Berger, Dorothy M., 240
Berk, Virginia B., 241, 242, 2289
Berkman, Myron, 243
Berkovitch, Merilu Mills, 244
Berkowitz, Diana, 245, 3268
Berman, M., 246
Berman, Robert, 247
Bermudez, Andrea B., 248, 249, 250, 251, 2364
Berns, Margie, 252, 253, 254
Bernstein, Janice, 3318
Berry, Terryn, 255
BESL Center, 256
Best, Linda, 257, 258, 259
Betancourt, Francisco, 260
Beyers, Joan, 261, 2188
Bhatia, A. T., 262
Bhatia, V. K., 263
Biaggi, Leslie, 264
Biber, Douglas, 1183
Bickner, Robert, 265
Bills, Betty F., 266
Birch, Barbara, 267
Birdsong, David, 268
Bitterman, Ellen, 269
Bjork, Lennart, 270
Blair, Linda, 271
Blair, Thomas E., 272
Blake, R. W., 273
Blanchard, Karen, 274
Blanton, Linda Lonon, 275, 276, 277, 278, 279, 280, 281, 282, 283, 284, 285, 286, 287, 288, 2765
Blasky, Andrew, 289
Blass, Laurie J., 290, 291, 292, 293, 1716, 1717

Blatchford, Charles, 1834
Blau, Eileen K., 294, 443
Bley-Vroman, Robert, 2877
Bliss, Bill, 2227
Bloch, Joel, 295, 296, 297, 298, 299, 300, 301, 302, 303, 304
Bloor, Meriel, 305
Bloor, Thomas, 99
Blot, David, 306, 307, 780
Blot, Richard, 650
Blue, George M., 308
Blumenthal, Anna, 309
Blumhardt, Doug, 2691
Blum-Kulka, Shoshana, 660
Boardman, Cynthia A., 310, 1087
Bodnar, Becky, 311
Bodner, Janet, 937
Boehm, Paul W., 312
Bofman, Theodora, 144, 145
Bolman, David Laurence, 313
Bonheim, H., 314
Bonner, Margaret, 315
Borkin, Ann, 316, 317
Borodkin, Thelma, 318
Bosher, Susan, 319, 320, 321, 1353
Boshoff, Phillip P., 823, 825, 2547
Boswood, Tim, 322
Bott, Donald E., 323
Bottoms, Laurie, 243
Bouchard, Donald L., 323, 1045, 2336, 2400, 2834, 2875, 2894, 3046, 3108
Boucher, Holly W., 324
Bouton, L., 1343
Bowen, J. Donald, 325
Bowie, David Greenfield, 326
Boyd, John A., 327
Boyd, John R., 328, 996, 2161
Boyd, Mary Ann, 328, 996
Boyd, Z., 329
Boyle, Owen F., 2416
Bracey, Maryruth, 330, 331, 332
Bradford, P. P., 333
Bradin, Claire, 217

Brady, Suzanne, 1535
Braine, George, 210, 211, 212, 334, 335, 336, 338, 339, 340, 341, 719, 1571
Brainer, Charles, 337
Braley, C. K., 2424
Branstine, Z., 2129
Brantley, John D., 1415
Brassard, Mary Lee, 2379
Bratt, Theresa D., 131
Braun, Shirley, 342
Breland, Hunter M., 343
Brenner, Catherine A., 344
Breyer, Jeffrey, 2216
Brickman, Bette, 345, 346
Bridgeman, Brent, 347, 348, 473, 474
Briére, Eugene J., 349, 350
Briggs, Sarah, 351
Brigham, Andrew, 525
Bright, William, 1679
Brinton, Donna M., 352, 353, 354, 2988, 2989
British Council, 355
Britton, Robin T., 356
Broadhead, Glenn L., 2180
Brock, Mark N., 98, 357, 358, 359, 360, 361, 362, 363, 364, 591, 2148, 2211, 2412, 2414, 3124, 3256, 3302, 3357
Brodkey, Dean G., 365, 366, 367, 2346
Bromage, Mary C., 368
Brookes, Arthur, 369, 370
Brookes, Gay, 371, 372, 373, 374, 375, 376, 377, 378, 978, 1106, 2084, 2587, 2588, 2589, 2985, 3132, 3133, 3352, 3353, 3435, 3436
Brooks, Elaine Barbara, 379, 380, 381, 382, 383
Brooks, Phyllis, 384
Broom, Mary Jo, 385
Brosnahan, Irene, 386, 387, 2346

Broukal, Milada, 388, 2765
Brown, Cheryl, 3262
Brown, D. F., 1460
Brown, H. Douglas, 389, 390
Brown, James Dean, 391, 392, 393, 394
Brown, Judith, 395
Brown, L. B., 1460
Brown, Linh Chan, 396
Brown, Martha S., 2388
Brown, R., 2067
Brown, Y. D., 397
Browne, Sammy R., 398
Bruder, Mary Newton, 399, 400
Bruno, Sam J., 641
Bruton, Anthony Stewart, 401, 402
Brutten, Sheila R., 2427, 2428, 2429
Bryant, W. H., 403
Buchanan, H. C., 329
Buchanan, Louis M., 404, 405, 406, 407
Buckingham, Thomas, 408, 409, 410, 411, 1166, 2400
Buell, Frederick, 412
Buker, Suzanne, 413, 874, 3292, 3293, 3294
Buley-Meissner, Mary Louise Catherine, 414
Bull, Wendy E., 415
Bullock, Chris, 2056
Bulos, Alice, 416
Buras, Khalifa Mehdi, 417
Burger, Sandra, 418
Burkhalter, Nancy, 419, 420
Burmeister, H., 419
Burnaby, Barbara, 216, 1764
Burns, Anne, 421, 422
Burns, Jane Unaiki, 2661
Burns, William T., 423
Burruel, Jose M., 424
Burt, Marina K., 76, 93, 2857
Burtoff, Michele J., 425, 426
Butler, Anita Jana, 429
Butler, Jeffrey, 427

Butler, Jonathan, 428
Butler, Sydney, 429
Butler-Nalin, K., 430
Butler-Pascoe, Mary Ellen, 431
Byrd, Donald R. H., 432, 433, 434, 435, 1102
Byrd, Patricia, 436, 437, 438, 439, 440, 441, 442, 443, 444, 463
Byrne, Donn, 445
Byrne, R., 446

Cabello, Beverly, 447
Cadet, Nancy Erber, 448, 1106
Cadiz, Yvonne, 449
Caesar, Susan, 1191
Cai, Guanjun, 450
Caldeira, Sandra M. A., 1025
Caldwell, Victoria, 2999
Calkins, Lucy McCormick, 451, 452
Call, Mary Emily, 2392
Camp, Roberta, 343, 474, 475
Campbell, Cherry C., 453, 454, 455, 456, 1643
Campbell, Deborah, 1311, 1560
Campbell, Donald, 457
Campbell, Russell, 1770
Canagarajah, A. Suresh, 458
Canale, Michael, 459, 460, 660
Candlin, Christopher N., 2019
Cannilao, Paz N.D.A., 461
Cannon, Beverly, 462
Canseco, Grace, 442, 463
Capobianco, Patricia, 1112
Card, Patricia, 464
Cardelle, Maria, 465
Cargill, Carol, 449, 466, 3071, 3085
Carlisle, Robert Stephen, 467, 468, 469, 470
Carlson, Sybil B., 347, 348, 471, 472, 473, 474, 475, 662, 1302
Carney, Helen Louise, 476

Carpenter, Cristin, 477, 478
Carr, Donna H., 479
Carr, Marion, 480
Carr, Richard, 481
Carrasquillo, Angel, 3234
Carrell, Patricia L., 482, 483, 484, 485, 486, 487, 488, 489, 490, 491, 492, 493, 494, 495, 496, 500, 501, 650, 651, 652, 735, 824, 3188
Carrier, Michael, 261, 2188
Carroll, Jeffrey, 497
Carroll, Sherrie, 2856
Carson, Joan E., 211, 279, 498, 499, 500, 501, 824
Carson, Joan G., 170, 220, 277, 502, 503, 504, 505, 506, 507, 508, 509, 510, 624, 652, 822, 957, 1007, 1100, 1572, 1813, 1929, 2275, 2610, 2807, 3004
Carter, Candy, 273, 416, 749, 2953, 3196, 3236, 3238, 3451
Carter, M. E., 511
Carter, Ronnie D., 512
Carthy, V., 513
Carver, Tina, 514
Casey, Barbara Irving, 515
Castellano, M., 516
Castille, Philip, 517
Cato, Julie, 1717
Cavalcanti, Matilda C., 620, 621
Cave, George, 518
Cech, Eve, 519
Celce-Murcia, Marianne, 520, 521, 522, 1077, 1582, 1815, 2328
Cerniglia, Constance, 523, 653
Cervantes, Raul, 1879
Chalaysap, A., 524
Chambers, Fred, 525
Chamot, Anna Uhl, 526, 527

Chan, Michelle M., 528, 529, 530, 531, 1850
Chance, L. L., 532
Chandrasegeran, Antonio, 533
Chang, S. J., 534
Chang, Winona Lee, 535
Chapin, Ruth, 536
Chapman, J. B., 537
Chappell, Virginia Ann, 538, 539, 540
Chappelle, Carol, 3001
Chargvis, Gwendolyn V., 541
Charles, Arthur H., 542
Charles, Maggie, 543
Charoenrath, P., 544
Charry, Myrna B., 545,
Chaudron, Craig, 546, 547, 548, 549, 650
Chelala, Silvia Ines, 550
Chen, Dar Wu, 551
Chen, Eileen Shu Hui, 552
Chen, Shih Jin, 3440
Chen, Sun I., 553
Chen, Tingguang, 3139
Chen, Yu F., 554
Chen, Yueh Miao, 555
Cheng, Peggy Geok Poh, 556
Chenoweth, Ann, 557, 953, 1781
Chen-yu, F., 558
Cheong, Peggy, 972
Chernick, Sarra D., 961
Cherry, Roger D., 1637
Chessin, L., 559
Cheung, Evelyn, 53
Cheung, K. K., 560
Chi, Marilyn Mei Ying, 561
Chiang, Yuet Sim Darrell, 562, 563
Chimombo, Moira, 564, 565
Ching, L. P., 566
Ching, Roberta J., 567
Chirinos, S. L., 568
Chisholm, Jane, 569, 1167
Chiste, Katherine Beaty, 570
Choi, Yeon Hee, 571, 572, 573, 574,

575
Christensen, J. Perry, 576
Christensen, Torkil, 577
Christopher, Virginia, 578, 735
CILT, 579
Clair, Elizabeth, 580
Clanchy, John, 135
Clark, B. L., 581
Clark, Carolyn, 457
Clark, Gregory, 582
Clark, J. A. R., 583
Clark, William G., 584
Clarke, Diana L., 585, 586
Clarke, Mark A., 539, 587, 588
Clarke, William G., 589
Clasen, Mary Pat, 590
Clayton, Thomas, 591
Cleary, Christopher, 592
Cleary, Linda Miller, 593, 594
Clifford, Marian, 595
Clifford, R., 1291
Clintron, Ralph Eliot, 596
Cloud, Nancy, 597
Clough, Martha, 598, 2258, 2259
Clouse, Barbara F., 599
Clymer, Diane, 2844, 2845, 2846
Clyne, Michael G., 600, 601, 602, 603, 604, 605
Cobb, Charles Miguel, 606
Coe, Richard M., 387, 607, 608
Coffey, Margaret P., 609
Cohen, Andrew D., 610, 611, 612, 613, 614, 615, 616, 617, 618, 619, 620, 621, 3121, 3435
Cohen, Deborah S., 390
Cohen, Leon J., 622
Colby, Jim, 623
Collignon, Fran Filipek, 624
Collins, Timothy G., 625
Colman, Lee (Rosalie M.), 626
Colton-Montalto, Bonita, 627
Concepcion, Blanca Esther, 628
Concepcion, Gladys, 1103
Condon, William, 629, 1299

Cone, Dennis, 630
Congrave, Cynthia, 3257
Conklin, Alicia, 631
Connor, Ulla M., 41, 42, 43, 107, 143, 484, 489, 490, 491, 523, 549, 632, 633, 634, 635, 636, 637, 638, 639, 640, 641, 642, 643, 644, 645, 646, 647, 648, 649, 650, 651, 652, 653, 654, 655, 656, 657, 658, 659, 660, 661, 662, 663, 664, 665, 666, 667, 668, 669, 670, 709, 920, 947, 948, 965, 1179, 1307, 1325, 1397, 1531, 1585, 1683, 1893, 1894, 1944, 2127, 2350, 2851, 3093, 3319
Connor-Linton, Jeff, 522, 671
Conrad, Susan M., 672, 1155, 1156, 2976
Constantinides, Janet C., 673, 674, 675, 676, 2646
Cook, Catherine, 1849
Cook, Janice, 677
Cook, Marjorie L., 678, 679, 680
Cooper, Rhonda, 681
Cooper, Thomas C., 682, 683
Corbett, John, 684
Corio, Ron, 685
Corno, Lyn, 465
Cortese, Giuseppina, 686
Costello, Jacqueline, 687, 688, 689
Couch, Pamela, 690
Coulibaly, Youssoupha, 691
Courter Berry, K., 1301
Courter, Karen S., 1300
Cowan, J. R., 1706
Cowart, Ray, 1752
Cox, Patricia, 692
Cramer, Nancy Arapoff, 693
Craven, Mary Louise, 2293
Crawford, Jeffrey, 694
Cray, Ellen, 752
Crerand, Mary E. Lavin, 695

Crew, Louie, 696
Crewe, William J., 697, 698, 699
Criper, C., 1335
Crismore, Avon, 700
Croft, Kenneth, 2967
Cromwell, Carole, 2812
Cronnell, Bruce, 701, 702, 703, 1488, 2506
Crookall, David, 704
Crookes, Graham, 705
Cross, J. C., 706
Crowe, Chris, 707
Crowell, Sheila C., 1660, 1661
Cruickshank, Donald, 708, 709, 710, 711, 712
Cruz, Jane, 713
Cruz, Mary Carmen E., 714
Crymes, Ruth, 84, 2903, 3401
Cukor-Avila, Patricia, 715, 1234
Culbertson, Patrick, 716
Culhane, T., 2424
Cullup, Michael, 717
Cumming, Alister H., 718, 719, 720, 721, 722, 723, 724, 725, 726, 727, 728, 729, 730, 731, 732, 733, 734, 735, 736, 737, 738, 739, 1945, 2189, 2190, 3209, 3435
Cummings, Martha C., 374, 375, 740, 741, 742, 3352, 3353
Cummings, Victor, 743, 744, 745, 746, 747, 3269
Cummins, Jim, 735, 748
Cummins, M. Z., 749
Cunha, Maria Isabel A., 797
Currie, Pat, 750, 751, 752
Curry, Dean, 753
Curtis, Wynn J., 1188

da Rocha Bastos, Lilia, 935
Dagenais, Diane, 754
Dahbi, Mohammed, 755
Dahnke, David, 756
Dailey, Beverly, 757, 3121

Dale, E., 1291
Dalgish, Gerard M., 758, 759
Dalle, Teresa, 760, 761, 762
Dally, P., 763
Damen, L., 764
d'Anglejan, A., 1706
Danielson, Dorothy W., 765
Danish, Barbara, 766
D'Annunzio, Anthony, 767
Dantas, Maria, 2665
Dantas-Whitney, Maria, 768, 1185
Das, Bikram K., 769, 2561
Date, Masaki, 770
Daubney-Davis, Ann E., 771, 772, 773, 774
Davidson, David M., 307, 775, 776, 777, 778, 779, 780
Davidson, Fred, 781, 782, 783, 1302, 1311, 1380
Davidson, Joseph O., 784, 785, 786
Davidson, Lori, 735
Davies, A., 1335
Davies, Eirlys E., 787, 788
Davies, Florence, 789
Davies, Norman F., 790
Davis, Betty J., 791
Davison, Chris, 1311
Day, Michael, 792
de Alvarado, Christine S., 793
de Andres, Robin, 794
De Jesus, Sicorro, 795, 796
De Masi, Mary, 2840
De Miller, Ines Kayon, 797
de Oliveira, Lucia Pacheco, 797
de Quincey, P., 136
Deakins, Alice H., 798, 799
Dean, Michael, 800
Dean, Terry, 801
Deane, Debra, 254
DeCarrico, Jeanette S., 2271
Dechert, Hans W., 1292, 1322
Decker, D. M., 802, 803
Deckert, Glenn D., 804, 805
Dedo, David R., 806, 807, 1456

Degenhart, R. Elaine, 808, 809, 1174, 3111
Dehghanpisheh, R. Elaine, 810, 811
Delaney, St. John, Sr., 812
Deligiorgis, Ionna, 813
DeMauro, G., 1305
Deming, Mary, 233
Denick, Maria, 443
Dennett, Joann Temple, 814, 815
Denzer, Debra, 233
DePourbaix, Renata, 816
Derrick-Mescua, M., 817
Desbonnet, Kenneth, 818, 1972
DeSilva, Robert, 819
Dessner, Linda Eckhardt, 820
Devenney, R., 821
Devine, Joanne, 822, 823, 824, 825, 2547
Deyoe, R. M., 826
Diaz, Diana M., 827, 828, 829, 830, 831, 832, 1408
Diaz, R., 3192
Diaz, S., 3192
DiCamilla, Fred, 833, 834
Dicker, Susan Jane, 835, 836, 837, 838
Dickson, Marcia
Dieckman, Elizabeth Ann, 839
Diffley, Frank, 1878
Dillon, Judy, 266
Dimond, Edith d'Olive, 840, 841
DiPietro, Robert J., 92
Dissayanake, Asoka S., 842
Divine, Beatice, 843
Dixon, D., 844
Dobra, Susan, 845
Dole, R., 846
Dolly, Martha Rowe, 847, 848, 849, 850
Dominquez, D., 2048
Donaldson, Anne S., 2899
Donaldson, John K., 851, 852, 853
Donley, Michael, 854, 855

Donnelly, Rory, 856
Donovan, Richard A., 473
Dooley, Mary S., 857
Doorn, Dan, 858
Dorrill, George T., 859
Dotson, Kim, 860
Douglas, Dan, 861, 1480, 3001
Douglas, Felicity, 862
Doushaq, Mufeeq H., 863
Dowd, Janice L., 2337
Dowling, Joe, 864
Downing, Bruce, 757, 3121
Downing, Pamela, 2600
Doxey, Carolyn, 865
Dreyer, Diana Yvonne, 866
Drobnic, Karl, 3077
Drunagly, Joan, 867
Druny, Helen, 868
Dubetz, Nancy, 3145
Dubin, Fraida, 869, 870, 871, 872
Dubois, Betty Lou, 873, 874
Dudley-Evans, Tony, 212, 875, 876, 877, 878, 879
Duffin, B., 880
Dulay, Heidi C., 76, 93, 2857
Dulmage, Juliana K., 881
Dunbar, Shirley, 882
Dungey, Joan M., 883
Dunkel, Patricia, 2468, 3188
Dunkelblau, Helene S., 884, 885
Dunlop, I., 886
Duquette, Georges, 3389
Duran, Richard P., 887, 1150
Durighello, Joy, 290
Dwyer, Margaret, 14
Dwyer, Robert, 322
Dwyer, S., 3122
Dyck, Patricia B., 888
Dyer, Patricia M., 889
Dykstra, Gerald, 890, 891, 892, 893
Dziombak, Constance E., 894

Earle-Carlin, Susan, 1498
Early, Margaret, 895

Easton, B. J., 896
Ebaru, Oru O., 897
Ebel, Carolyn, 898
Echeverria, Ellen W., 899
Edalat, Hassan, 900
Edelsky, Carole, 901, 902, 903, 904, 905, 906, 907, 908, 909, 910
Edge, Julian, 911, 912, 913
Edlund, John R., 914, 915
Edmondson, Marti, 916
Edmondson, Phillip, 916, 917
Edwards, Barbara Hall, 918
Egbert, Joy, 919
Ege-Zavala, Bernice, 1243
Eggington, William G., 920, 921, 1185, 2665
Eisenstein, Miriam R., 2824
Eison, Diane M., 922
Eisterhold, Joan C., 116, 492, 923, 924
Ekmeçi, F. Ozden, 925, 926
El Gamil Abdel Fattah, Ali, 927
El-Badri, Leila, 928
El-Daly, Hosney Mosafa, 929
Eleftherlou, Anna, 3297
El-Ezabi, Y. A., 930
El-Hibir, Babikir I., 931
El-Khatib, Ahmed Shafik Abdelwahab, 932, 933, 934
El-Komi, Mohamed, 1802
Elliot, Ligea G., 935
Elliott, M., 936
Elliott, Norbert, 937
Elsasser, Nan, 938, 1001, 1521
El-Sayed, A., 939
El-Shafie, Ahmed Salama, 940
El-Shushabi, Muhammad Attia Hasan, 941
Emel, L. J., 942
Engber, Cheryl A., 943
Engel, Dean, 1566
Engelbrecht, Guillermina, 944
Enger, Edward, 2994
Enginarlar, Husnu, 945

England, Lizabeth, 946
Enkvist, Nils E., 947, 948, 949, 950, 1988, 3321
Enright, D. Scott, 650, 1472
Epes, Mary, 951, 952
Era, Kathleen, 953, 1781
Erazmus, Edward T., 954
Erazo, Edward, 955
Erbaugh, Mary S., 956
Erwin, Bermarda, 2324
Eskey, David E., 824, 957, 958
Etheridge, John, 959
Etter, Alison, 2893
Evans, Linda S., 960
Evans, Mary, 961
Evans, Norman W., 962, 963, 964
Eveersen, L. S., 662
Evensen, Lars S., 34, 965, 966
Everson, Philip, 967
Evolva, Jill, 968
Ewen, E., 1143
Ewoldt, Carolyn, 969
Eyring, Janet, 970
Ezer, Hanna, 971

Fagan, Edward R., 972
Fagan, William T., 973
Faigan, Sybil Barbara, 974
Failer, Susan, 3063
Falk, B., 975
Fan, Lan Ying, 1978
Fan, Wen Juan, 976
Fang, Xuelan, 977
Fanselow, John F., 376, 978, 2583
Farghal, Mohammed, 979
Farmer, Mary, 654
Farnsworth, M. B., 980
Farrell, Alan, 981
Fathman, Ann K., 982, 983, 984, 985
Fayer, J., 986
Fein, D., 987
Fernández, Rodrigo Carmona, 2079
Ferris, Dana Rider, 988, 989, 990,

991
Ferris, M. Roger, 992
Ferris, Randall, 993, 994
Fieg, John Paul, 995, 996
Field, Yvette, 997
Fillerup, M., 2295
Findley, Dorothy Farris, 998
Fine, Jonathan, 460
Fink, Darlynn, 999
Finn, Perdita, 452
Finocchiaro, Mary, 1000
Fiore, Kyle, 1001
Fischer-Kohn, Elaine, 1002
Fitzgerald, Jill, 1003
Flahive, Douglas E., 130, 1004, 1005, 1006, 1007, 1008, 1009, 1010
Flanagan, Kristin, 2607
Flanigan, Beverly Obon, 1011
Flashner, V., 1643
Fleming, Sandra Monroe, 1991, 1992
Flood, James, 50
Flores, B., 1012
Florez Tighe, Viola, 1013, 1014
Flowerdew, John, 1015, 1016
Fluitt, Jan M., 1017
Foley, Dolores, 1018
Folman, Shoshana, 735, 1019, 1020, 1021, 1022, 1023
Folse, Keith S., 1024
Fontana, Niura M., 1025
Ford, Carol Kasser, 1026, 1148
Ford, Janet, 1027
Forester, Jeanne Marie, 1028
Forster, J. H., 1029, 1030
Fortes, Maria Beatriz, 797
Fotinis, Sandra Douglas, 514
Foulkes, John, 1302
Fox, C. Jay, 1031, 1032
Fox, Diane N., 2248, 3156
Fox, Helen, 1033
Fox, Janna, 1034
Fox, Len, 1035, 1036, 1037, 1038
Fox, Robert P., 2860

Foxall, Justine, 2104, 2105
Frager, A. M., 1039
Francis, Gladys Berro, 1486
Frank, Marcella, 1040, 1041, 1042, 1043, 1044, 1045, 1046
Franken, Margaret, 1047, 1048
Frankenberg-Garcia, A., 1049
Franklin, Elizabeth A., 1050, 1051
Franklin, Ellen, 1052
Franklin, Sharon, 1053
Fraser, C., 1054
Frawley, William E., 92, 1055
Freedman, Aviva, 1056, 1688, 2573, 3311
Freedman, Sarah Warshauer, 65
Freeman, Aviva, 1618, 1665
Freeman, C., 1039
Freeman, Colleen F., 1085
Freeman, David E., 1057, 1058, 1059
Freeman, Yvonne S., 1057, 1058, 1059
French, Charles R., 1060
Frenette, Normand, 460
Frestedt, M., 1061
Friederichs, J., 1062
Friedlander, Alexander C., 662, 1063, 1064, 1065, 1066, 1067, 1068, 1069, 1070, 1071, 1072, 1119, 2138
Friend, Jewell A., 1073, 1074
Fries, Peter H., 824
Frindethie, Martial K., 2691
Frodesen, Jan Marie, 1075, 1076, 1077, 1078, 1079, 1080, 1081, 1082, 1083, 2976, 2977
Frolich-Ward, Leonora, 1084
Fruger, Alan M., 1085
Frydenberg, Gro, 1086, 1087
Frye, Bruce T., 2008
Fryman, Jeleta, 2378
Fuentes, Jesus, 1088
Fulton, Mary, 1089
Furey, Patricia R., 399, 1090, 2392

Gabrielle, Susan Farr, 1091
Gadbow, Kate, 1092
Gadda, George, 1093, 1094, 1095
Gaer, Susan, 289
Gaies, Stephen J., 1096, 1097
Gajdusek, Linda, 1098, 1099, 1100
Galantai, F. L., 294
Galindo, Luis Rene, 1101
Gallingane, Gloria, 432, 433, 434, 435, 1102
Gallo, Rhodalyne Q., 1103
Galvan, Max, 1104, 1105
Gantzer, Jack, 374, 1106, 2985, 3352
Ganz, Dianne S., 1107
Garcia de Riley, L., 1108, 1109
Garcia Duran, Sara Solead, 1110
Garcia, E. A., 1012
Garcia, Ricardo L., 1111
Gargagliano, Arlen, 1112
Garkov, Julie George, 2856
Garretson, Kate, 1210
Gartz, Irene Tondorf, 1113
Gaskill, William H., 549, 1114, 1115, 1116, 2587
Gass, Susan M., 159, 169, 3031
Gates, Anna, 1270
Gates, Roberta Dixon, 1117
Gaylord, Wendy, 1167
Gebhard, Jerry, 3386
Geisler, Cheryl, 1118, 1119
Genesee, Fred, 1120
Gentry, Larry A., 1121
Genzel, Rhona B., 742, 1122, 1123
Gertzman, Alice, 1945
Getkham, Kunyarut Toy, 1124
Ghadessy, Mohsen, 1125, 1126
Ghaleb, Mary L., 1127
Ghani, Salwa Abdel, 1128
Ghazalah, Hasan, 1129
Giansanti, Susan P., 1130
Gibson, Deborah, 1131
Giesecke, William Bruce, 1132
Gilbert, J. W., 1133
Gilbert, Randi, 1134, 1135

Gilbert, Reta A., 1136
Gilboa, Carolyn C., 1137, 1138
Giles-Lee, Margaret, 1554
Gill, Jaswinder, 736
Gillette, Susan, 3121, 3122
Gilman, Charlotte, 1139, 1140
Gilman, Roberta, 1141
Ginn, Doris O., 1142
Gipps, C., 1143
Giroux, Nicki S., 1144
Glendinning, Eric, 3358, 3359
Gmuca, Jacqueline L., 817
Godsen, Hugh, 1145, 1146, 1147
Goffman, Richard, 3270, 3271
Goldberg, J. P., 1148
Goldberg, John R., 1476
Golder, Patricia L., 1149
Goldman, Sarah R., 887
Goldman, Susan R., 1150, 1151
Goldstein, Lynn M., 1152, 1153, 1154, 1155, 1156, 2346, 2976
Goldstein, Wallace L., 1157
Gollin, Sandra, 868
Golson, Emily Becker, 1158
Golub-Smith, Marna, 1159
Gomez, Ida, 1160
Gomez, Mary Louise, 1161
Gonshack, Sol, 1162
Gonzales, Roseann Duenas, 1163, 1164
Gonzalez, Ann, 1165
Gonzo, Susan, 1166
Goodfellow, Paula, 1167
Goodin, G., 1168
Goodrum, Rosemarie, 942, 1169, 2754
Goodwin, Alice Anne, 1170
Goodwin, Janet M., 353, 354, 1095, 1171,
Gordon, Deborah, 1879
Gordon, Helen Heightsman, 1172, 1173
Gorman, Thomas P., 1174, 3111
Gorrell, Donna, 1175
Gosden, Hugh, 1176, 1177
Grabe, William, 655, 660, 768, 1134, 1135, 1178, 1179, 1180,

1181, 1182, 1183, 1184, 1185, 1707, 2665
Graber-Wilson, Geraldine Louise, 1186
Graham, Janet G., 1187
Graham, Sheila Y., 1188
Granfors, T., 1189
Grant, Carl A., 1161
Grant, Judith, 1190
Grant, Michael, 1191
Grant, Sylvia, 197
Graves, Margaret E., 1192
Grayshon, M. C., 1193
Green, Colette, 1195
Green, J. F., 1194
Green, John, 1195
Green, Peter S., 1196
Greenall, Gerard M., 1197, 1453
Greenberg, Karen L., 473, 1197, 1198, 1199, 1200
Greene, Maxine, 1201
Gregg, Joan, 1202, 1203
Gregor, Lorena, 694
Gregory, George Ann, 1204
Gregory, James F., 2774
Groden, Suzy, 1205, 1846
Groenewald, Jeannette, 1206
Groff, Charlotte E., 1207
Groot, Ingeborg, 1208
Gross, Christine Uber, 1209
Grossman, Alberta N., 1210, 2136
Groves, Peggy Ann Lamon, 1211, 1212
Grubb, Melvin Harrel, 1213
Grundy, Peter, 370
Gubbay, Janet M., 2753
Guenther, Barbara, 1214
Guerra, Veronica A., 1215
Gueye, M., 1216
Guice, Stephen, 2954
Gundel, Jeanette K., 1217
Gunderson, Lee, 735
Gungle, Bruce W., 1218
Gurnee, Deborah, 1219
Gurrey, P., 1220

Gutierrez, Christine Diane, 1221, 1222
Gutstein, Shelley P., 1223, 1224, 1225
Guy, Anne Marie, 2821

Haas, Teri, 1226, 1227
Haber, Steven B., 1228, 1229, 1230, 2219
Hadaway, Nancy L., 1013, 1014, 1231, 1232, 1233, 1234, 1235
Hafernik, Johnnie Johnson, 1236, 1237, 1238, 1239, 1240, 1241
Hagemann, Julie Ann, 116, 1242
Hagen, Stacey, 1243
Haggan, Madeline, 1244
Haghighat, Cathy, 1245
Hagiwara, Anne L., 1246
Hahn, Cora, 1247
Hale, Gordon, 1248, 1249
Halimah, A., 1250
Halio, Marcia P., 1251
Hall, Ann, 1252
Hall, Barbara, 2754
Hall, Charles, 1253
Hall, Chris, 675, 676, 1253, 1254, 1255, 1256, 1257, 1258
Hall, David, 1259
Hall, Ernest, 1260, 1261, 1262, 1263
Hallau, Margaret, 969
Hallett, Brien, 1264
Halsell, Sharon Weber, 1265, 1266
Hamayan, Else V., 279, 1267
Hamdallah, Rami W., 1268
Hamden, Abdullah Shakir, 1269
Hamilton, Irene Nakal, 1270
Hammond, J., 1271
Hamp-Lyons, Liz, 42, 167, 469, 471, 629, 637, 708, 781, 1272, 1273, 1274, 1275, 1276, 1277, 1278, 1279, 1280, 1281, 1282, 1283, 1284, 1285, 1286, 1287, 1288, 1289, 1290, 1291, 1292, 1293,

1294, 1295, 1296, 1297, 1298, 1299, 1300, 1301, 1302, 1303, 1304, 1305, 1306, 1307, 1308, 1309, 1310, 1311, 1377, 1438, 1583, 2528, 3230
Hanania, Edith A. S., 122, 1312, 1313
Handscombe, Jean, 3427
Handscombe, Mary, 539
Hansen-Stain, L., 1314
Hanson-Smith, Elizabeth, 217, 1315, 1316, 1317
Hantrakul, Chanpen, 1318
Haque, A. R., 1319
Harder, B. D., 1320
Harding, Mary Beth, 1993
Hared, Mohamed, 994
Hargett, Gary Ray, 1321
Harklau, Linda, 2835, 2836
Harley, Birgit, 1322
Harlow, Linda L., 2024
Harmatz-Levin, Carol, 1225
Harrell, Betsy, 1323
Harrington, Michael, 1324
Harris, David P., 656, 1325, 1326
Harris, Muriel, 1327
Harshbarger, Bill, 1328, 1329
Harss-Covaleski, Sandra L., 2338
Hart, Mary Joanne, 3136
Harter, Carol, 125
Hartfiel, V. Faye, 1330, 1482, 1485, 1529, 3372
Hartford, Beverly S., 1331
Hartmann, Pamela, 1332, 1333
Hashemipour, P., 1573
Haskell, J. F., 2161
Hatch, Evelyn, 1334, 1335
Haugen, E., 1336
Hauptman, Philip C., 1337, 1338
Hawisher, Gail E., 709
Hawkes, L., 1339
Hawkey, Roger, 1259
Hawkins, Thom, 384
Hawrani, S., 1340

Hayden, Helen Mary, 973
Hayer, John, 351
Hayes, Curtis W., 242, 1341, 1342, 2198, 2289
Haynes, Laurie A., 1343, 1344
Hayward, Malcolm, 1345
Hayward, Nancy M., 1346, 1347, 1348, 1349, 1350
He, Agnes Weiyun, 1351
He, Gang Qiang, 1352
Healy, Dave, 1353, 2691
Heasley, Ben, 1303
Heath, Robert, 1354, 1355
Heath, Shirley Brice, 1356
Heaton, J. B., 1357
Hecht, Karlheinz, 1196
Hedge, Tricia, 1358
Hedgecock, John, 110, 190, 1359, 1360, 1361
Heim, Alice Lederman, 1362
Heiser, Patricia, 1363, 1364
Heller, M. D., 1365
Henderson, Kim, 1366
Henderson, Robert T., 1367, 2392
Hendrichsen, Lynn E., 1368, 1369, 1370, 2361, 2362
Hendrickson, James M., 1371, 1372, 1373, 1374
Henner-Stanchina, C., 1375
Henning, Grant H., 783, 1304, 1305, 1376, 1377, 1378, 1379, 1380, 1381, 3135
Hepworth, George R., 1382, 1383
Herendeen, Warren, 1384
Hermann, Andrea W., 1385, 1386
Hernandez, Jose, 1227
Herzog, Martha, 1387
Heuring, David L., 1388, 1389, 1879
Hewins, C., 1390
Hickey, Conchita C., 1391
Hicks, Diana, 2019
Higa, T. K., 1392
Hildenbrand, Joan L., 309, 1393, 1394

Hilferty, Ann, 325
Hill, S. S., 1395
Hinds, John, 1396, 1397, 1398, 1399, 1400, 1559
Hines, Mary, 675, 2153, 2583
Hinkel, Eli, 1401
Hirokawa, Keiko, 1167, 1402, 1403, 1404
Hirsch, Linda M., 1405, 1406, 1407, 1408
Ho, Belinda, 1409
Ho, W. K., 1410
Hobelman, Paul, 1411
Hochstein, Deanna, 1412, 2102
Hodor, Mary Jean, 1413
Hodson, J., 1414
Hoey, Michael, 1454
Hoffer, Bates, 559, 1415
Hoffman, Ludger, 1416
Hoffner, B., 160
Hogue, Anne, 2339, 2340
Holdrich, D. L., 1417
Holes, Clive, 1418
Holliday, Cynthia W., 522, 1419
Holm, J., 1420
Holmes, Dick, 1421
Holmes, J., 1422
Holshuh, Louis W., 2071
Holt, Sheryl, 1423
Holten, Christine A., 353, 354, 522, 1082, 1083, 2976
Holtzknecht, Susanne, 1424
Holtzman, W. Jr., 2048
Holwitz, Elaine K., 1425
Holzknecht, Susanne, 2980
Homburg, Taco Justus, 1426, 1427, 1428, 2430
Homer, Merlin, 1429
Hood, Mary Ann, 1430
Hood, Sue, 422, 1431
Hooper, Nancy, 1432
Hoot, J. L., 1624
Hoover, W., 2048
Horn, Vivian, 1433, 1434

Hornberger, N. H., 1435, 1436
Horning, Alice S., 1437
Horowitz, Daniel M., 1022, 1306, 1438, 1439, 1440, 1441, 1442, 1443, 1444, 1445, 1446, 1447, 1448, 1449, 3098
Horsella, Maria, 2956
Hottel-Burkhart, Nancy, 1450, 1451
Houghton, Diane, 1452, 1453, 1454, 3244
Houston, R. Daniel, 1455
Howard, Tharon, 1456
Howatt, A., 1335
Howe, Pat M., 1457, 1458
Hoye, Marjorie, 1459
Hozayin, Russanne, 126
Hu, Yang, 452
Hu, Zhuang Lin, 1460
Huang, Harry J., 1461
Hubbard, Phillip, 1462, 2397, 2398
Huckin, Thomas N., 212, 662, 1072, 1463, 1464, 1465, 1466
Huddlestone, Rodney D., 1467
Hudelson, Sarah, 48, 279, 470, 908, 909, 1468, 1469, 1470, 1471, 1472, 1473, 1474, 2675, 3133, 3207
Hudson, Thom, 1643
Huebner, Thom, 1475
Huffman, Donald T., 1476
Hugg, Sandy, 1477
Hughes, Arthur, 1286, 1478
Hughes, Eril, 1479
Hughey, Jane B., 1330, 1419, 1480, 1481, 1482, 1483, 1484, 1485, 1529, 3372
Huizenga, Jann, 1486, 1487
Humes, Ann, 1488
Hunt, Kellogg W., 1489, 1490
Hunter, Judy, 477, 478
Huntington, Lucia B., 1491
Huntley, Helen S., 1492
Huntsinger, Jami L., 1493
Huot, Brian A., 1546

Hurley, Daniel Sean, 1494
Hurt, Phyllis, 843
Huss, Rebecca L., 1495, 1496
Hutchinson, Carolyn, 2498
Hutchinson Weidauer, Marie, 1497
Hutchinson-Eichler, Marie, 1498
Hutton-Yoshihara, Susan, 708
Hvitfeldt, Christina, 1499, 1500
Hwang, Hae Jin, 1501
Hyland, Ken, 1502, 1503, 1504

Icke, V., 3122
Idris, Abdul Aziz, 1505
Ike, Ndubuisi J., 1506, 1507
Ilson, Robert, 1508
Ilyin, Donna, 47
Indrasuta, Chantanee, 1509, 1510
Ingberg, Maria, 1511
Inghilleri, Moira, 1512
Ingram, Beverly, 1513, 1514, 1515, 1516
Inman, Marianne E., 1517
Inness, Donna Kay, 1518
Intaraprawat, Puangpen, 1519
Irons, Glenwood H., 327, 1337, 1564, 2120, 2369
Irvine, Patricia, 1520, 1521
Isidro Y Santos, Antonio, 1522
Iskander, Mona, 126
Isserlis, Janet, 871
Italia, Paul G., 1523

Jacobs, George, 1524, 1525, 1526, 1527, 3443
Jacobs, Holly L., 1330, 1485, 1528, 1529, 2646, 3372
Jacobs, Roderick A., 1530
Jacobs, Suzanne E., 1531, 1532, 1533, 1534, 1535, 2587
Jacoby, Jay, 1536
Jafarpur, Abdoljavad, 1537
James, C., 1538
James, Jean Portnoy, 1539
James, Kenneth, 1540, 1541
James, Mark O., 1542, 1543
Jamieson, Joan, 1544
Jang, Margot, 1545
Janopoulos, Michael, 1546, 1547, 1548, 1549, 1550, 1551, 1552
Jaramillo, Barbara Lausberg, 1553
Jarrett, Joyce M., 1554
Jayaswal, Shakuntala, 1555
Jeannet, Julia, 102
Jenkins, Mark, 1556
Jenkins, Susan M., 1557, 1558, 1559, 1560, 1561
Jensen, Christine, 1562
Jensen, Julie M., 50
Jeske, Doreen Pat, 1563
Jewinski, Judi, 1564
Jex, William W., 1565, 1566
Jiang, Weiping, 2599
Jie, Gao, 1567
Jilbert, C., 910
Jilbert, Kristina A., 1568
Jisa, Harriet, 1569
Jobe, Patricia, 1252
John, Barbara, 1570
Johns, Ann M., 143, 211, 387, 655, 657, 658, 662, 947, 965, 1022, 1302, 1531, 1571, 1572, 1573, 1574, 1575, 1325, 1576, 1577, 1578, 1579, 1580, 1581, 1582, 1583, 1584, 1585, 1586, 1587, 1588, 1589, 1590, 1591, 1592, 1593, 1594, 1595, 1596, 1597, 1598, 1599, 1600, 1601, 1602, 1603, 1604, 1605, 1606, 1607, 1893, 2127, 3093, 3319, 3435, 3436
Johns, Tim, 3059
Johnson, Carol Virginia, 1608
Johnson, Donna M., 748, 901, 1059, 1184, 1218, 1468, 1609, 1610, 1611, 1612, 1613, 1614, 1761, 1868, 2073, 2149, 2214, 2228, 2456, 2622, 2719, 2819, 2846
Johnson, Janet, 3218

Johnson, Judith Anne, 1615, 1616
Johnson, Karen E., 1617
Johnson, Keith, 1618, 1619, 1620, 1621, 1622
Johnson, Martha, 1623
Johnson, Mary A., 1624, 1625
Johnson, Patricia, 1626, 1627, 1628, 1629, 1630, 1631, 1632
Johnson, T., 1633
Johnston, Sue Ann, 1634
Johnston, Susan S., 1635, 1636
Jollife, David A., 1637
Jolly, David, 1638
Jones, C. Stanley, 660, 1307, 1308, 1639, 1640, 1641, 1642, 1643, 1644, 1645, 1646, 1647, 1648, 3160, 3161
Jones, D., 1649
Jones, Janis, 1650
Jones, Patricia E., 1651
Jones, Paul McClure, 1652
Jones, Robert J., 343
Jordan, Geoff, 3059
Jordan, Mary Kaye, 1560, 1561, 1653
Jordan, R. R., 1654, 3244
Josephson, M. I., 1655
Judd, Elliot L., 1356, 2377
Jurich, Donna, 3221, 3222

Kachru, B., 1706, 1343
Kachru, Yamuna, 1656, 1657
Kaczmarek, Celeste M., 1658
Kadar-Fulop, Judith, 1659
Kadesch, Margot C., 1660
Kadesh, Margot C., 1661
Kalaja, Paula, 1662
Kalivoda, T., 683
Kamanya, Ella, 1663
Kambal, Mohamed Osman, 1664, 3456, 3457
Kameen, Patrick T., 1665, 1666, 1667, 1668
Kamel, Boshra Naguib, 1669
Kamel, Gehan Wahid, 1670

Kamisli, Sibel, 1671
Kang, Shu Min, 1672
Kangas, J. A., 1673
Kantor, Robert N., 1674, 1675, 1676, 1677, 3052
Kaplan, Judith D., 1678
Kaplan, Robert B., 484, 643, 656, 659, 660, 661, 662, 667, 920, 948, 1179, 1184, 1185, 1397, 1679, 1680, 1681, 1682, 1683, 1684, 1685, 1686, 1687, 1688, 1689, 1690, 1691, 1692, 1693, 1694, 1695, 1696, 1697, 1698, 1699, 1700, 1701, 1702, 1703, 1704, 1705, 1706, 1707, 1708, 1894, 2350, 2354, 2665, 2968
Karle, Deepika, 2521
Kassen, Margaret Ann, 268
Kasser, Carol, 1709
Katchen, Johanna E., 1710
Katz, Ann, 1711, 2976
Katz, Anne Marie, 1712, 1713, 1714
Kaufer, David S., 1119
Kaufman, Lionel M., 1715
Kayfetz, Janet L., 1716, 1717
Kearney, Barbara Anne, 1718
Keenan, John B., 2278
Keh, Claudia L., 1719, 1720, 1721, 1722
Keller, Maria A., 1723
Kellerman, Eric, 34
Kelly, Craig A., 1724
Kelly, Peter, 1725
Kelly, William, 412
Kempf, M. K., 1726
Kenkel, James, 1727
Kennedy, Barbara L., 1728, 1729, 1730
Kennedy, Graeme D., 977, 1731
Kenny, Brian, 1259
Kenyon, Dorry, 1732, 3039
Kenyon-Nord, Anne, 1733
Kerr, J. Y. K., 1734
Kerrigan, W. J., 1735

Kessler, Carolyn, 1342, 1736
Keto, T., 3395
Keyes, Joan Ross, 1737
Keyes, Jose Luis, 1738
Khalil, Aziz M., 1739, 1740, 1741
Kharma, Nayef N., 1742
Khattak, M. Ibrahim, 1743, 1744
Khered, M. O. H., 1745
Khouri, Sandra, 2473, 2474
Khranke, Keiko, 1796
Kifle, Yimer, 1746
Kikuchi, K., 1747
Kim, Ik Hwan, 1748
Kim, Weol Soon, 1749
Kimball, Jack, 1750
Kimball, Margot C., 1751
Kimmelman, Joan, 2095
King, Carol, 1513, 1514, 1515, 1516, 1752
Kinsella, Paul L., 1753
Kirk, Ann, 536
Kirkhoff, Kristen, 1754
Kirkland, Eleanor R., 1755
Kirkland, Margaret R., 1756, 1757, 1758, 1759, 2609
Kirkland, Mary L., 59
Kirkman, J., 134, 1540, 3096
Kirkpatrick, Carolyn, 951, 952
Kirn, Elaine, 1760
Kirsch, Gesa, 2074
Kitagawa, Mary M., 1761
Kitchin, Deborah Anne, 1762
Klassen, B. R., 1763
Klassen, Cecil, 1764
Kleber, Rodney E., 1765
Klein, Gema K., 1766
Kleinmann, Howard H., 1767, 1768
Klingenberg, Felicia, 2744
Klobusicky-Mailander, Elizabeth, 1769
Knapp, Donald, 1770
Knapp, John, 1771
Knepler, Henry, 1772
Knepler, Myrna, 1772, 1773, 3056

Knowles, Marji, 1219
Kobayashi, Hiroe, 1774, 1775, 1776, 1777
Kobayashi, Toshihiko, 1778, 1779
Koch, Barbara J., 1780
Koch, Rachel Spack, 3397
Kocher, Susan, 953, 1781
Koda, Keiko, 1782, 1783
Kohn, James, 871, 1784
Kolb, Maureen McDonough, 1210
Kolba, Ellen D., 1660, 1661
Kolls, Mardel R., 1785
Konecni, Evica, 1786
Konneker, Beverly H., 1787, 1788, 2431
Kopec, John, 881
Kosel, Leslie, 1789
Koshi, Annie K., 1790, 1791
Kotecha, Piyushi, 1792
Kowal, Kristopher H., 1793
Kowitz, Johanna, 1794
Kraft, Cheryl, 1795
Krahnke, Karl, 1796
Kramer, Melinda G., 663
Krantz, Harriet, 2095
Krapels, Alexandra Rowe, 1797, 1798, 1799, 1800, 1801, 1802
Krashen, Stephen D., 1803, 1804
Kreeft, Joy Elaine, 1225, 1805, 1806, 3044
Kresovich, Brant M., 1807, 1808, 1809
Kreutz, H. J., 605
Krishnaswamy, Revathi, 1810
Kroll, Barbara, 453, 499, 500, 1281, 1064, 1586, 1799, 1811, 1812, 1813, 1814, 1815, 1816, 1817, 1818, 1819, 1820, 1821, 1822, 1823, 1824, 1825, 1826, 1827, 1828, 1829, 1830, 1831, 1832, 1833, 1834, 1938, 2619, 2646, 2937, 3052, 3223
Kroll, Barry M., 1835, 1836, 1837, 1838

Krumm, M. Louise, 2415
Kuehn, Phyllis A., 311, 500, 508
Kuhlman, Natalie A., 870, 871, 1839, 1840
Kumaravadivelu, B., 2871
Kumpf, Lorraine E., 1841, 2823
Kunz, Linda Ann, 1842, 1843
Kupper, Lisa, 2331
Kupper-Herr, G., 1844
Kuromiya, Y., 9
Kurylo, Carolyn, 3164
Kutz, Eleanor, 1845, 1846
Kuure, Leena, 1847
Kwachka, Patricia E., 167, 168, 169
Kwah, Poh Foong, 1848
Kwalick, Barry, 1903
Kwan-Terry, Anna, 1849
Kwok, H., 1850

Labarca, Angela, 2682
Lachman, Alice W., 1851, 1852
Lackstrom, John, 1853
Lacy, Richard, 1854
Lado, Ana Luise, 1855
Lado, Robert, 1856
Lai, Eva Fung Kuen, 1857, 1858
Lai, Fung Kuen
Lai, Phooi Ching, 1859, 1860
Laing, Donald, 1861
Lakshmanan, Usha, 2872
Lam, Clara Yin Ping, 1862
Lamp, Susan A., 1863, 1864
Lanauze, Milagros, 1865
Land, Robert E, 1866, 1867, 1868, 1869, 2588, 2589, 3435, 3436
Lane, Janet, 184, 185, 1870
Lange, Ellen, 184, 185, 1870, 1871, 1872
Lantolf, James P., 1055, 2682
Laothamatas, J., 942
Lapkin, Sharon, 1873, 3089
Lapp, Diane, 50
Lapp, Ronald E., 994, 1874, 1875, 1876, 1877, 1878, 1879, 1880
Larkin, Greg, 1881
Larsen-Freeman, Diana, 1882, 1883, 1884, 1885
Larson, Donald N., 1886
Larson, Doug, 2649
Larson, Penny, 1356, 2377
Larson, Richard L., 2429
Lascaratou, C., 1478
Latief, Mohammad Adnan, 1887
Latona, Maria, 1888
Latulippe, Laura Donahue, 1889
Laube, Linda, 1890
Lauer, Janice, 664, 665, 666,
Laurén, Christer, 876, 3076
Laurencio, Dalia Edelman, 1891, 1892
Lautamatti, Liisa, 1893, 1894
Lawgali, Kim, 1895
Lawrence, Mary S., 1896, 1897, 1898, 1899
Lay, Nancy Duke, 1900, 1901, 1902, 1903, 1904, 1905, 1906
Lazarton, Anne, 1907
Leach, Patrick, 1908
Leader, Lars, 1909
Leahy, Robert, 2432
Leake, Ann, 757
Leap, William, 1910, 2165
Leavelle, Cynthia A., 1911
Leavitt, Hart Day, 1912
Lebauer, Roni S., 1913, 1914, 1915, 1916, 2823
Lederman, Marie Jean, 1567, 1917
Ledwell, Monica, 738, 739
Lee, Chung Eun, 1918
Lee, Chunok, 2824, 2825
Lee, Gyoung W., 1919
Lee, Marta, 1920, 1921
Lee, Nancy Sandra, 1922
Lee, Sam, 1795
Lee, W., 1923
Lee, Yu Chang, 1924

Lefkowitz, Natalie, 1360, 1925
Lehman, Jean Purves, 2016
Lehman, Rainer, 1926
Lehmann, R., 808
Lehtio, Pekka, 3184
Leibman, Suzanne, 818
Leimkuhler, Meg, 1927, 1928
Leki, Ilona, 170, 212, 220,
  254, 502, 509, 510, 628,
  652, 822, 957, 1007, 1100,
  1572, 1813, 1929, 1930,
  1931, 1932, 1933, 1934,
  1935, 1936, 1937, 1938,
  1939, 1940, 1941, 1942,
  1943, 1944, 1945, 2275,
  2610, 2765, 2807, 3004
Lenz, Becky, 968
Leone, Elizabeth, 1946
Leonhardt, Nancy Lynn, 1947
Leppanen, Sirpa, 1662
Lesikin, Joan, 1948
Less, Philip, 1949
LeTourneau, Mark S., 1950
Leung, L., 1951
Levenston, E. A., 1952
Leverson, S., 1953
Levine, I. W., 1954
Levinson, Joan, 1955
Levy, Mike, 1956
Lewis, Margaret, 871
Lewis, Peggy, 1958
Lewitt, Philip Jay, 1957
Li, K. N. Y., 1959
Li, Nim Yu Kitty
Li, Xiao Ming, 1960
Li, Xiaochun, 1961
Liao, Thomas Shu Hui, 1962
Libben, Gary, 1963
Lidman, Walter J., 1964
Lieber, Paula Ellen, 1965,
  1966
Liebman, JoAnne D., 1967,
  1968, 1969, 1970, 1971
Liebman-Kleine, JoAnne D.,
  1973, 1974, 1975, 1976, 1977
Liebman, Suzanne, 1972
Light, Richard L., 802, 1102,
  1978, 2591
Ligon, Fred, 1979
Lim, Ho Peng, 1980, 1981, 1982
Lima, Susan, 2600
Lin, Chun Chung, 1983
Lincoln, Wanda, 3078
Lindblat, I., 1511, 1847,
  1984, 3184, 3320
Lindeberg, Ann Charlotte, 34,
  1984, 1985, 1986, 1987, 1988
Lindemann, Erika, 1989, 1990,
  1991, 1992, 1993, 1994
Lindfors, Judith Wells, 1995,
  1996, 1997
Lindsay, D. Beth, 1998, 1999
Lindstrom, Margaret, 2000,
  2647, 2648, 2649, 3070
Linnarud, Moira, 34, 2001,
  2002, 2003, 2004, 2005
Linse, Caroline, 2006
Lintermann-Rygh, I., 2007
Liontas, John I., 2008
Liou, Hsien Chin, 2009, 2010,
  2011, 2012, 2138
Lipp, Ellen, 2013, 2014
Lites, Emily, 2015, 2016
Little, Greta D., 2017
Littlejohn, Andrew, 2018, 2019
Ljund, M., 1511, 1847, 1984,
  3184, 3320
Lloyd, Donald J., 2020
Lo, Winnie Au Yeung, 2021,
  2225
Lockhart, Charles, 2022, 2023
Lombardi, Barbara, 1270
Long, Donna Reseigh, 2024
Long, M. N., 2025
Long, Michael H., 3306
Longmire, Kay L., 2026
Lope, Dalila, 2027
Lorenz, Frederick O., 3227,

3228
Lott, Bernard, 2028
Love, Alison, 2029
Love, Barbara, 2030
Loveday, Leo, 2031
Low, Martha, 2032
Lowe, Pardee, 1387, 1711
Lu, Min Zhan, 2033
Lubin, J., 1643
Lucas, Tamara F., 2034, 2035, 2036, 2037, 2038, 3360
Lugton, R. C., 1700
Lund, Steven, 2039
Luo, Yi Yun, 2040
Lux, Paul A., 2041, 2042
Lynch, Tony, 2043

MacDonald, Andrew, 2044, 2045
MacDonald, Gina, 2044, 2045
MacDonald, Marguerite G., 2046, 2047
Mace-Matluck, B. J., 2048
Macero, Jeanette D., 379, 2382, 3413
MacGowan-Gilhooly, Adele, 2049, 2050, 2051, 2052, 2732
Macha, Dyne H., 2053, 2054
Mackay, Ray, 170, 2055
Mackay, Ronald, 737
Mackie, Ardiss, 2056
Mackinson-Smyth, JoAnn, 2456, 2783
MacNealy, Mary Sue, 2058
Maculaitis, Jean D'Arcy, 2839, 2909
Madden, Carolyn, 169, 3031
Madden, L. R., 1029, 1030
Madrey, Lourie, 2698
Madsen, Harold, 325
Maftoon-Semnani, P., 2059
Magelsdorf, Kate
Maguire, Mary H., 732, 2060, 2061
Maher, J. C., 2062
Maher, Maria, 452

Mahmoud, Amal Aboul-Ghany, 2063
Maier, Paula, 2064
Makinen, Kaarina, 2065, 2066
Makino, S., 2067
Malave, William M., 3389
Malcolm, Diane, 2068
Maldonado, R., 1573
Malkoç, Anna Maria, 2069, 2324
Mallett, Barbara A., 1754, 2070, 2071
Mallony, Lee, 121
Mamer, Ellen, 968
Mangelsdorf, Kate, 2072, 2073, 2074, 2075, 2076, 2077, 2720, 2847, 3140
Mann, Richard Philip, 2078
Mantell, Helen, 3358, 3359
Manuel, Carmen Cuenca, 2079
Manus, Joy, 1270
Marenghi, Ele, 819
Marino, Martha, 2080
Markkanen, Raija, 700
Markley, Rayner W., 2081
Markstein, Linda, 2082, 2083, 2084, 2765
Marler, Michael G., 2085
Marquez, Ely J., 2086
Marsh, D., 3395
Marshall, Helaine W., 2087, 2088
Marshall, Margaret J., 2089
Marshall, Stewart, 2090
Martin, Aida Ramiscal, 2091
Martin, Anne Verbrugge, 2092, 2093, 2094
Martin, Charles, 2095
Martin, James E., 2097
Martin, J. R., 2096
Martin, Marilyn, 2098
Martin, Virginia Verbrugge, 1789
Martin-Betancourt, Mary Ellen, 2099
Martone, Denice, 2136

Maruta, Samuel, 2100
Marwin, Nancy, 2101, 2102
Maschler, Toni, 2103
Masny, Diana, 2104, 2105
Mason, Beniko, 2106
Mason, Cheryl, 2107
Massa, Janis L., 2108
Master, Peter, 2109, 2110
Matalene, Carolyn, 2111, 2112, 2113
Mather, Susan, 2114
Mathies, Claude, 2475, 2476
Mathison, Maureen A., 3146, 3147
Matsuhashi, Ann, 1647
Matsumura-Lothrop, Emiko, 2859
Matta, William Bruce, 2115
Mattar, Hameed Ebrahim, 2116
Matthews, Debra, 2117, 2118
Matthews, Suzi, 2119
Matthies, Barbara, 2120
Matusmura, Emiko, 2121
Mauranen, A., 2122
Maxwell-Paegle, Monica A., 2123
May, Barbara Ann, 2124
Mayes, Patricia, 1607, 2124
Mbalia, Doreatha D., 1554
McAlister, Eve, 2125
McAlpine, Lynn, 2126
McCaffrey, Maggie, 2649
McCagg, Peter, 667, 668, 669, 2127
McCall, D. Matt, 2128
McClure, E., 2129
McCretton, Elena, 2130
McCurdy, Pamela, 2131
McDaniel, Barbara A., 2132, 2133
McDevitt, Damien, 2134
McDonough, Jeanne, 2315
McDonough, Steven, 2135
McDonough-Kolb, Maureen, 2136
McDough, Vivian, 2137
McGarrell, H. M., 2138

McGirt, J. D., 2139
McGough, Jeanne, 410
McGrail, Loren, 2140
McGreal, Rory, 2141
McGroarty, Mary, 2142
McIver, Bruce, 2143
McKay, Heather, 2144, 2145, 3182
McKay, June R., 2146, 2346
McKay, Sandra Lee, 1836, 2147, 2148, 2149, 2150, 2151, 2152, 2153, 2154, 2155, 2156, 2157, 2158, 2159
McKee, Macey B., 1449, 2160, 2161
McKee, Sue, 567
McKenna, Eleanor, 469
McKenzie, Joanna, 1162, 2162
McKiernan, John, 2747
McKinley, Sharon, 443, 2163
McLaughlin, Daniel, 2164, 2165
McLaughlin, Jane, 2166
McLeod, A., 2167
McMurray, D., 2167
McMurtrey, Margaret, 2169, 2170
McNamara, Martha J., 254, 2117, 2171, 2172
McNamara, T. F., 2173
McNerney, Maureen, 261, 2137, 2188
McTeague, F., 2394
Meara, Paul, 1297
Meath-Lang, Bonnie, 2174, 2175
Medina, Suzanne L., 152
Medley, Frank W., Jr., 2008
Medsker, Karen, 523
Meiden, Walter, 2176
Mejia, Jaime Armin, 2177
Mellor, Elva R., 2178
Mellor, Kathleen L., 2179, 2180
Mellow, Dean, 735
Meloni, Christine, 1225, 2181

Menasche, Lionel, 1090, 2182, 2183, 2184, 2185, 2186
Mendelsohn, David J., 261, 2137, 2187, 2188, 2189, 2190, 2191
Mendiola, Sandra E., 2192
Menke, Gregory E., 2193, 2194
Menke, Sharon Allerson, 2195
Mentel, James, 1333
Mercado, Carmen I., 2196, 2197
Merchler, Gerardo, 2198
Merrill, C., 2199
Messerschmitt, Dorothy S., 1356, 2377
Metcalf, A. A., 1735
Mettler, Sally, 2200, 2201
Meyer, Daisy M., 3227, 3228
Meyer, Thomas, 239
Meyers, Alan, 2202
Michel, Andrew John, 2203
Mileham, Jean, 1632
Miller, D., 2871
Miller, Debra Cohen, 2204
Miller, Janie Rees, 2205
Miller, Leah D., 2206, 2207, 2429
Miller, Margo, 2208, 2209
Miller, Marianne, 2209
Miller, Ruth Ellen, 2210
Milman, Jacqueline, 2211
Min, Chan K., 2212
Mirano-Neto, Nelson, 1723
Missaghie, Soheyle, 2691
Mitchell, Candice Jane, 2213
Mittan, Robert, 2214, 2215
Mixdorf, Marcia, 2657
Mixon, Myron, 2216
Mlynarczyk, Rebecca K., 798, 799, 1230, 2217, 2218, 2219
Moe, H., 2220
Moesser, Alba, 2221
Mohamed, Mohamed Abdulla, 2222
Mohan, Bernard A., 2021, 2223, 2224, 2225, 3133

Mohr, Eugene V., 2226
Molinsky, Steven J., 2227
Moll, Luis C., 2228, 3192
Monroe, Laura B., 493, 494, 495, 496
Monroe, Sandra, 1994
Monson, Patricia Mary Ryan, 2229
Montalvan, Ruth, 67, 2230
Montano-Harmon, Maria Rosario, 1185, 2231, 2232, 2665
Montera, Aida, 451
Moody, K. W., 2233
Moore, Lucy, 2234, 2235, 2236
Moore, Rod, 2236
Moragné e Silva, Michele Lowe, 254, 2237, 2238, 2239, 2240, 2241, 2242, 2243
Morain, G., 683
Morcos, Dorothy A., 2244
Moreland, Kim, 899
Moreno, Adelaide, 2734
Morgan, Elisabeth Joan, 2245, 2246
Morow, Philip R., 2247
Morrell, Shirley, 2248
Morris, M. M., 343
Morrisroe, Sue, 146, 2249
Morrow, Keith, 1622
Morroy, Robby, 1806, 2250
Moser, Janet, 2251
Moten, Barbara, 2252
Mountainbird, Pauline, 2253
Mowat, Ruth, 2254
Muhlhousen, K. E., 136
Mukkatash, L., 2255
Mullen, Karen A., 2256, 2257
Munch, Helen, 1843
Munsell, Paul, 2258, 2259
Munson, Sharon, 2986
Murie, Robin, 3121
Murison-Bowie, Simon, 3059
Murphy, Barbara, 197
Murphy, Dermott, 2019

Murphy, John M., 2279, 2280, 2281, 2282
Murray, Denis, 2260
Murray, Denise E., 1579
Mustafa, Hassan, 3107, 3332
Mustapha, Sali Zaliha, 2261
Myers, Cindy, 862, 2262
Myers, Greg, 2263
Myers, Sharon A., 2264

Nakadate, Neil, 1637
Narain, Mona, 2265
Nashaat, Karima, 2266
Mathan Dryden, Irene June, 2267
Nathenson-Mejia, S., 2268
Nation, Patricia, 2269
National Clearinghouse on Literacy Education, 2270
Nattinger, James, 2271
Nayar, Usha, 842
Neff, Jo Anne, 2272
Negrey, Beth, 2976
Neill, David R., 2273
Nelson, Eric S., 2274
Nelson, Gayle L., 2275, 2276, 2277, 2278, 2279, 2280, 2281, 2282
Nelson, Marie Ponsot, 2283
Nelson, Marie W., 2284, 2285, 2286
Neu, Joyce, 2287, 2829
Neumann, Anna, 2288
Neuwirth, Christine, 1119
Nevarez, Hector O., 241, 242, 2289
Nevo, David, 2290
Newsham, Gwen S., 2291, 2292
Newstetter, Wendy C., 1944
Newton, Janice, 2293
Ney, James W., 424, 2294, 2295
Ng, Benton, 2296
Ng, Peggy, 2022, 2023
Ngooi, Chiu Ai, 566, 1860
Nickell, Samila Sturgell, 2297

Nickson, Andrew, 3244
Nishimura, Yukiko K., 2298
Nishio, Yvonne, 2299
Nkamana, D. G., 2300
Noguchi, Rei R., 2301
Noonan, Michael, 2600
Nord, Martha, 2311
Nordman, Marianne, 876, 3076
Norloff, Charl, 3170
Norman, Unal, 2302
Norment, Nathaniel, 2303, 2304, 2305, 2306
Norris, William E., 84
Norrish, John, 99
Norton, Robert F., 2307, 2308
Notess, Mark H., 2309
Nourse, Jennifer, 3338
Nunan, David, 1945
Nurss, Joanne R., 2310

Obah, Thelma Y., 2311
Obeidat, Hussein Ali, 2312
O'Brien, Maryann, 2313, 2314, 2315, 2650, 2651
O'Brien, Teresa, 2316
O'Conner, Frederick, 2317
O'Day, Jennifer, 390
Odenthal, Joanne, 2318
Odlin, Terence, 2319, 2320
O'Donnell, Teresa D., 2321, 2367, 2368
Ohannessian, Sirapi, 2322, 2323, 2324
Oi, Kyoko Mizuno, 2325
Oi, Yip Lee Mee, 997
Okamura, F., 2326
Oller, John W., 1010, 1658, 2256, 2327
Olsen, Leslie, 1466
Olshtain, Elite, 872, 1022, 2328
Olson, Christie Kay, 514
Olson, David R., 2329
Olson, Gary, 1071
Oluwadiya, Adewumi, 2330

O'Malley, J. Michael, 527, 2331, 2332, 3213
Omberg, Margaret, 790
Onaka, Natsumi, 2333
Ong Kiam Ann, Albert, 2334
Oppenheim, Carol, 690
O'Quinn, Terri, 1994
Orem, Richard A., 3427
Orge, C., 2335
Orkin, Nell S., 3204
Ortblad, Dennis, 2336
Osburne, Andrea G., 2337, 2338
O'Shea, Judith, 570
Oshima, Alice, 2339, 2340
Osman, Alice H., 802, 1102, 2591
Oster, Judith, 2341, 2342, 2343, 2344, 2345, 2346
Oster, Sandra, 3454
Osterloh, K. H., 2347
Ostler, Shirley E., 660, 1789, 2348, 2349, 2350, 2351, 2352, 2353, 2354, 2355, 2356
Ostler-Howlett, Catherine, 735
Ouaouicha, Driss, 2357
Ounvichit, T., 2358
Ovaiza, S., 2359
Owens, Jonathan, 109
Owens, R. J., 2360

Pack, Alice C., 1370, 2361, 2362, 2363
Padron, Yolanda N., 248, 2364, 3275
Pagurek, Joyce, 2365
Paine, M. J., 2366
Paiva, Judith L., 395, 2321, 2367, 2368
Palhinha, Eduarda M. G., 1678
Palmberg, R., 1189
Palmer, Joe D., 2369, 2370
Paltridge, Brian, 2371
Pandharipande, R., 2372

Paramskas, Dana, 2293
Parasher, S. V., 2373
Pare, A., 732
Paris, Jerry, 937
Parish, Charles, 2433
Park, Young Mok, 2374
Parker, Barbara, 2123
Parkhurst, Christine, 2375, 2376, 2377, 2378
Parks, Susan, 2379
Parry, Kate, 1311
Partridge, Katheyrn L., 2380
Paschal, Gregory, 2381
Patkowski, Mark S., 2382, 2383
Patrie, James, 2384
Patthey, G. Genevieve, 994
Patthey-Chavez, G. G., 2385
Paul, Michael, 2386
Paul, Peter, 2387
Pauliukonis, Nancy R., 2388
Paulston, Christina Bratt, 893, 2389, 2390, 2391, 2392
Pavelich, J. L., 2393
Pavlik, Cheryl, 717, 2865, 2866
Payne, R., 2394
Paznik-Bondarin, Jane, 2395
Pearson, Christine Casanave, 1475, 2396, 2397, 2398
Pearson, Sheryl, 2399
Pease-Alvarez, Lucinda, 279
Pech, William C., 411, 2400
Pedtke, Dorothy A., 2324
Peirce, Bonny Norton, 3051
Peitzman, Faye, 1095, 2401, 2402
Penfield, Joyce, 2403
Penfield-Jasper, S., 160, 559
Pennington, Martha C., 2404, 2405, 2406, 2407, 2408, 2409, 2410, 2411, 2412, 2413, 2414, 2646, 2472, 3059
Peppin, Suzanne M., 2415
Peregoy, Suzanne F., 2416
Peretz, Arna S., 2417
Perez, Charlene G., 2418

Perkins, Kyle, 104, 709, 968, 1010, 1168, 1382, 1658, 1787, 1788, 2256, 2346, 2419, 2420, 2421, 2422, 2423, 2424, 2425, 2426, 2427, 2428, 2429, 2430, 2431, 2432, 2433, 3224
Perkins, Leroy, 2434
Perrin, Carol, 1879
Perry, William, 2435, 3179
Persky, Charles, 2586
Pervin, Carol, 1880
Pery-Woodley, Marie Paule, 2436, 2437, 2438, 2439
Peters, B., 2440
Peterson, H. M., 2441
Peterson, Mark P., 2442
Peterson, Pat Wilcox, 2443
Peterson, R. D., 2444
Petraglia, Joseph, 1789
Pettinari, Catherine, 2445
Peyasantiwong, Patcharin, 265
Peyton, Joy Kreeft, 49, 2036, 2174, 2446, 2447, 2448, 2449, 2450, 2451, 2452, 2453, 2454, 2455, 2456, 2457, 2458, 2459, 2460, 2461, 2783, 3043, 3221
Pfingstad, Nancy, 2462
Phap, D. T., 2463
Pharis, Keith E., 2464, 2465
Phillipson, Robert, 34
Phinney, Marianne, 260, 2138, 2466, 2467, 2468, 2469, 2470, 2471, 2472, 2473, 2474, 2475, 2476
Phooi, Ching Lae, 2477
Pica, Teresa, 2478, 2479
Pickard, Valeria, 2480
Picus, Mark, 2481, 2482, 2483, 2484, 2532
Pierce, Lorraine Valez, 2332
Pierson, H. D., 1062
Pike-Bakey, Meredith, 291, 292, 293
Pilgreen, Janice, 2761
Pimsarn, Pratin, 2485

Pincas, Anita, 2486, 2487, 2488
Pindi, Makaya, 2963
Piper, Alison, 2489, 2490, 2491, 2492
Piper, T., 2493
Pitcher, Barbara, 2494
Pitillo, Angelo, 2987
Plaskoff, Josh, 152
Platt, E., 2129
Poggi, Claudine, 2495
Poh, Shin C., 2496
Polak, Jeanne, 2497
Polio, Lharlene, 462
Politzer, Robert L., 992
Pollitt, Alastair, 2498
Polycarpou, Susan, 2499
Ponder, Roger, 2500
Port, Richard J., 2501
Porter, Delma McLeod, 2502
Porter, Don, 1286
Porter, D. W., 2503
Porter, Dwight, 2504
Posner, B., 2505
Potter, L. D., 2506
Poulsen, Eric, 2507, 2508
Povey, John F., 2509, 2510, 2511
Powell, Joyce, 2512, 2513
Powell, William W., 2500, 2514
Powers, Judith K., 2515, 2516, 2517, 2652
Praninskas, Jean, 2518
Prater, Doris L., 249, 250, 251, 2519
Preston, Denise, 169, 3031
Preston, W., 2520
Pretzer, Wallace L., 2521
Price, J. E., 1197, 1453
Price, Karen, 2378
Price, Pat, 481
Price, Susan, 2084
Price, Victoria, 2522
Prince, Eileen, 2523, 2524
Pringle, Ian, 1056, 1618,

1665, 1688, 2573, 3311
Prior, Paul Arthur, 211, 1944, 2525, 2526
Prochnow, Sheila B., 1302, 1309, 1310, 2527, 2528
Proctor, Susan, 2529
Prodromou, Luke P., 2530
Pruna, Ruth Goodgall, 2531
Pryzant, Peggy, 2532
Pucci, Sandra, 1361
Purves, Alan C., 265, 472, 666, 709, 808, 809, 1174, 1307, 1509, 1657, 1659, 1682, 2374, 2533, 2534, 2535, 2536, 2537, 2538, 2997, 3111, 3210

Qoqandi, Abdulaziz Mohammed Yar, 2539
Quinn, Mary Ellen, 1736

Ra, Jung B., 2494
Rabideau, Dan, 2540
Rabura, Tamera G., 2541
Radecki, Patricia M., 2542
Radell, Ralph, 2543
Radford, W. L., 2544
Raffel, Suzanne, 3202
Rafoth, Bennett A., 3438
Ragan, Peter H., 1849, 2545
Rahman, Muhammad Asfah, 2546
Railey, Kevin, 825, 2547
Raimes, Ann, 2548, 2549, 2550, 2551, 2552, 2553, 2554, 2555, 2556, 2557, 2558, 2559, 2560, 2561, 2562, 2563, 2564, 2565, 2566, 2567, 2568, 2569, 2570, 2571, 2572, 2573, 2574, 2575, 2576, 2577, 2578, 2579, 2580, 2581, 2582, 2583, 2584, 2585, 2586, 2587, 2588, 2589, 3131, 3132, 3435, 3436
Rainey, Kenneth, 2590
Rainsbury, Robert, 2591, 2592

Rakijas, Mirjana, 229, 2733
Ramaglia, Judith, 2593
Ramani, Esther, 2594
Ramirez, Maria G., 2178, 2276
Ramos, Rosinda Guerra, 1422
Ramsey, R. D., 2595
Rankin, D. S., 2596
Raphael, Caroline B., 2597
Raphan, Deborah, 2251
Rapp, Linda Chan, 2598
Raupach, Manfred, 1292, 1322
Raupp, Magdala, 447, 3239
Ray, Bonnie MacDougall, 2599
Ray, Ruth Elaine, 861, 2600, 2601
Rayburn, Kellie R., 2602, 2759
Raymond, Robert, 2603
Read, John, 2604, 2605, 2606
Rebuffot, Jacques, 738, 739
Reed, Leslee, 1806, 2457
Reeder, Nancy J., 2607
Reese, Clyde, 1159
Regent, O., 2608
Reichelderfer, N., 1673
Reichelt, Melinda, 2945, 2946, 2947
Reid, Francis C., 1757, 2609
Reid, Joy M., 136, 1306, 2346, 2587, 2610, 2611, 2612, 2613, 2614, 2615, 2616, 2617, 2618, 2619, 2620, 2621, 2622, 2623, 2624, 2625, 2626, 2627, 2628, 2629, 2630, 2631, 2632, 2633, 2634, 2635, 2636, 2637, 2638, 2639, 2640, 2641, 2642, 2643, 2644, 2645, 2646, 2647, 2648, 2649, 2650, 2651, 2652, 2653, 3052, 3070
Reitzel, Armeda, 2654
Rentz, Mark D., 2654
Retten, Susan, 2656
Reutten, Mary K., 2970
Reynolds, Ed, 2657
Reynolds, Patricia R., 2658

Reynoso, Wendy Demko, 2659
Rhynes, Elinor J., 2660
Rice, Martha K., 1219, 2661
Ricento, Thomas, 921, 1185, 2662, 2663, 2664, 2665
Richard-Amato, Patricia, 2666
Richards, B., 1339
Richards, Jack C., 2667, 3306
Richards, R. T., 2668
Richards-Apatiga, Ann R., 2669
Richardson, Gina, 2458, 2461
Richmond, Jack W., 2670
Richmond, Kent C., 2671, 2672, 2673
Rider, Nigel, 2130
Ridpath, Sandra, 2674
Rigg, Pat, 452, 902, 1472, 2675
Riggles, John, 2852
Riley, Kathryn I., 2676, 2677
Riley, P., 2608
Ringbom, Hakan
Rinnert, Carol, 1775, 1776
Rinvolucri, Mario, 2679
Rissanen, M., 1985
Rittershofer, John S., 2680
Riverol, Armando, 2681
Rivers, Wilga M., 2683, 2762
Rivers, William J., 2682
Rizzo, Betty, 2684
Roach, William L., 2685, 2686
Robb, Thomas N., 2687, 2741, 2742
Robbins, M., 2688
Robertson, Michelle M., 152
Robinett, Betty Wallace, 2391, 2689
Robinson, James H., 2690, 2691
Robinson, Janet O., 2692
Robinson, Pauline C., 370, 877, 1287, 1654, 2043, 2316, 2693, 3283, 3305
Robinson, Peter, 305, 789, 2694
Robinson, Timothy H., 2695, 2696, 2697, 2698, 2699
Robinson-Fellag, Linda, 2700
Rock, D. A., 343
Rodby, Judith, 539, 540, 2118, 2701, 2702, 2703, 2704, 2705, 2706, 2707, 2708
Roderman, Winifred H., 2709
Rodman, L., 2710
Rodoni, Ellodoro, 2711
Rodrigues, R. J., 2712
Rodriguez, Elizabeth, 2715
Rodriguez-Diaz, Douglas B., 2716
Rodriques, Raymond J., 2713, 2714
Rodriquez, Andres, 2717
Roen, Duane H., 748, 901, 1059, 1184, 1218, 1468, 1613, 1614, 1761, 1868, 2073, 2074, 2149, 2214, 2228, 2456, 2622, 2718, 2719, 2720, 2819, 2846
Rojas, Pauline M., 2721
Rollin, Maria Farias, 2722
Rooholamine, Simin Dokht, 2723
Rooks, George M., 2724, 2725
Root, Christine, 274
Root, Christine B., 2726, 2727, 2728
Rorschach, Elizabeth G., 229, 230, 2729, 2730, 2731, 2732, 2733, 2734
Rosario, Gertha Dunlevy, 2735
Rose, Michael, 1641
Rosen, L. J., 198
Rosow, La Vergne, 2736
Ross, C. N. G., 2737
Ross, David A., 2738
Ross, Jacqueline
Ross, Janet, 2739, 2740, 3037, 3038
Ross, Steven B., 2429, 2687, 2741, 2742

Rosser, Carl Frederick, 2743
Rothenheber, Paul, 2907
Rothschild, Dennie, 2744
Rottweiler, G. P., 2745
Roulon, Kathy, 1880
Rounds, Patricia L., 171, 172, 419, 1412
Rowe Henry, Alexandra, 1945
Rowland, J. Carter, 2746, 2747
Rowoth, James D., 457
Roy, Alice M., 2748, 2749, 2750, 2751
Rua-Larsen, Marybeth, 2752
Rubenstein, Judith S., 2753
Rubin, Donald L., 2754, 3438
Rubin, Joan, 613
Ruetten, Mary K., 279, 2755, 2756, 2757, 2758
Rupp, James H., 2759
Russell, Alicia, 2760
Russikoff, Karen, 2761
Russo, Gloria M., 2762
Rutherford, William, 675, 2153
Rutkowski-Weber, Rita K., 590
Rybowski, Tadeusz, 2763

Sa'adeddin, Mohammed, 2764
Sadow, Catherine, 3018, 3019, 3020
Sage, Howard, 2765
Sajavaara, K., 3395
Saksena, Anuradha, 2766
Salebi, Mohammed Yusuf, 2767
Salimbene, Suzanne, 2768
Sally, O., 2769
Saltzman, Shelley A., 2770, 2771
Sammander, Abdul Raziq, 2772
Samonte, Aurora L., 2773
Sampaio De Moraes, Marcia, 935
Sampson, Donald E., 2774
Sampson, Gloria P., 2775, 2776
Samuda, N., 2777
Samuel, M., 2778

Samway, Katharine Davies, 49, 470, 824, 2779, 2780, 2781, 2782, 2783, 2784, 2785
Sanaou, R., 2786
Sanborn, Jean, 2787
Sanchez, Lilian L., 2788
Sanchez, M., 1061
Sanchez-Escobar, A., 2789, 2790
Sanchez-Villamil, Olga Irene, 2791
Sanctis, Dona De, 2792
Sandberg, Karl C., 2793, 2794
Sankovich, Arthur A., 1754
Sansone, Richard, 2795
Santana-Seda, O., Sr., 2796
Santiago, Ramon, 2797
Santos, Terry Ann, 2798, 2799, 2800, 2801, 2802, 2803, 2804
Sarantos, Robin L., 2805, 2806
Sarig, Gissi, 1022, 1023, 2807, 2808
Sarkar, S., 2809
Sarwar, Zakia, 2810
Sasser, Linda, 2812
Sato, Charlene J., 2813
Sato, Taeko, 2814
Saunders, Mary Anne, 1758, 1759, 2815, 2816, 2817
Savage, Susan, 961
Saward, Christopher, 2818
Sayers, Dennis, 2819, 2820
Sayre, Joan, 2586
Scane, Joyce, 2821
Scarcella, Robin C., 660, 1569, 1915, 1916, 2287, 2434, 2822, 2823, 2824, 2825, 2826, 2827, 2828, 2829
Schachter, Jacqueline, 104, 968, 1382, 1834, 3224
Schaetzel, Kirsten, 2830, 2831
Schafer, John C., 1836, 1837, 1838, 2832
Schafer, John S., 2833
Scharer, Gillian D. E., 2834

Schecter, Sandra, 2835, 2836
Schenck, Mary Jane, 2837
Scheraga, Mona, 2838, 2839
Schick, Ruth M., 2840
Schiller, Janis L., 2841
Schlumberger, Ann L., 2075, 2076, 2842, 2843, 2844, 2845, 2846, 2847
Schneider, Melanie L., 670, 709, 2235, 2848, 2849, 2850, 2851, 2852
Scholtz, Celeste M., 2853
Schreiber, Mona, 2854
Schroder, Hartmut, 600, 1707, 2855
Schroen, Charles, 2856
Schumann, Francine M., 2857
Schwabe, G. T., 2858
Schwarte, Barbara, 1794, 2121, 2859
Scott, Charles T., 2860
Scott, M. S., 2861
Scott, Mary Lee, 3039
Scott, Suzanne, 2142
Scull, Sharon, 2862
Secord, M. A., 2863
Seda, Ileana, 2864
Segal, Margaret Keenan, 2865, 2866
Seidhofer, Barbara, 2867
Seitz, James E., 2868
Sekara, Ananda Tilaka, 2869
Selekman, Howard R., 1767, 1768
Selinker, Larry, 34, 159, 169, 1853, 2870, 2871, 2872, 2873, 2874, 2875, 2876, 2877, 3029, 3031
Seltzer, Sandra, 2095
Semen, Kathy P., 967
Semke, H. D., 2878, 2879
Sender, Barbara, 1922
Seng, Mark W., 2880
Serna, Irene A., 470, 3207

Severino, Carol, 2881, 2882, 2883
Seward, Bernard H., 2884, 2885
Seyoum, Mulugeta, 2459
Shabrami, Carol J. Thymian, 2886
Shaffer, M. J., 2887
Shakir, Abdullah, 2888
Shank, Cathy C., 2889
Sharma, V. Alex, 2890, 2891, 2892
Sharpsteen, Lorraine, 2893
Sharwood Smith, Michael, 34, 2894, 2895, 2896
Shaw, Peter A.
Shaw, Philip M., 1708, 2897, 2898, 2899
Sheal, P. R., 2900
Sheehan, Thomas, 2901
Sheetz-Brunetti, Y., 1633
Shen, Fan, 2902
Shen, Yao, 2903
Shenkarow, Ellen, 3
Sheorey, Ravi, 2904, 2905, 2906, 2907, 2908
Sheppard, Ken, 838
Sheraga, Mona, 2909
Sherman, Jane, 2910
Sherrard, Carol, 2911
Sherwin, A. T., 294
Shezi, Goodman T., 2912
Shih, May, 2913, 2914, 2915, 2916, 2917, 2918
Shikhani, May, 1313
Shindler, Jack, 2919, 2920
Shinoda, Y., 2921
Shishin, Alexandar, 2922
Shoemaker, Connie, 2499, 2923, 2924, 2925
Shook, Ronald, 1881, 2926
Shortreed, Ian, 2687, 2742
Shreve, D. H., 30
Shuman, Judith A., 1011
Shuy, Roger, 1806, 3044
Sides, Margaret N., 2927

Silber, Patricia, 2928
Silberstein, Sandra, 506, 507
Silva, Tony, 254, 708, 1327, 1544, 2929, 2930, 2931, 2932, 2933, 2934, 2935, 2936, 2937, 2938, 2939, 2940, 2941, 2942, 2943, 2944, 2945, 2946, 2947, 2948
Silver, Carole, 2948
Silver, Marcia, 1903
Silver, Nettie W., 2949
Silverman, A., 1148
Silvern, S. B., 1624
Silverstein, R., 2430
Simanu-Klutz, Luafata, 464
Simmen, Edward, 2950
Simmonds, Paul, 2951
Simon, S. T., 2952
Simpson, Elizabeth, 2953
Sims, Brenda R., 2954
Sims, Diana Mae, 2955
Sindermann, Gerda, 2956
Singh, Frances B., 2957
Singleton, C., 2958
Singley, Carol J., 324
Sinyor, Roberta, 2293
Siripham, Salakjit, 2959
Sistrunk, Sarah A., 2960
Sitko, Barbara, 4
Siu, Kwai Peng, 2961
Sivall, John, 2962
Skelton, John, 2963
Skibniewski, Lesnek, 2964, 2965
Skibniewski, Maria, 2965
Skidmore, Charles, 2966
Skinner, Anna A., 2699
Slager, William R., 2967, 2968
Slaughter, Randi, 180
Slaughter, Virginia, 1903
Smadi, Oglah M., 2969
Smalley, Regina L., 2970
Smalley, William A., 1886
Smith, Allison, 2971, 2972, 3131
Smith, Edward L., 1794
Smith, Jean Mullen, 2346
Smith, Larry E., 3124
Smith, Louise Z., 3416
Smith, M. S., 2973
Smith, Maggy, 2974
Smith, Rosalyn M., 2975
Smith, Wendy, 2976, 2977
Smithies, Michael S., 1424, 2978, 2979, 2980
Smoke, Trudy, 1226, 1227, 2981, 2982, 2983, 2984, 2985
Smolten, Lynn, 2986
Snell, Debra, 2987
Snellings, Courtenay Meade, 1486
Snipper, Grace C., 3330
Snow, Becky Gerlach, 1010
Snow, Catherine, 1865
Snow, Marguerite Ann, 211, 2988, 2989
Snyder, Beth, 111, 2990
So, Sufumi, 2413
So, Wu Yi, 2991, 2992
Soden, Betsy, 2252
Soh, Beelay, 2993
Sohn, David A., 1912, 2994
Sokmen, Anita Almansa, 2995
Sokolik, Maggi, 2996, 3180
Soon, Yeeping, 2993
Soppelsa, B. F., 1395
Soter, Anna O., 709, 2997, 2998
Southard, Bruce, 2999
Southard, Sherry G., 2999, 3000
Southwell, Michael G., 952
Spaan, Mary, 351, 3001, 3002
Spack, Ruth, 2589, 3003, 3004, 3005, 3006, 3007, 3008, 3009, 3010, 3011, 3012, 3013, 3014, 3015, 3016, 3017, 3018, 3019, 3020, 3132, 3133, 3435, 3436
Spaventa, Louis J., 1045, 2336, 2400, 2834, 2875, 2894, 3046, 3108
Speers, Kathleen, 3021
Spencer, D. H., 3022, 3023

Spiegel-Podnecky, Janet, 3024
Squire, James R., 50
Srivastava, R. N., 3025
St. John, Maggie Jo, 305, 3026
Stack, Jim, 3027
Staczek, John, 3028
Stahlheber, Eva, 3029
Stairs, A., 3030
Stalker, Jacqueline W., 3031, 3032
Stalker, James C., 3031, 3032
Stall, Julianne, 3033
Stanley, Jane, 3034
Stanley, M. H., 1120
Stanley, Nancy, 3035
Stansfield, Charles W., 1302, 1308, 1387, 1711, 2634, 3036, 3037, 3038, 3039, 3040
Stanton, Marge, 3041
Stanulewicz, Danuta, 3042
Staton, Jana, 1806, 2460, 2461, 3043, 3044, 3258
Staub, Don, 3045
Steed, James F., 3046
Steer, Jocelyn, 3047, 3048
Steffensen, Margaret S., 700, 3049, 3050, 3343
Steinhaus, Karin, 1159, 3051, 3052
Steinmann, H., 2067
Stenstrom, A. B., 3053, 3054
Stephens, Martha Kay, 3055
Stephens, Rory, 3056
Stephenson, Bessie C., 3057
Stern, H., 1690
Stern, Susan, 1916
Stevens, Vance, 2412, 3058, 3059
Stevenson, D. K., 2424
Stevenson, Dwight W., 3060
Stewart, Denise, 269
Stice, Randy, 3061
Stokes, Elizabeth, 3062
Stone, Betty, 3063
Storer, Graeme, 1259

Storla, Steven Redding, 3064, 3065, 3066, 3067
Stout, Barbara, 3068
Stratton, F., 3069
Stratton, Linda, 3070
Strei, Gerald J., 3071, 3072, 3073
Strevens, Peter, 1690
Strom, V., 1885
Strother, Judith B., 3074, 3075, 3076, 3203
Strunk, Vicki L., 2653
Sugimoto, Eiko, 3077
Suid, Murray, 3078
Suksaeresup, N., 3079
Sullivan, Kathleen E., 3080
Sullivan-Tuncan, Susan, 710
Sulzmann, H., 3081
Sumagaysay, Grace, 1103
Sun, Michelle C., 3082
Sunday, Betty R., 3083, 3084
Sunde, Karen, 196
Sunderman, Paula W., 3085, 3086
Susini, Sheila, 3087
Swain, Merrill, 34, 3088, 3089
Swales, John M., 134, 212, 715, 879, 1404, 1540, 2542, 3090, 3091, 3092, 3093, 3094, 3095, 3096, 3097, 3098, 3107, 3332
Sweedler-Brown, Carol O., 3099, 3100, 3101, 3102, 3103
Sween, M., 3104

Tabor, K., 3105
Taborek, Elizabeth, 3106
Tadros, Angele A., 3107, 3108
Tagong, Kanchit, 3109, 3110
Takala, Sauli, 809, 3111, 3112, 3113
Takano, Shoji, 3114
Takashima, Hideyuki, 3115
Taki El Din, Shaker Rizk, 3116
Talburt, Susan, 3117

Tamez, Jonathan D., 3118
Tanchotikul, Saovanee, 3119
Tannebaum, Elizabeth, 1979
Tapla, Elena, 3120
Tarini, Carla, 3021
Tarone, Elaine, 757, 3121, 3122
Tarpley, Fred, 3123
Tawake, Sandra, 3124
Taylin, Vicki, 3125
Taylor, Barry P., 2587, 2588, 2589, 3126, 3127, 3128, 3129, 3130, 3131, 3132, 3133, 3427, 3435, 3436
Taylor, Carol, 1302, 1381, 3134, 3135
Taylor, Charles M., 3136
Taylor, Dorothy, 2783, 2784
Taylor, E. A., 3137
Taylor, Gordon, 3138, 3139
Taylor, Steve, 1880
Taylor, Victoria, 1218, 2074, 2077, 3140
Tebbets, Diana, 919
Tedick, Diane J., 1306, 3141, 3142, 3143, 3144, 3145, 3146, 3147
Teel, T. L., 3148
Tegey, Margery, 3149
Teich, Nathaniel, 3150, 3151
Temperley, Mary S., 2683
Templin Richards, Rebecca, 3152
Teng, Chunhong, 3153
Teng, Wen Hua, 3154
Terdal, Marjorie S., 3155, 3156
Terdy, Dennis, 3157
Terry, Robert M., 3158
Tesdell, L., 3159
Tetroe, Jacqueline, 1647, 1648, 3160, 3161
Thabet, Ahmed Anwar, 3162
Thaipakdee, Supaporn, 3163
Thaiss, Christopher J., 3164
Tharu, Susie, 3165
Thibadeau, Sandra, 2379

Thomas, Gordon K., 3166
Thomas, Helen, 3167
Thomas, Jacinta, 3168, 3169, 3357
Thomas-Ruzic, Maria, 1487, 3170, 3171, 3172, 3176, 3177
Thompson, Carolyn, 2209
Thompson, Mertel, 3173
Thompson, Roger M., 3174, 3175
Thompson, Shirley, 916, 917
Thompson-Panos, K., 3171, 3172, 3176, 3177
Thonus, Terese, 3178
Thornburg, Linda, 2435, 3179
Tickle, Amy, 3045
Tillyer, Anthea, 2734, 2996, 3180
Tippetts, Robert, 1032
Tipton, S., 3181
Tish, Viola Florez, 1235
Todd-Trimble, Mary, 2873, 2874, 3077
Tom, Abigail, 2145, 3182
Tomlinson, B., 3183
Tommola, Jorma, 3184
Tooker, Nancy, 567
Tormakangas, Kari, 3185
Torres, Marceline, 2197
Touchie, H. Y., 3186
Towell, Janet, 3347
Townsend, Kimberley T., 757
Tracy, Glenn Edward, 3187
Tragant, Elsa, 3204
Tragardh, Thomas, 47
Traugott, Elizabeth Closs, 3188
Traurig, V., 3189
Traxler, Carol Bloomquist, 3190
Treuba, Henry T., 887, 1151, 3191, 3192, 3237
Tribble, Christopher, 522, 3193
Tricomi, E., 3194
Trimble, Louis, 1853, 2873, 2874, 2875, 2876, 2877, 3077,

3195
Tripp, Ellen L., 3196
Trump, Kathy, 26
Tsao, Fen Fu, 3197, 3198
Tucker, Amy, 689, 3199, 3200
Tucker, G. Richard, 1706, 2861
Tucker, Richard W., 3201
Tumposley, Nancy, 379, 2382, 3413
Turner, Kitty, 2166
Tyacke, Marian, 261, 2188, 2191
Tyler, Andrea, 3202

Ueta, Yumiko, 3262
Ulichny, Polly, 871
Ulijin, Jan M., 3076, 3203
Ultsch, Sharon, 3204
Urquhart, Alexander, 1302
Urzua, Carole, 49, 3205, 3206, 3207
Usovicz, Elizabeth, 3208
Uzawa, Kozuo, 3209

Vahapassi, Anneli, 3113, 3210
Valdes, Guadalupe, 3211, 3212
Valdes, Joyce Merrill, 1685
Valdez Pierce, Lorraine, 3213
Valeri-Gold, Maria, 233
van den Hoven, Adrian, 1861
van Dommelen, Deborah, 1100
Van Essen, Arthus, 1084
Van Gelder, Lizette O., 2746, 2747
Van Haalen, Teresa G., 3214, 3215
van Naerssen, Margaret, 1573
Van Peer, Willie, 1416
van Pletzen, Blane F., 3216
Van Schaik, Jennifer D., 3217
Van Slyke, Ann, 818, 1972
Van Wart, Montgomery, 3218
Vance, Kathy, 3219
Vande Berg, Michael, 711
Vander Lei, Elizabeth A., 3220

Vanetti, Lauren, 3221, 3222
Vann, Roberta J., 3223, 3224, 3225, 3226, 3227, 3228
Varonic, Evangeline M., 3229
Vaughan, Caroline, 3230
Velasquez, Clara, 3270, 3271
Verdi, Gail, 2734
Verdorn, Berthea J., 3231
Vergara, Elvira C., 3232
Vernick, Judy A., 1367, 2186
Vetter, Donald, 3233
Vilagra, Olivia, 2512, 2513
Vilamil, Olga, 3234
Villafane, Santiago, 2684
Villamizar, Clara, 1207
Villareal, Ida A., 2198
Vincent, Andre, 90
Vincent, Susan, 3235
Vitanza, Y. J., 302
Voltmer, Barbara, 1311
Voth, Charles, 735

Waanders, Janet, 474
Wagner, Helen, 3236
Wald, Benji, 3237
Walker, Carlene, 3238
Walker Defelix, Judith, 1892
Walker, Dianne, 586
Walker, Michael, 3239
Walker, P., 3240
Wall, Allie Patricia, 3241
Wall, Dianne, 3242, 3243, 3244
Wallace, David, 3245
Wallace, Ray B., 3246, 3247, 3248, 3249, 3250
Walsh, Catherine, 3251
Walsleben, Marjorie C., 3252
Walters, Keith, 3253, 3254
Walters, Larry W., 98, 359, 364, 591, 2148, 2211, 2414, 3124, 3255, 3256, 3302, 3357
Walton, Carolyn, 3257
Walworth, Margaret, 3258
Wang, Changhua, 3156

Wang, Chaobo, 3259
Wang, Moxi, 3260
Wang, Samuel H., 2010
Wang, Shaqui, 3386
Ward, MaryAnn, 2908
Wardell, David, 3261
Watabe, Masakazu, 3262
Waters, Karen, 3263
Watkins-Goffman, Linda, 245, 747, 3264, 3265, 3266, 3267, 3268, 3269, 3270, 3271
Watson, Laura T., 2700, 3272
Watson, Nadine, 650
Watson-Reekie, Cynthia B., 3273
Watts, M., 3274
Weaver, Laurie R., 3275
Webb, Sarah Jone, 3276, 3277
Webb, Susan, 861
Webb, Suzanne S., 3277
Webster, R., 3040
Weeks, Rosanne, 3278
Weiland, Patricia O., 1561, 3118
Weiner, Lauren R., 3279
Weinstein, Gail, 3280
Weinstein-Shr, Gail, 2159, 3281, 3282
Weir, Cyril, 1286, 1308, 3283, 3284
Weissberg, Robert C., 212, 3285, 3286, 3287, 3288, 3289, 3290, 3291, 3292, 3293, 3294
Wenden, Anita L., 613, 3295, 3296
Wenstrom, Laren, 2821
Wenzell, Vanessa, 3297
Werner, Agnes B., 3298
Werner, Patty, 2235
West, G. K., 444, 1395, 3299
Whalen, Karen, 3300
Whalley, Elizabeth, 170, 984, 985, 3301
White, Ronald V., 2587, 2588, 2589, 3302, 3303, 3304, 3305, 3306, 3307, 3435
White, Sheila, 3308
Whitehead, Catherine, 3309
Whitley, Catherine A., 1868, 1969, 3310
Whittaker, Priscilla F., 963, 964
Whittemore, Robert, 2248
Widdowson, Henry G., 522, 1022, 2587, 3131, 3311, 3312, 3313
Wiener, Harvey S., 473
Wiener, Lauren R., 3314, 3315
Wigfield, Jack, 3316, 3317
Wiggin, Barbara, 3318
Wigglesworth, David G., 2740, 2793
Wikborg, Eleanor, 3319, 3320, 3321, 3322
Wilcott, P., 3323
Wilcoxon, Hardy C., 3324
Wilcoxson, Barbara M., 3325
Wiley, Terrence G., 3326
Wilkins, David, 632
Willcott, Paul, 3327, 3328
Williams, Beverly, 3263
Williams, Elaine, 400
Williams, James D., 3329, 3330
Williams, Malcolm P., 3331, 3332, 3333
Williams, R., 134, 1540, 3096
Williams, R. M. E., 3334
Williamson, Julia, 3335
Williamson, Michael M., 1546
Willoquet-Maricondi, Paula, 3336
Wilson, Elaine, 3337, 3338
Windsor, A. T., 3339
Winer, Lise, 3340, 3341, 3342, 3343
Winfield, F. E., 3344
Winfield, Marie Yolette, 3345
Wingfield, R. J., 3346
Wink, Joan, 3347
Winser, Bill, 422

Winter, Esther, 3348
Wintergest, Ann C., 3349
Wiriyachitra, Arunee, 1411
Witbeck, Michael C., 3350
Withrow, Jean, 374, 375, 377, 378, 2084, 3351, 3352, 3353
Witt, Beth, 3354
Witte, Stephen P., 1637
Wohl, Milton, 3355
Wolff, Lisa, 717
Wolfram, Walt, 2461, 3356
Wong, Lian Aik, 3357
Wong, Rita, 3358, 3359, 3360
Wong, Ruth Yeang Lam, 3361
Wong, Sau Ling Cynthia, 3362, 3363
Wong, Shelley D., 3364
Wong, Yim King, 3365
Wongkhan, Siriporn, 3366
Wood, A. S., 3367
Wood, Susan, 2900
Woods, Devon, 3368, 3369
Woodward, Marcia R., 3370
Woodward, Suzanne W., 3371
Wormuth, Deanna R., 1330, 1419, 1483, 1484, 1485, 1529, 3372
Wrase, Judith, 70, 3373
Wright, John T., 3374
Wu, Jingyu, 3386
Wu, Teh Yuan, 3375
Wu, Yiqiang, 3376
Wulf, Kathleen M., 140, 141
Wyatt-Brown, Anne M., 3377, 3378, 3379

Xu, George Q., 3380, 3381, 3382, 3383, 3384

Yalden, Janice, 1056, 1618, 1665, 1688, 2573, 3311
Yamashita, Sayoko Okada, 3385
Yan, Zhuang, 3386
Yao, Luch Chunkun, 3387
Yap, Arthur. 3388

Yates, Robert, 712
Yau, Margaret S. S., 3389, 3390, 3391, 3392, 3393, 3394
Yli-Jokipii, H., 3395
Yobst, Julia, 3396, 3397
Yoder, Linda, 3398
Yontz, Ruth Ann, 164, 3399
Yorio, Carlos A., 104, 968, 1382, 3224, 3400
Yorkey, Richard, 3401
Yoshida, N. J., 3402
Yoshihara, Karen, 3403
Young, Angharad Bransford, 3404
Young, Lynn, 816
Young, Rodney K., 367, 942
Young, Terrell A., 3405
Youngkin, Betty N., 356
Youngquist, Julia A., 264
Yu, Zhen Zhong, 3406
Yuli, Hung Yeh, 2010

Zacker, Judith, 3407, 3408
Zaki, Abdellatif, 2207
Zamel, Vivian, 549, 650, 824, 1846, 2587, 2588, 2589, 3131, 3132, 3133, 3409. 3410, 3411, 3412, 3413, 3414, 3415, 3416, 3417, 3418, 3419, 3420, 3421, 3422, 3423, 3424, 3425, 3426, 3427, 3428, 3429, 3430, 3431, 3432, 3433, 3434, 3435, 3436
Zeider, Moshe, 3437
Zellermayer, Michael, 662, 3438, 3439
Zhang, Dongmei, 2414
Zhang, Feng Xing, 3440
Zhang, Mingsheng, 3386
Zhang, Shuqiang, 1527, 3441, 3442, 3443
Zhang, Xiaolin, 3444, 3445
Zhao, Heping, 3446, 3447
Zhou, Minglang, 3156
Zhu, Hong, 3448

Zhu, Wei, 3449
Ziahosseiny, Seid M., 2327
Zidan, Atta Taha, 3450
Zinkgraf, Stephen A., 1528, 1529
Ziv, Nina D., 3451
Zizi, Khadija, 3452
Zuck, Joyce Gilmour, 2252, 3453, 3454
Zuckerman, Gertrude, 3455
Zughoul, Muhammad R., 3456, 3457
Zukowski-Faust, Jean, 1635, 1636
Zutell, Jerry, 3458, 3459

INDEX OF SUBJECTS

Academic Writing 52, 54, 73, 155, 205, 207, 208, 210, 211, 295, 305, 308, 319, 341, 370, 463, 474, 604, 605, 657, 665, 798, 799, 801, 810, 877, 920, 1016, 1033, 1048, 1146, 1294, 1302, 1307, 1345, 1375, 1382, 1441, 1445, 1447, 1449, 1462, 1541, 1571, 1575, 1578, 1589, 1593, 1596, 1604, 1607, 1634, 1654, 1756, 1759, 1845, 1984, 2089, 2135, 2159, 2213, 2217, 2218, 2216, 2356, 2398, 2512, 2525, 2537, 2587, 2600, 2605, 2617, 2622, 2625, 2691, 2693, 2829, 2910, 2914, 2915, 2918, 2982, 2989, 3004, 3007, 3009, 3010, 3048, 3092, 3096, 3097, 3128, 3142, 3179, 3242, 3244, 3283, 3290, 3387, 3409, 3411

Acculturation 2229

Accuracy 92, 367, 838, 980, 1069, 1070, 1166, 2898

Adjunct 352, 1152, 1581, 2988

Administration 908, 2346, 2749

Adult Education 112, 177, 178, 180, 216, 256, 443, 595, 725, 767, 831, 974, 1102, 1332, 1760, 1958, 2091, 2137, 2142, 2227, 2460, 2513, 2524, 2540, 2753, 2838, 2889, 3024, 3231, 3316, 3317

Advanced 14, 30, 92, 96, 97, 103, 116, 137, 171, 182, 202, 247, 261, 276, 290, 293, 300, 342, 390, 404, 405, 408, 438, 478, 528, 537, 547, 554, 558, 599, 609, 675, 676, 693, 742, 751, 766, 787, 819, 834, 840, 854, 868, 873, 916, 951, 1029, 1030, 1035, 1037, 1040, 1041, 1042, 1043, 1086, 1194, 1237, 1241, 1246, 1258, 1283, 1303, 1320, 1330, 1450, 1497, 1556, 1646, 1698, 1708, 1751, 1754, 1787, 1849, 1874, 1889, 1895, 1898, 1955, 1978, 2013, 2017, 2032, 2045, 2054, 2070, 2076, 2077, 2089, 2093, 2095, 2098, 2167, 2172, 2194, 2203, 2219, 2258, 2259, 2273, 2392, 2395, 2425, 2426, 2500, 2639, 2698, 2725, 2787, 2805, 2806, 2856, 2916, 2919, 2920, 2944, 2952, 2981, 3008, 3009, 3021, 3067, 3069, 3136, 3167, 3202, 3208, 3241, 3261, 3268, 3270, 3271, 3291, 3327, 3355, 3363, 3373

Affect 174, 234, 271, 590, 932, 986, 1570, 2036, 2104, 2206, 2253, 2470, 2782, 3163, 3168, 3169, 3252, 3253, 3376

Alaskan 167, 168, 169, 3263, 3301

Amer-Indian 4, 128, 159, 160, 161, 162, 163, 559, 702, 857, 888, 1061, 1134, 1135, 1204, 1270, 1493, 1520, 1910, 2163, 2164, 2506, 2509, 2510, 2511, 3030, 3354, 3356

Anxiety 260, 414, 846, 1218, 1232, 1233, 1458, 2105, 2468, 2573, 2751, 3400

Approaches 76, 254, 327, 369, 370, 411, 714, 948, 1031, 1045, 1058, 1089, 1161, 1279, 1866, 2117, 2120, 2150, 2156, 2284, 2335, 2400, 2427, 2478, 2553, 2776, 2778, 2801, 2928, 3126, 3306, 3416

Arabic 2, 7, 8, 9, 35, 36, 37, 38, 39, 61, 108, 109, 118, 122, 132, 144, 147 195, 242, 415, 417, 426, 513, 592, 755, 817, 863, 923, 929, 930, 932, 933, 934, 936, 939, 940, 941, 990, 1128, 1244, 1250,

1268, 1312, 1340, 1379, 1418, 1664, 1669, 1670, 1702, 1704, 1739, 1745, 1796, 1798, 2063, 2078, 2116, 2209, 2244, 2255, 2289, 2312, 2348, 2350, 2355, 2357, 2379, 2537, 2539, 2600, 2601, 2623, 2696, 2764, 2772, 2841, 2861, 2888, 2890, 2891, 2960, 2969, 2997, 3107, 3116, 3162, 3171, 3172, 3176, 3177, 3186, 3219, 3225, 3226, 3254, 3300, 3323, 3328, 3331, 3332, 3333, 3401, 3450, 3452

Argumentation 164, 317, 553, 564, 572, 573, 574, 575, 637, 639, 643, 648, 649, 684, 692, 747, 845, 879, 991, 993, 1502, 1576, 1669, 1670, 1727, 2658 2961, 3269, 3314, 3365

Asian 319, 364, 497, 707, 976, 1314, 1397, 1793, 2055, 2109, 2146, 2210, 2265, 2496, 2532, 2599, 2659, 3121, 3124, 3206, 3255, 3301, 3357

Asian American 3256

ASL 1130, 2387

Assessment 22, 23, 40, 42, 43, 53, 100, 104, 105, 135, 167, 222, 311, 343, 367, 379, 391, 397, 474, 475, 476, 494, 495, 496, 532, 545, 570, 592, 597, 610, 629, 637, 644, 652, 708, 709, 710, 746, 757, 776, 778, 779, 781, 783, 786, 802, 806, 807, 808, 809, 842, 897, 917, 925, 967, 969, 987, 1002, 1057, 1078, 1093, 1094, 1174, 1192, 1198, 1200, 1272, 1273, 1274, 1275, 1276, 1277, 1278, 1280, 1281, 1282, 1284, 1285, 1286, 1287, 1289, 1291, 1292, 1294, 1295, 1296, 1298, 1299, 1302, 1304, 1305, 1306, 1307, 1308, 1309, 1310, 1311, 1313, 1378, 1381, 1387, 1415, 1419, 1426, 1427, 1438, 1479, 1480, 1485, 1528, 1529, 1545, 1546, 1550, 1551, 1567, 1583, 1612, 1632, 1636, 1650, 1665, 1666, 1667, 1675, 1692, 1711, 1716, 1717, 1740, 1781, 1785, 1791, 1794, 1816, 1819, 1821, 1835, 1839, 1864, 1869, 1917, 1926, 1946, 1980, 1981, 2082, 2084, 2132, 2148, 2171, 2189, 2190, 2191, 2257, 2290, 2332, 2382, 2422, 2423, 2428, 2432, 2433, 2465, 2494, 2498, 2522, 2527, 2528, 2533, 2534, 2550, 2558, 2605, 2606, 2645, 2650, 2651, 2695, 2697, 2744, 2780, 2803, 2830, 2840, 2996, 2999, 3001, 3002, 3022, 3027, 3036, 3038, 3039, 3040, 3051, 3052, 3101, 3102, 3113, 3120, 3134, 3135, 3142, 3144, 3146, 3185, 3188, 3190, 3213, 3230, 3243, 3338, 3348, 3349, 3372, 3457

Assignments 340, 442, 465, 577, 582, 733, 750, 844, 1131, 1237, 1282, 1368, 1384, 1448, 1482, 1809, 1820, 1824, 1827, 1830, 1831, 1854, 1933, 2032, 2071, 2128, 2183, 2212, 2217, 2415, 2442, 2719, 2728, 2738, 2843, 2919, 3137

Audience 208, 339, 461, 699, 1165, 1214, 1241, 1346, 1442, 1443, 1555, 1591, 1743, 2074, 2151, 2168, 2169, 2612, 2617, 2622, 2642, 2653, 2719, 2730, 2768, 2827, 2962, 3092, 3125, 3249

Background Knowledge 456, 591, 1064, 1067, 1280, 1558, 1590, 2604, 2874, 2877, 3143, 3344, 3446

Bantu 2300

Beginners 3, 10, 13, 124, 174, 176, 190, 216, 229, 240, 274, 283, 285, 312, 315, 327, 328, 371, 375, 377, 383, 388, 400, 421, 432, 433, 514, 542, 598, 631, 753, 780, 883, 919, 996, 1091, 1175, 1209,

1247, 1332, 1333, 1337, 1338, 1363, 1364, 1366, 1370, 1486, 1487, 1513, 1514, 1515, 1516, 1539, 1553, 1753, 1760, 1842, 1843, 1855, 1912, 1925, 1979, 2085, 2227, 2233, 2299, 2315, 2328, 2379, 2396, 2480, 2486, 2499, 2524, 2591, 2592, 2628, 2677, 2682, 2709, 2721, 2838, 2901, 2923, 2990, 3033, 3071, 3126, 3129, 3130, 3239, 3358, 3359

Bibliography 355, 407, 579, 603, 1157, 1631, 1706, 1856, 1989, 1990, 1991, 1992, 1993, 1994, 2054, 2069, 2270, 2322, 2323, 2324, 2692, 2746, 2747, 2836, 2855, 2903, 2945, 2946, 2947, 3277, 3382

Bilingual 718, 901, 908, 909, 944, 992, 1101, 1265, 1285, 1336, 1468, 1488, 1651, 2060, 2221, 2296, 2418, 2717, 2788, 2819, 3192, 3211, 3212, 3330

Brazil 326, 1025, 1540

Business Writing 368, 442, 463, 628, 636, 640, 641, 663, 853, 1559, 1601, 1602, 1605, 2015, 2018, 2064, 2083, 2247, 2593, 2595, 2694, 2788, 2954, 3261, 3314, 3395

Cambodian 1435, 2953

Chemistry 1167

Children 49, 50, 65, 156, 250, 460, 470, 527, 535, 602, 701, 716, 883, 901, 904, 905, 906, 907, 910, 971, 973, 976, 1003, 1014, 1050, 1051, 1120, 1135, 1266, 1270, 1355, 1468, 1469, 1470, 1472, 1473, 1495, 1496, 1522, 1531, 1535, 1624, 1755, 1805, 1873, 2061, 2096, 2129, 2197, 2268, 2296, 2328, 2416, 2493, 2675, 2712, 2780, 2782, 2783,

2784, 2785, 2857, 2864, 3030, 3157, 3205, 3206, 3207, 3213, 3281, 3394, 3458, 3459

Chinese 57, 78, 99, 100, 144, 205, 213, 295, 297, 298, 299, 301, 302, 357, 359, 362, 450, 498, 501, 504, 508, 531, 552, 553, 554, 556, 558, 561, 583, 607, 608, 687, 696, 763, 804, 836, 884, 885, 923, 956, 972, 990, 1076, 1116, 1151, 1236, 1254, 1352, 1396, 1410, 1460, 1567, 1594, 1599, 1634, 1637, 1684, 1701, 1720, 1726, 1754, 1798, 1821, 1850, 1857, 1859, 1881, 1902, 1903, 1904, 1905, 1906, 1908, 1917, 1921, 1923, 1924, 1951, 1959, 1960, 1961, 1962, 1983, 2009, 2010, 2011, 2012, 2021, 2033, 2040, 2078, 2101, 2111, 2112, 2113, 2147, 2149, 2224, 2225, 2296, 2304, 2305, 2306, 2337, 2341, 2414, 2477, 2482, 2623, 2696, 2737, 2828, 2853, 2902, 2935, 2961, 2982, 3029, 3055, 3061, 3082, 3106, 3139, 3153, 3154, 3156, 3166, 3197, 3198, 3259, 3324, 3361, 3362, 3364, 3365, 3376, 3384, 3386, 3387, 3389, 3392, 3440, 3442, 3447, 3448

Classroom Activities 159, 256, 287, 416, 477, 587, 760, 766, 854, 892, 902, 926, 1024, 1062, 1229, 1390, 1425, 1433, 1508, 1767, 1773, 1897, 2028, 2085, 2186, 2228, 2383, 2389, 2394, 2444, 2462, 2574, 2700, 2708, 2809, 2880, 2967, 3042, 3064, 3081, 3130, 3238, 3249, 3272, 3410, 3932

Classroom Research 372, 650, 912, 1542, 2277

Cognition 20, 88, 89, 121, 504, 719, 724, 730, 825, 958, 1206, 1617, 1803, 1898, 2114, 3421

Coherence 34, 56, 143, 223, 425, 459, 477, 485, 487, 488, 550, 572, 574, 575, 607, 645, 649, 654, 655, 658, 670, 949, 965, 966, 1125, 1126, 1168, 1325, 1338, 1434, 1442, 1511, 1532, 1534, 1593, 1598, 1599, 1621, 1626, 1789, 1893, 1894, 1966, 1984, 1986, 1987, 1988, 2133, 2438, 2662, 2663, 2827, 2851, 2888, 3093, 3289, 3319, 3321, 3322, 3324, 3448

Cohesion 34, 38, 39, 56, 72, 73, 74, 117, 122, 127, 316, 317, 365, 366, 485, 487, 488, 513, 569, 571, 649, 697, 843, 852, 853, 941, 968, 977, 979, 997, 1076, 1126, 1312, 1335, 1340, 1418, 1460, 1533, 1534, 1537, 1569, 1602, 1603, 1605, 1606, 1626, 1653, 1739, 1847, 1907, 1911, 1927, 1928, 1998, 1999, 2003, 2005, 2007, 2063, 2078, 2087, 2088, 2101, 2127, 2162, 2222, 2247, 2306, 2325, 2370, 2530, 2596, 2614, 2737, 3745, 2772, 2826, 2850, 2863, 3046, 3084, 3162, 3222, 3324, 3331, 3332, 3333, 3429, 3442, 3448

Collaboration 4, 25, 41, 114, 448, 464, 499, 531, 624, 733, 749, 799, 827, 834, 878, 894, 1012, 1047, 1052, 1227, 1231, 1360, 1515, 1846, 1913, 1914, 2107, 2260, 2311, 2459, 2507, 2515, 2529, 2616, 2618, 2626, 2652, 2812, 2927, 3221, 3354, 3380, 3419

Collocation 3445

Communicative Writing 114, 1618, 1619, 1621, 1622, 2894, 2895, 2896, 3071, 3158, 3307, 3311, 3312, 3313, 3315

Computers 44, 133, 136, 152, 154, 193, 217, 227, 228, 236, 237, 304, 346, 357, 358, 360, 361, 362, 363, 427, 431, 448, 523, 567, 631, 653, 685, 758, 759, 882, 894, 919, 988, 1004, 1016, 1025, 1028, 1053, 1088, 1118, 1119, 1127, 1316, 1317, 1385, 1386, 1565, 1624, 1625, 1662, 1733, 1749, 1762, 1769, 1795, 1858, 1862, 1871, 1909, 1913, 1914, 1956, 1959, 2009, 2010, 2011, 2012, 2107, 2124, 2138, 2141, 2287, 2293, 2297, 2318, 2377, 2378, 2406, 2408, 2410, 2411, 2412, 2456, 2466, 2467, 2468, 2469, 2471, 2472, 2473, 2474, 2475, 2476, 2480, 2491, 2492, 2507, 2546, 2620, 2630, 2633, 2634, 2636, 2637, 2641, 2648, 2649, 2674, 2716, 2760, 2819, 2820, 2823, 2829, 2907, 2949, 2993, 3058, 3059, 3063, 3162, 3163, 3184, 3193, 3215, 3218, 3257, 3405

Conferencing 32, 200, 266, 308, 337, 481, 538, 672, 740, 741, 982, 994, 1034, 1080, 1082, 1083, 1154, 1155, 1156, 1160, 1327, 1339, 1347, 1348, 1349, 1350, 1492, 1627, 1629, 1662, 1712, 2039, 2089, 2136, 2213, 2269, 2297, 2516, 2813, 2976, 2995, 3070, 2118, 3370, 3383

Content 10, 52, 352, 505, 840, 1095, 1408, 1533, 2091, 2211, 2580, 2893, 2989, 3005, 3147, 3151, 3258, 3290

Contrastive Analysis 1189

Contrastive Rhetoric 1, 8, 9, 57, 78, 148, 265, 296, 297, 298, 302, 303, 317, 408, 512, 534, 553, 556, 573, 575, 600, 601, 603, 634, 635, 640, 648, 656, 660, 662, 667, 668, 678, 679, 680, 687, 709, 763, 768, 811, 819, 879, 885, 896, 921, 934, 972, 990, 991, 1023, 1179, 1180, 1183, 1184, 1185, 1203, 1236, 1251, 1340, 1396, 1397, 1398, 1399, 1400, 1452, 1453, 1454, 1499, 1509, 1557,

1559, 1633, 1656, 1657, 1670, 1679, 1681, 1682, 1683, 1684, 1685, 1686, 1687, 1688, 1689, 1691, 1693, 1694, 1695, 1696, 1697, 1699, 1700, 1701, 1702, 1703, 1704, 1705, 1706, 1707, 1710, 1727, 1742, 1747, 1754, 1774, 1777, 1780, 1781, 1789, 1797, 1801, 1802, 1810, 1923, 1937, 1967, 1970, 1975, 1977, 2017, 2021, 2030, 2041, 2056, 2059, 2067, 2076, 2097, 2122, 2133, 2149, 2223, 2224, 2225, 2231, 2246, 2292, 2298, 2303, 2305, 2306, 2307, 2326, 2333, 2347, 2348, 2349, 2354, 2355, 2358, 2372, 2463, 2535, 2536, 2602, 2608, 2619, 2622, 2623, 2629, 2663, 2664, 2665, 2690, 2691, 2796, 2797, 2828, 2842, 2847, 2881, 3072, 3073, 3106, 3114, 3139, 3166, 3171, 3172, 3176, 3177, 3197, 3198, 3233, 3309, 3314, 3362, 3364, 3365, 3401, 3452

Control 47, 51, 87, 119, 131, 175, 176, 331, 332, 417, 518, 622, 765, 890, 893, 1045, 1046, 1173, 1433, 1544, 1722, 1751, 1761, 1767, 1972, 2028, 2062, 2123, 2233, 2258, 2315, 2389, 2391, 2501, 2518, 2583, 2584, 2721, 2739, 2740, 2967, 2968, 2979, 3023, 3126, 3149, 3291

Conventions 164, 316, 630, 2309, 2369

Courses 220, 418, 481, 531, 624, 880, 961, 998, 1036, 1086, 1102, 1131, 1430, 1541, 1616, 1709, 1752, 1877, 2043, 2102, 2273, 2352, 2425, 2480, 2531, 2853, 2915, 2918, 2958, 3152, 3335

Creative Writing 46, 82, 794, 1193, 1414, 1850, 2062, 2103, 2165, 2178, 2509, 2510, 2520, 2727, 2857, 3240, 3274

Creole 1185, 1420, 3173, 3341, 3342

Critical Thinking 1423

Culture 41, 58, 134, 165, 167, 168, 169, 170, 188, 243, 364, 472, 499, 600, 601, 604, 605, 608, 643, 666, 677, 762, 764, 801, 845, 870, 871, 1020, 1023, 1061, 1104, 1142, 1161, 1165, 1170, 1212, 1292, 1296, 1320, 1323, 1416, 1456, 1510, 1575, 1579, 1659, 1685, 1730, 1765, 1784, 1904, 2031, 2037, 2042, 2113, 2351, 2434, 2481, 2535, 2536, 2601, 2702, 2723, 2731, 2754, 2759, 2843, 2858, 2902, 2950, 3049, 3083, 3123, 3254, 3258, 3344, 3345, 3366, 3438

Curriculum 84, 89, 125, 130, 140, 221, 226, 233, 245, 280, 318, 331, 380, 396, 399, 412, 521, 551, 568, 580, 673, 748, 829, 891, 902, 1036, 1205, 1259, 1338, 1473, 1494, 1523, 1600, 1659, 1876, 1887, 2153, 2284, 2344, 2377, 2393, 2399, 2440, 2441, 2630, 2639, 2644, 2649, 2668, 2686, 2710, 2715, 2723, 2749, 2752, 2805, 2845, 2984, 2985, 3009, 3014, 3065, 3157, 3329, 3384

Danish 2508

Description 489, 3057

Development 470, 903, 936, 966, 1120, 1203, 1501, 2264, 2341, 2448, 2864

Dialogue Journals 197, 353, 354, 423, 462, 762, 847, 848, 849, 850, 857, 927, 1012, 1101, 1139, 1207, 1210, 1223, 1224, 1225, 1649, 1652, 1805, 1806, 1995, 1996, 1997, 2036, 2173, 2174, 2181, 2208, 2250, 2270, 2446, 2447, 2448, 2449, 2450, 2451, 2452, 2453, 2454, 2455, 2457, 2458, 2459, 2460,

2541, 3043, 3044, 3048, 3049, 3117, 3221, 3245, 3258, 3343, 3405

Dictionaries 91, 2599

Discourse Analysis 35, 191, 262, 522, 706, 921, 1113, 1125, 1168, 1334, 1383, 1640, 1180, 2252, 2437, 2680, 2906, 3031, 3035, 3032, 3399, 3454

Discourse Communities 134, 203, 206, 207, 507, 640, 657, 750, 816, 1093, 1137, 1439, 1588, 1718, 2108, 2600, 3010, 3012, 3090, 3140, 3251, 3410

Drafting 413, 838

Drills 2793

Dutch 1463, 3076, 3203

EAP 750, 1579, 3098

East Asian 2690

Editing 6, 15, 71, 103, 106, 190, 228, 251, 328, 404, 441, 541, 837, 1028, 1079, 1081, 1238, 1417, 1737, 1863, 1924, 1939, 2121, 2377, 2552, 2598, 2859, 2900, 2913, 3045, 3194

EFL Elementary 48, 90, 197, 424, 464, 467, 468, 515, 526, 530, 580, 597, 794, 858, 895, 898, 903, 983, 1012, 1028, 1053, 1134, 1160, 1213, 1265, 1341, 1435, 1474, 1488, 1614, 1625, 1733, 1806, 1865, 1964, 2006, 2198, 2229, 2294, 2310, 2366, 2451, 2452, 2458, 2541, 2779, 2781, 2998, 3078, 3214, 3236, 3265, 3266, 3325

ELTS 1276, 1277, 1286, 1289, 1291, 1295, 1298, 1304

Engineering 1561, 1576

Error 3383

Error Analysis 60, 77, 81, 128, 179, 185, 255, 313, 511, 559, 583, 701, 758, 868, 918, 929, 939, 995, 1030, 1081, 1132, 1194, 1196, 1199, 1216, 1268, 1321, 1391, 1410, 1424, 1518, 1606, 1655, 1693, 1726, 1784, 1837, 1838, 1919, 1921, 1952, 1962, 2116, 2139, 2199, 2255, 2288, 2294, 2312, 2373, 2483, 2678, 2688, 2861, 2891, 2959, 2963, 2980, 3053, 3058, 3308, 3328, 3341, 3342, 3363

Error Gravity 28, 294, 734, 788, 1478, 1538, 1547, 1549, 1741, 1748, 1778, 1779, 2000, 2130, 2802, 2803, 2804, 2904, 2905, 2908, 3099, 3115, 3154, 3227, 3228

Error Treatment 248, 320, 321, 465, 520, 533, 541, 732, 782, 803, 826, 911, 985, 1098, 1187, 1371, 1372, 1373, 1374, 1432, 1858, 1935, 2087, 2088, 2121, 2134, 2204, 2598, 2603, 2670, 2687, 2859, 2979, 3159, 3204, 3346, 3350

Errors 5, 18, 27, 61, 66, 172, 194, 195, 248, 268, 311, 323, 403, 419, 420, 427, 540, 592, 691, 863, 900, 1026, 1029, 1079, 1215, 1234, 1253, 1331, 1415, 1603, 1664, 1740, 1826, 1830, 1910, 1950, 2098, 2482, 2555, 2562, 2673, 2684, 2767, 2769, 2772, 2878, 2900, 3013, 3054, 3102, 3138, 3148, 3323, 3356

ESP 75, 149, 200, 204, 263, 305, 322, 336, 338, 339, 340, 529, 569, 876, 877, 878, 961, 1005, 1150, 1167, 1177, 1250, 1288, 1298, 1382, 1383, 1395, 1457, 1464, 1466, 1467, 1477, 1531, 1532,

1561, 1582, 1584, 1601, 1672, 1853, 2029, 2109, 2110, 2122, 2220, 2247, 2263, 2301, 2313, 2336, 2375, 2376, 2445, 2608, 2668, 2693, 2834, 2855, 2871, 2873, 2874, 2875, 2876, 2897, 2975, 3026, 3029, 3076, 3085, 3093, 3096, 3107, 3108, 3122, 3152, 3195, 3219, 3232, 3243, 3246, 3248, 3288, 3291, 3292, 3294, 3299, 3318, 3367, 3379, 3386, 3406, 3452

Ethiopia 1746

Ethnographic Research 178, 529, 831, 839, 976, 1103, 1104, 1127, 1222, 1228, 1265, 1802, 1974, 2108, 2263, 2525, 2848, 3168, 3191, 3255

Evaluation 23, 24, 66, 69, 147, 150, 252, 314, 323, 347, 351, 367, 394, 397, 459, 469, 471, 473, 480, 532, 548, 565, 578, 642, 722, 734, 775, 784, 785, 802, 818, 826, 856, 860, 886, 968, 975, 1009, 1010, 1017, 1026, 1032, 1070, 1096, 1097, 1198, 1261, 1288, 1297, 1313, 1319, 1377, 1379, 1380, 1422, 1480, 1485, 1529, 1537, 1584, 1639, 1655, 1658, 1770, 1868, 1875, 1883, 1885, 1887, 1947, 2137, 2139, 2187, 2234, 2256, 2320, 2371, 2419, 2420, 2421, 2426, 2429, 2430, 2464, 2538, 2554, 2621, 2631, 2656, 2732, 2755, 2756, 2757, 2785, 2802, 2849, 2850, 2904, 2940, 2951, 2971, 2986, 3090, 3100, 3111, 3112, 3141, 3174, 3210, 3337, 3437, 3456

Examination Essays 1197, 1262, 1402, 1403, 1440, 1458, 1585, 2043, 2118, 2170, 2337, 3022, 3097

Exercises 1972, 2505, 2653

Expertise 551, 719, 722, 728, 729, 730

Exposition 80, 556, 667, 668, 669, 868, 884, 895, 933, 1181, 1182, 1250, 1355, 1672, 1927, 2059, 2272, 2308, 2350, 2358, 2562, 2662, 2826, 2886, 3200, 3252

Expressive Writing 289, 1407, 2726

Farsi 811, 1710

Feedback 61, 98, 151, 239, 247, 322, 323, 330, 543, 547, 611, 613, 614, 615, 616, 617, 619, 620, 621, 623, 821, 945, 980, 982, 985, 989, 1048, 1253, 1260, 1261, 1284, 1492, 1503, 1524, 1525, 1527, 1721, 1838, 1862, 1952, 1961, 2126, 2131, 2214, 2234, 2380, 2384, 2406, 2475, 2479, 2542, 2555, 2687, 2689, 2758, 2878, 2917, 2987, 3021, 3244, 3441

Filipino 1522

Film 2125, 2155

Finnish 700, 1189, 1511, 1847, 2122, 2678

Fluency 92, 119, 350, 417, 518, 577, 586, 588, 954, 1166, 1542, 1773, 2052, 2583, 2729, 2732, 2734, 2898, 3189, 3245, 3390

Form 755, 1337, 1368

Free Writing 1247, 1982, 2175, 2501, 2879, 3129

French 460, 754, 973, 1120, 1254, 1322, 1451, 1557, 1559, 1861, 1873, 2061, 2292, 2438, 2439, 2608, 3300, 3452

Freshman Composition 334, 584, 862, 1137, 1562, 2053, 2521, 2676, 2929,

3173

FSP 1505, 2245, 2246

Gender 421, 422, 806, 807, 1611, 1612

Generative Rhetoric 83, 162, 2180

Genre 490, 491, 876, 1015, 1176, 1177, 1271, 1351, 1502, 1571, 1580, 2038, 2271, 2381, 3092, 3094, 3098, 3286

German 33, 600, 601, 602, 603, 604, 605, 1196, 2381

Grading 1596, 2689

Graduate Students 100, 210, 813, 1033, 1752, 1824, 1924, 2102, 2301 2397, 2398, 2414, 2515, 2525, 2897, 3379, 3386

Grammar 19, 59, 68, 245, 386, 431, 439, 520, 521, 628, 672, 756, 864, 928, 929, 1035, 1042, 1077, 1090, 1099, 1102, 1188, 1420, 1421, 1498, 1554, 1564, 1615, 1677, 1709, 1719, 1871, 1905, 2009, 2010, 2012, 2086, 2265, 2362, 2363, 2557, 2591, 2766, 2813, 2913, 2970, 3397, 3403, 3432, 3446

Greek 1478, 1734, 2303

Group Projects 2144

Group Work 249, 590, 913, 1128, 1228, 1364, 1535, 2285, 2489

Haitian 235, 2303

Handwriting 3, 132, 241, 242, 415, 437, 2081, 2119, 2254, 2289, 2884

Hearing-Impaired 33, 969, 1148, 2114, 2388, 2456

Hebrew 971, 1023, 3438, 3439, 3455

Hindi 583, 1656, 1657, 1810, 2373

Hispanic 12, 65, 144, 153, 189, 194, 205, 250, 260, 273, 313, 333, 424, 467, 468, 511, 593, 596, 669, 678, 679, 680, 701, 702, 716, 744, 747, 795, 796, 797, 817, 932, 836, 887, 901, 903, 904, 906, 907, 910, 929, 944, 986, 992, 1013, 1076, 1088, 1104, 1105, 1108, 1109, 1110, 1113, 1114, 1115, 1117, 1134, 1135, 1151, 1164, 1165, 1185, 1207, 1215, 1221, 1257, 1266, 1321, 1341, 1393, 1415, 1435, 1474, 1488, 1608, 1625, 1647, 1651, 1712, 1715, 1738, 1764, 1798, 1839, 1840, 1841, 1865, 1954, 2041, 2042, 2048, 2078, 2099, 2129, 2159, 2176, 2192, 2199, 2229, 2231, 2232, 2288, 2294, 2305, 2364, 2403, 2418, 2445, 2502, 2531, 2623, 2659, 2684, 2696, 2713, 2714, 2722, 2788, 2789, 2790, 2796, 2797, 2886, 2904, 2956, 2974, 3026, 3039, 3072, 3073, 3174, 3191, 3192, 3215, 3234, 3237, 3238, 3251, 3293, 3444, 3458, 3459

Hmong 3282

Holistic 393, 480, 651, 652, 1426, 1479, 1546, 1550, 1711, 2382, 2650, 2651, 2756, 2971, 3027, 3099, 3349

Hong Kong 2023

Hungarian 2128, 2435, 3167, 3179

Ideology 1201, 1574, 2145, 2798, 3409

IEA 808, 1174, 2533, 2538, 3113, 3210

IEP 126, 399, 449, 480, 1144, 1412,

1716, 2345, 2356, 2500, 2650, 2655, 2817, 2830, 2944, 3168

Imitation 2671, 2672

India 262, 2905

Indochinese 2463

Indonesian 1887, 2502

Instruction 20, 26, 257, 402, 458, 505, 526, 546, 713, 720, 790, 793, 818, 843, 914, 1056, 1110, 1123, 1164, 1329, 1526, 1818, 1936, 1966, 1969, 2117, 2176, 2266, 2490, 2512, 2548, 2553, 2556, 2564, 2565, 2571, 2588, 2620, 2624, 2646, 2683, 2767, 2790, 2791, 2839, 2860, 2937, 2943, 2949, 2991, 3260, 3384, 3404, 3435, 3450

Interaction 151, 462, 484, 486, 543, 741, 820, 849, 850, 999, 1512, 1609, 2455, 2762, 3118

Interlanguage 147, 1845, 2872

Intermediate 82, 104, 111, 138, 173, 180, 230, 261, 275, 284, 286, 291, 292, 307, 331, 378, 411, 433, 434, 435, 439, 449, 490, 491, 606, 683, 717, 752, 765, 774, 793, 800, 803, 835, 837, 873, 918, 952, 954, 1035, 1043, 1044, 1045, 1087, 1090, 1122, 1172, 1237, 1243, 1330, 1357, 1375, 1411, 1635, 1638, 1668, 1735, 1757, 1765, 1842, 1843, 1874, 1896, 1901, 1916, 1925, 2016, 2018, 2105, 2188, 2302, 2317, 2321, 2339, 2340, 2361, 2365, 2367, 2368, 2392, 2400, 2491, 2520, 2523, 2581, 2644, 2647, 2648, 2661, 2681, 2706, 2724, 2817, 2822, 2866, 2920, 2924, 2958, 2994, 3080, 3102, 3335, 3351

Introductions 155, 299, 1654

Invention 85, 129, 139, 203, 204, 413, 771, 772, 773, 774, 1027, 1046, 1329, 1462, 1507, 1517, 1526, 1660, 1844, 1874, 1920, 1974, 2144, 2152, 2154, 2155, 2330, 2543, 2635, 2640, 2666, 2718, 2751, 3015, 3016, 3020, 3241, 3380, 3396

Iran 120, 1117, 1453, 1537, 3308

Italian 2910

Japanese 9, 213, 403, 426, 498, 503, 641, 669, 671, 792, 812, 814, 815, 896, 953, 990, 1132, 1185, 1223, 1236, 1318, 1320, 1396, 1397, 1398, 1399, 1400, 1557, 1559, 1608, 1747, 1774, 1776, 17777, 1781, 1796, 1807, 1808, 1821, 1841, 1949, 1957, 2067, 2298, 2325, 2326, 2333, 2348, 2603, 2662, 2663, 2680, 2737, 2741, 2814, 2886, 2921, 2922, 2987, 3077, 3114, 3115, 3200, 3209, 3261, 3304, 3334, 3366, 3385

Journal Writing 566, 690, 858, 859, 881, 1191, 1192, 1195, 1409, 1809, 1860, 1888, 1942, 1943, 2034, 2035, 2037, 2038, 2711, 3017, 3018, 3222, 3256, 3339, 3406

Journals 2728, 2736, 2742

Korean 28, 144, 213, 427, 534, 571, 572, 573, 574, 575, 594, 920, 1070, 1396, 1501, 1748, 1918, 1927, 1928, 2212, 2307, 2308, 2824, 2825, 3399 L1

Influence 118, 159, 160, 419, 420, 460, 500, 501, 502, 503, 701, 724, 727, 747, 923, 1066, 1067, 1109, 1111, 1322, 1336, 1451, 1608, 1647, 1663, 1775, 1776, 1869, 1903, 1906, 2199, 2237, 2288,

2403, 2696, 2806, 3082, 3089, 3109, 3110, 3209, 3262

L1-L2 Comparison 7, 9, 796, 825, 930, 988, 1049, 1065, 1066, 1067, 1134, 1135, 1796, 1983, 2239, 2240, 2241, 2242, 2243, 2338, 2797, 2841, 2931, 2932, 2964, 2965, 3276, 3376

Lab Report Writing 336, 338

Laboratory 395, 894, 1795, 2793

Language Development 144, 1163, 1270, 1800, 1806, 1837, 1881, 1882, 1982, 3392, 3421

Laotian 1575, 1579

Large Classes 625, 844, 913, 1506, 2810, 2811

Law 127

LEA 13, 216, 410, 767, 1755, 1958, 2675

Learning Styles 493, 494, 495, 496, 870, 1971

Letter Writing 79, 423, 763, 959, 1112, 1231, 2006, 2248, 2654, 2795, 2834, 3042, 3233

Lexis 91, 343, 933, 943, 2001, 2002, 2802, 3357

L1 Influence 1064, 1105, 1951, 2805, 3300

Listening-Writing Relations 1190, 1491, 1750, 1768, 2334, 3250

Literacy 50, 112, 157, 199, 211, 272, 278, 501, 502, 498, 508, 516, 561, 596, 695, 718, 721, 725, 736, 738, 764, 870, 871, 887, 905, 937, 938, 956, 957, 1001, 1003, 1051, 1101, 1151, 1169, 1178, 1245, 1342, 1356, 1431, 1435, 1436, 1439, 1453, 1473, 1495, 1521, 1583, 1736, 1764, 1783, 1855, 2033, 2048, 2052, 2142, 2145, 2158, 2166, 2196, 2197, 2229, 2319, 2329, 2353, 2387, 2401, 2403, 2454, 2460, 2506, 2675, 2701, 2703, 2704, 2707, 2717, 2748, 2750, 2889, 3025, 3089, 3104, 3157, 3207, 3237, 3263, 3276, 3280, 3281, 3282, 3297, 3326, 3330, 3411

Literature 115, 527, 688, 690, 1100, 1136, 1421, 1439, 1746, 2026, 2055, 2103, 2161, 2302, 2495, 2530, 2686, 2770, 2854, 3003, 3014, 3124, 3199, 3336

Logs 231, 2699

LOR 1143, 1784, 2434, 2824

Macedonian 1786

Malawi 564, 565

Malay 144, 563, 591, 817, 1499, 1500, 1505, 1626, 2245, 2246, 2267

Malaysia 2261

Mali 1216

Marathi 2372

Materials 68, 405, 515, 537, 540, 869, 872, 873, 946, 1005, 1132, 1191, 1230, 1300, 1358, 1362, 1577, 1601, 1620, 1638, 1730, 1738, 1828, 2008, 2024, 2142, 2157, 2561, 2566, 2591, 2658, 2887, 2955, 2983, 3056, 3083, 3098, 3217, 3231

Mechanics 1417, 2328

Media 1136, 2343, 2809

Medicine 842

Metacognition 152, 319, 822, 823, 1242, 1519, 1749, 2547, 2624, 2791, 3267, 3295

Methods 83, 446, 841, 935, 1018, 1362, 2322, 2336, 2584, 2794, 2816, 2992, 3183

Micronesia 1211, 1212

Middle School 385, 416, 992, 1737, 2198, 2300, 3191, 3192, 3297, 3375

Models 176, 576, 735, 1891, 1892, 3273, 3288

Monitoring 837, 2603

Motivation 79, 519, 795, 1350, 1352, 1390, 1641, 1852, 2045, 2079, 2216, 3165, 3235

Narration 31, 80, 326, 429, 812, 1006, 1014, 1326, 1343, 1509, 1510, 1715, 1810, 1841, 1965, 1983, 2305, 2502, 2682, 2961, 2998, 3119

Narrative 161, 306

Needs 585, 702, 1833, 2210

Networking 133, 2456, 2819

Newspaper 2024

Nigerian 5, 897, 2330

Norwegian 966, 1236, 1254, 2007, 2220

Note-Taking 246, 1208

NS-NNS Comparisons 29, 70, 80, 90, 99, 133, 150, 183, 185, 188, 194, 214, 225, 232, 233, 313, 343, 372, 386, 389, 391, 392, 393, 398, 406, 414, 430, 454, 456, 535, 538, 555, 571, 589, 667, 677, 712, 744, 769, 788, 814, 815, 823, 860, 861, 866, 880, 888, 937, 946, 955, 987, 991, 993, 997, 998, 999, 1006, 1008, 1011, 1029, 1034, 1047, 1055, 1078, 1086, 1116, 1117, 1133, 1150, 1183, 1196, 1197, 1213, 1233, 1256, 1350, 1401, 1402, 1403, 1437, 1459, 1469, 1478, 1532, 1534, 1547, 1549, 1558, 1592, 1611, 1640, 1673, 1694, 1714, 1715, 1766, 1778, 1779, 1812, 1835, 1960, 1968, 1970, 1975, 1998, 1999, 2001, 2020, 2053, 2063, 2064, 2068, 2078, 2094, 2101, 2115, 2129, 2130, 2132, 2139, 2148, 2196, 2245, 2246, 2283, 2329, 2349, 2374, 2375, 2397, 2436, 2443, 2470, 2493, 2505, 2526, 2559, 2563, 2582, 2614, 2713, 2714, 2882, 2905, 2933, 2934, 2935, 2936, 2954, 2972, 2998, 3028 3061, 3087, 3115, 3175, 3220, 3225, 3283, 3381, 3389, 3393, 3399, 3402, 3416, 3420, 3421, 3426, 3428, 3430, 3434, 3445

Objective Measures 93, 142, 145, 153, 192, 311, 475, 637, 639, 775, 778, 779, 1010, 1096, 1180, 1378, 1426, 1427, 1428, 1530, 1632, 1636, 1665, 1666, 1667, 1882, 1883, 1885, 1980, 1981, 2187, 2192, 2422, 2424, 2430, 2432, 2433, 2890, 2892, 3278, 3456

Organization 264, 426, 1633, 1841, 2093, 2225, 2298, 2304, 2308, 2325, 2789, 3229

Orthography 1367, 1886

Output Hypothesis 1328, 3088

Pakistani 1319

Papua New Guinea 1424, 2090, 2978

Paragraph 51, 70, 175, 264, 272, 478, 854, 934, 1110, 1325, 1511, 1698, 1705, 1786, 2067, 2086, 2333, 2370, 2486, 2544, 2740, 2871, 3031, 3108, 3128, 3259, 3288, 3319, 3381

Paraphrase Writing 545, 668, 1324, 2816

Peace 267

Pedagogy 187, 1392, 1417, 2429, 2431, 2777, 2887

Peer Response 107, 166, 204, 209, 215, 238, 239, 312, 357, 358, 541, 790, 866, 1107, 1238, 1260, 1351, 1492, 1500, 1520, 1527, 1555, 1610, 1737, 2022, 2023, 2072, 2075, 2214, 2215, 2234, 2276, 2279, 2282, 2479, 2529, 2618, 2744, 2856, 2977, 3034, 3045, 3443, 3449, 3451

Perceptions 288, 2093, 2364, 2758, 2932

Persian 1, 18, 63, 64, 81, 583, 900, 1245, 2059, 2723

Persuasion 63, 489, 641, 642, 664, 665, 666, 1519, 1781

Phillipines 67, 2230, 2773, 3232

Placement 334, 392, 469, 578, 785, 786, 1141, 1412, 1692, 1934, 1946, 2044, 2371, 2929

Plagiarism 804, 805, 1170, 3371

Planning 152, 1239, 1647, 3160, 3161, 3390

Polish 512, 1254, 1331, 2964, 2965, 3235

Politics 359, 748, 2586, 2676, 2799, 2800, 2883

Portfolios 40, 345, 629, 1032, 1057, 1299, 1311, 1650, 1711, 1785, 1895, 2082, 2084, 2332, 2554, 2966, 3213

Portugese 56, 611, 768, 1185, 2238, 2239, 2240, 2242, 2243

Pragmatics 196, 2031, 2097

Preferences 3204, 3301, 3437

Process Instruction 25, 37, 149, 199, 321, 374, 375, 395, 447, 451, 512, 598, 625, 653, 681, 689, 830, 917, 922, 1004, 1054, 1088, 1206, 1209, 1221, 1235, 1290, 1358, 1363, 1444, 1446, 1484, 1516, 1623, 1720, 1732, 1771, 1875, 1876, 1877, 1880, 1902, 1976, 2011, 2286, 2379, 2409, 2416, 2499, 2587, 2589, 2643, 2660, 2694, 2719, 2844, 2885, 3132, 3304, 3369, 3398, 3402, 3408, 3415, 3423, 3424, 3427, 3428, 3431, 3434, 3436

Process Research 49, 189, 381, 382, 383, 550, 973, 1065, 1072, 1105, 1114, 1262, 1263, 1393, 1512, 1643, 1644, 1645, 1646, 1648, 1725, 1977, 2099, 2182, 2203, 2237, 2238, 2239, 2240, 2243, 2267, 2413, 2508, 2568, 2569, 2570, 2572, 2781, 2964, 3026, 3105, 3153, 3161, 3265, 3266, 3273, 3305, 3412, 3413, 3414, 3417, 3422, 3425

Professional Writing 1015, 2667

Proficiency 351, 728, 729, 842, 960, 1099, 1213, 1379, 1428, 1745, 1782, 1791, 2058, 2256, 2824, 2890

Programs 1, 140, 252, 361, 471, 537, 588, 708, 882, 958, 1073, 1377, 1900, 1922, 1954, 1956, 2057, 2300, 2441, 2471, 2634, 2734, 2869, 2988, 3400

Project Work 219, 223, 305, 342, 385, 448, 686, 733, 960, 970, 2140, 2497, 2705, 2818, 2996, 3180, 3235

Prompts 168, 570, 651, 1078, 1159, 1276, 1306, 1309, 1310, 1345, 1404, 1440, 1445, 3001, 3002, 3051, 3120, 3146

Prose Models 2671, 2672

Psychology 1055, 1072, 1513, 1568, 1714, 2331, 2748, 3377

Punctuation 436

Punjabi 721, 725, 736, 974, 1495

Questioning 3264

Raters 126, 391, 393, 1299, 1528, 1717, 2132, 2465, 3099, 3141

Rating 53, 1159, 1376, 2189, 2190, 2257, 2382, 2695

Reader 1661, 1869, 1960, 3353

Reading-Writing Relations 12, 15, 22, 45, 47, 86, 101, 110, 116, 130, 156, 170, 217, 220, 267, 277, 279, 281, 282, 306, 374, 376, 453, 454, 479, 483, 484, 486, 489, 490, 491, 492, 501, 502, 503, 504, 509, 510, 624, 651, 652, 653, 684, 686, 688, 718, 735, 738, 739, 760, 789, 799, 822, 824, 848, 857, 872, 924, 957, 1005, 1007, 1008, 1009, 1019, 1021, 1022, 1024, 1084, 1095, 1100, 1106, 1118, 1119, 1124, 1140, 1152, 1171, 1186, 1242, 1255, 1341, 1359, 1375, 1384, 1395, 1434, 1436, 1442, 1448, 1459, 1461, 1482, 1552, 1572, 1573, 1577, 1627, 1628, 1660, 1673, 1704, 1803, 1804, 1813, 1848, 1857, 1901, 1913, 1915, 1929, 1930, 1931, 1953, 2027, 2051, 2106, 2127, 2143, 2209, 2261, 2271, 6675, 2313, 2353, 2396, 2442, 2485, 2519, 2540, 2609, 2610, 2613, 2615, 2722, 2741, 2752, 2760, 2761, 2765, 2784, 2807, 2812, 2853, 2867, 3004, 3019, 3049, 3065, 3066, 3103, 3155, 3156, 3325, 3352, 3438, 3453, 3455

Reformulation 54, 55, 1085, 1952, 2733, 2742, 2786, 3170

Refugees 1052, 2927

Register 218, 626, 1241, 1369, 1404, 1531, 1630, 1731, 2369, 2745, 2870, 3203

Report Writing 2090

Research 244, 337, 1275, 1293, 1562, 1818, 1867, 1873, 1931, 1944, 1945, 2046, 2223, 2314, 2327, 2345, 2419, 2427, 2588, 2682, 3037, 3044, 3211, 3212, 3347, 3419, 3435

Research Writing 44, 102, 123, 201, 212, 344, 453, 455, 456, 457, 552, 590, 627, 636, 692, 707, 715, 816, 1145, 1147, 1176, 1246, 1252, 1300, 1301, 1395, 1413, 1441, 1540, 1544, 1718, 2183, 2184, 2185, 2205, 2207, 2262, 2352, 2390, 2594, 2770, 2792, 2815, 2817, 2831, 2869, 2899, 3047, 3091,

3094, 3095, 3152, 3286, 3360, 3378, 3379

Resistance 1890, 2435

Responding 184, 251, 268, 300, 428, 476, 536, 560, 732, 737, 820, 821, 847, 984, 1155, 1187, 1214, 1264, 1276, 1277, 1292, 1524, 1712, 1723, 1878, 1879, 1938, 1949, 2025, 2060, 2098, 2173, 2250, 2449, 2560, 2574, 2673, 2718, 2743, 2804, 2883, 2888, 3221, 3230, 3272, 3283, 3301, 3368, 3422, 3443

Review 482, 549, 632, 638, 647, 723, 947, 950, 1121, 1178, 1335, 1471, 1587, 1706, 1793, 1799, 1814, 1817, 1937, 2196, 2275, 2404, 2436, 2514, 2567, 2717, 2835, 2855, 2931, 2933, 2937, 2939, 2940, 2941, 2942, 2943, 2951, 3025, 3043, 3112, 3131, 3133, 3305, 3362, 3418

Revision 36, 43, 54, 55, 151, 213, 214, 238, 300, 430, 523, 533, 536, 547, 548, 557, 577, 612, 613, 614, 615, 616, 617, 618, 619, 620, 621, 623, 631, 654, 820, 853, 940, 994, 1075, 1114, 1115, 1116, 1121, 1254, 1257, 1364, 1365, 1388, 1389, 1394, 1593, 1594, 1749, 1859, 1862, 1982, 2077, 2131, 2279, 2402, 2473, 2474, 2476, 2777, 2483, 2674, 2730, 2761, 2771, 2814, 2952, 2917, 2972, 2977, 3021, 3041, 3067, 3109, 3110, 3127, 3161, 3181, 3205, 3215, 3264, 3267, 3431, 3449

Rhetoric 68, 87, 359, 497, 582, 664, 696, 761, 769, 792, 810, 916, 932, 1020, 1142, 1619, 1637, 1709, 1819, 1825, 1853, 2031, 2074, 2085, 2111, 2112, 2113, 2291, 2304, 2350, 2357, 2870, 2873, 2875, 2922, 3195, 3367, 3396

Russian 2251, 3117

Samoa 1314

Schema 57, 58, 196, 492, 1258, 1594, 1628, 2662, 3366

Scientific Writing 705, 1062, 1259, 1354, 2263, 2594

Scoring 69, 1002, 1278, 1304, 1307, 1479, 1816, 2420, 2421, 2426, 2498, 2527, 2528, 3113, 3457

Secondary School 4, 5, 29, 90, 120, 131, 140, 141, 146, 158, 186, 193, 243, 312, 401, 429, 430, 530, 542, 556, 565, 593, 594, 757, 839, 881, 885, 898, 940, 972, 983, 1124, 1140, 1162, 1211, 1212, 1220, 1311, 1614, 1722, 1736, 1785, 1857, 1858, 1892, 1951, 1953, 1954, 1959, 2100, 2166, 2220, 2227, 2232, 2318, 2330, 2385, 2488, 2520, 2524, 2539, 2544, 2681, 2752, 2839, 2912, 2925, 2949, 2953, 2990, 3084, 3119, 3121, 3155, 3182, 3237, 3257, 3342, 3392

Senegal 691

Sentence Combining 2, 77, 409, 682, 683, 777, 1044, 1149, 1166, 1489, 1617, 1631, 1668, 1757, 1763, 1787, 1788, 1808, 1881, 2160, 2193, 2194, 2295, 2503, 2742, 2787, 2926, 2958, 3116, 3187, 3334, 3373, 3433

Singapore 698, 699, 1354, 2413, 3361, 3388

Social 11, 277, 324, 398, 915, 1613, 2701, 2703, 2704, 2707

Socio-Cultural Factors 1222, 2033, 2146

Sociolinguistics 253, 259, 309

Socio-Political Theory 1948

South Africa 2912

South Pacific 3233

Southeast Asian 757, 3205, 3280

Spanish 6, 213, 516, 550, 583, 628, 839, 923, 990, 1234, 1855, 2268, 2272, 2306, 2348, 2385, 2712, 2935, 3148, 3214

Speaking-Writing Relations 6, 7, 11, 48, 72, 73, 108, 109, 139, 159, 166, 249, 255, 309, 326, 332, 356, 422, 542, 596, 676, 741, 743, 744, 745, 791, 812, 833, 890, 938, 975, 981, 986, 1013, 1111, 1123, 1169, 1204, 1217, 1226, 1266, 1314, 1346, 1344, 1356, 1369, 1405, 1406, 1407, 1408, 1475, 1483, 1496, 1499, 1508, 1563, 1669, 1784, 1847, 1893, 1907, 1910, 1918, 2058, 2073, 2136, 2163, 2200, 2201, 2226, 2269, 2315, 2369, 2434, 2543, 2666, 2712, 2714, 2754, 2772, 2833, 2864, 2872, 2973, 2978, 3028, 3088, 3201, 3216, 3223, 3224, 3225, 3226, 3285, 3286, 3298, 3331, 3345, 3385, 3439

Spelling 194, 333, 389, 703, 716, 791, 931, 1103, 1244, 2204, 2268, 2274, 2327, 2359, 2678, 2769, 3159, 3458, 3459

Sri Lanka 2769

Standards 630, 671, 698, 699, 746, 1521, 1595, 1604, 1941, 2201, 2360, 2601, 3388

Strategies 172, 250, 527, 727, 731, 738, 739, 1642, 1647, 1908, 2484, 2563, 3064, 3275, 3278, 3361

Student Publications 519, 694, 704, 867, 942, 963, 964, 1144, 1543, 1909, 2165, 2249, 2497, 2727, 2909, 2962, 3354 Style 21, 75, 93, 94, 192, 314, 613, 614, 615, 616, 617, 620, 743, 787, 809, 863, 1020, 1060, 1129, 1416, 1418, 1611, 1674, 1676, 1678, 1702, 1713, 1746, 1923, 2000, 2004, 2182, 2195, 2236, 2316, 2355, 2423, 2487, 2532, 2579, 2632, 2789, 2959, 2998, 2123, 3167, 3208, 3216, 3383, 3439

Sudanese 1664

Summary Writing 36, 123, 165, 171, 172, 525, 622, 855, 1008, 1422, 1459, 1465, 1590, 1591, 1597, 1607, 1758, 1759, 2092, 2235, 2417, 2504, 2607, 2763, 2807, 2808, 2867, 2911, 3371

Swahili 2222

Swedish 270, 758, 1189, 1511, 2001, 2002, 2003, 2678, 3053, 3054, 3319, 3320, 3321, 3322

Syllabus Design 789, 2679, 2995, 3069, 3279

Syntactic Development 18, 66, 145, 524, 683, 1133, 1428, 1490, 1530, 1731, 1745, 1805, 1861, 1884, 2891, 2892, 3226, 3334, 3374, 3393, 3394, 3404

Syntactic Structures 94, 142, 218, 232, 343, 349, 539, 930, 1075, 1467, 1658, 1697, 1738, 1955, 1965, 2070, 2195, 2244, 2439, 2632, 2960, 2074, 3075, 3076, 3145, 3186, 3262, 3389

Tagalog 27

TAS 775, 776, 778, 779, 2424

Task 301, 339, 347, 348, 663, 1200, 1287, 1438, 1447, 1450, 1572, 1585, 1595, 1596, 1613, 1776, 2019, 2032, 2071, 2161, 2238, 2386, 2398, 2452, 2461, 2526, 2604, 2605, 2609, 2625, 2775, 2854, 2912, 3295, 3391

Teacher Education 354, 1153, 2821

Teacher Preparation 67, 141, 184, 187, 325, 329, 335, 353, 372, 373, 387, 401, 402, 445, 452, 466, 589, 708, 711, 719, 720, 726, 862, 927, 978, 1011, 1108, 1349, 1392, 1429, 1466, 1690, 1724, 1811, 1813, 1815, 1822, 1823, 1825, 1828, 1829, 1834, 1846, 1868, 1872, 1890, 1932, 2046, 2047, 2096, 2124, 2230, 2283, 2407, 2457, 2574, 2576, 2611, 2642, 2844, 2846, 2930, 2986, 3053, 3079, 3170, 3307, 3340, 3343

Technical Writing 181, 202, 294, 444, 517, 585, 673, 674, 814, 815, 852, 1463, 1464, 1560, 1570, 1630, 1653, 1743, 1744, 1786, 1792, 2110, 2193, 2278, 2309, 2393, 2399, 2590, 2595, 2877, 2921, 3000, 3060, 3077, 3163, 3195, 3203, 3293, 3294, 3299, 3318, 3378

Text Analysis 299, 387, 484, 486, 607, 608, 658, 659, 661, 948, 949, 988, 1179, 1181, 1182, 1269, 1401, 1416, 1592, 1605, 1686, 1700, 1707, 1727, 1928, 1984, 1986, 1987, 1988, 2002, 2094, 2381, 2436, 2437, 2438, 2439, 2545, 2633, 2636, 2637, 2764, 2832, 3093, 3107, 3184, 3332, 3381

Textbook 3, 10, 14, 59, 96, 97, 106, 111, 124, 137, 138, 173, 180, 182, 186, 198, 229, 230, 240, 261, 274, 275, 276, 283, 284, 285, 286, 290, 291, 292, 293, 307, 315, 368, 377, 378, 388, 390, 400, 432, 433, 434, 435, 437, 438, 439, 440, 514, 528, 606, 609, 693, 717, 751, 752, 753, 766, 780, 800, 835, 864, 951, 996, 1035, 1037, 1038, 1040, 1042, 1043, 1087, 1090, 1091, 1122, 1162, 1172, 1175, 1188, 1202, 1243, 1283, 1301, 1303, 1324, 1330, 1332, 1333, 1357, 1366, 1370, 1464, 1486, 1487, 1497, 1514, 1539, 1553, 1554, 1556, 1615, 1635, 1735, 1753, 1760, 1772, 1790, 1842, 1848, 1849, 1896, 1898, 1901, 1912, 1916, 1925, 1940, 1978, 1979, 2013, 2016, 2018, 2049, 2050, 2081, 2083, 2095, 2144, 2172, 2184, 2188, 2202, 2219, 2227, 2259, 2299, 2317, 2321, 2323, 2324, 2340, 2342, 2361, 2365, 2367, 2368, 2392, 2395, 2466, 2488, 2523, 2524, 2551, 2552, 2557, 2561, 2567, 2581, 2592, 2597, 2627, 2628, 2647, 2655, 2657, 2661, 2698, 2706, 2709, 27242725, 2753, 2822, 2837, 2838, 2862, 2865, 2866, 2884, 2901, 2903, 2923, 2924, 2925, 2966, 2970, 2981, 2990, 2994, 3003, 3006, 3024, 3078, 3080, 3086, 3182, 3199, 3217, 3239, 3268, 3270, 3271, 3277, 3292, 3316, 3317, 3351, 3353, 3355, 3358, 3359, 3417

Thai 113, 265, 524, 544, 995, 1117, 1124, 1259, 1396, 1411, 1509, 1510, 1524, 1700, 1748, 2080, 2358, 2520, 2959, 3079, 3109, 3110, 3119, 3366

Theory 889, 1068, 1328, 1587, 1818, 1832, 1969, 2228, 2575, 3056, 3280, 3420, 3435

Time 1248, 1249, 1794, 1807, 1820, 1827, 1830, 1854, 2118, 2316

Tonga 1314

Topic 155, 191, 192, 308, 349, 1006, 1064, 1240, 1306, 1450, 1481, 1637,

1675, 1676, 1695, 1729, 1852, 1933, 1947, 2045, 2065, 2066, 2149, 2149, 2151, 2181, 2374, 2451, 2452, 2458, 2461, 2577, 2606, 2619, 2738, 2950, 3052, 3074, 3075, 3142, 3143, 3145, 3198, 3322

Transfer 500, 508, 691, 1297, 1321, 2828, 2858, 3114, 3150, 3151, 3160, 3290, 3444

Translation 17, 925, 1461, 1775, 2338, 2956, 3039

TSA 523, 646, 654, 670, 1893, 1894, 2065, 2066, 2851, 2852, 3181, 3254, 3289

T-Unit 153, 1010, 1097, 1143, 1501, 1666, 1667, 1668, 1884, 2192, 2418, 2539

Turkish 945, 1671, 2302

Tutoring 62, 95, 244, 581, 767, 865, 1034, 1071, 1327, 1353, 1406, 1536, 1728, 1950, 2014, 2285, 2674, 2691, 2953, 3178, 3196, 3244, 3370

TWE 633, 967, 1248, 1249, 1376, 1381, 1675, 1816, 2290, 2494, 2549, 2550, 2558, 2621, 2631, 3036, 3037, 3040, 3051, 3134, 3135, 3188

University 14, 37, 59, 64, 96, 111, 135, 137, 163, 188, 198, 215, 221, 222, 224, 225, 226, 229, 230, 257, 259, 262, 270, 273, 278, 280, 301, 318, 338, 344, 347, 350, 368, 380, 390, 412, 440, 441, 444, 453, 528, 529, 544, 555, 558, 583, 599, 609, 674, 680, 740, 752, 755, 776, 793, 795, 796, 806, 807, 836, 874, 880, 932, 937, 939, 949, 951, 952, 953, 965, 987, 1083, 1087, 1099, 1102, 1106, , 1113, 1115, 1127, 1132, 1133, 1186, 1224, 1430, 1447, 1455, 1464, 1494, 1498, 1514, 1519, 1597, 1598, 1603, 1615, 1661, 1664, 1772, 1811, 1831, 1833, 1859, 1876, 1927, 1940, 1946, 1978, 2013, 2049, 2050, 2051, 2084, 2099, 2153, 2168, 2202, 2205, 2253, 2267, 2295, 2325, 2342, 2344, 2380, 2435, 2441, 2496, 2531, 2545, 2551, 2552, 2570, 2585, 2597, 2627, 2697, 2698, 2722, 2730, 2777, 2792, 2796, 2837, 2845, 2862, 2914, 2936, 2970, 2974, 2982, 3006, 3007, 3008, 3062, 3069, 3083, 3085, 3086, 3136, 3149, 3176, 3196, 3199, 3202, 3234, 3238, 3242, 3246, 3292, 3336, 3352, 3355, 3414, 3449, 3451

Usage 888, 1041, 1318, 1674, 1676, 2264, 3055

Vai 2319

Variation 169, 472, 700, 1475, 1612, 2035, 2374

Vietnamese 1103, 1584, 2303, 2482, 2483, 2484, 2832, 2997

Vocabulary 1016, 1074, 1138, 1609, 2115

Voice 563, 1201, 1455, 1851, 2660, 3216

WAC 135, 201, 203, 209, 224, 418, 507, 828, 851, 1405, 1548, 1560, 1600, 2416, 2586, 2743, 2899

West Africa 1220

West Indian 1143

Whole Language 883, 1058, 1059, 1267, 1361, 1469, 2051, 2178, 2310, 2729,

2736

Word Processing 136, 154, 227, 228, 236, 237, 269, 567, 631, 685, 1053, 1315, 1316, 1317, 1385, 1386, 1976, 1504, 1565, 1671, 1762, 1956, 2107, 2141, 2287, 2404, 2405, 2408, 2409, 2410, 2411, 2412, 2469, 2470, 2472, 2473, 2474, 2475, 2476, 2491, 2492, 2508, 2546, 2774, 2829, 2948, 3214, 3215, 3218, 3257

Workshop 562, 1107, 1226, 3011, 3035, 3062, 3407, 3408

Writing Center 62, 684, 481, 899, 962, 1039, 1071, 1085, 1092, 1219, 1327 1353, 2014, 2293, 2378, 2515, 2516, 2517, 2669, 2881, 2882, 3063, 3164, 3178

Writing Groups 2277, 2280, 2281

Zairean 2963

Zimbabwe 2029, 2100, 3057

Zulu 1995, 1996, 1997